NEWSWEEK CONDENSED BOOKS

ARNOLD C. BRACKMAN

ANDREW TOBIAS

JOSEPH C. GOULDEN

EVERETT S. ALLEN

THE SEARCH FOR THE GOLD OF TUTANKHAMEN

FIRE AND ICE
THE STORY OF CHARLES REVSON— THE MAN WHO BUILT THE REVLON EMPIRE

THE BEST YEARS
1945–1950

A WIND TO SHAKE THE WORLD
THE STORY OF THE 1938 HURRICANE

NEWSWEEK BOOKS, New York

NEWSWEEK CONDENSED BOOKS

Herbert A. Gilbert, Editor
Janet Czarnetzki, Art Director
Elaine K. Andrews, Associate Editor

Alvin Garfin, Publisher

The original editions of the books in this volume
are published and copyrighted as follows:

The Search for the Gold of Tutankhamen
Published by Mason/Charter Publishers, Inc.
Copyright © 1976 by Arnold C. Brackman

Fire and Ice
Published by William Morrow & Company, Inc.
Copyright © 1975, 1976 by Andrew Tobias

The Best Years
Published by Atheneum Publishers
Copyright © 1976 by Joseph C. Goulden

A Wind to Shake the World
Published by Little, Brown and Company
Copyright © 1976 by Everett S. Allen

Volume V Number 2
Printed and bound in the United States of America

CONTENTS

THE SEARCH
FOR THE GOLD OF
TUTANKHAMEN

A condensation of the book by

ARNOLD C. BRACKMAN

Part I

THE SEARCH

CHAPTER 1

In 1922, as summer waned in England, George Edward Stanhope Molyneux Herbert, fifth earl of Carnarvon, came to a painful decision. For eighteen years he had underwritten annual expeditions in desolate Upper Egypt in search of an archaeological will-o'-the-wisp: the lost, but perhaps intact, tomb of an Egyptian pharaoh. Carnarvon decided to abandon the quest.

Although his expeditions, field-marshaled by Howard Carter, a self-taught Egyptologist, had turned up an occasional bush-league trophy—for example, a stele overlaid with hieroglyphics, the so-called Carnarvon Tablet—the search no longer seemed worth continuing. Fifty thousand pounds ($250,000) had so far been gambled on the venture.

Except for the war years, 1914–1918, when he converted his picturesque family seat of Highclere Castle—built in the twelfth and thirteenth centuries—into a military rest and rehabilitation center, Carnarvon spent half a year or more annually in the cramped, depressing bungalow he had built for himself in Upper Egypt. It was at a point directly across the Nile from the site of ancient Karnak. Perched on a lonely hill, the house was situated at the entrance to Biban-el-Moluk, the Arabic name for "Gate of the Kings" or for what foreigners called the Valley of the Tombs of the Kings.

Unlike the cared-for lawns, pastures, and woodlands of Highclere, Carnarvon's cottage here had not a tree, not a shrub, not a blade of grass anywhere near it. The sun beat down unmercifully. The cottage provided a panoramic view of the Valley of the Tombs of the Kings; of its brooding, somber precipices and escarpments in different shades of raw and burnt umber; of its bleak, lifeless peaks, some rising 1,800 feet above the surface of the blue Nile.

In this remote setting, the pharaohs built their hypogea: rock tombs or sepulchers cut directly into the rock, often replete with hidden passages, secret chambers, stairwells, and annexes. Since the beginning of the last century, sixty-four tombs had been discovered in the Valley. The largest, designed to house the mummy of Seti (Sethos) I and built more than thirty centuries ago, was 470 feet long and plunged 180 feet below the earth's surface. "The atmosphere is suffocating," wrote a traveler who descended into its depths almost a hundred years ago. "The place is ghostly and peopled with nightmares."

The traveler was not the first to render this judgment. In 1843, the Reverend Stephen Olin, the president of Wesleyan University, visited the Valley and recorded a corresponding sentiment. "Our way led us for more than an hour through a region of sterility and desolation," he wrote. Not a shrub, not a bird, not an insect, enlivened the "gloomy, dreary retreat." And he added as an afterthought: "It is a singular fact that when first explored by modern [sic] travellers, all the royal tombs had been broken open and rifled of their contents."

Manifestly, this was an odd place for an English lord to spend most of the year, much less the autumn and winter of his life.

Lord Carnarvon's daily pattern had always been much the same. He rose just before daybreak, around 5:30, to avoid the heat of the day; and after a breakfast of tea and *totleh*, an Egyptian jelly encrusted with blanched almonds, he set out for the Valley. He rode by donkey over the rock-strewn trail, covered with chips of limestone and white and black flint, which led by his house and into the core of Biban-el-Moluk. At the dig, he joined his ringmaster, Howard Carter, who actively supervised crews of as many as 275 men, clad in their traditional gallabiyas (long, loose, and billowing white robes), painstakingly removing more than 200,000 tons of debris by wicker basket in search of a clue to that prize of prizes, the inviolate, treasure-filled tomb of a pharaoh. The men, fellahin from neighboring villages, worked for as little as three piasters (fifteen cents) a day. They worked every day except Tuesday (by tradition, no digging was done on this day) and for only a half day on Friday, the Moslem Sabbath.

At the end of the work day, Carnarvon remounted his donkey for the trek back to his double-domed bungalow, which the impoverished Egyptians dubbed "Castle Carnarvon." At sundown, he sat on the second story terrace, a whiskey in hand, and gazed out on the forbidding landscape. At that latitude (20°N), the sun sets rapidly, leaving a crimson line along the horizon for only a few minutes. The countryside is plunged into darkness. Carnarvon dined lightly either on canned goods imported from England or on local mutton. A bottle of red wine was always on the table. Exhausted by the day's work, he usually retired early.

For years, Carnarvon almost unfailingly followed this pattern. By 1922, however, he felt there was no longer any chance of his and Carter's discovering an intact king's tomb.

In point of fact, no such tomb had ever been found. Indeed, there was a spreading conviction among Egyptologists that one never would be found. Sir Gaston Maspero, who served as Egypt's director general of excavations and antiquities, was convinced that Carnarvon's great enterprise, however worthy, was a futile one. The American millionaire, Theodore M. Davis, like Carnarvon an amateur archaeologist, had also spent a fortune in the same pursuit without success. In 1912, after more than a dozen years in the field, Davis quit. "I fear," he concluded, "that the Valley of the Tombs is now exhausted."

That, to the mind of Carnarvon (and Carter), was precisely the trouble. Every time somebody declared the Valley exhausted, something else was later found, a despoiled tomb or a clue to the existence of other tombs. For example, in 1815 Giovanni Belzoni, the first modern excavator of the Valley, uncovered the plundered tombs of Seti I, Rameses I, and other great pharaohs. When he left the field, he expressed the "firm conviction" that he had found everything there was to find. "I exerted all my humble abilities in endeavoring to find another tomb," he wrote five years later, "but [did] not succeed."

Twenty-four years later, a Berlin expedition led by the celebrated Karl Richard Lepsius took the first detailed measurements of the Valley. Archaeologically speaking, Lepsius announced the place was "exhausted." Yet in 1898 Victor Loret, a Frenchman, stumbled on several new tombs. But, as with all twenty-nine hypogea found in the Valley since Belzoni's days, each tomb had been rifled and ravaged in antiquity. In some cases, the cream-colored linen wrappings of the mummies were shredded by thieves in their frenzied search for treasure. In other cases, the tombs were stripped of everything except immovable wall paintings, annotated with hieroglyphics, works of inestimable historic and artistic value. Yet Loret's find generated new hope that more tombs, possibly an untouched tomb, might yet be found.

11

For Carnarvon and Carter, during their annual winter campaigns in Egypt, usually between October and April, their occasional discoveries served to whet their appetites. But as the years swept by and the grand prize still eluded them the Valley took its psychological toll. The harsh heat and the grim reality of the terrain eventually drained Carnarvon, if not yet Carter, of ambition, energy, and hope.

Although Carnarvon wearied of his own endless search, he did gradually amass the world's finest private collection of Egyptian antiquities. He not only scoured the Valley of the Tombs of the Kings and other sites for finds—Luxor, Thebes, Karnak—but he combed the thieves' market in Cairo and maintained regular contact with antiquity dealers throughout the Near East. The clou of his collection was a solid gold statue, about a foot high, of Amen-Ra, who had emerged by the beginning of the Eighteenth Dynasty as the supreme god of Egypt, a melding of Amen, the ram-headed god of Thebes, and Ra, the sun-god of Memphis. Neither Carnarvon nor Carter actually found the figure. It was recovered from the sand amid the ruins of the fabulous temple complex at Karnak like so many other objects of art by a nameless Egyptian fellah. In those days, the gold alone was worth almost £10,000 ($50,000). Today, on the wildly fluctuating Zurich gold market, it is probably worth many times that figure, exclusive of its artistic value.

By the summer of 1922, the fifty-six-year-old Carnarvon concluded that the archaeological establishment was probably right: another pharaoh's tomb would never be found. Even if it were, it would most assuredly be empty, looted in antiquity.

It was equally assured that an inviolate tomb would contain a treasure trove. The ravaged tombs were evidence of that—and so was Egyptian tradition. For thousands of years, in accordance with their religious beliefs about the existence of a hereafter, the Egyptians buried with their monarchs gilded chariots and funerary statues, weapons, furniture, and urns filled with food. The coffins of the dead were made of solid gold, it was said, and the mummy wore a mask of gold inlaid with semiprecious stones. Within the folds of the mummy's wrappings, the high priests tucked jeweled amulets and charms. "That the body should not waste or decay was an object of anxious solicitude," explained Samuel Birch, curator of Egyptology at the British Museum, as early as 1867, "and for this purpose various bandlets and amulets, prepared with certain magical preparations, and sanctified with certain spells or prayers, or even offerings and small sacrifices, were distributed over various parts of the mummy." Thus, gold rings adorned the mummy's fingers; gold bracelets, the wrists;

gold necklaces, the throat; and gold pendants, the chest. Even the finger-nails and toes were sheathed in gold. A papyrus of the Middle Kingdom, written four thousand years ago, during the classic period of Egyptian prose and poetry, provided convincing proof that a pharaoh's tomb was literally worth its weight in gold. The papyrus described the moment of a pharaoh's burial as "the night devoted to oils with bandages [when] thou art reunited with the earth in the mummy case of gold with head of lapis-lazuli."

Obviously, such descriptive passages in the funerary rites of the day were an open invitation to the local mafia. The Amherst Papyrus, a por-tion of a roll containing three and one-half columns of hieroglyphics, which was acquired shortly before the turn of the last century by Lord Hackney—like Carnarvon, a "collector"—astonishingly contained the court record of the prosecution of a band of tomb robbers in the time of Rameses IX, who lived and died more than a millennium before the ap-pearance of Christ. Here was the world's first account of organized crime. The despoilers, the papyrus reported, consisted of a gang of thirty-nine grave robbers, about half of whom were "insiders," members of the Es-tablishment, including eight sacred scribes and seven high priests. The latter knew the secret location of the royal tombs. For good measure, they had access to the offices of the royal architect and stole floor plans. The papyrus provides hard evidence that the Establishment had neither faith nor respect for the system.

"We opened their coffins and unwrapped their mummies," a ringleader confessed in court. ". . . There were numerous amulets and ornaments at the mummy's throat. Its head had a mask of gold upon it. The august mummy of the king was overlaid with gold throughout. Its coverings were wrought of gold and silver within and without. . . . We found the king's wife likewise. We stripped off all that we found. . . . We set fire to their wrappings. We stole their furniture, which we found with them, and vases of gold, silver and bronze."

But however attractive the thought of gold, Lord Carnarvon was forced to abandon the search in 1922 for sound financial reasons. Although the pound, like Britain herself, ruled the world, England was caught up in the inflationary squeeze that followed World War I. Lord Carnarvon felt the pinch as he struggled to maintain the standard of living to which he was accustomed after inheriting his father's title and estate, which included 36,000 acres of land.

No question about it. The string had run out on his expensive hobby, Egyptology.

CHAPTER 2

As was their autumnal custom, Carnarvon and Howard Carter were to confer at Highclere—a setting of crenellated walls and towers, formal gardens and hunting preserves—to review the year's work in Upper Egypt and map their upcoming winter campaign. In 1922, Carnarvon dreaded the interview.

An extrovert who made and kept friends easily, an attractive personality, in many ways a free soul despite his overlay of British reserve, Carnarvon realized that his decision to abandon the quest would crush Carter, a lonely bachelor whose entire life was given over to Egyptology. Carnarvon feared that quitting the pursuit at so late a date was not quite the gentlemanly thing to do.

Carter came to call, as usual, at Highclere Castle. Although he was slightly broader and heavier than Carnarvon and eight years his junior (it seemed much more), the collaborators bore a striking general resemblance to each other in mien, an air of English aplomb and civility, and in physical appearance—medium height, ample dark hair, trim moustaches. They even dressed similarly, in tweedy jackets, white shirts, and bow ties. As an ancient Egyptian would have expressed it, Carter appeared to be Carnarvon's *ka*, his other self, his double, his soul, his spirit, his aura.

But beneath these similarities were completely different personalities.

Carter was an introvert: shy, diffident, retiring, more comfortable in the background than in the forefront. Uneasy in large groups, he lacked the ability to make small talk. Whereas Carnarvon made friends easily, Carter made enemies easily. Carter was a man of uncompromising, inflexible integrity and honesty. If he were in the right, as he saw it, he was obstinate to the point of sheer pertinacity. His character was explosive. It was perhaps an inferiority complex, springing from his low estate on the social ladder in a feudal-minded society, that he covered with a quick temper. High-strung and taut, constantly on the defensive, he was, among his countrymen and among Europeans generally, aggressive. With Egyptians, however, he felt at ease, among peers.

He was a lonely man whom one of his closest friends described as "a strange fellow in many ways." He lived alone in a small adobe house he had built near the Valley of the Tombs. "Castle Carter," the fellahin called it. He was unmarried, and there were no women in his life. He had received no formal education in his youth, and, like his father, a superior draftsman and unheralded water colorist who painted the portraits of the

14

aristocracy's favorite animals—a Derby winner, a pet retriever—Carter had a long record of employment by the leisure class. Carnarvon was not his first benefactor. He also worked for Theodore Davis, the Rhode Island millionaire who had left an Egyptological legacy.

The one thing Carvarvon and Carter unquestionably shared was a genuine passion for Egyptology. This dedication was enough to bridge the social abyss between them. They genuinely liked and respected each other beyond the patron-client relationship. Nevertheless, there was an unavoidable master-servant relationship between them, however subterranean, and they both knew it. Not that Carter felt that by working for Carnarvon he had accepted a grant, a free ride. Carnarvon's wealth may have underwritten his employment, but the job was hardly a sinecure.

While Carnarvon thought of archaeology as a hunt in which the player tracked for high stakes, Carter thought of archaeology as a game. On one occasion he confessed publicly that he had taken up archaeology because of his strong inclination toward the science of deduction. "If I hadn't gone for archaeology," he explained, "I might have entered Scotland Yard."

That afternoon at Highclere, over whiskeys probably, the two men reviewed the year's "barren labor." This was Carter's own descriptive phrase for the last campaign. He did not try to hide the fact. Yet barren though it had been, Carter's hopes were unquenchable, in large part because his very way of life depended upon an endless quest, an interminable search. Thus, Carter began to talk with customary excitement about the upcoming winter season.

Carnarvon interrupted him, albeit gently. Postwar economic conditions, he said with discomfort, precluded continuing the quest. In a word, the search for the lost tomb of a pharaoh must be abandoned.

Carter was stunned. Despite those barren years, he was unshakably convinced that "at least one more royal tomb," as he frequently expressed it, would be found. That was the tomb of the youthful pharaoh Tutankhamen of the Eighteenth Dynasty. He had ruled in Egypt's Golden Age, more than thirty centuries earlier. The existence of such a tomb, Carter never tired of pointing out, was confirmed by clues that the Davis expeditions had unearthed in the Valley before World War I. Indeed, Davis actually claimed to have found the tomb; rifled, of course. Carter was convinced that what Davis found was not a pharaoh's tomb, but a hint of things to come. The evidence was circumstantial, Carter conceded, but would Scotland Yard abandon a case because the evidence was inconclusive?

Carter fought to control his poise. Then, in a desperate effort to win back his patron, he spread on the table before them the now familiar, smudged and frayed map of the Valley they had used over the years. He conceded that they had probed virtually every foot of the Valley. But he pointed to one square, the area just below the entrance to the empty hypogeum of Rameses VI, with its plundered passages, chambers, gaily painted walls, and hieroglyphics. This particular area, shaped more like a triangle than a square because of the cliff's configuration, had never been excavated. Twice Carter had opted to dig at that very spot, but had been interrupted. For one thing, the Rameses tomb was a highlight on guided tours through the Valley during the winter tourist season. Carter was reluctant to close down the area, disappoint tourists, and interfere with the business of the Egyptian guides whose meager livelihood depended on free access to the tomb. Moreover, the spot was strewn with the ruins of stone huts and the rubbish of laborers and artists who had worked on the Rameses tomb. It was, therefore, a most unlikely spot to probe because it was inconceivable that the workers erected their shelters across the opening of a pharaoh's tomb—unless, of course, the entrance was lost in *their* antiquity, possibly as the result of a rock slide, an earthquake (such as the one in 27 B.C.) or one of those rare torrential rains that flooded the gorge and raised havoc among the boulders and loose rocks. These violent downpours, accompanied by thunder and lightning, periodically converted the Valley into a cascading canyon of foaming water that lifted and transplanted great stones with ease.

During Carter's thirty-five years of wandering in the Egyptian desert, he could recall only four rainfalls in the Valley, one in 1898, another in 1900, and two in 1916, one of which he personally witnessed at 4:00 P.M., November 1, 1916, when the Great Northern Ravine, north and collateral with the Valley and confluent at the mouth, was transformed into a bursting dam as literally tons of wildly crashing water tumbled headlong through the canyon, redesigning the shape of the Valley.

Carter clung to the remote hope that the entrance to the tomb of Tutankhamen had been covered over in such a fashion. "We had now dug in the Valley for several seasons with extremely scanty results," he later wrote, "and it became a much debated question whether we should continue the work." This line, incidentally, is the only hint Carter ever dropped that he and Carnarvon "much debated" the question at Highclere in 1922. "After these barren years," Carter asked, "were we justified in going on with it?"

Carnarvon's answer was adamant. He refused.

Because Carnarvon's license to dig in the Valley did not expire until November 16, 1923, and was, therefore, good for another year—no dig could be undertaken in Egypt without a government-awarded concession—Carter drew himself upright and formally requested permission from Carnarvon to work the concession once more at his, Carter's, expense. Carnarvon must have suppressed a smile. It cost a bare minimum of £2,000 ($10,000)—easily the equivalent of $50,000 today—to organize a season's work, and he knew Carter simply did not have that kind of ready cash.

Carter said that if he found nothing, he would agree that the Valley was indeed exhausted. If, however, he found the lost tomb, the discovery was Carnarvon's, as they had agreed when they shook hands and began their collaboration in 1907.

Carnarvon thought Carter's offer was too unselfish, too generous. As a gentleman, as a sportsman, Carnarvon could not accept that offer. It was simply not cricket to dump, not so much the project, but Carter and their team of *reises* and diggers, so abruptly after so many years of teamwork. Very well, then, he would give Carter notice; he would agree to one— "one," he repeated—more campaign at his, Carnarvon's, expense.

The collaborators once again shook hands to seal the new compact. Shortly thereafter, Carter left for Cairo to organize the last campaign in the Valley of the Tombs of the Kings.

CHAPTER 3

As was his custom, Carter returned to Egypt circuitously via the Dover-Calais ferry, the Calais-Marseilles express, and thence by a Messageries Maritimes steamship to Alexandria, Egypt's principal port of entry. Even at sea, he was not far from Egyptology. The best-known Messageries steamships making the run were the 12,500-ton, 495-foot long, twin-screw, 17½-knot *Champollion,* named for the man who first deciphered the Rosetta stone, and her sister ship, the *Mariette Pasha,* named for the French Egyptologist, except that she did not have a Maier bow and was, therefore, two knots slower. The journey, made in late October of that year, marked the last time he ever traveled in anonymity.

Carter's initial interest in Tutankhamen had begun in 1891 during his first year in Egypt, when he was sent to work in Flinder Petrie's camp.

Petrie described himself in this period as working to "fill in the blanks" of the history of the Eighteenth Dynasty. At Gurob, Petrie had satisfied himself that Tutankhamen ("He who serves Amen") was originally named Tutankhaten ("He who serves Aten") and that he changed his name when he restored the seat of the Egyptian throne to its former capital at Thebes. Thus, Tutankhamen's reign marked the transition from the experimental belief in one Creator to a return to the tradition of worshiping the old sun-god, Amen-Ra, and a coterie of other gods.

At the time seventeen-year-old Howard Carter joined Petrie, only a few facts were known about Tutankhamen's personal history. From the number of small objects he found while digging at Akhetaten, the place of Tutankhamen's coronation, Petrie concluded that the young pharaoh had lived there only briefly, perhaps six years, before the capital was returned to Thebes. Petrie found neither a palace nor a tomb fit for a pharaoh at the new capital and therefore concluded—correctly, as it later developed—that Tutankhamen had reverted to tradition and was buried with the other pharaohs in the Valley of the Tombs of the Kings.

Because pharaonic court records about plundered tombs made no mention of Tutankhamen's tomb's being robbed, Petrie also drew the conclusion that tomb despoilers had overlooked his burial place or, more likely, that the location of the tomb had been lost in the antiquity of antiquities.

At the outset of the present century, the consensus among archaeologists was that all the major pharaohs of the Eighteenth Dynasty buried in the Valley were accounted for except three. Poetically, the three were the principal figures in the Akhenaten heresy. Among them were Akhenaten himself, the heretic, who changed his name from Amenhotep IV when he discovered the true and only God, Aten; Tutankhamen, the great compromiser, whose reign sought to bridge the abyss between Thebes and Akhetaton; and Harmhab, the archrevisionist who fully restored the old gods to Egyptian religious belief. Many archaeologists doubted that the heretic's mummy would ever be found; as Sir Alan Gardiner, the English Egyptologist, observed, "Conceivably Akhenaten's body had been torn to pieces and thrown to the dogs." As for Harmhab, the evidence at that time strongly suggested that the general was buried at Memphis or at some place in lower Egypt. This left only the mummy and tomb of Tutankhamen unaccounted for. Because neither had been recovered, there was a persistent hope, albeit frail, that perhaps his tomb had eluded the "curse of Egypt," the tomb robbers.

Tutankhamen's name had been familiar to archaeologists since Napoleon's day. In the British Museum the pharaoh's cartouche adorned the lions found at Gebel Arkal: somehow they had escaped the hammers of Harmhab's stone masons. Early Egyptologists speculated a great deal about how this phantom pharaoh fitted into the historical matrix of ancient Egypt. Was he a commoner or a member of royalty, possibly related to Amenhotep III, Akhenaten's predecessor? The only point on which the scholars were in full agreement was that a king by that name once held the flail and crook and ruled Egypt at a crucial time in her development.

Fifteen years after Carter first landed in Egypt, a French Egyptologist provided the first tangible record of events attributed to Tutankhamen's reign. Digging at the base of a temple in Karnak on June 28, 1905, Georges Legrain recovered intact a red sandstone stele from under several feet of sand. The tablet had fallen from the pillar upon which it had been fixed and had been partly shattered by the fall. Apparently nobody noticed it at the time; perhaps a sudden sandstorm swirled through Luxor. Whatever the case, centuries of sand accumulated at the spot and preserved the pieces in excellent fashion. Harmhab's agents of destruction missed it completely.

The stele provided the initial insight into Tutankhamen's rule. Because in that age works were often written to flatter the ruler, it is sometimes difficult to distinguish between fact and fiction, but such records are evidence of the values and thoughts of 3,500 years ago.

When, in the aftermath of the Akhenaten heresy, Tutankhamen assumed the throne on the death of Akhenaten, the stele recorded "the land was overridden with ills." The shrines of the gods "ran to destruction." In turn, "the gods neglected the land." The farthest frontiers of the empire were reoccupied by barbarians. Tutankhamen appealed to the gods and goddesses for assistance, but they shunned him. Accordingly, the new pharaoh embarked on a vigorous program to win back the forsaken gods. "His majesty made rules for the land every day without cease," according to the stele. Tutankhamen restored the worship of Amen and "made his august image in pure gold"; he "raised monuments to the other gods"; he increased the number of sacred vases "in gold, silver, copper and bronze without limit to their number"; he multiplied the riches of the temples "by two, by three, by four, in silver, gold, lapis-lazuli, malachite, precious stones of every kind, royal linen, white linen . . . no end of all precious things"; he built new ships to sail the waters and "covered them with gold . . . so that they lighted up the Nile." He surrounded himself, the high priests, and nobility with "slaves, male and female, singers and tumbling girls." He was benevolent and dispensed justice evenhandedly.

As a consequence, everyone everywhere "exulted, shouted, struck their chests and danced for gladness."

Maspero, one of the earliest students of Tutankhamen's reign, held that the picture of the young pharaoh's life and times was probably accurate. "There is no doubt that the great mass of the Egyptian population must have experienced strong joy when the persecution [of former gods] ended, and the old order of religion was reinstated," he observed. And yet the archaeologists of Maspero's day were more mystified than ever because the stele showed, as had some of Petrie's earlier finds, that although Tutankhamen restored Amen, he also remained faithful to Akhenaten's vision of Aten, the one and only god, the sole creator of the universe. A representation of the rays of the solar disk bathed the stele.

The Legrain discovery attracted the attention, of course, of Carter, who was then, as an outcast among Egyptologists, eking out a meager living through the sale of watercolors at Luxor's Winter Palace Hotel. Convincing proof of Tutankhamen's former existence came at a time when Carter's life had reached a low point.

Two years later, in 1907, when Carter's fortunes changed dramatically and he embarked upon his journey into history with Carnarvon, Legrain published a book containing a photograph of the rare stele. While the book was on the Parisian press, the authenticity of the stele was confirmed beyond doubt. The shattered fragment of a duplicate was recovered at Thebes.

At almost the same time, Theodore Davis turned up new evidence that Tutankhamen had indeed been buried in the Valley.

"While digging near the foot of a high hill in the Valley of the Tombs of the Kings," Davis reported, "my attention was attracted to a large rock tilted to one side, and for some mysterious reason, I felt interested in it." With the aid of an assistant, Edward Ayrton, Davis carefully extracted from beneath the rock an exquisite faience cup, pigeon blue in color. The Egyptians were (and are) masters of faience: a process in which clay is heated with glass. The glass melts and imparts a lovely color to the clay.

"The cup bore the cartouche of Touatankhamanou," the elated Davis reported. (*Touatankhamanou* was the accepted spelling at that time.)

The following season (1907–1908), Davis, assisted by E. Harold Jones, returned to the dig. In the course of a preliminary resurvey of the Valley, Davis and Jones came upon the unmistakable signs of a lost tomb. They put their fellahin to work immediately. "At the depth of 25 feet we found a room filled almost to the top with dried mud, showing that water had entered it," Davis recalled. They carefully sifted through the mud and, in great excitement, Davis said, "we found a broken box containing several pieces of gold leaf stamped with the names of Touatankhamanou and his wife Ankhousmanou. . . . We also found under the mud, lying on the floor in one corner, a beautiful alabaster statue."

The discovery caused a sensation in Luxor and Cairo. Some of the gold pieces, very thin and flat, apparently had been stripped by plunderers from the furniture and funerary articles buried with the dead pharaoh; other pieces of gold leaf, slightly thicker, contained engraved scenes and had probably been nailed or stitched to other objects, such as a chariot. "After spreading [them] out," said George Daressy, then a Davis aide, "I succeeded in reconstructing some designs, more or less incomplete."

A number of pieces of leaf, some measuring eight by five inches, bore the cartouche of Tutankhamen and depicted his life-style. In one scene, the pharaoh stood erect in his chariot, bow poised, in the midst of a hunt. The scene was unique; for the first time a pharaoh was shown accompanied not by lions but by a greyhound. Another fragment of gold leaf bore the legend, "Lord of the two lands giving life forever like the sun." Still another scene depicted Tutankhamen with his youthful wife, her seductive figure discernible through a diaphanous negligee. She wore the headdress of Hathor, the cow-headed goddess of Amenti, a deity of the Egyptian Hades. Standing behind her husband, as he smote an enemy with a sword, she declaimed: "All protection of life is behind him, like the sun." Still other vignettes showed black Africans, with short frizzy hair, and western Asians, with curled beards, paying homage to the new pharaoh.

The alabaster funerary statue was a delight in itself, fifty-nine inches tall, carved from fine, translucent stone. The figure was that of a man in mufti, his arms crossed upon his chest. Unfortunately, the figurine bore no inscription.

Warming to the dig, Davis accelerated the pace of the excavation. Again he was rewarded with success.

"A few days after this we came upon a pit, some distance from the tomb, filled with large earthen pots containing what would seem to be the debris from a tomb, such as dried wreaths of leaves and flowers, and small bags containing a powdered substance," Davis reported. "The cover of one of these jars had been broken and wrapped about it was a cloth on which was inscribed the name of Touatankhamanou."

Davis did not recognize the monumental nature of his discovery. Instead, disappointed by the contents of the jars, he brushed them aside, storing them in the camp's warehouse.

Some months later, however, Herbert E. Winlock, who became curator of Egyptology at the Metropolitan Museum of Art and was then a member of the museum's Egyptian Expedition, examined the Davis find. His pulse quickened. Winlock considered the discovery incontrovertible proof that Tutankhamen was buried in the Valley. With the American millionaire's approval, Winlock repacked the jars and shipped them to the Metropolitan for a thorough examination. The New York word came back: "Extraordinary."

The articles packed into the jars included several clay seals of the royal necropolis; the dried leaves and flowers were of the style of floral collars worn at Egyptian funerals more than three thousand years earlier; and the piece of linen used to hold together the contents of the broken jar bore the inscription ". . . year of the reign of Tutankhamen." The conclusion was manifest: Davis's find was part of the funerary debris from Tutankhamen's burial service. In the dry climate of Upper Egypt, the objects were so well preserved that it seemed they were thrown aside only the day before—not, as in fact they were, literally, more than a million days earlier. Obviously, a mourner, perhaps a servant or a necropolis official, tidied up after the funeral, stuffed the odds and ends into the jars, and shoved them into a crevice in the rock—sweeping them under the rug, so to speak.

The excitement at the camp was transmitted to Carter and Carnarvon. "With all this evidence before us," Carter said, "we were thoroughly convinced in our own minds that the tomb of Tutankhamen [was] still to be found." Although he did not say so, he probably felt Davis would beat him to it and turn up the lost tomb. Davis probably thought similarly.

Then, in 1908, Davis's decade of digging in the Valley was crowned with an irritating mix of triumph and failure.

On February 25 of that year, the Davis crew discovered signs of another tomb. After a day's feverish digging, they uncovered a stairway leading sharply down a few feet, where broken rock and sand filled the space almost to the top. "It was impossible to advance except by digging our way with our hands," Davis reminisced, "and, as we were most anxious to find whose tomb it was, my assistant, Mr. Ayrton, in spite of the heat, undertook the difficult task of crawling over sharp rocks and sand for some distance [to look for an inscription]."

Arthur Weigall, then working for Davis, recalled in his memoirs that they first thought they had discovered the tomb of Tutankhamen. "The size and shape of the entrance left no doubt that the work was to be dated to the end of the eighteenth dynasty," he said.

But their buoyancy was quickly deflated when Ayrton read the hieratic inscription on a supporting beam of the tomb: it contained the name of Harmhab, the general who had sought to blot Tutankhamen's name from history.

Davis described the party as "astonished" by the discovery, as no doubt it was. But Weigall focused on another emotional reaction. "We were disappointed," he wrote.

Wriggling and crawling through the tunnel, accompanied by a small avalanche of stones, Davis, Weigall, and Jones joined Ayrton and continued to squirm deeper into the tomb's passageway.

"It was necessary to drag ourselves over the stones and sand which blocked the way, with our heads unpleasantly near the rough roof," Davis recounted. "There was little air, except that which came from the mouth of the tomb 130 feet above, and the heat was stifling."

The party dropped into a large room and in the center of it stood a red granite sarcophagus, 9 by 4 by 4 feet. Weigall provided this eyewitness account of the excitement: "Looking into the sarcophagus, the lid having been thrown off by plunderers, we found it empty except for a skull and a few bones." As usual, plunderers for profit had preceded the plunderers for art and science—by centuries, if not millennia.

Harmhab's stripped tomb was the last find Davis ever made in the Valley of the Kings, although he continued the search for Tutankhamen's tomb through 1912. Then, drained of his hopes and too tired to dream, Davis abandoned his quest.

The aging, eccentric millionaire consoled himself, however, with the conviction that the discovery of the blue faience cup and the gold leaves was proof positive that he had found Tutankhamen's tomb. "[These discoveries] lead me to conclude that Touatankhamanou was originally buried in the tomb," he wrote, "and that it was afterwards robbed, leaving the few things that I have mentioned."

Davis published his findings in *The Tombs of Harmhabi and Touatankhamanou.* It was a four-part collaboration. Davis wrote the section on the discovery of the tombs, Maspero provided the historical background on both pharaohs, Daressy prepared the catalog, and Lancelot Crane illustrated the folio. Daressy did not mirror the confidence Davis had reflected in the title of the book. He called his section of the work "Catalogue of the Objects Found in an Unknown Tomb, Supposed to be Touatankhamanou." This was the same Daressy who later, as acting director of the government's antiquities service, signed the Carnarvon-Carter concession of the Valley.

Carter scoffed at Davis's claim, which he termed "ludicrous." The Davis theory was "quite untenable," he said. No pharaoh, Carter argued, would be buried in a shallow pit grave. Inwardly, he must have been relieved that Davis had not found the tomb. History was still to be written.

CHAPTER 4

Before receiving the cherished permit to dig in the Valley proper, but in the course of initial excavations, Carnarvon and Carter had, in the latter's words, "the good fortune" to locate the empty tomb of Amenhotep I, the second ruler of the illustrious Eighteenth Dynasty. The find, like so many others, was largely a matter of luck.

"The entrance was secreted under a huge boulder," Carter reported in his account of the discovery in the *Journal of Egyptian Archaeology* in 1915, "and a unique feature is that the debris coming from its excavation was removed in its entirety to a considerable distance away, and hidden in a depression in the ravine below.

"Thus," he wrote, "when the tomb was sealed up there could have been practically no visible indication of its existence."

They expected to find Amenhotep's tomb looted, and they did. Early in the Eighteenth Dynasty, after a series of frightful plunders in the Valley, the mummies of several sovereigns, including Amenhotep, were removed from their original resting place and deposited, family style, in a mausoleum. The location of the mausoleum remained hidden in the Valley until Loret's discovery in 1881, thirty-five centuries later.

Despite its being a plundered tomb, Carnarvon and Carter burrowed into it with zeal. There was always the off-chance that some of the treasure buried with the pharaoh might still be recovered intact, perhaps in a secret, walled-up chamber in the tomb. But the Amenhotep tomb was shorn not only of its mummy and treasure—its galleries, passageways, and chambers were a shambles, evidence of extensive depredation. "All that was left of the king's funeral equipment was the debris of broken vessels and statuettes, fragments of alabaster, green feldspar, yellow limestone, red conglomerate, serpentine, and basalt," Carter reported. "They were broken with such method that hardly a fragment larger than six square inches was found among them, though apparently many of the vases had been of large dimensions." Some of the fragments contained inscriptions, including the cartouche or elliptical frame bearing the name of Amenhotep I.

In July 1914, Carnarvon was officially informed that he would receive the permit to dig up the entire Valley. He and Carter set about to draw up their "elaborate campaign," as Carter called it. They crisscrossed their map of the Valley with plotting lines, like a mariner's chart; authorized their *reises* to raise a force of 275 men; ordered fresh supplies from Cairo to be shipped to Luxor and then onto the dig; and developed a scheme to dig up the Valley to bedrock. Their starting point: the area of Davis's discoveries.

In August, however, war broke out in Europe, and all was uproar and confusion in the Near East. The "elaborate campaign" was suspended.

With the failure of the Turkish invasions of 1915–1916, the war receded from Egypt, affording Carter an opportunity to carry out single-handedly the search for Tutankhamen's tomb. In point of fact, as early as 1915, the year he formally signed the Valley concession on behalf of Carnarvon, after the failure of the first Turkish offensive, Carter was dispatched to Upper Egypt to assist unofficially in policing the Valley. The absence of officials and the diversion of regular guards from Upper Egypt, owing to the war, spurred a revival of activity among what Carter called "local native tomb robbers."

In 1916 a group of "local native tomb robbers" from a village near Luxor made a spectacular find in the Kurna hills adjacent to the Valley of the Tombs. In the prewar period, the area, which included peaks rising 1,800 feet above sea level, had been known to Egyptologists as the "lost cemetery of royal families"—the last resting place of the wives and children of the pharaohs. Why the archaeologists dubbed it "lost" is inexplicable.

At that time, the region was relatively unexplored except for one valley, Gabbanat-el-Qirud, in which tombs abounded, hidden in clefts and crevices. Some tombs were cut high up into the rock faces of the perpendicular cliffs. All the known tombs had been ravaged in antiquity.

Through his contacts among the fellahin at Luxor, who respected his integrity, Carter learned of the fresh discovery. Acting on the intelligence, he gathered together a handful of former workers, including several, he later admitted, "who had escaped the Army Labor Levies." This was an extraordinary admission on the part of a British official during wartime: a clue perhaps to his intimate relations with the Egyptians in the colonial period. He and his men set off for the Kurna hills.

From the crest of a precipice, "Carter's irregulars" heard voices and noise below and saw the occasional flicker of a kerosene lamp. The robbers had found a hypogeum cut into the face of a cliff and were hard at work. The tomb's opening was cleverly concealed 130 feet from the top of the cliff and 220 feet from the floor of the valley.

Studying the scene, Carter observed that the thieves had descended to the opening by a worn rope. He cut the rope, then secured his own stout line and shinnied down until he was parallel with the tomb's opening, dangling in space. "Shinnying down a rope at midnight into a nestful of industrious tomb-robbers," he recalled dryly, "is a pastime which at least does not lack excitement." Eight thieves were at work; at his sudden appearance, they dropped their tools in shock. "There was an awkward moment or two," Carter said.

He boldly offered them a choice: either ascend on his rope or remain where they were. They probably recognized him. After twenty years in Upper Egypt, the former chief inspector of antiquities was known in every village; more important, in this situation, he was also respected. The culprits departed peacefully—and Carter never reported them to the authorities.

To Carter's utter amazement, given the location of the tomb, he entered a lateral passageway that ran straight into the cliff for 55 feet and then opened onto a stairway. In a periodic report to Carnarvon to keep him abreast of developments in Egypt, Carter wrote, "I found that they had burrowed into it like rabbits as far as the sepulchral hall. The burrow made by them was some twenty-nine meters long and would allow but one man to pass at a time and then only by creeping upon his stomach. They had widened and deepened the burrow for further operations."

On his return to Luxor, Carter promptly notified the antiquities service in Cairo of the discovery and, with the approval of British headquarters, the department arranged for him to carry on at the spot.

For the next twenty days, relays of fellahin labored day and night to clear the tunnel and chamber. The job was arduous and dangerous. Because coming and going by a single rope was impractical for a large body of workers, Carter jerry-rigged an "elevator" that operated on pulleys. "For anyone who suffers from vertigo," he remarked later, "it certainly was not pleasant." He himself always made the descent in a net!

As the work progressed, excitement at the camp rose. Surely so well-hidden a tomb, Carter reasoned, must be intact and must contain wonderful treasure. But the tomb contained only an empty, crystalline sandstone sarcophagus, which bore hieratic inscriptions and the cartouche of Hatshepsut, whose body had already been found in the Valley of the Tombs.

In hieroglyphics he read the queen's moving, eloquent appeal: "Place me among the stars imperishable . . . that I may not die."

Clearly, this was the original tomb of the radiant queen of the terraced temple of Deir-el-Bahari, who usurped the throne at her husband's death and proclaimed herself pharaoh. "It is to be presumed," Carter wrote in a report that appeared in the *Journal of Egyptian Archaeology* in 1917, "that on her definite adoption of the dignity and predicates of the pharaohs, this great queen felt it beneath her dignity to be buried in the distant spot consecrated to the royal *harim,* and transferred her sepulchre to the same valley which was to become the regular burial place of the kings of the Eighteenth Dynasty."

If she had been buried in this secret place, her mummy would have remained undisturbed, at least into the early part of the twentieth century, three and one-half millennia later. Then it would have been plucked clean. A pharaoh she would be, Carter mused, and a pharaoh's fate she shared.

But how in the name of Aten (or Amen) did the ancient Egyptians cut the tunnel halfway up the face of the cliff? How did they move the sarcophagus, which weighed tons and whose lid alone measured six and one-half feet by two and one-half feet, into the burial chamber? The engineering feat was as puzzling as it was astounding.

"I have endeavored to discover whether it was lowered into the tomb from the cliff above or whether it was hauled up from the valley below," Carter said, "but I have been unable to discover indications pointing either way. Far away on the lower foothills west of the valley, I think I can trace a possible road by which it may have been brought, but the traces are too slight to be more than hypothetical."

The excitement surrounding the discovery incited Carter to transfer his search for an intact tomb from the Valley of the Tombs to the adjacent Kurna hills.

With his band of *reises* and unreported deserters from the labor battalions, he undertook extensive soundings in the area at Carnarvon's expense and with the approval of the wartime authorities in Cairo. He uncovered potsherds of the Eighteenth Dynasty—Tutankhamen's dynasty—and fragments of granite, basalt, crystalline sandstone, and alabaster, the raw materials frequently found in and near Egyptian burial grounds. He also took rubbings of many inscriptions carved into the cliffs and chiseled "H.C. 1916" alongside them so that future explorers would know that they were already copied and cataloged. The initials, a lasting monument to his life and times in Upper Egypt, are still there. "On one of the ancient roads of the upper plateau," he wrote matter-of-factly, "I picked up a large copper coin of Ptolemy II Philadelphus."

But these finds were lowlights. As in the past, he wrote Carnarvon with an air of disappointment, "in this small valley I have been unable to find any traces of [intact] tombs." Nevertheless, he returned to the Kurna hills in early 1917 and pressed his dig. The end result was the same, and he ruefully concluded, "Though at present there are no visible traces, I believe there must be other tombs in this bay." His report was accompanied by a map, which illustrated the relationship of the Kurna hills to the Valley of the Kings and identified important finds in both places. There was a notable exception. Carter did not put an X to mark the spot where Davis contended he had found the tomb of Tutankhamen.

At this point, Carter realized, as sometimes happens to one in the midst of research, that he had backed off the main track and, out of curiosity, wound up on a siding. That summer, with the Americans now in the war and the Central Powers hard-pressed along the western front, Carter went back to the main line. "In the autumn of 1917 our real campaign in the Valley opened," he wrote in the 1923 edition of *The Tomb of Tutankh-amen*, employing the modest first person plural. By describing the new expedition as "our real campaign," he implied that all their other campaigns constituted an idle effort, which was hardly the case. Most likely, Carter hoped to keep up Carnarvon's spirit—and keep up the flow of pounds from his treasury.

"The difficulty," Carter said later, "was to know where to begin, for mountains of rubbish thrown out by previous excavators encumbered the ground in all directions." Worse, no sort of record had ever been kept as to which areas had been properly excavated and which had not.

For a start, he tackled the square encompassing the known and plundered tombs of Rameses II and VI and Merneptah. He drew blanks. The following year, with the war over, Carnarvon joined him; and, in a renewed burst of ardor, the pair spent the next seven months digging in the Valley. They found nothing.

In 1919 they made their first important postwar find, a cache of thirteen alabaster jars bearing the names of Rameses II, the widely acknowledged pharaoh of the Captivity, and Merneptah, his successor and the ostensible pharaoh of Exodus. Both had lived centuries *after* Tutankhamen. "As this was the nearest approach to a real find that we had yet made in the Valley," Carter later wrote, "we were naturally somewhat excited."

Lady Carnarvon had joined them for this campaign, and Carter said, "I remember [she] insisted on digging out these jars—beautiful specimens they were—with her own hands."

The 1920 campaign was launched with fervor, given their minor success the year before. They spent eight months digging daily—in terrible heat and on inhospitable terrain. The following year, they dug for seven months. They found nothing, absolutely nothing. "We were again disappointed," Carnarvon told friends.

Was Davis right after all? Had he really found Tutankhamen's empty, plundered tomb? Was that the last tomb to be found in the Valley? Doubts even plagued the optimist Carter from time to time. "We had now dug in the Valley for several seasons with extremely scanty results," he wrote, "and it became a much debated question whether we should continue the work, or try for a more profitable site elsewhere."

After these barren years, were they justified in going on with it? Carter later observed, "We had worked for months at a stretch and found nothing, and only an excavator knows how desperately depressing that can be." And, he continued, "we had almost made up our minds that we were beaten . . . " The operative word is *almost*.

Stubbornly, Carter clung to the slender hope that his powers of deduction would win the day, that an inviolate pharaoh's tomb was yet to be found—Tutankhamen's—and that he would find it.

The year 1922 was eventually at hand, fifteen years and $250,000 after Carnarvon first took up Egyptology. He reached the decision at Highclere to abandon the whole business—only to be trapped by Carter into organizing one last dig in the vaunted Valley of the Tombs of the Kings.

As their close friend and colleague, the English Egyptologist Sir Alan Gardiner, put it, Carter's return to Upper Egypt in the autumn of 1922 was his "last chance."

As it turned out, all else was prologue.

Part II

THE DISCOVERY

CHAPTER 5

Before his departure from England, Carter casually mentioned to Carnarvon and others, including friends at the British Museum, that after living alone in Egypt for thirty years, he planned to return with a companion.

Cairo's foreign community was agog with speculation that October. Who was she? British, of course. Where had he met her? Nobody could recall a woman in his life until then. Well, as they said, life begins at forty. Most probably a sudden encounter.

At the Messageries Maritimes dock in Alexandria, Carter stepped off a French steamer with her in hand; that is, her cage. The "she" turned out to be a gold canary that chirped happily and sang almost incessantly.

On October 28 the odd couple arrived at Luxor, and the canary's cage was suspended from a stand on the second floor veranda of "Castle Carter." The house was situated between Carnarvon's and the Nile, within a thousand yards of the former. The internal layout of both bungalows (or mausoleums) was about the same, although Carter's cottage had one dome to Carnarvon's two and Carter's house was situated on a lower rise than Carnarvon's. When the two houses were viewed within one perspective, their size and location seemed to reflect the higher and lower social statuses of their owners at the time of their construction in the days of a still heavily stratified Edwardian England. In one respect, however, Carter's house was far superior: on the south side it boasted three trees, a thorny, small-leaved acacia, and a couple of tamarisks, which required little moisture and provided excellent shade. Carnarvon usually tethered his donkeys, with Carter's, in the shade of those trees, the only touch of green—of life—between the riverine village of El Gournah and the barren, desolate Valley of the Tombs.

After arriving home on the west bank of the Nile, Carter spent the next several days arranging for the movement of fresh supplies into the Valley, working out the payroll for his new labor force, conferring with his *reises*, and so forth. On November 3, with his frayed map of the Valley in hand, Carter outlined to his new assistant, A. R. "Pecky" Callender, who took up his residence at "Castle Carter," the final campaign. They were to excavate exclusively around the entrance to the tomb of Rameses VI, concentrating on the spot where some old artisans' huts of the Twentieth Dynasty (circa 1181 B.C.) protruded from the sand. Twice before Carter had been deterred from digging at this location—which was only 100 yards from the spot where Theodore Davis, in 1907, found the funerary cache he mistakenly identified as Tutankhamen's tomb.

In an experiment that evening, the gallabiya-clad men removed enough sand from the location to indicate that they would have to clear the area to about three feet to reach bedrock. Carter ordered his labor force to dig a trench right through the spot. Arrangements were completed for the work to begin at daybreak the following day.

Most archaeological digs, including Carter's, follow a set pattern. The moment a pickman finds something of interest, he notifies the nearest *reis*. The foreman, taking pick or shovel in hand, satisfies himself as to what was found and either instructs the man to carry on or, in turn, summons the field archaeologist. As Sir Charles Leonard Woolley, the excavator of Ur of the Chaldees, once observed, "The Arab foreman is, next to the archaeologist, himself, the most important person on the excavation, for on him depends the conduct of the whole gang of diggers."

On the morning of November 4, 1922, Carter rose shortly before dawn and took his customary tea on the veranda, feeding his cheerful yellow companion a small biscuit. Then he set off for the dig. But as he approached, he was greeted with complete silence. All work had stopped. The turbaned foreman, Ahmed Gurgar, who possessed a quaint but excellent command of English, was impatiently waiting for him, a group of fellahin clustered nearby. They had begun work about forty-five minutes earlier and had cleared the first hut for about two feet when they came upon a step cut directly into the limestone bedrock.

With Carter and Callender, who had now joined the group, supervising the operation, the workmen cleared the step completely. Creamy white, the first step led to another and then another, descending deeper and deeper into the floor of the Valley. Without the usual midday break, the work party labored on through the day, a fiery sun overhead, and into the cool twilight. "Think of it," Carter often said afterwards. "Twice before I had come within a yard or two of that first step."

Sifting the limestone chips that blocked their way, chip for chip, Carter and his men had cleared sixteen steps by the following day. Suddenly, astoundingly, their way was blocked by a sealed wooden door. The door bore the clay impressions of the high priests of the royal necropolis, a couchant jackal with nine prostrate prisoners. Anything, Carter realized, *anything* might lie behind that door. His first wild impulse was to smash the seals and tear down the door. But in the end, Carter, the archaeologist, the man of training, triumphed over the impulsive man of action.

To the utter astonishment of Callender, the *reises*, and the workmen, he ordered the staircase and entrance refilled with debris (mostly limestone chips), posted Callender at the spot with a loaded rifle, and ordered the *reises* to construct a wooden hut nearby for sentries. Then he rushed off for Luxor and arranged with the local authorities to have armed soldiers from the Sudanese Camel Coast Guard brought to the scene. These details completed, on November 6 he sent off to Highclere, from the Eastern Telegraph Company's office, the following cable: AT LAST HAVE MADE A WONDERFUL DISCOVERY IN VALLEY. MAGNIFICENT TOMB WITH SEALS INTACT. RECOVERED SAME FOR YOUR ARRIVAL. CONGRATULATIONS.

Carnarvon was at dinner when the cable arrived. He promptly telephoned Gardiner, who later recounted the subsequent conversation to Leonard Cottrell, a writer on archaeology who is best know for his work with the B.B.C. "When Carnarvon had told me the news," Gardiner recalled, "his first question was, 'Do you think this could be the tomb of Tutankhamen?'" Gardiner was noncommittal.

In those days, it usually took a fortnight to make the journey by boat from Liverpool to Alexandria. Carnarvon spent the next day arranging passage on the first available steamer. On November 8 he dispatched the following cable to Luxor: PROPOSE ARRIVE ALEXANDRIA TWENTIETH.

For Carter, the ecstasy of discovery turned into two weeks of almost unbearable torment. He was too excited to eat or sleep properly. After each restless night he revisited the scene of the discovery, but there was, of course, nothing to see, no tangible evidence of the find except the picturesque detachment of armed camel coastguardsmen with the stolid Callender in command. "The tomb had vanished," Carter later wrote, " . . . and I found it hard to persuade myself at times that the whole episode had not been a dream." On November 18, Carter left for Cairo to greet Carnarvon, who was accompanied on this historic journey, not by his wife, but, as usual, by his daughter, Lady Evelyn.

Gentleman and loyalist that he was, as fitting tribute to his friend and benefactor, Carter erected on the site of the discovery a slab of rough stone, shaped like a stele, on which he drew in black paint a crude representation of the House of Herbert's coat of arms, a crest with three lions rampant, a panther with flames issuing from the mouth and ears, and a roaring lion standing upright on its hind legs. The crest bore the legend: *Ung je serviray* ("One I shall serve").

CHAPTER 6

In anticipation of Carnarvon's impending arrival, Carter ordered the staircase reexcavated November 23. The following afternoon, Carnarvon and his twenty-one-year-old daughter, in a broad-brimmed, black hat (she preferred that color, the repressive sun of Upper Egypt notwithstanding), reached the Valley. Both were in an understandably acute state of excitability, their British reserve jettisoned.

Closely reexamined, the sealed door had two different sets of seals. One bore the cartouches of Tutankhamen, both his nomen and prenomen;

the other belonged to the officials who policed the royal necropolis. Hope was dashed when minute inspection of the door revealed that its bottom half had been rebuilt. Carter was mortified: the tomb had undoubtedly been broken into and then resealed in antiquity. Like Cinderella's golden coach at midnight, Carter's great discovery dissolved into a pumpkin.

With utmost care, Carter removed the seals and systematically dismantled the door, taking measurements and other notes and preserving as much of the door as possible for later reexamination. Behind the door, burrowed deeper into the earth, lay a passageway, dark and forbidding, blocked up with limestone chips. After a night's digging, Carter and Carnarvon cleared the passage. Among the rubble, they recovered fragments of broken boxes, vases, and jars—plunderers had beat them to it again. "Damn it," Carter cursed softly, convinced that they had found only the entrance to a funerary cache similar to Davis's discovery.

Then, on November 26, 1922, Carter went through what he later described as "the day of days, the most wonderful that I have ever lived through." In midafternoon, thirty feet from the outer door, the last stone chips were removed from the tunnel—revealing a second sealed door. It bore only the seals of Tutankhamen.

The moment of truth was at hand. Painstakingly, Carter made a small opening in the second door, and, his hand trembling slightly, he thrust in an iron testing-rod. The rod struck nothing. Whatever lay behind that door, was not filled with debris. As a test for noxious gases, Carter widened the breach and inserted a lighted candle. It flickered briefly as a rush of hot, entrapped air poured through the opening. But the candle remained lit. There was no poison gas behind the door; there was oxygen. Oxygen meant there was life. Just as death could not be avoided above the ground, apparently life could not be eluded below the ground.

His hands now trembling uncontrollably, Carter again widened the breach, reinserted the candle, and this time poked his head in. He was, as he remarked later, "dumbstruck with amazement." An eternity passed. He was paralyzed, speechless.

Carnarvon stood behind him, impatiently waiting for a firsthand report. "A long silence followed," Carnarvon recounted later, "until I said, I fear in somewhat trembling tones, 'Well, what is it?'"

Both men recalled different replies. Carter said, "It was all I could do to get out the words, 'Yes, wonderful things!'" Later that year he explained: "As my eyes grew accustomed to the light, details of the room within emerged slowly from the mist, strange animals, statues, and gold—everywhere the glint of gold."

Carnarvon remembered a slightly different response. He said Carter replied, "There are some marvellous objects here!"

Lord Carnarvon stepped chivalrously aside to permit his daughter to take the next peek into the kaleidoscope of the dawn of civilization. She did so and gasped. Then Carnarvon took his turn, while a dazed Carter and a dumbstruck Lady Evelyn stood transfixed. "At first sight, with the inadequate light," Carnarvon said, "all one could see was what appeared to be gold bars!"

Egyptologist Arthur Weigall, apparently drawing on Pecky Callender's recollection of the historic scene, offers a slightly different account.

"Wonderful! Marvellous!" Carter is said to have exclaimed as Carnarvon pulled at his arm, shouting, "Hey! let me have a look." But Carter was immobilized by astonishment at all he saw.

"At last," Weigall wrote, "Mr. Carter was pulled from the hole, so the scene was jestingly represented to me, 'like a cork from a bottle,' and Lord Carnarvon took his place."

Whatever the case, the party's immediate impulse was to rip down the door and rush pell-mell into the antechamber and touch the gold before the mirage disappeared, to fondle the gleaming bars as tangible proof that they were not living through a fantasy.

Some archaeologists refuse to admit it, but the spirit of the treasure hunt pervades the discipline. To his credit, Carter conceded the point forthrightly in *The Tomb of Tut-ankh-amen,* the classic account of the discovery he published the following year. The first sensation on entering a tomb, he wrote, is that time is annihilated and you are an intruder. Other sensations quickly follow—"the exhilaration of discovery, the fever of suspense, the almost overmastering impulse, born of curiosity, to break down the seals and lift the lids of boxes, the thought—pure joy to the investigator—that you are about to add a page of history, or solve some problem of research, the strained expectancy—why not confess it?—of the treasure-seeker."

Carter, Carnarvon, and his daughter had seen something incredible: the antechamber was packed, helter-skelter, with alabaster jars, strangely shaped boxes, gilt-covered furniture, including three colossal gilt couches with the heads of animals (which Carnarvon mistakenly took for "gold bars"), magnificent faience vases, statues and statuettes in gold and alabaster, golden chariots and a gold throne with exquisite, inlaid semiprecious stones depicting Tutankhamen and his lovely queen, Ankhesenpaaten—a tableau that has since ranked as one of the world's greatest known works of art.

On the right-hand side of the room, along the north wall, the onlookers could see two life-sized statues of the king. These monarchial sentinels, facing each other, were attired in gold sandals and gold skirts. They brandished golden staves. Upon each of their foreheads was the sacred uraeus, the coiled cobra, whose magic powers had protected the tomb for more than thirty-three centuries.

Carnarvon, like Carter, fought to control his impatience. "It was a severe tax on one's curiosity not to demolish part of the door," he later admitted.

On a personal level, the discovery meant different things to each man. Archaelogy aside, for Carnarvon it meant that he would recoup losses spread over almost twenty years. For Carter, it meant that he had at last come into his own; he, the commoner, was now rightfully Carnarvon's peer.

Howard Carter promptly exercised leadership. He redoubled the guard at the entrance; sent to Cairo for a steel door to be shipped to Luxor by train (then, as now, a journey of twelve or more hours); and hired his own platoon of ghaffirs, or watchmen, to watch over the guards who were guarding the tomb, in the hope of resolving the age-old problem: *Quis custodet custodes?*

He also issued an appeal for outside help, cabling A. M. Lythgoe, curator of Egyptology of the Metropolitan Museum of Art: "DISCOVERY COLOSSAL AND NEED EVERY ASSISTANCE . . ." The cable, partly garbled, is still in the possession of the Metropolitan in New York. In it, Carter specifically requested the services of Harry Burton, the Museum's staff photographer, who was then a member of the Metropolitan's expedition at the adjoining site in the Theban necropolis.

Lythgoe promptly cabled back: "ONLY TOO DELIGHTED TO ASSIST IN ANY POSSIBLE WAY." Thereupon, the Metropolitan's team descended on the Valley and put themselves selflessly at Carter's disposal. Among them was the aforementioned Winlock, then the leader of the expedition; Burton; and A. C. Mace, Petrie's nephew. It was a refreshing example of international cooperation in a field given to academic and national jealousies.

Among others who rushed to Biban-el-Moluk was the intrepid James Henry Breasted, accompanied by his son, Charles. "All my life I shall remember the picture," the son wrote in his memoirs, describing his descent with his father, Carter, and Winlock down the sixteen steps into that other world. "Through the steel bars we saw an incredible vision," he said, "an impossible scene from a fairy tale."

His father and Winlock, he recalled, turned and looked into Carter's face. Words failed the trio, and tears streamed from their eyes. They shook hands and, in a state of wild hysteria, broke into uncontrollable laughter.

Charles Breasted wrote that his first and lasting impression of the cache was the fantastically superb quality of the art and craftmanship of the ancient Egyptians, a craftmanship that made a mockery of Lorenzo Ghiberti and Benvenuto Cellini, artistic detail that surpassed Albrecht Dürer. "It made me fairly dizzy," he wrote.

An uneasiness that they could not articulate also overcame them, a mood that Carter had earlier described as the feeling of the "intruder." This sentiment persists in Egyptology to this very day. Working among the dead perhaps makes it unavoidable.

"There is something peculiarly sensational in the examining of a tomb which has not been entered for some thousands of years," wrote Weigall, Theodore Davis's former aide, in 1923, after a visit to Tutankhamen's tomb. "One cannot describe the silence, the echoing steps, the dark shadows; the hot breathless air; nor tell of the sense of lost time and the penetrating of it which moves one so deeply."

Breasted, in particular, entertained extraordinary experiences within the tomb. Left in the antechamber to study, decipher, and copy the 150 almost illegible seal impressions on the walls, working alone and in silence, he suddenly heard strange rustling and murmuring sounds that rose and fell. For a moment, fear spread through him, and he had the impulse to flee. But the sounds were not those of ghosts, he reasoned; there had to be an explanation. Suddenly he hit upon it: the injection of fresh air into the hermetically sealed room had altered the antechamber's temperature and humidity. Wooden articles like the spoked chariot wheels and the furniture groaned, creaked, and snapped as they adjusted themselves to the new atmosphere.

But for Breasted, the most terrifying experience was yet to unfold. In a scene out of the last act of Mozart's *Don Giovanni,* when the statue of the Commendatore comes to life to summon Giovanni into hell, Breasted reported a "curious incident."

As he labored over the seals in the half-dusk, he happened to glance up at the face of one of the royal, life-sized sentinels. Unmistakably, he saw the eyes move. "For a moment," he later wrote his son, Charles, "this was strangely disturbing." That moment must have lasted an eternity. Once again he sought a rational explanation—and realized that as the humidity and temperature in the antechamber altered, some of the pigment used in coloring the eyes of the twin statues dropped off in iridescent, shiny, mica-sized flakes. The flakes caught and reflected the light from his flashlight and gave the statues a frightening animation.

Eventually, a triumphant, albeit shaken, Breasted emerged with exciting news. The seals on the walls were indeed those of Tutankhamen. Thieves had broken into the antechamber, as Carter feared, but they had been caught, and the tomb had been resealed. There was a reasonable chance, therefore, that the rest of the tomb was still intact.

At this point, Carter and the others realized that the most important object of all was missing from among the jumble of articles in the antechamber—the mummy of the king. Then they made another astounding find. Between the sentinels of the king was the bare outline of a plastered-over, hidden door. Behind that secret door, they surmised, lay the mummy of the pharaoh. "My God!" Carter exclaimed.

In their first joint public statement, issued on December 3, 1922, and written by Carter, the discoverers boldly declared, "We shall find Pharaoh Tutankhamen." They then gave a detailed description of what lay beyond the secret door. This foreknowledge confounded many observers and started rumors that the pair had been led to the spot by some secret papyrus rolls that had somehow fallen into their hands. In truth, they had reached their conclusions on the basis of having studied the Turin, Abbott, Meyer and Amherst papyri. The Turin papyri, for example, specifically stated that the mummy of a pharaoh was housed not in one coffin but in the nest of three coffins, like a Chinese puzzle. Of course, nobody had ever found a mummy in such a state.

"We know that the custom was that the king would not only be buried in his sarcophagus enclosed in the three coffins, but that the sarcophagus itself was protected by a series of funeral canopies which, from the details in these papyri, seemed to have been constructed of wood," they said in their statement. Avoiding the use of the tantalizing word "gold," the pair forecast that within these canopies or shrines, within the sarcophagus, within the three coffins, "we shall be confronted with an unimaginably rich . . . result."

And Carter inserted a commonplace Moslem expletive into the statement. "*Inshallah* (May it please God), our expectations will be realized."

Invited by the London *Times* to write an article about their discovery, Carnarvon rushed into print with Carter's conclusion. In the article, Carnarvon wrote: "There is little doubt behind this wall there exists a chamber of chambers, and in one of those probably reposes, in his coffins and sarcophagus, the body of King Tutankhamen." Carnarvon used the plural, "coffins," as had Carter in the joint statement.

Part of the Valley of the Kings, the ancient royal necropolis of Thebes, in Upper Egypt. The entrance to the tomb of Rameses VI is at center. The opening to Tutankhamen's tomb had been hidden by the debris of the huts of workmen and artisans who worked on the tomb of Rameses VI.

The second coffin within the first (outside), shown with rigging for removal. In cramped quarters, the job of opening Tutankhamen's tomb was complicated.

When the lid of the second coffin was raised, the sight Carter beheld left him numb. The third, and last, coffin, weighing 2,248 pounds, was of solid gold.

The back of the funerary mask of the young pharaoh. The mask, made of gold, was placed over the head and shoulders of the mummy. Below, the antechamber contained a jumble of articles. The disorder was created by tomb robbers in antiquity.

Howard Carter, left, and Lord Carnarvon wrapping up one of the two statues of Tutankhamen found in the antechamber. The mummy of the young king, right, was in an advanced state of decay, probably due to a too lavish use of oils and unguents.

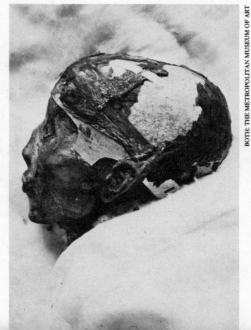

So meticulous were Carter and Carnarvon in their work that it took the party ten weeks to photograph, draw to scale, and remove, piece by piece, each object from the antechamber. With the room cleared, the group was confronted by the mysterious seven-foot-high door that had been guarded by the life-sized sentinels.

Carter had a raised platform built at the base of the door and a series of wall supports erected on either side like the reinforcement of a coal mine facing. Then on Feburary 16, 1923, he and Carnarvon and the rest of the team reassembled in the empty antechamber. "Carnarvon was pale as he stepped slowly into the darkness and was lost in the shadows of ancient Egypt," a London *Daily Express* correspondent wrote from a vantage point outside the entrance to the tomb. "No matter how little superstitious a man may be, the act of breaking into a tomb must cause an emotion which time can never efface."

Within the antechamber, Carter mounted the scaffold, sledgehammer in hand. As he struck the wall, the sound reverberated through the stillness of the underground vault. He worked for ten minutes, his white shirt drenched with perspiration. He had hammered out a small opening along the lintel of the doorway, a jagged hole large enough to take a flashlight. The beams of his Eveready played, in his own words, "on a solid wall of gold!"

It proved to be a gilded shrine of wood. The sepulchral chamber was 21 by 13 feet, the gleaming catafalque, or canopy, 17 x 11 feet. It all but filled the burial room, with a space of only 2 feet separating it from the walls on all four sides; above, it almost brushed the chamber's ceiling.

Then, along the right wall, beyond the burial chamber, he found the entranceway to another room, later dubbed the "treasury." Within it, Carter discovered the Canopic chest containing the king's viscera, guarded by four delicate little golden goddesses sculptured in transparent gowns; a great effigy of Anubis, the jackal god; strange-shaped, oviform boxes; golden chariots; and a heap of objects, looking like large white eggs, thrown under a gilded piece of furniture. As for the latter, Carter later explained to the press that they contained food for the dead— trussed ducks, haunches of mutton, all mummified. "The Egyptians," Carter said, "boxed food as Americans tin it today."

And Sir Alan Gardiner, who was a member of the party that memorable day, recalled to Cottrell his own impressions. "Beyond the burial chamber we found on the right the entrance to another room. . . . It was full of marvels . . . [including] a number of caskets. Carter opened one of these and on the top lay a beautiful ostrich-feather fan. The feathers were perfect, fluffing out just as if they had recently been plucked. Those feathers completely annihilated the centuries for me. It was as if the king had been buried a few days before . . . they made on me an impression such as I had never experienced before and never shall again."

It was a refrain echoed by each member of the party.

Said Weigall, who was present as the wall was breached: "There was something very solemn, and even tragic, in this awakening of the once great king now when his empire was long fallen to pieces and his glory departed. And as I took my place at the mouth of the tomb I felt, if I may say without affectation, a sense of deep sadness weighing upon me."

A number of those on hand, overwrought by the excitement of the moment, became jocular under stress. When cane chairs were carried down into the empty antechamber for the special observers, Carnarvon joked that it looked as if he and Carter were preparing to give a concert. "His words, though of little moment, distressed me, for I was absorbed, as it were, in my own thoughts, which were anything but jocular," Weigall recalled. "And I turned to the man next to me and said, 'If he goes down in that spirit, I give him six weeks to live.' I do not know why I said it . . ."

By now, of course, Carter and Carnarvon realized that they had arrived at the end of the rainbow and that there was indeed a pot of gold. Realizing that the discovery would draw the attention of every grave robber in Egypt, Carter moved to outwit them. In addition to the armed guards ensconced in the Valley, he arranged for the installation of a new, electrically charged steel door at the mouth of the tomb. A warning was issued: "Any tomb-robber who touches the door will be killed instantly."

Carter and Carnarvon also decided to end the season. Within a few days, the temperature in the Valley would rise above 100°F, and, until the following October, it would be humanly impossible to work in the suffocating, stifling rock tomb. Indeed, one newspaper correspondent reported that when Carnarvon emerged from the tomb on February 16, "he came up slowly into the air looking grey and old."

Accordingly, on February 26, the tomb was officially closed; scores of fellahin, acting as a fire-bucket brigade, discharged basket after basket of sand and limestone chips into the shaft. A cloud of dust hovered over the site, and from a distance, according to one eyewitness, a plume of "cloud-like smoke as from a great fire" rose over the Valley. Carter then busied himself for the next two months crating the objects for shipment to the Cairo Museum. In a neat hand, he wrote up a descriptive index card for each item.

Between the discovery of the tomb's first limestone step in November and the discovery of the shrines in February, the worlds of Carter and Carnarvon turned topsy-turvy. Just as Tutankhamen never rested in peace again, neither would they.

When news of the discovery of the tomb swept up and down the Nile, the fellahin attributed the find to Carter's pet canary. "The golden bird has done it," the villagers said. "The bird has led him to the tomb." Indeed, the Egyptians dubbed the sepulcher "the Tomb of the Bird."

Shortly after the discovery, however, a soft cry—"almost human," Breasted senior said—was heard from Carter's house. A cobra had slithered onto the veranda and entered the bird's cage. Among the Egyptians, the incident was widely viewed as an ill omen. "The serpent from the crown of the king has swallowed the golden bird," they lamented. The fellahin were convinced that the king's uraeus had struck to avenge itself against the bird for betraying the secret of the tomb.

Nor was it only the fellahin who drew this conclusion. The world's press splashed the story on the front page; *The New York Times* termed the canary-cobra affair "an interesting incident."

For the record, in Luxor and its environs today, there is another story still in circulation about the discovery of the tomb and the death of the canary. "Carter," an aged resident, who was thirteen at the time, told me emphatically in early 1975, "does not deserve the incredible fame he had achieved."

According to this version, a British soldier during World War I purchased a roll of papyrus from an Egyptian farmer who had found it accidentally. Later Carter acquired the roll. The soldier could not read it, but Carter could. The papyrus pinpointed the location of Tutankhamen's tomb and even listed its contents. Thereafter, keeping the knowledge of the papyrus a secret to himself, Carter concentrated his search around Rameses' tomb. It was not until 1922 that he succeeded in removing the thousands upon thousands of tons of limechips that covered the area. It was then that the tomb was "discovered."

Moreover, my informant declared, shortly before, in the course of a trip to Cairo, Carter visited the Khan-el-Khalili, the fourteenth-century marketplace that still ranks as among the most spectacular oriental bazaars in the Near East. For a reason that even Carter could not fathom, he was attracted to a canary at a bird dealer's stall. The merchant realized that Carter found the canary irresistible and, accordingly, sold the ten-piaster bird for 100 piasters (one Egyptian pound). On the day Carter "discovered" the tomb of Tutankhamen, a six-and-a-half-foot-long cobra—so the story goes—emerged from the tomb and killed the canary. "The yellow bird shrieked so loudly that its cries reverberated through the hills of Biban-el-Moluk," the Luxor resident recalled. Tradition, he added, held that Tutankhamen's queen was the last to leave the tomb and that she carried the robes of mourning on which there was a scarab bearing the drawing of a golden bird. "Tutankhamen's soul did not die on the day Carter broke into the burial chamber," I was told with great sincerity. "It died on the same day as the canary, with the discovery of the golden shrines." My informant attributed these fantastic events to the powerful magic practiced by the high priests of ancient Egypt, especially Tutankhamen's successor, Ay, the grand vizier at the time, who held power briefly before General Harmhab usurped the throne.

Whatever the case, the consensus, then as now, was that the bird's death was a disquieting development. "There was almost universal concern," wrote Breasted more than a half-century ago, "that something terrible will happen."

Part III

THE AFTERMATH

CHAPTER 7

News of the tomb's discovery traveled more than the length and breadth of the Nile. Wild rumors soon followed: three airplanes were said to have landed clandestinely in the Valley, loaded up with treasure, and taken off for a secret destination. Another rumor held that several mummies were found in the tomb, each covered with gold. Some said there were three mummies; others, eight.

With a view to "overtaking these rumors," as Carter termed it, he and Carnarvon decided to have a formal opening of the tomb on November 29, 1922. They invited a number of senior British and Egyptian officials and, from the press, the Cairo correspondent of the London *Times,* Arthur Merton.

In young Breasted's memoirs there is evidence that whereas Carnarvon favored admitting only the *Times* reporter to the tomb, Carter leaned towards a general invitation to Cairo's press, including both Egyptian and foreign correspondents. Whatever the case, the first story about the discovery, written from within the tomb, was a London *Times* exclusive. Merton, characterizing the find as "the most sensational discovery of the century," said, "The remarkable discovery announced today is the reward of patience, perseverance and perspicacity."

Reuters, the principal British news agency, and also the Egyptian and the world press, caught with their headlines down, recouped their loss the following day. In a Cairo dispatch, Reuters described the discovery as "astounding" and quoted Egyptologists terming the tomb's contents "beyond the dreams of avarice." The treasure found in the antechamber alone, the news agency reported, was worth "millions of pounds sterling." The American Associated Press described the find as "the most sensational in Egyptology" and reported "important papyri were also found" (as it later developed, to the dismay of Egyptologists, no papyrus was ever found).

With these dispatches in print, the journalistic dam burst; and shortly thereafter, in the manner of the protagonists in Evelyn Waugh's brilliant *Scoop,* to mix a metaphor, the world's press descended on the Valley like owls hunting nocturnal rodents.

To reach the Valley, correspondents had to ferry across the Nile, and enterprising newsmen hired by the month the few feluccas available— riverboats with lateen sails, which had been working the Nile even before Tutankhamen's day. As news of the shoreside boom at Luxor spread up and down the river, a veritable flotilla of feluccas converged on the scene. To some it looked like a new Battle of the Nile was underway.

Once across the river, on the west bank, the intrepid correspondents found that the principal mode of travel to the Valley was by donkey, a journey of six miles, which took a half-hour or more. At the site of the dig, chaos reigned. The London *Daily Telegraph* described the setting as reminiscent of Derby Day. "When the day's work was completed [at the tomb], involving the careful removal of treasure from the antechamber," the paper reported, "correspondents began a spirited dash across the desert to the banks of the Nile upon donkeys, horses, camels, and chariot- like sandcarts in a race to be the first to reach the telegraph office."

By the time the vanguard of the world's press descended on Luxor in mid-December, Carnarvon had left for England to report the discovery directly to the king. During an audience with George V at Buckingham Palace on December 22, a spokesman solemnly disclosed later, the king "listened with great interest to a description of the important discoveries made recently by him and Mr. Howard Carter as the culmination of the excavations which they have carried on for nearly sixteen years." Carnarvon, the spokesman said, assured the king that the mummy of the pharaoh would be found when each of the gilded shrines was dismantled, something yet to be done.

Carter, the commoner, was never invited to Buckingham Palace. Nor did he even make the New Year's Honors List, although such obscure personages made it in January 1923 as the head of the customs department in New Zealand.

For that matter, King Fuad of Egypt decorated neither Carnarvon nor Carter for their work, although, in a formal statement, he lavishly praised them. "The names of Lord Carnarvon and of Mr. Carter and of their zealous collaborators whom I am delighted to congratulate on their brilliant success," he said, "will remain ever linked with the archaeological splendor of our ancient country, and Egypt will always retain for them feelings of deepest gratitude."

Significantly, perhaps, on the very day that George V granted Carnarvon an audience, Carter flung open the tomb and invited all newsmen, including the "native" Egyptian press, to inspect the hypogeum firsthand.

The London *Exchange Telegraph* reported that the treasure, not counting what might be found inside the sarcophagus, was already valued by art experts at £3,000,000 ($15,000,000). And a front-page story in *The New York Times* on February 18, 1923, datelined Luxor, began, "The gem-studded cavern of Ali Baba seems to have been a trinket shop in comparison, and Aladdin's lamp never realized such treasures as the flashlights from the torches illuminated to the lucky few who entered [Tutankhamen's] mortuary chambers yesterday."

Not only was there interest in the treasure for the sake of treasure, but also excitement in religious and art circles. "As Tutankhamen lived in the period of the Exodus," one British daily declared, "perhaps there is buried with him an account of Israel and Biblical times from the Egyptian standpoint. Possibly also a full account of Akhenaten . . . [who] preached Christian doctrines."

Pierre Lacau, the French director of the department of antiquities, told the Cairo press that the discovery was the "greatest find in the history of archaeology, and probably in the history of art." And the senior Breasted openly declared, "The craftsmen of Greece were mere hacks compared to the masters who designed and adorned [Tutankhamen's] throne."

Neither Carter nor Carnarvon anticipated the world's reaction to their discovery. Clearly, they inherited a monumental public relations problem. But the problem was hardly insurmountable.

The obvious solution was to form a rotating pool at Luxor, picking the name of a correspondent out of the hat each day and having him or her cover the tomb and share the resultant report with the rest of the press. But Carnarvon, perhaps in part disposed to consider newsmen scavengers and also in part to earn a justifiable return on his enormous investment, entered into an exclusive and controversial agreement with *The Times*. He gave the London daily a news monopoly in return for £5,000 ($25,000) in cash and three-fourths of the profits from the syndication of *The Times'* reports abroad. As Carnarvon's agent, *The Times* promptly sold its coverage around the world.

Carter was horrified by his colleague's decision. "Over Carter's emphatic protests," Charles Breasted wrote later, "he [Carnarvon] presently entered into an agreement with his friend, John Jacob Astor, chairman of the London Times Company, Ltd., where *The Times* was given a world copyright on all news, pictures, etc."

"The tomb is not his [Carnarvon's] property," the London *Daily Express* howled. "He has not dug up the bones of his ancestors in the Welsh mountains. . . . By making an exclusive secret of the contents of the inner tomb he has ranged against him the majority of the world's most influential newspapers."

Six days later, on February 16, 1923, *The Times* went to Carnarvon's rescue. Critics, the paper said, had charged him "with creating a monopoly of news from Luxor, and even of commercialism [although] he supplied the news through *The Times* solely because he thought it would be the best way, in fact the only practical way, of supplying it fully and independently to all newspapers."

As the protests mounted, *The Times,* in a second defense, denounced "misleading statements" about the transaction and said "it seems desirable to place on record the fact that the financial proceeds of *The Times'* arrangement . . . are wholly devoted to the cost of the work at the tomb. The sole beneficiary is the cause of scientific research."

The Times also wheeled in a battery of "experts" to support its stand— among them, Jean Capart, secretary of the Royal Cinquantenaire Museum of Brussels and one of Belgium's outstanding Egyptologists.

"No obstacle whatever must be allowed to intervene between examination of the pharaonic treasures and the immediate distribution of the news to all the papers," Capart wrote in a special article. "If Lord Carnarvon does not give way, if he does not cancel the agreement with *The London Times,* the Egyptian government must intervene and the concession must be declared forfeit!" he continued. "One would almost think one were dreaming when one reads such things. On the contrary, archaeologists feel Carnarvon has given the public daily information through the intermediary of the greatest newspaper in the world."

Events at the tomb sometimes belied these words. For example, when an American newsreel company arrived in the Valley, a gilded chariot was in the course of being removed from the tomb. The cameramen had no sooner set up their equipment than a sheet was thrown over the chariot. The Americans complained bitterly that they were standing in a public roadway, but Carnarvon and Carter were unmoved. A European camera company proved more resourceful. After arriving in the Valley, its team perched their camera equipment atop a nearby cliff and, according to a local report, "with the aid of a telescope [undoubtedly a telescopic lens] took some pictures." Even so, the report said, "A warm discussion ensued."

By the end of the year, there was "an extraordinary invasion of visitors from the North, due, to a great extent, to the Christmas festivities"—Luxor was drawing trade from Bethlehem. An agent for the International Sleeping Car Company announced in New York that Carnarvon had guaranteed the company that American tourists would be permitted to view the tomb. (Carnarvon had promised no such thing.) But the Egyptian State Railway did open a new train service between Cairo and Luxor, officially christened "the Tutankhamen Special."

Few tourists, of course, ever negotiated the mysterious sixteen steps into the tomb. Carter made sure of that. At best, the curious clustered around the entrance to the tomb and, amid gasps of astonishment, clicked their inevitable cameras as objects were carefully removed from the tomb by the fellahin workers.

There was always a festive air around the pit entrance. Women in filmy light summer dresses ensconced themselves on the walls of the tomb—holding green, red, blue, and yellow parasols to shade them from the burning sun overhead. European men wore pith helmets; the Japanese, despite the oppressive heat, were in black suits. A sprinkling of Egyptians in flowing white gallabiyas completed the picturesque scene.

By January 1923, on the eve of Carnarvon's return from England—again, in the company of his devoted daughter, Lady Evelyn, and not his wife—a besieged Carter showed signs of strain. Terribly irritable, he frequently snapped at colleagues and workers and simply refused to talk to the press. The constant flood of "celebrities" to the tomb, the glare of the press, and the circus atmosphere had interrupted his routine. For thirty years, largely in solitude, he had labored in Upper Egypt. Now he suddenly found himself at stage center, and quite unable to work. Worse, he was inwardly infuriated by the realization that most of the visitors to the Valley were not even mildly interested in archaeology. They had come to Luxor, he wrote later, "because it is the thing to do."

Carter was especially annoyed by newsmen who, barred from the tomb by the Carnarvon agreement, seized on every scrap of news and blew it out of proportion. On one occasion, as a case in point, the perennially cloudless, blue sky of Upper Egypt turned black. Fear spread in the Valley that a rarity of rarities—a rain storm—might erupt and send tons of cascading water crashing through the chasm and into the open tomb. European and American newspapers, not privy to the London *Times*' reports, played up the angle. A New York headline read: "PANIC SPREADING: GRAVE POSSIBILITY PRICELESS ANTIQUITIES MAY BE HOPELESSLY DESTROYED BY TOMORROW."

While this commotion was in progress, a correspondent from the London *Daily Mail* reported that an attempt to photograph the treasure in the tomb *in situ* had failed completely. There was fear, he wrote, that the flashlight powder would ignite the intensely dry, inflammable wooden objects in the sepulcher, turning the tomb into a bonfire. This, of course, was nonsense.

When Carnarvon returned that January from his audience with the king at Buckingham Palace, he brought with him a new motorcar, a Ford. It was ferried across the Nile, one of the first automobiles to appear along the west bank of the Theban necropolis. The London *Times* treated it as a major event, observing that the vehicle "created no little excitement among the people." Barred from publishing its own photographs, the *Illustrated London News* had a field day with imaginative woodcuts of Carter and Carnarvon at work within the tomb. And the rest of the press kept up its assault on Carnarvon.

"So far," said the *Daily Express* at one point, "Lord Carnarvon's treatment of King Tutankhamen [is] suggestive of a gentleman who has hit upon a patent corn cure."

CHAPTER 8

A postwar upsurge of Egyptian nationalism coincided with the discovery of Tutankhamen's tomb. Its highlight was the return to Egypt in 1923 of Zaghlul Pasha, the nationalist leader who had been imprisoned by the British at Gibraltar and elsewhere. Only the year before, after riots in Cairo and the assassination of several British officials, London had sought to placate Egyptian ire by lifting the British protectorate and formally declaring the country independent—that is, except in matters of defense and foreign affairs. The Egyptians denounced this "independence" as a sham.

The country was divided politically into two camps: the popular Wafdist (nationalist) party of the returned Zaghlul was supported by a coalition of intellectuals, students, and the mass of politically credulous and unsophisticated fellahin; King Fuad was backed by the wealthy pashas and their middle-class effendi allies. In the intricate maneuvering for political advantage, each side accused the other of permitting itself to be used as a pawn by the British.

Carnarvon, as noted earlier, was largely apolitical. (Had he inherited a modicum of the brilliant political skill of his father, the fourth earl of Carnarvon, he probably would have thought twice about selling exclusive rights to a British newspaper, however prestigious a journal.) In any event, as a result of the arrangement, the Egyptian press was in the awkward position of relying on an English newspaper for stories about a marvelous discovery in its own country. The Egyptian government was as outraged as the Egyptian press. By the time Carnarvon realized his error, he felt compelled, as an English gentleman, to stand "loyally by his bargain," as one observer said. (It was this same strength of character that induced him to underwrite Carter's last expedition in the Valley of the Kings.)

To compound matters, the Egyptians felt slighted in other ways. Most of the visitors invited inside the tomb were European VIPs. A random day, picked from the visitor's log, showed that on February 12, 1923, a Tuesday, when the fellahin laborers took their traditional day of rest, thirty-four "celebrities" and "personalities" visited the tomb. Six were Egyptians.

In defense of Carnarvon and Carter, it should be observed that at first the Egyptians did not realize the significance of the discovery. A check of the Egyptian press for the first week after the discovery reveals that the story of the find was downplayed in favor of politics. But as the world beat a path to Luxor, the Egyptians, especially those studying abroad, recognized its import and felt themselves reduced to the role of spear carriers.

As they came to realize that there was nothing bogus about the treasure, Egyptian nationalists publicly advocated that the treasure be sold and the proceeds used to pay off the national debt. Indeed, in his formal statement on the discovery, in which he congratulated Carnarvon and Carter, King Fuad, in a poetic sense, had used the word *profit*. "As an Egyptian I also could not fail to reflect on the weighty inheritance which imposes on every Egyptian the duty to show himself worthy of such a great past. I am certain that this discovery is one of the greatest and most fruitful ever made, and Egypt's history will derive from it the greatest profit."

Meanwhile, a struggle was incubating over the ownership and disposition of the treasure. Earlier, overcome by euphoria, Carnarvon unintentionally touched off the battle for possession of the treasure. During his London sojourn, he told newsmen that since the tomb had been rifled in antiquity, half the treasure was his by the terms of his contract with the Egyptian government. He also indicated that he would donate part of his share to the British Museum and the Metropolitan Museum of Art.

Those remarks enraged Egyptians. *El Ahram,* an influential Egyptian journal, expressed "doubt whether the government will take the same view." And the Ministry of Public Works, of which the department of antiquities was a branch, put out an official statement that claimed the treasure on behalf of the Egyptian government.

Although regulations provided that the discoverer should receive half of the objects found in a rifled tomb, except for articles that the Egyptian government reserved for itself, the Ministry claimed that Carnarvon's license expressly provided that he should have no right to any objects that he might find. In a subtle ploy, the government appealed to Carnarvon's sense of fair play. Carnarvon, the statement alleged, had "accepted with pleasure a condition in the license that he was entitled to nothing [thereby] giving a clear proof that he did not entertain any material ambitions in the matter and that he was devoted to the service of science and art."

This was news to Carnarvon and also to Carter.

On December 23, Carter announced that he and his assistants, including the outside archaeological help he had recruited, conclusively established that the tomb had not been entered into since about twenty-five years after Tutankhamen's death, circa 1377 B.C. "When the inner [sealed] chamber is opened," Carter said with relish, "we shall find the king [unmolested] in all the magnificence of his state religion."

Cairo promptly interpreted Carter's statement to mean that the tomb itself was undisturbed and that the contents were therefore outside of Carnarvon's contract and that he was not entitled to a single object. Like the *Daily Express* before it, on the other side of the Atlantic, *The New York Times* also concluded that Carnarvon was "partly to blame" for this state of affairs because he advanced the claim that because the tomb had been rifled in antiquity, half the contents belonged to him.

Then, in the realization that part of the treasure was slipping from their grasp, museum directors rallied to Carnarvon's side. The British Museum's Sir Frederic Kenyon declared that Carnarvon's share of the objects was his "own private property" and that he could keep the objects, sell them, or give them away, as he saw fit.

"If a country owning ancient sites adopts a policy of rigid exclusion or refuses to permit ancient objects to leave the country," Sir Frederic said with contempt, "it means that the hunting of old sites will be done largely by natives and art dealers." Under such circumstances, he said, "museums, private archaeologists and wealthy men would be deprived of fair incentive."

"Regardless of Lord Carnarvon's agreement, under which he was to have one half of what he found," Breasted said, "there is little possibility that Egypt will give up any material part of the spoils from the tomb of Tutankhamen, and the splendid things there will either fall into the hands of natives and be sold off piecemeal to dealers, or they will be placed in an Egyptian museum."

Meanwhile, just as Carter had disagreed with Carnarvon over his arrangement with *The Times,* Carter now took issue with his benefactor over the disposition of the treasure. In view of the magnitude of the discovery, Carter felt that the tomb's contents should remain intact and should not be scattered indifferently around the world in public museums and private collections. The treasure should never leave Egypt, he argued; it should be housed in a special wing of the Cairo Museum. The sporting thing to do was for Carnarvon to renounce all rights and claim to the tomb with which ever thereafter the name of the House of Herbert would be associated. Compensation for Carnarvon's investment could be worked out with the Egyptian authorities, Carter contended. The Egyptians, Carter reasoned, would behave responsibly; it was in their interest to promote tourism, goodwill, and future digs.

Both men were so distraught at this point that they sometimes acted irrationally. By spring their friends thought each was on the threshold of a nervous breakdown. The rapture of discovery, the joy of accomplishment, had given way to heartache—and even agony. It seemed that Carter and Carnarvon could never again confide in each other without winding up in a row. The senior Breasted was so disturbed by this "painful situation," as he called it, that in a private letter dated March 12, 1923, he expressed concern that "a complete break seems inevitable" between the two longtime friends and associates.

The break was not long in coming.

A few days later, in the course of a visit at Carter's house, they got into a shouting match. In a burst of fury, Carter ordered Carnarvon from his home. Carnarvon stormed out and never again went back.

The two houses were the only signs of life between the Valley of the Tombs and the Nile village of El Gournah—six miles of desolate, inhospitable wasteland. In the days that followed, the only two neighbors in that no-man's land ignored one another completely.

Then, suddenly, a new and wholly unexpected development restored the focus of attention to the tomb itself and provided the Tutankhamen story with a dimension that guaranteed its place in the annals of the Roaring Twenties.

To the credulous students of the occult sciences of the ancient Egyptians, the next development came as no surprise. As the various storms swirled overhead that March, like the khamsin or sandstorms that periodically sweep the Nile, Carnarvon was bitten on the right cheek by an insect. The bite turned septic.

Carnarvon himself believed he was bitten by a mosquito. Others thought he had been bitten by an insect and then, while shaving, he had accidentally removed the scab. Another belief was that he nicked himself one morning while shaving and that a mosquito or fly had alighted on the wound. Professor Newberry, for one, dismissed the mosquito thesis. In the Valley itself there were no mosquitoes, he pointed out, so that the poisonous bite must have occurred at Luxor, on the other side of the Nile.

After penetrating the antechamber in November 1922, Carter and Carnarvon had pursued a meticulously scientific program before going into the sealed burial chamber. The morning after they breached the secret door, five sterile swabs, obtained from Dr. A. C. Thaysen of the Bacteriological Laboratory of the Royal Navy, were carried into the farthest corners of the burial chamber, to a point where no human had trod for more than 3,000 years. The swabs were wiped on the walls and floor and then sent to the Royal Navy's Wareham laboratory for examination by H. J. Bunker, a senior chemist. Four swabs were sterile. The fifth, reported A. Lucas, a Fellow of the Institute of Chemistry, contained several organisms that had probably been wafted into the tomb with the circulation of outside air. Lucas concluded, "No life of any kind, even of the lowest form, existed in the tomb when it was first found." The fungus growths on several walls were dry and "apparently dead."

For the scientific record, specimens of dead insects in the burial chamber were sent to entomologists at the Egyptian Ministry of Agriculture and to members of the Royal Egyptian Agricultural Society. The insects proved to be small beetles of the kind that feed on dead organic matter.

All were of a common variety still prevalent in Egypt; despite more than thirty centuries, there had been no evolutionary change or modification in their size or structure. The remains of small spiders and their webs were also found.

Whatever the case, Carnarvon's health had so worsened by late March that his daughter, Lady Evelyn, rushed him by train to the Cairo Hospital. Five physicians were consulted, and Lady Evelyn cabled her mother, the Countess Almina, at Highclere, and also her brother, Lord Portchester, who was then in India on military duty, to come to Cairo. The first announcement of Carnarvon's illness had been officially made on March 19: it was an infection attributed to "an insect bite." The news hit the front pages worldwide.

Dramatically, Lady Carnarvon flew to her husband's side. This was news in itself, for flying was still a novelty. But after crossing the English Channel, Lady Carnarvon's plane put down at Paris' Le Bourget airfield—the scene of a wild celebration four years later when Lindbergh crossed the Atlantic. Apparently Almina had taken ill in flight, and she was forced to complete the dash to Cairo by boat from Marseilles.

With his family at his side, Carnarvon rallied magnificently, displaying the remarkable desire for life that had carried him through his automobile accident of almost twenty years earlier. His physicians were astonished by his progress and, with confidence, announced to the press that he would recover completely.

During this period, a remorseful Carter visited his stricken friend's bedside and made peace. Both men realized that their harsh exchange reflected not so much hostility and antagonism towards each other as the strains they had been put to by one of the world's great discoveries.

But, suddenly, barely a week after Lady Carnarvon arrived at the Cairo Hospital, her husband suffered a relapse. Anxiety alternated with hope as his life ebbed. He remained conscious to the end, his wife, son, and daughter at his side. His last words were: "I am ready."

At 2:00 A.M., April 5, 1923, at the age of fifty-seven, less than twenty weeks after he first emerged from the mummy's resting-place, Carnarvon followed Tutankhamen into the netherworld of Amenti. Officially, his death was attributed to lobar pneumonia, complicated by pleurisy, both the result of blood poisoning from an insect bite.

"The excitement of his discovery and the lamentable worries it brought him," a London commentator said, "must have done much to sap the vitality which was needed so sorely this last week."

At the exact moment of death, something strange happened in Cairo.

The city's electric lights flickered and went out. Briefly, the Egyptian capital was in total darkness; the only visible light was that overhead of the stars imperishable. "This curious occurrence was widely interpreted by those anxiously awaiting for news as an omen of evil," wrote H. V. Morton, a veteran foreign correspondent.

The incident caused a sensation in Cairo. Lord Allenby, the British high commissioner, ordered a British Army colonel, an engineer in charge of the Cairo Electricity Board's generating plants, to launch an official inquiry into the power failure. After a thorough investigation, he could not explain what had caused the outage.

Deeply shaken by the loss of a companion of so many years, Carter swore, "This tomb has brought us bad luck." But the work of excavating the tomb, he announced, would go on.

The archaeological establishment was dazed. "In the history of archaeological research, no such tragic event has taken place as the death of Lord Carnarvon," said Professor Newberry, who had picked Howard Carter for the assignment in Egypt thirty years earlier. "The fatigue and heat which he experienced in the Valley of the Kings no doubt contributed to lower his vitality." And the aging Sir William Matthew Flinders Petrie described Carnarvon's death as a calamity. "He financed the whole of that expedition and as far as one knows at present there is no one to carry it on," he said. Professor E. G. Elliot Smith, who undertook the first scientific study of royal mummies in the *salle des momies* of the Cairo Museum, said, "That his death should have followed so closely upon the dramatic culmination of his sixteen years' task in Egypt is indeed poignantly tragic. But that it should happen now, when the years of difficult work and delicate negotiation in connection with the discovery demand in a very special sense his personal presence, makes it nothing less than a calamity."

Ironically, Carnarvon died without knowing whether or not the shrines in the burial chamber contained the vaunted mummy of the king. For that matter, he died without ever gazing on the features of Tutankhamen, the pharaoh, who, in the end, exercised such a profound influence on Carnarvon and the House of Herbert.

Carnarvon's body was embalmed and made ready for shipment to England for interment at Beacon Hill, Highclere. In the midst of these preparations, Carter took ill. Appalled, the Countess Almina postponed her departure for England with the body of her late husband. Although Carter threw off his strange illness within a few days, this sudden development gave rise to a popular view that the tomb was cursed, that Tutankhamen and/or the high priests of ancient Egypt sought to punish those who violated the dead.

Rational men sought to dam the flood of speculation. Said Dr. Leonard Williams, an eminent London physician, "Mr. Carter has undoubtedly been working very hard and working, too, in underground passages which cannot be particularly healthy. On top of all this, the anxiety caused by Lord Carnarvon's long illness and its fatal termination must have tolled very heavily upon Mr. Carter. It is no wonder he should become ill. I think the same thing would probably have happened to any one of us."

When Carter recovered, the Countess Almina accompanied her husband's body to England. The voyage was made without incident, although several people who had booked passage on the same ship canceled their plans, fearing that some disaster might befall the steamer.

On April 7, two days after Carnarvon's death, the London *Times* published Carnarvon's last article on the Valley, which he had mailed at Luxor. "Almost at the moment of its arrival," a *Times* editor wrote, "came the first news of the illness which had so tragic an issue." The opening line of Carnarvon's piece was: "We have come to the end. . . ." He referred, of course, to the closing of the tomb for the season.

If, as the ancient Egyptians firmly believed, the heart of the dead must be weighed against a feather to determine whether it is light enough to journey into immortality, then Carnarvon, to his infinite credit, may have absolved himself in Osiris' eyes for desecrating, in the name of art and science, the tomb of Tutankhamen.

"I very much hope," he wrote in that final article, "I can say I almost feel sure [that the king's body] will be allowed to remain where it was placed so many, many centuries ago." Carnarvon's last hope from his own grave, as it were, was that Tutankhamen would be provided the opportunity to rest in peace through eternity.

With interment at Highclere, memorial services were held in London and Cairo. At St. Margaret's, Westminster, the service was attended by the nobility and the military, by archaeologists, and by the curious. In Cairo, the service was attended by Egyptian officials; Pierre Lacau and members of the department of antiquities; British officials; and the diplomatic corps. Howard Carter was not present.

At Biban-el-Moluk, where the temperature had climbed to over 100°F, Carter was busily supervising the last-minute details of closing the tomb until the start of the next season. He estimated that only a fourth of the work of excavation had been accomplished. The mummy, of course (if there were one), was still to be found, and there were probably other hidden chambers to explore in the hypogeum.

Like a shadow over Carnarvon's tragic death was the persistent popular belief that he had been stricken by an ancient Egyptian spell. Indeed, ever since the death of Carter's canary, there had been talk of a curse. To the credulous, Carnarvon's death simply confirmed it, and the world's press pulled out all stops on this angle.

Clare Sheridan, a columnist, wrote in *The World*: "Lord Carnarvon had to pay the price each one pays who dares to touch the Oriental dead. Other men have paid the penalty before. There is hardly a mummy in any museum in Europe that has not its sinister record for those who crossed its path. In my own family there is the same tale of disaster attached to the relic that a great uncle brought from Luxor."

In Paris, the world-famous Parisian seer, M. Lancellin, declared: "Tutankhamen has taken his revenge!" His rival, Madame Fraya, observed in turn that Egyptian occult science was highly developed and that Carnarvon had been the victim of the *ka* "or what is known in Egyptian and Oriental occult science as the 'doctrine of the double.'"

Sir Arthur Conan Doyle, a London literary giant of the era, held that an Egyptian mummy could radiate evil "elements." "It is impossible to say with absolute certainty if this is true but if we had proper occult powers we could delineate it," he contended. "In Lord Carnarvon's case, human illness was the primary cause of death. Yet the 'elementals' may have brought about the conditions which caused his illness." Accordingly, "a malevolent spirit may have caused Lord Carnarvon's fatal illness."

When Sir Arthur spoke, an enraptured public, perhaps naturally enough, did not hear *his* voice, but that of Sherlock Holmes. And one word from Holmes was enough to cause a panic. A front-page headline in the London *Daily Express* of April 7, 1923, read: "EGYPTIAN COLLECTORS IN A PANIC—SUDDEN RUSH TO HAND OVER THEIR TREASURES—GROUNDLESS FEARS."

However groundless the fears, parcels containing Egyptian relics poured into the British Museum; a number of owners acknowledged fear that Carnarvon had been killed by Tutankhamen's *ka* or double. "These fears are, it is hardly necessary to state, absolutely groundless," a museum spokesman said. Packages containing the shriveled hands and feet of mummies, faience, and wooden statues and other Egyptian antiquities arrived daily for the Egyptian rooms, the entrance to which, as one London guide put it, was marked by a "gruesome . . . vitrified corpse, in crouching posture, of a man of the Neolithic period, probably 7000 B.C."

The British Museum, said the *Express,* had become a "godsend to the superstitious."

Algernon Blackwood, a popular writer of the twenties whose best-sellers included *The Lost World* and *Pam's Garden,* both of which were set in the world of dreams and the supernatural, scoffed at the idea of a curse. "To credit any Egyptian magician of several thousand years ago with sufficient power to kill a man today is to lay a heavier burden upon a 'curse' than it can bear," he said.

There was a theory that ancient high priests had impregnated some objects in the tomb with poison and that Carnarvon had accidentally nicked himself.

But a French professor provided a more titillating answer to the question of why Carter was not felled by the same curse. Carter himself, he implied, might have been responsible for Carnarvon's death. A pharaoh's tomb could not be explored with impunity by inexpert hands. Carter was a professional Egyptologist, an expert. Thus, under identical circumstances, Carter lived and Carnarvon died—because Carter knew what to touch and what not to!

Carter refused to dignify any of these tales with denials or libel suits. But in Volume II of *The Tomb of Tut-ankh-amen,* which was published in 1927, Carter felt compelled to abandon a position of reticence and refute the wild stories. "The sentiment of the Egyptologist . . . is not one of fear, but of respect and awe," he wrote. "It is entirely opposed to the foolish superstitions which are far too prevalent among emotional people in search of 'psychic' excitement."

He denounced the storymongers as "mischievous . . . unpardonable . . . mendacious . . . and . . . malicious." "If it be not actually libellous," he wrote, "it points in that spiteful direction, and all sane people should dismiss such inventions with contempt."

But Carter's bid to end the rumors failed; the stories were too good. The theme of the mummy's curse not only persisted, but developed an uncontrollable ground swell. The explanation for its durability was given by Morton, one of the serious journalists at Luxor. "The queer atmosphere which clings to all things Egyptian is responsible for the widespread story that in opening the tomb of Tutankhamen Carnarvon exposed himself to the fury of some malignant influence, or that he was poisoned by materials left in the tomb thousands of years ago."

Indeed, the mummy's-curse theme was so captivating that *The New York Times,* on its front page, employed an *A* head of three decks of 30-point type with ten additional banks as follows: "CARNARVON'S DEATH

SPREADS THEORIES ABOUT VENGEANCE." In an adjoining column, a modest two-deck *Y* head in 18-point type reported: "Lenin Critically Ill, May Die Any Minute But Moscow Says He Still Keeps Control."

CHAPTER 9

After a restful summer, Carter returned to Upper Egypt in October 1923, as he had done for thirty years, to mount the new season. With the assistance of "Pecky" Callender and the Metropolitan staff, chiefly Mace and Burton, Carter reopened the tomb of Seti II, a pharaoh of the Nineteenth Dynasty, which Carter had converted the previous year into a laboratory and warehouse. At the tomb of Tutankhamen, under the direction of Carter's chief *reis*, Ahmed Gurgar, the limestone chips used to block it up were painstakingly removed, chip by chip; the job took about a month. In late November, additional power lines were installed in the tomb for the battery of klieg lights Burton imported from America—with the idea of making a frame-by-frame photographic record of the dismantling of the shrines and the opening of the sarcophagus of the king. (That there would be one was no longer doubted.)

In the Seti lab, Carter and his collaborators labored to preserve, in various chemical vats, the art objects that had been removed earlier and stored. They also crated objects for shipment to Cairo. Meanwhile, the dust from the Tutankhamen tomb was sifted for odds and ends. This effort produced spectacular archaeological results. In removing the gold and inlaid throne from the antechamber, Carter had discovered that one of the four upreared uraei on the backrest was missing. In the tomb's dust, the missing piece was recovered.

With a view to dismantling the nest of shrines in the burial chamber, in order to get at the sarcophagus and the mummy, Carter planned to demolish the plaster wall that separated the antechamber from the burial vault. Putting the project in motion in the limited space was an engineering feat. Once the wall was torn down, Carter's team erected scaffolding in the tomb and an elaborate series of chain hoists, with differential gears, for lifting multiton loads.

Carter and his aides worked from 8:00 A.M. to 1:00 P.M., took a one-hour break for lunch, and then returned to work until 4:00 P.M. By late afternoon everyone was physically and emotionally drained.

Outside the laboratory, the Valley took on the appearance of a logging camp as teams of fellahin toiled in the burning sun, sawing freshly imported lumber and making shipping crates and scaffolding. Quiet descended during the lunch hour. Each day's luncheon, prepared at the Winter Palace Hotel and carried to the site, was like a working session between a field marshal and his staff. Promptly at 1:00 P.M., Carter, wearing a bow tie and a homburg, and his white-sleeved crew assembled in Tomb No. 10 at a long table covered with an immaculate white tablecloth. A year before, Carnarvon had been at the head of the table. Now Carter sat in that place.

It took Carter and his men eighty-four days to dismantle the four gold-sheathed shrines. The catafalques were composed of eighty separate pieces, each shrine of exquisite goldwork (the largest shrine, the outer one, was also inlaid with blue faience). The sides and ceiling of the shrines were dotted with religious texts and symbols and overlaid in gilt.

The largest shrine, known as the first shrine, was 10.6 feet long, 10 feet wide, and 9 feet high. The smallest, fourth shrine within the nest measured 9½ by 4½ by 6 feet. Each shrine fitted snugly into the other.

Upon dismantling the outershell, Carter was elated to find a rope around the second shrine, the intact knot bearing unbroken seals. The shrines had not been opened since the day they were sealed millennia earlier—these were genuine time capsules. "We had at last found what we had never dreamed of attaining—an absolute insight into the funerary customs followed in the burial of an ancient pharaoh," Carter wrote. "Years of toil had not been wasted."

In each succeeding shell, the gold was brighter. "The sight was dazzling, superb, almost blinding in its effect," Merton of *The Times* wrote on January 4, 1924, when the third shrine was opened to reveal still another. Indeed, Merton, perched in the catbird seat (with "Mecham" at his elbow), ran out of superlatives as one shrine after another was dismantled. Here are samples of descriptive passages from his reports on the opening of the last three shrines:

Carefully the cord was severed, the bolts drawn and the doors opened, and a third shrine was revealed, exactly similar in design, of gold throughout, like the other two, with similar ebony bolts across its doors, and its cord and sealing still in position. . . .

Once more the bolts were drawn and the seal cord cut, and then the doors of this third shrine were opened, revealing yet a fourth shrine, also of gold, brighter and more dazzling than the last. . . .

The decisive moment was at hand, and we all watched with tense excitement. The bolts of the last doors swung slowly open and there, filling the entire area within the fourth shrine, and effectively barring all further progress, stood an enormous sarcophagus of crystalline sandstone, intact, with the lid still firmly in its place.

Carter, the mummy-seeker, had found his mummy. The quest of a lifetime had ended in triumph.

On the door panel of the first shrine Carter and his band read: "Lord of Diadems, Tutankhamen . . . living forever . . . in the Region of Silence."

And on a panel in the second shrine, Isis, mother of Osiris, lord of the underworld, pledged: "I have come to be thy protection, thou are my son . . . May thou lift thy head to see Ra, to stand on thy feet, to walk about in the forms thou likest, to move as before . . . To never decay!"

In the third shrine: "I have come to be thy protection, thy head is attached to thy body . . . I have given thee the day of eternity. . . . May thy house [tomb] prosper eternally as Ra himself . . . Thy *ka* is stable, remaining forever in thy castle [tomb] . . . Thy heart is pleased . . . Thou livest forever and eternally . . . son of Ra, Tutankhamen . . . Thou livest!"

The last shrine contained the most sorrowful lines found in Egyptian theology. "I have seen yesterday," the ancient Egyptian scripture concluded. "I know tomorrow."

With the shrines dismantled, a magnificent mural depicting Tutankhamen's passage into Osiris' world of the dead stood, totally unobstructed on the north wall for the first time in thirty-five centuries. The mural's color and vitality were such that it looked as if it had been painted only the day before. Within the shrines, Carter discovered a treasure trove of smaller objects: silver walking sticks, models of Nile barges, gold statuettes—each designed to serve Tutankhamen in the afterworld.

Since the discovery of the sixteen steps fifteen months before, one supreme moment had dizzily succeeded another. Carter and the world now breathlessly awaited the most supreme of all moments—lifting the lid of the sarcophagus. Compared with this prospect, the treasure that had already been found—and estimated to be worth $15 million—seemed relatively unimportant.

For the occasion, which fell on February 12, 1924, Carter invited nineteen guests: a mix of archaeologists, government officials, and VIPs. The group included two token Egyptians (the local governor and the undersecretary of state in the Ministry of Public Works), and three token Frenchmen (Lacau and the directors of the French Archaeological Institute and the French Expedition in Egypt). The other guests were Anglo-American—Gardiner, Newberry, Breasted, Mace, Callender, and others. Among the VIPs were two controversial figures, Major Astor and Edward S. Harkness, the American railroad mogul who would acquire Carnarvon's Egyptian collection right from under the noses of the British. Present, but not listed in the register of official guests, was Merton.

Carter spent the morning checking the makeshift contraption he had constructed in the burial chamber for lifting the one-and-a-half ton lid, a series of blocks and tackles, ropes, and chain hoists. Iron clamps had been attached to the lid.

Promptly at 1:00 P.M., the guests assembled in Tomb 10 for a bit of lunch. As usual, wine and tea were served, the tea in deference to the religious sensibilities of Moslem guests.

At 3:00 P.M. the guests descended into the tomb. Klieg lights were turned on. As the temperature soared into the upper nineties, Burton's motion picture camera, poised on a tripod, began to whir. Carter signaled Callender, who was in charge of the blocks and pulleys. The chain hoists clanked, and the ropes grew taut. The lid trembled. Inch by inch, the rose granite cover, glistening under the klieg lights, was raised from the sarcophagus. When the lid was about two feet above the sarcophagus, Carter ordered a stop to the operation. Like a boat cradled aloft in a travel lift, the lid hung in midair.

Carter approached the sarcophagus, turned on his flashlight, and peered into its interior. For a fraction of a second, cold disappointment surged through his body. He saw nothing. Nothing, that is, except a discolored linen pall that covered the contents like a blanket. Gingerly, with Mace's assistance, Carter began to roll up the shroud. Sections of linen crumbled in their fingers. Their hearts pounded; their blood pressure rose; their mouths were parched. Perspiration streaked down their faces and stained their white shirts.

As they removed the linen, the gleam of burnished gold momentarily blinded them. Both men gasped aloud. A gold effigy of the youthful pharaoh filled the sarcophagus, rich goldwork on gesso. The face of the effigy was covered with a solid gold mask, brilliantly sculptured in Tutankhamen's image. On the forehead were the reared cobra and the vulture's head, symbols of Lower and Upper Egypt, poised to strike.

"Everywhere the glint of gold," Carter said in awe.

Upon the effigy was a graveside touch as common today as it was then: a wreath of withered flowers. Were they placed there by Tutankhamen's queen, Ankhesenpaaton? She had been the loveliest of the three daughters of Akhenaten, the heretic who destroyed the idols and preached the existence of one God, and his radiant queen, Nefertiti. Tutankhamen has given us license to dream.

In a memoir to his son, Breasted recalled the moment:

As they [removed the pall], we suddenly saw the gleaming gold of the vulture's head and the up-reared cobra on the king's forehead. We saw his eyes, which seemed to look out upon us as in life; and soon the king's whole figure was revealed to us in all the splendor of shining gold. His gold-covered arms and hands were crossed upon his breast; in his right hand he grasped a crook or staff, wrought of gold and colored stones; in his left, he held the ceremonial fagellum or scourge [flail], also of gold. His figure was swathed in the gilded plumage of a protecting goddess.

What Breasted and the others saw was simply the outer coffin, cunningly wrought by the sculptor with the aid of lapidary and goldsmith into a portrait figure of a king lying, again in Breasted's words, "as if stretched out upon the lid like a crusader on his tomb slab in some cathedral."

"I looked at my watch," Breasted remembered, "—scarcely an hour had passed since we had entered the tomb, yet we came away with a sense of having glimpsed the era and the last rites of Tutankhamen."

The party emerged from the tomb in a daze, unable to work further, the lid still suspended aloft some twenty-four inches directly above the sarcophagus. "Our one haunting regret," Carter remarked, "is that Lord Carnarvon was not spared to witness the fruits of his undertaking."

In Tomb No. 10, Carter and his guests toasted each other in champagne and tea.

The following morning, Carter led members of the press on a firsthand, two-hour inspection of the interior of the tomb and sarcophagus, partly a post-Carnarvon public relations campaign designed to assuage the press and partly in compliance with the newly negotiated contract between Almina, the countess of Carnarvon, now Mrs. Dennistoun, and the Egyptian government.

The press was also overcome. "I have never seen and never hope to see again such a magnificent sight," Merton cabled his paper. Reuters reported that "the view was dazzling . . . a more wonderful discovery has not yet been made." And the correspondent of the *Egyptian Gazette* wrote, "The great Tut stunt has reached and passed its climax. . . . It was a thrilling moment."

With the departure of the correspondents scheduled for noon, Carter originally had planned to escort the wives of his collaborators into the tomb and then proceed to a luncheon in honor of his staff. But then came a directive from the ministry of public works barring the women, and Lacau informed Carter that police had been dispatched to the site with instructions to bar the women if they sought to enter.

For Carter, the order evoked memories of his run-in, some twenty years earlier, with the French over the presence of women at Petrie's dig. Carter was visibly agitated, and on leaving the tomb that morning the correspondent of the *Egyptian Gazette* reported that he looked "strained and worried."

As noon approached, Carter told his aides what had transpired earlier. They, in turn, announced that they refused to work further in the tomb unless their wives were accorded the common courtesy of inspecting the object of their fifteen months' toil.

In character, Carter acted impulsively. He went directly to the tomb, cut the power lines, slammed shut the steel door, and pad-locked it. He deposited the only set of keys in his tweed jacket, adjusted his bow tie, pulled his homburg down on his head, and, in a rage, headed for Luxor. At the Winter Palace Hotel Carter posted the following notice on the bulletin board:

NOTICE

Owing to the impossible restrictions and discourtesies on the part of the Public Works Department and its Antiquity Service, all my collaborators in protest have refused to work any further upon the scientific investigations of the discovery of the tomb of Tutankhamen. I am therefore obliged to make known to the public that immediately after the press view of the tomb this morning between 10:00 A.M. and noon the tomb [was] closed and no further work can be carried out.

[signed] Howard Carter
February 13, 1924.

If Carter was outraged by his treatment at the hands of the ministry, Morcos Bey Hanna and Lacau were livid. Lacau summarily ordered Carter to hand over the keys. He refused.

Meanwhile, the mummy of Tutankhamen lay stretched out in its nest of coffins. Overhead was more than a ton of granite sarcophagus lid, suspended by a series of multiple hoists designed to lift and lower the lid—not to hold it in suspension indefinitely.

In Boston, the staid *Christian Science Monitor* carried a headline that read: "LUXOR WRANGLES AS SARCOPHAGUS LID IS HELD IN AIR."

Fiction could not have created a more unbelievable plot line.

At this juncture, another crisis developed. Lord Allenby, British high commissioner and commander in chief of the British army in Egypt, was scheduled to make a formal visit to the tomb on March 6. The Egyptian government was thus confronted with three options: rescind the order against the wives and have Carter reopen the tomb, which would have constituted an intolerable loss of face; inform Allenby that the tomb was closed and that the visit would have to be canceled, implying that Egypt lacked the authority to open it; or break into the tomb and sequester it in the name of the Egyptian government.

Zaghlul Pasha opted for the third alternative.

The cabinet authorized Lacau on February 20 to "reopen the tomb and resume work at the earliest possible moment." Lacking Egyptologists of its own, the government sought to make a deal with Lythgoe, Mace, and other members of the staff of the Metropolitan Museum of Art: the Museum was invited to take over work in the tomb. Acting as spokesman, Mace indignantly rejected the offer and termed it "an insult to all concerned."

In another maneuver, Lacau publicly announced that Carter might resume the work in the tomb at the expense—but under the control—of the Egyptian government. Still in a rage, Carter refused.

And so, in a formal statement, the government delivered Carter an ultimatum: return to work in forty-eight hours or face cancellation of the concession. ("Such a step is quite impossible," Lady Carnarvon said. "The license cannot be revoked after my signature is attached. No government would be so discourteous.")

Discourteous or not, on February 22, Lacau, accompanied by several Egyptian officials; the chief of police; a detachment of armed police; and a squad of workers armed with chisels, crowbars, axes, and hacksaws arrived at the tomb. They filed through the locks securing the outer door and then smashed the bolts of the steel inner gate and succeeded, finally, in opening the tomb.

"They descended into the tomb with lighted candles," a correspondent wrote, "like a band of conspirators."

In the burial chamber, the lid was still suspended in midair. Lacau and his men gently swung it aside and lowered it to the floor of the tomb. Their sigh of relief could be heard around the world.

On March 6, Zaghlul Pasha turned the incident to political advantage by deciding to visit the tomb himself. He and the Allenbys traveled to

Luxor in separate trains. Along the route, tens of thousands of fellahin lined the tracks to shout their support of the prime minister and chant anti-British slogans. As the London *Times* dryly put it, the demonstration "removed from the minds of the government's guests any doubt in regard to the political sentiments of the populace."

Zaghlul Pasha had invited, in addition to Lord and Lady Allenby, a number of other luminaries to the official reopening of the tomb. There were several members of European royalty, including Prince Frederick Leopold of Prussia.

Like commoners before them, the celebrities descended the sixteen steps and gasped at the scene of golden grandeur before them. Tutankhamen still rested peacefully within his coffins, secure in the massive, open sarcophagus. The British guests applauded the excellent condition of the tomb and the superb theatrical lighting effects arranged by Lacau. Everything went smoothly. But all the Egyptologists in the country boycotted the ceremony, except M. Foucart, the director of the French Expedition and, of course, Lacau. That night the prime minister presided over a gala banquet at the Winter Palace Hotel. The Allenbys were conspicuous by their absence: they had gone directly from their special armored train to the tomb and then back to the train, leaving immediately for Cairo.

For ten days following the formal opening of the tomb, more than 2,000 visitors, including large numbers of fellahin, trooped down the limestone steps. Given the width of the passageway into the tomb, no wider than a subway car, the tomb must have taken on the appearance of a Times Square rush hour.

In Cairo, Carter and Lady Carnarvon brought legal suit against the Egyptian government.

Gradually the principals hammered out an acceptable compromise: Carter was guaranteed freedom from harassment as he completed his work in the tomb, and in turn, he and Lady Carnarvon renounced all claims to the treasure. "I hereby voluntarily relinquish all claims on the part of Almina, Countess of Carnarvon, and the trustees and executors of the estate of the late Lord Carnarvon, to the antiquities in the tomb of Tutankhamen, and agree to withdraw all legal actions, as far as they relate to the enforcement of such claim," Carter and Lady Carnarvon declared in a joint letter sent to Morcos Bey. The settlement provided that the government would compensate the Carnarvon estate for its expenses in the Valley; a figure of £50,000 ($250,000) was bandied about. Finally, as a token repayment to the Egyptologists who worked on the tomb, Cairo also agreed to present "duplicate objects in the tomb" as gifts to the British Museum and the Metropolitan Museum of Art. Final details were put to paper March 11.

Egypt had yet to regain complete independence from foreign control, and the court system reflected the roiled state of affairs. Because the case involved foreigners, the suit came before a mixed tribunal presided over by a British judge. The judge appointed Breasted, Sr., as mediator. Even so, Carter and Lady Carnarvon engaged in overkill. In the selection of counsel, they retained General Sir John Maxwell, the former British commander in Egypt, executor of Carnarvon's estate, and an old friend of the family. Unfortunately, they also retained as counsel F. M. Maxwell, an able English solicitor in Cairo. An expert in Egyptian law, he had been, alas, the public prosecutor in the treason case that had put Morcos Bey Hanna, now Zaghlul Pasha's minister of public works, behind bars. During the treason trial, Maxwell had demanded the death penalty for Morcos Bey.

Carter's pact was about to be signed when Maxwell, talking aloud to himself, characterized the Egyptian government's behavior in the affair as "the action of bandits." Morcos Bey Hanna flew into a rage and broke off negotiations. Breasted and Carter hurried to repair the breach. Carter, at Breasted's urging, sent the minister a note of apology. "I wish to dissociate myself absolutely from the use of the word 'bandit' and to express my profound regret that such language should have furnished the just occasion for the termination of our negotiations," he said. But it was useless. The negotiations were never resumed.

An outraged Maxwell threatened to sue Breasted, the author of Carter's apology, for defamation of [Maxwell's] character. But nothing came of it.

"Heaven deliver me from ever again attempting to act as peace-maker in a lawsuit over the possession of a royal tomb of ancient Egypt!" Breasted, the court's mediator, wrote his son.

The consequences were profound. Neither the British Museum nor the Metropolitan received a single duplicate object from the tomb of Tutankhamen for their collections.

On March 12, the mixed court found in favor of Carter and Lady Carnarvon on all legal points in their applications for the tomb's sequestration. But it was a bootless award. The Egyptian government refused to discuss the matter further, and the court was unable to enforce its judgment without touching off a political crisis of incalculable dimensions.

The pendulum of political power was swinging in Egypt's favor, and, accordingly, later in the month the Egyptian government appealed the mixed court's ruling. A mixed court of appeal, sitting in Alexandria, reversed the lower court's decision. Egypt had won the day; indeed, the war had been won the day the government asserted its sovereignty and broke into the tomb.

Emboldened by its courtroom victory and probably prodded by Lacau, who sensed the opportunity for a kill, the Egyptian government barred Carter and members of the Carnarvon family from ever reentering the tomb of Tutankhamen.

The blow came that spring as Carter reached his fiftieth birthday. He was now at the crest of his fame and creative energy. He should have been in a position to savor his triumph. Instead, he was completely demoralized. Cairo's decision first stunned him and then plunged him into a state of deep depression.

At a loss over his next course of action, Carter reluctantly accepted an avalanche of lucrative offers to hit the lecture trail in the United States. In a daze, during the last week of March, he sailed for England. At Southampton he booked passage for the United States aboard the Cunard White Star liner *Berengaria*.

In the course of his voyage, he came to the sickening realization that his work in the tomb of Tutankhamen was finished—he would never return to his beloved Valley and would never gaze on the mummy of Tutankhamen.

By the time the black-hulled, red-booted liner tied up on April 20 in her slip on Manhattan's West Side, Carter had decided to embark on another fantastic voyage of discovery, an archaeological campaign he had once filed away in his mind for an unspecified future. This was to organize an expedition into eastern equatorial Africa in search of archaeology's missing link—a civilization originating in the heart of darkness that might have been the common mother of the civilizations that flourished in the valleys of the Nile, the Tigris, and the Euphrates. Carter's objective was the jungle-clad interior of Somaliland and Ethiopia, then called Abyssinia. He was moved in this direction, he later explained, by the results of archaeological research in northern Africa and western Asian valleys, each of which contained drawings and sculptures of animals found only in black Africa.

In the United States, Carter was accorded honors of the sort his own country denied him. Never received at Buckingham Palace, he was invited to the White House, where he and Calvin Coolidge struck it off well. Both of them shared basic characteristics—frugality, modesty, and unpretentiousness. They were also plain in speech, appearance, and habit.

Finally, both were self-made men. As he left the Oval Office, Carter told newsmen that he was "amazed and flattered" by Coolidge's familiarity with his work in Upper Egypt. Indeed, Coolidge was so impressed with his visitor that he invited Carter to return to the White House for dinner on May 9. That evening, in the warmth of the East Room, Carter enthralled the presidential circle with a talk about his search and discovery of the tomb of Tutankhamen. And although no university in England ever accorded him even an honorary degree, Carter was invited to Yale, which in the course of a ceremony that drew a large crowd to New Haven, bestowed upon him an honorary doctor of science degree. (He appended the title to his name with the publication three years later of the second volume of his trilogy, *The Tomb of Tut-ankh-amen*.)

Despite the accolades he received in the United States, Carter returned to England that summer a lonely, defeated, and embittered man. His depressive mood deepened when he found a letter waiting for him from Ahmed Gurgar, his chief *reis*. In English, in a shaky hand, Gurgar wrote: "Beg to write this letter hoping you are enjoying good health and ask the Almighty to keep you and bring you back to us in safety." All the *reises* and ghaffirs "beg to send their best regards." The letter ended: "My best remarks to your honorable self . . . longing to your early coming."

In the House of Commons, questions were raised about the government's role in the Tutankhamen affair. Ramsay MacDonald, the Labour party's first prime minister, washed his hands of the matter. "Howard Carter," he told Parliament, "in his excavation work in Egypt [is] a private individual and subject to the provisions of the Egyptian law of antiquities." In the face of militant nationalist sentiment in Egypt, 10 Downing Street had enough trouble without getting involved in so sticky a wicket as Tutankhamen.

And so, by all rights, Carter's search and discovery of the tomb of Tutankhamen should end at this point.

CHAPTER 11

While Carter sulked in England, the political situation in Egypt deteriorated rapidly. Sir Lee Stack, the sirdar, or commander, of the Egyptian army and the governor-general of the Sudan—the most important British official in the area next to Lord Allenby—was assassinated on November 19 in the streets of Cairo. London seized on the incident to restore its pre-Wafdist authority in Egypt.

Britain leveled a series of demands at Zaghlul Pasha's government, including an apology, the prosecution of the murderers, a $2.5 million indemnity, an end to public meetings in Egypt, and, as *The Times* neatly characterized it, "a free hand for the protection of foreign interests" along the Nile. Egypt's prime minister accepted some of the demands and rejected others.

In a no-nonsense mood, the British moved. British troops seized the Alexandria Customs, the principal source of Egypt's financial strength, and carried out maneuvers in downtown Cairo. To the music of fife and drum, units of the Duke of Wellington's Regiment marched down the avenues, fixed bayonets gleaming in the sun; then came the Highland Light Infantry, with kilted pipers and scarlet and white hackles tucked into their helmets; and the Hampshire Regiment, with machine guns packed on mules. While the columns paraded around Cairo, British forces along the Suez Canal were ordered to stand alert, and British gunboats took up positions in the roadsteads of Egypt's main ports, Alexandria and Port Said.

In the face of this show of force, Zaghlul Pasha resigned. He was immediately replaced by a British puppet who submitted readily to London's demands. Forthwith, political rallies were banned, the elected parliament prorogued, and scores of anti-British personalities detained in a series of sweeping razzias. British imperial power was restored over Egypt.

Whether Howard Carter pulled strings in the Foreign Office and/or Colonial Office and/or used the influence of the British Museum and the academic establishment in the bargain is still open to question. But the fact is that Britain had no sooner reasserted itself in Egypt than Carter turned up in Cairo. On January 13, 1925, a report from the Egyptian capital disclosed that the dispute over the tomb had been suddenly and "amicably" resolved. The settlement, it said, resulted from "the more reasonable attitude shown by the Egyptian authorities."

The accord was along the lines of the compromise agreement originally negotiated by Breasted. Carter and Lady Carnarvon renounced the treasure; the Egyptian government promised not to harass Carter in his work; Egypt pledged to compensate the Carnarvon estate to the amount of the expenses the late lord incurred in searching for the tomb; and, in recognition of the "admirable discovery," the government offered the Carnarvon estate a choice of duplicate objects from the tomb to either keep at Highclere or give to museums, as it saw fit. Publicity arrangements concerning the tomb were placed in Cairo's hands.

With the settlement, an overjoyed Carter, oblivious to the political upheaval around him, rushed off to Luxor and his home on the west bank of the Nile. There he was warmly greeted by his *reises* and ghaffirs. It is a measure of the Egyptian character that in personal relationships the Egyptians are blind to politics, although politics is a strong suit in their nature.

In a simple ceremony on January 25, the tomb of Tutankhamen, which had been closed for eleven months, was reopened. To Carter's relief, only a few hardy tourists were on hand; the murder of Sir Lee Stack and the turmoil that followed had done in the tourist trade.

Within the laboratory and the tomb, Carter found everything in good order except the pall that had covered the coffin. It had been completely ruined as a result of exposure to the air.

CHAPTER 12

To begin a new season's work is a less simple task than is perhaps generally imagined," Carter once modestly observed. Nineteen-twenty-five was not an exception. He and his collaborators spent the first half of the year mapping a strategy for the realization of three terminal objectives: opening the coffins, removing the mummy, and unwrapping it.

New scaffolding was erected in the burial chamber for handling the coffins, new power lines were laid for X-raying the mummy, and a veritable laboratory was installed in the tomb for immersing the mummy's wrappings in vats of chemical preservatives.

In the light of Carnarvon's fate, Carter took one interesting, little publicized precaution. On several occasions, after detecting an invasion of "minute insect life," he sprayed the tomb with the primitive pesticides of the period.

It was the problem of preservation that especially worried the team. At the Cairo Museum, for example, where articles of gold from the previous season were on display, Carter found, to his dismay, that they already exhibited signs of discoloration. Worse, some of the wooden oviform boxes, chariot wheels, and statuettes developed cracks. "Everything may seem to be going well until suddenly, in the crisis of the process [of preservation], you hear a crack . . ." Carter wrote later. "Your nerves are at an almost painful tension. What is happening? . . . What action is needed to avert a catastrophe?"

He summoned a battery of experts to help: A. Lucas, the director of the Egyptian government's chemical department; Alexander Scott, the British Museum's director of scientific research; Douglas Derry, a professor of anatomy; and Dr. Saleh Bey Hamdi, the former director of Egyptian University. In addition, Carter mustered one hundred experienced *reises*, ghaffirs and fellahin.

On October 10, 1925, work inside the tomb had regained its old momentum. With two sets of three-sheaf pulley blocks, the heavy gilt wooden lid of the first anthropoid coffin, measuring 7 feet 4 inches in length, was slowly lifted by its original silver ornamental handles. With the lid raised, the curious band of archaeologists peered expectantly into the coffin. As their eyes adjusted to the shadows, they saw a linen pall covered with garlands of dried flowers.

When Carter drew back the shroud, he looked upon a magnificently gilded mummiform coffin, 6 feet 8 inches in length, the head and shoulders of the effigy covered with a burnished, glistening funerary mask of solid gold.

At this moment of jubilation, Carter was confronted by one of the two great disappointments that clouded his discovery. The first and greatest disappointment was the failure to find a scrap of papyrus, even a hint of the life and times of the entombed pharaoh. The other disappointment was that, on closer inspection of the second coffin, Carter discovered evidence of dampness. "A rather ominous feature," he commented with typical understatement. ". . . Disconcerting." Moisture, of course, could destroy not only the linen bandages in which the king's august body was swathed, but the mummy itself as well.

On November 11, an odd work day because Armistice Day was universally and reverently observed globally, the lid of the second coffin was raised. Although Carter and his associates expected to find a third coffin in the nest, the sight that they beheld left them numb. The third coffin, 6 feet, 1¾ inches long, was solid gold.

Between 2½ and 3½ millimeters thick, it was an enormous mass of pure bullion, weighing 2,448⅛ pounds. At the fluctuating price of gold today—around $150 per ounce—the third coffin was worth $6 million. (The weight of the three burnished gold masks found in the next was, altogether, 581⅞ pounds.

Patently, these cost-price figures are absurd. The masks and third coffin represent, to this day, an unmatched pinnacle of art and craftsmanship. Judging their value by weight is as ludicrous as judging the value of a Rembrandt by the cost of canvas and pigment.

Carter and his assistants were suddenly overwhelmed by the implications of their astonishing discovery. Tutankhamen, whose name would forever outshine and outlive the names of all the other kings of pharaonic Egypt combined—unless another intact tomb was discovered—was, in historical terms, a lesser pharaoh who died, X rays later showed, at the age of eighteen. Yet, if the treasure buried with him was so fantastic, how much more fantastic must have been the amount of treasure buried with such great pharaohs as Rameses VI, whose rock tomb, situated above Tutankhamen's, was a hundred times more cavernous?

Gold was, of course, not all there was to the third coffin. There was the mummy itself—literally covered in jewels.

"At such moments," Carter confessed, "the emotions evade verbal expression . . . Three thousand years and more had elapsed since men's eyes had gazed into that golden coffin. Time, measured by the brevity of human life, seemed to lose its common perspective before a spectacle so vividly recalling the solemn religious rites of a vanished civilization. But it is useless to dwell on such sentiments . . ."

Here is a partial count of what Carter recovered from the mummy after he removed the gold mask that covered the face, shoulders, and heart.

On the head, a royal diadem of gold with cobra and vulture, signifying Lower and Upper Egypt; *about the neck,* a pectoral of bejeweled gold and silver charms and amulets; *on the breast,* a series of small pectorals, arranged in sixteen layers, displaying extraordinary cloisonné work; *on the arms,* eleven magnificent bracelets, studded with semiprecious stones; *on the hands,* thirteen rings; *on each finger,* a gold sheath; *around the waist,* two girdles of gold and jewels; *at the hip,* a gold-handled dagger with an iron blade (of great archaeological worth, for it demonstrated that Egypt was already in the Iron Age); *around the legs,* a royal apron of inlaid gold; *on the feet,* gold sandals; *on each toe,* a gold sheath.

All told, Carter found 143 objects within the linen folds of the mummy. Each was worth a terrorist's ransom.

As for the mummy, Carter entertained great expectations that it would be found, as he put it, "in almost perfect condition." But "we found him [sic] in a terrible state," Carter said.

The high priests had treated Tutankhamen in death as in life with reverence and respect. Swathed in yards of the finest cambric bandages, the mummy had been protected by a series of shells, seven in number, the four shrines, and the three coffins.

When the last rites were performed, apparently, as sometimes happened in the case of other mummies, something had gone awry. Humidity—"a sore decayer of your whoreson dead body," as the gravedigger put it to Hamlet—was locked into the gold coffin. As a result, the unguents poured over the mummy before sealing the coffin had turned, with chemical action, into a pitchlike substance with the consistency of marine epoxy glue. This started a form of spontaneous combustion that destroyed the linen wrappings and caused the skin and underlying tissues of the mummy to become extremely brittle. Tutankhamen's mummy was stuck fast to the bottom of the coffin, and all of Carter's ingenuity could not move it.

Accordingly, the mummy had to be examined *in situ* as it lay in its gold coffin. The charred linen wrappings, which often crumpled to powder at the touch, had to be removed in bits and pieces, some no larger than a Band-Aid.

After seven consecutive days of work, with temperatures in the tomb in the high nineties, "the youthful pharaoh was before us at last: an obscure and ephemeral ruler, ceasing to be the mere shadow of a name, had re-entered . . . the world of reality and history!" Carter wrote. "Here was the climax of our long researches! The tomb had yielded its secret!"

Following the examination of the mummy, Carter directed his attention to a small opening along the west wall of the burial chamber. When he had first discovered it two years earlier, he had boarded it up so he would not be tempted to explore it until the shrines and coffins were dismantled and examined. This decision is a testimony to Carter's self-discipline and devotion to archaeology—a devotion to the past and the future at the expense of the present.

Dubbed the Treasury, this room, more than any other chamber in the rock tomb, a British Egyptologist recently pointed out, "was concerned with the mysteries of the world beyond the tomb." Roughly 15 by 12 by 7 feet, the room had a gilt-wood shrine as a centerpiece. On each side of the canopy, facing inward, were golden figures of slender, seductive goddesses in transparent gowns, their hands outspread, their countenances serene.

When Carter opened the shrine, he discovered an alabaster chest with a sculpted head divided into four compartments. Each compartment contained, in pure gold, a miniature coffin. This was the so-called Canopic chest, which contained the viscera of the mummy. Carter gently opened the coffins: one contained Tutankhamen's liver, wrapped in linen; another, his lungs; the third, his stomach; and the fourth, his intestines.

Nearby were two small anthropoid coffins, each casket containing a second coffin. Within each of the second coffins was a stillborn child.

One was the mummified body of what appeared to be a five-month-old female fetus, carefully wrapped in linen. But there was no abdominal incision and no indication of how the body had been preserved. The skin was gray; the body, shrunken and brittle. The second child, also believed to have been a girl, was also wrapped in bandages. The eyes were open; the eyebrows, distinct; a few eyelashes, still intact. The abdominal wall had been opened by an incision and closed with a sealing resin. The abdominal cavity was stuffed with saline-impregnated lime. The baby had been about seven months old at the time of death.

"With little doubt," Carter wrote, "they were the offspring of Tutankhamen." If so, it is intriguing that the stillborn children were buried with the father and not with the mother (Ankhesenpaaton's tomb has never been found). Actually, to this day there is a dispute among Egyptologists over the parentage of the two babies: "Why should royal children, dying before their father, have been buried in his tomb?" asks Christiane Desroches-Noblecourt of the Louvre.

In this same chamber, Carter also found scores of clay and wooden *ushabti* figures. *Ushabti* were the answerers—the slaves, servants, and soldiers—destined to do Tutankhamen's bidding in the afterworld. The room also contained a fleet of model ships: solar barges in which the pharaoh might cruise in the wake of the sun-god Ra on his daily voyage through the heavens.

When he cleared the Treasury, Carter turned to the fourth and last chamber within the tomb. The Annex, he called it. Serving as the tomb's warehouse, this storeroom was filled with objects of every description in gold, silver, ivory, glass, and wood, from backgammon-style boards and toys to bedsteads, clothing, weapons, and literally hundreds of other items. They were thrown about helter-skelter.

Carter's meticulous work in the Treasury and the Annex occupied him for five seasons until 1932. One thousand seven hundred and three objects from the tomb are still on display in the Cairo Museum. To this day, their numbers follow the order in which Carter dutifully shipped them to the Museum between 1923 and 1932.

Carter's finds, after the reopening of the tomb in 1925, continued to make headlines and to draw even larger crowds to Upper Egypt. In the first three months of 1926 alone, as the political situation momentarily stabilized, more than 12,000 persons visited Tutankhamen's crypt.

Next to the discovery of the tomb itself, the public was captivated most by Carter's discovery of the solid gold coffin and the mummy. Of the two it is difficult to judge which created the greater sensation. As Dr. Derry, who examined the mummy with Dr. Hamdi, observed on November 17, 1925, in his press report, "The preservation of the dead body . . . had always excited the greatest interest."

In their report, the two anatomists placed Tutankhamen's age at about eighteen, certainly under twenty. They estimated that in life he stood about five feet six inches tall. His skull bore a close resemblance to that of Akhenaten, the heretic who first conceived of his creator in monotheistic terms. Like Akhenaten, Tutankhamen had a platybasia skull, that is, flat-based: in profile, it resembled a lima bean. This abnormality is found in patients who have Paget's disease and in other conditions associated with a softening of the skull bones. However, such an odd-shaped skull is not conclusive evidence of a disease of the central nervous system. Platybasia per se is not necessarily associated with symptoms. In Tutankhamen's case, the deformity may be ascribed in part, perhaps, to incest.

The Derry-Hamdi report observed that all of Tutankhamen's limbs were wrapped separately; all his fingers and toes, bandaged individually. The eyes had been left partly opened; the eyelashes were very long and intact. The skull cavity was empty. The nose—a portion of it, flattened permanently by the pressure of the head bandages—was stuffed with resinous material in the manner employed by mummy makers after extracting the subject's brains through the nasal passage, as observed by Herodotus. Another note: Tutankhamen's penis had been drawn forward, wrapped independently of other parts of the body, and then kept in ithyphallic position on pelvic bandages.

In a final paragraph, the examiners noted: "On the left cheek, just in front of the lobe of the ear, is a rounded depression, the skin filling it, resembling a scab." A scab? "It is not possible to say what the nature of his lesion may have been," they said.

The insect that bit Carnarvon, it will be recalled, had struck him on the cheek and left a scab. Thereafter, there was no stopping the legend of the curse of Tutankhamen.

CHAPTER 13

Breaking into the tomb and stripping the mummy initiated an unprecedented debate over the relationship between archaeology and the rights of the dead. Moral outcry was heard from the pulpit, the press, and parliament.

From the grave, Tutankhamen seemed to have wreaked his vengeance upon Carter: each successive controversy left him more drained, more embittered, more irritable, and more isolated.

Moral outrage at the treatment of Tutankhamen came from unexpected sources: the prospect of the body's removal from the tomb stirred the death merchandisers, the Associated Undertakers of Greater New York. Frank E. Campbell, whose New York mortuary facilities rivaled those of ancient Thebes, led the assault. "It is not pleasant to contemplate the prospect of having the bodies of Washington and Lincoln dug up after a couple of hundred or a thousand years and placed on exhibition in a public museum," Campbell asserted. "It is no less revolting to think of a similar indignity being inflicted upon the remains of King Tutankhamen."

At a meeting of the embalmers' organization, Campbell went a step further: "The mummies already in our museums have no business being there. They should be restored to the tombs from which they were removed."

In London, Sir John Maxwell, who had handled Carter's case before the mixed courts, scoffed at this line of reasoning. "If public opinion in this matter is germane, then, to be consistent, all bodies of rich and poor alike should be recommitted to the earth, and all national museums should take steps to return their mummies to Egypt for reinterment," he said. "But it might be as well to remind the good people at home," he added dryly, "that at all museums on a Bank Holiday the crowd dearly loves its mummy."

"The incident holds one moral," the London *Star* said editorially, "the superiority of incineration over embalming if a poor old king wishes his dust to rest in peace."

Arthur Weigall, the former inspector general of antiquities in Upper Egypt, acknowledged that he was besieged by people who asked: "How would we like it were foreigners to come to England and ransack our graveyards?"

He ascribed this widespread feeling against meddling to religious convictions. Some churchmen, he observed, held that the bodies of the dead should not be trifled with because they would rise again at the call of the last trumpet. To others, a corpse represented the total collapse of human expediency, the absolute paralysis of human systems and devices; and thus, in the mind's search for permanency, the bones of the deceased become consecrate. Indeed, Weigall, who was present when Carter broke down the wall and entered the burial chamber for the first time, recalled that he, Weigall, was "overwhelmingly conscious of the presence of God at that hour, and with all my heart I wanted the awaking king to know that he was safe in His hands, and that there was nothing to fear."

Nonetheless, as an Egyptologist, Weigall argued that the dead are the property of the living and that the archaeologist was truly the agent for the estate of the grave. The archaeologist is a gravedigger, if not of bygone individuals, then of bygone civilizations.

Even the critics were wont to admit that what was done cannot be undone. Once Carter discovered the tomb and unwrapped the mummy, the question of what to do with "it" became a matter not so much of ethics as of urgent practicality. Carnarvon before his death, as noted earlier, had expressed publicly the hope that the mummy would not be removed from the tomb. Carter, of course, entertained similar sentiments. During his American lecture tour, Carter told critics, "I believe myself that it is a wrong thing to disturb the dead." But, he added, "In no other way can we learn anything about unknown civilizations." In hedging, Carter implied that somewhere in time a line must be drawn beyond which the rights of the dead are terminated.

Carter's own moral dilemma runs as a submerged current throughout the trilogy he published in 1923, 1927, and 1933. In the first volume, he took issue with critics "who call us vandals for taking objects from the tombs." He argued that by removing antiquities to museums, Egyptologists really assured the safety of the objects, given the record of plunder in Egypt since antiquity. Four years later, in his second volume, he acknowledged that when he and his collaborators gazed on Tutankhamen's coffin, "many and disturbing were our emotions awakened by that Osiride form." Most of these emotions were voiceless. "But, in that silence," he wrote, "you could almost hear the ghostly footsteps of the departing mourners."

Yet what was to become of Tutankhamen's remains? One suggestion was that Tutankhamen's mummy should be mewed up in one of the empty chambers inside the Great Pyramid of Giza, on the outskirts of Cairo.

But Luxor was unhappy with the idea. Local merchants and others put pressure on Cairo to keep the mummy in its tomb. Luxor's interest was not so much ethical as commercial: as long as the mummy was within its tomb, the Valley would attract endless legions of tourists.

Many archaeologists subscribed to Luxor's position, but for different reasons. Professor Newberry, sounding more like a man of the cloth than one of the spade, observed, "The exhibition of mummies in our museums serves no useful purpose, and personally I should like to see all the bodies of the pharaohs of Egypt, which now fill a large gallery in the Cairo Museum, taken back to their tombs and reinterred." Sir Martin Conway, former vice-president of the London Society of Antiquarians, agreed: "I think that after Tutankhamen's body has been examined and all desirable information obtained as to his age, racial type and religion, it should be decently buried out of sight and with such precautions as will prevent disturbances in the future."

Other Egyptologists were against leaving the mummy in its tomb. "The problem . . . is a very serious one," Flinders Petrie warned, "much more so than the average layman [and academic] imagines." Unless an armed guard were maintained around the clock, he said, "I believe an attempt will be made by robbers to despoil the tomb. Even electric wires and the sealing of the door with heavy rocks would be of no avail alone." Petrie pointed out that every Egyptologist had experience with grave robbers, and cited the case, from a generation earlier, of Amenhotep II. That pharaoh's bones, of no intrinisc value, were returned, because of public pressure, to their tomb, and an iron gate was placed across the entrance. "What happened?" Petrie asked, providing the reply: "One night an Egyptian ghoul smashed the tomb open and tore the whole mummy to pieces. It is astonishing how the idea of gold or treasure will tempt a ghoul in any country."

Elliot Smith, the renowned anatomist-Egyptologist, concurred with Petrie. "There has been a good deal of not altogether relevant discussion about the ethics of desecration, which is none the less unfortunate because it is inspired by ignorance of the real facts of the case."

"If archaeologists did not open and examine these tombs," Smith said further, "there is no doubt that in time the native [sic] tomb-robbers of Luxor, the most experienced members of their craft to be found anywhere, would in time discover the hidden tombs, plundering them and destroying historical evidence. There can be no question that the work of the archaeologist, when conscientiously done, saves the ancient tombs from willful destruction and gives the mummies and the furniture a new lease of assured existence."

These arguments aside, for scientific reasons, Petrie and Smith, among others, favored keeping Tutankhamen in Upper Egypt. For one thing, the mummy was in poor shape, and a long journey might do further damage. For another, the climate of Upper Egypt was better suited for the mummy's continued preservation. Carter agreed. So did Lacau.

They won the day. On October 31, 1926, after four years of debate, Carter rewrapped the mummy and placed it in the first, or outermost, wooden coffin. Then he lowered it into the great quartz sarcophagus, which had remained, unmoved, exactly where it had been placed in the burial chamber at the time of Tutankhamen's interment.

It is still there.

The sarcophagus is open, and the lifelike, mummiform coffin peers up at visitors, bathed by a cluster of floodlights. In a sense, Tutankhamen lies eternally in state.

CHAPTER 14

The discovery and excavation of the Tutankhamen tomb was, of course, the high point of Howard Carter's life—more of an escarpment than a peak, and a plateau that lasted ten years. At 59, in early 1933, he completed the removal of the more than 2,000 objects he found in the hypogeum.

Like most men, Carter had plans that never materialized. He reconsidered his plan to explore Ethiopia; but, perhaps influenced by the gold he had found, he announced that he would instead search for the tomb of Alexander the Great. Carter was convinced that it was located in the environs of Alexandria, Egypt's great port city whose very name evoked memories of that imperishable conqueror. Many scholars were skeptical; unimaginatively, they argued that even if the tomb were found, no important relics would be recovered. According to tradition, the tomb was rifled first by Cleopatra to settle her debts and then by her Roman paramours, Caesar and Antony. But, just as Carter had been certain that Davis had not found Tutankhamen's tomb and that the Valley of the Kings was not exhausted, he was convinced that Alexander's lost tomb could be uncovered. And he forecast that Alexander would be found entombed in a "coffin of pure gold."

But when the work in Tutankhamen's tomb was finished, as if on signal from Osiris, Carter took grievously ill. For the next six years he suffered in great torment and agony. On March 2, 1939, on the eve of his sixty-sixth birthday, a year that is best remembered for marking the outbreak of World War II, he died.

In truth, however, Carter was not thus accepted by the archaeological establishment of his time. He lacked formal training; he was self-taught. He had no old school tie. In the class-conscious Victorian and Edwardian England in which he reached his majority, his origins worked against him—he never truly came up from downstairs. After all, his father had painted animal pictures for the fox-and-hound crowd, who thought of him on a level only slightly above that of their stableboys.

Like his father, Howard Carter also was in the employ of the nobility. But it was not only his lack of formal education and his class origins that worked against him—it was also his explosive personality. Carter was essentially a self-contained loner, fiercely proud, fiercely independent of mind and sharp of tongue. He did not make friends easily.

In one respect, Carter's plight resembled that of Heinrich Schliemann, who unearthed the gold of Troy. Through archaeology, both men groped for social status. But Schliemann, the extrovert, was a crafty, worldly trader and skilled public relations practitioner in an age before the term was invented. Schliemann, who, perhaps more than any other individual, had a right to the sobriquet of "founder of modern archaeology," made certain that he was rewarded for his finding of Troy. He was dined and wined by the kaiser in his native Germany and lionized in England, where he was a guest at No. 10 Downing Street and where he was accorded a doctor of canon law degree by Oxford University and was made an honorary fellow of Queen's College. By contrast, Carter never enjoyed an audience with either his king or prime minister, and no university in Britain bestowed upon him even an honorary degree.

The attitude of the Egyptological and English establishments is best mirrored in the assessment of Carter by his friend and colleague, Sir Wallis Budge, keeper of Egyptian antiquities at the British Museum. Sir Wallis said he possessed "very special qualifications for the work he undertook for Lord Carnarvon, namely, a good knowledge of colloquial Arabic, great experience in dealing with the natives [sic] and the 'antica' dealers in the country, [and was] skilled in the practical work of excavation." Budge also paid him the high compliment of being "a gentleman." But then Budge put him down forever, although he probably never thought of it that way. Carter, Budge said, possessed a "keen interest in Egyptian archaeology." So much for Carter's work over a span of forty-plus years in Egypt. He was not an Egyptologist.

Among the Egyptians, Carter fared no better with the elite than in his own country. In the Cairo Museum, the corridors are lined with busts of great and small Egyptologists, the giants and those "keenly interested in Egyptian archaeology," Brugsch, Mariette, Lepsius, Wilkinson, Maspero, and many others. Carter is conspicuously absent.

When I inquired about a bust of Carter (and of Carnarvon, who, if nothing else, most assuredly was "keenly interested"), I was told by an important Museum official, "Ah, the busts on display were all made before

1922." Perhaps. But in the courtyard I noticed, as I left the threadbare, rundown building, the latest addition to the collection, the bust of Zakharia Gnomein, the splendid Egyptologist who died suddenly in 1959 at the age of 48, apparently a suicide.

Of even greater interest, on the second floor of the Museum, where the treasures of Tutankhamen are on display in a shabby and dingy setting—reflecting the economic strains and stresses through which Egypt passed during the turbulent Nasser period—a placard in three languages retells the story of the discovery and excavation of the pharaoh's tomb. The names of Carter and Carnarvon do not once occur.

Egypt's treatment of the English explorers is explicable, given the spirit of troubled nationalism that has possessed the Nile for the past half century. But for England, a nation of explorers, the failure to honor one of its indefatigable sons is not so readily explicable.

Carter died at home, in physical agony but in peaceful surroundings, amid Egyptian artifacts, at Albert Court in the southwestern section of London. His last days attracted no such attention in the press as Carnarvon's had. At his death, the king sent no message.

In the retrospect of millennia, there was perhaps no one richer in experience nor more suited than Carter to have managed the excavation of the tomb; for that, Tutankhamen's ka should at least be grateful, even if Carter was the instrument of fate in shattering the hopefully eternal peace of its corporeal mold. It was as if thousands of years had to pass before the world produced a Carter to undertake the task of locating and restoring to Aten's rays the artistic triumphs of Tutankhamen's epoch.

Four days after his death, on March 6, Carter was laid quietly to rest at Putney Vale Cemetery, a burial place now largely forgotten. Among those few on hand was Lady Evelyn Beauchamp, who had not forgotten. She remembered him well as the tempestuous figure from her girlhood, when she was her father's companion on his forays into Upper Egypt.

By coincidence, a month after Carter's death, following a silence of more than three thousand years, Tutankhamen's trumpets reverberated around the world. At the Cairo Museum, in an experiment that was broadcast live to every continent, the two trumpets Carter had found in the tomb, one of silver and the other of copper, were played. Described as shrill and piercing by those in attendance, in a poetic sense the three short blasts on each bugle were, fittingly, taps—Tutankhamen's farewell to Carter above the earth and his welcome to Carter below.

Carter's ka, eternally hovering in the twilight zone between light and darkness, was probably pleased.

85

Lauren Hutton, one-time Playboy bunny, signed an exclusive modeling contract with Charles Revson and earned about $200,000 annually.

FIRE AND ICE

THE STORY OF CHARLES REVSON—
THE MAN WHO BUILT THE REVLON EMPIRE

A condensation of the book by
ANDREW TOBIAS

CHAPTER 1

NEW YORK ON $5,000 A DAY

It is the fall of 1972. Charles Revson is on the phone with the assistant manager of Campbell's funeral parlor, trying to arrange for the burial of Norman Norell, namesake of a major Revlon perfume. He is used to dealing with the manager at Campbell's, not the assistant manager, but the manager has stepped out. "This is Charles Revson," he says. "Do you know who I am?" The man apologizes. "Charles Revson, Charles Revson—don't you know who I am?" Sorry.

Revson tries another tack: "Mr. Norman Norell. Do you know who *he* is?" He doesn't know Norell, either. "Norman Norell! You don't know who Norman Norell is?" He is supposed to be making funeral arrangements, but he hasn't been able to make contact with this man. He says, "You don't know Revson, and you don't know Norell. *You live in New York?*" The man says something about the suburbs.

Charles's inclination is to hang up and wait for the man's boss to return, but he still has to make the funeral arrangements. He says: "Norman Norell. He's a leading name in fashion, if you don't know him. He's just died at Lenox Hill Hospital and I want to make arrangements. Go over and get him. I don't know what he is." By which Charles means religion. Norman *Levinson* was his real name, from Noblesville, Indiana. He was half Jewish, half something else. "I don't know what he is," Charles says, "so I don't know what the service is going to be. How big is that chapel of yours?" The man says it seats however many people, and Charles says, "No, it doesn't." He's arguing with the guy. "Oh, it has a balcony? You have to *tell* me that when you talk to me. How big is your air-conditioning unit? It's going to be very hot there." The man says it's whatever it is, and Charles says, "I don't know if that's enough, couple of thousand people going to be there . . ." The man reassures Charles that they've had plenty of people there and the system has been adequate. So Charles says, "Well, I don't know yet if we're going to have it at your place, but you go pick him up and fix him up and we'll see. I'll be down in a little while to pick the box. My name is Charles Revson—don't you know who I am? Well, when I get there make sure the other guy's there." Click.

The point is that there certainly were people who didn't know who Charles Revson was. On the other hand, Charles Revson was not the sort of person whom, once you had met him, you would easily forget. "I know that man," a waitress at the Sands in Las Vegas said as she refused to allow his party at her table. "I can't deal with him."

Shortly after noon on a Sunday in August 1975, with only a nurse in attendance, Charles Revson himself died. He left:

One cosmetics and pharmaceuticals empire—Revlon, Inc.

Three ex-wives—including one whose name he couldn't remember, one on whom he had cheated like a cardsharp, and one—Lyn—on whom he walked out days after giving her $30,000 in a tin can for their tenth anniversary.

One brother—with whom he had feuded bitterly for thirteen years.

Two sons and two stepsons—all working for their father, none entrusted with the execution of his estate or the direction of his charitable foundation.

One granddaughter—on whom he was able to lavish the affection he denied everyone else.

Hundreds of shell-shocked, verbally assaulted, overworked, overpaid, and in some cases wiretapped executives.

Scores of intimate one-night acquaintances.

And, withal, a great many more admirers than is commonly thought.

He left, too, an estate valued at barely $100 million. It would have been more had he not been given to spending money on a par with men five and ten times as wealthy. Raised in a cold-water flat in Manchester, New Hampshire, he had fought his way up to a standard of living that was New York on $5,000 a day. Literally.

His mahogany-paneled living room was by no means the world's largest, but it was ample (26' × 36'), particularly when you appreciate that it was the living room not in his triplex penthouse but on his triplex yacht. Air-conditioned so vigorously as to require electric blankets on every bed, the *Ultima II* was 257 feet long—a full New York City block; slept fifteen guests; and employed a year-round, full-time, uniformed staff of thirty-one—nine officers and twenty-two crew. It was powered by the equivalent of ten Cadillacs and a Toyota. Its propellor blades measured eight feet from tip to tip. A thirty-foot air-conditioned launch, a twenty-four-foot speedboat, and a little motorboat sat on one corner of the deck like bicycles on the back of a Lincoln. Sixteen bathrooms, twenty-two touch-tone telephone extensions . . . a walk-in freezer for the several hundred pounds of specially-cut meat flown down from New York before each cruise. Without taking into account its adjoining study and enormous dressing room, the Revson stateroom occupied 391 square feet—more than twice the size of the master stateroom on the presidential yacht *Sequoia*. After Onassis's *Christina* and Niarchos's *Atlantis*, Revson's was the largest private yacht in the world.

Revson bought the *Ultima II* in the summer of 1967 from D. K. Ludwig, the secretive billionaire shipbuilder, and then went about a major overhaul and total redecoration. The Burma teak decking alone, hand-laid in Naples, cost $125,000. Also: forty-eight sterling silver place settings from England, forty-eight gold-plated settings from France; two movie projectors for nightly movies; engraved, gold-lettered Cartier stationery with the blue, green, and white "R" flag flowering in the wind, at $1.75 or so for each sheet and envelope. . . .

You wish pizza? Sweet and sour pork? Lobster Newburg? Filet mignon? Fresh-squeezed juice in your Dom Perignon? Chief steward Wu would positively *run* to bring what you desired. And not out of fear, either, but pride. He would watch you take your first cup of coffee and, if it met with your pleasure, deliver every cup that followed precisely that way.

The *Ultima II* cost $3.5 million to buy and refurbish. The maintenance and crew, the transoceanic phone bills, the Gucci Bingo prizes, the fuel ($20,000 for a tank of gas), the steaks, the buckets of golf balls whacked off the bridge—by 1975 expenses were averaging $1,800 a day. Add in the cost of tying up $3.5 million, plus depreciation, and the ship cost Revson, personally, better than $3,000 a day. Four days out of five no one used it.

Yachts aside, there were scores of $650 suits and $1,000 tuxedos, dozens of pairs of $300 shoes. Each custom-made Jules Holden button-down shirt cost $42 (there were ninety-eight at his apartment); each pair of pajamas, also custom-made, was $68 (his last order was for a dozen pairs); each pair of custom-made undershorts—$26.50 (one executive tells of having had to transport an order of sixty pairs from Switzerland). These, plus eighty-six monogrammed handkerchiefs, ninety-five pairs of black socks, etc., were stored in glass-fronted drawers he designed to be able to tell at a glance what was where. And the custom-made drawers were just a small part of a custom-made cooperative apartment that easily qualified as one of New York's most expensive. It was sold after his death—in a terribly depressed real-estate market—to the Shah of Iran's twin sister for $1.4 million. But even at that it represented no capital gain. He had purchased the Park Avenue triplex from the estate of Helena Rubinstein for a mere $390,000 in 1967, but spent thirty months and $3 million gutting it and redoing it to his gold-everything taste. It had been an extremely open, airy, cluttered, eclectic apartment. His first step, characteristically, was to seal shut all the windows and provide a controlled, artificially-lighted, air-conditioned environment. Fans ran at all times, blowing warm or cool air; the electric bill alone approached $100 a day. Maintenance charges came to another $200. And that did not include the eight live-in servants or odds and ends like food.

If anything, the apartment was too large. The boardroom-like dining room seemed embarrassingly empty with fewer than twenty-four guests, so most dinners were served in the library. The third-floor marble-and-mirror ballroom and its adjoining industrial-sized kitchen cost $750,000 to do up, but were used not even once.

And then you had the country estate at Premium Point; the $200-a-day Waldorf Towers suite (formerly Herbert Hoover's) he camped in while the Rubinstein apartment was being made over; the masseur, the medical bills, the phone bills, the florist's bills, the $50,000 fifteen-minute gambling losses, the million-dollar U.J.A. pledges, the chartered jets . . . plus Lyn's chauffeur, Lyn's $3,000 dresses, Lyn's jewelry, Lyn's pinball machines, Lyn's daisy chain of $100 bills, Lyn's lunches at Lutece . . . there was no way Charles could make ends meet on his $1,650,000 annual salary-plus-dividends. He had occasionally to sell a few of his million-plus shares of Revlon stock.

A Revson secretary who lived "in constant fear" from 1968 to 1971, by which time the man had mellowed a good deal, put together a handbook for her successor. It ran 108 pages and included instructions on flowers ("If Mr. Revson is invited out, always include $150 for flowers as his gift to the hostess"); on every detail of office decorum ("Check that Kleenex boxes are at least half full . . . Curio shelf should be dusted. Mr. Revson is concerned about the items on this shelf . . ."); and on the daily nap ("It is the responsibility of the second secretary to prepare his sofa for rest . . . The sofa pad is to be kept in the bathroom closet on a hanger with clips"). The manual specified that the Revson bathroom be checked hourly, and that there always be "two glasses, his brush and three combs" out on the sink. Only twice in the previous year, the author noted, had Revson deviated from Geisha-brand tuna salad at lunch in the office; but for the occasional sorties out to the plant the secretary was to order a "double, double corned beef on rye, very lean with no fat, with mustard, wrapped in tinfoil. Also ask for a very old pickle . . ." An elaborate telephone procedure included the information that all Revson's phones have "a cut-off switch. The moment Mr. Revson picks up on any wire, you cannot hear the party on the other end." One frequent caller, the manual advised, was Lyn Revson. "He always takes her calls no matter who he is with or where he is." Still, "Mr. Revson is fully entitled to his privacy. Therefore, any caller, including Mr. Revson's immediate family, should never be informed concerning Mr. Revson's whereabouts or who he is meeting with."

CHAPTER 2

SEPARATING MYTH FROM LEGEND

No one who grows up in a tenement, starts a business in the middle of the Depression, and ultimately builds a half-billion-dollar global corporation, is ordinary, or even "normal." Charles Revson least of all. His business style was so abrasive, his personal style so eccentric, and his success so stunning, that he became something of a legend not just "in his own time" but, indeed, midway through his career.

In forty-three years he built one of the 300 largest industrial enterprises in the United States, and one of the 200 most profitable. He managed to do this not by capitalizing on a single great invention—which is easy once you have the invention. Nor by acquiring the ongoing enterprises of others and merging them into his own, as were built so many of our largest corporations, from General Motors and United Airlines to Gulf & Western and ITT. He was granted no monopoly, he was no bootlegger-turned-legit, he struck no oil—he didn't even have friends in high places.

Instead, Revson built Revlon product by product, shade promotion by shade promotion, country by country, year by year. Most men would have sold out and retired by the time the first $10-million plateau had been reached. The kind of entrepreneur who can take a company from nothing up to $10 million in sales is often not suited, either by temperament or training, to take it the next step, or the next or the next. But Revson, like very few other entrepreneurs, took his company all the way to the top. He sold the first bottle of nail enamel personally, and he was deeply involved with the selling of the half-billionth bottle. He wasn't just nominally in charge, after a while, checking in from the golf course to see how his young dynamos were doing. *He* was the dynamo, and he was running the place. To the day illness forced him to stop, he was the chief executive officer of the company—and, for all intents and purposes, the chief operating officer, the creative director, the marketing director and, for that matter, the *board* of directors.

This is not to say that he was a creative genius or an executive superman. He was not. You could even make the case that after a certain point his company would have been better off without him. But he did have a deeply probing, agile mind, incredible dedication and tenacity, a genius for color, an eye for detail, and an instinctive marketing sense. He also had the rare capacity, at least in part, to broaden himself and his horizons as the company grew. The extent to which he was *not* able to do this was, largely, what made for his peculiarities and for the byzantine way in which he ran his company.

Revson's handpicked successor, Michel Bergerac, will not be a legend, because he is just the kind of highly accomplished multinational business executive you would expect to find at the head of a company like Revlon. But put into the same spot a Charles Revson, whose father was a cigar-roller in Manchester, New Hampshire (Bergerac's father was an executive in Europe), who never got further than high school (Bergerac collected graduate degrees in Paris and Los Angeles), and who never even worked for any other large company to see how it was done (Bergerac was executive vice president of $11-billion ITT), and you have the stuff of quite a story. Not to mention massive insecurities, two hushed-up "heart attacks," and a nervous stomach.

In the annals of American business, Revson has to be compared not with Helena Rubinstein and Elizabeth Arden, though those comparisons are themselves fascinating, but with staggering egomaniacs like Walt Disney or even the original Henry Ford. *Big*-time sons of bitches. He entered a fledgling, highly unprofessional industry of one-man shows (one-woman shows, really) and, more than anyone else, was responsible for building it into a $5-billion industry. While his social impact was obviously not as great, nor as practical, as that of Henry Ford, he nonetheless changed the appearance of women throughout the world—both in how they looked to others and how they looked to themselves. He injected a little excitement into what Martin Revson, borrowing from Thoreau, liked to call the "quiet desperation" of the average housewife's daily life.

The irony is that he held women in such contempt. And that he himself, the beauty-maker, was so unbeautiful.

The paradox is that, for all the warts, many of the people who knew him well—women particularly, but men, too—fell in love with him. Literally, or as a sort of father figure.

It would be too easy to paint Revson only as a bullying egomaniac who would scratch his crotch or stand up and break wind in the middle of a meeting. In fairness, one tries to understand *why* a man as concerned with his image and dignity, and as afraid of being embarrassed, would do such things. He *was* the terror of Madison Avenue, but it's not enough to say that he would degrade his subordinates or that he was often hopelessly inarticulate. The question is, why? What was he trying to say?

The problem with legends-in-their-own-time is that it is sometimes difficult to tell where truth leaves off and legend begins.

"There are so many myths built up around this man," his friend and executive assistant, Irving Botwin, told me, "such as, to be perfectly frank with you, that he's tough, he's a prick. He's not. He finds it tough to fire somebody. He's the softest-hearted and most compassionate guy in the world."

Like any man, and perhaps more than most, Revson had different sides, different moods, acted differently with different people, and changed somewhat over the years. It's hard enough, then, to pin down the "real" Charles Revson, as though all his actions could have been predicted by a simple formula. And it's made all the more difficult by having to see him through the eyes of others, who have their own axes to grind. Needless to say, one doesn't hear too many stories in which the narrator himself comes out the fool or the blackguard. More often, the narrator is the hero with the clever tongue who, alone, would stand up to Charles and set him straight.

Revson loyalists go to great lengths to laugh off as "myth" anything that might seem the least bit unbecoming. Beware, they say, of talking with people who have left the company and who ascribe their own lack of success to some failing in Charles. Meanwhile, people outside the company dismiss those within as a coterie of lackeys not worth talking to.

But to a larger extent than either group might have expected, the basic pictures that emerge from each are not so very dissimilar. The main difference is in point of view. Both groups agree, for example, that Charles frequently tore his executives apart (though the loyalists deny he would bring grown men to tears). But the loyalists ascribe this to his desire to teach, while others ascribe it more to a need to bully and degrade. Both groups, with a few exceptions, concede the man's basic honesty. But the loyalists attribute this to pureness of heart, while some others see it as an inordinate fear of being caught doing something dishonest. One group sees him as having been generous; others concentrate on the motives behind the generosity. And so on. Certainly, though, apart from differences in point of view, stories abound which are simply untrue.

So, to begin with, one must disregard almost any information that is not, in some way, at least, first-hand. But that by no means suffices to screen out the unicorns. A key Revlon executive told me that Lyn Revson had given him a tour of their Park Avenue apartment and had shown him their huge bed—which, he said, had been fitted out with special flaps to prevent Charles from falling out at night. Charles tossed and turned a lot, Lyn told him, and these flaps would automatically come up at two in the morning to form a sort of cradle, and recede at six. Lyn pressed a button on the wall that activated these flaps "before his very eyes," he said.

Yes, there was a button on the bed that would elevate the head-and-shoulders portion of the mattress up to a TV-viewing angle. And, yes, there was a button concealed in the side of the bed that summoned the police, who would come dashing up to the apartment every time it was pressed accidentally. But—and I inspected this bed at some length—there were no automatic side flaps. Yet this man (and only this man) swears he saw them.

Similarly, when Revlon was moving into new offices at 666 Fifth Avenue, Charles did have the manufacturer of the boardroom chairs come to him for a "sitting," and did go through four different handmade models before he was satisfied. But he did *not* have them built so that all the directors, regardless of height, would end up at eye level—or, as the story is best told, with him one inch above the others. On the other hand, it *is* true that, presented with a series of valuable eighteenth-century Piranesi etchings for his approval, he said, "Shit, Sam, couldn't we get the artist back to put a little color in them?"

Most of the Revson stories that first-hand witnesses tell are probably true, if often embellished. But many of them, considered objectively, are less damning than they seem.

For example, one day Revlon was rehearsing a commercial that would be performed live in front of 50,000,000 people a couple of hours later on *The $64,000 Question*. There was no one in the theater but the technical crew, the model, the agency people, and the people from Revlon.

Charles was in the control booth. As they were running through this commercial, Charles's voice boomed out through the empty theater: "GET RID OF THAT GIRL, SHE LOOKS TOO JEWISH!" ECHO, Echo, echo. And the model, naturally, burst into tears and went running off the stage, with two hours to air time.

What no good storyteller will bother to point out, and neither of the eyewitnesses who told me the story did, is that Charles almost surely did not know that the mike in the control room was open or that anyone outside would hear him. Which, if so, makes his conduct (a) a good deal more believable and (b) a good deal less offensive.

Thus, there were often unreported circumstances which retrieve the man from utter caricature. He *would* take his pulse during meetings, he *would* check the color of the phlegm in his handkerchief, and he *did* have an electrocardiogram taken daily when he traveled. But he had also had two mild "heart attacks" in his midforties, which were kept very quiet. Knowing that, his hypochondria seems a little less outrageous. Likewise his bizarre eating habits.

There is the temptation to take sides. To say, with Victor Barnett, perhaps the least-liked executive at Revlon and the loyalest of the loyalists, that Charles Revson was "a truly great human being." Or to say with Josh Rothstein, former president of one of the companies Revson bought, and one of his most passionate detractors, that Revson was "the worst bastard who ever lived." Not surprisingly, the truth lies somewhere in between. Many spoke in terms of love/hate feelings. As one former Revson associate summarized: "He could do it all; he could make you want to die and he could make you want to live."

However his virtues and motives might be debated, and however murky the details surrounding certain of his affairs, the basic outline of Charles Haskell Revson's life is clear enough. He was born in Somerville, Massachusetts, outside Boston, on October 11, 1906. He grew up with his older brother, Joseph, and his younger brother, Martin, in Manchester, New Hampshire. There his father worked rolling cigars by hand, and his mother worked on and off as a saleswoman and supervisor at a novelty and dry-goods store. Both were Russian-born Jews. His mother, Jeanette Weiss Revson, was brought to America by her family while still an infant. His father, Samuel Morris Revson, emigrated in his early twenties to avoid conscription into the czarist army.

In Manchester the family lived in a six-unit tenement house on Conant Street. Their apartment faced the rear on the first floor. They had running cold water, a coal-burning stove for cooking and heat, and always plenty to eat. Oatmeal or Cream of Wheat with Dutch hot chocolate for breakfast, lamb chops or steak for dinner many nights, fish on Friday, and a roast of some kind on Sunday.

Almost everyone else on the west side of Manchester, the wrong side of the Merrimac River, was Gentile. Martin can remember only one other Jewish family. The Revsons kept largely to themselves. They virtually never entertained, virtually never went out to eat, attended no synagogue, and had no telephone.

Joseph, who in his own way was even stronger than Charles, fell behind in school because of illness. Though sixteen months older, he and Charles were in the same class in elementary school and throughout high school. Martin trailed four years behind. Charles and Joseph got along well and would often do their homework together, although physically and emotionally Charles and Martin seemed to come from one mold, and Joseph, from another. Joseph, red-haired and pasty-faced, was the aloof one, off in his own room; Charles and Martin, although further apart in age, palled around more and shared the same room.

The boys walked to school, nearly two miles each way, on even the coldest New Hampshire winter mornings. Joseph, miraculously, graduated second in their class of 127. The best explanation for Joseph's academic success would seem to have been his memory, his delight in detail, and his ability to learn by rote. Charles, who was more outgoing than Joseph and whose intelligence was sharper and more intuitive, graduated third or fourth. The Manchester High yearbook listed Joe's hobby as "reciting" and Charles's as "argumentation." The parrot versus the fox.

Charles was "Slotkin, a tailor" in the senior class play, worked on the school magazine and the yearbook, and helped organize a school debating team. A classmate remembers him as having been popular with the girls in the class, mischievous and, even then, sometimes curt or cutting with his sense of humor. Joseph, she says, kept more to himself.

Class president Rufus King, who starred on the football and baseball teams and still lives up in Manchester, says that the Revson boys kept pretty much to themselves. They weren't on any of the school teams. He remembers that "Chick," as Charles was then called, was "a real peewee." He was still just sixteen when he graduated, and it was only afterward that he shot up several inches to his full five-foot-eight or so. He subscribed to Charles Atlas to build up his body, but never in his life weighed much more than 140 pounds.

The Revsons were a proud family. Charles's father, whom all three sons called "the Major" (none could remember why), was a five-foot-one, balding, distinguished-looking man, and an introvert. But proud, and forever talking about his family in Russia who had been "purveyors of grain to the czarist government." A Litvak Jew, he took pride in the supposed superiority of the Litvaks over the Galicians. And while he obviously was not a great success, the job he advanced to—packing the various shades of tobacco attractively—did require a modicum of artistry. He didn't look like he belonged on the west side of the river, people said; he looked more like a banker. When the family moved to Brooklyn in 1925 in the hope of bettering its financial situation, he became a life insurance salesman. But, being neither especially aggressive nor articulate nor personable, he did not excel.

He was not a practical thinker. He was, instead, an ill-equipped intellectual. Martin remembers him as having been "very curious and interested in world affairs, but not too sound in his conclusions." Whether he was more a frustrated Russian aristocrat or a frustrated Socialist revolutionary, or just confused, the Major had no difficulty adapting to the luxuries his son provided him later in life.

Charles's mother was the taller and the more outgoing of his parents. Many years younger, more practical, more dynamic. A fair cook, but not much interested in the house. Where the Major led a secluded life, always reading, her prime interests were on the outside. She died of a strep throat in 1933. It may have been from his mother that Charles inherited much of his drive; the rest would have stemmed from a need he felt to supply the success his father's pride cried out for.

Upon graduating from Manchester Central High School in 1923, "Chick" left Manchester for New York, where he went to work selling $16.75 dresses for a cousin's Pickwick Dress Company. With that, the family's hope that he would become a lawyer began to fade. He was getting an education in women's fashion instead. By the time he left Pickwick he had worked his way up to being a piece-goods buyer, a job he preferred because it gave him the opportunity to work with materials and colors.

The story goes that Charles was fired from Pickwick in 1930 for buying too much of a pattern he fell in love with. By the time it was apparent the pattern would sell out, he had already found himself other work. Supposedly, he went right into selling nail polish for a company called Elka, in New Jersey. *Actually,* he ran off to Chicago with Ida Tompkins, the daughter of a farmer from Pennsylvania and a show girl, and married her instead of the lovely girl at Pickwick he'd been expected to wed. His parents were heartbroken when they found out.

99

In Chicago, he signed up with an outfit that sold sales-motivation materials. Sales plans. The year 1930 was not the most auspicious time to start selling them, however, and for the six or nine months he was in Chicago things were very bad. There were days when he had hardly anything to eat. He returned to New York with his wife, but had no better luck selling the sales plans. They soon separated. Charles enjoyed confiding to intimates that it was because the girl's parents were sure he would never amount to anything.

Whoever Ida Tompkins was, she should have tried to stick it out a little longer, as from here things started to go right for Charles. He moved back in with his family, by then living at 173rd Street and Amsterdam Avenue, and began selling nail polish for a firm in New Jersey. Then, with his brother Joseph and a man named Charles Lachman, now described as "the world's luckiest man," he formed Revlon. The "l" was for Lachman, who says they were first going to name the company Revlac, but it didn't sound good.

Revlon was born on March 1, 1932, when Charles Revson was still only twenty five. Unfocused to this point, his life would be, for the next forty-three years, 100 percent Revlon.

CHAPTER 3

THE OBSESSION

Whatever else he was—nasty, crude, lonely, virile, brilliant, inarticulate, insecure, generous, honest, ruthless, complicated—Charles Revson was a man of single-minded persistence and drive, entirely dedicated to his business. And a perfectionist. You could even say he was a fanatic, in the same way Bobby Fischer is, or J. Edgar Hoover was. Each lived exclusively for his own particular "business," and each knew his business better than anybody else.

"To Charles, Revlon was not a business, it was a religion," explains Irving Botwin. And while, unlike Fischer and Hoover, Revson had enough sexual diversions to fill one of those FBI file cabinets, even these were carried on with a certain market researcher's detachment. Women were his business. And nothing distracted the man from his business. The day John Kennedy was shot, Charles was in a meeting in New Jersey at the offices of Evan-Picone, a sportswear company he had bought the year before. A secretary came into the conference room with the news. Revson looked up, got up, walked around the room, and then continued with the meeting. The secretary was instructed to keep them posted. What good would it do to listen to the radio or call off the meeting? Would that help Kennedy? Not everyone would have been able to concentrate on the spring fashion line after hearing such news, but Charles Revson could.

Nor was he one to sit around at home wallowing in the national tragedy. On the official day of mourning, when businesses were closed and families throughout America were sitting sadly around their television sets, Charles Revson was at Revlon headquarters presiding over a marketing meeting. There was too much work to be done to take the day off. Because no matter how large or profitable Revlon grew, it was always nothing compared to what it could be. Nothing was ever right. It was one continuous crisis (a state of affairs he fostered), which only he could straighten out. "Why am I the only one who thinks around here?" he would complain to his people, most of whom were killing themselves on his behalf.

Revson was just too absorbed by his own world to pay much attention to the schedule of the world outside—and so close to the business he sometimes missed what was going on. There is the story, for example, that he once called a meeting of all his top people to discuss the problem of executive turnover. *Why couldn't Revlon keep its goddamn executives?* The meeting was called for six o'clock on the Friday of a July Fourth weekend; Charles walked in at eight o'clock; and he proceeded to tell the assembled that the *reason* they couldn't keep their goddman executives was that they weren't *training* them properly.

He knew about national holidays and events like Christmas, of course. But for him holidays were interruptions in the urgent work to be done. He hated holidays and vacations and did his best to keep his people from taking them. As for Christmas, that was no holiday—it was the pivotal selling season and, always, the greatest crisis of all. More than once he called meetings late on December 24—because to him it was just December 24. One yuletide meeting was called to discuss how heavy the returns of unsold Christmas-promotion merchandise might be. The bells of St. Patrick's down the street chimed eight . . . nine . . . ten times. But he was oblivious.

To some extent, of course, Revson would feed his voracious ego with such displays of power over his people. But it wasn't that *they* had to stay late while *he* was home decorating the tree. He was right there at the head of the table with them. Which suggests, inasmuch as he was highly competitive with his men, that such meetings were also a way of testing their stamina and devotion to the business against his own. Two tests he could never lose. Then, too, he may simply have been trying to milk every last ounce of effort out of them, as was his standard procedure. Finally, he and at least a few of the other men at such meetings must have taken some pleasure in the self-sacrifice involved in working late on Christmas Eve. By implication, it made their work seem that much more urgent, that much more important.

Still, whatever other motives may have been involved, Charles's basic obliviousness to time and complete absorption in his own empire was genuine. Like a sports addict with the score tied in the last inning of the last game of the World Series, he wondered how anyone could have his radio tuned to anything else. And for Charles the score was *always* tied, at best. He never felt secure enough in his lead to sit back and relax a little; egotist though he was, he did not think of himself as "a winner." He was constantly, irrationally afraid he might lose . . . which is to say, fail.

He made little effort to remember where business began and left off. Asked to say a few words at a farewell party for one of his international executives—a man with whose performance he was uncharacteristically pleased—he turned it into a half-hour harangue of the others present, chiding them for not performing as well. This was hardly the occasion for such a lecture. He could almost never bring himself to verbalize praise or thanks or affection. Such warm and positive sentiments did not fit his tough, manly, street fighter's self-image, or his generally negative outlook on life. So that on those few occasions when he *did* say something nice, he generally accompanied it with something cutting or sarcastic.

He did not waste time going out to lunch or socializing over executive martinis in the middle of the day. Instead, he ate lunch at the office with one group or another of his executives. These working lunches would sometimes run until four or five in the afternoon. All business.

Charles had no patience for small talk. One day Pope Paul was in town and scheduled to pass right by Revlon's office as lunch was underway. Charles excused himself to go into his adjoining sitting room for a minute or two, and while he was gone somebody says, "Isn't it great? We have perfect seats to see the Pope—a once-in-a-lifetime thing." And as he is rambling on about how the Pope has never set foot in America before, Charles comes back into the room. "What the hell are you guys talking about?" Charles asks testily (for him a standard entrance). So somebody says, "We were talking about the Pope's visit." And Charles says, "What the hell for? We don't sell to the Vatican."

One may guess that when Charles said things like this he was only half serious, in the sense that he was conscious of the role he was playing. And, for that matter, he may have assumed the others were conscious of it, too. But two things are certain: First, he wasn't just trying to be funny. He almost never tried to be funny. Second, though he may in fact have understood perfectly well why his people were talking about the Pope, he didn't want them wasting their—which was really *his*—time with it. Is that what he was paying them so well to talk about! Besides which, Charles could be comfortable in a group of people only if he was dominating it. The Pope's visit was not a subject on which he was the authority, so he would want to belittle its importance and return to the game at which he was, in both senses of the word, master.

Why couldn't these guys concentrate? Christ, you leave them alone for three minutes and they're talking about the Pope. Well, Charles Revson could concentrate. Not just on the business in general, but on individual details, as well. He would home in on a nail enamel bottle and study it and study it long after everyone else in the room would have run out of things to study, and *nothing* would be more important than that bottle. Or that lipstick shade. Or that advertisement. Needless to say, he often drove less exacting people (which is to say, everybody) crazy.

There was no disputing his ability to concentrate. He could spend an hour and a half going over one engraving proof trying to decide what color red the lipstick on the model's lips should be. He could go through thirty drafts of an ad before he was satisfied. And then make a change at the last minute.

He could see subtleties in color, in particular, that few laymen could see and even fewer printers reproduce. On nothing did he so stickle as on color. There was a meeting of salesmen and distributors at a hotel in Asbury Park, New Jersey, in the forties at which he was to be the main speaker. Everyone was already seated when he arrived. The regional manager made a brief introduction, but Charles refused to speak. He was offended by the tablecloths. They clashed with the rest of the room. This was Revlon, a color-conscious company; he was Revson, the color genius; he owned the goddamn company and was paying the hotel for the goddamn meal . . . and he wouldn't start talking until the tablecloths were changed. It took at least half an hour for the waiters to find acceptable tablecloths, remove all the silverware, dishes, glasses, water pitchers and so forth, switch the tableclothes, and then put everything back again. Then, and only then, could the luncheon begin.

Charles was not being theatrical; he was being typical. He wanted things right.

He set up a full-scale laboratory and sophisticated quality controls long before anyone else in the industry had them; he recalled batches of products long before—thirty years before—product recalls and "consumerism" were invented. Revlon's Sheer Radiance, a recent example, was selling very well when Charles, having first approved it, began to have second thoughts. "It could be better," he said. Right in the middle of a promotion he made them empty every bottle in the house, wash them all, and refill them with an improved formula. Sheer Radiance was out of stock for three months. Any other company that had a product selling so well would either have left well enough alone or gradually changed the formula as new batches were prepared. Not Charles.

If you were a bank president or an advertising hotshot or a potential supplier, you couldn't get him on the phone. But if you were a woman with a Revlon lipstick that smeared, you got through to him like *that*. "The reason I talk to them," he used to say of such consumer calls, "is that they are the real boss."

Even his friends were all business. He had no "life-long" friends as some people do. The only boys from Manchester with whom he kept in close contact were his brothers . . . and that was business. In fact, after Joseph (1955) and then Martin (1958) left, or were forced out of, Revlon, Charles froze them out of his consciousness altogether. He said barely a word to Joseph from 1955 until he died in 1971. And though Charles and Martin settled their differences around that time, for years they would pass each other in public places without so much as a nod of recognition.

The few close friends Charles did have over the years all worked for him in one way or another:

For many years, he and his second wife Ancky would socialize with Harry and Helen Meresman. Meresman was Revson's accountant from Day One and remained his closest financial adviser.

Lester Herzog was Charles's closest friend from the late thirties to the early fifties. He and Charles shared a "bachelor's" pad on Central Park South (the quotation marks in recognition of the fact that Charles was not a bachelor). Lester worked for Revlon as one of Charles's key yes-men, despite his lack of any apparent talent. But he was thoroughly devoted to Charles, and Charles was genuinely fond of him. Yet even Lester was pretty well forgotten when he married and could no longer spend his evenings out on the town.

Lester Herzog's successor in this role, Bill Heller, was first brought in as Revlon's controller, and later became head of the fledgling international operation. Divorced, he was for some years Charles's closest companion. Another friendship that was born of the business.

Particularly in later years, Charles was too much consumed with Revlon to have any interest in or time for making friends outside the business. For the better part of his life, most of the people Charles knew worked for him. Which may have had something to do with his autocratic outlook. He did not feel comfortable outside his own environment, or with equally forceful, successful men or women whom he could not dominate. Nor were the corporation heads, financial men, political figures, and New York cultural people you might expect to find in the circle of the chairman of a leading fashion company beating down his doors to gain entry. He was not first on everyone's guest list, since before each appearance his wife or his secretary would call up once or twice to dictate his menu and to check that it would be cooked specifically as required. And woe to the hostess who was not prepared with the Dom Perignon. True to his need to be in charge, he was a better host than he was a guest.

He belonged to Old Oaks Country Club in Purchase, New York. But he had no friends there. Sometimes people from the company would join him. But often he would play alone with the pro. He wasn't there for the game, anyway; he played a few holes to stay in shape for the business.

As for the *Ultima II,* a sensational yacht which should have served to win *anyone* friends, of a sort, anyway, the guest list was less impressive than the vessel. For many people the idea of being set adrift in large but nonetheless confined quarters with Charles Revson was . . . unappealing. The regulars on the yacht were a group from which he could expect absolutely no competition or argument.

How would Charles Revson spend much of his time in the middle of the Mediterranean? On the radiophone back to the office or the laboratory in New York. And was his yacht named after his wife? Naturally not: it was named after his prestige product line.

Even more than with most entrepreneurs, the story of the man is the story of his business.

CHAPTER 4

YES, HE PAINTED HIS NAILS

In Revson's last full year at the helm, 1974, Revlon reported sales (rounded off to the nearest $1,000) of $605,937,000. By contrast, in its first nine months of existence, in 1932, sales were $4,055.09—and there was no thought of rounding off the $55.09, because it was enough to pay his salary for two weeks, or two months' rent.

The following year, sales rose smartly to $11,246.98. Of this, expenses were as follows:

Merchandise purchased (nail enamel, bottles, caps, brushes, etc.)	$4,792.26
Wages	813.80
Rent	330.00
Miscellaneous taxes	161.29
Trucking and parcel post	345.67
Shipping supplies	71.71
Advertising (in trade journals)	978.32
Telephone	136.88
Traveling and miscellaneous	772.13
	$8,402.06

That left $2,844.92 for the three partners: Charles and Joseph Revson, with 25 percent each, and Charles Lachman, with 50 percent. (The profit in 1974 was $50 million.)

In 1974, Charles Revson had a home in the country, a triplex at 625 Park Avenue, a chauffeur-driven Rolls, and a personal staff (including the crew of his yacht) of forty-four people. He drew a $300,000 salary and collected $1,300,000 in dividends. He made more than $1 million in charitable donations and paid $131,000 in federal income tax. In 1934, he lived with his father and brothers at 625 West 164 Street in Washington Heights and rode the subway to work. He earned a total of $2,521.60 for the year, $50.79 of which was paid in federal income tax.

Like most companies, Revlon had a humble beginning. What gets lost in the comparison of 1934 and 1974 is the speed with which the company, and with it Charles, became secure. By 1937 he had—by most standards, and certainly by those of the Depression—"made it." In that year he drew a princely $16,500. Sales had multiplied forty-fold in just four years. Even after plowing $62,000 back into advertising, there was an $18,000 profit.

The next year, 1938, the company merely tripled in size. Charles's salary-plus-bonus jumped to $39,000—a lot for a single fellow in those days of the nickel subway and the $1,695 Cadillac. Thus, from 1930, when he left his cousin's dress company at the age of twenty-four, to 1937 or so, aged thirty, Charles Revson was struggling to make it; and for the rest of his life he was just struggling to make it bigger.

The year lipstick was added to Revlon's line of nail-care products, 1940, sales more than doubled over the previous year, to $2.8 million. They sextupled in the forties, septupled in the fifties, and nearly tripled in the sixties, reaching $371 million in 1970. By 1980, one might guess, even though Charles bowed out around the $600-million level, the figure could easily surpass $1 billion or more, particularly with the acquisitions Revson's successor, the man from ITT, is likely to make.

One naturally wonders how this great enterprise was launched. A company press release from the fifties, leaving out Charles's first wife, his trip to Chicago, and his brief career in the sales-motivation field, romanticizes the founding of Revlon as follows:

It was a bleak November morning back in the depression year of 1931, and Charles Revson, then in his very early twenties, badly needed a job. Over a cup of coffee in the Automat, young Revson scanned the sparse Help Wanted ads in the paper—a perusal that similarly occupied thousands of other jobless men at the time.

Two of the ads were for selling jobs; one for a man to sell household appliances—the other, a man to sell cosmetics. Each required applicants to appear in person, and at the same time the following morning. Charles knew there would be a long line at both places. He had never sold either household appliances or cosmetics. So, tossing a nickel in the air, he let chance decide where he would go: heads—cosmetics, tails—household appliances.

The coin landed on the table, heads up, and at dawn the next morning, Charles Revson was waiting for the offices to open. He got the job. A little more than a year later, Revlon was born.

That was the last time anything concerning Revlon was left to chance.

So maybe he didn't flip a nickel at the Automat to determine his fate. Maybe it was a dime. But the fact remains that he did go to work selling nail polish for a Newark, New Jersey, firm called Elka sometime in 1931. His territory was "Greater New York" and soon he had his older brother Joseph quit work at the General Motors assembly plant in Tarrytown to join him.

At first some of their friends and relations looked askance at the nail polish business. They considered it "sissyish." And cosmetics in those days were reserved largely for actresses and whores. What's more, this Elka firm in Newark did not have a great deal of class. There were just two of them at Elka, an older man who owned the place, and his demonstrator, a hunchback. She would go around the beauty shows pushing Elka's polish. "It was pitiful," Martin recalls.

Elka's product, however, was revolutionary. It was opaque. All the other nail polishes on the market were transparent. Charles saw the potential in this difference. The others were made with dyes and were limited to three shades of red—light, medium, and dark. Revlon felt that polish —"cream enamel," it came to be called—made with pigment so that it would really cover the nails, and made in a wide variety of shades, could capture the market.

He and Joseph were given a few feet of space in a cousin's lamp factory at 38 West 21 Street (the Revsons were never at a loss for cousins), and the tiny firm of Revson Brothers limped along for a year or so selling and distributing Elka nail enamel to beauty salons around New York. Charles began learning everything he could about nail enamel and about the beauty salons that were his customers. He wouldn't just deliver the product and collect cash. He would find out what was right about it, what was wrong, and what they liked about competitive products. He would put the stuff on his own nails to get the feel of it and he learned to apply it to others' nails by way of demonstration. He became, in effect, one of the few guys in the locker room who could give a really good manicure.

His ability to immerse himself in a subject was about to pay off. He began to see that the cosmetics industry, such as it was, was run by weak people; and he began to sense its potential. He asked Elka to expand his distributorship to include the entire country. When Elka turned him down, he went out on his own.

Which brings us to Charles Lachman, who had had the good fortune to marry into a small chemical company—Dresden—in New Rochelle, New York. Dresden made nail polish for other firms to sell. Lachman was interested in selling the stuff direct to beauty salons under his own label. He had heard about the Revson brothers, and he got in touch with them. Or else, as *he* remembers it, they were looking for a supplier, had heard of Dresden, and got in touch with *him*. Either way, it proved to be a very good thing for C.R. Lachman, then thirty-five years old. He and the Revsons agreed to form a separate company—Revlon—which would buy its nail enamel from Dresden. The Revsons were able to scrape together $300, for which, it was agreed, they were entitled to half the new company. Lackman would provide his technical expertise, such as it was, and see that Dresden supplied nail enamel to Revlon on credit. But because Revlon collected cash on delivery, Lachman's "financing" never amounted to more than a few thousand dollars.

It was Charles's first, and undoubtedly his worst, big deal. People used to ask Lachman what he did for the company. "I've got a rake," he would say, "and I rake it in." Still, a deal is a deal, and Charles was not one to renege. Many people have called Charles a son of a bitch, but few ever called him a "lying, cheating son of a bitch." He lived with his deal for a while; and then—and you can hardly blame him—he renegotiated it.

Lachman was described in some stories about Revlon as "a brilliant young chemist." Looking back on Revlon's early days, Martin Revson qualifies that description. "He didn't know his ass from a hole in the ground about chemistry," Martin says. Dresden did not have a better nail polish than Elka; what the Dresden deal offered the Revsons was a stake in their own business. Charlie Lachman did not develop any magic formula; in fact, it was his senior partner at Dresden, a chemist named Taylor Sherwood, who cooked up the enamel to the Revsons' specifications. Sherwood's mistake was in not wanting to participate in Revlon himself.

Now, if Charlie Lachman was not a brilliant young chemist, he was not a brilliant young marketing man, either. He did not share Charles's instinct for color, for fashion, or for the consumer. Nor was he by any means as driven. As a result, the brash young Revson and his slower-moving senior partner clashed. "To the point," says Martin, "where Lachman was asked to do nothing. After the first year, he did nothing and was put on the shelf. Absolutely nothing." For the next thirty-odd years he drew a substantial salary—plus "bonuses"—and he let Charles make the decisions and do all the work.

Fairly soon, of course, Lachman was smiling broadly. "He was very grateful for his good fortune, I must admit," says Martin. But two of Charles's decisions around 1937 did not sit so well.

The first was his decision to find a new nail enamel supplier. He was not satisfied with the quality of the product coming from Dresden. Charlie Lachman and his wife, Ruth (not to be confused with his second wife, Ruth, or his third wife, Rita), still owned Dresden, and his share in Revlon had not yet made him even his first million (let alone the $100 million or so it came to be worth at its peak)—so he was miffed. A company called Maas & Waldstein, located like Elka in Newark, was given the business and has kept it ever since.

To make matters worse, it was around this time that Charles said to Lachman, in effect: "We're doing all the work and you've got half the company. We ought to be equal partners." Lachman was persuaded to cut his own share back to a third, so that Charles and Joseph would each have a third. At the same time, however, two classes of stock were created in such a way that Lachman retained 50 percent of the voting rights. He could not be ganged up on.

Later, Lachman recalls, both he and Joseph wanted to cut young Martin into the company, but Charles, he says, was reluctant to go along. They persuaded him, and in the summer of 1938 each of the one-third partners was cut back to 30 percent, freeing up 10 percent of the company for Martin. But this was done in such a way that Lachman *still* controlled half the votes.

Unlike a silent partner, which is what Charlie Lachman in essence became, an entrepreneur has to work his ass off. He fills eleven jobs himself, he worries about everything, he is driven by a vision, and he is constantly selling different versions of that vision to customers, employees, investors, suppliers—to himself—and to anyone else who will listen. Yet the vision he is selling is not quite the same as the vision that drives him. He can endlessly extol the virtues of his product or service, evoking images of a world of whiter washes, fewer cavities, or more brilliant fingernails. And he can be intimately involved, as Charles was, in the creation and the quality of his products. But it is the business, not the product, that obsesses him. He just sells the product; he *owns* the business. He has a vision, quite simply, of hitting the jackpot and winning, along with money: independence, power, and respect—the game.

By one account, Charles Revson was "nurtured on Horatio Alger books." Whether or not this is so—in later life he stuck mainly to paperback Westerns—it is true that he always wanted to make a lot of money and that he never pretended otherwise. He harbored no fond memories of the simple life in Manchester; he got out of there as fast as he could. He harbored no left-wing sympathies, either. His thoughts ran more to the practical than to the intellectual. Looking out the window early one Depression morning as limousine after limousine passed by on the way from Westchester to Manhattan, he was not repelled by such opulence in the midst of widespread national suffering, as some of his peers might have been. Instead, he said, determinedly: "Some day *I'll* have a Cadillac limousine and be driven by my chauffeur to *my* office."

In the meantime, he and Joseph would take the subway from West 164 Street down to the drab, $25-a-month room they had rented at 15 West 44 Street, a few doors down from the Harvard Club and diagonally across from *The New Yorker*.

Charles would carry a soft black sample case full of nail enamel from beauty salon to beauty salon while Joseph remained in the office, keeping meticulous records, watching every penny and paperclip, and seeing that Revlon bills were paid on time. If Joseph told a vendor he would have a check by Monday morning, he could bet his life it would be there.

Martin was still working for the brokerage firm of E. A. Pierce, a fore-runner of Merrill, Lynch, and did not quit his $35-a-week job to become Revlon's sales manager until 1935. So the only other Revlon employee for much of 1933, not including the boys' mother, who would come down to help out, was a shipping clerk by the name of George Hastell. Hastell came to Revlon fresh from high school and was still with the firm in 1975, a manager in Revlon's large Edison, New Jersey, factory.

George Hastell

I started working [for Revlon in June 1933], and I had to get there at seven o'clock every morning. Mr. Joseph would open the door and then we would work and leave around five or six. They started me out at $7 a week and said if I worked out they would raise it to $9 after a month, which they did. Then the N.R.A. came in and everybody had to be paid $15 a week.

The office was very small. You walked through the door and there was like an eight-by-eight reception area, with a desk and a typewriter. Behind a partition was a room with two tables, a telephone and a window at the end that looked out on the street. When the four of us were in there— Charles, Joseph, Mrs. Revson, and me—it was crowded.

Our "warehouse" was a metal file cabinet. We had very little stock. We didn't make it ourselves; it came in to us from Dresden in eight-ounce bottles, and we would pour it into quarter-ounce bottles. You held the bottles in your hand and poured from one to the other without spilling. The one thing about nail enamel then was that it had a base, unlike the other nail polishes you could see through, and you had to keep this base in circulation. You couldn't always get it off the bottom, but Mr. Charles taught me how to shake a bottle to get it off.

After we filled the bottles and made up the packages, I would go down to the post office. They used to advertise in a beauty shop magazine, in which you sent in sixty cents and we would mail out a bottle of nail enamel. Or we would send it out C.O.D. My first day I came down to the post office loaded with packages and got in line, and when I got up to the window the man says to me, "Oh, you're from Revlon." I said, "Yes." "Another new kid, huh?" I said, "Yes, why?" I thought I was the *only* new kid. He said, "You're not going to last there. Nobody does. They always have a turnover. They work you too hard." Apparently, I was the third or fourth shipping clerk they had had that year.

Another job of mine was to deliver. I had a little black suitcase in which I'd pack the bottles, and I used to travel around on the subway or the trolley car and deliver. Everything was C.O.D.: if I made twelve deliveries, I'd come back with something like $12 or $15.

Mr. Joseph worked with me in the office. Mr. Charles was always out selling. Their mother worked in the office, too. She would drop in and help out, filling bottles, putting labels on them—all that sort of thing. Their father would drop in, also, but he didn't take an active interest. You could see he was proud of his sons because they had a going business, though.

Then we started to get busy, and I could see day after day the business kept growing. They got so busy they asked me if I knew anybody who wanted a job, and I said, "Sure." They said, "If you know some nice young guy, bring him in." I brought one in and this is the way it went, bringing in more and more people as we got bigger and bigger.

In that tiny building, 15 West 44 Street, there was a furrier called Sally Studios, and they were growing, too. And pretty soon there became a competition between the two companies of who was going to take up most of the building. Finally, we got so big that we said, "You keep the building and we'll move." And we moved to 125 West 45 Street, above Caruso's Restaurant.

We must have had twenty or thirty people in the factory by the time we moved to Forty-fifth Street, and five or six people in the office. It just grew continuously. It never stopped. On Forty-fourth Street we had no machinery whatsoever. On Forty-fifth we had two machines that I recall—old machines bought secondhand. One was a makeshift filling machine, so we wouldn't have to fill the bottles one at a time by hand. We put the bottles on wooden trays under a hopper full of four or five gallons of nail enamel. You pushed a pedal and the filling spouts would open up; when the bottles were filled, you'd lift up on the pedal and go to the next row.

And we got a labeling machine. At first we had to put labels on by hand. We had one of those ceramic rollers with water in it that you passed the labels over to wet the glue, and then you positioned the labels on the bottles and the boxes. The dexterity of the people doing this was amazing, that they could put them on straight all the time. If we had one that was slightly crooked, we'd scrape it off with a razor blade. But at Forty-fifth Street we got this big old-fashioned machine that would whirl and whirl around and a big arm would come down and put glue on and then come back up again.

When we moved the factory up to [525 West] Fifty-second Street [in

1938], we started getting things like conveyor belts. That's where we did all our assembling. That's when we started with our Christmas sets. We'd make a manicure set with bottles of nail enamel, a tweezer, an orange stick, an emory board . . .

In the early days, I remember particularly Charles always having nail polish on his fingernails, all different colors—a different shade on each nail. [This saved the expense of printing up a color chart]. Every time a nail polish came in, I'd see him sitting there, putting it on. Then all the girls in the office would have to wear the nail enamel. Same thing with the factory girls: he put the nail enamel on them and said, "You wear that." When we started with the assembly line operations, this got to be a problem. When a girl was called upstairs, it would disrupt the line.

He was particularly fussy about trimming the applicator brushes. He wanted them even, no straggly bristles on the sides, perfect. He made a fetish of perfection. He wanted perfection and quality. And even then we were throwing batches out if they weren't right.

In the early days, Charles and Joseph seemed to be very equal. It wasn't until later that Charles began to dominate. They each took a different area of responsibility . . . Charles was always the salesman, Joseph was the controller, the bookkeeper, the plant manager. Charles had the vision; he always knew that we would grow bigger and bigger.

CHAPTER 5

CHARMING CHARLIE

When I started," Charles Revson is supposed to have told Revlon sales managers on more than one occasion, "I used to sell bullshit. I used to walk around—I didn't have anything, didn't even know where I was gonna eat. I used to walk into a store and sell some bullshit, and walk out of the store and say, 'Hey, that's pretty good.' So I went back and bought the bullshit back for more than I sold it for so I could use it again to sell it for even more than I paid for it."

Though he had failed with the Chicago sales-motivation outfit he briefly represented, Revson apparently learned something about selling and about motivating salesmen from the experience. He was not the smooth-talking, carnation-lapeled hero of *The Music Man*, but his enthusiasm was equally great, and in his youth he cut quite a figure. "Charles personally went out and did the selling," a long-time associate asserts, "personally got the distribution, personally slept with half the girls around the country to get counter space for Revlon. He was very human, very charming, very witty, smoked three packs of cigarettes a day, and drank bourbon neat. His charisma is what built Revlon—and the rest of the industry as well. All this other stuff . . . his impeccable behavior, dark suits, not laughing, not drinking, not smoking, being very staid and proper and so on . . . all that came later, after the company was of a very sizable dimension."

Although most of them go unrecorded, Charles Revson had some wild times in the thirties—and the forties and the fifties, and the sixties, right up until the time he married Lyn. "Charlie was terrific," says one of his first salesmen. "We used to travel together sometimes and get laid every night and have a fantastic time."

Instead of loosening up as he became more successful, he stiffened. Instead of becoming more comfortable with the big world outside, he became more introverted.

Almost everyone has tried selling something at one time or another—Girl Scout cookies or Christmas cards, yearbook ads or encyclopedias—and the experience for most people is unsettling. It is lonely, it is embarrassing, and the inevitable rejections are deadening. Tough enough when, in your sales pitch, you can blame your pushiness on a "good cause," like the yearbook; or when you are backed by a well-known name; or when you are calling on people you know; or when you have a supportive sales manager helping to guide you along. But try going cold, a young Jew from Manchester, New Hampshire, on the shortish, thinnish side, into beauty salon after beauty salon where nobody knows you, nobody's heard of you or your product; and try selling it at a premium price, cash on delivery, in the depths of the Depression. Those first few years took the kind of motivation few people have. If Revson hadn't had three big pluses going for him, he might never have made much of a name for himself. But, first, he really did have a much better product; second, he was an attractive young man calling, for the most part, on women (bringing out sexual instincts in some and motherly instincts in others); and third, if he didn't keep selling, how was he going to eat?

The lean years paid off. Beauty salons that tried the product reordered. Word spread within the beauty trade and among women. Soon Charles was hiring salesmen, attending beauty shows, and signing up beauty supply jobbers to distribute Revlon products in other parts of the country.

Charles could not afford a booth at the 1933 beauty show. A young man he had met while calling on beauty salons, Robert Hoffman, inventor of the Hoffman professional hair drier system, gave him a corner of his own. Charles set up a card table and painted all the nails he could. He collected cash in a cigar box from the sales that resulted. Later, as Revlon grew and the Hoffman hair drier system ran into stiff competition, Hoffman went to work selling for Charles Revson. But for a while he was one of several more established men in the beauty field who took a liking to Charles and tried to help him along (and then wound up working for him).

Hoffman remembers going down to Atlanta to attend the beauty show there. "We drove down to Washington in my old Ford, and took the train from there," he says. "While we were in Washington, he stayed with one of my cousins, and I stayed with another. (Neither one had enough room for both of us, and we couldn't afford a hotel.) He stayed on the couch. The next day, my uncle, who had a potato-chip plant, gave us a huge tin of potato chips to take along on the train. When we got to Atlanta, Charles checked us into the best suite in the hotel, to make an impression . . . but he had no cash. He believed in the best even when he was broke. He was buying made-to-order shoes long before he could afford to. [One of the first tenets of salesmanship: Look successful.]

"He wired Joe for money, and Joe wired back just one word: 'No.'

"We had to entertain, so we went out and bought the cheapest bottle of whiskey we could find, and all our entertaining was done in this big suite with a giant can of potato chips in the middle of the floor."

Charles was the smartest, most dynamic man at the show, all of twenty-seven or twenty-eight years old. People gravitated to him. The phone in their hotel suite never stopped ringing; the women loved him. The only thing that put people off a bit—even then—was that, as Hoffman recalls, "He was the most miserable eater I have even seen. He would think nothing of sending eggs back three of four times. You know: 'I ordered two-minute eggs, and these are two-and-a-half-minute eggs.' And he would make a scene sometimes."

There was still the matter of the hotel bill to be cleared up, not to mention the train fare he had gambled away at a series of convivial late-night poker games. Joseph had been careful to give his brother a series of future-dated checks, one for each of the weeks he was to be on the road, and he wouldn't send more money. (Without Joseph's small-mindedness and conservatism, Revlon might not have made it through those first difficult years.) Charles managed to borrow some money from another of his mentors at the beauty show, a man named Mike Sager.

Sager used to travel around the country in his Chevrolet selling cosmetics for Hyman & Hyman. He met "Charlie"—as the real old-timers knew him—at a beauty show and, like Hoffman, helped him get in to see the right jobbers. Eventually, Sager left Hyman & Hyman for Revlon. For a while he had the entire West Coast as his territory. He also helped the company find new products to copy. "Copy everything and you can't go wrong," he remembers Charles telling him. That way—and it was basically Charles's formula for forty-three years—you let the competitors do the groundwork and make the mistakes. And when they hit with something good, you make it better, package it better, advertise it better, and bury them.

Another salesman who traveled with Charles was Jack Price. To conserve funds, one of them would check in and give the bellboy all their luggage; the other would wait a few minutes and then sneak up to the "single" room. "Charlie never went to bed without putting lipstick on his lips and nail polish on his nails," Price says. "He would leave a call with the desk to wake him at two and at four and at six to see how it was wearing."

A small booth at the Midwest Beauty Show, in Chicago's Sherman Hotel in the spring of 1934, resulted in Revson's first big sale. As he told the story to a trade paper years later, with some stilted editing and perhaps just a touch of honest fiction:

"I started my sales talk by showing the prospect how to apply our cream nail polish, then a new type. Before the week was out, I was teaching beauty shop operators and clerks how to demonstrate and use the polish. That group grew so big I had to rent the booth next to ours, and that additional space made my exhibit larger than our entire plant.

"One afternoon, when I had seven or eight pupils demonstrating, the manager of the beauty salon at Marshall Field & Company stopped by, watched our practical schooling, and from the size of the operation evidently got the idea that we were a big concern. She gave me an order that nearly exhausted our stock. [Later,] I dropped into Marshall Field's and told the salon manager we always followed up our orders and asked could I be of further service . . . She asked about other colors in our line, and I pulled out my order book.

" 'Your company must be a pretty big concern to hold a man over here just to service accounts,' she remarked as she placed an order for a dozen of one number.

" 'Not as large as we hope to be,' I replied, wondering how Joseph was going to package and ship show orders alone, not counting this one.

" 'Next time I'm in New York I'd like to go through your plant and meet your chemist,' was her clincher as she added three dozen of another item to the order, darn near filling that sheet.

" 'Yes, do that, but I hope it's not too soon. We are working out an expansion program and the place will be cluttered up for a while.' Of course, I hoped her trip would be delayed.

"I sent the order to Joseph by wire. It was the biggest we'd ever had. [Around $400, by most accounts.]

"He wired back: 'Is this an error in transmission? I couldn't fill it in weeks.' I wired, 'The order is correct.' Then I caught the train back to New York.

"The last of that order went over to the post office at midnight Sunday. Joseph and I dragged our weary bones for a sleep around the clock. We hadn't seen a bed in nearly a week. But we had made our promised shipping date."

And they all lived happily ever after. In fact, there was another big coup at that 1934 beauty show. It was at that show that Charles met A. C. Bailey, of the Bailey Beauty Supply Company in Chicago, which has been distributing Revlon products in that city ever since. Bailey remembers Charles selling alone in a tiny booth a tray of five shades of enamel at $1.25. But he went with Charles nonetheless.

"I went with him," Bailey says, "because I had checked with some of the finest beauty shops in the east, like Michael of the Waldorf, and found that this polish was incredible. It was chip-proof and had more stay-on power, had more gloss and luster, the colors were beautiful, and the formula was just terrific. We were carrying at that time about five brands of nail polish. We threw it all out and carried only Revlon."

Forty-three years later, Mr. Bailey appreciated the chance to characterize Charles Revson: "The most charming man that ever lived, the most dynamic man that ever lived, the greatest salesman that ever drew breath; very charitable, very knowledgeable, a dynamic personality, and a great human being." Which suggests that Charles acted differently with people who bought from him than with people who worked for him. And that he was easier to love from a thousand miles away than from down the hall. But Bailey's warm feelings are understandable. Revlon *built* jobbers like A. C. Bailey. The demand among beauty salons for Revlon nail enamel became so great, to the virtual exclusion of any other brand, that the jobber in each city fortunate enough to have the Revlon line was almost assured of success. As Revlon grew and added more products, so did the jobber. Even so, many of them hated Revson. He pushed them for all he could.

In 1935, Martin joined Revlon full-time as sales manager. If Joseph was the old-fashioned elementary-school teacher, explaining everything very slowly, twice, and putting a great premium on neatness . . . Martin was the demanding but popular high-school football coach, who "actually believed all the things he said," as one incredulous associate put it. Martin had many of Charles's dynamic qualities, but not the brilliance—or the mean streak. Martin was more ebullient, would shout, throw things out the window, pound the table; Charles never raised his voice. Yet people feared Charles; they liked Martin.

"I traveled all over the country with Martin and he was fantastic," says ad man Norman Norman. "It was our job to give sales presentations to department stores. We'd go to a city, take the biggest suite in a hotel and meet with nobody but the president of the store. 'I'm Martin Revson, V.P. of the company. I'm entitled to see you. We're going to be the biggest cosmetic company in the country and I'm here to work out with you the details of how that's going to happen.' First the president would laugh, then he'd take him seriously, and before you knew it, an hour and a half later they were working out the details . . . Martin was one of the most brilliant sales managers I've ever seen in my life and it was all home-grown and natural."

Martin developed "Psycho-Revlons," where salesmen would act out selling situations in front of a group and have their performance criticized. At the time, this sort of role-playing exercise was novel. (Charles would not subject himself to group citicism, but in the early days he did keep a recording device in his apartment to practice pitches and pep talks.)

Martin's sales force quickly grew to cover the whole country. By 1937, they were selling to department stores, and then drugstores, as well as beauty salons. It was an aggressive sales force; slackers were not tolerated. The pressure from the top came right down through the ranks to the salesman. One district sales manager required a lagging salesman to call in *every two hours* to report on his progress until his performance improved. And since drugstores were often open until ten at night, salesmen were expected to work very long days, if necessary, to meet their quotas.

Periodically, other cosmetic firms would attempt to encroach on Revlon's territory, and competitive battles would ensue. The Revlon salesmen were expected to win. If a Chen-Yu nail enamel color chart somehow walked out of a store in a salesman's briefcase . . . well, it could always be replaced by a Revlon color chart. If the bottle caps on some Chen-Yu nail enamel were loosened a bit and the enamel hardened

. . . well, the store, or the consumer, would know not to buy an inferior brand again. If, in an attempt to secure counter space, a salesman should spread his arms out, accidentally sweeping the competitive product off either end of the counter onto the floor . . . well, the salesmen were authorized to buy up the damaged merchandise at the retailer's cost and replace it with Revlon product. And if there were a particularly intractable marketing problem, Mickey Soroko might be sent in to take care of it.

Mark D. Soroko—the strong-arm man, the problem-solver, the enforcer, the house dick. A character lifted straight from the pages of Damon Runyan. Soroko was in some ways the most valuable player in the company, after Charles, for twenty-five years. He was first a process server, tracking down people to serve with subpoenas, and next ran a collection agency, frightening or threatening people into paying off their debts. He was the kind of guy who would go out of his way for a fight.

Mickey met Charles through a cousin—the mind boggles at all Charles's cousins—and then, when he was going through a messy divorce and was down on his luck, in the midthirties, he moved in with the Revson boys, who were sharing a suite at the Cameron Hotel on Eighty-sixth Street. Martin and Charles slept in one bedroom, Joe slept in the other, and Mickey slept on the couch. At first Mickey was reluctant when they asked him to join Revlon. "I thought it was a feminine business," he says. "I was surprised later on when I found out it was one of the roughest businesses you can have. Especially due to the fact that outside of Helena Rubinstein, we were the only Jews in the business. And we were not welcome."

If the beauty business was a "pretty rough one," it was partly because Mickey Soroko was in it. Mickey was the kind to shout and threaten and slam his fist on the table . . . even, some said, to carry a gun (though not to use it)—or, at least, to show up on occasion with someone who did carry a gun. Yet most people could not help liking him.

Fiercely loyal to Charles and to the company, he would always wait around at night until Charles left the office. And Charles, though undoubtedly a little afraid of Mickey, recognized his indispensability and rewarded him appropriately. He made a gentleman of Mickey: Hand-tailored suits, Havana cigars, and yellow Cadillacs that were his trademark in Larchmont. As a final gesture, in 1971 Charles made him a member of Revlon's board of directors.

Charles liked street fighters, liked to think of himself as one, and had his man in Mickey Soroko. No one knew exactly how Mickey did what he did—there were plenty of rumors—but he got things done. Presumably, those people he couldn't scare into doing what he wanted he could cajole, and those people he couldn't cajole he could pay off. He had signing privileges on a special Revlon bank account. And no Revlon controller was about to question any of his expense vouchers. In one town ages ago there was a problem with fire regulations, which would not permit the sale of nail enamel, a flammable substance. A couple of weeks later, one of the *fire trucks* went around delivering the nail enamel that had been held up. How did this happen? Mickey won't say.

He was responsible for all Revlon's product liability cases, which is why he became so thick with the dermatologists. They could alert him to problems; they would be loathe to testify against Revlon in court. (A Revlon base-coat called "Ever-On" in the early days was so effective that it may have been responsible for the devastation of a great many fingernails and perhaps even one amputation. The product was withdrawn, of course, and Mickey went dashing around the country settling what might otherwise have been scores of costly lawsuits. Without Mickey, Revlon might then and there have gone the way of Bon Vivant vichyssoise.) He was responsible for dealing with the Food and Drug Administration. He was responsible at first for labor negotiations. And for internal security. And for enforcement of Revlon's selective distribution policies—cracking down on black market operations in Revlon merchandise. Anything that needed doing where you might have to get your hands a little dirty, Mickey stood ready to do.

Clearly then, despite Revlon's reputation as a one-man success story, Charles had some invaluable help. In the early years, brother Martin and Mickey Soroko were among the major contributors. Others came on board as the company grew. And there were also a great, great many minor contributors.

One such was David Kreloff, who in 1975 was completing his thirty-sixth year of service to the company, about as loyal a soldier as one could find. He was around early enough to see Revlon in its adolescence.

Dave Kreloff

When I first joined the company in March of 1939, Revlon was already substantial. They had enamels and the manicure products, but they did not have lipstick. They came out with lipstick in 1940, and it was unbelievably exciting. I was in the mail department and it was a six-day week, until noon on Saturday. I'm always thinking of ways to improve things, and I went to the controller and said I wanted to make some suggestions but I didn't know who to talk to . . . and a week later I was made head of the mail department. And six months after that I was brought up into the sales department.

In those days, Charles would hold a sales meeting every Saturday on the fifth floor of our offices, at 125 West 45 Street. The conference room was right next to the mail room on that floor. He would come in in the morning, take off his jacket, roll up his sleeves, and stay in there for the whole day. The meetings lasted all day. When I finished my work I would go in there and do whatever they wanted me to do. I used to run over to the Gaiety Deli off Seventh Avenue, and get them all sandwiches.

He was the greatest salesman ever. Martin was the sales manager, but Charles was the salesman. I'd listen to him talk about why you can be successful and how you can be. He always said you had to have the will to win. And you couldn't help yourself—you had to believe him. I watched him sell his bottle of nail enamel to two department store buyers one day. They just couldn't resist him. He didn't scream or badger; he told them what the future would be. That the whole fashion world was going to come along, and that this is what it would be like. They believed him and he was right.

Can you remember anything about Joseph?

Well, if something was on the floor, even a piece of paper, he'd have a meeting and make a big fuss about it. He would make an issue over it. I remember rubber bands. But he was a nice guy . . .

What about Martin?

Well, I remember one day I was sitting in on a sales meeting he had called . . . and Charles walked in. And you could see it and you couldn't: a little flicker of change came over Martin because big brother was looking over his shoulder, Charles being as critical as he is. As Charles walked in Martin kept talking, but his tone had changed. Less self-confident. And Charles just wandered around making everyone feel uncomfortable; the meeting went nowhere until Charles left the room.

CHAPTER 6

LIFE WITHOUT FATHER

Johanna Catharina Christina de Knecht, the beautiful daughter of an important Dutch publisher and the former wife of a French count, sailed from Europe in 1939 with a group of friends aboard a yacht belonging to Baron Johnnie Ampain. The baron was a European banker/industrialist, said to have an income even then in excess of a million dollars a year, and it had been his intention to sail to the Philippines via the Suez Canal, with a brief layover at his home in Egypt. Bad weather precluded passage in that direction, however, and so the party sailed the other way, via Monte Carlo, to Cuba instead. From there young Johanna had gone with some friends to New York, staying at the Sherry-Netherland Hotel and planning to return in two weeks to Paris.

But war broke out, and travel plans were again up-ended. Worse, the flow of funds from abroad was interrupted, and the twenty-five-year-old ex-countess found herself modeling for Saks Fifth Avenue.

She and some other models were returning from a photo session at the 1939 World's Fair one March day when they stopped at a beauty show being held in the Sixty-fifth Street armory. While waiting for one of the models to have her picture taken, Johanna Catharina Christina de Knecht, who spoke four languages, was approached by a kinky-haired gentleman who introduced himself as Lester Herzog. He invited her to have her nails done at the Revlon booth. Ancky Christina, as she was known for modeling purposes, accepted.

"The first time I saw her," Charles recalled ten years later, "she had the wrong shade of lipstick. She needed an education and I had a lot of trouble with her." Perhaps—but he was taken with her nonetheless. He asked her out for the evening. In fact, he took eight or ten people out on the town that night, as he often would in those days (many of them buyers), darting into one nightclub for a drink or two and then out to another and another and another—and another. "I said to myself, 'This man must be rolling in money. He's crazy!' " Ancky recalls.

Charles took Ancky home. "He gave me his card and said, 'Call me.' And that was the beginning, I vood say."

At first, though Charles seemed like "a very nice man, very dynamic," it was really the opportunity of modeling for Revlon that interested Ancky. "It was a working arrangement, you might say." (Ancky was neither the first model nor the last to have such an arrangement with Charles.) But over a period of about a year—and a great many American Beauty roses, which were his trademark, three dozen at a clip—Ancky began seeing more and more of Charles Revson.

Sitting on the veranda of her magnificent Palm Beach home, a few doors down from Estée Lauder's place, fifteen years divorced from Charles but in love with him still, Ancky recalled the unorthodox way he went about wooing her:

"Charles kept on saying, 'I'm never going to get married, I'm never going to get married.' So one day after about six months I said to him, 'Charles, I'm not getting any younger, you're never going to get married, it's been nice knowing you, we had a marvelous time—think we've got to say bye-bye.'

"So he kept on saying, 'I'm never going to get married.' So I said, finally, good-bye. And we got married four days later."

The wedding was held on October 26, 1940, in a judge's chambers in New York. Charles was thirty-four. During the course of the ceremony, he started to laugh. Heh, heh. "He wasn't laughing purposely," Martin recalls, "or making fun of the ceremony—he was laughing nervously." But Judge Eder didn't know that. He departed from the traditional text long enough to remind the groom of "the seriousness of marriage."

Marriage was not Charles Revson's forte; he was not entirely enthusiastic about the concept. No doubt this was partially the result of his first one. Indeed, when Charles and Ancky went for their marriage license and Charles was asked by the clerk for the name of his first wife, Charles—though he readily admitted there had been a first wife—simply could not remember her name. Ancky had to supply it for him.

Their week-long honeymoon was in Hot Springs, Arkansas, where, perhaps not coincidentally, Charles was also able to take care of some business with an important department store. "I think that was our trouble," Ancky reflects. "It was always business. Always business. I think he lived his whole life for business."

"The first year," Ancky remembers, "we used to go to lots of good places. We saw every show. Charles was a big theater-goer, and we used to sometimes get into a little argument. If the play was no good, he'd say, 'C'mon, let's go.' I'd say, 'Oh, let's stay, it might get better.' Maybe that's why he made three or four nightclubs in one night—he was impatient. He didn't like something, he'd walk out and go to the next place. He was usually right when he said, 'It won't get any better.'"

The Revsons always ate out—at Pavillon, the Colony, or at Ronnie's Steak House, a Revson favorite. "He'd say, 'Let's have dinner around seven-thirty.' I'd say, 'Fine,' and show up at the office at seven-thirty. And I vood sit and sit in the waiting room, sometimes until nine o'clock, and it was getting to be a little . . . So I said, 'Charles, I won't come, I won't pick up, I won't wait, I'll meet you in a restaurant. And if you say we are going to have dinner at eight, we meet at the restaurant at eight.' Then he came on time, I suppose because he didn't want me there by myself."

Every so often the dashing young couple would go to Ben Marden's casino, a big nightclub over in Jersey well known for its activities upstairs. "Everybody went there," says Ancky, "all of New York." They used to let Ancky win at blackjack just to keep her away from Charles, who was playing on the "real" table for big stakes. By dealing Ancky winning hands, they had her begging Charles to stay just a little longer. Later he learned to set in advance exactly how long he would play—rarely more than half an hour—and when time was up, he quit. He would win a lot and he would lose a lot, but he would never get carried away.

Several times a year they would go out to the track, and for a short period in his life Charles became absorbed in the horses. He would sit in the office betting twenty races a day. He enjoyed gambling on tips in the stock market, too. He was not one to buy and hold, he was after *action.* Yet in business, he was not a gambler. The business was not to be fooled with or jeopardized in any way. Without the business, the rest of this would not have been possible and Charles knew it.

In 1942 Ancky became pregnant with John. "I was excited about it," she says, "because from the day I got married I wanted to get pregnant— and it wasn't easy." One reason must have been that for a time Charles didn't want to have children. "I wanted to have five," Ancky says, "but he said it wasn't a good idea to bring children into 'this miserable world.' The war was going on and there was a lot of tension." High as Charles was riding by 1942, it still seemed to him a miserable world. Ancky had John, then a miscarriage, then Charles, Jr., then another miscarriage. But later she adopted a daughter (as a final attempt, some said, to regain Charles's attention before their divorce in 1960); and later, with her new husband, she adopted two more children—so she wound up with five after all.

During the war, Martin was in the navy and Joe was in the army. Ancky worked for the Red Cross every day from ten to four and would sometimes get up at five in the morning to go down to the boats that were arriving with wounded soldiers and accompany them in the ambulances to lift their spirits. For recreation, she attended aviation college two nights a week. She learned to fly, but not yet being a citizen could not get her license.

While Ancky was working day and night on her charities, her husband was working day and night on the government contracts Mickey Soroko had somehow managed to land him, and on Revlon. Besides assembling first-aid kits, he was charged with producing dye-markers for the navy and hand-grenades for the army. To do this he set up the Vorset Corporation in Oxford, New Jersey. The plant was carefully divided into eighteen separate buildings so that a mistake in one would not necessarily obliterate all the others.

Vorset was not unprofitable and it kept Charles out of the army. It also performed for the war effort with such distinction as to receive, in July 1944, the army/navy "E"—an "award of excellence" for "achievement in production." Charles was justifiably proud. He had set out to make the best damn dye-markers the navy had ever seen, and he had succeeded. Dye-markers are not as easy to make as they sound, given, for one thing, the varying colors and temperatures of water in different parts of the ocean, and given—as Charles later demonstrated to the navy that he had been—faulty specifications. He had had to come up with his own recipe for dye-markers.

There is a story that when Charles was in Washington discussing one of his contracts, a procurement officer asked him whether he knew anything about "powder." Meaning gunpowder. Charles, thinking in his own terms, said he knew "everything" about powder, and so was given the go-ahead.

Revlon, meanwhile, was in a holding pattern. Distribution was extended and sales grew, but supplies were scarce. Glass bottles were rationed. Lipsticks were deemed important for morale, but their metal cases had to be replaced, first with plastic, then with paper.

The Revsons didn't see each other much during the war years; both were working hard. But they didn't see all that much more of each other after the war, either. Ancky slowed her pace; Charles did not. Ancky would come up to the Squibb Building and say: "Charles, Charles—when are you coming *home?*"

It was his routine throughout life to sleep late and work late. When he was first married he would rise around ten-thirty. But once up, he was too preoccupied to take time for the breakfast Ancky soon stopped bothering to make. He would work until ten-thirty or eleven at night.

They lived in Manhattan, first in the Warwick Hotel, then across the street in a gigantic three-bedroom, three-bath duplex apartment at the Dorset, on Fifty-fourth Street just off Fifth Avenue. The bedrooms were upstairs, overlooking a huge two-story living room.

Martin, meanwhile, was living in Westchester with his wife, Julie, whom he had married in 1938, and with their young son, Peter. Julie Phelps Hall had been a nightclub singer before she married Martin. One of the men she had dated before Martin was (just to keep things interesting) . . . Charles. For years the two families were very close; it was Julie, by one account at least, who helped persuade the Charles Revsons to move up to Westchester. Shortly after Johnnie was born in 1943, Charles plunked down $90,000 for a ten-acre home in Rye. Charles described "Holly House" as "early Tudor." It came with a tennis court and they soon added a pool. Not for Charles, who was too embarrassed by his skinny legs ever to wear a swimsuit or short pants, but for Ancky, who loved to swim. To help her keep Holly House in order, she had a cook, a butler, and an upstairs maid. To help with the children there was Katie Lowery, a governess who came to help out for six weeks in the summer of 1945 and wound up staying thirty years.

The Revsons were now Westchesterites, but they did not give up the apartment at the Dorset until the late fifties, when they moved into the Pierre. In addition, for a dozen years or more Charles shared an apartment at 240 Central Park South with his bachelor friend Lester Herzog ("the king's pimp," as some knew him). Charles would stay in town Monday, Tuesday, and Thursday nights; by the fifties, he would often stay in town Wednesday nights, too. Ancky would come in Monday nights for the opera. Both boys attended Rye Country Day School from the age of four through the ninth grade, when they were sent to Deerfield.

On weekends, Holly House was like a country club: There were always twenty cars in the driveway . . . people would be playing tennis or taking lessons from a local pro, Joe Sobek . . . swimming . . . "always big parties, sandwiches for everybody," Ancky recalls. "It was lots of fun in those days." In the wintertime there were sleigh rides followed by hot chocolate.

Saturday nights they played gin. Charles didn't like bridge. "We'd have maybe four tables, sixteen people would come over," says Ancky, "and then at eleven o'clock or midnight we'd have a big buffet with all kinds of food and everybody would stop playing. And after that everybody would go back to playing cards. Charles was very good at gin."

Sunday for Charles would begin with a late-morning perusal of the papers, noting the news and poring over his own and competitors' ads. Then there might be more tennis, or possibly a trip to the factory or the lab. Ancky had to try on all the lipsticks, and then wear them into the hotbox to see how they stood up in heat and humidity. It was hell, she says.

For a time Charles had a box at Yankee Stadium, and would take his boys out to the ball park. "He liked to go shopping at the A and P also," says Ancky—"Can you imagine that? Charles Revson shopping at the A and P? Going to the ball game? So he wasn't always the way he became later on." He would play Monopoly with the children. He once built a rowboat with them, from a kit, with the help of the tennis pro. On rare occasions, he would drive the family up to Moosehead Lake, in Maine, to go fishing. "I must say," Ancky says, "when he was home he spent a lot of time with the children. The trouble was, he wasn't home that often."

Christmas was a warm family occasion. The Revsons always had two trees. Max, the gardener, would string the lights, but Charles insisted on decorating the main tree with Ancky on Christmas Eve after the boys had gone to sleep. Even on Christmas day he would not rise until around eleven, while the boys, naturally, if they could sleep at all in the face of such impending munificence, were up at seven. Thus, the second, smaller tree upstairs. It was stocked with just enough minor attractions to keep the boys occupied until Charles was ready for Christmas to begin.

Santa was good to the Revsons. They were never a deprived family. The boys had to wash cars for their allowance, it's true—but look what they were washing. The family fleet consisted, around 1957, of a chauffeured limousine; a tangerine-colored Eldorado Charles had had specially made for Ancky to match one of his new lipstick shades (years earlier there had been an ultraviolet Chrysler); a Corvette and a Thunderbird both purchased in one day; a station wagon; an old three-wheeled Cushman scooter they called "the putt-putt," which Charles enjoyed driving into town for a laugh; and a lawn-mower-motor "car" for the kids to drive around the property.

Charles was thirty-nine when his second son arrived, in March 1946. He wanted to name him Joseph, as he did not expect his brother to marry and have a son of his own. (Joe did marry, the following year—Charles was the best man at the wedding—and had two sons and a daughter.) But Ancky hated the name Joseph . . . had never liked her own name, Johanna . . . and so, for the first week of his life, the second son was known as "Mr. X." Finally, they agreed to name him Charles Haskell Revson, Jr. His mother has always called him Boochie; others know him as Boochie, Junior, or Charles. For the longest time he felt uncomfortable being introduced as "Charles Revson," with all that that implied.

"I never really knew my father," Charles, Jr., says. "I would see him one out of every five or six nights maybe. He'd come home Friday night, we'd be watching television or something and would come down to say hello to him, kiss him on the cheek, and then go back upstairs. I'd see him maybe Saturday. He did always insist on our kissing him, but he wasn't the type you'd just put your arms around and hug. If anything was wrong, I could always count on his help; but when I was growing up, I didn't see him that much."

Nor was Ancky what Charles, Jr., would call a "mother's mother." "When she was younger," he says, "she was a glamorous, beautiful-looking woman. She didn't want to sit around. She always wanted to go out and be seen . . . I'm very close to my nurse, Katie—she brought me up." Charles left it to Katie to provide the discipline. He never spanked the children or commanded them to do anything. "What he would do," Charles, Jr., says, "is nag and nag and keep at you. And when he stopped nagging, then you knew you were in trouble. Because then he'd cut you off completely. He was like a headmaster, like a teacher who's always right. You never got to know him. He never let you get close."

There were two impediments to a perfect marriage between Charles and Johanna Revson. First, Charles was never home. Second, they were both strong, stubborn people. Charles could—and did—spend two hours arguing with Ancky on a trans-atlantic phone call. Usually their disagreements related to the children.

For one thing, Ancky wasn't Jewish. Charles himself was not particularly religious (even though "Revson" means "rabbi's son"); but he was not about to have his sons singing "Jesus Loves Me," either. Imagine his surprise, as they say, therefore, when he came downstairs unusually early one Sunday morning, around eleven, to see his two boys all dressed up. Where were they going? More to the point, it turned out, where had they been? Indeed, *where had they been going every Sunday morning for two years* while their father was asleep upstairs? Sunday School. (This despite the fact that Ancky was not particularly religious, either.) They never went again.

Charles didn't want his sons going to a Protestant Sunday School, but he did want them to go to camp. Ancky did not, and they wound up not going. He also wanted them to go to prep school, which they did. Charles wanted Boochie to take Saturday morning boxing lessons. Ancky was unalterably opposed to the idea. (Charles, Jr., didn't like it either.)

But the biggest problem was competition from the business. "Charles, why do you *work* so hard," Ancky would ask as he got richer and richer. "It's easy to get to the top," Charles would reply. "The hard thing is to stay there." Ancky was itching to go to the parties and balls that, years later, Charles would begin to go to with his third wife, Lyn. "If he might have been more social," she says, "I might still be married to him. It's just that I got tired of sitting at home and not doing anything. I feel if you sit home too much your life is passing you by completely."

He was, besides being tired when he got home from work, shy. He felt uncomfortable making small talk with polished New York socialites. He was more at home with Lester and a couple of broads. And that brings up the painful issue of Charles's fidelity. Charles never had any serious affairs while he was married to Ancky—and *that,* one of his long-time associates and screwing buddies told me, is the important thing. But there is little doubt that on a night-to-night basis he was a firm believer in the double standard. He called Ancky frequently to find out just what she was doing at all times, but did not hold himself equally accountable.

Sales manager Jack Price, now retired in Scottsdale, Arizona, with his wife of forty-seven years, claims to have been one of Charles's chief procurers until he left Revlon in 1944. "Charlie Revson never lived a healthy day of his life without screwing at least three times," he says. "He did it anytime he wanted, and he always paid for it. He never romanced any of the girls—he didn't have the time or the interest." He did it in the office, he did it on the road, and most of all he did it up in the apartment at 240 Central Park South that was registered in Lester Herzog's name.

The apartment, to which only Price, Herzog, and Revson had keys, consisted of a large living room, a large kitchen, and a long bedroom with three beds. It was used to entertain visiting buyers as well as Revson and his inner circle. There was the evening, for example, that Charlie, Lester, Al Katz, a Revlon salesman, and a jobber from out of town were all sitting on the floor playing strip poker. Four women whom Price had arranged for were already stripped and looking on. Price himself, of course, was only an observer: "He never saw me naked unless I had just come out of the shower." Charlie, on the other hand, was exceptionally well endowed, Price says (holding his hands apart as though boasting about a fish he had caught) and he was not averse to letting people in on the secret.

The poker game progressed and the Revlon salesman, a New England family man, was losing badly. Finally, Price says, he loses everything, "and he has to lay one of the broads in front of everybody." He doesn't want to. He says, "Charlie, look, I've been married fourteen years . . . Please . . ." Revson says "You got into it, you started with it, you gotta go through with it." Then he turns to Price and says: "If he doesn't, I want him canned tomorrow morning." He turns back to the salesman and says, "What the hell do you care? These girls aren't going to say anything. They don't care. Take off your clothes and fuck. If I were you, Maurie," he advises icily, "I'd do it. You got yourself into this."

So he did.

Charles did not grow more faithful to Ancky with time. Yet he didn't want Ancky to leave him, as she began threatening she would. In fact, when in 1960 she decided to get a divorce, he offered her her full $2.5 million settlement plus a magnificent ruby necklace if she would stay.

Revson attributed his marital problems to his marrying women less intelligent than he, and with whom he thus had difficulty communicating. But given his character, it would be a rare woman indeed who could have satisfied him and maintained her dignity at the same time.

"He liked to tell you everything you should do," Ancky says. "He didn't want to have any aggravation; he wanted you to agree with him on everything."

He would tell Ancky how to make up. "I have big eyes and I wanted to make them look larger and he always said, 'You shouldn't do that.'" He would tell her not to go water-skiing. "But Charles, I *love* to go water-skiing! Why shouldn't I go water-skiing?" He would tell her where she could and could not go. "I was on a trip once with friends. I went to Holland and Paris, but I could not go any farther south than Paris. He made great stipulations. It was silly—if you want to do something bad in Europe it's very easy; you don't have to go to the Riviera."

Charles became more demanding and difficult as he got older. It got to be his way or no way. "He was a man," Ancky says, "who always wanted to be right. That was his character. And nine out of ten times he *was* right!"

Though she divorced him, Ancky loved Charles to the end. "How can I explain?" she reflects. "Charles expected you to be completely in the background. I am not a background girl. You must be a person. That's the way I feel, anyhow. You cannot be somebody's slave . . . that's very difficult. For me it's difficult. And yet I don't know how to describe him, because he could be the most thoughtful man. I remember once he was in Europe and he brought me back beautiful Dutch Delft. Or he'd bring me caviar from Paris. I never felt left behind with Charles—I really mean that." Yet Charles would never allow Ancky to accompany him on business trips. It was a strict company policy that wives be left at home, regardless of who might pay their travel expenses.

Near the end, Ancky frequently threatened Charles with divorce. Finally she went into his office one day and saw a photograph of him and the Princess Borghese, namesake of one of his cosmetics lines. Charles was wearing tails. "I was so mad," Ancky says, "because so many times I had asked him to wear tails for some function I had arranged, for one of my charities or something—and he would never do it for me. But for the business, he was wearing tails. I looked at him and I said, 'I want a divorce.' And that was it."

CHAPTER 7

BUT YOU WOULDN'T WANT TO WORK THERE

By the late forties, Revlon was already ensconced in the Squibb Building, at 745 Fifth Avenue, and had more than a thousand employees on the payroll, there and at the plant. The Revsons had had fifteen years or so to learn how to deal with employees. Yet turnover of clerical personnel was running at 166 percent a year—the average girl lasted seven months—and executive turnover was nearly as bad.

People were like checkers in the Revson style of management. One personnel man from the early fifties, now head of personnel for a *Fortune*-500 company, would have to fire thirty people in the office when business slacked off, then go out and hire thirty more on Monday when business picked back up.

Receptionists were chosen to match the decor—and since the decor of the reception area was changed at least twice a year to match each new shade promotion, the average receptionist was fortunate to last six months. To Charles, she was the central character in what was really one enormous walk-in window display. But rather than have Personnel line up a dozen prospects for him to audition, Charles would just requisition "a blonde" or "a brunette." Then, in passing through the reception area, he would decide that the woman was no good—she wasn't a *natural* blonde, or her complexion was too dark, or she wasn't tall enough—get rid of her. By the time the right girl had been installed, a new promotion would be on its way, and the call would go out for a redhead.

Longevity with the firm was inversely proportional to proximity to Charles. You get close to the fire, you get burned. With a few notable exceptions, like Ruth Harvey, Charles went through secretaries like a leper through a crowd. One of his secretaries had a mustache of sorts. Get rid of her. Another was the "Secretary of the Year" before he hired her. It was a disaster. Here she was, all efficient and organized and professional; and here was Charles, always running late, keeping his records in his head, and expecting her to take his shirts and his dirty handkerchiefs to the laundry. He virtually never dictated a letter and virtually never wrote—or read—memos. If his secretary gave him mail that had to be answered, he'd say, "Give it to so-and-so . . . find somebody to take care of it." The letters that did go out over his signature were all written by her. Besides sorting his dirty laundry, she would go down to the kitchen three times a day and prepare his special tray of food—which he would sometimes just push away in disgust.

One of his secretaries had a law degree, great secretarial skills, and a knowledge of several languages. He hated her with a passion. But as he never fired anyone himself, he called Mickey in to do it. Mickey supposedly walked up to her desk and said, simply, "Get out of here." See how easy it is to communicate with people?

You would think that a secretary would require very little urging to leave such a boss, despite the money and status that went with the job. But it was difficult to get a secretary for Charles Revson who would not fall in love with him. However inconsiderate or abusive he could be, he had that tremendous magnetism.

At Revlon, fear was the dominant emotion, particularly among those whose intercoms might crackle at any time with a call from Charles. The tension started at the top. Each of the brothers was strong-willed and outspoken, even if Charles was clearly dominant. Their battles were frequent and bloody. To quote Carl Erbe, their public-relations counsel of many years, and a close friend of Martin's: "There was a tremendous emotional clash among the brothers. They would fight and not talk for three or four days. But the end result was good, because what they were fighting for was a better business." Physically, the fraternal summit meetings were extraordinary. Joseph was a sniffler. He had allergies. Martin had a nervous cough and kept a spittoon nearby. And Charles, who had digestive problems, belched a great deal. Together, they sounded like a sputtering Model T. Ford.

Charles wanted the fabric of his organization to be tight. If a girl went to the ladies' room, she was goofing off. "You treat your secretary like a sister," he often chided executives. He spent his own money lavishly and was generous with salaries, but he was also capable of saying to a woman who tossed a paperclip into the ashtray of his conference table, "I *paid* for that paperclip!" And mean it.

He had a great fear of being taken. He would go to any expense to get an ad perfect, yet he hated to let his creative people shoot ads on location. Locations tended to be in rather sensational vacation spots, and Charles was afraid he was being taken. At one meeting up in his skyscraper office with a bunch of advertising and agency people, he stopped in midsentence when a passing jet plane caught his eye. "There goes another art director," he said ruefully. A New York photographer's studio once had to be transformed into a Caribbean paradise, palm trees and all, at enormous cost, because Charles refused to have three or four of his people fly down to shoot the ad.

Not only were people "fucking on the company," as Charles put it; they weren't coming in to work on time. This may have had something to do with the fact that Charles himself never arrived at the office much before eleven or twelve, but it was no less deplorable. (Charles knew about the lateness of others through his network of informants.) At various times in the company's history, therefore—and as late as 1971, when Revlon was supposedly a modern corporation—everyone was required to sign in in the morning. *Everyone.* Even Charles signed in.

If Revlon was a difficult place to work, particularly in the forties and fifties, it was not without its rewards. Upper-echelon executives were treated to stock options along with their salaries; but particularly before Revlon went public, and afterward as well, the Christmas bonus was used as the chief expression of appreciation. Charles never praised anyone's work. But the fact that an executive was still on the payroll meant he was doing okay, and the size of his Christmas check signified just how well. Joseph would distribute the checks promptly to the operations people who worked under him. Charles would keep *his* batch of checks in his vest pocket for months. People were standing around with their tongues hanging out. Christmas went by, New Year's went by, Washington's Birthday . . . Then Charles would pull out one of the crumpled checks, with the ink practically worn off, and he'd say, "Here, kiddie, here's a check for you." By the time the guy actually got the bonus, he'd lost his taste for it. But Charles looked on these bonuses as gifts. Nobody should tell him when they were to be given. If they were required of him, they weren't gifts. This way, he had everyone on a string.

The clerical and factory workers, at first, got no Christmas bonuses. They got Thanksgiving turkeys. A choice: kosher or non-kosher. Anytime anything came up, no matter what, Charles and Joseph would say to Walter Ronner, the personnel man, "Look at these goddamn people. We give them turkeys and look what they do to us."

"I was getting kind of tired of hearing about turkeys all the time," Ronner says, "and Dave Livingston, the head of District Sixty-five, knew it. He said to me one time in the middle of our negotiations, 'You know, Ronner, we only have to eat those turkeys once a year. You've got to eat them all year round. Why don't we discontinue the turkeys? We don't want them.'"

The next time Charles said something about the turkeys, Ronner told him that the union had requested that they be discontinued. "You mean they don't want them?" Charles asked. "Why not?" "Because they don't think they should sell their soul for a turkey," he replied. "Would you?"

Unions made Charles uneasy and he never dealt with unions himself, leaving that first to Mickey Soroko, and later to his personnel managers.

The first attempts to organize Revlon workers came in the late thirties, while the company was still on Forty-fifth Street. The union organizers had gotten some Revlon employees along with some noncompany people to form a picket line. Mickey Soroko arranged to have all the nonstrikers meet at the Bloomingdale's subway exit and drive across town to Revlon's offices in cars he had hired, walk through the jeering picketers and into the building. After about a week, the picketers threw in the towel. In the midforties, however, Revlon was organized by District 65 of the Distributive Workers of America, then a very left-wing outfit.

Mickey's dealings with the unions ranged from the heavy hand to the glad hand. During a strike in 1947, he came down with the flu and had the entire union negotiating committee bussed up to his home in Larchmont. Someone suggested to Charles that this might not be so smart, bringing the workers to posh surroundings to tell them the few cents an hour raise they were demanding was excessive. But Charles supposedly said, "What are you talking about, posh? His home is a nothing. It's a piece of junk." As, by Charles's standards, it was. But the workers were impressed. They liked the swings in the yard—just the kind of playground they wanted for their kids—and they were delighted to find a bartender in a white jacket waiting for them inside with an open bar, hors d'oeuvres, and the like. Indeed, rather than feel any great sympathy for Mickey, who came down in his pajamas and bathrobe for the negotiations, some of them began to feel nine feet tall from the drinks.

Still, even if it cost a little more than it might have to settle the strike, Revlon could afford it. And it was worth the money to get those workers to stop slipping little "fuck you" notes into the compacts, the way in later years disgruntled automotive workers would toss a loose bolt into the deep recesses of the odd Cadillac or Continental.

Charles himself never attended labor negotiations and rarely visited the factory. He was much more interested in the laboratory and in the marketing end of his business—the creative side. Joseph was at least nominally in charge of overseeing Operations.

Joseph would arrive at the 134th-Street plant every Tuesday for inspection. Knowing Joseph's routine, the workers, who arrived at the plant at eight, would spend the morning cleaning and sweeping and dusting until Joseph came. They would not run any of their production lines, because there was no way to do so without messing things up. Management cooperated in this farce because management's neck was on the line, too.

As Joseph's car pulled up to the plant, the word would go around to get ready. And as soon as he approached a work area, the conveyer belts would be started up. Joseph would go through and see everyone working and everything spotless, just the way a plant should be. No boxes on the floor, nothing out of place.

Joseph's method, if you made a mistake, was to make you live with it (or fire you). Martin's philosophy was frequently articulated this way: "Kiddie, I'm running a bank. You make deposits, you make withdrawals—you're human. You got enough deposits to cover your withdrawals? You got an account." Once he called in a man who had really blown it and was expecting big trouble. Martin walked over and put his hand on the man's shoulder and said, "Kiddie, you've got the deposits; don't make no more withdrawals." And that was the end of it.

Charles could take an equally broadminded view of mistakes if they were made honestly and were admitted openly. But Bill Mandel, who worked head to head with Charles for fifteen years, makes an additional point, regarding Charles's sense of proportion: "I've often said," he says, "that I could come up with a product that would sell twenty-two million dollars' worth. And the next night I could go to dinner with Charles, and if I order the wrong champagne—that's one for me, the twenty-two-million-dollar product; and one against me, the champagne. They're equal. That's my description of Charles."

It was Joseph's conservatism combined with a clash of stubborn brotherly pride that led to his departure from the company in 1955, shortly before the public offering. Joseph thought it might be risky to take Revlon public and was against the move. His partners were for it. Furthermore, Charles had decided he had had enough of arguing. There could only be one man in charge. If his partners wanted to stay in the company, they would have to enter into a voting trust agreement, assigning the voting power of their stock to him. Joseph refused. He offered to buy Charles out. But he couldn't afford to buy out Lachman as well—and Lachman, wisely, was not about to entrust the company to Joseph. So it was agreed that Revlon would buy back Joseph's stock.

Harry Meresman was sent up to Joseph's place in the country to try to mediate and persuade Joseph to sign the voting trust agreement so that he could remain in the company, but he still refused. Meresman recalls asking Joseph how he would feel if, after the company went public, the stock proved to be worth much more than he would be getting for it from the company. Joseph said that sometimes a man had to put principle ahead of money. And so he sold his 30 percent share in Revlon back to the company for $2,528,000, leaving his brothers and Lachman with all the stock.

Revlon went public on December 7, 1955, at $12 a share, six months after *The $64,000 Question* debuted. Within weeks it hit $30. By mid-1956 it had split two-for-one (as it did again in 1961, and three-for-two in 1969) and by the end of 1956 it was listed on the New York Stock Exchange.

That Charles, Martin, and Charlie Lachman had not expected this kind of instant success was evidenced by their selling 101,833 shares as part of the public offering. Thirty-four Revlon employees, meanwhile, were permitted to buy an average of 3,000 shares each at $11 a share, $1 below the opening price. Those who held on for just four years realized a 1,000 percent gain, or something more than $300,000 apiece—which was separate and apart from the stock options they were soon granted.

Had Joseph waited four years, his Revlon stock would have brought $35 million. Joseph later said that if he had known Charles wanted him to stay in the company, and that it was Charles who had sent Harry, he would have stayed. Meresman asks, dryly, "Who did he *think* was sending me?"

But unlike Charles, Joseph could live easily off the income from $2.5 million. He led a very quiet, lonely life after leaving Revlon. It was not long afterward that his wife, Elise, separated from him, leaving him even more isolated. He spent much of his time in his apartment at the Carlton House, on Sixty-first and Madison. He liked to paint.

One evening in December 1971, Carl Erbe saw him walking down Fifty-seventh Street. "Joe, for Christ's sake, you don't look good," said Erbe. "Have you been to the doctor?" Joe said: "I'm going now." He died of a heart attack the next day. Charles attended the funeral but did not speak. Joseph's estate was valued at $2,531,873, almost exactly what he had received for his share in the business sixteen years earlier.

CHAPTER 8

FIRE AND ICE AND EVERYTHING NICE

Marketing is strategy. Instinctively or consciously, Charles plotted a shrewd one. From the beginning, Revlon's approach was that nail enamel was a fashion accessory, not a mere beauty aid, and that women should use different shades to suit different outfits, moods, and occasions. This automatically broadened the market. Where before a woman might not have bought a new bottle of nail enamel until the old one was empty, now she might keep half a dozen or more on her dresser . . . particularly because fashions, and with them Revlon's colors, kept changing so fast. Like General Motors, a company Revson greatly admired, Revlon instituted the model change and, with it, planned obsolescence. Revlon would bring out a new color every fall and spring. By the midforties, its semiannual shade promotions were as much an event to women as Detroit's new-car introductions were to men. The most popular colors would remain in Revlon's line for years; but when the new color was announced, smart women just had to add it to their collection.

Later, with General Motors as his model, Charles developed separate cosmetic lines, similar to GM's divisions, to go after each segment of the market. Revlon itself was the popular-priced line (which Charles preferred to liken to Pontiac rather than Chevrolet); Natural Wonder, the youth line; Moon Drops, the dry-skin line; Etherea, the hypoallergenic line; Marcella Borghese, the high-class line with an international flavor; and Ultima II, the top of the line. Likewise the fragrance lines. And the strategy worked as well for Revlon as it had for GM.

Although Revlon was born of the Depression, Charles chose to compete not on price (there were nail polishes around for a dime), but on quality. Furthermore, he understood what he was really selling. He wasn't selling the fact that his polish was made with pigment, and thus fully covered the nails; he was selling the chance that it might turn the right head, or lend "a touch of class." He wasn't selling a very deep red polish; he was selling *Cherries in the Snow* or *Fire and Ice*—and with the colors, excitement, fun, and a fantasy. Since it didn't cost any more to make dark red polish called *Berry Bon Bon* than to make plain dark red polish, and the one could be sold for six times the price of the other, this was not a bad strategy.

In order to sell the excitement, fun, and fantasy—indeed, in order to create it—Revlon always advertised very heavily in relation to its sales. One result was that beauty salons and competitors got the impression Revlon was a much larger concern than it really was—which was part of the idea. (The company borrowed privately for years before going for its first bank loan, in order not to reveal its modest balance sheet. Only the Revsons, Charlie Lachman, and Harry Meresman knew the figures; and it was Harry who arranged for the early financing, at 2 percent a month, through an arm of his accounting firm.)

Revlon's first ad outside the trade journals appeared in the summer of 1935 in *The New Yorker*. This may have had something to do with Charles's passing their offices each day on the way to and from his own, but more likely it was that *The New Yorker* woman was exactly the kind of "classy dame" with which he wanted Revlon associated. The ninth-of-a-page ad referred to "The House of Revlon." It's the image that counts, never mind the fact that "the House of Revlon" was a few bare rooms where people poured from big bottles into little ones and trimmed applicator brushes; or that that ad, which cost $335.56, was Revlon's total consumer advertising budget for the year. (In 1975, Revlon was spending $75,000 in *The New Yorker*, and perhaps $65 million elsewhere.)

Whatever profit Revlon made was plowed back into advertising. At first the company even borrowed to advertise. The result was enormous demand at the beauty salons for the latest Revlon color. And the mechanics of a manicurist's tray being what they were (particularly the trays Revlon designed), it was much easier to carry just one line of nail enamel than several. It was also less of an investment. Revlon became not just the General Motors of nail enamels in the field; it became the AT&T.

In its first five years, Revlon dealt exclusively with the beauty trade. That in itself was a selling point to the beauticians; and since the company couldn't sell everyone at once anyway, it was good strategy to start here. What better advertisement than to have Revlon used by the professionals? What more ideal arrangement than to have women *pay* to have ten samples of the product painted onto their nails, to be shown around town for the rest of the week?

It was only natural that women whose nails were done with Revlon enamel upstairs in a department store beauty salon would then demand the product downstairs at the cosmetics counter. Revlon soon obliged. And after selected department stores were opened, selected drugstores were offered the opportunity of carrying the Revlon line, as well. "Selected," because a Revlon product was not just any commodity, like soap powder, to be found on every corner. The trick was to make it nearly as available and yet maintain the aura of exclusivity. By limiting the Revlon "franchise" to the best outlets, Revlon also gained more leverage with each one, and the ability to demand the kind of attention and promotion it could not otherwise expect.

Revson understood the difference between a differentiable product and a commodity. It is the difference between Morton's salt, at ten cents a pound, and Lawry's seasoned salt, at $1.79. Both have brand names, true, but there is not much you can do to distinguish one pure salt from another. You compete on price and on the efficiencies of your operation. Revson didn't want to compete on price, and his operation was not all that efficient. He wanted to compete on the creativity of his products and on his company's marketing skill.

"Cost-of-goods"—the cost of the product itself and its packaging—was the fundamental number in Revson's business equation. Charles liked products that cost little to make, relative to what he could sell them for. If his cost-of-goods was low enough, he could advertise heavily; he could afford severe quality standards; he could make mistakes; he could operate his impressive research facility; and he could still make a good profit.

Many manufacturers will sell a product for twice what it costs them to make, applying the rest of the money to indirect costs like advertising, sales commissions, management, overhead, interest and, they hope, profits. Revson tried to sell his products for quadruple, not just double, their cost. The distributors and stores to whom the products were sold would then approximately double the price once more.

In 1962 the materials in a seventy-five-cent bottle of cream nail enamel cost Revlon only one tenth of that. (The enamel itself, minus bottle and box, cost practically nothing.) A two-ounce bottle of Eterna 27, the magic wrinkle remover, sold for $8.00 and cost just fifty cents (plus labor and overhead) to produce. Other products allowed less generous markups (like the hair sprays), while some allowed more. Nail polish remover didn't allow as good a markup, presumably because it's not what you'd call a high-fashion item. *This* commodity, however, had the very considerable advantage of being carried along by the rest of the Revlon line. Futurama lipstick cases, including one in sterling silver for $47.50, had modest markups relative to those of the lipstick refills—the old "give away the razors to sell the blades" ploy, only not quite so generous.

There was also the dynamics of "economy sizes." In 1962 you could buy three times as much Revlon Velvety Nail Enamel Remover for sixty cents as you could for thirty-five. But you weren't hurting Revlon; the extra two ounces, including the larger package, cost 3.3 cents. The markup on the extra two ounces was even greater than on the first ounce.

One reason for Revlon's hefty markups is that the consumer is paying for a lot of advertising. Professor Theodore Levitt of Harvard Business School, among others, argues that advertising and packaging are as much a part of cosmetic products as alcohol or lanolin, and so a justifiable, albeit very large, part of the cost. Would an unadvertised private-label lipstick in a plain package afford a woman as much satisfaction as a Revlon lipstick at twice the price? Would she be participating in the fun and fantasy? If the answer is yes, then Safeway is missing a bet. But women, by and large, don't want elegance on sale. It is a marketing cliché that with certain ailing products the way to boost sales is not to cut prices but to *hike* them.

Revlon's fashion strategy came into its own in 1940, with the "Matching Lips and Fingertips" campaign and the introduction of Revlon lipstick. For the first time, Revlon ads, like its products, were in full color, and spread over two pages in such magazines as *Vogue* and *Harper's Bazaar*. "Pick up a tea-cup, light a cigarette, draw on a glove. Your slightest gesture delights the eye . . . with lips and fingertips accented vitally, fashionably by Revlon." Crudely put, Revlon was selling "class to the masses"; a chance to be fashionable for the price of a lipstick.

Matching lips and fingertips was a canny way to enter the lipstick business. The only way to match your lips with Revlon fingertips was, of course, with Revlon lipstick. Neat. Interestingly, "matching lips and fingertips" was not an original Revlon idea. Another firm had used the theme in its ads a few years earlier. The difference was, as with so many other things he copied—Revson made it work.

It wasn't until 1944 (*Pink Lightning*) that the full-scale color promotions were begun. Prior to that there had been campaigns like "Expect Great Things From Revlon," and "Morale Is A Woman's Business."

The shade promotions allowed for total "theming" of the marketing effort. To introduce *Fatal Apple* in 1945—"the most tempting color since Eve winked at Adam"—color spreads were placed in the fashion magazines; department stores were furnished with window displays; the Revlon showroom was decorated to match; and Revlon's publicity director, Bea Castle, arranged an elaborate dress party that featured not only Maurice the Mindreader, but also a snake and snake charmer from the William Morris Agency, a hollow gold apple door prize from Cartier, a grove of miniature apple trees from the Washington State apple-growers' association, and fashions from Forever Eve. All New York's top editors and publishers were invited to this party and some of them came. Charles himself remained in the background, but loved it. He had taken particular interest in the menu: lobster and rice, meatballs and spaghetti—this was a cocktail party, but he felt that people coming from work wanted more than just cheese on a cracker. They wanted entertainment and something good to eat along with their drinks.

When *Plumb Beautiful* was introduced in 1949, Bergdorf Goodman devoted eight windows to the promotion, where Russian sables, chinchilla, ermine, and mink were the background for Revlon's sixty-cent nail enamel. Such was (and is) the power of a Revlon promotion in the fashion world.

In 1950, Revlon kicked off its new color with a full-page teaser in *The New York Times*. Smoke was curling from the burning edges of a hole in

The partners, circa 1950: Charles, Charlie Lachman, Martin and Joseph. Below, Charles presents the first $64,000 check to a Marine captain named McCutchen who knew all about food. The $64,000 Question, sponsored solely by Revlon, was seen by 55 million weekly and lifted the company's sales by about $64 million.

Christmas, circa 1947. There was a tree upstairs as well, with gifts to keep the boys occupied until Charles was ready for the holiday to begin. Below, Charles with Lyn, his third wife. Their wedding took place in February, 1964.

Graduation day. John Revson had two shadows to grow up in, not one: his father, right, and his cousin Peter, below. Peter, Martin Revson's son, was killed at thirty-five when his racer crashed into an iron railing and burst into flames.

Charles's 257-foot yacht, Ultima II, carried a staff of 31, had 16 bathrooms, 22 phones, and a tank of fuel cost $20,000. Tuesday was, for years, lab day—and Charles, left, loved every minute of it. Right, Charles, caught in a reflective mood.

Revlon unleashes an Angry Young Pink—the <u>killer-color</u> of the year!

'stormy pink'

a wild-and-arrogant pink...cross-bred with red
...raging Fall fashion for lips and fingertips!

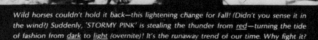

Wild horses couldn't hold it back—this lightening change for Fall! (Didn't you sense it in the wind?) Suddenly, 'STORMY PINK' is stealing the thunder from <u>red</u>—turning the tide of fashion from <u>dark</u> to <u>light</u> (overnite)! It's the runaway trend of our time. Why fight it?

'stormy pink' in Sculptura, Super Lustrous II, Lustrous and Lanolite Lipsticks. Also in matching Nail Enamel. (both Cream and Frosted).

146

Suzy Parker posed for six hours at night in the water off Montauk Point for Stormy Pink. Her older sister, Dorian Leigh, modeled Fire and Ice.

Above, Suzy Parker again—1962. Lauren Hutton, right, for Ultima II. The Ultima line was created for Charles's department store, carriage-trade answer to Estée Lauder.

w down | beach | pink | nouveau | super-
pink | peach | cognito | peach | natural!

Revlon's (not a cliché in a carload)

'colors avant garde'

10 new <u>potent</u> <u>pales</u> for lips and nails!

New <u>low-key</u> <u>look</u> for today's <u>new</u> <u>breed</u> of
beauty... bored with yesterday's fashion
clichés, restless for tomorrow's look today!

mes the evolution! No harsh or hackneyed reds, no pedestrian pinks! These
<u>low-key</u> colors—so new they're barely born! Sensuously soft. Shatteringly chic.
u'll love them on sight. Scoop up Revlon's **'COLORS AVANT GARDE'**—all 10 at a clip!

It's hard to believe a makeup
that feels this light and looks this natural
could cover this well.

'Beautiful Creme Makeup' is so natural-looking you never
look 'made up', even in sunlight. And even if your skin isn't perfect, this
exclusive gel formula makeup covers perfectly. It wears beautifully in
humid or rainy weather too,
because it's waterproof.
'Beautiful Creme Makeup' is
matte enough for normal or even
oily skin. Yet it's moist enough for
dry skin with tiny lines to hide. The
result is believably beautiful skin.
For hours and hours.

'ULTIMA' II
CHARLES REVSON

OUTFIT DESIGNED BY JACQUES BEL...

Charlie

A most original fragrance

He had always resented the fact that Revlon wasn't named after him, as "Arden" was Arden or "Lauder," Lauder. In later years his name became more prominent.

Concentrated Perfume Purse Spray. 5.00

Concentrated Perfume Spray. 7.50

Concentrated Cologne Spray. 3.50 to 8.50

Concentrated Perfume-in-a-Pot. 4.50

It's Charlie's first Christmas!
(So it's one gift she never
found under her tree before.)
Give it to her now—any one of
six beautiful ways.

by REVLON

Concentrated Perfume Oil. 6.50

Concentrated Cologne. 6.00

the center of the page. At first glance, the hole and the smoke looked real. The headline was, WHERE'S THE FIRE? And that's all. No Revlon signature, no copy, nothing. Shortly thereafter, *Where's the Fire?* was introduced as Revlon's new shade.

The shade promotion to end all others was Revlon's *Fire and Ice*, in the fall of 1952. "You could hardly pick up a general-circulation or fashion magazine this week," *Business Week* led off a major story, "without seeing the [*Fire and Ice*] advertisement . . . To much of the industry, this was one of the most effective ads in cosmetics history. In a sense, it marked a new height in an industry where advertising is all-important (cosmetics are second only to food in advertising volume). Perhaps more than any previous ad, this one successfully combines dignity, class, and glamour (a trade euphemism for sex)."

The two-page spread consisted of a dazzling model, Dorian Leigh, in an icy silver-sequin dress with a fiery scarlet cape; and on the facing page, the headline, ARE YOU MADE FOR 'FIRE AND ICE?' You were, the ad stated, if you could answer eight of the following fifteen questions in the affirmative:

Have you ever danced with your shoes off?

Did you ever wish on a new moon?

Do you blush when you find yourself flirting?

When a recipe calls for one dash of bitters, do you think it's better with two?

Do you secretly hope the next man you meet will be a psychiatrist?

Do you sometimes feel that other women resent you?

Have you ever wanted to wear an ankle bracelet?

Do sables excite you, even on other women?

Do you love to look up at a man?

Do you face crowded parties with panic—then wind up having a wonderful time?

Does gypsy music made you sad?

Do you think any man really understands you?

Would you streak your hair with platinum without consulting your husband?

If tourist flights were running, would you take a trip to Mars?

Do you close your eyes when you're kissed?

The response to the promotion was sensational. (It didn't hurt the other forty-eight shades of lipstick and nail enamel in the Revlon line, either.) Nine thousand window displays were devoted to *Fire and Ice*. Every newspaper and magazine wrote about it and every radio announcer made reference to it. *Fire and Ice* beauty contests were conducted around the country. Disc jockeys and newspaper editors were sent questionnaires. ("In your field, you are a pulse-taker and an opinion-maker. Your ideas are very important . . . "); and the uncynical responses that were returned, by the hundreds, were consistent with the times.

Twenty-two hotels, from the Plaza in New York to the Cornhusker in Lincoln, Nebraska, were induced to stage *Fire and Ice* preview parties. Rudy Vallee, starring at the Sheraton Biltmore in Providence, talked about the *Fire and Ice* party all week.

Judges in the Hollywood *Fire and Ice* beauty contest included David Niven, Robert Stack, and Ray Milland.

Arthur Godfrey, Jimmy Durante, and Steve Allen managed to play on the promotion. Dave Garroway gave the *Fire and Ice* quiz to one of his secretaries on the *Today* show; *Beat the Clock* and *Search for Tomorrow* also found ways to work it in.

Revlon's advertising muscle never hurt in getting plugs like these. "Those things are done sort of inadvertently," Martin once explained to *Business Week*. "What you do is go to see Hope or Skelton or somebody of that nature and tell them about your new product coming out with, oh, a couple of million dollars in advertising, and then the script writer writes it in . . . So that's the way we get it in—sort of inadvertently." Commented S. J. Perelman: "The easy negligence of the whole thing is truly captivating. For sheer insouciance, nothing could surpass the spectacle of an incipient Mark Twain grinding out cosmetic yaks with a two-million-dollar pitchfork lightly pinking his bottom."

The *Fire and Ice* campaign definitely had "the Revlon touch." "There's a little bit of bad in every good woman," Revlon marketers felt, and it was to this that Revlon always tried to appeal. It was a matter of giving women "a little immoral support." Revson wanted his models to be "Park Avenue whores"—elegant, but with the sexual thing underneath. The *Fire and Ice* copy asked: "What is the American girl made of? Sugar and spice and everything nice? Not since the days of the Gibson Girl! There's a *new* American beauty . . . she's tease and temptress, siren and gamin, dynamic and demure. Men find her slightly, delightfully baffling. Sometimes a little maddening. Yet they admit she's *easily* the most exciting woman in the world! She's the 1952 American beauty, with a foolproof formula for melting a male! She's the '*Fire and Ice*' girl. (Are you?)"

"Our ads were more strongly read than the editorial copy in the magazines where we advertised, and that was given to us as a goal," says Norman B. Norman, who headed Revlon's advertising from the agency side in the late forties and into the midfifties. "All Revlon advertising had to do with emotions . . . how women thought, how they lived, how they loved . . . and we wove in our products. That's quite different from what most companies do, where they describe their products, the benefits of them. Revlon never did that, which was a brilliance of its own."

Now, the question naturally arises, who was the genius behind this campaign and the others? And the first part of the answer is that it was not Charles. Yes, Charles had the judgment most of the time to know what was good and what was not, in itself no small talent. But he was no David Ogilvy. As a copywriter, Charles could not have commanded $100 a week. It was not he who came up with names like *Paint the Town Pink* or *Rosy Future* or *Pink Vanilla*. His creativity lay in the product end. As a marketer, he was shrewd rather than creative. He liked to think of himself as a great editor. "The trick isn't to know when you have it," he used to say, "the trick is to know when you don't." His forte was criticism, not enthusiasm.

No one could match his scrutiny of the color in an ad, or his sense of how the model's eyebrows should look, or his patience in endlessly improving a package design. But he needed a good deal of coaching when it came to words. Those who worked with him closely say that his editing had two consistent and allied characteristics. The first was to make things "safer." Where he made change after change, the trend was often away from the daring or the risky or the bold to the more conventional. Secondly, his renowned "perfectionism" to some degree was, rather, the grip of indecision. He would redo and redo and change and change past one deadline after another, not so much to make each version better than the last—which they often were not—but because of the fear of letting loose something that might be no good. He was a terrible procrastinator because, egotist though he was, like anyone else he was unsure of his judgments and afraid of making a mistake.

Charles was an instinctive rather than a professional marketing man. He had little regard for a company like Procter & Gamble, even though to most marketers P&G is about as good as you can get. The modus operandi at Procter & Gamble is market research and testing. Testing new products, testing new ads, testing alternative promotions . . . the science of marketing. The modus operandi at Revlon was instinct . . . the art of marketing. Fashions changed too fast to allow test marketing. Where P&G might take four years to launch a new product, Revlon could be in national distribution in six months. Charles had to anticipate the market and run on instinct. He would get the opinions of those around him—Revlon secretaries were particularly important in this regard—and that was it. (He did test market, in a sense, by allowing his competitors to make many of the innovations—and the mistakes—for him.) Nor did he bother to commission market research to determine by questionnaire what women wanted, what they liked about competitive products, and how they thought of Revlon. He relied largely on his own intimate understanding of his products and of his market. He was his own walking market survey, asking questions of retailers and consumers wherever he went. He did credit himself with "sensitivity," but lost patience with people who ascribed his success to some sort of magic touch. As he himself put it: "The only thing you can say about me is that if I have something to do, I'll learn everything about it—that I will. I'm nosy as a son of a gun. I am nosy. There's nothing about it I won't learn."

Charles had to know how things *worked*. If man is motivated by his need to control his environment, Charles seemed to be doubly so. And to control things, one must first understand how they work. What's more, he was an enormous reader. Cowboy books for escape, yes, but piles of magazines of all sorts, too. "He was more up to date than anybody," says Bill Mandel.

Better than anything else, Charles knew women. Not how to live with them, maybe, or how to respect them, but how they should look and what they would buy.

"I always felt that when Charles looked at a woman, and I'm including myself, it was like being behind an X-ray machine," Kay Daly says. "Charles knew if I had a slip on, if my underwear was clean . . . He had terrible taste in furniture and decor [gold on gold], but the way a woman should look was native to him."

This remarkable sensitivity, combined with his Pygmaliomania, led him to "redo" tens of millions of women throughout the world.

CHAPTER 9

THE REVLON GIRL(S)

As one of the largest advertisers in the fashion business, Revlon's appetite for beautiful women was insatiable. Just as a great many of New York's ad men and designers passed through Revlon's mill at one time or another, so did a great many models. Candice Bergen was at school in Philadelphia when Revlon's Sandy Buchsbaum "discovered" her and spread her across the pages of *Vogue*. Barbara Feldon came rolling out of a rug in a commercial for Chemstrand when Revson happened to be watching television. She was signed to an exclusive contract. Mary Bacon was a jockey—and, it turned out later much to Revlon's embarrassment, a Ku Klux Klanswoman—before she became a "Charlie girl." Just four women—Dorian Leigh and her sister Suzy Parker, Barbara Britton and Lauren Hutton—became so closely identified with the company over a period of years that they were, in effect, "the Revlon girl."

Dorian Leigh, the stunning redhead in the *Fire and Ice* ad, was already a top model when she did *Fatal Apple,* her first Revlon spread, in 1945. From then on Revson considered her "lucky" and used her in shade promotion after shade promotion. But he barely knew her while she was "the Revlon girl." "He only became very friendly with me," she says, "when I came to Europe and he came here." In Europe still, running a restaurant she calls Chez Dorian about an hour outside Paris, she says that in the fifties Revson became "very romantic" with her—but that he didn't get very far. "He was used to buying everything he wanted," she says, "and in me he met someone he couldn't buy."

As Revlon spokeswoman, Barbara Britton anchored nine commercials a week: three each on *The $64,000 Question, The $64,000 Challenge,* and *The Walter Winchell File.* Models would play out the scenes in the ads, but she did all the talking. In her busiest year she earned $130,000—more than twice what the president of TWA was making. Her work load diminished after the quiz-show era passed, and when taped commercials replaced live. But her famous line—"If its the finest of it's kind it's by Revlon—Revlon London, Paris and New York"—opened *The Ed Sullivan Show* week after week. "And now here's the *star* of our show," she would continue, a gracious version of jolly Ed McMahon, "Ed *Sullivan!*"

While Barbara was integrity-grace-and-beauty on television, Suzy Parker was the same, only with a dollop of elegant come-hither thrown in, in print. Born "Cecilia" Parker (in 1932), she now lives in California with her husband, actor Bradford Dillman. She became an even better-known model than her older sister, Dorian. *Life* magazine devoted a cover to her in 1957, and no less an authority than *The New York Times,* in their obituary of Kay Daly, incorrectly credited her with the *Fire and Ice* ad.

Charles was wild for Suzy Parker, at least professionally. "They don't make combos like that anymore," he said of the two sisters. But when B.B.D.&O., the ad agency, suggested that she be put under exclusive contract—a novel concept at the time—he said no. The agency was talking about a lot of money; Charles wouldn't even throw out a counteroffer. "He thought I should be working for the sheer joy of working for Revlon," she says. Her $120-an-hour fee might have been more than fair for most kinds of work, but these Revlon shade promotions involved a single session, three or four hours, and that was *the* ad for the season. "So I finally said screw him," she says. "The next time they wanted me for an ad I said no thank you. Then the war was on. He absolutely hated me. He said, 'I can't stand the girl's face, I don't want to see it anymore.' Which was okay by me—I had other accounts and I was interested in movies.

"As time went on it became really very funny. They did this particular Cleopatra ad and shot it with ten or twelve different black-haired girls, at great expense. It wasn't the photographer's fault; it was just that they couldn't choose the model. So they had to keep paying Avedon for the pictures. It was a disaster. Finally, at the last minute, they brought me in and put a black wig on me and they never let Revson know it was me in the ad. He never realized." (He doubtless realized full well. Out of pride he may have pretended he didn't.)

Earlier she had done a similar last-minute bailout retake on *Stormy Pink*. "We worked at night [double the fee] off Montauk Point, in the ocean, and I had to hold a stallion. We really did that. It was very dangerous because it was windy and the pebbles kept rolling out from underneath the horse's feet, and I'm trying to hold him down. We worked on that for almost six hours in the middle of the night, in the middle of the ocean [well, not quite], and I was in a chiffon dress. I think the reason I was such a good model wasn't that I was such a particular beauty or anything, but that I was as strong as a horse. And that occasion proved it!"

And yet, even after he turned her down for the contract she wanted, she kept doing the ads. "It was my own vanity, I suppose . . . my own challenge that I could come in after they'd spent all that time and money trying with other girls and in two or three hours do the ad."

In terms of exclusive contracts, she says, she paved the way for Lauren Hutton. "But," she adds, laughing, "Lauren should really get her own expression. She's still using mine."

Mary Laurence "Lauren" Hutton, as practically any red-blooded American knows, *is* Ultima II and gets a bit more than $200,000 a year to play the role.

Contrary to publicity photos, and certainly contrary to rumor, there was nothing between Lauren Hutton and Charles Revson beyond a friendly mutual respect. She was not Revson's discovery; she was, she says, just the logical choice: "I was the only big brand-name model in the country." Nor did she meet him during the five months of negotiations that led to her exclusive Revlon engagement. It was only at the signing, in 1973, that they met for the first time—and established a rapport.

It was photographer Richard Avedon who had sold Revson on the twenty-eight-year-old one-time Playboy bunny. And now, for the signing, he was asking her to be on her best behavior—to appear, not in jeans, which was more her off-camera style, but in "high drag," as she puts it. She complied. She even agreed to wear her "tooth," the dental falsie that bridges the gap in her smile. She didn't want to, "because it always creates an artificial situation," but she wore it anyway.

They were all sitting around stiffly—she and Avedon, Charles and Paul Woolard, agents and lawyers—having tea. When the crumpets came around, she grabbed one, completely forgetting about her tooth. Naturally it got caught in a wad of crumpet—and she cracked up. She looked over at Avedon, who was a nervous wreck, and gave him a grin—with a big black gap in the middle of her teeth. He sort of choked on his tea. Not knowing what else to do, she just made an announcement. "You'll have to forgive me," she said in her backwoods-Florida, liberated-hip mellow-dy, "but my tooth is stuck in a wad of crumpet here and we'll have to do something about it because it cost fifty dollars and I'm not going to lose it." Charles laughed. (Yes, Charles laughed.) Lauren retrieved her tooth. She went back to behaving, she says, and sitting there silently.

As for her having an affair with Revson, she says that their total contact was confined to five or six "high teas," like the first, and to one dinner at the Beverly Hills Hotel—at which several others were present. Lauren Hutton is one of the few who credit Revson with having had "a wonderful sense of humor. We always joked back and forth," she says. She also appreciated what she saw as his courtliness.

If only he had been as charming with everyone else.

CHAPTER 10

BUT YOU STILL WOULDN'T WANT TO WORK THERE

As good as Charles Revson was with products, that's how bad he was with people. He was a savvy marketing man and a lousy boss. He had qualities of great leadership, and could milk the most out of many of his people, but he was about the last man in the world any but a very special breed would want to work for. He was a sort of a cross between a Vince Lombardi—tough, demanding, but you would give your life for him—and a Captain Queeg—petty, demeaning, paranoid. He also paid well.

A lot depended on you:

If you were a bright guy with a flashy résumé, a wife and kids in Mamaroneck, and a nine-to-six professional executive's mentality, you could be in for trouble. You represented a challenge to Revson, for one thing—a chance for the crude, self-educated, self-made Revson to take on your Princeton B.A. and your Chicago M.B.A. and your upper-middle-class upbringing, and win. Could you possibly be as good as you had cracked yourself up to be? Could you offer the kind of dedication this fanatic wanted of all his people? Could you even understand what it was he was trying to say to you?

But if you were street-smart, and tough, and not easily cowed, but ready to give your heart and soul for the company; if you never tried to bullshit him, but knew how to "handle" him nonetheless; if the chemistry were right and you really had the talent . . . then you might last for some time.

If the "divorce" did come, be you wife, brother, or executive, you might never talk to him again, no matter how long you had known him. (He wouldn't let Ancky or Lyn visit him when he was dying.)

Generally, if you were a hotshot, you peaked remarkably early. And then, even if it were not for another year, you were as good as gone. Revson would fire you in his mind a year before anyone else knew it, explains Bill Mandel, for years the heir apparent.

Many men should probably never have been hired in the first place. But Revson was always after some brilliant new executive or creative talent whom he just *had* to have; whom he had to overpay to get; and with whom he would quickly become disenchanted. One out of ten might pay off, he figured, and the other nine were just the necessary cost of finding the tenth.

The turnover among executives was unbelievable. Part of the problem may have been Charles's need to eat executives for breakfast, to feed his own ego and assuage his insecurities. Part of it must also have been his impatience with men not as bright as he and not nearly as knowledgeable about the business. He would frequently feign a sort of sarcastic simplemindedness when he wasn't satisfied with the answers he was getting. "La-aa-arry?" He would force people to repeat their statements three and four times—which begins to crack anyone's self-confidence. Or sometimes he would just forget their names.

One Wall Street analyst was working on a report titled, "Twelve Coming Executives at Revlon," to prove that the company had developed depth of management. Only two of the twelve were around by the time the man finally gave up in disgust. *Ad Age* referred to it as "the grand march from Revlon."

By the midsixties the turnover slowed, in part because Charles was directing some of his attention to other things, such as acquisitions. He acquired and then disposed of—hired and fired—almost as many companies as executives. And then there were Revlon presidents to court, marry, and divorce (three of them, between 1965 and 1971: George Murphy, Dan Rodgers, and Joe Anderer); hair stylists in the extravagant Revlon salon to get rid of; Lyn and the yacht and the triplex apartment to remodel, all at great expense; and international operations and the pharmaceutical company to oversee. It was only natural that Charles would have less of an impact on the nuts and the bolts of each ad and the hiring and firing of each middle manager. Moreover, the brilliant-if-abrasive marketing whiz, Bill Mandel, had risen in the company to the point where he could stand up to Charles and, largely, keep him away from the rest of the troops.

Despite Revson's fearsome reputation for chewing people up, a lot of very talented men and women were attracted to the company over the years (women were restricted to creative posts). Revlon represented the challenge of the big leagues, and never hurt anyone's resume. What's more, you could actually form quite an affection and respect for this dynamic, single-minded, slightly insane, often infuriating, galloping egomaniac, even if he never did say thank you. His aloofness and never being satisfied enhanced his magnetism. "You got the feeling from him," Kay Daly said, "that no matter what you did, you were never going to please him. And this is something that is very interesting to women."

And then there was the money. Revson paid premium wages (coupled with lucrative stock options) because he could never have gotten top people to work with him, and to work those hours, if he had not. And once a man worth $25,000 anywhere else had gotten used to a $35,000 lifestyle, Revson owned him. He could abuse him all day long, and the man would take it because he couldn't afford to leave. "It was the most overpaid company in the business," asserts an alumnus, "and that was Revson's luxury for telling them anything he wanted."

Additionally, he would pay almost any price for what he wanted; never wanted to be thought of as cheap; and lacked the patience to negotiate. When he wanted something, he wanted it now—and that costs money.

"If the job is right and the money is right," he asked one man who had left Revlon, "will you come back?"

"Well, I, uh—" stuttered the man, caught by the directness of the question.

"Not, 'Well, I, uh,' goddamn it—*yes or no?*"

"If the job is right and the money is right? Well, yes!"

"Okay, Jay," Charles said to Jay Bennett, who was sitting with them, "take care of it."

"What would it take to get you back," Bennett asked one such man. "Sixty? Seventy? Eighty?" To which the man replied, "Well, you just ruled out sixty and seventy."

In a marketing business like Revlon or a research business like U.S.V., Revlon's pharmaceutical company, it pays to get the top creative talent, because what you are really selling, as opposed to raw materials or labor, is the product of a few good brains. But talent always seemed brighter outside the company. Once it was working for Revlon, it lost much of its mystique. So there was little advancement from within the ranks, and the salary increases were not nearly as lavish as that initial deal. And here was the catch: In order to get a big raise or a promotion, you generally had to threaten to leave for the competition (or actually do so and then be wooed back). But once you did that you were a marked man. Charles took that sort of thing personally. Your disloyalty to him and to Revlon would not be forgotten. Your salary would be raised, and the search would begin for your successor. He would get even with you and regain the dominant position in the relationship by paying enough to keep you—and then forcing you out. It was the old "You can't fire me; I quit" syndrome, in reverse. There were exceptions, but it was a familiar Revson pattern.

Charles was a demanding, often abusive employer, no question about it. He had this relentless intensity . . . like a man too excited by his ideas and his work to fall asleep as, in fact, Revson had difficulty doing. He would call Ray Stetzer at the lab every day without fail. And then he would call him at home on Sunday night. Sunday night conversations with Stetzer could run nonstop from seven-thirty to eleven—three and a half hours on the phone—because Charles had that many questions to ask, that many products to discuss, and that much stamina. And then Monday morning, as every other morning, the phone would ring up at the lab at ten o'clock, and Charles would be asking Ray what progress had been made on the things they had discussed the night before.

He even offered Stetzer two acres of his own property in Rye if he would only build a house there. It wasn't enough that he would call Stetzer at three or four in the morning from Tokyo (well, it wasn't three or four in *Tokyo*); or that once in the late forties he had the Royal Canadian Mounted Police track the Stetzers down in the midst of their vacation to have him rush back to the office; or that in 1952 a police gondola in Venice came out to get them in the middle of the Grand Canal for the same purpose. He wanted them to live next door.

That Stetzer died of a heart attack at forty-nine (as did Bill Heller) was not entirely unrelated to "the Revlon experience." Said an ex-personnel manager: "I left because I just didn't think I could take the Charles Revson routine. You know, a lot of the people who were close to him are dead now. I'm not sure I'd be alive today if I had stayed."

That's putting it strongly, to be sure—but what *about* all these charges of "owning" executives and "murdering" them and such? Someone once confronted Charles directly on these points:

Charles was dining at The Four Seasons with this man, whom he very much wanted to hire—the woo-ee, we'll call him. Now a top Revlon executive, the woo-ee was then quite comfortable and secure where he was, thank you, and so felt he had nothing to lose by being frank.

"Mr. Revson," he said, "I'm intrigued by what you're offering me, but—excuse me for being blunt—I hear you're a real shit. That you devour people, that you think you own them seven days a week. . . . You've got a lousy reputation, and I really would like your response to that."

The thrust of Revson's answer was that he's honest, he's straight, and, yes, he is demanding. And he thinks he got his reputation because he is a perfectionist and he gets rid of people if they don't live up to his expectations. He said there are an awful lot of millionaires walking around the street today that he made millionaires, and you never hear from *them*. Which was true.

"But then," says the woo-ee, "he began rambling around the subject and—you know, he's always an hour late, and we didn't meet at The Four Seasons until ten. The restaurant closed at one, but he got up and tipped somebody to keep the place open—the kitchen and everything—and we must have sat there until at least three o'clock talking, and he was still answering that question. He's very defensive about it.

"And Charles says: 'Now, as to this thing about owning people, that's bullshit. I don't own my people. Why, I just hired a guy—fantastic, a real professional manager, just came in a few months ago. I don't follow him at all—I don't even know what he did last week. I don't own him. Jay

[Bennett, his personnel man], call Harry and have him get his ass on down here.'

"So Jay gets up and calls Harry, who lives out in Connecticut, and wakes him up. And he drives in, sleep in his eyes—it must be well past three A.M. by now—and Charles says, 'Kiddie, tell him I don't own you.'"

CHAPTER 11

THE $64,000,000 QUIZ SHOW

It seemed like a good idea. Chrysler is supposed to have turned it down because they were afraid of labor problems: how would it look to their rank-and-file to be giving away huge sums of money on the air while fighting pennies-an-hour increases at the bargaining table? Madame Rubinstein turned it down because, not then owning a television herself, she thought "only poor people watch those awful machines." Revson, too, had supposedly passed on it the first time around. He was getting awful tired of investing in one "stiff" of a TV series after the next. He had a natural bias against television advertising anyway. It was black and white, and he was selling colors. Nor could he control TV ads the way he could control print. Yet Hazel Bishop had been murdering Revlon's lipstick business with its sponsorship of *This Is Your Life,* and Revson was not about to lose a competitive battle. So with a good deal of prodding from Walter Craig, of Norman, Craig & Kummel, Charles agreed to sponsor a new show, to be called *The $64,000 Question.* He insisted, however, on the unusual right to pull out after thirteen weeks if it proved a dud.

After the first night, Charles, Martin, and Norman retreated to Charles's table at Billy Reid's Little Club, the first table on the right past the bar. Charles was morose. It was another goddamn dog, and he wanted out. Norman and Martin had to stay up with him late into the night defending the show's potential. "I think he thought it was a long way from cosmetics and wasn't conducive to the emotional aura and surroundings in which he'd like to see his products," says Norman. He was proved wrong.

First aired June 7, 1955, within four weeks *The $64,000 Question* was number one in the ratings. Some of the products featured on the show were experiencing 300 percent and 500 percent sales increases. One lipstick shade sold out in ten days. What was advertised on Tuesday night was sold out Wednesday morning.

On an average Tuesday night at ten, nearly twice as many people—55,000,000—were watching Revlon's ads as had watched Nixon's "Checkers" speech. At its peak an unbelievable 82 percent of the television sets switched on around the country were tuned to emcee Hal March, the famous "isolation booth," Revlon spokeswoman Barbara Britton, and the latest Revlon promotion. Movie theaters complained of sparse attendance on Tuesday nights. Restaurant business was off.

The ten-thirty to eleven time slot following *The $64,000 Question* suddenly became very valuable. General Motors won out in the bidding for it, and Edward R. Murrow's *See It Now*, which had occupied the time, was forced to move to make way for a more commercial show. Imagine— General Motors bidding to capitalize on Charlie Revson's success! It would have swelled his chest with pride . . . if only he could have taken credit for having discovered, or at least not bad-mouthed, the show. Instead, it rankled him—which may have been the underlying reason for his dumping Norman, Craig & Kummel in 1956, despite the fact that Revlon's sales and profits were exploding as a direct result of NC&K's having brought in *The $64,000 Question.*

Soon Revlon had captured Sunday night audiences with a spin-off, *The $64,000 Challenge.* And in an effort to make it a triple sweep—Sunday, Monday, and Tuesday—it was announced that *The Most Beautiful Girl in the World* would debut at 9 P.M. Eastern Daylight Time, October 22, 1956. The show was to be a sort of weekly Miss America pageant, with $250,000 thrown in as top prizes to keep the contestants smiling. Revson set as criteria for contestants that they be beautiful, talented, and intelligent. After screening hundreds of potential contestants, the last of a string of producers assigned to create a pilot went to Charles: "Would you say Judy Garland is talented?" Of course. "Intelligent?" Yeah. "Beautiful?" No. He then proposed Hedy Lamarr, whom Charles faulted on a different count. "Well," concluded the producer, "how do you expect us to come up with three contestants a week if Judy Garland and Hedy Lamarr wouldn't qualify?" The show never made it to the air.

It may be argued that *The $64,000 Question* was the difference between Revson's becoming just another successful businessman and his becoming a superstar. Up until this time, Revlon had risen to the level of its competitors, but did not dominate the field, except in nail polish. It had to fight costly battles with competitors. It did not have huge advantages of scale. Profits were modest. The company was not home free. There was no IBM-versus-everybody-else relationship here.

The Question raised Revlon sales, profits, and consumer awareness so dramatically as to put it miles ahead of its competitors. And that sort of edge tends to be self-perpetuating, or even self-expanding. The rich get richer. The companies with the most resources, other things being equal (not better, just equal), can swamp the competition.

Sales, which had been growing at from 10 to 20 percent a year in the first half of the fifties, suddenly shot up 54 percent in 1955—even though *The Question* was only on the air for the second half of the year. Profits tripled. It was a fine way to kick off Revlon's public stock offering.

The next year, sales were up yet another 66 percent, to $85 million, profits better than doubled. The pretax profit on every sales dollar had widened from eight cents in 1954 to twenty cents. Helena Rubinstein, Max Factor, Coty, and Hazel Bishop, which had all been at least within striking distance of Revlon before *The Question* went on the air, were left bitterly in the dust. Revlon was number one in lipstick, number one in hair spray, number one in nail products, and number one in makeup. The chairman of Hazel Bishop had to report a surprising $460,000 loss for 1955, "due to circumstances beyond our control," as he put it. Hazel Bishop had been swamped by Revlon.

By 1957, a spate of competitive quiz shows, most notably *Twenty-One*, with its Charles Van Doren, had begun to cut into *The Question* craze, and Revlon found itself doing things like upping the top prize money from $64,000 to $256,000. And a year later quiz shows had become old hat—the subject of a budding national scandal. *The $64,000 Question* was quietly folded. But not before it had lifted Revlon sales by about $64,000,000.

Revlon's weekly cost of producing *The $64,000 Question,* including prize money, which averaged a mere $14,000 per show, was $27,800— about half what it cost Hazel Bishop to produce *This Is Your Life.* Another $40,000 went for each half hour of network broadcast time. In total, Revlon got more than three minutes of national attention for less than $70,000 a week. By contrast, three minutes of commercial time when *The Godfather* was shown on TV in 1974 cost a sponsor $675,000.

But it was better than that. *The Godfather* dragged on for hours, with countless sponsors, one after another. People were riveted to *The $64,000 Question,* for which there was only one sponsor. Identification of Revlon with *The Question* was very close; Charles himself appeared to present the first $64,000 check (to a U.S. marine who knew all about food). The commercials were all done live. The studio audience oohed and aahed at Revlon's extravanganzas just as they sat in tense silence during the show's most suspenseful moments. Barbara Britton was almost as much a part of the show as Hal March. The electricity was shared. Constant national publicity mentioned Revlon again and again.

Doing the commercials live had a number of advantages, not least of which was that it allowed Revlon to steal television time. Each of Revlon's three commercials per show was supposed to run one minute. Few, if any, ran less, and a great many ran longer. Says a key figure from that period, still with Revlon: "We would run 'sixty-second' commercials for *three minutes* and there was nothing they could do to stop us because we were live. What were they going to do? Run to the middle of the stage and yell, 'Stop!'?"

Another reason Charles insisted on live commercials (which were not unusual in those days) was the flexibility it gave him in deciding almost up to the last minute what to pitch and how. He could drive everybody crazy, and did.

"All during *The $64,000 Question* and *The Challenge*," a veteran of these wars remembers, "he would never start a script until maybe a week before air, which made life impossible. You would get approval—alleged approval—generally no more than forty-eight hours before the air. You'd be at rehearsal at six o'clock for the first run-through. Mandel would walk in with a long face. 'Bad news.' 'What's the matter?' 'Charles hates it.' Then you'd rewrite, starting at six-thirty, seven o'clock, and you'd have a prompter crew there to redo the prompter. Go and dress at nine; on the air at ten. Charles felt there was greater spontaneity by doing that."

Miraculously, nothing dramatic went wrong with any of Revlon's productions. Models were given few lines to say, so there was little they could flub. One model was charged with looking up indignantly at the camera and saying—"Soap on my face? Never!"—in connection with an ad for Clean & Clear. This very sexy model studied and studied her line, and when the great moment came she looked up indignantly at America and said, "Face on my soap? Never!"

Working on the Revlon account was like riding in a rodeo. It was a challenge, you could win some money, and the ride generally ended fairly quickly anyway. From 1944 to 1957 Revlon used nine separate ad agencies. "Revlon's then small $600,000 account," *Time* reported, "was first snagged by McCann-Erickson's John McCarthy—who lasted a stormy six months with Revson. The two men finally fell out over McCarthy's dirty fingernails. When Revson needled him, McCarthy snapped: 'What do you want me to do, use nail polish?' Revson laughed—and ordered McCarthy thrown off the account." Reportedly, sixteen or seventeen other top account men followed McCarthy until, in 1948, the account moved to the William Weintraub agency. There it was handled by Norman B. Norman, who later formed Norman, Craig & Kummel. Norman managed to work with Charles for seven years. He, too, was a "street fighter" not universally loved. He drove a white Silver Cloud with NBN plates, dressed like Charles, acted like Charles, and came from much the same mold. He was, however, taller, more articulate, and able to work for someone else, which Charles would undoubtedly have found extraordinarily difficult. After seven years he was canned.

Norman attributed his downfall to George Abrams, a Revlon V.P. he felt was out to get him—and on whom, accordingly, he placed a private detective. Abrams was propped up at Revlon by Bill Mandel, whom he had brought over from his former company, Block Drug, as his assistant. After a while, Mandel decided to let George fend for himself, and that was the end of George.

When Abrams left Revlon, Mandel quickly became the most important man in the company after Charles. It was Mandel, largely, who presented the marketing side of Revlon to Wall Street security analysts; Mandel who developed much of the theming for Revlon campaigns; Mandel who would battle with Charles over the proper positioning of new products and the proper strategy for the company as a whole. He filled the gap left by Martin Revson's departure, and he served as the interface between Charles and the rest of the marketing and agency people. He would take their work and sell it to Charles. The underlying logic of this arrangement was simply that in a group Charles would bully people, whereas one-on-one he was not bad. He was reasonable. The agency, Grey Advertising this time, managed to steer clear of Revson for so long—years—that one day Charles looked up, as if struck by a sudden thought, and asked Mandel: "Where's Grey?" Structured this way, Grey has managed to keep the account for seventeen years.

Similarly, Mandel never showed Charles TV advertising in advance—"because we would never have gotten it on the air." Charles had mixed feelings about TV commercials, anyway, even though they had contributed so directly to his success. When he once asked to see a review of all the advertising that had been done in the prior six months—"everything"—Kay Daly and Mandel organized it and decided to start with the most recent commercials. Charles arrived, impatient as always—"Come on, come on"—and they started to run the commercials. Charles said, "I didn't want to see television, I told you I wanted to see *advertising*."

Print would hold still and he could perfect it. It was a permanent statement. A TV commercial, good or bad, evaporated. It was more important to him to get the ad for the Sunday *Times* perfect, even if it reached fewer people, because (a) they were the people he cared about; and (b) an imperfection would not evaporate—it would just sit there and embarrass him.

CHAPTER 12

HEARTBURN

Not long after the debut of *The $64,000 Question,* and not long before the public offering of Revlon stock—in June and December 1955, respectively—Charles had a mild heart attack. As a result, he quit smoking and embarked on a fanatically strict low-cholesterol diet.

The only thing Charles Revson took more seriously than his business was his health. Compulsive about his products, he was an out-and-out nut about his health. "He swallowed every pill in the world," says Irving Botwin. "The guy was a walking drugstore." His doctor objects to use of the term "hypochondriac," on the grounds that any man who has survived two heart attacks has reason for concern. But the intensity of his concern far exceeded the severity of his attacks. They were so mild his ex-wife doesn't even believe he ever had them.

He had a variety of digestive complaints throughout his life, including at one time a small ulcer; and also a variety of attempted cures, many of them self-devised. In the early forties he went on a baby-food diet. Around the same time, he consumed great quantities of halvah. At Billy Reid's Little Club he would order Bumble Bee salmon and baked beans (neither was on the menu); and if the beans were not kept properly separate from the salmon, he would send the plate back to the kitchen to be rearranged. He didn't want salmon juice mixing with his beans. For many years he would pour a gloopy white liquid into a glass of water before every meal and gobble a fistful of antacid pills after, leaving the corners of his mouth chalky white. It was for his stomach, also, that he gave up hard liquor.

"He never had any heart attack," scoffs Ancky, who was married to him when both were alleged to have occurred. "He had two," says Dr. Steiner, much of whose livelihood lo these thirty-six years was derived from Revson and Revlon. Katie Lowery, attempting to reconcile these seemingly contradictory views, suggests Charles may have talked Steiner into agreeing that his minor heart probelms were "attacks." After all, beyond a point what purpose is served by arguing with your patient? Particularly when he has you on retainer and is helping to fund your research. If he wants to exaggerate his brush with death, why aggravate him by insisting on a less dramatic interpretation?

It is fair to conclude that Charles had at least two mild cardiac episodes—call them what you will; that one occurred in late 1955, so as to land him in the hospital the day his stock went public and to require a longer than usual stay in Arthur Godfrey's suite at the Kenilworth Hotel in Miami to recuperate; that at the same time as he may have been exaggerating their importance in his own mind, he was simultaneously doing his best to conceal them from the public; and that mild as they may have been, they scared the shit out of him.

Accordingly, he brought extraordinary self-discipline to the task of caring for his heart. To begin with, he gave up smoking. The three to five packs of Phillip Morris regulars he smoked each day were cut, immediately, to nil. Cigars were likewise discarded. To ease his withdrawal he placed jars of hard candy all over his office. And from time to time he would dangle an unlit cigarillo from his lips. Naturally, the uninformed were forever lunging to light it and had constantly to be fought off.

On instructions from Dr. Steiner, he also swore off cholesterol. These days such a diet (less stringently observed) has gained wide acceptance. In those days people thought he was crazy. Always a picky eater, he now became impossible. He shunned eggs and dairy products, of course, and was buying margarine in the days when it was still sold in tins at the drugstore. He developed the habit of running his finger over his steak and his vegetables and then sniffing it to be sure the chef or hostess had followed his butter-free instructions. He would seat himself, when possible, with a view of the kitchen to watch his food being prepared. It would be ridiculous to suggest that he thought people were trying to poison him—but neither did he trust them. Even at home he would suspect that contraband had been slipped into a particular dish.

On flights abroad he sometimes carried a soft athletic bag with two of his specially trimmed steaks and two bottles of Dom Perignon, to be sure of truly first-class treatment. In his last year on earth he had his meals chauffered all the way up to the hospital in the Bronx from his apartment on Sixty-fifth Street.

Much of the Revson legend stems from quirks in the way he took care of himself. One could paint quite a sad picture of a man with grave health problems whom others unfeelingly ridiculed. Imagine his embarrassment at having to ask for special treatment in a restaurant! At having to have a special plate at a party! Except his health problems weren't grave; and if he felt embarrassment over his special requirements, he never showed it. Nor were they truly necessary. To be on the safe side, however, he would frequently take his own pulse; he kept electrocardiographs in the city, the country, and on his yacht; he had electrocardiograms taken daily when he traveled (a doctor was always aboard the yacht); and to remain fit, he exercised six mornings a week for twenty years with his private trainer/masseur/chiropractor, Dr. Mac—a Jewish ex-fight-trainer and semipro football player from Rumania.

His exercise room at 625 Park Avenue was small but elegant, with naked Greeks cavorting on red wallpaper. Dr. Mac would in later years arrive from Levittown every morning a little past nine. Charles was usually on the phone by then or, occasionally, asleep. A quick shower was followed by ten or fifteen minutes on the Mr. Jogger Cadette, twenty or thirty minutes on the electric bike, a minute or two under the sun lamp, and twenty minutes of exercise with tension cables. Mac was careful not to have Charles work up a heavy sweat. "But sometimes he'd give a sneeze or two and say, 'Gee, I think I'm catching a cold.' And I'd say, 'You don't have a cold.' And he'd say, 'Well, I'll go and see Dr. Steiner anyway.' Each time I'd bet him a dime he didn't have a cold—and I won myself quite a pile of dimes."

After the exercises, a massage, a gentle rubbing/kneading "treatment." Then he would shower or bathe and pick out one of his hundred or so Fioravanti suits that all looked the same, anyway (so much so that the butler had to number them to be sure which jacket went with which trousers), and have breakfast. Saturdays, this routine would go on up in the country. Sundays, Mac's day off, Charles would go through it alone.

Once at work there was another routine. "Charles had the most routinized life of any man I've ever met," says a man who got a call from him every Sunday night in the middle of *Mission: Impossible*.

He paced himself. His anger, for example, was always controlled. He would never leap out of his chair and start shouting. He would uncoil himself slowly, like a rattler, if he rose from his seat at all. There would be a slight tremble to his lower lip, which could curl up over his upper lip. His eyes drilled you. And if he was really furious, a little foam might show through his lips. But that's all. Never any quick or violent movement.

During his daily marathon lunch meetings, he would rest his head in his hands or on the table. He had the habit, too, of closing his eyes—you could never tell whether he was with you or not. But the sleepy look was deceptive. Watch out. After the marathon lunch, a nap.

By five or six in the afternoon he would be just beginning to catch his stride. His creative people, who arrived earlier and took no naps, were beginning to flag. Meetings would last another couple of hours, after which he would walk the few blocks to his apartment, shower, take another nap, dine, and around half past ten he would be ready, at last, for the meat of the day, the things he really wanted to do. "I had some fascinating evenings with him," one former associate says, "but they would most of the time run well past midnight. Charles was really a very lonely person who wanted company, and I guess the night was the loneliest period. He found it difficult to sleep. He was very much a night person."

With all the time he spent worrying about his heart, one marvels that he still found time to worry about other parts of his body. He would run up to Dr. Stovin, his ear, nose, and throat man of forty years, at the slightest provocation—often accompanied by executives so he could work on the way up and back. He suffered from allergies, was given to fairly frequent nosebleeds, and liked to have his sinuses X-rayed periodically.

He was concerned with his skin. He used Eterna 27, his wondrous wrinkle remover, every night. (He also ordered the tip of his nose and the tips of his "devil's ears" airbrushed out of all photos.) He would "collect" his blackheads, and the bumps that come with old age, and every couple of months have Revlon's staff dermatologist remove them. "I would send all my tools down to his office by messenger," says Dr. Brauer, "and then at the end of the day, when everyone had left, he would show me the areas and I would remove them. He was aware of every square inch of his body, including his back."

For all this (and I have spared you his ophthalmologist, his throat specialist, and whoever else)—for all this the man was hardly sick, *really* sick a day in his life. He almost never missed a day's work. Which proves either that his self-attentiveness paid off or that it was unnecessary.

CHAPTER   13

WHO—ME?

The headlines were extraordinary. This whole quiz show mania, touched off by the *The $64,000 Question* and gripping the country for three years, had turned out to be a fraud. The front page, eight-column headline of *The Washington Post,* November 5, 1959, ran: EX-

REVLON AIDE ADMITS TV FIX. This referred to an affidavit sent down to the congressional hearings by George Abrams and it came at an embarrassing moment for the Revsons, each of whom was testifying that they had been flabbergasted—just flabbergasted—to learn that their shows, *The $64,000 Question* and *The $64,000 Challenge* had been rigged. Meanwhile, the producers of the shows, who actually did the rigging, were blaming the Revsons, Martin in particular, for pulling the strings. President Eisenhower likened "this whole mess" to the Chicago Black Sox scandal of 1919 and said nobody would be satisfied until it was cleared up. Dave Garroway broke into tears on the *Today* show and had to leave the show half an hour early when his cohost, former quiz-show star Charles Van Doren, was dismissed from NBC for his role in the scandal. Revlon stock fell five points in one day.

Revlon loyalists will tell you it was *Twenty-One*, a rival show, and not *The Question* that was fixed. They will tell you, with a note of resignation at having been unfairly wronged, that most people think Charles Van Doren was on *The Question,* when in fact he was on *Twenty-One.* Dig a little deeper and you arrive at this somewhat subtle distinction: *Twenty-One* was fixed; *The Question* and *The Challenge* were "controlled." Charles Van Doren and others on *Twenty-One* were actually given answers before the show, and were taught to stammer and stutter for dramatic effect. ("Let's skip that part of the question till later, please.") The air conditioning in the isolation booth was purposely left off so that contestants would sweat under the hot lights, as if from tension. Contestants on *The Question* were *not* handed the answers; instead the producers ascertained in advance just what they did and did not know and devised their questions accordingly. It amounted to the same thing.

The *Daily News* headline on November 5, 1959, read like a parody of a *Daily News* headline: HAD BANK VAULT KEY, SAYS GIRL TV FIXER. The girl TV fixer (not a TV repairwoman, you understand) was none other than thirty-six-year-old Shirley Bernstein, Leonard's sister. (The Bernsteins' father, coincidentally, was a Revlon jobber in Boston.) Ms. Bernstein was associate producer of *The Challenge.* She was in reality the producer, she testified, only Revlon "felt very strongly that a woman should not get the producer credit." Her statement was taken by Richard N. Goodwin.

Ms. Bernstein would have extensive discussions with the contestants to find out the range of their knowledge, she said, "so that in writing the questions I could, with some degree of success, prognosticate the outcome of the match." She would ask questions almost identical to those to be asked on the show when Revlon requested a particular outcome.

Goodwin: Was this request made of you?

Bernstein: Not directly, but through Mr. Carlin [the executive producer].

Goodwin: Was it your complete understanding from the start that you were receiving instructions from the sponsor as to how a match should come out?

Bernstein: Yes, completely. There were many meetings with the sponsor where Mr. Carlin would come back white with anger.

Goodwin: Did Mr. Carlin ever tell you directly that the sponsor had requested a particular outcome to a match?

Bernstein: Yes.

Goodwin: With what degree of accuracy would you control the outcome of a match?

Bernstein: At the peak of my efficiency, about 80 percent.

Ms. Bernstein said that both she and her assistant had keys to the famous Manufacturers Hanover Trust vault (Revlon's bank of long standing), and that they would go in and get the questions at any time.

No one disputed that there had been weekly meetings between the producers, the agency people, and Revlon, chaired by Martin. Yet Charles and Martin denied any knowledge of the controls. PROBERS SEE PERJURY OVER $64,000 "FIX" ran the *Herald Tribune* headline, with the subhead: Revsons Deny Ordering Rigging; Producers Swore Sponsor Did.

Martin admitted that he would voice opinions at these meetings as to which contestants had audience appeal and which he hoped would lose. He admitted that his opinions could be forcefully stated. But he claimed to have *no idea* that his wishes would be taken as orders, or that the producers had some way of carrying them out. Neither was he apparently surprised to notice, as the weeks and months went on, the remarkable consistency with which his idle wishes, expressed innocently at these meetings, seemed to be fulfilled.

Mr. Carlin, executive producer of the show, told the subcommittee they would discuss "every possible phase of the show . . . in the minutest detail." Martin admitted that, but testified he "never once suggested that a contestant win or lose." He went so far as to say that *had* he ever known that the shows he sponsored were controlled in any way—he would have dropped them . . . even though they were catapulting his company's sales and profits beyond even his wildest hopes.

Charles, meanwhile, had all but escaped coming under this embarrassing congressional spotlight. Subcommittee staffers had sifted through a great deal of material and decided it was not necessary to call him to testify. At the last minute, he sent a telegram to the committee *insisting* on his right to do so. It was not the smartest thing Charles Revson ever did. In his defense, it should be said that he sent the telegram on advice of a public-relations expert. The thought was that all the other witnesses would doubtless try to shift the blame onto Revlon, so Charles should have a chance to defend the company's good name. It's quite possible Charles really didn't know the extent of Revlon's implication in the controlling of the shows, and accordingly feared less than he should have.

One problem was that the congressmen assumed Charles knew what Martin knew—that if one brother was fibbing, the other was, too. Charles couldn't come right out and tell the congressmen that he and Martin had not been on speaking terms for some time—that they would pass each other at these very congressional hearings without so much as a nod. That would have been embarrassing.

Charles spent three days at the hearings waiting to be called. Mandel, who was with him, says he was magnificent in a crisis. "He taught me not to panic."

When it finally did come time for Charles to testify, he said that he never missed watching *The Question* if he could possibly help it. He would walk out of a theater in the middle of a play just to watch the show on Tuesday nights to see whether the Italian shoemaker would win $32,000 by answering a question on Italian opera. "Sure, I was the sponsor," he said, "but I was just like the rest of the millions of Americans caught up in the drama of this program. If I had known that these shows were fixed, crooked, rigged, do you think for one minute that I would have watched or bothered this way?" A cynic might point out that watching the shows was the only way Revson could see his own live commercials, which may have been of more interest to him than the questions and answers; and that even people who fix prizefights generally turn out to watch the contest.

Revson concluded his statement deftly: "Remember that [the producers] admitted to this committee yesterday that they also rigged *The Big Surprise* . . . [That show and ours] had only one thing in common. It was not the sponsor, it was the producer. This producer would have you believe that sponsor pressure from Revlon drove him to do what he did on our show. Then what caused him to rig *The Big Surprise?*"

It was a neat twist—but not enough to appease the congressmen, who were by this time in the hearings feeling their self-righteous oats.

Mr. Rogers: You made a lot more [from these shows] than any of the contestants or all the contestants put together, didn't you?

Mr. Revson: . . . Yes, we did.

Mr. Rogers: Since you have branded these as deceitful practices, have you made any efforts or thought of any way to make restitution of that money to the American people?

Mr. Revson: I would not truthfully know how to answer that question, sir.

Mr. Rogers: I don't either, Mr. Revson.

Mr. Revson: Pardon me?

Mr. Rogers: I would not know how to answer it either. I just wonder— you and your brother come up here and say you were victims of fraud, too, but you were the kind of victims of the fraud that some of the winners on these contests were—that is, you profited very well by being a victim. You brand these other people as deceitful, and I agree with you, they were deceitful; but you are the one who profited the most by the deceitful practices that were played upon the American people. I am wondering what is in your mind and the mind of the Revlon Company, to try to make restitution or correction of a wrong which you admit occurred.

Mr. Revson: We have never given any thought to that. . . .

Mr. Rogers: You have branded this, you and your brother both branded this as a deceitful practice and a reprehensible practice. Yet you are willing to accept the profits from it and let the contestants take all of the blame. Both of you said you had nothing to do with the running of it. The most you did was to make suggestions, isn't that correct?

Mr. Revson: Yes, sir.

Mr. Rogers: Were those suggestions subtle suggestions, Mr. Revson?

Mr. Revson: The suggestions made as far as I am concerned had no relativity to that.

Mr. Rogers: You mean they were about as subtle as a blow by a baseball bat?

Mr. Revson: I certainly do not.

Mr. Rogers: That is what the evidence would indicate, as you know. You heard the testimony.

Mr. Revson: I heard it, yes.

Mr. Rogers: It would indicate [that] when . . . Mr. Martin Revson made a suggestion, there was not any question in his mind or anyone else's mind as to what he meant and what he intended to have.

Mr. Revson: That is correct.

Mr. Rogers: That is actually what happened. A suggestion was made and you expected it to be carried out?

Mr. Revson: Pardon me?

Mr. Rogers: A suggestion was made in one of these meetings you expected to be carried out, didn't you?

Mr. Revson: I didn't get the first part, then. I thought I got it.

Mr. Rogers: I say, that in these meetings you had, when you made a suggestion, which you claim you had the right to do under your contract, you expected that suggestion to be carried out, didn't you?

Mr. Revson: The few infrequent times that I was there, I don't remember discussing anything about a contestant or anything like that. The times that I would be in there would have relation to the format of the show, or possibly a change in the plateau aspects of the money part, or the show could be more interesting, or something such as that.

As if the congressional hearings hadn't been bad enough, they were followed only four months later, in March 1960, by an even more embarrassing controversy. Brother Martin, by now two years gone from the company, was suing brother Charles for fraud, seeking $601,460.80, and alleging (rather irrelevantly), that Charles "humiliated," "mistreated," and "abused" executives to the point that working conditions at Revlon had become the subject of "widespread ill-repute and ridicule."

A tenet of Charles's existence was to avoid embarrassment, let alone ridicule, and this suit dished up both. Ordinarily, Charles went out of his way to avoid legal problems. Revlon attorneys were faced with the fact that their star witness simply refused to go into court or even to give a deposition. "He had a fear of the law and certainly a fear of being a witness—he was almost paranoid in this respect," says one of the lawyers who was instructed to settle out of court many cases that could easily have been won. Yet in the case of Martin's suit—although it eventually *was* settled out of court—pride for a while got the better of paranoia.

Martin's attorney, William G. Mulligan, professed "amazement and dismay" that the suit had hit the papers, and swore that he and his client had "maintained absolute silence." In the then prevailing atmosphere, however, one must assume that Martin was more pleased than mortified to see his charges widely quoted, and that Charles was more mortified than pleased. Charles would state only that the suit was without merit, and that he regretted it. "It is unfortunate," he said, "that the language of the complaint contains the kind of emotional statements which sometimes characterize suits involving members of the same family."

The suit was an offshoot of Martin's leaving the firm. Doubtless it could have been settled amicably had Martin left on amicable terms but such was not the case. The suit concerned 231,000 shares of Revlon stock which Martin owned, but which he had assigned to the famous "voting trust." Martin owned the stock, but Charles, as sole trustee, controlled it.

Martin wanted to remove his stock from the trust; Charles was in no hurry. He didn't want Martin to be in a position to dump a lot of stock on the market and thereby depress the value of Revlon shares; and, more importantly, he was determined to keep at least 51 percent of the company under his own control. With Martin's 231,000 shares in the trust, Charles controlled about 55 percent of the stock. Without it, he would have controlled less than half.

As a practical matter, Charles would have had effective control of the company with less than a majority of the stock. However, Charles's "neurotic anxieties" on this point—as Martin's lawyers referred to his concern—may have stemmed from the frustrating years when Revlon was still a private company and Charles had to submit decisions to Lachman for approval. Or perhaps they stemmed simply from Charles's general paranoia.

Nonetheless, control over a majority of Revlon stock could hardly hurt, and Charles was determined to have it. Martin came up with a possible solution: 131,000 of his shares would be released to him, which would still leave Charles control over a majority of Revlon stock. The remaining 100,000 shares would be sold back to Revlon itself in exchange for stock in Schering Corporation, a pharmaceutical company Revlon had for a time been trying to acquire.

Charles decided this wasn't such a bad idea . . . only he wanted Martin to agree to give up $6 a share in figuring the value of his Revlon stock. In other words, for Revlon stock that was selling at $35 a share in the open market, Martin would be given only $29 worth of Schering stock. Charles claimed to have inside information that Schering stock would very likely do better than Revlon stock over the coming year, so Martin would come out ahead.

Martin said a $6 discount was too much; Charles agreed to cut it to $4. Martin said a $4 discount was too much; Charles agreed to cut it to $3. What's more, according to Martin, Charles promised that in the unlikely event Schering stock did *not* out-perform Revlon over the following year, he would see to it that Martin got the extra Schering stock he was forfeiting by accepting the $3 discount.

As it turned out, Schering stock appreciated a stunning 71 percent over the designated time period (August 15, 1958 to July 15, 1959). Only, Revlon stock appreciated even a bit more—by 75 percent. And Martin, notwithstanding his $2 million profit on the Schering stock, expected Charles to stick to what he understood their agreement to be: namely, to deliver the Schering stock Martin had forfeited by accepting the $3 discount on his Revlon shares. He demanded either 7,518 Schering shares or $601,460.80 in cash. (The amount to which those shares would have appreciated by the time the suit was filed.)

Charles claimed he had never made any such promise. "Show it to me in writing," was his position, and Martin had nothing to show.

After a modest amount of backing and forthing, barking and frothing, they settled out of court. Charles paid Martin $300,000 out of his own pocket.

The suit itself was really just a battle in a larger war between the brothers. Many said that the provocateur of this war had been Julie Revson, Martin's wife. Julie knew both men well, and it was her opinion, no doubt biased as a consequence of her marriage, that Martin should be running the show. She wanted him at least to be president, with Charles kicked upstairs to the chairman's seat. After some pressure Charles had actually agreed to such a change in titles, to go into effect by 1959, but Martin did not stay around that long. He explains why:

"I'm not going to tell you all the inner feelings that I had, because I don't want to reveal them. I'll give you a general answer. While he and I got along very well when it came to merchandising and products . . . we didn't always agree on finances. My compensation. Also, while I had tremendous latitude, certain things still had to be cleared to his opinion. And sometimes, whether it was the name of a product or something like that, it became kind of sticky. I felt, after we had so many meetings, if he said, 'No' and 'Why don't you fellows go back and look at it again?'—it became a little irritating. Things like that.

"I irritated him and he irritated me on certain things . . . It wasn't a point of wanting to run the company myself or supersede him or kick him out of the business. I never thought of that. I always knew his value . . . I felt that these personal irritants had grown to such a degree it would be better for us to go our separate ways . . .

"So I made my decision in February [1958]. When Charles and I sat down on a Monday morning I opened the meeting by saying: 'I have it in mind of leaving.' He asked why. I said: 'It's got to the point where our views are different. There's no sense in going through any details—why don't I leave amicably?' If he was surprised, he didn't indicate it. He was calm through the whole matter, which he had a way of being during matters like this."

They agreed that Martin would stay until a replacement could be found. When Charles kept stalling on the question of releasing Martin's stock from the voting trust, Martin told him, "I'm not discussing anything else until we settle this matter." He collected a few papers and never appeared in the office again. But because his resignation was in a sort of limbo, his office at 666 Fifth Avenue—never occupied—was kept empty, but fully furnished and dusted daily, in case he should one day show up back on the job.

It took thirteen years for the fraternal rift to mend. During those years Charles was nothing short of frigid on the subject of his brother. "What brother?" he once said. "I don't have a brother."

Charles blamed wives; Martin maintains this was not so. But he does credit wives—a new set—with bringing about the reconciliation. "That's the happy thing, that we got back together," he says. "I think Lyn was an important instrument in getting us back together. She and Eleanor [Martin's second wife] got along fine. I think she convinced Charles; and Eleanor convinced me."

CHAPTER 14

"WOMEN ARE LIARS AND CHEATS"

Beset by deep-seated insecurities, Revson was a different man in many respects from the image he chose to project. Manly, stern, tough, crude—much of this was a front. He had an almost pathetic yearning at times to be a warmer, more accepted person. He once did manage to compliment an executive on a job well done—jaws dropped—then said: "There. I did it. Now don't ask me to do it again."

His emotional straitjacket, like his extraordinary drive, stemmed from insecurities the basis of which are not hard to imagine. His size, his lack of athletic prowess, the femininity of the products he always seemed to be selling (ladies' shoes, dresses, cosmetics), the nail enamel he wore, his self-styled "sensitivity," his hypochondria—reasons aplenty to have to prove oneself a man. Then there were his growing up Jewish among Gentiles, his lack of education or polish, his tenement upbringing, the narrowness of his interests—added to whatever less obvious reasons he may have had to feel insecure, it was a lot for a man on the forty-ninth floor of New York's General Motors Building to cope with. He was even insecure about his breath, gargling Cepacol by the gallon.

His insecurities fell roughly into two sets: those that led to the striving for manliness and those that led to a striving for class. He would be rough and crude to be one of the boys; proper and genteel to be classy. The friction between these not entirely compatible sets of insecurities must have generated some psychological heat.

Insecure, Revson hid behind his business in a world he created for himself, venturing outside only with trepidation, sticking closely to established routines and familiar places and, as far as possible, taking his environment with him. Riding down in the office elevator he seemed almost to shrink into himself. Up there, he was king of the mountain. Outside, he was alone.

He was lonely because he couldn't open up; he couldn't open up because he didn't trust people; and he didn't trust people because he wouldn't believe they liked him—or even could like him.

The years between his estrangement from Ancky and his marriage to Lyn were, with the year of his death, the loneliest. "I don't know how many times I walked the streets and had dinner with him because he had no place to go," Mandel says. But even married he was a lonely man. His wives did not share his life—his life was his business, and they were carefully excluded. He had never learned to make friends with women—they served a different purpose.

He went about lovemaking, women who slept with him said, as though he were going through an exercise class: ten minutes of this, fifteen of that, five of the other, orgasm, no repeats, off to the showers. Whether this was true where his wives were concerned, one has not the temerity to ask. When Eugenia Sheppard asked him at dinner one evening on the yacht what he thought of women, he said: "I think they're all liars and cheats."

"Women in the abstract he idolized," an associate from the forties feels certain. "He put her on a pedestal and paid tribute. But individually, women were to be trampled on and cast away like you would a cigarette."

With his parents both long gone, Joseph and Martin out of the company, the boys off at Deerfield, Lester Herzog married and Ancky actually going through with the divorce, in the spring of 1960 Charles relied for companionship most heavily on Bill Heller and then George Beck.

As Lester had, Heller would eagerly do anything for Charles. He waited around the office every day until "C.R." was ready to leave, often went out to eat with him, served as his "beard" (so Charles could pass off as Heller's the girl he was with), ran out for sandwiches, carried the money and the margarine, secured and paid off women, took the wiretapping rap, wrote Johnny's term papers for Deerfield—anything. If he wasn't as altruistic in his devotion to Charles as Lester had been, Charles didn't seem to notice. Heller became his closest companion—not to mention secretary/treasurer of Revlon, and then head of its international operations. It was not your standard intercorporate relationship, as might prevail between the chairman and the international vice president of General Motors or Xerox, but neither was Revlon your standard corporation.

For ten years Heller's life was simple. Then in 1959 he met Iris Segal. They fell in love. Suddenly Heller found himself torn between two much stronger, more talented people, each vying mightily for his devotion. It took him all of three years to collapse and die under the strain.

Heller was forty-seven when he met Iris, then vice president and director of Seligman & Latz, the leading beauty salon operator (headquartered, like Revlon, at 666 Fifth Avenue). Charles had known Iris since 1933. He respected her success and ability; but because he didn't want her breaking up his relationship with Bill, he was given to making derogatory remarks behind her back. He told several of his executives to try to discourage Heller from seeing her.

Bill, for his part, was so terrified of displeasing Charles—and, incidentally, jeopardizing his chances for the top spot in Revlon's international division—that he underplayed considerably the love he felt for Iris. He didn't mention, for example, that they had gone off and secretly gotten married.

After the wedding, Charles may not have demanded from Bill more than his standard measure of fanatical devotion, but it seemed for all the world to the new Mrs. Heller that her old friend Charles was doing his best to break up her marriage. "Charles," she even claims to have confronted him once, "are you trying to break up our marriage?" "Yes," he replied.

He was forever calling Bill at home—"the call of the wild," the Hellers used to call it—and, naturally, whenever Charles went abroad, he expected the head of his international operation to come with him. Not for business reasons so much as to keep him company. They enjoyed gambling and kept joint safe-deposit boxes in some of Europe's finest hotels. They were given to other vices as well, which led Iris to place detectives on Bill's trail, and then to write poison pen letters to a number of Left Bank bar girls.

It was a highly charged situation, and it took its toll.

"I was married twenty-five years the first time," Iris recalls, "and only

twenty-five months the second time. [To Bill.] It was a rather tempestuous marriage. Bill would get calls from Charles at two in the morning asking him to come down to his apartment. He used to tell me it was because
Charles wanted to discuss something, but later he admitted that Charles
used to get midnight frights." Iris says Bill would sometimes sleep with
Charles in his huge bed—a matter not of sex but of loneliness. On such
occasions Bill would come home with a little 'chr' monogram on his shirt
instead of the 'wdh' he had left with. (Their shirts were in other respects
identical.)

The upshot of all Bill's trudging and traveling and trying to keep
Charles happy and trying to keep Iris happy was a massive coronary.

And now life was lonelier than ever. Fortunately, there was George
Beck to help fill the void. George was a swinger among swingers. He was
married five times. It was nine weeks after marrying his fifth wife on
Christmas day, 1970, that he (fifty-one) and she (thirty-one) were mur-
dered in the nude aboard Beck's fifty-seven-foot houseboat, the *Bachaven*
(short for "Bachelor's Haven"). Some of his children met each other at
his funeral for the first time.

Beck's remarkable life-style was facilitated by his good looks—"the
blond Adonis," he was called, though his hair would go gray around the
roots from time to time; by his access to a twin-engine Beechcraft Queen-
Air that each financial official in turn tried to persuade Charles to unload,
but which George always managed to persuade him to retain; and by his
influence over Charles himself, the basis of which was a source of considerable rumor-mongering.

Revson was drawn to Beck for his youth and good looks, his intelligence, his war record, his self-confidence, his zest for women, and his
ability to get things done. Others in the company resented his instant success and influence.

On a strictly business level, Beck was soon running a sales program to
the military and was later given charge over certain department stores.
But George Beck's importance to Charles lay elsewhere.

George was too good at his work to leave many traces, but a reliable
source states categorically that he arranged, on Charles's behalf, for
scores of bugs and wiretaps, both in the office ("every major executive was
tapped"), at homes, and at various apartments Revlon executives had occasion to frequent. He would not actually place most of the bugs himself;
he would direct one of Revlon's security men to do the work. "There is no
question about it," this source states.

It was Beck, too, who helped mastermind the capture in midindiscretion of the third Mrs. Revson . . . but that came later. For the moment, Charles was very much a bachelor, and George helped keep him company and keep him entertained. He channeled a great many attractive women Charles's way.

What George or Bill Heller couldn't come up with Billy Reid did. Billy Reid's Little Club was by far Charles's favorite hangout when he outgrew Bill's Gay Nineties. It was described by one occasional patron as "a high-class pimping academy."

It was only with his marriage to Lyn, in 1964, that his days as ladies'-man-about-town came to an end. In the meantime, his most intense emotional relationships were probably with his executives.

CHAPTER 15

DIVIDING AND CONQUERING

Nobody gets along around here," says one current Revlon vice president. "Bergerac is trying to change that, but if you took all the other executives and put them in the same room, nobody would be left alive. Under stress conditions, they dislike each other sometimes to the point of embarrassment."

How can a company run like that?

"With a whip and a chair and Charles as the lion tamer. Each is very strong in what he does, each jealous of his prerogatives, and each goaded on by Charles, to a degree, to get the other."

The fear and even hatred that was engendered in some Revlon executives, both of Revson himself and of the men he pitted them against, led to the expenditure of great effort on Revlon's behalf, and to constant self-evaluation. Am I doing this right? Where could I be criticized? How can I do it better?

Certainly such an atmosphere led as well to ulcers and unhappiness and to the famous rate of executive turnover. But the system seemed to work and it weeded out the "soft sisters." Furthermore, the cause of the turnover—having two bodies for each job—was also its solution. Someone was always panting to take over where whoever-it-was left off. Revson ran a heavy inventory of executive talent, but there wasn't as much duplication as there seemed: in his mind one group was earmarked as coming, and the other as going.

"I must truthfully say," says Dr. Harvey Sadow, formerly of U.S.V. Pharmaceuticals, "that the most unsavory human relations evolved in the Revson/Revlon organization, largely because of the conditions created by Charles's driving need for total acknowledgment. It was almost divide and conquer rather than unify and succeed. This is my singular criticism of the man."

For mental stress, Revlon's corporate jungle must have been the match of any ongoing nonpenal institution in the western world. If the hours didn't kill you, the blood pressure might. Take the classic tension between the marketing department and the lab—between Ray Stetzer and Bill Mandel. Both men strong, brilliant, blunt, egotistical. Charles had Mandel sample opinions on a proposed new product. The opinions were unfavorable. On Tuesday—lab day—Revson asks Stetzer: "Raymond, what do you think of this product?" Stetzer thinks it's fine. Charles says, "Bill, tell Raymond what you found out with your testing." Mandel reports the comments he's gotten, and Stetzer gets out of his chair and goes wild. "He claimed I had made up all the comments and hadn't really done the testing—that he had had a report from someone downtown that I hadn't really done it . . . He went wild. That's what killed him. Five or ten years later he went wild in a meeting and died that night."

Even Mandel did not escape unscathed. Revlon took a terrible toll on his fingernails, and worse. A man who radiates loads of energy but very little warmth, Mandel would start shaking Sunday afternoon in preparation of Monday morning management meetings. He actually *passed out* at one such meeting, it became so heated. He had to be carried out. He was rushed to Doctors Hospital, all of thirty-four years old.

Just as the jitters started for Mandel Sunday afternoon, so Suzanne Grayson remembers her Friday nights for the feeling of relief they brought her. She and her husband never scheduled social engagements for Friday night, because she was just too wrecked from the week to go out and face the world. One Friday night, however, they did go out with friends. All of a sudden, in the middle of a restaurant and with reference to nothing, she just burst into tears.

It was only nail polish and hair sprays, just as football and chess are only games, but when you get into the big leagues, you are not just playing. If you can't measure up, as inevitably many people at Revlon couldn't, the toll on your self-esteem can be brutal.

It was, of course, precisely the toughness, seriousness, and brutality of Revlon that made it so satisfying to those who could cope. (Also the money.) To some of them, Revson was a father figure. To others, he was the unsympathetic mirror of their own inadequacy.

Revson thrived on innuendo, gossip, and infighting, so that's what he got. He paid more attention to whispers in the ear than to factual memoranda. He delighted in calling the head of the plant and making him squirm: "I hear the Aquamarine lotion isn't being filled to the top," he would say. "How come?"

"I don't know anything about that, Mr. Revson. I'll investigate right away."

"I don't know," Charles would moan. "I sit here on Fifth Avenue and I know about it and you don't? Maybe we should trade places."

Just how much internal spying there was at Revlon is hard to assess. Begging rumors ran rife, and when the company moved out of 666 Fifth Avenue, a network of wires was discovered in the walls—installed, the story ran, for an intercom system that was never hooked up. After the 1955 New York State wiretap hearings, one good-humored executive took to cupping his hand over his mouth and leaning down into the space beneath his desk: "You hear that, Charles?" he would ask.

A dozen years later, Revlon's president, Dan Rodgers, noticed some clicking sounds on his phone and asked his secretary to ring the phone company and have it fixed. Jokingly he suggested that his line was tapped. Indeed it was, the phone company discovered. But as there was no conclusive proof, the grand jury was persuaded not to indict anyone, which would only have hurt Revlon's innocent shareholders. How would it look to Wall Street to suggest that the chairman of the board had been tapping the president's phone?

Revson may or may not have ordered the tap, but it was he who set the tone of his administration. "We don't have any friends," Nixon told his closest aides soon after being elected by one of the largest majorities on record. Revson, too, never knew whether people were really on his side, which he doubted, or whether they merely wanted something from him. Revlon executives were nicknamed "the Jewish Mafia" by one of their number; Charles was the Godfather. As anyone who goes to the movies knows, a Godfather can never be too careful.

Like the Godfather, he had a certain presence. Short and lean, more head than shoulders, "lovely nails," "amazing eyes," hairy arms, skinny legs, he was voted one of America's ten best-groomed men and featured in full-page, full-color ads as a Calvert Man of Distinction. He was not handsome so much as he was arresting. A 135-pound presence. When he was introduced to a two-star admiral, it was the admiral who was awed.

Like the Godfather, he was hard to read. Martin was a reactor; Charles was impassive. Except for those occasional thin smiles, signaling trouble, you never knew for sure what he was thinking.

Like the Godfather, he was hard to fool. He could walk into a room and tell immediately who was prepared and who wasn't, who believed in his convictions and who didn't. Those who tried to tell him what they thought he wanted to hear got burned. "Don't try to second-guess me," he warned associates, who kept trying anyway. It's true that he had his penchant for yes-men—Lester Herzog and others—but from most of his executives he expected strong opinions and a good fight. Then, rather than saying, simply, "Well, I've listened carefully to what you all have to say and weighed both sides and decided to do it my way . . ." he would keep at the argument and keep at it and keep at it, relentlessly, until he either wore them down into submission or persuaded them of his position. More than wanting them to carry out his bidding, it seemed, he wanted them to acknowledge he was right. In this respect, he was less like the Godfather and more like *der Führer*.

Like any dictator, Charles had occasionally to put down a coup. Mandel all but left for the top spot at Helena Rubinstein at the end of 1966, and key marketing people were ready to leave as well, when Charles and Jay Bennett lured him down to the Bahamas for a week-long negotiation that was concluded on New Year's Eve. "How could you *do* this to me?" Charles wanted to know. He was always good at playing the victim—clutching his heart in mock pain at the obstinacy or stupidity of those around him. But on this score with Mandel he was quite serious: he didn't want to lose him; he considered it an act of great disloyalty; and he was afraid of all the "secrets" Mandel would be taking with him.

Mandel agreed to cancel his contract with Rubinstein in return for greater authority within Revlon (plus a handsome compensation package). But the authority didn't last long, and soon Mandel, passed over for the presidency he so badly wanted, was working part-time as a consultant to the company, and then not at all.

And then there was the famous facial hair conspiracy: While Charles was on his August cruise one year, in 1969, Norman Greif, Stan Kohlenberg, Bill Mandel, Larry Wechsler, and Joe Freedman all grew beards. Just to see what would happen. Charles returned and called a lunch meeting. His secretary, in an inspired moment, had seated all the beards on one side of the table, all the nonbeards on the other. Charles walks in without so much as a double take or a smile and proceeds to rip everyone apart for four hours . . . never mentioning beards. The next day each man received a rare C.R. memo. "I would appreciate it," he wrote, "if you would test the enclosed product as soon as possible." Enclosed was one can of Braggi shave cream. Off came the beards.

Somewhat more serious was the mutiny two summers later, again conceived during Charles's August cruise, as though only then could the executives summon the required nerve and only then manage to work together. A committee of Revlon's six top executives flew to Ashdod, Israel, to confront the chairman on his yacht. "We just can't keep running things this way," was the gist of their message.

The conference lasted two or three days. "In retrospect," says Paul Woolard, "I think the committee was well-intentioned, somewhat immature in its attitudes, and expecting more than was feasible. These were men who were themselves fathers and mature in their own right—but with Charles somewhat immature. Looking back on it, Charles held all the cards. Not because he wanted anybody on the committee to leave the company, or that he could have lived without their services, but *emotionally* he held all the cards. The people at Revlon are very emotionally involved with the company and with Charles himself."

While Israeli coastguardsmen were exploding depth charges in the harbor to jar alien frogmen, Charles was telling his children: You want to form a management committee? Terrific idea! By all means! Notify the press! (Which they did.) . . . And within days of his return he had everyone back at each other's throats and business as usual."

"While Charles was away," one of the committee members says, "considerable momentum and enthusiasm were built up. I think Charles found this unity among his people very disconcerting. Things fell apart pretty fast when he got back."

CHAPTER 16

EMPIRE BUILDING

The standard ways to build a business into an empire are to acquire other companies and to set up operations abroad. Revson did both. Armed with a high multiple of earnings and the conviction that he could run any business there was, he acquired more than a score of them. And believing that "if it's good enough for America, it's good enough for Japan," he launched operations in ninety-seven countries.

His first major acquisition came as the result of an office warming he and Martin attended in the fall of 1957 at the new digs of one of Revlon's smaller ad agencies.

At lunch they met Sam and Al Abrams, founder/owners of Knomark, Inc., which made Esquire shoe polish. Charles quickly assessed their business and told them they should be selling their shoe polish for fifty cents, not fifteen, the same way he had entered the nail polish market. Three weeks later Revlon bought Knomark. (One can just hear the boys clustered around the Dow Jones ticker: "Nail polish . . . shoe polish . . . it's a fit!") With some $15 million in sales, it was Revlon's first major acquisition.

Revson put Irving Bottner, his treasurer/controller, in charge of Esquire. (That's Bott*ner*—Bot*win* you've already met.) The Abrams brothers, despite huge salaries, soon quit. It was the basic acquisition syndrome: You buy a small company that depends on the energy and expertise of a couple of highly motivated people. You make them millionaires, which kills much of their motivation. And you meddle in their business, which drives them up a wall—or out the door.

What Irving Bottner wanted to do, in accordance with Revson's vision, was "to take shoe polish out of the kitchen and put it in the bedroom." Make it a class product, in other words, just as Revson had done with nail enamel. Change its image and double its price. However, this proved difficult. It was hard to sell a sexy, romantic, glamorous shoe polish.

Lady Color was introduced in the hope that women would paint their shoes to match their attire. Instant Patent Leather and an application that made leather look like alligator skin were also introduced. But none of these products revolutionized the instep.

Estimates of Revlon's lack of success with Esquire vary, but it was enough that Revson decided eventually to get rid of the business. As he told *Forbes* in May 1969, several months after disposing of it and a couple of other acquisitions: "We've had it . . . We're not running a hospital [for ailing businesses] here."

It may have been more trouble than it was worth, but Esquire was by no means a disaster. Evan-Picone, a sportswear manufacturer, was. Acquired in 1962 for $12 million as it rode the crest of popularity for its women's slacks, it was sold back to one of the original partners (Picone) for $1 million four years later. The $11 million difference, plus operating losses along the way, retarded Revlon's growth. Women who felt they "had" to have the latest Revlon lipstick did not feel the same about Evan-Picone's fashions. Even Revson, had he devoted his full attention to this business, might not have been able to make every season click. He foresaw the sportswear boom, but was wrong to think he could capitalize on it with Evan-Picone. "This will be my first failure," he said when he agreed to take his losses and get out.

Then there was an importer of silk dresses, a plastic molder, a large investment in Schick shavers, an artificial flower importer—and others, most of which proved that businessmen should stick to the businesses they know best.

It has been said of William Paley's disastrous acquisitions at CBS that broadcasting is such a lucrative business his mistakes were smothered in profits. Much the same was true of Revson's acquisitions and the cosmetics industry. It is the seller, not the buyer, who generally holds most of the cards in this game. He knows exactly what he's selling and is not likely to undervalue it. Revson paid very full prices for his acquisitions. He was not bargain hunting; he wanted businesses that returned at least 16 percent pretax profit on each dollar of sales—businesses with margins like his own. Financial pros look at return on *investment,* not sales, but Charles was a merchant by instinct and a financial man only by the accident of his success.

Where he did shine was in his determination to buy U.S. Vitamin and Pharmaceuticals Corporation, in 1966. Attracted by the profit margins and by his own hypochondria, he had long been after a drug company. He had found the industry closed to him, however, not least because of his religion. U.S. Vitamin was one of the few Jewish drug companies around—and even at that he had to pay $67 million for a lackluster company with a mere $20 million in sales. But pay it he did, and in nine years U.S.V. grew nearly tenfold.

Revlon's overseas distribution was first handled by the United States Government. During World War II, post exchanges all over the world carried Revlon products. At least one GI would give his local ladies Revlon lipstick cases, promising the lipstick itself if the relationship . . . matured. Thus the gospel spread. American cosmetics—many of them Revlon's—became the envy of the rest of the world. As Inez Robb wrote in a syndicated column (March 15, 1952)—that Carl Erbe, Revlon's brilliant, roughhewn publicist, no doubt planted: "What Scotland is to tweeds and tipple, Ireland to linen and blarney, France to perfumes and Switzerland to cheese and chimes: that is what America is to cosmetics in the eyes of the world."

Beyond the PXs, however, sales abroad were slight. Revlon had operations only in Mexico and England at first, and in other areas merely exported goods to distributors over whom it exercised little or no control. Bill Heller was put in charge of selling Revlon to the world in 1960, but at the time of his death, in 1962, the world had yet to catch fire. Foreign sales were then running around $20 million. A dozen years later, they would be ten times as great.

Except for translating ad copy, it was Revson's idea to sell abroad exactly as he was selling at home. American cosmetics, like American denims and soft drinks, were in great demand. Eventually, he came to allow each foreign subsidiary enough independence to adapt their marketing to their market. But to a large extent, what worked in the U.S. was equally successful abroad. One much noted TV commercial, for example, included in its sixty-second message a silent, forty-seven-second kiss. The ad was for Intimate perfume, the message universal.

Still, each country had its quirks. The Spanish would not allow such a kiss to violate the pureness of their airwaves. In Italy, at least in 1960, commercials had to run two minutes—but only twenty seconds of that time could be devoted to "the sell." The rest had to be entertainment of some kind. In Venezuela, the announcer had to be a Venezuelan national, which meant re-recording everything.

When Revlon went into Japan, the largest cosmetics market in the world after the U.S., Revson decided to stick not only with his western products, but with his western ads, western product names, and western models. Only the ad copy was translated. Factor, already well established in Japan, quickly countered with a "Japanese cosmetics for Japanese women" campaign—but Revlon sales took off. Eventually, Factor had to switch to the same Americanized strategy.

Charles visited the fledgling Japanese operation in 1962. The trip included a ride up into the provinces in a private railroad car, complete with geisha girls. Revson was quick to grasp that the geishas were among the country's most avid and affluent cosmetics buyers, and fashion-setters to boot. Accordingly, he spent considerable time studying them and urged his marketing people to do likewise.

Sailing from Capri to the Holy Land aboard his 257-foot yacht, with thirty-one in help and cases of Dom Perignon in the hold, finding his products regally displayed in every port along the way, and telephoning instructions to his generals back in New York, Charles Revson in his later years was indeed an emperor. And self-made at that. An odd sort of emperor when you looked beneath the robes—but what emperor wasn't?

Twice a year, beginning in the late sixties, Revlon would gather its international executives for a three- or four-day dog and pony show. One of the meetings was generally scheduled during Revson's annual month-long Mediterranean cruise, in the fervent hope that he would break up his vacation to attend. He invariably did.

It wasn't that he lacked valuable experience to impart to the international staff, it was just the way he imparted it. The executives from New York who were used to him could ignore the profanity, follow the analogies and endure the digressions. Not so the hundred-odd international managers, sales managers, and chief beauty consultants. It was like listening to a verbal Jackson Pollack.

Charles would sit with a box of Kleenex beside him, periodically clearing his throat; push his glasses up onto his head and rest his elbows on the table, supporting his temples with the heels of his palms; look out over his audience of stuffy Englishmen, genteel Frenchmen, stilted Germans, exceedingly well-mannered Latin Americans and Japanese—well, *any* American entrepreneur would likely come off as something of a cowboy before such a group . . . and he would proceed to talk. And talk. And talk. No prepared text, a few key words on a napkin. He always believed that a man who could not speak extemporaneously was not worth much.

One talk ran five hours. Says one Revlon bigwig: "These were the most rambling, unstructured, give-'em-hell, cover-the-waterfront, crude speeches you can imagine. Regardless of whether the audience was ninety percent men, entirely men, or what, it was an entirely unnecessary display of who was boss. I don't know how much damage they did, but I'm sure Bob Armstrong [head of the international division] spent the next six months picking up the pieces." Wasn't Revson aware of the impression he was making? "Yes, I'm sure he was." Then why did he do it? "I think Charles still thought in many ways that he was just a poor boy from Manchester, dealing with polished foreign talent. He felt very much at a disadvantage and had to gain control of the situation. The only way he could do it was to shock them, to embarrass them—to show that he was the boss and could get away with it."

One reason Charles's ramblings were hard to follow was his unfamiliar use of language. Revsonisms: "Stop beating around the rosary bush." "I want it done one, two, six." "Asshole to asshole." (Like peas in a pod.) "What you guys have to do is re-upholster your thinking." "Remember the dumb lady." (The typical consumer—things must be kept *simple*.) "It should be *at least* twenty-four-karat gold." "Mediocricy." "Don't answer that—that's a historical question." "Who hit Annie in the fanny with the flounder?" (Who started it?) "I'm the kind of a guy who burns his graves behind him." "It's too Jewish." (Said of a packaging design—too gaudy.) "Is it clearer than mud?" (Perfectly clear?) "It's as plain as the five fingers on your face." "Don't make a case celerb out of it."

Charles was an inadvertent master of non sequitur. "If you had all the money in the world," he counseled once, "whatever it may be, you can't have it all. You can't have all the window displays and all the advertising you want, and all this and so forth. It's impossible. And so therefore, you must find out what are the most important things that you need, and what are the winning numbers. What are those numbers that pay off the best? [I.e., the most profitable marketing formula.] Is it seven? Is it eleven? Or is it three? Or whatever it may be. *Because what do we want fundamentally?* [Profit? Share of market?] We want the least amount of turnover as far as people is concerned . . ."

After viewing the results of a decision he himself had made, he would say, "How could you let me do this to myself?"

Launching into one topic, but wanting first to cover another, he began "Might I say before I say what I am about to say. . ."

He would say: "The first thing is that the color must be right, and the second thing—which is really the first thing—the texture must be right." He tried to crowd everything up into the number-one position. *Everything* had to be right, so *everything* was number one. The idea of ranking bothered him because he didn't want to accept a lipstick, even if it had great luster, if it didn't have great wear. The two are somewhat incompatible and he had a tough time making a choice—so he put them both first.

"The reason I am opening my talk this morning of marketing," he said once, about a thousand words along in his preface, "is because I think it is one of the key—that does not mean and I don't wish to infer that operations are not important. They are. Administration is important and it is. But it does mean that you can have great administration and great operations, but if you don't have great marketing, you will not make it. You do have some chance with great marketing and mediocre administration and mediocre operations to make it, but vice versa, you will not make it . . ."

As Mandel says, he had a hard time setting priorities. Paul Woolard suggests this was also the reason for his frequent use of the phrase "in turn"—everything relating to everything else at the same level. Others saw the "in turns" as a nervous stalling mechanism, like "uh . . ." Revlon personnel occasionally ran pools based on the number of "in turns" counted in a given speech.

Because his foibles contrasted so sharply with his position and success, they drew attention. But attention should be drawn, too, to the cold competence his success was based on. There was his much noted preoccupation with detail, but also the ability to see the big picture. He could ramble endlessly, but also cut through to the heart of a matter. He could choose an odd assortment of friends and confidants, but also frequently tell when he was being conned. The power behind this emperor's throne was his own inner strength. The brains behind his operation were, notwithstanding the hundreds of good minds in his organization, his own.

CHAPTER 17

FOLLOW THE LAUDER

It was easy to forget, if you knew Charles Revson, that Revlon was not the world's largest cosmetics company. In 1975, it trailed Avon, L'Oreal and Shiseido. But Avon's sales were exclusively door-to-door and thus not directly competitive. To Charles, Avon barely existed. And neither L'Oreal nor Shiseido was important in the U.S. market. His real competitors through the years were companies and brands such as Blue Bird, Chen-Yu, Hazel Bishop, Helena Rubinstein, Elizabeth Arden, Max Factor and—his arch rival in the last decade of his life—Estée Lauder.

He felt the same inner rage toward competitors an apartment dweller feels toward a burglar. They were encroaching on *his space*. "If you come into my ball park," he warned Gulf & Western's Charlie Bluhdorn, "I'll kick your ass."

He made a point of never mentioning his competitors by name. They did likewise. Arden, a poor Canadian truck driver's daughter made good, called him, simply, "that man." (To tweak her, he brought out a men's line by the same name.) Rubinstein, a Polish immigrant-via-Australia, called him "the nail man." He referred to them, and to Lauder, a social climber whose first rung varies from interview to interview, only as "competition." Or, if he wanted to become very specific, he would say, "she."

He had a CIA-like intelligence network and—because he assumed his competitors did, too—a fetish for closed doors. All his products were assigned code names prior to introduction—"Park Avenue" (Cerissa), "Cosmos" (Charlie). The Ciara fragrance was designated "March," its targeted launch date. It was seven months late. "If we don't get the engravings by July," people were saying, "March won't go out before November." It was enough to confuse the canniest competitor.

From his yacht, Revson was unusually cryptic for fear competitors might be tuned in to his radio frequency. Nail enamel was "n.e.," lipstick, "l.s."—pronounced fast, like "any" and "else." Projects and companies were referred to by code; people, as "what's his name." "Have what's his name call me about that other matter," he would tell Jay Bennett, fully expecting him to comply. (And because they had such a close working relationship, Bennett usually could.)

But if Estée Lauder did not have a cadre of ham radio operatiors scanning the Mediterranean for trade secrets, she could still find out a thing or two. When Etherea, Revlon's hypoallergenic line, was being launched to compete with Lauder's Clinique, a memo was circulated to four trusted employees listing the names to be used for each item in the line. Top secret stuff. Lauder ran an ad for Clinique in *Women's Wear Daily* using every name in the memo as an adjective, and underlining each one lest there be any doubt in Revson's mind that he'd been stuffed. Etherea was to have an item called "B.C.O."—biologically correct oils; Lauder's ad said, "our night cream is *biologically correct.*" And so on.

Revson had a conniption. But all manner of sleuthing by his FBI-trained security chief failed to reveal the leak.

At any given time in Revlon's history there was some one competitor in particular Revson felt he had to destroy. Blue Bird, the first, was easy: Revlon had a demonstrably better product. It was that simple. Revson was soon able to demand that jobbers drop Blue Bird—and all their other competitive lines—if they wanted to carry Revlon. The jobbers didn't like it, or other tough policies that followed, but they had no choice. By the time the FTC ruled some of Revlon's exclusive agreements out of order, the company had acquired a lock on the beauty salon market.

During the war, Chen-Yu was the brand to beat. One quirk of wartime rationing was that glass allocations were issued to companies that made the bottles rather than to the companies, like Revlon or Chen-Yu, that used them. Charles wanted to know what Chen-Yu's Chicago-based bottler might require to steer Chen-Yu's allocation of bottles his way. Jack Price arranged to fly the co-owners of this bottling firm to New York. He says he watched as Charles settled with them for $15,000. Chen-Yu suddenly found itself scrambling for upwards of half a million bottles. After the war, Revlon offered to replace all the substandard inventory it had out, such as those cardboard lipstick cases, with new, quality merchandise. It took money to do that, and Chen-Yu hadn't the resources to match the offer.

Hazel Bishop—"stays on you, not on him"—was another dragon to be slain. This upstart had built a huge lipstick business overnight through the use of television. Merv Griffin, a young singer, started pitching the nonsmear brand on *The Kate Smith Show* in 1952. "People couldn't understand how with only three salesmen we managed to get such massive distribution," Raymond Spector, who owned the company, says. "But Revson personally sent a memo around to his salesmen saying, 'Wherever you go, find out how Hazel Bishop is doing and send the information directly to me.' At that time we were still in only a few major markets. People started calling us from all over. They figured that if Revlon was interested, they should be too."

Charles got him in the end, though. The biggest marketing blow was *The $64,000 Question.* The biggest psychological blow was Spector's discovery that someone—he states categorically it was Revson—had been listening in on his most private conversations for more than a year. He first grew suspicious when information that could not possibly have leaked to the trade did. Revlon kept beating him to market with his own ideas, he says. He then tried planting false tidbits to see if they, too, would come back to him and *they* did. Alarmed, he retained the services of two eavesdropping experts who found that several of Spector's phones were indeed tapped, and his office bugged as well.

Revson's market timing was uncanny, Spector alleges, at least in part because he had advance knowledge of his competitors' plans. "I think Revson was a prick," he says, simply. Among Revlon competitors, this was not an uncommon view.

Madame Rubinstein thought the nail man was "heartless." She was anguished by the way he would copy her products ("only better!"). But he fascinated her. She couldn't help admiring him. She even bought Revlon stock.

They were not so dissimilar, Madame and the nail man. She, too, was an earthy, idiosyncratic, impossible, tyrannical Jewish founder/one-man-show. She hired people, milked them, and fired them. She played one off the other. She burped unabashedly and blew her nose on her bed sheets. She felt surrounded by ingratitude. *Un*like Revson, however, she was not out to prove herself to anyone, she did not live in fear of being embarrassed, and she was thoroughly—ludicrously—cheap. Yet far better liked than Charles, for all his lavish entertaining. Her quirks were seen as amusing rather than gauche or offensive. No one called her ruthless, although she had the same obsession with her business that Charles did.

For many years it was not he but "the other one"—Arden—whose competition most irked Madame Rubinstein. Arden once raided virtually the entire Rubinstein sales staff. Madame retaliated by hiring Arden's ex-husband as her sales manager. At least the nail man and she were in largely separate fields. He had the lipstick and nail enamel markets, yes, but Madame was queen of the treatment creams. It was only in 1962, when Revson launched Eterna 27, the remarkable skin cream, that Madame felt really threatened. A Rubinstein executive walked into her office that day to find the window open wide and Madame leaning out, screaming and shaking her first. Her third-floor office was directly opposite 666 Fifth Avenue, where Revson ruled the twenty-seventh floor. This tiny ninety-year-old woman was screaming at him in a very heavy Polish accent, "What are you *doing?* You're killing me, you rat!"

In 1965, she died. A year and a half later, Arden died as well. That left two: Revson and Lauder. Most of the other companies had been or soon were merged into conglomerates, with results that ranged from fair to poor.

Max Factor, swallowed by Norton Simon in 1973, had done better than most since the death of its founder/namesake decades earlier in 1938. It was Factor that in 1967 challenged Revlon's privileged position in the fashion magazines. Revson had always demanded that his ads precede those of his competitors and Factor lodged a protest. Bill Fine, then in charge of three Hearst magazines, had to agree that the policy was unfair. With much apprehension, he told Revson he was sorry, but Revlon could no longer be first in every issue. "We made our stand," Fine says, "and Charles said, in simple terms: 'Fuck you. I'll pull my advertising out of all Hearst magazines.'" Which meant not only Fine's three, *Harper's Bazaar, Town & Country* and *House Beautiful,* but *Cosmopolitan* and *Good Housekeeping* as well. Revlon's annual outlay in these books approached seven figures.

There was a period of two or three weeks' impasse. And as word of the confrontation spread, Fine found himself in a box. He had to win *some* concession lest other of his major advertisers revolt. It got so that Fine used to have a man come massage his neck and arm each time before he went over to see Revson, because he would start to get a tingle and an ache in his back.

Fine managed to emerge with at least this much: When Revlon had a black and white page, it would run first. When Revlon had a color page, it would be the first color page—but another cosmetics ad, in black and white, could come first. As Revlon was not running black and white ads at the time, it was what Fine calls "maybe a fifty-one percent victory—which is pretty good when you're dealing with Revlon."

The changed policy worked to the advantage of Estée Lauder. Lauder *was* running black and white ads. Revson soon followed. In fact, *whatever* Lauder did, Charles soon followed. She offered "gift with purchase"; he offered gift with purchase. She went to using a single model exclusively; he followed with Lauren Hutton for Ultima—and one-upped her by signing Richard Avedon as her exclusive photographer. She went to sepia ads; he went to sepia. She switched back from sepia; he switched back. She brought out Aramis; he brought out Braggi. She brought out Clinique; he brought out Etherea. She brought out a fragrance called Estée; he brought out Charlie. To add insult to unoriginality, he would put copied products in one of his less-than-Ultima lines, to cheapen the originals by association.

Stan Kohlenberg, who runs the Ultima line, Charles's department-store, carriage-trade answer to Estée Lauder, keeps Lauder's photograph on a dart board in his office. He says he sometimes thinks she is just Charles in drag.

Of all the women in his life, although he never spoke more than two words to her, it was probably Estée Lauder who had the greatest impact. She was the one competitor he set out to beat but couldn't. It had taken her a full fourteen years, from 1946 to 1960, to reach $1 million in sales— but a mere fourteen more to reach $100 million. Revlon was still much larger, but she had captured exactly the segment of the market that mattered to him most. As Revlon owned sex and fashion in the fifties and Arden owned pink, so Estée Lauder by the late sixties owned class. Suddenly she was beating him in all the best department stores, *she* had the houses in Palm Beach and the South of France, *she* was dining with the Duke and Duchess of Windsor. The Park Avenue socialite he had always had his eye on had found a counter at Bloomingdale's she liked better than his. Never mind what a small segment of the market she represented. As a result, Mandel says, "his priorities came all out of whack. The whole corporation was working on one percent of its business ninety percent of the time to satisfy this ego of his: Ultima, Borghese, and Braggi. He left a hole wide open in the marketplace for Factor to make a comeback and for others to get into the business as well."

Revson argued that the quality image of his top lines would enhance the image of basic Revlon. But pride, not profit, was his fundamental motivation in taking the course he did.

And so it was Lauder, not Lyn, who led Charles to be more "social." Lauder, not Lyn, who lured him to the black-tie affairs Ancky had always longed to go to. It was to combat Lauder, not to amuse Lyn, that he landed on the Breakers Hotel golf course in a helicopter, photographers and reporters lined up on the fairway, where he was to judge a very hotsy-totsy, uppercrust (read: Gentile) Palm Beach beauty contest. That Lyn was young, beautiful, vivacious, and extraordinary in bed were sources of genuine pleasure and great allure. That she helped him project the glamorous image and generate the *Women's Wear* coverage he wanted to combat Lauder was perhaps even more important to him. And why not? Lyn's motive for marrying this notoriously difficult fifty-seven-year-old must have included an element of practicality, also.

CHAPTER 18

THE BRONX NEFERTITI

Finally Charles was marrying a nice Jewish girl. Lyn Fisher Sheresky Revson, born in New York around the time the Revlon firm was, may not have had all of Ancky's European sophistication, but she was younger, she had been around—and she, too, had an accent: thick New Yorkese. She had splendid qualities, witness her popularity, her three lovely children (by her first husband), and the fact that of all the women he could have married, Charles chose her. Except for her Liza-Dolittle-of-the-Grand-Concourse speech, and her use of little rabbit punches as exclamation marks, she had all the Park Avenue elegance and earthy sexiness Charles could possibly have wanted in a woman. What elegance she lacked initially he soon built in. And, according to his son John, he was not looking for a woman who would do a lot of talking, anyway. "He thought he'd marry a 'Yes, Charles; sure, Charles' kind of woman, but it didn't work out that way. There's a marriage that should have ended after two months but didn't."

But almost did.

The first few weeks after the wedding in February 1964 were not pleasant ones for Charles. On the one hand, he had this gnawing suspicion that his young bride might not have terminated affairs she had been having prior to their wedding. There had, apparently, been some difficulty in this regard during the courtship, and Charles had made it very clear that it was to stop.

The other thing was the impending marriage of his son John, just turned twenty-one, to Ricki Brody, nineteen-year-old daughter of a prominent New York restaurateur. Remembering his own early mistake, Charles was dead set against it. John, however, had become quite used to getting what he wanted. So, apparently, had Lyn.

While preparations were being made for the Brody-Revson wedding at the Plaza, Charles was working with George Beck to satisfy his suspicions. If he was suspicious by nature, in this case at least it was not without cause. At one point he arranged to be out of town solely for the purpose of leaving his wife to her own devices. It became clear to him that Lyn was still seeing two men. (It goes without saying that had he been cheating on *Lyn,* that would simply have been the male prerogative).

It was touch-and-go for a while as to whether the fledgling marriage would come to an abrupt halt. Either way, Charles's pride had to suffer. It was handled this way: Lyn was given, in the words of one insider, "some very heavy papers" to sign as a supplement/amendment to the prenuptial agreement they had already drawn up. In these, allegedly, Lyn abrogated all rights to Charles's estate. There was even a termination clause, as one might find in an employment contract. Moreover, Lyn was moved out of the Revson suite at the Pierre and into one of her own at the Stanhope. She was on probation, in a sort of purgatory. It was like dating all over again. Charles would send the car for her in the evening, take her home at night, and spend weekends with her up at Premium Point. (The cover story was that the Pierre was simply too small for everyone.) He would even take back her jewelry at the end of each evening.

Meanwhile, John was getting married at the Plaza. Charles arrived late to the wedding, as he was late to everything. John, typically, was later still. "The tailor delivered my tails late," he explains. But what is forty-five minutes when you have a lifetime ahead of you? The tragedy was that the young Mrs. Revson did not. She and John were divorced five years later. During their years together, John managed to go through much of his wife's substantial wealth. Like his father, he was always a big spender— Ancky thinks he went through $2 million in one year—but he lacked the personal fortune to back it up. Charles wound up bailing John out to the tune of several hundreds of thousands—at least. The marriage had turned out to be even worse than he had feared; in *this* case he took no pleasure in having been proved right. Jill, his granddaughter by this marriage, became the single most important person in the last years of his life. He was able to lavish on her the kind of pure love he had never been able to offer anyone else.

John's second marriage, to Alexis Turpin, ended in divorce as well.

Oddly, while John's marriages were crumbling in direct testimony to the difficulty of growing up Charles Revson's son, Charles and Lyn were managing to make a go of it, after all. They became, in fact, quite the loving couple. "I think he was really devoted to her," Suzanne Grayson says, echoed by others. "The only time I ever saw him soft in any kind of personal relationship was with her." He would be at his most bilious, lambasting an executive . . . his gold phone would ring—as it did a dozen times each day—and he would switch instantly to a tender, "*Yes,* my darling. Where are you *now,* my darling? Of *course,* my darling." Without missing a beat, he would then return to the man's jugular. It had never been that way with Ancky. Time had turned the tables on him. He had never taken Ancky with him on business trips; he would never leave Lyn behind. His possessiveness came most openly into view at public affairs when the uninitiated would occasionally, and in all innocence, ask Lyn to dance. "Nobody dances with my wife other than myself," he would say icily for all to hear.

For her part, Lyn became "very attentive—maybe even too attentive," to Charles. When they traveled, her friend Jerry Zipkin says, she would do everything—"his pills, his arrangements, she would order his proper breakfast, sit right there as it was brought in to make sure it was right (because it was a very complicated breakfast)—she was unbelievable."

When it came to the larger matters, such as Lyn's wardrobe, Charles was in charge. "He ran the house, he ran the yacht, he ordered the meals, he decorated the apartment. Lyn very wisely stayed out of it," Zipkin explains, "because then he wouldn't have anything to criticize. He treated her more like one of his executives than his wife."

His first order of business was to make Lyn over. Out went the high heels, the wad of chewing gum, and the heavy makeup. He took Lyn to *his* tailor for slacks, to get them just right. Very man-tailored, very simple. Norell would send his latest offerings up to the office and Charles would choose Lyn's wardrobe. The "look" he gave her was austere. Always a high neckline. "She has the most beautiful bosom in the world," Kay Daly confided, "and it was never again seen after she married Charles."

Lyn had loads of life and vitality. Charles toned her down and took some of the life out of her. She became somewhat hostile and bitchy, people said. She was not beloved by the crew of the *Ultima II.* She did, however, become a great hit with the press. About a year after they were married, the Revsons went on what was, in effect, a national publicity tour.

Before Lyn's first interview, Charles kept coming in to ask, "Sweetie, are you nervous?" "I'd be a lot less nervous if you went away," she said. And the next day, where he got a couple of paragraphs buried in the business section of the paper, there was a half page of Lyn on the women's page with quotes and pictures. It happened that way all over, and was great for Revlon.

Charles taught Lyn to blend her makeup. "Now," she says, "people don't even think I wear any. Actually, my makeup list is a yard long." His feeling about makeup was—ironically—that most women use too much To achieve her natural look, Lyn merely scrubbed with Ultima II Skim Milk Liquid Facial Soap followed by Ultima II Astringent Toner followed by Etherea B.C.O. Face Oil followed by Ultima II Transparent Bronzing Tint, Ultima II Blushing Creme (in Deep Sienna), and Ultima II Color Gel Stick in Bronzelit Copper to tint the chin, cheeks, and forehead. She listed twenty other Revlon products for the eyes, lips, scent, sun, and bath.

Lyn told an interviewer how, when she finished making up, Charles would come over to her and pat her forehead and cheeks with a Kleenex. "It is his way of telling me, 'Now you look perfect,'" she said. "On the other hand, when I tell him I like his hair when it is longer, he gets a haircut. And that's his way of telling me that he is the authority."

But," said Lyn, "he knows that I appreciate everything I have and that nothing would mean anything without my husband. For instance, I have this thing about bathing and perfume. I can take as many as three baths a day, and I use practically a bottle of bath oil a day. And I love perfume. I spray Ultima when I feel sexy and Norell when I feel elegant . . . Sometimes he watches me using the bath oil and the perfume, and he smiles and says, 'You know, it's a good thing I'm in this business.'"

It was probably most fun being Mrs. Charles Revson aboard the *Ultima II*. There were the cowboy movies under the stars . . . The Christmases in Acapulco . . . the excitement of not knowing where you would be going from one day to the next (in later years, Charles took to telling the captain only the night before which port to steam for) . . . the crew lining up on deck, in uniform, with foghorn sounding, whenever the Revsons arrived or left for a cruise . . . the hot Mediterranean breezes, freezing staterooms, and warm-as-toast electric blankets . . . the fabulous service and unmatched cuisine . . . the Bingo and backgammon . . . the special television hookups for prizefights and presidential addresses . . . and, of course, the parties. Guests aboard the

yacht included the likes of Alec Guinness, Princess Grace and Prince Ra-
nier, Faye Dunaway, the Earl of Litchfield, Count and Countess Bis-
marck, Merle Oberon and the Cornelius Vanderbilt Whitneys.

How had he suddenly become so popular—so *social*? Any suggestion
that Earl Blackwell, owner of Celebrity Register, and gossip columnists
Eugenia Sheppard and Aileen Mehle (Suzy Knickerbocker) were on the
payroll for this purpose is outrageous. But they were regular guests on the
yacht (flown to and fro) and good friends, and so very helpful. Aileen
Mehle was named Revlon's first female board member, at an annual compensation of $6,500, in 1972. Also, by happy coincidence, her column be-
gan appearing in the *Daily News* right around the time Revlon began advertising in that unlikely publication for the first time, to the tune of
$50,000 or $100,000 a year. Anyway, the Revsons began appearing in the
columns with some regularity.

Eat your heart out, Estée Lauder: The Revsons had become international socialites, too . . . with a little help from their friends.

Back in dreary old Manhattan, they would often have dinner in bed
watching TV. *The Sonny and Cher Comedy Hour* was a favorite, not least
because Revlon sponsored it. Lyn, however, preferred to go out. Sunday
nights there was often an argument because Charles wanted to get something over at the Sixth Avenue Deli, while Lyn had in mind Elaine's or
Pearl's. Charles had a low tolerance for New York social life. If it was for
the business, it was one thing; but a lot of small talk at Elaine's . . .

He preferred to dine at home with a business-related guest. It seemed
to one such guest, whom Charles was trying to hire, that at least eight
people were waiting on them. The only thing he found offensive about
the Revson library/dining room, he says, was "a really awful portrait of
Charles staring down from over the fireplace." Over dinner, there was little discussion of the job he was being offered, much discussion between
Charles and Lyn as to the crispiness of the french fries—was it sufficient?
After dinner they spent two or three hours showing him the apartment,
"a symphony in beige." The foyer, he thought, looked like the lobby of
the Squibb Building. Charles made a point of the fact that the ceiling in
their bedroom was genuine gold leaf. As they left one room and walked
into another, Charles would grab hold of Lyn and kiss her. In all, the evening went on until three A.M.

Saturday was the ritual silent movie at Premium Point. Silent, because
nobody talked to anybody. Two features would be shown, with one in reserve in case Charles decided (unilaterally) to kill one in midrun. He

wanted a good action plot, but he also watched with an eye for the appearance of the actors and actresses; the styles, clothes, houses, cars . . . At the end of one movie he said: "If I were going to make an acquisition, it would be in sunglasses. From now on women are going to walk around in slacks, fur coats, flowing hair and sunglasses." According to a fashion maven who recalled the incident, his timing was perfect.

Mildred Custin, former president of Bonwit Teller, is one of many who thought that all in all it was "a lovely marriage." "He treated her like a child," she says. "He babied her. He always wanted her to be happy and cheerful." When he was first romancing her and they had had a little spat, he went out to Cartier and bought what might easily have been a hundred grand in gems. When he returned to their suite at the George V, in Paris, Lyn asked where he'd been. He said he'd been out working on some business. Then he said, "Here—I found a little candy store and bought you some candy." And he tossed her the jewels, which he had put in a little brown paper bag. She dumped them out on the bed—flabbergasted.

Eight years into their marriage, Charles celebrated his sixty-fifth birthday in Las Vegas with Lyn, Eugenia Sheppard, and one other couple. As they were driving in from the airport he reached into his briefcase and took out—yes, another paper bag. "Here's something I forgot to give you," he said over his shoulder, from the front seat. He tossed it into her lap and Lyn pulled out a beautiful aquamarine and amethyst necklace.

But there was no telling with this man . . . you never knew what he was thinking. At their tenth anniversary party he presented her with a tin can containing a check for $30,000, plus five little Van Cleef & Arpels bracelets she had always wanted—and began divorce proceedings two days later.

Charles had been planning to leave Lyn for about a year. Things had kept happening to delay him. There was his son's divorce, for example. He didn't want both to be going through divorce proceedings at the same time. It wouldn't look good.

He had gradually gotten fed up. "She was bugging him," Irving explains; "he didn't want to get dragged into her hysterics." And he was tired of being dragged to one affair after another. One executive overheard Charles's end of a phone conversation not long before he left her. They were having quite an argument, the gist of which was that she wanted him to go to a party with her that night, but he had already invited some of his marketing people over to the apartment for dinner and a meeting. He was telling her to go to the party herself, if she wanted to, because he was going to be busy all evening. She apparently didn't understand, because he then said, "Look, I've got *business* to do." And then it escalated to, "Look, I didn't want to go to France but I did what you wanted and I'm getting *tired* of this kind of thing." He sounded beleaguered, as though he were not winning. That evening, he had his meeting and she went to the party herself. About a month later, he left her.

He must have known at the time of his tenth anniversary party that he would have Judge Rifkind call Lyn the following Monday to break the news. (He never fired anyone himself.) But there was not even a hint of trouble at the party. The story goes that as he left for work that Monday morning he told the butler, "Take good care of Mrs. Revson today—she'll need it." Lyn told Eugenia Sheppard that he was wearing the tie she had given him for Valentine's day.

Like all his decisions, this one had been mulled and mulled. ("Charles would fire you in his mind a year before anyone else knew it," Mandel had said.) According to Botwin, by this time one of his closest confidants, he had decided to change his life-style and gradually withdraw from the business, spending more and more time on his yacht, dating beautiful women, having last flings. The tenth anniversary timing may have been revenge, retribution for the embarrassment she had caused him some ten years before—the kind of grudge it was by no means beyond him to bear. Or it may have been out of considerateness—waiting until after the event so as not to embarrass her and as if to say: "There. We've had a good ten years, all in all, but now it's time to end it." Or it may simply have been that the occasion itself triggered a final decision.

Whatever it was, he left Lyn to break the news as she wished. She waited a full three weeks to do so. When she finally did talk to friends, after the news had been leaked in Earl Wilson's column, she said she could offer no explanation for his leaving her, and that it had come as a total surprise.

Eugenia Sheppard is quite certain that the rumor of Lyn's having had another affair was untrue. "I'm sure of that. Lyn would not be that foolish. And whatever you say, she was really devoted to Charles in her own way."

Supposedly, the prenuptial agreement, or its amendment, called for a settlement of $1 million on severance, but Charles gave her, according to John, "a lot more than she deserved on the basis of her prenuptial agreement" but "much less than $5 million." The most reliable rumor places Lyn's settlement at $2 million. One provision in the divorce agreement was that Lyn could not speak with anyone from the press about her marriage, nor write anything herself.

CHAPTER 19

LAST RITES

The man from the temple had arrived promptly for his appointment with Charles Revson, which meant that he could have a long wait. He was sitting in Revson's office with Irving Botwin.

"Revson always had me sit with people," Botwin explains, "because he was always an hour late for any meeting. Rather than have someone sit in the office all by himself, he'd say, 'Irving, sit with the guy; I'll join you shortly.'"

The man Irving was sitting with had come on behalf of Temple Emanu-El, of which Revson was an inactive member, to solicit money for a building fund. He was new to this, Irving recalls his saying, had never approached anyone for a contribution before . . . but, being a C.P.A. and active in the temple, they had made him chairman of the drive. He was understandably nervous about meeting Revson, and wanted to know what he was like.

"He's not going to bite you," said Irving. "The worst that can happen is that he says no."

Charles comes in, Irving introduces them, and Revson says, "I suppose you're here on behalf of the temple?" The man says, "Yes, we have a drive on for the building fund." Revson says, "I'm in between meetings and I know you're busy and I don't want to waste your time and you probably want to get home to your dinner . . . " It was by now around six-thirty. " . . . Irving, give him twenty-five thousand dollars." And he shook the man's hand and walked out.

"The guy started to tremble," says Irving. "He probably would have been happy to get two thousand. I started to walk him back to the elevator and I could see he couldn't put his coat on; he couldn't find the sleeves. He said: 'That's the most remarkable guy I've ever met in my life.'"

The man from the temple, Alfred Bachrach, remembers the incident a little differently, though with much the same result. He wasn't chairman of the building drive, he was president of the temple. He wasn't new to the fund-raising business, he had already received $25,000 and $50,000 donations from several prime donors. Charles said he was interested in the temple, even though he wasn't able to attend as often as he would have liked, and asked what "they" were giving, meaning the other prominent members. They were giving $25,000 or $50,000, Bachrach said, using some names he'd been given permission to use, and Charles generously offered $25,000, the amount for which a classroom would be named in his honor. But the essence of the story—Charles's generosity—holds. Over the years he gave many millions of dollars to Jewish, medical, and educational causes. Roughly fifty million more—half his estate—was placed in a charitable foundation upon his death.

The block-long "Revson Plaza" that spans Amsterdam Avenue and connects Columbia Law School with the rest of the campus was his $1-million-plus gift, as was the $750,000 black marble computerized (to compensate for shifts in the wind) fountain at Lincoln Center.

Like most donors, Charles was both embarrassed by, and eager for, recognition of his generosity. Those who spoke of his "buying his way into heaven" were simply unfair. If he was no more purely altruistic than the next guy, he was also no less. He believed, as he stated often, that "we who take have got to give." He felt particularly strongly about supporting the state of Israel. Why should he build a factory there when it looked as though it would be more economical to ship goods in from other markets? "Because we're Jews, that's why," he told his financial vice president. He was not one for prayers, and he knew little of the history of his people—but he knew who his people were.

And now, August 26, 1975, after a year-long struggle with pancreatic cancer, he was being credited by the rabbi at Temple Emanu-El with having been a "a giant" among those people. Nearly a thousand of them—many current and former employees—had come to his funeral. And when former judge Simon Rifkind, who delivered the eulogy, characterized Charles's unbending perfectionism as having been "both his greatest strength and his greatest failing," nearly a thousand heads nodded imperceptibly.

Lyn's among them. She had arrived at the temple in a white, low-cut dress, her hair disheveled—looking exactly as her former husband would not have wanted her to look. No seat had been reserved for her. Unlike Ancky, she was not considered a member of the immediate family.

In other respects, everything was just as Charles would have wished. Quietly impressive. (Well, he would have had something to say about the lack of air conditioning, numerous of those assembled remarked, but other than that . . .) The casket was smothered in red carnations. At Ferncliffe, the nonsectarian cemetery where he was laid to rest beside his parents and his brother Joseph, each of the 150 onlookers was given a red carnation to place on the casket upon leaving, by way of farewell. Charles had arranged the same farewell for the Major years before, only with white carnations.

It was widely assumed that Charles had divorced Lyn (and hired Bergerac) only after he learned of his terminal illness, thereby to assure that she would be cut out of his estate. This was not the case. He may have sensed that he was entering the last phase of his life, but he did not know how short that phase would prove to be.

By his sixty-eighth birthday, however—October 11, 1974—he had already been in the hospital for an operation on "an obstructive jaundice due to a gallstone"—they thought he had hepatitis at first—and he knew he would soon be going back for more treatment. The ritual surprise party held for him in the office each year thus took on a special significance.

There was champagne and low-cholesterol cake, and some gag telegrams the advertising people had come up with, as well as a handsome oriental chest for which they had all chipped in. Charles began to say something, but his voice was quivering. "I didn't think I was going to make it this year," he started to say—and he began to cry. He actually began to cry. He quickly left the room. "Well, that proves he's human," someone said, to break the uncomfortable silence.

"It was very touching," says Charles, Jr. "Although people respected and feared him, they could feel sympatico towards him. The telegrams and the gift were not what choked him up, because he'd seen this for thirty-five years. It was his having just had the operation, and the fact that he would never hold the same position in the company that he had had. Bergerac would be coming in, and it was going to be a new era for him."

It was the beginning of the end of what had been a life-long, all-consuming love affair. But it was also a measure of his remarkable self-discipline and clear thinking that he *had* decided to begin a process of orderly succession. Other founder/chief-executives run their companies halfway into senility and halfway into the ground rather than relinquish the reins to an able successor—Elizabeth Arden was a case in point.

In Revson's judgment, no one man within the company stood out sufficiently to be certain of commanding unquestioned respect and unchallenged authority. Revson shrewdly decided to go after a man head and shoulders above the rest.

He hadn't been much interested in his first three presidents. Indeed, when the board of directors chose Revlon's first, George Murphy, they did so knowing he would never last. It was, in one director's words, just a way to get Charles used to the idea of having someone between himself and the rest of the company. But now that *he* wanted Revlon to have a president—a post that had been vacant for five years—he wanted the best that money could buy. After considering a number of possibilities, he decided on Michel Bergerac.

A result of Bergerac's leadership skill, and of some enormous financial incentives, was that none of Revlon's veterans left the company.

Revlon won't fall apart without Revson, in part because of Bergerac, but also because—despite all the turnover—he built an organization with depth. He reproduced himself. It wasn't always the most pleasant training, but it pervades the entire cosmetics industry. When Suzanne Grayson, who left Revlon to build her own company, examines a product, her question is always: "Would Charles approve this?" As one observer put it, he carved his initials into everyone he ever worked with.

Most men derive satisfaction and a shot at immortality of sorts by leaving the world offspring. Whatever reservations Charles felt about his own, he had Revlon to leave as a monument to his memory. In later years he had, increasingly—and under the guise of its having been necessary for business—become more and more to Revlon what Colonel Sanders is to Kentucky Fried Chicken. A constant struggle went on within him between his shyness (insecurities) and his ego, with the latter winning more and more of the battles as he got older. He had always resented the fact that his company was not called Charles Revson, the way Arden was Arden; Factor, Factor; Rubinstein, Rubinstein; and Lauder, Lauder. But he couldn't come right out and *say* that—he wanted others to goad him into stardom for the good of the company. A woman who worked for Revlon first in the late fifties and then again in the early seventies noticed a huge change in Charles: his ego had inflated tremendously. She recalls a package designer presenting a new carton, with the product name in large type above CHARLES REVSON, smaller. Charles didn't like the package. The elements were not in balance, he said. The designer, who knew all about elements, begged to differ. Charles said the design looked top-heavy. The designer said it was just right. Charles tried every way to say it without saying it: *screw the design; he wanted his name bigger.*

A few years earlier, Revlon had gotten a terrific write-up in *Women's Wear*—it was all "Revlon says this" and "Revlon is bringing out that"—a very positive piece—and Charles called his PR man, Warren Leslie, livid. Furious. Why? "It should be personalized! I want it personalized!" Mandel had been trying to convey just the opposite image—that Revlon was an ongoing corporation, not a one-man show—so that Wall Street would have more confidence. But Charles wanted to be portrayed as the last word in fashion and marketing. Wall Street would keep buying the stock, he said, as long as they kept showing the earnings. And he was right.

And so it was that month by month the CHARLES REVSON grew into Charles Revson into *Charles Revson* into CHARLES REVSON, in ads and package designs. By the time of his death, there was a CHR line, a Charles Revson, Inc., a wildly successful perfume called Charlie (which blossomed into a full cosmetics line), and a men's line that would be introduced called Chaz. No one will say whether Jontue, a fragrance that followed Charlie, was a coy bow in the direction of "John, too."

Probably not, but the question of John's future role in the company is often raised. And that, in turn, raises the question of Charles's will—a curious document. Neither John nor Charles was given a seat on the board of the Revson Foundation, into which half Revson's estate was placed. Nor were they given control over much of the other half.

Others named in Charles's will were his stepchildren, Steven, Jeffrey and Susan Sheresky, his granddaughter, Jill; Katie Lowery, to whom he was always grateful for having in large measure brought up his children—and who, accordingly, will receive $10,000 a year tax-free for the rest of her life; and Irving Botwin, his friend and executive assistant, to whom he left $250,000 in cash.

Had he wanted to, with a mere 2 percent of his estate he could have bestowed $10,000 on each of 200 people toward whom he felt kindly, or by whom he particularly wished to be remembered—but that was not what he had in mind. Beyond pointing out that Bill White had been on the corporate payroll all those years, not on Charles's personal staff, neither Irving Botwin—dumbfounded by his good fortune—nor Harry Meresman, who helped prepare the will, could offer any explanation or rationale for the seeming omissions. "You never knew what that man was thinking," Botwin says of his departed friend and benefactor.

Far from bringing on a rush of vituperative revelations, Charles's death elicited an outpouring of fond and respectful remembrances—some hypocritical, to be sure, but many genuine. One of the nicest came from Marlene Beck, George Beck's fourth wife. She had not been a key figure in his life, of course, but in a way her impression is all the more significant for that. "Charles was the most fantastic man I ever met," she told me quietly. "It's just sad he allowed so few people to know him. He expected you to understand the feelings he couldn't express, and if you didn't, that was just too bad. You never had to ask people whether he was in the office or not—you just knew from the electricity. Now people don't run any more. The urgency is gone."

So are the fear and chaos.

THE BEST YEARS

A condensation of the book by

JOSEPH C. GOULDEN

PROLOGUE: HOW WE BEGAN

In August 1944, Hollywood producer Samuel Goldwyn was leafing through *Time* magazine when his eye fell upon a photograph of eleven travel-soiled soldiers hanging from the window of a grimy Pullman car—some smiling, some seemingly bewildered, some almost grimly expectant. Below the window were chalked two words: "Home Again!"

A shrewd movie-moneyman, Goldwyn immediately saw a potential market in those faces; after all, some 15,000,000 men and women would be "home again" once the war ended. Later that day he telephoned writer MacKinlay Kantor in Palm Beach and said he wanted a story about the "living, loving people, working, playing, loafing, in the American way of peace." Kantor liked the idea, and over the next year he wrote a novel entitled *Glory for Me*, about three homecoming veterans. Pleased, Goldwyn turned the book over to playwright Robert Sherwood for a script, and signed up top director William Wyler.

But Sherwood had problems with the script. One of Kantor's veterans had come out of the war with an injury that made him spastic, a condition difficult to portray on the screen. He and Wyler tried several approaches to a screen treatment but couldn't satisfy themselves or Goldwyn. They kept working.

Meanwhile, a young paratrooper named Harold Russell was undertaking a movie experience of an entirely different sort. Russell was in Walter Reed Army Hospital in Washington, painfully learning to use the cold metallic hooks that were to substitute for the hands he had lost during a training accident, and worrying about whether he could hold down his prewar job as a meat cutter.

One day officials from the Veterans Administration came around Walter Reed scouting for a lead character for a film about rehabilitation of crippled soldiers. "I was the only double-arm in the place, and a four-star general, the first one I ever seen, told me I would make the movie," Russell says. "I replied, 'Yes, sir.'" The twenty-five-minute film, *Diary of a Sergeant,* traced Russell from an opening scene on the operating table, where he anguished over his future, through his struggle with the artificial hands, to a tolerably upbeat homecoming and entry into college, with a girl friend. "It was a damned good job," Russell said of *Diary*.

The film was so good, in fact, that the government decided to use it at war bond rallies. Wyler, still working with Sherwood on the Kantor script, saw it in Hollywood one night, borrowed a print, and took it home and called Goldwyn. The next day Goldwyn's office called Russell, by now attending Boston University, and persuaded him to come west to star in the movie.

The story was of three servicemen returning to the fictitious Midwestern town of Boone City, and the way they went about picking up the threads of their prewar existence: Dana Andrews, a bombardier captain with ambitions beyond his old job as a soda jerk, and tired of his addle-brained wife, Virginia Mayo; Frederic March, who found his bank job stuffy after serving as a middle-aged infantry sergeant; and Russell, cast as former sailor Homer Parrish. The movie did not pretend that homecoming was easy, but, of course, all the snarls are resolved, and toward the end of the movie, someone concludes that they are really enjoying "the best years of our lives."

Robert Sherwood thought those six words more aptly expressed the thrust of the movie than Kantor's original *Glory for Me*. Goldwyn cautiously hired the Gallup polling organization to do a survey on what the public considered to be "the best years." The answers were most upbeat. A thirty-year-old housewife answered, "This year—right now. My husband's come home from the army, I'm having a baby, and this is the most challenging time I've yet seen. If I don't have any more years, this one [1946] is fine." A twenty-three-year-old veteran agreed: "Oh, boy, this last year will be hard to beat. Got discharged from the army, got married, got back into college . . ." As RKO General Pictures later exclaimed in releasing *The Best Years of Our Lives,* "These and scores of other answers had a special significance for Mr. Goldwyn. They told him that America was still living, loving, dreaming."

Nonetheless many persons in Hollywood told Sam Goldwyn he was a damned fool even to consider such a movie. "The 'professionals,' whoever the hell they are," Harold Russell said, "told Sam: 'This thing will never go. With all your good intentions, you just can't show an amputee in a motion picutre. This movie is not good box office.'" If Goldwyn ever worried or listened, no hint of it came through to the cast.

The Best Years, released in October 1946, won nine Academy Awards including an Oscar for amateur actor Harold Russell, and the New York film critics called it the best movie of the year. After the promotional tours Russell thought about staying in Hollywood, either as an actor or as a public relations man for Goldwyn's organization. But his friend Wyler discouraged the notions. "How much future is there in the motion picture industry for a guy without any hands over a period of five or ten years?" he asked. Russell agreed, and went back to Massachusetts, where he is a businessman in a Boston suburb.

"I can look back at that period now and say they truly *were* 'the best years,'" Russell says. "The guys who came out of World War Two were idealistic. They sincerely believed that this time they were coming home to build a new world. You'd hear guys say, 'The one thing I want to do when I get out is to make sure that this thing will never happen again.' We felt the day had come when the wars were all over, we were going to break down the bonds that separated people."

Russell shook his head. "I could give you a long lecture on what went wrong. But the important thing is that the postwar years *were* a great period for our country, and you had a tremendous feeling just being alive. Periods of readjustment are always difficult, but they are also interesting. We had problems, sure, but they didn't dominate us; we face the same things now, and we despair."

The Best Years is an attempt to re-create what was happening in and to America from the end of World War Two to the start of the Korean War. August 1945 to June 1950. What years! Two vivid flashes of light over Japan, two ugly, churning mushroom clouds, and suddenly the war was over, a full year ahead of expectation. Americans rejoiced in the ultimate euphoria of victory over people whom even our schoolchildren had been taught to hate, in a conflict where defeat meant national and personal subjugation. Four years of common sacrifice gave Americans a reason for shared joy, and a rare sense of national unity and superiority, reinforced with an overriding moral righteousness only slightly diminished by the fact that the penultimate events of the war were the first uses of nuclear weaponry. Once again we had bailed out the British and the French in the nick of time, and the Russians as well. Oh, the Allies helped, certainly, but *we* provided the decisive striking power, when all appeared lost for the rest of western civilization. So America basked in collective self-glory.

August 1945 found America victorious on places other than the battlefield. The Great Depression fell along with the Axis powers, and the word "want" took on a new and not entirely negative meaning: when citizens wished to buy something, the shortage was not of dollars, but of articles to carry home from the stores. When the war ended, Americans had jobs (53,000,000 of them, with unemployment less than two percent) and money ($140 billion in liquid savings, in war bonds and in banks and in their wallets, about three times the national income in 1932). Although most people expected some inevitable painful bumps as the economy shifted from war to peace, Americans nonetheless entered the postwar era confident the bread lines were gone forever.

Prewar "normalcy" meant 8,000,000 men out of work, and a take-home pay, for the average industrial worker, of less than $25 weekly (versus $44.39 on V-J Day). Now Americans read the Sunday supplement features about the future, and they believed it would work: futuristic automobiles and jet planes that would whisk them around the world, even to the moon, as they luxuriated in the twenty-five-hour week made possible by the arcane technologies developed in secret war laboratories. The American's new house—and Americans needed them, about 15,000,000 in all, to make up for construction lost during the Depression and the war, and to catch up with the population jump—would be made of glass and plastic, with perhaps a supporting slab or two of steel or aluminum. Radiant heat would keep the house warm in freezing weather, even with the windows open for fresh air, or comfortably cool in the summer. No outside noise, no dust, no termites, no germs (ultraviolet lamps would take care of them). New plastic clothing would be so cheap a man would wear a suit two or three times and toss it in the trash.

The wonder drugs of the battlefield, those long clumsy words ending in "my-o-cin," would rid society of most illnesses. Another chemical proven in Burma and the swamps of the South Pacific, dichloro-diphenyl-trichloro-ethane (DDT, the scientists mercifully abbreviated it), would rid the outdoors of flies and mosquitoes and other flying bugs. There would be consumer goods in abundance: after all, had not American industry built 297,000 planes and 86,338 tanks and 71,060 ships during wartime? Did not this mammoth industrial capacity mean a surfeit of autos and refrigerators once a few gauges were changed on the machines?

A restiveness to return to the peacetime economy and to begin enjoying the material fruits of victory was highly visible even before the formal peace. As hundreds of thousands of GIs streamed from the European to the Pacific theater, and naval bombardments of Japanese coastal cities reinforced the steady air bombings, defense officials had trouble keeping the public's mind on the fact that civilians still had a role in the war. The lassitude was reflected in sudden and unfillable job vacancies in war plants. In California, a shortage of shipyard workers became so critical that the United States Employment Service (USES) resorted to shock tactics. Rather than continuing to conceal the extent of shipping damages, they threw open Terminal Island and Los Angeles harbor to visitors so citizens could see the effects of kamikaze attacks on the destroyer USS *Zellars* and the hospital ship USS *Comfort.* The USES set up booths to recruit shipyard workers. On a single weekend, 250,000 persons visited the ships. Only 2,500 paused at the USES stands, and of these only a handful expressed an interest in defense jobs. In Michigan City, Indiana, an army plane dropped thousands of leaflets seeking 300 workers for the local Pullman plant, which was doing defense work. As a Labor Department official commented, "Workers in war plants have had their noses to the grindstone for three or four years now. Many have been foregoing vacations, working overtime, sacrificing home life. They are told that continued work is necessary to win the war against Japan, but they see war plants closing down. . . . They want to blow off steam." The July 30 *Newsweek* cover, two weeks before peace, revealed the deepening public dichotomy: the cover photo was of a scrawny Japanese soldier with a three-day stubble of beard, with the caption: "The Jap: How Long Can He Take It?" Page nine was a full-page color ad from General Motors on "What's ahead at Oldsmobile." The text noted that production lines released from war work were being swifly converted to private cars: "Under this new 'combined operations program,' America's Oldest Car Manufacturer soon will be serving the home-front as well as the war-front—building vitally needed motor cars for essential transportation." Americans read the car ads (few could buy autos, however; even after a partial conversion following V-E Day, Ford produced only ten vehicles per day) and they had their first fleeting taste of consumer goods (when a Philadelphia department store advertised 100 electric irons at $9.20, the supply lasted fifteen minutes). And so the citizenry waited, with whetted appetites and overflowing wallets, for the economic cornucopia of peace.

Looking abroad, Americans also saw reasons for optimism. A series of Gallup polls found their confidence about winning the war matched only by their confidence in keeping the peace. A clear majority did not expect war again for at least twenty-five years. Americans believed in the United Nations, in the Yalta agreement, even in the Russians, to the extent that public sentiment favored a continuing military alliance. "The war for human decency is done," *Fortune* editorialized in September 1945, "and now the United States stands out as the inheritor of more power and more responsibility than any nation on earth. . . . Partly against its will—certainly without seeking the prize—it has become the guardian and standard-bearer of western civilization."

And, above the general euphoria, a broad national confidence, both in the future of individuals and the country's ability to solve any postwar problems, arose. The mood was caught by a young Swedish exchange student named Olof Palme, later his nation's prime minister. "I wrote the first review for the Swedish press of Mailer's *The Naked and the Dead*. I remember the thrust of the last paragraph: 'The spirit of the world is ours for the taking.' This statement was typical of postwar American youth. America was a country with a lot of social and economic problems, and ideological differences. But it was not a divided country. I returned [to Sweden, in 1948] with a deep affection for America, for the vitality, for the openness." Hear, too, Les Cramer, a navy veteran of the South Pacific who went back to college in Ohio: "You had a mixture of feelings. I wanted to make up for the fun I had missed while overseas, and I also wanted to start moving professionally. I had not the slightest doubt that I would be able to do both, and that I would make a comfortable living when I graduated." Charles Lehman, a Missouri veteran, remembers, "I was a twenty-one-year-old lieutenant with a high-school education, and my only prewar experience was as a stock boy in a grocery store. But on V-J Day, I *knew* it was only a matter of time before I was rich—or well-off, anyway." (Lehman is now an insurance man in a Kansas City suburb— "comfortable, but by no means rich.") Stan Monto, who grew up in rural northern California, says, "The war taught me there was another world out there, beyond the vegetable patch." When he was discharged from the marines in 1946, he remembers, "I never gave a thought to going back to the country; I headed straight for San Francisco, because I wanted something better out of life than a permanent assignment at the end of a hoe. If I hadn't been exposed to something else, I never would have had the confidence to leave home."

Peace. The return of more than 15,000,000 men and women from war. The strong probability of continuing economic plenty. National confidence. A high degree of unity, born of the shared adventure and triumph of war. An acceptably popular President, even if Harry S. Truman himself recognized that, for the moment at least, he wore the mantle of FDR by inheritance only, not by mandate of the electorate. Americans truly had reasons to anticipate the best years of their lives.

By contrast, five years later the national mood had done a complete turnabout. Discord was widespread. The unions and the corporations fought one another with savagery, as America suffered the most crippling series of strikes in its history. In the South, racists forgot about the "brotherhood" of war, and stories about lynchings of blacks sprinkled the nation's newspapers. Only a threatened black boycott of the Selective Service System, organized by A. Philip Randolph, the unionist, forced the military forces to abandon segregation.

The fear of a nuclear confrontation with the detested Russians—the same people who, five years before, were courageous, all-sacrificing allies—permeated national thinking, so much so that one's Americanism was gauged by the ferocity of his denunciation of any ideas even vaguely parallel to Communist ideology. In the United States Senate, the mere mention of a government functionary's name by a jowly, long-ignored back-bencher named Joseph R. McCarthy sent newspaper makeup men scampering for their largest, blackest type. Although McCarthy was some months away from his demagogic apogee, by 1950 he was a most visible menace to Americans in general and to the Truman Administration in particular. And more than any other public person he symbolized the anxieties, the fears, the outright hatreds that marred what Americans had hoped, had expected, would be an era of tranquility and prosperity.

So the best years led to Joe McCarthy. They were also the birth of national television and the concurrent death of national radio. The best years were builder William Levitt converting a Long Island potato patch into a mass of production-line houses—portending the suburbization of America and the deification of the automobile. The best years were the give-'em-hell-Harry campaign of 1948, the one Truman couldn't win, and Taft-Hartley and Alger Hiss and frozen foods and the long-playing phonograph record. *Forever Amber,* the first lurid national best-seller a woman could read under the hair dryer. The discovery of flying saucers. The Boudreau shift. Lena the Hyena. Kaiser-Frazer. Computers. Billy Graham. Borden's Hemo. The Ingrid Bergman-Roberto Rossellini affair. *Death of a Salesman.* William ("Catch me before I kill more") Heirens. "Open the Door, Richard." Howard Unruh, the Camden killer. Glenn McCarthy and the hydrogen bomb and the "Friendship Club" pyramid chain letters. The first drive-in bank and the Berlin airlift. The Coke machine and Thomas E. Dewey. Gorgeous George and the Kinsey Report. The o–o tie between Army and Notre Dame in 1946. *Bongo bongo bongo, I don't want to leave the Congo.* . . .

CHAPTER 1

COMING HOME

Once the din of victory celebrations subsided, GI and civilian alike demanded BRING OUR BOYS HOME—NOW! America had its victory; now it wanted its fathers, sons, and brothers. On V-J Day slightly more than 12,000,000 men and women served in the military, about 7,000,000 of them in foreign countries and on the high seas. The vast majority were volunteers and draftees eager to shed their uniforms as swiftly as possible, but disbanding such a mighty force, the military learned, is almost as difficult as assembling it.

In what order should men be discharged? Administratively, the easier course would be to dismiss intact units. But wouldn't first-in/first-out be fairer? How about older men and fathers? Shouldn't they receive more consideration than single men in their early twenties? So the argument went, with planners trying to strike a fair balance between length of service, combat experience, and a multitude of other factors. Finally, someone suggested asking the soldier what discharge system *he* preferred.

So in the summer of 1944, as the Allies pushed across Europe, opinion specialists from the Research Branch of the War Department's Information and Education Division buttonholed soldiers at posts around the world and asked questions. When tabulated, the survey showed 54 percent listing overseas service the highest (even among troops polled in the United States). Next were the number of dependents, time in the military, and age. These findings in hand, the War Department announced its first demobilization policy on September 6, 1944: that discharges would be on an individual, not a unit, basis; and that surplus soldiers would be mustered out as quickly as possible after Germany fell. It warned that some men fighting in Europe might be shipped to the Pacific and said that details of the point system would be announced in due course.

That demobilization was going to make a lot of people unhappy, regardless of how the military carried it out, became painfully obvious beginning with the German capitulation in May 1945. The mechanics of the point system, revealed the day after V-E Day, gave one point for each month in the service; one for each month overseas; five for each campaign star or combat decoration; and, if the GI was a father, twelve for each child under age eighteen, to a maximum of three children. The army's first "magic number" for immediate discharge was eighty-five points, and GIs the world over scrambled for pencil and paper to compute their totals.

The flow of discharges, once it began, quickly became a gush. Between V-E Day (May 7) and mid-September the army alone mustered out 700,000 men, surging toward a goal of 25,000 daily. The navy, preparing to return some 4,000,000 men from abroad in the first year of peace, hurried landing and cargo craft into yards for conversion to troop carriers (three weeks and $280,000 were required to transform a stubby Liberty ship, workhouse of the navy's freight fleet, into an ersatz liner capable of holding 550 men). In July the *Queen Mary* sped westward across the Atlantic with its lights ablaze for the first time since 1939, carrying 15,278 troops happy to crowd into space designed for 2,000. By autumn of 1945, the navy had 843 troop and combat ships ferrying men to the states. "It took us three and a half years to get the men overseas, and it will take us only ten months to get them back," Admiral William M. Callaghan, the director of naval transportation, told an inquiring Senate committee.

But for the individual GI, the troop ship home could be the last great adventure—and frustration—of the war. Some of the civilian-soldiers managed to laugh about the round-the-clock chow lines, the crowding (bunks were stacked six and eight deep in the holds of some freighters), the lack of exercise space (on some ships enlisted men were allowed fifteen minutes daily above decks), the shipboard discipline enforced by officers and noncoms bent on demonstrating that, peace or no peace, the GI remained government property.

One person repelled by the diehard hold of the military caste system was the American Communist leader Elizabeth Turley Flynn, who got passage aboard the troop transport USAT *Edward M. Alexander* en route home from a European meeting of the International Congress of Women. Mrs. Flynn said that even though the enlisted men ate franks and sauerkraut for breakfast while officers enjoyed eggs and fresh fruit, they were "initially philosophical." But morale took a nasty turn on Christmas Eve when enlisted men lined up for a USO show for which tickets had been distributed. "The announcement came over the loudspeaker that the performance was 'for officers only,' and military personnel [enlisted men] would return to quarters. They drowned out the voice in catcalls and boos." The men glumly returned to the hold; the next day, the ship commander ordered a rerun of the entertainment for them. Mrs. Flynn concluded, somewhat jubilantly, "Agitation pays even on an army transport, especially one headed towards home."

C. K. Hollomanberg worked as an executive for a New York hotel chain before going to Europe as a fighter pilot. A man who appreciated his com-

fort, Hollomanberg recoiled from the possibility of traveling home in the hold of a troop ship. "I spent much of my military career keeping out of uncomfortable mob situations," he said. "Uncle Sam had given me a fighter plane to ride in for more than fifty combat missions, and I really thought he could find one for me one more time." Uncle Sam couldn't, at first, because Hollomanberg was neither ranking brass, a VIP, wounded, nor facing a family crisis that warranted priority transport. But one asset Hollomanberg did possess was ingenuity.

"At the main demobilization terminal in Roussefls, I scouted around until I found a guy, a lieutenant, who controlled the shipping rosters. I laid it down for him directly: 'You get me a plane ride home, my good young man, and when you get home, I expect you and your wife to spend a week in New York as a guest of my hotel.'

" 'Sit right there,' the lieutenant told me, and hurried away. I was scared shitless. I expected him to come back with an MP and have me hauled off to Lichfield for attempted bribery. I almost got up and sneaked out. Then here came the lieutenant, with a file of papers. 'Here is the drill,' he said. 'You are a compassionate case, so you get priority, that's what these orders say. If anyone asks any questions, you turned all the papers over to the shipping center here, and "the sergeant" insisted that he had to keep them. See you in New York this fall, Captain.'

"I went off without a question. Fifty-three hours later I was in the states, and within a week I was back at my desk. The lieutenant? Well, I got a letter from him later that year. He was out, but he couldn't afford to come to New York just then, so I told him any time. I got a Christmas card from him each year, and he'd jot on it, 'Soon, I hope.' When he did come East, in 1953, I had left the hotel business and moved to Erie. But I kept my bargain: I had the chain send me the bill for his week, and I laid out something like $140 for him and his wife. Troop ships were pretty far from my mind by that time, but what the hell, you make a deal, you keep it. I sure the hell would have handed him $140 in the summer of forty-five."

For men in the Pacific, the vast expanses of water separating them from home caused seemingly ceaseless weeks of tedium. Under optimum conditions, a transport required more than a month from Manila to San Francisco. But the ships didn't always sail the more direct route at top speed for they had to pick up servicemen from dozens of remote Pacific atolls where war had scattered them. One GI, home from the Philippines, wrote his senator: "I have just arrived here [San Francisco] on October 14, 1945 . . . with 1,200 other enlisted men. We spent 81 days from July

26 to October 14 in arriving at our destination. I carried my seabag and personal gear across the gangplank 27 times." Another reported living aboard a ship at anchor for twenty-seven days in the Olithi islands group, awaiting sailing orders that were dealyed for some reason never made clear to the troops. During his spare time—which was considerable, as the GI wrote—he counted no less than 200 ships of varying sizes in the anchorage, and asked why the navy could not put them to use ferrying men home. The navy, responding to scores of such complaints before the Senate Naval Affairs Committee, said many small ships didn't carry enough men to make such use worthwhile. The navy could not sail a 40,000-ton vessel, with a 40-man crew, 12,000 miles over 2½ months "just in order to return twenty or thirty passengers," said Admiral Callaghan.

Stateside transportation had problems as well. With most of America's autos and buses worn out during four years of war and air passenger service a novelty, the railroads handled the bulk of long-distance traffic. Restless civilians, eager for long-delayed vacation trips, competed with returning servicemen for the few available seats—so vigorously, in fact, that by late summer the railroads and government attempted to keep them at home. The Association of American Railroads advertised: "If it comes to a choice between your taking a trip—and a returned soldier getting to see his home folks—we know you will understand who deserves the right of way."

In terms of getting men home and out of uniform, the War Department performed well; but in terms of long-range policy goals, demobilization proved a disaster, one that effectively wrecked the U.S. military.

The reasons are several. President Truman spoke repeatedly of the United States' intention to assume vast peacetime responsibilities for world security—language that could mean only that hundreds of thousands of American troops would remain on foreign soil indefinitely. In a letter to the House Military Affairs Committee in August 1945, he noted that since Generals Eisenhower and MacArthur needed 1,200,000 men for occupation duty, planning for the postwar army should start from that base figure. He estimated an army of 2,500,000 men by July 1946. Even so, Mr. Truman foresaw problems. At the then-rates of induction and demobilization, the army would have only 800,000 volunteers and draftees at that time. Thus he said the difference of 1,700,000 men "must be made up by holding additional numbers of veterans in the service."

After stating the policy, the Truman Administration proceeded to ignore it. Instead, it bowed to public and congressional pressures and set about dispersing the army as rapidly as possible. A scant month after Mr.

Truman's pronouncement about the 2,500,000-man army, General Marshall was telling a congressional committee that the demobilization rate "has been determined by transportation facilities and the availability of trained personnel to carry its administrative requirements out. It has no relationship whatsoever to the size of the army of the future."

In fairness to the Truman Administration, its surrender to expediency could have been avoided only at great political cost. As early as March 1945 the chief Pentagon lobbyist had warned General Marshall that "the attitude of Congress is beginning to approach that which exists towards the military establishment in normal times of peace. . . . Until recently, Congress has responded to the army as the desperate householder whose home is in flames welcomes the fire department: drive over the lawn, chop down the doors, throw the furniture out the window, but save the house. Now, with the flames under control, the Congress, like the householder, is noting for the first time the water damages and thinking that if the fire department had acted differently, the lawn would not be torn up, the doors smashed, and the furniture broken." The lobbyist counseled that the Pentagon treat Congress gingerly if it expected passage of such priority legislation as an extension of the draft.

Congress's major offensive against the military commenced August 4, 1945, only days before V-J Day, in a letter from Senator Edwin C. Johnson of Colorado to Secretary Stimson, demanding an immediate reduction in the size of the armed forces. Johnson, a self-elected point man for the congressional dissidents, asserted there was a "widespread feeling in Congress and the country now that the War Department is tenaciously holding millions of men it does not need and whom it cannot use."

Editorial criticism, although scattered, was from influential sources. The Chicago *Tribune* asked in an editorial, "Has the army heard of peace?" and demanded force reductions. Returning to the same "outrage" a few days later, the *Tribune* saw no explanation other than "incompetence and selfishness. . . . It often has been pointed out that the more rapidly the army is reduced from its wartime strength the more rapidly its higher officers will be reduced in number, rank and influence. It would be hard to imagine a worse reason than this one for keeping millions of men in the army, but what other reason is there?" The *Wall Street Journal,* noting that the army alone would still have 6,000,000 men by the end of 1945, declared, "On the basis of any information available to the public, that is a policy that is perfectly idiotic. If the United States saw any other country pursuing a similar policy, we would be crying to high heaven about 'militarism' and what not." The *Journal* charged that the army "is deliberately pursuing a policy of 'gradual' demobilization. . . . We wonder if anyone in Washington has any adequate idea of the resentment that is being built up in this country."

Washington was not deaf. Under Secretary of War Robert P. Patterson, called before the Senate Military Affairs Committee to account for the "slow pace of demobilization" (at a time, ironically, when discharges ran 30 to 45 percent ahead of schedule), protested that the Pentagon was doing the "best job possible," mustering out 10,000 men daily. "We are getting 10,000 *letters* a day," shot back Senator Johnson, who complained that former combat troops were "mowing lawns with bayonets" to kill time awaiting discharge. Representative Homer V. Ramey of Ohio complained that he and colleagues spent so much time handling citizen gripes about the military that they acted as "harried errand boys at a time when other vital questions" demanded attention. All that the Pentagon could do was avow that it was trying and plead for patience.

The climax came in January 1946 when the War Department was forced into a grudging admission that it had promised faster discharges than it could deliver and pushed the discharge of two-year men back to July 1, 1946.

And it also pushed GIs and the Congress into open revolt. The unfortunate Patterson was just beginning an inspection tour of Pacific bases when the statement was released. When he arrived in Guam, angry demonstrating soldiers burned him in effigy. At each stop thereafter worried local commanders arranged for him to meet soldier delegations to vent the GI ire. But on successive days in Manila he faced shouting mobs of up to 10,000 soldiers and sailors. The Pacific edition of *Stars & Stripes* bannered PATTERSON CALLED NUMBER ONE ENEMY BY JEERING MOB. Other GIs marched through Manila with banners protesting the cancellation of ship sailings that were to take them home. "We want ships, we want to go home," they chanted.

The protests spread rapidly around the world. Virtually every U.S. command witnessed demonstrations against the "slow-down" order. Soldiers booed their commanding officers at mass meetings and passed their service caps for money to buy ads in state-wide newspapers. Military police noted sharp increases in arrests for drunkenness, reckless driving, and slovenly dress. In Frankfurt, 2,000 soldiers gathered outside the quarters of the occupation commander. "Service yes, serfdom no," they called. "Japs go home—how about us?"

The spectacle of an army in near mutiny jarred the military. On the other side of the world, General MacArthur said the turmoil made it difficult to turn Japan toward true democracy because "real democratic leaders are afraid to speak, not knowing how long U.S. troops will be here to protect them." After General Eisenhower ordered an end to demonstrations upon pain of court martial, the Milwaukee *Journal* called some of the GI complaints "fantastic," especially those that soldiers were being kept overseas to enforce "imperialism" and to enable the "brass hats to maintain large commands to keep their own rank or to 'play at war.'" The *Journal* did not believe that President Truman, "who must answer to the American people and the 15 million American vets at the polls, would dare to resist the clamor of these soldiers overseas unless he was convinced that the welfare of the nation and the world required him to do so."

The immensely popular General Eisenhower finally invoked his personal prestige and charm to hush Congress. On January 15 he appeared before members assembled in the Library of Congress. Ike went right to the point: the military was slowing demobilization because if the present rate continued "we would literally run out of soldiers." The military had been told by "higher authority" to perform certain functions. If Congress insists on cutting the military's strength, it should also specify the functions to be discontinued. Ike professed sympathy for the women pickets and other aggrieved relatives of servicemen, but added, "If we should take every father today, authorize his discharge, and start him home, the army simply cannot do his job."

Eisenhower convinced the congressmen. Critics thereafter complained of isolated instances of supposed injustice, but never again attacked the overall demobilization policy. But by the end of 1945 the once-mighty American fighting forces were a hollow, echoing shell. Even President Truman conceded in his memoirs, "The program we were following was no longer demobilization—it was disintegration of our armed forces." Truman did his part to speed along the process: in January 1946 he told the Pentagon he wanted an overall military strength of 2,000,000 men, about a million fewer than planned. The army, Mr. Truman directed, should be cut to 1,000,000, or some 50,000 less than what the brass had called the minimum "bedrock requirements." Congress went even further. During debate over the draft extension in the spring of 1946, the military was cut even deeper, to 1,070,000 men effective July 1, 1947.

To career military men the cuts portended disaster. The army desperately cut training cycles for recruits from seventeen to thirteen weeks, then to eight: once a soldier finished basic training, he was shipped directly to Germany or Japan. By mid-1946 the army was not a closely integrated military machine but large groups of individual replacements. General Carl Spaatz, the army air force commander, reported that only two of fifty-five air groups passed their 1946 proficiency tests: "Airplanes were stranded in all parts of the globe for lack of maintenance personnel to repair them . . . serviceable and even new aircraft, equipment and material were left to deteriorate for lack of personnel to prepare them for storage." In June 1946 the army's four "active" divisions in the United States included the 2nd Armored Division, with only 20 percent of its authorized personnel; and the 3rd Infantry, "which existed only on paper with a complement of sixteen officers and twelve enlisted men."

In its postmortems on demobilization, years after the war, the army itself could not decide whether the operation was a success. An army study, published in 1968, took a middle view, saying:

In terms of what were actually the national objectives during the 1945–46 period—rapid return of soldiers to civilian life and rapid reconversion of a wartime to a peacetime economy—it was a success. From the vantage point of preserving necessary American forces to support American diplomacy, it was a failure.

But to America of 1945–46, the long-range implication of rapid demobilization was a question to be ignored. The public demanded the physical presence of its loved ones as proof that peace had truly returned to America. But the civilians, concurrently, were in the midst of their own preparations for the best years, earnestly studying how to cope with that mysterious creature known as The Veteran.

CHAPTER 2

PREPARING FOR ULYSSES

As the war drew to a close, the American public awaited the return of its combat servicemen with a curious ambivalence: could the "veteran" abandon overnight his blood lust for killing? Was it really safe to put bayonet and judo experts into civilian society? Such talk was encouraged by pop experts on veterans in the press and the supposedly learned professions. The Boston *Post* found a psychologist at Boston University who warned that unless the government started a program "of reeducating the soldier, sailor and marine not to kill, we will endure a crime wave of proportions that will exceed by far that which followed World War One."

Luncheon-club speakers and feature writers fretted over the subject, and literally hundreds of magazine articles titillated, alarmed, reassured, and informed the public on what to expect. "Don't Go Sympathizing," counseled *Time*. "Don't Let the Veteran Down," pleaded the *Saturday Evening Post*. The armed services, concurrently, ran their own orientation programs to prepare the veterans for their reintroduction to civilians. A slim, pocket-sized booklet, "Coming Home," prepared by a team of air force psychiatrists and published in 1945, suggested that becoming a civilian might be tougher than anticipated: regardless of whether the vet felt an immediate need for the booklet's counsel, he should retain it for later days when he feels "good or bad or just mixed up." One strong recommendation was that men feeling restless should vent their stresses by boxing, hunting, chopping wood, or "jitterbugging, too. . . . Of course, it would be fine if he [the veteran] could have all of his former values restored by just blowing a whistle. But it takes time, sometimes lots of it, to 'decondition' or 'detrain' after a session of combat." The booklet also emphasized that any man who felt stress while still on active duty should seek immediate psychiatric counseling.

Once in civilian clothes again the veteran could be distinguished by his eagle-in-circle discharge button—the "ruptured duck" as it soon became known. To insure wide publicity for the emblem the War Department urged corporations to refer to it in their advertising. Ford and Texaco explained, "In the days to come, the ranks of those who wear this proud insignia will grow. Let all of us give them our grateful thanks and recognition." But J. C. Furnas, who studied returned veterans in Elmira, New York, for the *American Legion Magazine* shortly before the war ended, found few vets would wear the button. "The public doesn't know what it means," one vet told Furnas. "It's too small—you can't tell what it is two feet away." If a vet wore the button he was apt to be asked "how you got shipped home when the other guys are still out there somewhere fighting." Furnas commented, "One dischargee, veteran of Tarawa, you hear, leaves his button off because he takes special pleasure in socking busybodies who ask him the wrong question. More of him would help a lot."

Thousands upon unhappy thousands of men returned "home" to discover that it had not survived their absence; that their marriages no longer existed, in emotion or in reality. Hurried, lonely people made frightful mistakes in choosing mates, and in 1945 and 1946 discovered they really didn't care that much about their spouses. During 1945 the United States achieved the highest divorce rate in the world—thirty-one divorces for every 100 marriages, double the prewar rate, a grand total of 502,000. The record surpassed even that of the First World War, when the divorce rate jumped 40 percent for 1918–1920, then settled back to prewar norms.

In their instant analyses marriage specialists cited separation as the largest single factor. Another was the increased economic independence of women. For the first time in her history, the American woman learned she could find and hold a job, drive and maintain the family car, keep the checkbook in balance—without the help of a man. Because they had learned to fend for themselves, women did not view divorce with the stark terror of earlier generations: if a marriage didn't work, why ruin two lives by continuing it? The respectability of numbers stripped divorce of much of its old stigma.

By his own testimony, as revealed through sociological and other polls, the veteran saw the war as a direct loss, personally and professionally. The war cost him years away from school and/or a career; would he ever be able to regain the lost time and money? Many felt estranged from civilian life, even after mustering out: their friends weren't around anymore, food was scarce, prices high, and gasoline nonavailable. Many felt homecoming was a letdown. "Every guy thinks it will be the greatest thing in the world, but somehow I didn't quite get the thrill I thought I would."

Jerry———is a prosperous insurance agent in East Texas, a confident, poised man in his sixties who is high in his town's economic power structure. He spent four of the war years in the army as a noncommissioned officer:

"The draft board here didn't do an equitable job deciding who went into the service. I was nothing in ———, nor was my family. So I was among the first to go, right after Pearl Harbor. I was kind of burned, because many of the kids I'd gone to high school with got deferments on the grounds they were essential to the farm work, or to their father's business.

"When I came home I was even madder. Here these people were, who had sat out the war, they had made money hand over fist while the rest of us were away; they had a big head start and they made the most of it. I had some cash I had saved, and the first day or so I went down to a car dealer— one of those who had managed to slip around the draft, even though he was my age and in good physical shape—anyway, I asked him about buying a car, and he wanted money under the table, a subterfuge to beat the price freeze.

"I told him to go to hell, that I had fought a war for the cause of decency and honesty, and that I wasn't going to be shaken down by some damned profiteer.

"I guess I was pretty belligerent that first month. I wouldn't get a hair-cut, I shaved when I felt like it, which wasn't very often, I didn't even keep myself clean. I was saying to the slackers, 'To hell with you, I won't play your game.'

"Of course, I was only hurting myself, because I realized after a few weeks that going around mad wasn't helping me sell insurance. I cleaned myself up, and I started doing better. But I never did pay money under the table to get a car. I waited until the market straightened out before I bought.

"One thing, though, I still remember the bastards who thought the war was nothing more than another way of making money. I'm polite with them now, and socialize with them, and buy stuff from them. But I'll nev-er respect them."

GI antipathy extended even to homecoming fetes. Four sociologists who studied veteran problems in an Illinois town of 6,000 persons found the servicemen edgy when given too much attention. "I wanted to see the relatives all right, but I wanted to see them one at a time," one veteran told the interviewers. "So the first thing my mother does is haul us out to a picnic with all the relatives, and I had to stand around with all of them and answer their darn fool questions."

In some instances—apparently isolated—servicemen suffered from de-liberate cruelty. The journalist J. C. Furnas recounted some problems he found in the factory town of Elmira, New York: "In one shop a nerve-shattered boy's benchmates insisted it was fun to make sudden noises to make him jump and turn white. In another a veteran shrinking from the racket associated with his old job asked for outside work—only to be re-fused and eventually laid off as inefficient, even though he had offered to take a lower pay outside."

Another man, a quiet dischargee, worked normally until a low-flying plane came over the plant. "He dived under the desk in a panic of col-lapse and it was days before he could face work again. In case after case a boy back on his old factory job can't take the racket of nearby presses crashing down, and he has to be shifted to outside work." (Elmira had no psychiatrist to help such persons, nor were there VA facilities.)

Faced with these and other pressures, unable (or not ready) to find a job, flush with savings and mustering-out pay, many servicemen roamed—three or four friends pooling their resources to buy an old auto and the gas and oil for a leisurely drive to whatever spot on the map struck their attention.

Boredom. Ennui. An end to military regimentation, and the necessity for men to make their own decisions—men in many instances who had gone into the army straight from school with no experience in the adult world. The loss of group identification—first, the status and security of being a member of a specific military unit; next, the rapidly diminished novelty of the "ex-serviceman," who by the end of 1945, in public opinion, had been home long enough not to be considered anyone special.

The 52-20 Club. One benefit for vets was a "readjustment allowance" of up to $20 weekly for fifty-two weeks for men who either were unemployed or earned less than $100 a month. During the four years of its existence, the 52-20 Club had 8,500,000 members who drew $3.7 billion. The vast majority accepted benefits only briefly, while finding jobs and getting back into the economy. But a conspicuous number deliberately loafed away the entire year.

CHAPTER 3

VETERANS—OR CITIZENS?

The 52-20 Club flourished because Americans accept as a matter of faith that men who go to war should be rewarded when they return home. Land grants, cash bonuses, free medical and hospital care, pensions, gratis fishing and hunting licenses, preferential hiring for governmental jobs, streetcar passes, even lifetime movie passes—such is the largess a grateful country has bestowed upon its fighting men after battle.

Fiscal conservatives expressed wariness of locking the country into an open-ended program of cash benefits, fearing that euphoric generosity at war's end would burden future generations. The operative criteria, based upon congressional decisions beginning in 1944, were to give the veterans enough to "catch up" with civilians who had not gone off to war, but to avoid turning the national treasure into a cornucopia that would make former servicemen an overprivileged class.

In the clamor for benefits, the loudest voice of the organized veteran belonged to the American Legion. It boasted 2,000,000 members when the war ended, and a chapter system that made it visible in every American hamlet.

Incentives to join the Legion were many. Often the local Veterans Administration official was a Legionnaire and gave fellow members preferential treatment. The Legion had tight liaison with the VA at all levels, and its Washington office could expedite claims. In small towns, such local powers as the banker, insurance agent, leading merchants, even the police chief and sheriff, were often Legionnaires. For a young veteran, membership was the chance to hobnob with people who could give him a job or approve his loan. In the bone-dry towns of the Bible and corn belts, the Legion hall was the only place in town where a man could buy a bottle of beer and idle away a Saturday afternoon shooting pool. In larger cities, the Legion bar was popular because as a private, non-profit club it undersold competitors and followed loose closing hours. The Legion sponsored dances and picnics and showed movies; veterans (and their families) gravitated to the Legion hall often because the town offered no other social attractions.

Politically, the Legion's consistent demand was that the country "not forget" the veteran once the immediate postwar euphoria subsided and their first concern was the inability of the Veterans Administration to care for thousands of servicemen discharged because of disability. The law provided that they be hospitalized and given compensation. But the VA, a horror house of red tape and inefficiency, could not do its job, and thousands of veterans received neither money nor care for months.

Harry W. Colmery, an attorney from Topeka, Kansas, who had been both Republican national chairman and national commander of the Legion (both in the 1930's), took responsibility for writing specific legislation. When veterans returned to civilian life "they should be given the opportunity to reach that place, position or status which they normally expected to achieve, and probably would have achieved, had their war service not interrupted their careers." Secondly, Colmery thought it "sound national policy" to adopt a benefits program "to see us through the troublous times which [are] ahead of us, by giving stability and hope and faith to the men and women who would return." Veterans should be assured of their benefits before leaving the military. "When the time comes to get out," Colmery said, "most men will sign almost anything, without any thought of the fact or the future." So the bill contained a section to the effect that no predischarge declaration should be held against a veteran if he asked for benefits later.

Yet did the American Legion strike the best deal possible for the veterans it purported to represent? Returning veterans read in the papers of the splendid benefits being readied for them—only to find that in reality not all that much had been changed. And the American Legion, in the legislative infighting on the GI Bill, consistently took conservative positions that worked to the disadvantage of the veteran.

A prime example was housing. One section of the GI Bill provided financing for veterans who wanted to buy or build homes. The real estate lobby (specifically, the National Association of Real Estate Boards and the National Association of Home Builders) liked the concept of the bill, for it was certain to touch off a postwar housing boom. But the real estate people wanted a bill of their own design. A key issue was whether the home-finance section of the bill should be administered by the existing Federal Housing Administration or the VA. The FHA was the logical agency, for it had the staff and experience. The VA would have to create a duplicate bureaucratic apparatus. The real estate interests, however, distrusted the FHA because of its involvement in public housing (an un-pleasant association in their industry) and did not want to give it a toehold in the veterans' program. So the Legion fought alongside the real estate lobby for VA control. Another issue was a proposal in the original version of the GI Bill that the government make housing loans outright for three percent. Again, there was strong business opposition: the real estate in-dustry and its allies (including the Legion) argued for conventional financing through banks and savings and loan associations. As a result, the GI paid higher interest than necessary when he went into the home market.

Despite its defects, the GI Bill did avoid the obvious pitfall of simply paying off servicemen with a lump-sum bonus and leaving them on their own. And, in the long run, the approach of the GI Bill was economical to the nation as well as beneficial to the veteran. The total cost of the World War Two GI Bill, for education and training, was $14.5 billion when it ended July 25, 1956. During its twelve-year existence, 7,800,000 veterans (50 percent of the 15,600,000 eligible) received training: 2,200,000 in insti-tutions of higher learning; nearly 3,500,000 below college level; 1,400,000 on-the-job; and almost 700,000 in institutional on-farm courses.

CHAPTER 4

BOOKS AND BONUSES

In terms of sheer revolutionary impact upon American society, the most important feature of the GI Bill was higher education. Through its financial assistance, the GI Bill brought a college degree to within reach of millions of persons who otherwise would have gone directly into trades or blue-collar jobs. Between 1945 and 1950, according to VA figures, 2,300,000 veterans studied in colleges and universities under the GI Bill. It marked the popularization of higher education in America: after the 1940's, a college degree came to be considered an essential passport for entrance into much of the business and professional world.

America's postwar affluence and emphasis on technology undoubtedly would have boosted college enrollment even if the GI Bill had not existed. But the GI Bill was important because it was tantamount to a forced feeding of the universities: the veterans demanded schooling, and in a hurry, and their very presence jolted academia into a double-time expansion inconceivable to an earlier educational generation. Further, the GI Bill marked the first federal contributions to higher education since the establishment of the land-grant colleges in the late 1800's, a political precedent of no little significance.

Colleges realized even before the war ended that they faced unprecedented enrollments once the servicemen returned home. A War Department survey taken in 1944, before the benefits of the GI Bill were firmly set, showed that at least 8 percent of the 16,000,000 people in uniform intended to enter college. So the universities began to think seriously about what veterans would expect of them. Beginning in 1943, Columbia University sent its former students in the military a periodic "Memorandum from Morningside" to tell them what was happening on their old campus. Near the war's end, 1,200 servicemen were asked what they wanted from Columbia, both as students and as humans. Virtually every man who responded urged that he and fellow veterans be treated exactly like other students. They asked only that recognition be given their age, their varied experience, and their desire to make up for lost time. An officer aboard the USS *Chief,* in the Pacific, reported, "Much as I'd like to, I don't expect to take very much more liberal arts work. By the time I get back to school, I'll be getting on in years, and with several more years of professional study contemplated, the problem of when I'll start earning a living will begin to be a serious one." The officer nonetheless had mixed feelings about suggestions that Columbia accelerate its courses. "Education is too important to me now to be raced through. I want to have the feeling of leisure to do an honest job with the most valuable time of my life." Going to a year-round three-semester plan "would turn college into a factory." But a P-51 pilot was not worried about twelve unbroken months of classes: "I remember how we used to think that a full year would be a tough grind, but it was probably laziness that prompted that feeling."

A condescending tone frequently crept into college bureaucrats' house organs as they discussed what to do with the veteran. As was much else of

America, the educators were prepared to treat the veteran as somewhat of a special animal, and they didn't know quite what to expect of him, or vice versa. "Because the veteran fought our fight," President Paul Klapper of Queens College wrote in *School and Society,* "because the victory he brings is purchased all too frequently at the expense of his health and his integrated personality, ours is the obligation to make him at home in the society he has served." But Klapper warned that universities "must guard against mawkish generosity toward the veteran-student. If he receives a substandard education because of our mistaken kindness, he will become a substandard member of his vocational and cultural group."

The fretting of the academics, however, was beyond the earshot of the veteran student, who saw considerable visible evidence that the colleges were preparing for him. College after college created special programs tailored for the veteran. The University of Nebraska, for example, waived its entrance requirement of a high-school diploma for anyone who could prove his "capability" of doing college-level work; it created one-, two-, and three-year curricula for veterans wanting to rush through specialized courses. North Dakota Agricultural College added a "school of veteran education" to "provide for the returning veteran such training as will prepare him for a pleasant and profitable place in the post-war world." Chancellor Robert M. Hutchins of the University of Chicago worried about "educational hoboes" who would drift into school for lack of anything better to do. Western Reserve University in Cleveland set up a course in small business management for the veteran. At North Carolina State College, the navy closed its diesel engineering school, which had trained hundreds of technicians for sea duty, and the head of the ceramics department returned from service with the War Production Board. The universities were ready for peace.

Late in the war University of Texas sociologists Drs. Harry Moore and Bernice Moore speculated on what the returning veteran would think of the coed: "He will not be staggered if when he returns she has changed not at all; if she has refused to grow up; if she has not kept up with the times; if she has not learned what the war really meant. He expects and needs a *woman* [the sociologists' emphasis] when he returns." But did the coeds fit the veteran's definition of "woman"? And were coeds fresh from home prepared for men three, four, five years older, and experienced in subjects other than warfare? In retrospect, no other aspect of postwar campus life had such long-range insignificance as the debate over boy-girl relationships, an argument waged with windy fury in dormitory bull sessions, the letters columns of campus newspapers, college political campaigns, even in quasi-learned sociological tracts; so intense, in fact, that when the *New York Times* published an article by a veteran comparing American girls unfavorably with Europeans the storm of protesting mail was so immense that the *Times* self-defensively devoted two full pages to the females' rebuttal.

For veterans, a major irritant was the frequently outrageously one-sided male-female ratio. At the University of Texas, an archetypical large state university, the ratio was three males for each woman, a figure that provoked an ominous opinion from a professor of anthropology: "Not even warfare has ever put such a strain on any civilized or primitive society. There have been isolated cases of such a ratio, but it is definitely an artificial phenomenon." John Bryson, writing in a special issue of *The Texas Ranger* devoted to women, commented, "The contrast between ego-inflated young girls, blessed with such a ratio, and the women the veteran met in a realistic outside world has provided a comparison that only invites unpleasantness and hard feelings. The female excuse, 'Look how unhappy we were during the manpower shortage; we have to make up for lost time,' is hardly logical to men who spent their formative years enduring the loneliness of jungles, trenches, and barracks in similar lost time, intensified by the ultimate in suffering."

But where to live, and where to study? Increased enrollments staggered the capacity of colleges to absorb the gush of students. A *School and Society* survey of 450 institutions found increases of up to 580 percent in teachers' colleges; 125 percent in agricultural and engineering colleges; 280 percent in arts and sciences. The surge surprised even the educational bureaucrats: in early 1946 the U.S. Office of Education had estimated that college enrollments would reach 2,000,000 in 1949 and 3,000,000 some five years later. But by November 1946 enrollments were 2,062,000, of whom 1,073,000 were veterans (and 667,000 were women). Further, the demands came after more than a decade of financial starvation for the colleges, whose income dropped precipitously during the Depression and war years because of lower investment income and decreased enrollment and gifts.

So the colleges scrambled. Temple University in Philadelphia bought an old aircraft-parts plant and converted it into classrooms. The state of New York set up a college at a naval training station near Geneva, and enrolled 12,000 students. Colleges and universities in New York City combined to convert barracks at Camp Shanks into housing for 2,400 families, and buses hauled the students to and from classes. The Federal

Public Housing Authority dismantled more than 100,000 housing units built for war workers and transported them, complete with surplus furniture, to campuses. The University of Wisconsin established branches in thirty-four cities to give the first two years of college work; the University of Illinois managed to obtain an old amusement pier in Chicago, used for navy classes during the war, and squeeze in 4,000 students. Wisconsin bedded 1,866 vets in an old munitions plant thirty-five miles from campus, another 1,600 at an airbase.

Student ingenuities were no less active. At the University of Iowa, three students found living space in the basement of a funeral parlor. At the University of Southern California, two men lived in an auto for seven months, studying at night under a street light. At Auburn University in Alabama, two students persuaded a sympathetic Episcopal minister to let them live in the belfry of his church.

Gripe though they did, most student vets philosophically accepted the housing mess as an unpleasant extension of wartime hardship, a discomfort that could be endured because school, unlike war, had a definite completion date. The vets and their families lived in tight camaraderie: in "villages" of house trailers, Quonset huts, plywood houses, and old army barracks that had been hauled to campuses and converted into housing. Many of the dwellings were little more than sparsely furnished housekeeping rooms. At Northern Carolina State, for instance, the majority of couples lived in quarters without cooking facilities. But the vets built a markedly cohesive community.

Consider Monroe Park, an enclave of ninety-five house trailers for vet families at the University of Wisconsin, dubbed the "state's most fertile five acres" because of the high birth rate the year after former servicemen and their wives reunited and settled down to study. (In one week in the spring of 1947 babies were born to five Monroe Park families.) Monroe Park was as tightly organized as an army battalion, albeit on a more convivial basis. It elected a mayor (term: one semester) to serve as liaison with university and town officials. Six "constables" had arrest power but, aside from quieting roisterous Saturday night parties, spent most of their time handling such emergencies as defective oil heaters. The park's cooperative grocery store grossed $5,000 weekly and gave eight vets part-time work; its prices were about 10 percent lower than private stores'. The park sponsored a bowling league, a softball team, semimonthly dances at a community recreation center (with music by radio or jukebox), and classes on sewing, cooking, and child care. The Monroe Park vets skimped. Trailer rent ranged from $25 to $32.50 monthly, including electricity for light and cooking, and oil for heating (but no running water). Estimated expenses for a family with one child were $150 monthly, $60 more than the GI Bill stipend.

Dick Mullan was a freshman at Pennsylvania State College when drafted into the infantry for "three kind of grim years." At age twenty-one, he and his new wife, Peggy, returned to State College, Pa., in 1947 to pursue a degree in biochemistry. They lived briefly in a small upstairs apartment with no stove or refrigerator. "We kept things outside the window to keep them cool, milk and cream for breakfast. We tried to cook on a hot plate, cleaning the dishes in the bathroom sink." Mullan carpooled with neighbors to the campus, three miles distant, often waiting hours in the library for a ride home at night. Peggy had problems getting to and from her job in the graduate school. Hence they felt themselves lucky when a vacancy suddenly developed for an apartment on Beaver Street, State College's main thoroughfare near the campus.

"Our new apartment was really a front porch, right on the main street, with venetian blinds separating us from the outside world. The 'living room' consisted of a desk and a chair. The stove had three gas burners. We had some sort of tin contraption, a Dutch oven, which we put on top of the stove. But we did all sorts of wild things with it. We'd bake cakes and roasts. One time my brother came for dinner and said, 'Peggy, sometimes I think you are going to open that thing and take out a suckling pig!'

"But the bathroom was the real riot. There was no shower, no bathtub. We were never really sure how the landlady expected us to keep clean; I guess she really didn't. Everything in the bathroom was miniature—little tiny john, little tiny sink. The problem was to figure out how to take a bath. I could always go up the street and take showers at the fraternity house. But this really wasn't going to do for Peggy.

"I was down at Sears one day and saw a collapsible bathtub—a camping type of thing, which you opened up like a cot and filled with water, using a pan or a bucket. You had to be careful about scraping or tearing the thing—which we did at the end, anyway—but it worked, sort of. Since we lived right on the main street, if you wanted to take a bath you had to pull the blinds and lock the front door. If anyone came to the door, you quickly said, 'Sorry, I'm taking a bath.'" ("When I got pregnant, it was a real drag," recollected Peggy Mullan. "It was hard enough getting in and out, but there was no way I could fill or empty it, no way.")

"The landlady didn't even know we had the thing until we moved; I don't think she was particularly interested in how we kept clean, if we did.

I really felt we were not too welcome by the town, that the people wanted to exploit us. When we finally left, though, after one and one-half years, we sold it to her at the price we had paid for it, leak and all.

"The bedroom was approximately seven by eight feet, with a double bed six and three-quarters by seven and three-quarters feet. It took up the whole room. You walked in and fell right into bed—the bedroom was really that, a BEDroom." ("You crawled in from the end," Peggy Mullan said. "That got funny when I was pregnant—I needed Dick to pull me in from the foot of the bed.")

"The front porch had no insulation. We'd start a bridge game, and it would get colder and colder and colder; there was no answer but for everyone to go home. Sometimes we'd come in from a weekend outing when the temperature was ten below zero, and there was a big rush to get hot chocolate and crawl into bed and attempt to get warm."

Peggy Mullan was 8 1/2 months pregnant the snowy February day in 1950 when Dick received his degree. ("There was a real baby explosion the last year at State College, when everyone was finishing; most all of our friends were pregnant.") They returned to the apartment and crammed their belongings into a 1938 Plymouth. "The last thing we put in was the broom we used to sweep the snow off the top of the car. We had a drink with a fraternity brother and drove away in ten inches of snow, ready for the world.

"It was one of the best times of our life. We were young. What we had to contend with was more in the pioneer tradition of the country. We survived, and we learned, which was good for all of us."

As inflation pushed the cost of living steadily upward, Congress heard an increasing crescendo of cries by veteran students that they could not survive on GI Bill payments. A conference of veterans, labor, and education officials in January 1947 produced considerable data to support the complaints. The veterans' demands were irresistible: in 1948 Congress kicked up the benefits to $75 monthly for a single vet; $105 for a couple, $120 for a family with a child. Budgets nonetheless remained tight, but the veterans tugged their belts and kept at their studies.

Regardless of their desires to blend into the general student population, veterans did retain a separate identity. Because of their intensity of purpose, the conventional wisdom among college bureaucrats was that they accomplished far more academically than did nonveterans. But the difference was more imagined than real. The Educational Testing Service studied 10,000 veteran and nonveteran students at sixteen colleges during the late 1940's and arrived at the carefully hedged conclusion that among freshmen "there is a tendency for veterans to achieve higher grades in relation to ability than do nonveteran students." But ETS said the "actual magnitude of the difference is small, however. In the most extreme case, the advantage of the veterans would on the average amount to no more than the difference between a C and a C-plus." But for "interrupted veterans" (that is, those who had attended college before military service, and then returned) there was "marked superiority" at four of five large universities studied. ETS also turned up an apparent anomaly: despite their seriousness, the veterans "on the whole . . . attached less importance to college grades and to college graduation than the non-veterans." They attended college to obtain higher-paying jobs, not to prepare for a profession.

The veterans' emphasis on the practical offended many professorial sensitivities. Were the universities destined to be nothing more than academic factories, producing graduates in assembly-line fashion, with the emphasis upon speed rather than quality? Must the popularization of higher education mean also its vulgarization?

But according to S. N. Vinocour, a veteran who taught speech at the University of Nevada, "If pedagogic desks were reversed and the veteran now in college were given the opportunity to grade his professor, he would give him a big red 'F' and rate him as insipid, antiquated and ineffectual." Reporting on a 5,000-mile research tour of campuses in *School and Society* in 1947, Vinocour wrote that many vets feared an economic depression was imminent. Hence they wanted career training rather than theoretical courses. The veteran, Vinocour maintained, did not want to "fritter away his time cramming inconsequential facts, such as learning the names of all the signers of the Declaration of Independence, conjugation of the vulgar Latin verbs, memorizing the date that Shakespeare first said 'Hello' to Ann Hathaway, or how many hours Benjamin Franklin had to stand in the rain with his kite." The veteran felt he entered college as a full-fledged and mature citizen, "not as an adolescent high school graduate eager to participate in the old rah-rah days of Siwash." He considered the collegiate atmosphere "not only very stupid, but a definite hindrance to his acquiring an education." Vinocour argued that the veteran wanted more practical courses (such as radio technique) and "more realistic English courses," rather than the "minor poems of Milton" and "history of oratory." Concluding, Vinocour charged that veterans are "living and studying in a vacuum covered with the moss of the professor's yellow lecture notes."

Such a broadside, of course, could not go unchallenged. *School and Society* bristled with angry rebuttals from professors claiming that the indolent veteran was the major educational problem of the nation. Most of the vets, asserted the correspondents, would be better off in trade schools, not universities; they decried their lack of intellectual curiosity and abhorrence of serious scholarship. So frothful was the debate (or, more accurately, the attack upon Vinocour) that it eventually burst from the pages of *School and Society* into other academic trade journals. One must speculate at the magnitude of the classroom slight that prompted the retaliatory outburst of the venerable Professor Bayard Quincy Morgan, of Stanford University, in the *Pacific Spectator,* a West Coast intellectual quarterly. Morgan scoffed at the complaint about "professors mumbling from notes yellow with age" (a paraphrase of one of Vinocour's laments). He asked, "does that mean to you that the ideas embodied there are *necessarily* flyblown and fit only for the ash can? Must I write a fresh set of lecture notes every year, ignoring everything I said the year before?" Morgan continued: "They want a degree, oh yes, but about as a man buys a railway ticket or secures a passport. . . . [A]nything that doesn't contribute directly and demonstrably to the quickest acquisition of a degree is not only not wanted, it is resented." Veterans wanted "training" rather than "education." Morgan summarized their attitude: " 'Never mind the theory; that takes too long, and we won't understand anyway. What we want is the know-how.' So they demand just enough English to talk to a day laborer; just enough of a foreign language to order a meal or engage a hotel room; just enough mathematics to check the bills and the bank statement."

Beneath Morgan's wrath was a serious criticism of an ominous drift in American higher education. The new generation of students, he said, was resentful of courses that did not provide "results." Confronted with a course outside their narrow professional field, they asked, "What good will it do me?" The veterans, he maintained, were scornful of free discussion of political, economic, and social ideas. Morgan felt he knew why: "The armed forces were always intent on 'getting the job done,' and always in a hurry. They rushed the recruits through 'just enough' of everything, trusting . . . to the exigencies of actual fighting to augment the scanty education of the trainee. It is not surprising if the veteran thinks all education is like that, and expects the college to give him the same kind of training he got in the army or navy." (Critical as Morgan was of the veteran, he said academicians should listen to the complaints, and, "perhaps, with the veteran's help and counsel, improve on our present system.")

Summing up the first full campus year of peacetime, *The Texas Ranger* at the University of Texas noted, "All in all, it was a year of everyone trying to return to normal. Khaki leftovers from the army gradually disappeared from the campus as clothes became available to the new civilians. There was less and less talk about old outfits and more and more discussion of what lies ahead. All in all, it looked like American college life was on the way back."

So, too, was the American economy, but with a mass of problems that far surpassed any troubles faced by the academicians. The question, in essence, was whether business and labor could survive peace.

CHAPTER 5

POPPING THE CONTROLS CORK

Speaking from the White House a few hours after the Japanese surrender, Chester Bowles, the price control chief, happily announced the economy's first small move toward prewar normality. Gasoline rationing was at an end, Bowles said over national radio. "Now you can take your gasoline and fuel oil coupons and paste them in your memory book. Rationing has been lifted, too, on canned fruits and vegetables. It's a pleasure for us at last to be able to bring you good news."

Other announcements were more foreboding. In Philadelphia, the navy declared a two-day holiday for most civilians at the shipyard, not so they could sleep off victory celebrations, but to await word from Washington on the future. The navy had ninety-five ships under construction at Philadelphia and yards elsewhere, including a battleship, two aircraft carriers, and twenty cruisers. Quite obviously these vessels would never sail into battle, but what should be done with their partially completed hulls? Curtiss-Wright, the big aircraft firm, told 150,000 workers in sixteen plants to go home and wait for further instructions. In Seattle and Renton, Washington, skilled metal workers stood in the silent plants of Boeing Aircraft and listened to a company official's voice over the public address system: the air corps wanted 50 B-29s in September, instead of the 122 ordered; 10 rather than 20 in October. The official was sympathetic, but what could he really say? The war had ended, and with it the lush wages and premium overtime pay of defense work. In a single day, Boeing laid off 21,200 of the 29,000 persons employed in the two plants. Within forty-eight hours of peace the army sent manufacturers 60,000 form telegrams cancelling contracts worth $7.3 billion; the air corps, a few days later, kicked the totals to 70,848 contracts valued at $15 billion.

Thus the first impact of peace upon the American economy, a swift braking of an industrial machine that had pushed the gross national product, in dollar-dripping bounds, from $101.4 billion in 1940 to $215.2 billion in 1945. With Washington expecting the Pacific war to continue for another year or more, postwar economic planning was rudimentary. The sudden declaration and the overnight stilling of the factories sent chill tremors through many persons, once the initial relief of peace passed. Was the prosperity of wartime illusionary? With the gushing pump of defense spending halted, would civilian demand keep the economy churning? The frenetic pace of war had pumped average weekly earnings to almost twice their 1940 level—$44.39 versus $24.20, with much of the bulge due to the extra overtime pay in the standard forty-eight-hour week.

"There should be no mincing of words," said John W. Snyder, the Truman Administration's ranking reconversion planner. The end of war spending would cause "an immediate and large dislocation of our economy," with the "severity of this shock . . . increased by the sudden ending of the war." Nonetheless, Snyder made plain the Administration did not intend to "continue the manufacture of useless armaments for as much as one day to cushion the shock."

Some raw statistics show the challenge that peace brought to economic planners. Consider, first, the manpower problem. In August 1945 the civilian labor force was at a historic peak of 53,140,000, and some 12,120,000 persons remained in the armed forces, the bulk of them scheduled for swift mustering out. With the rapid paring of defense work forces, manpower experts somberly forecast that civilian industry could not possibly absorb homecoming soldiers. Before the sudden Japanese collapse, planners had hoped for a "frictional float" of perhaps 2,000,000 jobless persons during reconversion. But the uncertainty of August 1945 pushed the guesses even higher: 8,000,000 jobless, according to the government's stable of economists; anywhere from 10,000,000 to 20,000,000, by organized labor's guess. Labor, it must be noted, wanted tight controls and heavy government spending to cushion reconversion; hence its figure was more scare than science. The National Association of Manufacturers, conversely, which wanted all controls lifted immediately so that "industry can get back to work," pooh-poohed the prospects of massive unemployment.

And the persons who retained their jobs would be demanding more money. Because of rationing and tight price controls, the cost of living remained markedly stable in 1940–45, rising only about 30 percent. When overtime was excluded, however, base pays had been permitted to increase only 15 percent, hence labor was ready for catch-up bargaining once wage controls were lifted.

Another dangerous ingredient, paradoxically, was a cornucopia of spendable wealth that civilians and soldiers had piled up during the war.

For the last two years of the war, citizens socked away about 25 percent of their take-home pay, and by midsummer 1945 their liquid assets totaled an astounding $140 billion in savings accounts and war bonds—three times the entire national income in 1932. Add in the individual incomes of $120-plus billion for 1945, and Americans had a quarter of a trillion dollars to spend during the first year of peace—a mountain of wealth sufficient to make any economist blink. Citizens literally itched to spend their money—for homes, for cars to replace the 1930's clunkers they nursed through the war, for refrigerators and juicy red steaks and nylons and anything else that caught their eye.

Thus the ingredients for a monumental economic tangle: a threatened shaking out of the work force, with high unemployment; an avaricious public hunger for consumer goods, more by far than industry could produce in the predictable future; worker restiveness for higher wages; a gnawing fear that the Depression had only been interrupted, not ended; and the complex task of turning factories back to civilian production. As a complicating factor, peace brought a quickening of the ideological debate over whether government should "quit meddling" with the fortunes of its citizens and businesses, and permit the economy to "return to a free market." Many Americans had accepted economic controls only grudgingly because of the back-to-work aberrations of Depression and war, and a sizeable and outspoken minority still fondled hopes of reversing the New Deal. Conservatives made themselves jittery with a scholarly treatise entitled *The Road to Serfdom,* written just before the war ended by Friedrich A. von Hayek, an Austrian-born economist then living in Great Britain. Hayek, who was to be awarded the 1974 Nobel prize in economics, argued that Nazism and the New Deal shared the same headwaters of national economic planning. Any form of collectivism, be it socialism, communism, liberalism, or Nazism, led inevitably to totalitarianism (i.e., "serfdom").

Government planners' overriding concern as the war ended was what to do about the quaky mountain of cash savings that threatened to crash down upon the economy with avalanche force. By one estimate, Americans had the money to buy three times as much consumer goods as could be produced the first year of peace even if reconversion went smoothly. If free spending is permitted in such circumstances, run-away inflation inevitably results. Chester Bowles, the director of the Office of Price Administration, feared a repetition of the post-World War One situation, when Bernard M. Baruch, in charge of price and production controls, resigned the day after the armistice, saying his job was done. The economy fell with a thud the next winter, and the jobless total reached 8,000,000 before recovery. There were 110,000 business bankruptices and more than 400,000 farmers lost their land; nearly half the inflation took place after the guns stopped firing. In Bowles' estimate, "after World War One, economic fumbling delayed orderly peacetime conversion for more than two years." He called the situation in August 1945 "one of the most dangerous periods in our country's economic history." Bowles was pleased that "we had built a price, wage and rent control dam with surprisingly few leaks." Nonetheless the amount of savings behind that dam was "steadily growing. If the public should become convinced that the dam was about to be removed or to collapse, those savings would inundate the market to bid up prices, and the inflation would quickly get out of hand." The long-range solution was increased production, but it would take months until industry put out enough washing machines, autos, and radios to soak up the surplus purchasing power. The stopgaps of higher taxes and compulsory savings programs appealed to neither Congress nor the Treasury Department. So Bowles asked for continued controls, to help the economy over an expected two-year hump.

Mechanically, controls made much sense. Politically, they proved impossible. Americans endured wartime regimentation of the marketplace in the patriotic spirit of national emergency but now they wanted to shake off the restraining hands of Washington bureaucrats. And the American manufacturer eagerly egged on the protests. Controls ran counter to the American tradition. Full production could be achieved only in a free market: what sane businessman would strain himself producing trousers and bathtubs to be sold at cheap, controlled prices? (The same businessman envisioned all the while hordes of consumers bearing down on his store, war-savings dollars held aloft, eager to pay twice the controlled price for virtually anything on the shelf.)

Cheating the controllers became a boasted-about national pastime, with buyer and seller alike finding gimmicks to put a patina of legitimacy on bribes. Auto dealers would sell only to persons willing to buy odd accessories—a lap robe for $100, or an extra jack for $125, or another battery for $150. A New Yorker who wanted a fifth of Scotch might be required to buy, as well, bottles of rum, gin, and cheap wine. In San Francisco, a man who wanted a bathtub also had to purchase a medicine cabinet, an ironing board, a garage-door handle, and panel molding—and he still paid $8.25 above ceiling price for the bathtub.

Controls—scrap them or keep them?—gave the fledgling Truman Administration its first major political test. Uncomfortable with the newness of its power, the pecking order around the President not yet established, the Administration was already heaving with quiet but vicious jousting matches between FDR holdovers and Truman intimates. Many of the Roosevelt people treated the new President as somewhat of a bumpkin unworthy of the Rooseveltian mantle; their intrinsic loyalty was not to Truman, but to FDR's programs and ideals. The Trumanites, for their part, bridled at the notion that any decision must be prefaced with the question, "What would President Roosevelt have done?" And the divisions were acutely visible in the controls fight, one in which the Truman Administration seemed to be in a contradictory set of positions.

As an "overriding goal" the Administration declared it wished to return to civilian production as rapidly as possible, "vastly expanded over anything this or any other nation has ever seen," with the American people "as *individual customers* [determining] what businessman and farmer are to produce [the government's emphasis]." Yet the Administration was not quite ready for a totally free economy, and its policy guidelines on controls, announced the day the war ended, were wonderously subjective:

Wherever immediate removal of controls will help to get expanded production under way faster, they will be removed.

Wherever the removal of controls at this time would bring a chaotic condition or cause bottlenecks, or produce a disruptive scramble for goods, controls will be kept and used.

But how to draw the line on which controls should be lifted? On this question the President's men divided sharply. As his chief economic adviser Truman relied heavily upon John Snyder, an old National Guard friend who had held minor bank jobs in small-town Arkansas and Missouri before entering the Treasury Department bureaucracy during the New Deal. Snyder spent most of the prewar years in assignments outside Washington, and in many ways he embodied the Midwesterner's abhorrence of government "meddling" in other people's business. Snyder's favored path was containing least resistance; if someone complained loudly enough to be heard, Snyder's reflexive reaction was to yield, thereby relieving the pressure. The subtleties of controls were a concept that Snyder either did not understand or did not accept. "Snyder lacked an overall picture of what planners were trying to do with the economy," said a former associate, "and he was also averse to the idea of controls themselves."

Pitted against Snyder was Chester Bowles, whom President Roosevelt had summoned to Washington early in the war to oversee the price controls program. The energetic Bowles carried impeccable business credentials. A cofounder of the Benton & Bowles advertising agency, a Madison Avenue titan, he had earned his fortune, and he was personally friendly with the men who dominated American commerce. Nonetheless Bowles moved smoothly into the Democratic Administration. Cerebral, articulate, witty, skilled at bureaucratic and political infighting, Bowles felt not at all uncomfortable around government (even if he was a reluctant postwar carryover), and he did not shudder at the thought of Washington exercising power over business. Further, Bowles feared that the hard-won price stability achieved by wartime controls—an accomplishment of considerable personal pride to Bowles—could be washed away overnight. Although he publicly supported the White House's goal of a quick end to controls, Bowles thought they should continue through mid-1947. Bowles enthusiastically promoted the extension of OPA, due to expire New Year's Day 1946 unless Congress said otherwise. And here Bowles came into direct confrontation with yet another, even tougher, set of opponents: the business community and their titular spokesman in Congress, Republican Senator Robert A. Taft of Ohio.

Working through the National Association of Manufacturers and lobbying adjuncts, business laid siege to Washington beginning in the autumn of 1945 in a crusade with the victory-or-else fervor of an ideological war. Warning of a "regimented economy," industrialists and merchants marched by the dozens into the vast Senate Caucus Room, where a tolerably sympathetic Senate Banking Committee clucked over predictions of bankruptcy and ruin.

To Harry Truman the business assault on price controls was part of a broad Republican drive against his presidency. Some in the White House felt the GOP would risk economic chaos and runaway inflation as an acceptable price for discrediting the Democrats and beginning a systematic rollback of the New Deal. Conversely, citizen mail to the President was broadly supportive of continued controls.

But in Congress a working "Republocrat" majority, composed of Republicans and sympathetic southern and other conservative Democrats, had the votes to emasculate OPA. Truman vetoed their bill, and Congress promptly overrode Truman's veto, leaving OPA a powerless hulk.

247

Prices spurted. Sirloin steak went from fifty-five cents to one dollar a pound overnight; butter from eighty cents to a dollar; milk from sixteen cents a quart to twenty. The rent situation was even worse, with increases reported of from 15 to 1,000 percent.

By autumn of 1946 the control system was in near collapse. Meat virtually vanished from America's dinner tables, with farmers and ranchers keeping cattle off the market because of low prices, and stores closing because of lack of supplies. In one week in September 1946 Armour's main Chicago plant slaughtered 68 cattle rather than the average 9,000; two of three butcher shops in New York City were closed.

On the evening of October 14, Truman went on national radio to abandon price controls; he retreated under a covering fire of oratory, charging that a "reckless group of selfish men" in Congress gambled for political advantage on destruction of the controls programs. The people who killed controls, the President said, were the "same bunch which fought every attempt at social reform initiated by the New Deal" and "hated Franklin D. Roosevelt and fought everything he stood for."

The Washington *Times-Herald* saw the end of a political era: "[E]ven Democratic diehards admitted the New Deal concept of government was at an end . . . the planned economy of a past era is dead." So, too, was OPA.

CHAPTER 6

WE WANT MORE!

A month after the war ended, the *CIO News,* organ of the Congress of Industrial Organizations, reported a beguiling "five year study of war profits." Prepared by the United Steel Workers of America, it showed a 113 percent rise in after-tax profits in the steel industry between the five-year periods 1935–39 and 1940–44, from $576 million to $1.225 billion. Assets of the steel companies increased from $4.86 billion at the beginning of 1940 to almost $6 billion at the first of 1945; dividend payments those years amounted to $705 million. But the steel workers union cited these statistics not in praise of corporate efficiency, but as a war cry that set alarm bells to ringing in board rooms across the nation. Philip Murray, president both of the steel workers and the parent CIO, pointed to the billion dollars added to the companies' assets during wartime, and the near three-quarters of a billion paid out to stockholders. "Contrast this with the financial position of America's 475,000 steel workers," Murray said. "In five years of war work, they have accumulated only . . . $285 million in savings, or $600 a worker."

Management understood Murray's implied threat: now free of its no-strike pledge labor intended to fight for what it considered to be a fair share of the war profits hoarded by business. Further, the unions wanted to bring incomes into tolerable balance with the cost of living, essentially by gaining, for the standard forty-hour week, the same take-home pay workers made for forty-eight hours during the war.

Statistically, the unions had a strong case, but from management's viewpoint, the wage situation was considerably more complex. With price controls destined to sputter on indefinitely, the corporations argued they did not have the money for higher pay. The uncertainties of reconversion, the loss of defense contracts, an undefinable fear of the unknown ahead in the postwar years—these and other factors made manufacturers wary of locking themselves into high-pay contracts. Management's willingness to fight the unions led to a wave of strikes that was seemingly endless, with 3,500,000 persons involved in walkouts during 1945, chiefly the last few months.

The big confrontation was two months in the shaping, with the United Auto Workers and General Motors as protagonists. The UAW's choice of GM as a target was both tactical and political. The other industry giant, Ford, had fallen on hard times during the 1930's because of the eccentric conduct of aging founder Henry Ford, and was losing money heavily until the war started. The UAW feared that too vigorous a shove just might push Ford out of existence. GM, conversely, evoked no such cautions, for it had piled up vast wartime profits, much of them possible because of wage curbs. But GM was off balance. It lost $2 billion in defense contracts in a single swipe on V-J Day, and it was sweating and straining to convert its 102 plants to peacetime production, with the battle cry of "from tanks to Cadillacs in two months." To be shut by a strike during reconversion could throw GM behind competitors in the postwar market. Internally, the UAW feared its own very survival was at stake. Some 140,000 of its members went off GM payrolls when the war ended, and the surviving 180,000 found their pay envelopes shrunken by about 25 percent because of the loss of overtime. Hence the UAW had a militancy born of fright. And in Walter Reuther, the UAW's GM department had a leader to give firm voice to that militancy. Reuther was then only thirty-eight years old, a fastidious, slightly built redhead of German-socialist origins, a unionist whose head had been bloodied in organizing Ford workers a decade earlier. He was articulate, visionary, and highly ambitious. Reuther wanted the UAW presidency, and one route into the office was by establishing himself as a more forceful man than the incumbent, R.J. Thomas. So Reuther found his political aspirations in happy juxtaposition with a situation that veritably demanded that he, as a union leader, move vigorously to protect rank-and-file members.

When bargaining began, Reuther asked pay increases of 30 percent; specifically, a base pay of $1.45 hourly, versus the $1.12 then earned by the average GM worker. This would give UAW members $58 weekly, roughly equal to the take-home pay they earned with overtime during the war. After weeks of jockeying and public name-calling with the GM president, Charles Wilson, who decried "the monopolistic power of your [Reuther's] union," the UAW rejected a GM counteroffer of ten cents an hour and voted six-to-one to strike. In December 1945 some 195,000 men walked away from 95 GM plants, and the first big postwar strike was on.

To GM executives Reuther went far beyond the acceptable bounds of collective bargaining. Reuther's linkage of pay increases to GM's supposed "ability to pay" and his demand that GM's books be opened to an arbitration panel were ideas anathema to industry.

But in the end, happenings elsewhere cut the ground from beneath Reuther and UAW. In January 1946 panic rushed through the Truman Administration as industry after industry fell idle to strikes: the steel mills; the meat packing houses; the electrical equipment factories. Three key industries, with more than 1,600,000 workers, *plus* the 175,000 auto workers, plus dozens of smaller unions were idled. Truman realized normal bargaining techniques were not enough. So he intervened with fact-finding panels in the auto and steel disputes. In recommendations issued in the same January week, the panels made parallel findings, as follows: the cost of living had jumped about 33 percent since before the war, while the wartime wage freeze had limited pay increases to around 15 percent for the average industrial worker. Allowing for regional variances in the cost of living, and "circumstances peculiar to particular industries," the panels called for wage increases to a level 33 percent above that of January 1941. For the auto industry, the recommended increase was 19½ cents an hour; for steel, 18½ cents. But there was a major difference. The auto pay jump would not be coupled with an increase in car prices, whereas the steel panel recommended a $5 per ton increase in steel prices, which the Administration announced it would support. United States Steel, titular leader of the industry, at first refused to accept the panel's terms, with President Benjamin Fairless demanding a $6.25 per ton price increase. Whereupon labor heard support from some unexpected voices: *Life* magazine said editorially, "Mr. Fairless should pay 18½ cents; right or wrong, the President picked it, and we've got to get on with the job." Fairless and steel settled, and workers' pay went up an average $32 monthly, the largest single raise in the history of the industry. GM, however, would not be pressured. It refused to follow the "unsound principle" that a rich company should pay higher wages than a less profitable one (i.e., Ford) and offered the UAW 18½ cents on a "take it or leave it" basis.

Reuther suddenly found himself an isolated labor leader. His own rank and file bickered over continuing a "penny an hour strike," especially when other unions accepted the 18½-cent increase. Internal CIO politics were also involved: Reuther simultaneously jousted with a Communist faction in the UAW and with Philip Murray, president of both the CIO and the United Steel Workers, and a man deeply suspicious of his younger rival. Rightly or wrongly, Reuther felt the Communists and Murray would toss the GM strikers overboard for their own ends. The White House put the final squeeze on Reuther, refusing to reenter the negotiations and urging that he settle for 18½ cents. In March, after 113 days of bargaining, the UAW broke and signed while insisting, for purposes of face, that improved seniority provisions and a dues checkoff system were worth an extra penny. Within the next four months the government permitted GM and the other auto makers no less than three rounds of price increases. "The plain fact," commented *Time,* "was that the people everywhere, not caring much who got what, sensing that both higher wages and higher prices were in the air, wanted labor and industry to get back into production on almost any terms."

A few months after Harry Truman became President, labor specialist Louis Stark wrote that "organized labor had taken [his measure] . . . and found it to be friendly and disposed to be reasonable." But his differences with labor soon escalated—first with the railroads and then during his showdown with the bristly-browed John L. Lewis, of whom even a friendly biographer wrote in 1949, "No man in our history has been so hated for so long a period." To Americans of the 1930's and the 1940's, Lewis' coal strikes were as much an annual ritual as the first sighting of the ground hog, or a President throwing out the first baseball of the season. A forbidding, hulking man who glowered at the world between strands of tousled gray hair, Lewis made a theatrical production of each sentence, and his seemingly impromptu insults left the tarnish of public ridicule on several generations of prominent persons.

In the 1940's Lewis was the renegade of organized labor, his mine workers out of the CIO (which he was instrumental in organizing) because of his refusal to join its support of Roosevelt's third term in 1940, his feud with the AFL leadership so virulent that some members of its hierarchy feared him physically. But Lewis' power was real: he was callous and brutal to the public, but his miners revered him as a flesh-and-blood saint; in the homes of many miners, two pictures were on display: one of the Virgin Mary, the other of John L. Lewis. Further, America needed the coal these men produced. Coal heated more than half the houses in the country. Coal powered 95 percent of the nation's locomotives; coal fired steel furnaces and provided the thermal-electric power for most of American industry. Although press, public, and government hostility built against the miners, the auto and steel industrialists would counterpressure the coal operators to accede to the union's demands so that "their own fabulous profits will not be interrupted."

Perhaps prophetically, the second major news story in the United States the day Harry Truman succeeded to the presidency involved John L. Lewis: his grudging acceptance of a coal contract that temporarily put his miners back to work. He took his men out twice again before the year ended and then in April 1946, just as the nation was recovering from the auto and steel strikes, Lewis called yet another strike. This time the issue was a demand that a miners' welfare fund be financed by royalties on each ton of coal produced. As coal stockpiles dwindled that dreary spring, the government ordered dimouts of twenty-two eastern states; railroads laid off 51,000 men, the struggling Ford Motor Company another 110,000; New Jersey declared itself in a "state of emergency." But just as a general economic collapse seemed imminent, Lewis sent his miners back to work in a two-week truce—a tactic typical of the cunning Lewis, dancing away just as an infuriated nation prepared for drastc retaliation. Only Lewis didn't jump quite fast enough: when further negotiations stalled, Truman ordered Julius A. Krug, the secretary of the interior, to seize the mines. "Let Truman dig coal with his bayonets," jeered Lewis, and the miners ignored Krug's order that they return to work. The government capitulated in nine days, and Lewis got his welfare and retirement fund, financed by a five-cent levy on every ton of coal mined.

Lewis wasn't satisfied. In the fall he demanded that Krug reopen the negotiations and increase both vacation pay and contributions to the welfare plan. Rebuffed, he ordered another strike.

Truman saw the case as something much greater than a quarrel over wages, hours, and working conditions. He believed the sovereignty of the United States government was at stake, since the Interior Department still controlled the mines. Truman got a court order restraining Lewis and the UMWA from breaking the contract provision against strikes. The U.S. courts were an institution that Lewis could defy at his own peril.

U.S. District Court Judge T. Alan Goldsborough granted the injunction, and tossed Lewis completely off balance: the legalities of his walkout were to be resolved, not by political dictates, but in a court of law. And Lewis didn't like the prospects. When he came to court for sentencing, on December 4, according to one observer, his eyes were sunken, his skin flappy, his mop of hair gray, dry, and scraggly.

Lewis listened to Goldsborough's summation in fidgeting silence. "This is not the act of a low law-breaker," Goldsborough said, "but it is an evil, demoniac, monstrous thing that means hunger and cold and unemployment and destitution and disorganization of the social fabric. . . . It is proper for me to say . . . that if actions of this kind can be successfully persisted in, the government will be overthrown." He fined the UMWA the requested $3,500,000 (of a treasury of $13,500,000). Lewis ordered his miners back to work, his reigning days over. The next spring the U.S. Supreme Court reduced the fine to $700,000.

"Well, John L. had to fold up," Truman matter-of-factly wrote his mother. "He couldn't take the gaff. No bully can."

While the strife in big industrial centers commanded national headlines and presidential attention, quiet, most intense struggles disrupted old patterns in the backwaters of American labor—among unskilled and farm workers in the South. War industries siphoned hundreds of thousands of these persons out of low-pay areas. Once exposed to city life and shipyard and aircraft-factory wages, they were never quite the same again. To the South, especially, a major shock of peacetime was that the dirty work of agriculture and commerce no longer would be performed for pennies. The situation flabbergasted the South; and its business establishment spent many postwar months trying to convince the populace (and itself, for that matter) that the high wages of war were a transient phenomenon best forgotten by all concerned, and as rapidly as possible. The people who ran the South anguishedly cried out for a return of the remembered old days, when everyone knew his place—in the economy and elsewhere—and did not measure local wages against the benchmark of a shipyard in Pascagoula or an oil refinery in Houston. "Cotton Pickers, Where Are You?" pleaded the Memphis *Press Scimitar*. Mrs. Clara Kitts, director of the Memphis office of the United States Employment Service (USES), found it peculiar that farmers were "begging for pickers" even though they paid $2.10 per hundred pounds in Mississippi and $2.05

in Arkansas. "A good picker can average 300 to 400 pounds a day," Mrs. Kitts said. "A whole family picking can bring home lots of money. The weather has been warm and beautiful. There are lots of people idle. But still nobody comes out to pick. I don't understand why." In prewar days, she said, the office dispatched 16,000 pickers daily. Now only 3,000 could be found. Nor were men interested in working for sixty cents to $1 an hour in the citrus groves around Bradenton, Florida, a situation the local *Herald* could not understand: "They prefer to idle and spend their wartime savings. . . . [A] good many men now idle would be earning good wages right along if they could be persuaded that it is a more sensible thing to be in gainful occupation at reasonable pay than to indulge in a foolish hope that wartime wages and jobs are coming back and that one is warranted to wait for the return." In Jacksonville, Florida, where job seekers wanted "double the pay offered by industry," George Main, the local USES officer, commented, "The principal conversion problem in Jacksonville is the reconversion of our minds to current conditions."

Nor on the whole were black women eager to return to prewar conditions. The Associated Press, in a survey of southern cities in the fall of 1945, reported that "negro [sic] maids and cooks and yardmen aren't beating paths back to their old jobs." Persons who made ninety cents an hour or more in defense jobs preferred to "take the claim" (i.e., for unemployment compensation). Although one USES official expressed optimism about a "gradual return to their old jobs," the AP concluded that "very few people expect to see a return of the days when there was a cook in every kitchen in the south—when negro servants were paid as little as $3 a week for long hours." In Orlando, Florida, matrons found maids demanding fifty cents an hour, whereas prewar servants worked from 8 A.M. to 7 P.M., six days a week, for $4 to $7 (or 9 A.M. to 2 P.M. for $3). In West Palm Beach and Miami, a domestic wouldn't consider less than $25 weekly. In Manhattan cooks demanded $250 monthly, butlers $150 to $225.

Conservative southern editorialists fumed about the "free-loaders" and "parasites" who took unemployment pay rather than slipping back into their prewar jobs (at prewar pay, in many instances). The *Lakeland* (Florida) *Ledger* complained about southern blacks ("and some whites") who went north to "the defense plant employment and cosmopolitan living of centers like Detroit or Chicago, found contentment there, and have not come back." But the *Ledger* was confident that nature eventually would side with the citrus growers: "For one thing, colder weather will chase some of the hesitating blacks and whites southward to work. . . . Some [blacks] said in a kind of whisper that northern unions are discouraging southward migration of negro labor so as to tighten the shortage here." In Marion, South Carolina, the *Star* felt that cutting off unemployment pay would help speed the "loafers" back to work: "It will do the culls good to suffer for a short while and it will give them time to think it over and get off their high horse. Then when they realize who they are and why they are—that we are members of a society that lives by the sweat of its brow— then the period of transition will gradually begin to progress into a state of normality." The *State,* of Columbia, South Carolina, wished the jobless would go away. "Instead of scurrying home after losing their jobs in defense plants, thousands of the people are still hanging around the town for better jobs than they left and showing no disposition to return home until their unemployment pegs out. Perhaps six months hence when the free hand-outs have been spent, few jobs might be going begging."

Many southern states heatedly resisted paying unemployment compensation to persons unwilling to work for prewar wages. In Georgia, the State Department of Labor held that anyone refusing such a job was unemployed by choice, and hence ineligible for benefits. It cited a woman who refused a job paying $2.50 a day plus meals and tips. "This job would have paid her much more than she had made on any job before the war. Before going into war work as a riveter for 85¢ an hour she had worked for a laundry for $12 per week and as cashier in a filling station at from 30¢ to 35¢ an hour." In Tennessee, Commissioner W.O. Hake of the Tennesse Labor Department sent letters to unions and employers asking to identify persons drawing benefits to whom they had offered jobs. Unions replied that Hake was attempting to "induce employees to establish a state-wide spy system." Some of the jobs deemed "suitable" by Hake, the union said, paid the "miserably low wage" of $16 weekly, only $1 more than the unemployment benefit.

So adamant was employer resistance to higher wages, so intent the determination to bludgeon workers back to prewar conditions, that several industries even appealed to the War Department that German prisoners of war be kept in the United States for extra months past peace so that they continue in their assigned jobs. The pulp and paper manufacturers of Florida wanted a thousand POWs; so did citrus growers around the big POW camp at Winter Haven; so did the cotton barons of Virginia. The Pentagon refused, citing a policy of shipping the POWs home as rapidly as possible, and thereby denying the employers a pool of dirt-cheap labor.

For returning vets the pay disillusionment was especially jolting. For months these men had heard—and believed—the barracks gossip about the big money earned by war workers. Now they were home to share the new prosperity and could not seem to find it. So the restless vets skipped from job to job, unable to decide in advance whether they would really enjoy the work—many with no specific goal in mind other than the first paycheck, their gut-confidence shored by the knowledge that a 52–20 Club stipend was always there for the asking, resistant to menial jobs and often reluctant to return to their prewar employer. (Big New York companies, for instance, reported a scarcity of office boys—sixty to sixty-five cents an hour—in the immediate postwar months.) But the veterans found that the high war wages had melted away. A USES official in Florida, calling the GIs "disillusioned and disappointed," commented, "It's a terrible letdown for the veteran when he finds out what kinds of wages are actually being paid." One vet told the New York *Sun:* "One problem is that we got so used to bragging and lying to one another about the super jobs we were going to find after peace that we lost touch with reality. You heard more big yarns and dreams about the money you made than on almost any subject except women." What career could there be for a twenty-one-year-old fighter pilot who had earned $400 monthly during the war—but who had no college training and whose practical experience consisted of shooting down other people's airplanes? *National Aeronautics Magazine,* after study of the potential job market in late 1945, suggested that most of the 3,000,000 men and women in military aviation should forget about flying as a peacetime avocation, even though a survey indicated perhaps half of them wished to continue. "The peacetime aviation is governed, not by the law of national necessity, which justified the greatest expenditures in history, but by the law of economics, which decrees that an airplane or an air service must show some signs of paying for itself. . . . Aviation probably will be no more remunerative than the washing-machine business."

CHAPTER 7

MOVING ON

T he ending of the Second World War found the United States facing a "housing shortage of unparalleled magnitude," in the words of a government study. The Depression had staggered the home-building industry. New starts dropped to 93,000 in 1933, from a peak of 937,000 in 1926, and recovery was barely underway when the war sent construction into yet another tailspin.

The young veteran felt the shortage more keenly than any other group, for he was the person whose prewar home had been with his family or in an apartment. Now married and eager to form his own household, he found "no vacancy" signs plastered everywhere he looked. By October 1945, when only 3,000,000 persons had been demobilized, and another 11,000 000 awaited discharge, the government estimated that 1,200,000 families already lived "doubled up."

Veterans tried to joke about their situation, but the humor bore the frantic hollowness of desperation. A couple wanted to rent the bedroom set on the stage of a Broadway theater for use during nonperformance hours. Another couple actually moved into the display window of a Manhattan department store for two days, until sympathetic publicity brought them an apartment. Bill Mauldin's Willie and Joe, the doughboy characters of wartime, now "reconverting" along with everyone else, moved into a barn, where they told the inquiring farmer who came out with a shotgun and lantern, "If ya want character references, Mister, write to Signor Pasticelli, Venafro, Italy. We occupied his barn for seven weeks." In Chicago, GIs and families filled garages, coal sheds, and cellars; in San Francisco, vets "lived" in autos parked on city streets, using the restrooms in the public library and cooking over wood fires in the park. Chicago put 250 streetcars on sale for conversion into "homes."

The emotional volatility of the housing crisis was not lost on the White House. One poignant letter among thousands received was from a Los Angeles man who wrote President Truman:

Tonight coming home I met a first class medical sergeant and his wife. She was crying. She had a little boy on her lap. I said, "Sergeant, what's the matter?" and he said, "I've no place to go tonight and my wife is having another baby." I have them with me tonight.

The man expressed confidence in Truman's ability, but urged, "Do *something.*"

The Truman Administration tried a multipronged solution. Truman sought to continue rent controls for as long as possible, to prevent landlords from gouging tenants in the scarce market. "You can't turn the chiselers loose," he wrote a friend, John B. Pew, a Kansas City lawyer. If rent controls ended he feared "it will make the Florida boom look like a Sunday school picnic. . . . Naturally the landlords and real estate owners want to see the boom because they all figure that they can get out without being hurt—that simply can't be done." Truman directed that materials be channeled into construction of medium-income houses, rather than nonessential buildings such as restaurants and shopping centers. This order, in April 1946, halted an estimated $14 billion of construction in the blueprint stage, bringing an angry editorial grump from the *Wall Street Journal*: "The drastic order, if tightly enforced, will halt what is potentially the largest nonresidential building spree in history." And Truman tried to devise a program that would push the construction industry into mass production of houses that low- and middle-income families could afford, rather than concentrating on luxury homes.

But Truman recognized the practical problems. When an old friend, Bernard F. Hickman, the postmaster in St. Louis, complained about slow progress, the President replied in a personal note, "You must remember that there isn't any possible way of waving a wand and getting houses to spring up. For four years we have concentrated on the war effort and it will take time to get the necessary houses constructed. . . . The construction industry is disorganized—there are more strikes in the building trades than in all the other industries combined. . . . Making speeches and blaming somebody for something which can't be helped is not going to help the shortage."

But each initiative the Truman Administration attempted encountered vehement opposition. Builders claimed that inflation, both of wages and material costs, made it impossible for them to construct the low-cost housing demanded by veterans. By one 1946 survey, three-fourths of the persons searching for houses could pay no more than $50 a month, limiting them to houses costing $6,000 or less; only 6.8 percent could afford to pay $75 or more a month. Yet builders claimed they could not build a $6,000 house that anyone would want. Contractor Clarke Daniel in 1945 duplicated three two-bedroom houses he had put up before the war in suburban Prince Georges County, Maryland. The 1941 versions cost $6,230; the 1945 ones, $9,919, an increase of 59 percent. Daniel complained that although he paid laborers ninety cents an hour, rather than the prewar sixty cents, "they do only about two-thirds the work; they are very inefficient." Builders elsewhere reported similar escalations.

But even as they complained that economics prevented them from satisfying the low- and middle-income markets, the builders vigorously opposed any federal programs to encourage cheap housing. The industry, through its powerful Washington lobby, the National Association of Home Builders and the National Association of Real Estate Boards (NAHB and NAREB), fought any direct government role in housing, other than guaranteeing loans for housing units costing $10,000 and more. The NAHB argued that any government move to undercut interest rates of conventional lenders (banks and savings and loan associations) to spur low-cost homes would "lead to socialized housing." Even in the emergency months just after the war ended, when veterans slept on relatives' couches and begged for cold-water tenements, the NAHB scorned moves to give them temporary lodging in unused military barracks. Indeed, the thrust of the industry argument was that the problem was not so much a *shortage* of housing as it was an *oversupply* of people with the money to pay for decent places to live, an exercise in logic that many persons in official Washington and elsewhere found difficult to understand. For instance, the National Association of Apartment Owners, at its 1947 convention in Cleveland, complained that "stenographers and clerks" were earning so much money they lived alone in apartments that previously housed four or more persons, a situation possible because of rent controls. The association's president, John E. Owens, said that in Los Angeles alone the removal of controls would enable apartments to absorb 80,000 more tenants. "There are simply too many people occupying space they don't need," Owens said. "A rent increase would take care of a lot of that." (But a more objective observer could find evidence the problem went deeper than controls. In early 1946 the Des Moines *Register & Tribune,* cross-checking local realtors' claims that the housing crisis had passed there and controls could be removed, published an advertisement offering a nonexistent apartment for rent. During the next three days 351 callers asked for it. Of these, 56 told a reporter they lived in hotels or sleeping rooms, 68 with parents, 14 planned to be married, 137 "wanted something better.")

The salvation proved to be the GI Bill, with its guarantee of low-cost loans for veterans. From the program's inception in late 1944 through the end of 1947, some 1,056,771 veterans received home loans. The average GI house cost $7,300, although four of ten sold for more than $8,000, and one in twenty for more than $12,000.

The mass market opened by the low-cost loans ultimately was satisfied by a revolution in housing construction with several interrelated ingredients: standardization, the automobile, and the willingness of harassed buyers to pay for homes that an earlier generation would have scorned as junk.

Standardization resulted from an eagerness of builders to follow designs that could be erected swiftly by someone other than skilled carpenters, who, although they did good work, also demanded union wages. The most visible result was the proliferation of the so-called Cape Cod house in the immediate postwar years, not so much by buyer preference as by builder dictate. "Postwar homes," the *American Builder* said in 1945, "have to be designed for the greatest possible economy. This demands straight lines without many breaks in the foundation and roof. It means the elimination of dormers, almost to extinction." It meant "the almost unbroken foundation lines of the true Cape Cod, and the simplicity of framing . . . with which most carpenters are familiar."

Appliance manufacturers urged on the trend to standardization. In July 1945 the American Gas Association persuaded the entire appliance industry to agree upon standard sizes for both kitchen cabinets and appliances, maintaining that a streamlined kitchen should not belong exclusively to the housewife who could afford custom workmanship. Working space would be thirty-six inches above the floor. To prevent toe stubbing, cabinets, stoves, and other fixtures would have a "toe cove" three inches deep and four inches high. Counter tops could extend 25¼ inches from the wall, allowing half an inch overhang from the cabinet base. The agreement was perhaps the most significant thing to happen to the kitchen since the invention of the gas stove, in terms of aesthetics, convenience, and economy. Unsightly gaps and bumps between cabinet units and appliances would be no longer; new items could be bought without throwing the entire kitchen out of kilter. For the builder, standardization meant easier construction: manufacturers soon supplied packaged kitchen units that could be melded together, cabinet with sink with stove, with the ease of a child stacking toy blocks. The standard package concept spread to other parts of the house as well. For instance, in 1947 the Borg-Warner Corporation displayed what it called a "core unit" for heating, plumbing, and electrical facilities—essentially a console affair containing the central heating plant and the main terminals for the household plumbing and electrical outlets, compact enough to be rolled into the house by a single workman, at a considerable saving in both space and installation costs.

During the war years many builders gained experience in hurry-up production techniques when called upon to erect housing for defense workers. One such contractor, and a man whose name became synonymous with "post-war development builder," was William J. Levitt, who built nearly 2,500 units during the eighteen months after Pearl Harbor in the Norfolk, Virginia, area. Levitt then joined the navy and served the remainder of the war in the Pacific. Returning home at age thirty-nine, he sensed several things that were about to happen to America.

So Levitt and his father, Abraham, and brother, Alfred, bought hundreds of acres of potato fields on Long Island, scoured the country for scarce building materials, and set out to construct a 1,000-home new town. The supplies came into a railhead near his building site, and a "factory" rapidly assembled such standard components as interior partitions, roof trusses, and door and window units. Levitt split his work force into crews: one group built foundation forms down one side of the street, crossed over, and came back down the other side, followed by another crew pouring concrete that had been mixed in a central plant; next would come carpenters to erect the framework—crew after crew, each performing a specialized job, and then hurrying to the next house in line. Levitt used nonunion workers; thus his painters could work with sprayguns, rather than the archaic handbrush, for an estimated time saving of 60 percent. The unions, although unhappy, never succeeded in organizing Levitt. By the end of 1946, his first homes nearing completion, Levitt advertised in New York newspapers:

IT'S MISTER KILROY NOW . . . FOR $70 A MONTH.

By the hundreds the home-hungry veterans drove out to Long Island and listened to salesmen recite Levitt's offer: $1,000 down, $70 monthly, for a three-bedroom house with a log-burning fireplace, a gas range, venetian blinds, a gas heater, and a landscaped lot of 75 by 100 feet, all for a total price of $9,990.

Levitt's idea stood the test of the marketplace. He continued cutting costs (by cutting "frills" from the house, and refining his building procedure). In 1947 he gave the name Levittown to another thousand farm acres near Hempstead, Long Island, built 150 homes weekly, and sold them for $6,900—a 25-by-30-foot two-bedroom bungalow, to be sure, and austere, but the veterans bought them. Levitt had an eye for savings. He provided a "full basement," but an unfinished one; if the buyer wanted a recreation room, or a work room, he built it himself. The "third" bedroom in the fancier models did not have a closet; instead, Levitt stuck a metal cabinet behind the door, and told buyers this gave them "more usable space." There were differences in the exterior trim, in the colors, in the spacing of shutters and windows, in the setbacks from the street; yet anyone who looked closely could detect that there wasn't really all that much difference in the four basic Levitt houses. Levitt used asphalt tile for the floors, even in the living room and dining area (*area*, not room), and explained that the traditional hardwood floor was not available because of shortages. By 1949 more than 4,000 persons annually were buying Levitt homes, and he enjoyed a reputation as the "Henry Ford of the postwar builders."

Builders elsewhere used variations of the Levitt technique. In Dallas, for instance, Angus W. Wynne, Jr., produced a finished house in twenty days in his 2,200-home Wynnewood development. Developers of Oak Meadows, a low-priced development near Oak Lawn, Illinois, a Chicago suburb, used an overhead conveyor belt to haul fabricated sections from a central workshop to home sites, and they built 1,200 units in slightly more than a year. Traditional carpentry vanished: workmen used glue and automatic nailing guns to bind precut panels to precut frames, and the expectation of a six-man crew was to erect the frame and roof trusses of two houses daily.

The psychic toll and social costs of the jerry-built developments were another matter. The developments lacked a focus for community interest. Many did not have a single store, park, even a neighborhood school. Thus residents fell back upon one another to break the tedium of the day, with devastating effect. Howard Mendelson, of the American University Bureau of Social Research, concluded, "In these communities, there is no real privacy. The women become involved in one another's emotional problems. And, unless they take part in community activities, they are apt to be shunned and lead incredibly lonely lives, surrounded by the endless monotony of the development itself and trying to cope with the monotony of their children and housework. Their husbands may drive off to the city each day, but for the women, there is no escape. It's often a tough life for them." For surcease the women turned to television and the mass-market magazines—which, in turn, led to further emotional and intellectual inbreeding, because everyone else in the development watched and read the same things. Dr. Leonard J. Duhl, a staff psychiatrist for the National Institute of Mental Health, foresaw a long-range effect on children raised in a matriarchal society, knowing fathers only as "nighttime residents and weekend guests." Duhl wrote that the suburbs, with their one-class conformity, denied the child the chance to "try out new ideas, feelings and himself . . . to see what fits."

There was another drawback as well. Many veterans went into the quickie developments with the intention of moving on to more traditional housing as soon as it became available or affordable. Prewar Americans bought houses with the intention of living in them for a lifetime; in the 1940's, however, and thereafter, people thought of a house as they did an automobile: use it until the new wears off, or you see something better. John Keats, the social critic, wrote bitingly of what happened to the mass suburban developments once the first generation of veterans began moving elsewhere. "Secondhand development houses were sold to the kind of people who buy secondhand automobiles solely out of need. People, in other words, less financially responsible; less able to give the same degree of care to the house than the original veteran-purchaser gave to it."

In sum, the cheap developments gave the veterans—and other Americans—*houses*; all too frequently, however, they did not provide *homes*. And a vague unease was noted by sociologists and other students of the public: the American was discovering that all too often his "home" turned out to be the same overadvertised, overpriced, under-quality junk as did his car. Thus did his dream of a better postwar world slip a bit further toward disappointment.

CHAPTER 8

AFTERNOONS OF SOAP AND HOPE

Cultural historians are of a single mind about American diversions once peace returned. Americans opted for frivolity in literature and in film; they sang nonsense lyrics ("Bongo bongo bongo, I don't wanna' leave the Congo, I refuse to go. . . ."); they enjoyed bizarre national fads.

Crazes sputtered unpredictably across the land. In the winter of 1948-49, serious adults began forming "pyramid friendship clubs." To avoid postal strictures against chain-letter schemes, members met personally to exchange money. With local variations, the schemes worked as follows: at his first party, a new member handed over $4 and became one of many "number 12's" at the base of the pyramid. To the next meeting he brought two new members, each with $4. Subsequently, as new members multiplied and formed pyramids behind him, he was pushed toward the peak. On the twelfth night, if things went well, he received $4,096 for his original $4 investment. According to the newspapers, people won anywhere from $800 to $1,500, the jackpot depending upon the size of the opening ante. In a Los Angeles suburb a crowd cheered a judge who ruled the clubs violated no laws. By March 1949, when the craze reached New York, the first payment in some clubs soared to $5, with a possible payoff of $10,240; reporters chased rumors of a Wall Street club with a $100 ante and a payoff of $204,800. The clubs defied reason and mathematical tables. By one computation, 16,777,216 players would be required to keep a club going for 25 days. But no one listened to the warnings. Suddenly, in the spring of 1949, the clubs vanished overnight. Their replacements, at the teen-age level, included "slam books," in which New

Orleans schoolgirls exchanged brutally frank comments on friends; and "scratching," an automotive sport in which Atlanta youngsters put their fathers' cars in reverse, roared backward in a tight circle, then slammed into low gear and sped forward, at unestimated cost to gears and nerves of adult bystanders.

Radio proved the medium that struck a happy common denominator with the entire country. Radio had cemented itself in national popularity for years—as a curiosity during the 1920's; as the poor man's theater during the Depression; as a messenger with the voice of immediacy during the war. By 1947, 34.8 million of the 38.5 million households in the country had at least one radio receiver; there were 8.5 million in use in automobiles; and another 21.6 million in stores, hotels, and institutions.

What Americans heard fell into three broad daily cycles: beginning in midmorning, housewives could follow a most unique aural-literary form known as the soap opera—Balzacian tales of domestic tragedy, unrequited love, and medical curiosa. At three o'clock or thereabouts the programming switched abruptly to the juvenile serials—improbably high adventure and derring-do in which justice prevailed and girl-boy relationships were most platonic. Finally, during the dinner hour, radio reached out for every ear in the family with situation comedies, quiz shows, and music. According to polling data, the average American listened to radio about fourteen hours weekly.

The soap operas stood as an industry unto themselves, a merchandising dynamo that generated about 60 percent of advertising revenues for the four major networks, and sold more boxes of washing powder, more bathtubs of suds, more varieties of feminine gimmickry, than anyone ever bothered to count. Procter & Gamble alone spent $14.9 million in 1946 for the soap dramas "Road of Life," "Right to Happiness," "Life Can Be Beautiful," and "Ma Perkins." The "soaps," as they were known, existed for the sole purpose of making money, and money they indeed made. In the words of Mary Jane Higby, for eighteen years the star of "When a Girl Marries," soap opera "may well have been the lowest point ever reached by dramatic art . . . but dollar for dollar, it may well have been the greatest value the advertiser ever got for his money."

The brain trust of the soaps was the husband-and-wife team of Frank and Ann Hummert, veterans of Chicago advertising, who first experimented in the genre in the early 1930's with a serial entitled "Just Plain Bill," about a Midwest barber who "married out of his station." A folksy, decent chap, Bill endured condescending relatives and spent more time trying to solve other people's problems than he did cutting hair. Bill wasn't always successful, either, and seldom did his episodes have the heart-warming happy endings of conventional pulp fiction. Housewives worried about the Depression could empathize with poor old Bill, and his vast audience convinced the Hummerts that emotional voyeurism was a marketable commodity. They formed a production agency in New York that was a veritable factory for daytime radio "drama," producing fodder that by the end of the war filled about one-eighth of network air time.

The serials opened with distinctive theme music, Pavlovian in intention, to alert the housewife to put her radio alongside the ironing or sewing she could do as she listened to the daily installment. Usually a Hammond organ provided the overture, for its cathedral solemnity implied the program was serious business, not sheer frivolity. But there were other instruments as well. "Helen Trent" opened to the strains of a ukulele, "Just Plain Bill" to a plaintive mouth organ, "Mary Marlin" to a tinkly piano rendition of Debussy's *Clair de Lune*. The overture was invariably followed by a brief recap of the continuing story line—words that faithful listeners could recite along with the announcer:

And now—"Our Gal Sunday"—the story of an orphan girl named Sunday, from the little mining town of Silver Creek, Colorado, who in young womanhood married England's richest, most handsome lord, Lord Henry Brinthrope. The story that asks the question, Can this girl from a mining town in the West find happiness as the wife of a wealthy and titled Englishman?

"The Romance of Helen Trent"—the story of a woman who sets out to prove what so many other women long to prove in their own lives, that romance can live on at thirty-five and even beyond.

We give you now—"Stella Dallas"—a continuation on the air of a true-to-life story of mother love and sacrifice, in which Stella Dallas saw her beloved daughter, Laurel, marry into wealth and society and, realizing the difference in their taste and worlds, went out of Laurel's life.

Then the story bowed to the first commercial: laundry flakes ("Rinso White, Rinso White, happy little wash day song . . ."), or toothpaste, or bleach. This interruption, plus another commercial break at midpoint of the program and the close-out echo, left only eight minutes for the writer to remind the audience of what had happened yesterday; to make perceptible progress in the plot; and to contrive an ending suspenseful enough to entice people to "tune in again tomorrow, same time, same place on your dial, for another thrilling episode in the . . ."

Writers added dramatic girth to the soaps by lacing the basic story lines with subplots. Confusion reigned, but audiences loved complex situations. Moreover, the padding delayed the inevitable hour when the heroine must face a crisis and resolve it. Gilbert Seldes, the critic, wrote: "The woman at the center of the serial is a strong character, but if she were permitted to function in strength, the plot would blow up in a few days; she has to be harried and chivvied and above all prevented from taking action." Keeping these subplots in motion along with the main story required liberal use of scene shifts. A character might enter an elevator on Monday and not reach the seventh floor until Thursday of the following week. "Meanwhile, at the office of Dr. Nolan," or "Meanwhile, as the country club dance reaches a peak of gaiety," other characters went about their business.

One quality the soaps never achieved—nor intended—was reality. The soap world was a mélange of tense courtroom scenes as characters fought over wills and the custody of children; of lost mates who roamed the world; of treacherous lovers, invariably male, whose backgrounds were blurred by mysterious dark happenings; of an incidence of amnesia that would defy medical probability tables.

The soaps ended in mid-afternoon, clearing the air waves for the kid serials—sagas that were, in a sense, a continuation of the grand story-telling tradition that traced its origins to the campfires of antiquity, but also were a literary form devised to make the breakfast food industry profitable. Children love good stories, and always have. What difference if they are told by a village elder on the steppes of Asia Minor, by the books of Bret Harte or Mark Twain, or by a radio character who interrupts a wheezy organ rendition of Saint-Saens' symphonic poem *Le Rouet d'Omphale* with the mocking question-and-answer: "Who knows what evil lurrrrrks in the hearts of men? *The Shadow knows!* Hmmmmmmmmmmm-hmmmm-hmmmmm."

On the surface the cereal-serials that so fascinated youngsters had the same content, and intent, as the soap operas that mothers listened to four hours earlier in the day.

They buttressed the continuing national consensus that good *could* triumph over bad. Miniature morality plays, they taught us to brush off the dust of temporary defeats, and to persevere. Villains lied; heroes told the truth. The "decent townspeople" spontaneously banded together in adversity. Doctors were kindly old men who never lost a patient (nor dunned them about the bill). The serials even avoided the imminent sexual crises of adolescence: What really happened between Buck Rogers and his pretty copilot Wilma Deering during those weeks-long flights into space in a comfortable cabin? It never occurred to us to ask.

Nor did our mothers. For one thing, few adults could endure the gamma-ray battles and cattle stampedes for enough consecutive afternoons to become aware of what we were hearing. They reserved the same scorn for "The Green Hornet" that children did for "One Man's Family." Further, the serials convinced us to take spoons to otherwise unacceptable breakfast stuff. Buck Rogers' Cocomalt would have sold on its own, for it made milk palatable, even appealing; so, too, could Ovaltine, assiduously huckstered by Little Orphan Annie ("Leapin' lizards! For a swell summer drink there's nothing like a cold Ovaltine shake-up mug, eh, Sandy?" "Arf! Arf!") But Ralston shredded cereal was another matter entirely, a food without any redeeming culinary values whatsoever. Yet not only did Tom Mix persuade us to eat Ralston, we eagerly sang his theme song—a commercial—and convinced ourselves that the cereal *was* good.

The approach of dusk mercifully ended the daily soap/cereal drama; whatever kid-momma drama existed during the evening hours tended to be weeklies, longer shows that resolved a single plot situation within a tight half-hour. By custom, a large percentage of families listened to the radio together, often from dinner through to bedtime. Hence, the need to sell an all-ages market resulted in some programming that was substandard, in some other that was at worst escapist, and at the best entertainment of classic quality.

Through fortuitous circumstance, both the popular ratings and the dictates of good taste agreed upon the man who was the best, both as a salesman and as a master of his art. His name was Jack Benny, and he stood atop the ferociously competitive world of radio comedy for more than a decade. Benny mastered radio's special demand for a blend of intimacy and elusiveness. He conjured up a living, visual world in the listener's imagination through word and sound—and, frequently, silence, for the affronted pause was a Benny trademark. The disembodied voices of Benny's entourage became personal friends to the audience.

Laughter. Warmth. Immediacy. Radio personalities brought their friendly banter into the living room weekly. Bob Hope and Bing Crosby. Fred Allen. Senator Beauregard Claghorn.

Danny Kaye, thirty-three years old in 1946, soared to sixth place in the ratings with an act based on occasionally intelligible gibberish. His opening and closing signature went something like this:

Git-gat-gittle-giddle-di-ap-giddle-de-rap   gipple-de-tommy,   riddle-de-biddle-de-roop, de-reep, fa-san, skeedle-de-woo-da, fiddle-de-wade, reep.

Unfortunately for radio—and the people who relied upon it as their major medium of entertainment—the Bennys, the Fred Allens, the Danny Kayes were scarce, and radio suffered from a surfeit of the same old voices.

But radio *did* try some new programs in the 1940's—give-away shows and disc jockeys.

The progenitor of the give-aways was Ralph Edwards, whose popular "Truth and Consequences" inspired a succession of imitators. Under the "Truth or Consequences" format, a contestant who flubbed a question was dispatched on a treasure hunt bounded only by the vast imagination of the show's staff.

In another gambit, the show put the nation in a tizzy over the identity of "Miss Hush," who mouthed such clues as,

Second for Santa Claus, first for me, thirteen for wreath, seven for tree. Bring me an auto, a book and a ball, and I'll say Merry Christmas in the spring, not in fall. What does the wreath have to do with the tree? It's second for Santa Claus, first for me. Santa Claus comes by sleigh, but I prefer an auto.

Miss Hush kept the nation guessing for almost six months, with 10,000 letters daily fluttering down on the NBC offices, and an audience estimated at 20,000,000 persons. Tip sheets intended to decipher the weekly clues sold for $1. When NBC suggested that prospective entrants enclose $1 with their letters, with proceeds to charity, the March of Dimes amassed $325,000 very quickly. Finally, for prizes including a 1947 convertible and a trip to Hawaii, Ruth Subbie, a Fort Worth, Texas, housewife, named Miss Hush: Martha Graham. On the Mutual network, "Queen for a Day" offered "new future" prizes of a home in the San Fernando Valley north of Los Angeles, a Kaiser automobile, and a choice of jobs.

Next came the disc jockey. A stack of records, an Associated Press or United Press wire with items tailored for a three- or five-minute "newscast," an announcer who could read and speak English, an engineer, and an advertising salesman (especially the latter)—such was the staff of many a postwar radio station. The format of canned music interspersed with many, many commercials was a businessman's delight.

The ad men somberly attempted to pass some of them off as new and significant forms of artistic expression—humbuggery, of course, but enough to entice *Time* to give the firm of Batten Barton Durstine & Osborn a rating of "number one on the jingle-jangle hit parade" for a bouncy little ditty with a calypso beat extolling the care of bananas:

I'm Chiquita Banana and I've come to say
Bananas have to ripen in a certain way. . . .
Bananas like the climate of the very, very tropical equator
So you should never put bananas in the refrigerator.

A catchy tune, to be sure, but did not radio exist for reasons other than huckstering?

The most revelatory thing that can be said about the nonsense songs is that teen-agers loved them, and they learned them by listening to the radio. For months the people of the world's most powerful nation bestowed their collective approval on such "music" as:

Open the door, Richard,
Open the door and let me in,
Open the door, Richard,
Rich-ard, why *don't* you open the door?

A black jazz-band leader, Jack McVea, based the song on a vaudeville skit written in 1919 by John Mason, who got half the royalties after his lawyers coughed politely. Five versions of "Richard" went on sale the first month, with a dozen more performers rushing their renditions to the public (including The Yokels, who sang it in Yiddish). A mention of the word "Richard" by Bob Hope, Fred Allen, or Bing Crosby set radio audiences to guffawing. And the song's success commenced a scramble for yet more nonsense.

Musicians George Tibbles and Ramey Idriss, working with piano, a guitar, and their memories of a movie cartoon character, dashed off both words and lyrics in half an hour to:

Ha ha ha ha-ha
Ha ha ha ha-ha
Tho' it doesn't make sense,
To the dull and the dense
Ha ha ha ha-ha
That's the Woody Woodpecker song.

After four weeks the song topped *Variety*'s list of the most-played jukebox tunes.

James Anderson, of Port Arthur, Texas, spent much of his army career pushing a mop, and he got to humming as he worked:

"M, I say M-O, M-O-P, M-O-P-P . . .
R, I say R-A, R-A-G, R-A-G-G . . ."

Anderson didn't know how to write music on paper, so he just sang it, and sent the recording to a friend of Johnnie Lee Willis, a western singer. It soon topped the "Hit Parade" of popular tunes.

Despite the flash popularity of the nonsense songs, Americans were distinctly dichotomous in their taste for popular music. In October 1947, a not untypical month, four of the top ten tunes on *Billboard*'s list were at least sixteen years old ("That's My Desire," "I Wonder Who's Kissing Her Now," "Peg O' My Heart," and "When You Were Sweet Sixteen"). The year's best-selling record was Francis Craig's "Near You," followed closely by "Peg O' My Heart," which had been written in 1913.

Dance bands were an immediate casualty of the deejays and the jukebox. An eight-week period in 1947 saw the demise of the bands of Benny Goodman, Tommy Dorsey, Les Brown, and Jack Teagarden. So radio was king.

To close observers of the broadcast industry, however, the most significant event of the era was not the merits of the soap opera, nor the taste of commercials, but a prizefight. On June 19, 1946, some 45,000 persons watched heavyweight champion Joe Louis pound Billy Conn into unconsciousness in Yankee Stadium, while an estimated 100,000 others saw the same knockout on television receivers in New York, Philadelphia, and Washington. In the opinion of radio critic John Crosby, "RCA's miraculous new image orthicon camera brought the television audience a crystal-clear and far more intimate view of the fight than that of the stadium audience." Radio's days as the prime national medium of expression were rapidly dwindling away even as it enjoyed its golden hour of primacy.

CHAPTER 9

BIRTH OF THE TUBE

Television began as a diversion, a toy, an entertainment that few persons felt could challenge the preeminence of radio. It quickly grew into the *enfant terrible* of the best years, one radically revising not only America's entertainment patterns, but the conduct of politics, dissemination of news, the huckstering of consumer goods. Yet the promising new medium, viewed at first with unabashed idealism, was handed unquestioningly to the same men who had debased radio.

The broadcast companies had nibbled at TV several years before the war, with RCA producing the first commercial telecast on February 26,

1939, from the New York World's Fair. "Amos 'n' Andy" went before cameras in blackface, and a few weeks later Franklin D. Roosevelt became the first President to speak on TV. RCA began marketing sets with five- and nine-inch screens, at prices ranging from $200 to $600. Programming was rudimentary—variety shows from Radio City Music Hall, puppets and jugglers, an occasional cooking demonstration, snippets of drama. A mobile unit picked up everything from Columbia University baseball games to wrestling in Brooklyn, ice skating in Rockefeller Center, even pictures of planes landing at La Guardia Airport. CBS and DuMont joined in, and, by the end of 1941 about two score stations were on the air, on the East Coast and in Los Angeles. But with only 10,000 or so sets in the country, and the FCC and the industry unable to agree on the technology of the new medium, television was definitely a novelty. And, with the approach of war, civilian development stopped altogether as the government commandeered technicians to work on the ultrasecret radar.

RCA quickly resumed its lead in 1945, promising in August to have sets on the market by the next summer. RCA's ads reflected the uncertainty of TV technology. They lauded both "direct view" receivers, with persons looking directly at a six-by-eight-inch screen, for normal livingroom use; and a "projection screen" of eighteen-by-twenty-four inches for larger groups. RCA, employing the considerable lobbying prowess of President David Sarnoff, pressured the Federal Communications Commission to begin licensing immediately, and to let the industry work out the technical problems on the basis of operational experience. But a major difficulty was color television. The early work emphasized black-and-white transmissions, but experts prophesied that color could not be far behind. In the interim, such industry leaders as Zenith's Eugene McDonald complained it was unfair for the FCC to permit the sale of any black-and-white sets "without putting the public on notice that they will be obsolete." CBS was first with a color system in 1947, an incredibly complex one involving rotating color wheels, positioned in front of both camera and receiver, that sorted out the spectrum and produced strikingly vivid images. But the CBS system had practical drawbacks. A CBS home receiver required a cabinet three times as large as the picture tube because of what one TV expert called "this damn Ferris wheel that ran in front of the tube." A similar wheel spun in front of the camera. More grievously, the CBS system was not compatible with existing black-and-white sets, which meant that if the FCC accepted the CBS system, every set in the country would be obsolete. RCA's David Sarnoff told the FCC to bide its time, that his engineers would have a comparable color system ready in six months with the added advantage of being compatible with existing black-and-white sets. How did he know they would succeed? Erik Barnouw, the radio historian, quotes him as replying: "I told them to."

CBS, meanwhile, was content to let television develop at a leisurely pace, for several reasons: the high costs of putting TV stations on the air; the uncertainty of advertiser willingness to pay the higher prices when sight was added to sound; the postwar boom in radio profits. In a study given the Federal Communications Commission in 1946, CBS argued that whatever its ultimate values, television faced "seven lean years" of huge outlays and meager returns, with radio income dwindling as advertisers shifted to the new medium. In effect, CBS asked, why starve for seven years when you can continue to feast on radio profits? CBS's lack of faith was demonstrated when the network rejected four of the five station licenses allotted to it by the FCC.

In February 1946 NBC made the first Washington-New York transmission via 225 miles of coaxial cable, depicting General Dwight Eisenhower placing a wreath at the Lincoln Memorial. The image came into Radio City as blurred and jumpy as an old Charlie Chaplin movie, but no matter—RCA had proved intercity transmissions were technically feasible. By the summer of 1947 a "network" linked New York City with Philadelphia and Schenectady.

By the spring of 1947 NBC was on the air almost thirty hours weekly, and the predominant voice was that of an oldtime sportscaster named Robert S. Stanton. NBC covered all Giant baseball games at the Polo Grounds, it went to the United Nations for debate on the Palestine issue, it put together crude studio dramas, it doted on boxing, one of the few sports confined to a tight, easily photographed arena.

By the late 1940's, as the coaxial cable carried television across the nation, only one serious obstacle remained in its path: the price of a set. For less than $20 a family could buy a radio capable of picking up any network program with acceptable fidelity. Television prices, however, began around $300 and went about as high as a buyer's ambitions, with elaborate mahogany consoles retailing for $4,000. With median family income just over the $3,000 mark, not every family could afford to spend a tenth of its annual earnings on an unproven, nonessential appliance. The manufacturers tried hard to cut costs to bring television within range of the mass market. The Admiral Corporation in Chicago began stamping out plastic cabinets for about one-third the cost of wooden ones; still, by mid-1948 not more than one American in ten had witnessed a television program. There were only twenty-eight stations (radio had more than 1,600), and of the 325,000 sets in the nation, half were clustered around the New York metropolitan area. It was obvious that television needed a mass merchandiser.

During the first part of the 1940's, a Los Angeles auto dealer named Earl "Mad Man" Muntz acquired a national reputation for offbeat advertising gimmicks. Freeway billboards depicted a slightly cockeyed Muntz in Napoleonic dress, with such captions as "My wife says I'm crazy because I give such good deals on cars." When the auto boom began to die down, Muntz decided to explore the profitability of television.

"I got a permanent small suite in the Warwick, and I started playing around with television. I bought a line model of every kind of set I could find to see how they worked. RCA and all the rest were carrying thirty, maybe thirty-two tubes. I started taking out tubes and changing the wiring, and seeing how I could make them work with less—what the set really needed and what was padding. I finally got the set down to eleven tubes. Everybody called it 'the gutless wonder' but it worked like a son of a bitch. We built it with eleven tubes to save money. Funny thing, it worked better that way. The fewer tubes you had in the set, the longer it would run without trouble because heat was the thing that was raising hell with the cathode rays.

"But what we were doing was trying to build a set as simple as possible, and as low priced as possible. We got under the $200 barrier, then we put out a metal cabinet job we called the Pumpkin. A helluva good little set. We made a buck out of it, and we gave TV to people who wouldn't have it yet had they waited to screw around with RCA and the other companies."

Inaugurating its new television section in its issue of May 24, 1948, *Time* predicted that "chances are that it [television] will change the American way of life more than anything since the Model T." Jack R. Poppele, president of the Television Broadcasters Association, said that television "is as expansive as the human mind can comprehend. Television holds the key to enlightenment which may unlock the door to world understanding." Children would attend classes in their own living rooms, presidential candidates would win elections from the studio, housewives would see on the screen the dresses and groceries they wanted, and shop by telephone. Television—the educational, entertainment, and commercial nirvana of the future.

In 1949, 75 percent of the Americans who owned television sets

watched the weekly program of a comedian named Milton Berle, "Texaco Star Theater." Berle, age forty, had been in the "theater" and its environs for thirty-five years. He acted as master of ceremonies of the show: a
helter-skelter clown who could sing, dance, juggle, do card tricks, imita-
tions and acrobatics, ride a unicycle, and mug underwater. He changed
costumes at least five times each show—Superman, Li'l Abner, Santa
Claus, the Easter bunny, Father Time, Rosie O'Grady, an organ grinder,
and a snaggled-tooth rube. He loved to burlesque Carmen Miranda, the
explosive Latin singer. He took a horse on stage, and he persuaded the
Metropolitan Opera's Lauritz Melchior to appear in blackface and Gracie
Fields to sing in a bathing suit. Brash, obnoxious, Berle would do just
about anything to provide a laugh.

Berle didn't worry at scoffers, at critics who called his show warmed-
over vaudeville. He cared only for the television audience in the twenty-
four cities that carried "Texaco Star Theater." And close observers began
to note some patterns beginning shortly before eight o'clock on Tuesday
evenings, when Berle went on the air. Restaurant business dropped
sharply. Some stores closed altogether. Tuesday became "dead night" at
movie theaters. The other networks simply got out of the way. Three of
every four Americans watching television were tuned to comedian Milton
Berle—the most popular personality that television could offer to the
public.

CHAPTER 10

SOME BOOKS, AND A MAN NAMED KINSEY

Asked once why Book-of-the-Month Club membership increased by
more than 300,000 during the war years (from 508,000 in 1941 to
848,000 in 1946), founder and president Harry Scherman matter-of-factly
replied, "It was hard to get other things." Gasoline rationing forced people to stay at home. Shortages of consumer goods reduced the ways they
could spend money. Most competent professional athletes went away to
war, and their replacements, despite a certain novelty, didn't warrant
many trips to the ball park. Radio indeed had its mass audience, but there
were many Americans who didn't choose to squander their leisure hours
on soap operas and "Amos 'n' Andy." So they bought books, a trend that
continued after the war ended.

Initially, they continued the trend of escapist fare begun during the war to get their minds off events around them: Daphne du Maurier's *The King's General,* about a centuries-ago militarist, seemed more palatable than a novel on the realities of North Africa and Normandy. During the first three months of 1946 six new novels ran up sales of more than half a million copies: du Maurier's novel sold a million copies; *David the King,* by Gladys Schmitt, 825,000; *Arch of Triumph,* by Erich Maria Remarque, 750,000; and *The Foxes of Harrow,* by Frank Yerby, and *Before the Sun Goes Down,* by Elizabeth Metzger Howard, each 600,000. And despite the many earth-shaking events of 1945-46—the first use of atomic energy, the multifold problems of peace and reconversion—the best-selling nonfiction work was *The Egg and I,* by Betty MacDonald, a light-hearted account of life on a primitive Oregon chicken farm. The MacDonalds shared the countryside with such neighbors as the Kettle clan, dominated by Ma Kettle, a mountainously fat woman in a very dirty housedress. *The Egg and I* sold 1,038,500 copies; Hollywood bought it for a movie, and television later carved out Ma Kettle for a separate comic series.

The first distinctive shift in taste was to introspection on national problems. *The Snake Pit,* by Mary Jane Ward, gave a sickening portrait of conditions in mental hospitals. *The Lost Weekend,* by Charles Jackson, recounted the binge of a middle-class Manhattan executive, the sort of person with whom many bookbuyers could relate. Frederick Wakeman's *The Hucksters* ripped the paving stones off Madison Avenue and hurled them at the admen who worked there. "The public cavorted in this Hall of Mirrors," wrote Joseph Henry Jackson, book critic of the San Francisco *Chronicle,* "and the novels that did the reflecting, especially when they showed the reader to himself in poses of a downright unpleasant nature, found enormous audiences. Americans were in a mood to be told off, and they embraced most warmly the writers who scolded hardest."

Yet another phase, as the Cold War approached, was a keener interest in serious nonfiction about current world affairs, especially the Soviet Union. The war was one subject on which tastes changed slowly. Predictably, the first years brought a plethora of memoirs and I-was-there stories. Two best sellers mark the parameters of what Americans were willing to read (or write) about the war, and when. *Mr. Roberts,* by Thomas Heggen, published by Houghton Mifflin in 1946, was a jolly story about the experiences of a junior officer on the USS *Reluctant.* Boredom and cranky senior officers, not Japanese bullets, were the main danger. Two years later came Norman Mailer's *The Naked and the Dead,* a war novel of another genre entirely.

Built on an army platoon on an arduous and dangerous combat patrol across a Pacific island, the novel told of gut wounds and diarrhea, of grime and sweat and of savagery, by American and Japanese alike.

Critics and readers couldn't decide exactly what to make of this young man and his graphic realism, the cynicism with which his soldiers went about their killing, the libido-quickening sexuality of flashback remembrances. Nonetheless people bought the book. Its first year on the market *The Naked and the Dead* sold 137,185 copies in the bookstores and another 60,000 through book clubs.

That the public worried about sex being discussed explicitly, even in books, was indicative of a peculiar ambiguity that permeated American life. For centuries the accepted societal dogma was that sexuality remained dormant until a person fell in love and married. Any sexual activity prior to (or outside of) marriage was sinful, and perhaps illegal as well. Theologians insisted on these strictures, society approved them, the courts enforced them—and people ignored them.

The conflict was shoved out of the shadows in 1948 by a book that was a publishing and cultural phenomenon, *Sexual Behavior in the Human Male*, by Dr. Alfred C. Kinsey, a zoologist at Indiana University. In 1938 Indiana University asked Kinsey to coordinate a marriage course, and he found there was so little data about human sexual activity that he could offer only guesses to his students. So Kinsey set about gathering his own case histories, eventually compiling them on 5,300 white males. He asked about the incidence and frequency of orgasms through six sexual outlets: masturbation; nocturnal emissions; heterosexual petting; intercourse (premarital, marital, extramarital, post-marital, and with prostitutes); homosexual encounters; and animal contacts. The analysis was in terms of race, marital status, age, educational level, occupational class, familial and religious background, and place of residence. Kinsey's conclusions, after almost a decade of work, dashed about every prevailing conception of the seldom-mentioned subject of sex.

Aware in advance the book would create a furor, Kinsey arranged to have the book published under the dignified imprimatur of W. B. Saunders Company, an old and respected Philadelphia medical publisher.

The formal publication date was January 5, 1948. By the first week of March, 200,000 copies had been sold, and Saunders had two printing companies working around the clock to meet the demand. The book itself weighed three pounds and contained 804 pages of pedantic text and tables; the reviewer who called it a "dreary morass of technical jargon and statistical charts" knew whereof he wrote. But for anyone who poked through the material, what Kinsey had accomplished, quite simply, was to tell American men about their collective sexuality: that each man's fantasies, even his activities, were shared by a plurality of his neighbors.

The immediate response was what can be expected when a forbidden subject is mentioned in public: snickers. A radio comedian knew he could mention the Kinsey Report with the assurance of hearty guffaws. Theologians, scientists, and sociologists roundly denounced the report.

Stung by the criticisms, acutely sensitive to persons who attacked him as a charlatan or sensationalist, Kinsey remained generally aloof from the debate, content to confine his role to a continuing compilation of data. As the 1940's ended, he was well along on work on his second volume, *Sexual Behavior in the Human Female,* published in 1953. But his findings brought to Americans the first stirrings of what was to become the sexual revolution, a concept the public could talk about after his book, even if not accept.

The lively discussion about the Kinsey Report aside, did the American public really care about serious writing in the postwar period? In 1949 the nation brooded over the Berlin airlift, the Soviet acquisition of the atomic bomb, the fear of a "shadow government" of Communists and sympathizers in Washington. In this year of fear and trembling, the nonfiction best-seller list, based upon trade sales in stores, went as follows:

White Collar Zoo, by Clare Barnes, Jr., a series of animal photos humorously captioned to relate them to familiar office characters and situations.

How to Win at Canasta, by Oswald Jacoby, capitalizing on the current card craze.

The Seven Storey Mountain, by Thomas Merton, an autobiography of the Trappist monk.

Home Sweet Zoo, by Barnes, the photo book idea transported to the household.

Cheaper by the Dozen, by Frank B. Gilbreth, Jr., and Ernestine Gilbreth Carey, on how an efficiency expert raised a family of twelve children, and made the experience sound more fun than common sense would suggest.

The Greatest Story Ever Told, by Fulton Oursler.

Canasta, the Argentine Rummy Game, by Ottilie H. Reilly and Alexander Rosa. Yet another card book.

Canasta, by Josefina Aratayeta de Viel. And another.

Peace of Soul, by Fulton J. Sheen.

A Guide to Confident Living, by Norman Vincent Peale.

In sum, America's interest in these, the best years, was distinctly escapist: four religious books, three books on a card-game fad, three books of humor. Events beyond the individual American's control were gradually tugging him toward a share of a collective responsibility for the rest of the world. But he did not care to read about what this new obligation would require of him.

CHAPTER 11

THE MOVIES FLICKER OUT

The peace years almost killed Hollywood. The movies began the period in seemingly robust health, with a ready-built market of patrons apparently ready to pay a dollar to view almost anything projected on a screen. Crowded housing conditions encouraged people to get outside their homes for diversion, and millions of veterans had acquired the movie habit via constant exposure at USO shows and canteens. Movie box offices clicked out an average 95 million tickets a week during 1946, 10 million more than the best prewar year; industry profits doubled the first year after peace.

The boom didn't last. After those first golden months, the movies fell into a cost-quality squeeze which made the stock lavish musical too expensive to support. Restrictive taxes by foreign governments, notably the British, effectively sealed off a market that had given Hollywood about one-third its total profits. A Red scare over alleged Communist influence in filmmaking threw the entire industry into the jitters. Then, of course, the new bugaboo, television, caught the eye of the mob known as the American entertainment public and suddenly the movie houses stood empty on Saturday nights.

Movies about the war no longer fared well. But to Hollywood's credit, the industry boasted dazzling technical expertise. Lavish musicals, fluffy comedies, tough melodramas with maximum action and minimum message—studios ground them out "with skill and chromium-plated production finish," in the words of critic Howard Barnes of the New York *Herald Tribune.* Metro-Goldwyn-Mayer spent eight years adapting *The Yearling,* the Pulitzer Prize novel by Marjorie Kinnan Rawlings, about a small boy growing up in the Florida bayou country immediately after the Civil War. *The Jolson Story,* a glamorized biography of the mammy singer; *Blue Skies,* a happy musical with Bing Crosby and Fred Astaire; and *Night and Day,* with a profusion of Cole Porter tunes, showed the industry at its commercial best. *Gentleman's Agreement,* based on the novel by Laura Z. Hobson, exposed the social and economic sores of anti-Semitism. *Pinky,* about a black woman who "passed" for white, explored a new area of racial prejudice.

Years of acrimonious labor-management relations erupted into strikes in 1946-47, throwing production schedules into disarray and splitting the community asunder. When a truce came, the wounds remained, and the average picture cost twice what it had six years previously. As revenues dwindled, bankers and outside managers supplanted the flamboyant individuals who had long dominated Hollywood.

By 1950 the movies had degenerated to the point where drive-in theaters drew serious consideration as a salvation. A thousand or more were strewn around the country, offering all sorts of subsidiary attractions: barbecue pits so that families could come early and cook supper before the movie began; bottle-warming service for the baby; shuffleboard. Concession business ran around four times as high per ticket as at a sit-down movie. When business got really bad an operator would offer a weeknight game of "speedometer bingo," in which the prize went to the motorist whose odometer displayed the right sequence of digits.

All things considered, however, the drive-ins really weren't the movies.

CHAPTER 12

EXIT THE NEW DEALERS

What blurred image the general public had of Harry Truman, an image derived chiefly from his subdued vice-presidential campaign, was that of a not especially bright fellow who could be anyone's next-door neighbor; nice enough, in his own way, but did one really trust him with the country?

The hostility was deepest among certain Roosevelt intimates, for several reasons. Liberals resented Truman as the displacer of Henry Wallace on the 1944 ticket, an antagonism Wallace did nothing to quiet. "How I wish you were at the helm," Minneapolis Mayor Hubert H. Humphrey wrote to Wallace a few days after FDR's death. Eleanor Roosevelt, in a private letter to Wallace, expressed her own indirect misgivings about Truman. "I feel that you are peculiarly fitted to carry on the ideals which were close to my husband's heart," she wrote. Wallace, shoved far down the prestige ladder by Roosevelt to Secretary of Commerce, was left with nothing other than the titular leadership of American liberals. Although willing to credit Truman as an honest and devoted senator, the liberals dismissed him as representative of a narrow, small-town mentality, lacking any guiding ideology to handle the fundamental issues facing America and the world. Further, the Roosevelt Administration was so entrenched in Washington, after thirteen years, that the people serving it acted as if they owned the government. Truman was a newcomer, a usurper. It was not surprising then that Truman cleaned house. Within four months he accepted the resignations of all cabinet officers except Wallace, retained as a gesture toward the left wing, and Secretary of the Interior Harold Ickes, who resigned from the administration in 1946.

But the quality of HST's appointees caused stirs. Tom C. Clark, named as attorney general, carried such a reputation as a reactionary lightweight and a politician that his predecessor, the patrician Francis Biddle, pleaded with the President not to appoint him. Fred Vinson, who replaced Henry Morgenthau as secretary of the treasury, was another conservative of limited vision, frank in stating he didn't believe in "social experimentation." (Clark later followed Vinson onto the Supreme Court bench.)

Truman had begun his presidency with an "approval" rating of 87 percent. But as labor-management problems swept the nation, idling workers, and economic reconversion developed painful kinks, public opinion turned against the President, slipping to 82 percent in early November 1945, to 75 percent later in the month; then down to 63 percent in February 1946 and to 50 percent in April. Thereafter well over half the time a majority of the public disapproved of his performance in office.

The Henry Wallace firing involved one of the more mystifying figures ever to hold high public office in America. Not even the people closest to Wallace purported to understand him. A skilled campaigner, capable of arousing intense devotion among followers, he nonetheless was "shy, ill at ease in public places, sloppy in his dress, tousled of hair, and completely incapable of small talk," in the words of his biographer and contemporary, Frank Kingdon, who knew him well. Wallace lived on several planes simultaneously. A plant geneticist by training—and a good one, who developed several hybrid strains of corn—he followed his grandfather and father into the editorship of *Wallace's Farmer,* one of the most widely read and respected farm papers in the country. Wallace went into the Roosevelt cabinet in 1933 as secretary of agriculture and presided over the radical farm legislation of the early New Deal: chiefly, attempts to boost prices by controlling crop acreage and slaughtering calves and piglets. Wallace gradually expanded his interests beyond agriculture to become a leading spokesman for New Deal ideas; FDR, after making him Vice-President, also used him extensively to articulate American war aims.

But Wallace had problems. Were it not for his high office, his staggering inconsistencies of word and action and his predilection for foggy speech that masked even foggier ideas would have brought him swift dismissal as a classic Washington misfit. Foremost among Wallace's many preoccupations was religion, and while professing adherence to High Episcopalianism, he concurrently dabbled in mysticism and astrology. He would draw horoscopes for visitors, and he maintained that the future could be predicted from certain markings on the Great Pyramid. When a business delegation protested that a Wallace agriculture program couldn't possibly work, he stood upright and his flashing eyes looked toward Heaven: "I have faith that Divine Providence will provide a means to fit the times," he said. When pressed, he closed his eyes and lapsed into, or feigned, sleep, frequently during important conferences.

Mindful that Wallace was anathema to vast segments of the Democratic Party, Roosevelt decided in early 1944 to nudge him off the ticket, choosing Truman instead.

Although he continued as secretary of commerce in the Truman cabinet, Wallace was far from comfortable. In July 1946 Wallace sent Truman a long memorandum contending that U.S. actions were unnecessarily provoking hostile responses by the Soviets. He listed the atomic bomb tests at Bikini; continued production of B-29 bombers and plans to go ahead with the larger B-32; the proliferation of air bases around the world; a $28-billion defense budget; and indiscreet high-level talk about the possibility of preventive war. In this memo and in speeches Wallace pleaded for better understanding of the Soviets, and their better understanding of the United States. When columnist Joseph Alsop, in a private talk, warned Wallace that he was "in a completely indefensible position in the cabinet," Wallace deduced that "Joe in effect was a secret agent sent by the get-tough-with-Russia boys in the State Department to come over and sound me out. . . . Joe was on the verge of hysterics."

Truman was upset when Wallace intervened in a special Manhattan congressional election on behalf of Johannes Steel, an American Labor Party candidate running with Communist support, over a Democratic opponent with a solid progressive record who was backed by both the Liberal Party and the New York *Post*. But how would he get rid of Wallace without unnecessary fuss?

Wallace forced Truman's hand in the fall of 1946. On September 12 he was to address a Madison Square Garden rally sponsored by two leftist political groups, the National Citizens Political Action Committee (NCPAC) and the Independent Citizens Committee of the Arts, Sciences, and Professions. Both groups contained heavy infestations of Stalinists. The slant of the groups is important because it was to this forum that Wallace chose to make a major speech criticizing the Truman Administration's conduct of U.S.-Soviet relations.

Wallace knew he was venturing onto quaky ground. Rather than submitting the speech to the State Department for review, the usual procedure, he went directly to Truman. And, by Truman's account, Wallace hoodwinked him. After some talk about Commerce Department matters Wallace mentioned vaguely that he intended to make the speech, and read Truman some sample lines. For instance, he said, "I am neither anti-British nor pro-British—neither anti-Russian nor pro-Russian." Truman said Wallace suggested that was the way America should conduct its relations with the USSR, and the President nodded agreement. Wallace also read enough anti-Soviet lines to persuade Truman he was moving closer to the Administration policy. But Wallace's account is somewhat different. He claimed that he and Truman spent an hour together, and that Truman went over the speech with him "page by page," occasionally chiming, "That's right," and "Yes, that is what I believe." Truman didn't suggest a single change, and Wallace asked if he could say the White House endorsed the speech. Truman agreed.

The morning of September 12 Truman had a press conference, and William Mylander of the Cowles newspapers, holding high a text of what Wallace was to say that night, began asking about it. Truman interrupted; he could not answer questions about a speech that had not been delivered.

"Well, it's about you," Mylander said. "That's why I asked."

"What's the question?" Truman answered, smiling.

Mylander quoted from the speech, including a line following the sentence about Wallace being neither pro-British nor anti-British. Wallace had inserted, "When President Truman read these words, he said they represented the policy of the administration."

"That is correct," Truman said.

Mylander continued. "My question is, Does that apply just to that paragraph or the whole speech?"

"I approved the whole speech," Truman said.

Well, was the speech a departure from policies that Secretary of State

James Byrnes had been enunciating at the Paris Peace Conference that very week?

No, Truman said, Wallace's remarks were "right in line" with Byrnes's views.

The Madison Square Garden rally that evening was a hornets' nest of anti-Administration sentiment. One resolution charged that the "aims of President Roosevelt have been placed in jeopardy by the 'get tough with Russia' policy, the refusal to withdraw American forces from China, and support for British imperialism." Senator Claude Pepper of Florida urged a return to friendship with the Soviets, and accused Truman of appeasing "imperialists in the Republican Party." Pepper continued: "With conservative Democrats and reactionary Republicans making our foreign policy, it is all we can do to keep foolish people from having us . . . drop our atomic bombs on the Russian people." (Byrnes, it must be noted, at that very moment was trying to assure the Soviets at the Paris conference that the United States had no militaristic designs.)

By comparison Wallace sounded moderate; nonetheless, as a ranking figure in the Administration his direct criticisms of policies of the President he served were tantamount to political treason.

We are reckoning with a force which cannot be handled successfully by a "get tough with Russia" policy. . . . Throughout the world there are numerous reactionary elements which had hoped for Axis victory . . . and continually try to provoke war. . .

We have no more business in the political affairs of Eastern Europe than Russia has in the political affairs of . . . the United States. . . . We are striving to democratize Japan and our area of control in Germany while Russia strives to socialize Eastern Germany. . . .

[T]he danger of war is much less from communism than it is from imperialism, whether it be of the United States or England—or from fascism, the remnants of fascism, which may be in Spain or Argentina.

Let's get this straight, regardless of what Mr. Taft or Mr. Dewey may say, if we can overcome the imperialistic urge in the Western World, I'm convinced there'll be no war.

When Wallace ventured a mild criticism of the Soviet Union, many in the audience booed. He flinched but finished the sentence. Thereafter, however, he carefully dropped lines that the crowd might consider hostile—a sentence, for instance, about "native communists faithfully following every twist and turn in the Moscow party line." Another theme was that America should accept geopolitical reality and recognize that the Soviets would dominate a third of the world, the United States much of the rest, assisted by Great Britain. Three years previously Wallace had advocated "One World." Now he had retreated to "two spheres of influence," a change that sickened many long-time admirers.

For several stunned hours neither friend nor foe knew what to make of Wallace's speech. Conservative columnist John O'Donnell of the New York *Daily News* cheered Wallace (and seriously) as a late arrival among isolationists. The *New York Times* wondered how good an internationalist Wallace really was. Even the first editions of the *Daily Worker* denounced the speech.

Truman called in the press and rebuked Wallace, who remained unrepentant.

In preceding days Secretary of State James Byrnes and his delegation at the Paris Peace Conference had been filing an estimated 90,000 words daily of cabled reports (chiefly texts of speeches by the participants). But for three long days, the teletype machines fell silent, save for perfunctory traffic. On the fourth day, Byrnes sent a direct message to the President which said, in effect, Wallace or me. Truman quickly pacified Byrnes directly via a teletype "conversation." Then he called in Wallace and fired him.

The episode upset Truman, for it made a public fool of him at a time dangerously close to the congressional elections, and it encouraged the Soviets to behave obstinately on the assumption that American policy was confused. But Truman had no regrets as to the outcome.

CHAPTER 13

HAD ENOUGH? YES!

For the Democratic party, the exit of Henry Wallace loomed as the penultimate act of disaster in the November congressional elections. As early as June the Democratic National Committee, surveying the massive defection of labor and public anger over problems ranging from meat shortages and housing to the botched price control program, privately admitted the possibility of losing control of the House of Representatives. (The Republicans needed to win twenty-six new seats to control the House, and nine of sixteen seats up for election to gain the Senate.)

Republicans gleefully exploited every blunder and accused the Democrats of offering nothing more than "confusion, corruption and Communism." The GOP national chairman, Brazilla Carroll Reece, a Tennessee congressman, claimed the Democrats had fallen under the sway of "Red-fascists." The predominantly Republican daily press, sensing a chance to purge the nation of detested New Deal reforms, stated as unchallenged fact the charge that key Democratic units did the bidding of the Soviets. That such charges could be made without evidence more substantial than the obvious fact that many Americans disagreed with Truman's foreign policy, can be credited in good part to J. Edgar Hoover, director of the FBI. Hoover's ability to scent changes of public opinion contributed in great part to his long tenure, and in 1946 he forsaw a virulent swing against domestic communism. In a speech to the American Legion convention in San Francisco on September 30, Hoover allowed that at least 100,000 Communists were running loose in America—in "some newspapers, magazines, books, radio and the screen . . . some churches, schools, colleges and even fraternal orders." The number of out-and-out Communists didn't scare Hoover; his fear was that ten sympathizers stood behind every card holder, "ready to do the party's work. These include their satellites, their fellow travelers and their so-called progressive and liberal allies. They have maneuvered themselves into positions where a few Communists control the destinies of hundreds who are either willing to be led or have been duped into obeying the dictates of others." The Hoover speech evoked dismay at the Democratic National Committee. But no one in the Administration stepped forth to bell the redoubtable Hoover.

Valid or not, the charges struck home in voting blocs that traditionally went Democratic. The Washington Post's Edward T. Folliard found "hatred of communism rampant" in all the states he visited. In Detroit, a Republican politician of Polish ancestry told Folliard, "You political reporters are overlooking something in this campaign. That's the foreign-born. They are off the reservation, and I mean off. Why, I can take you to clubhouses here where they have torn Roosevelt's picture from the wall." The politician cited clubhouses of Poles, Lithuanians, Estonians, and others who felt Roosevelt had betrayed their country to Russia at the Yalta Conference. In Pennsylvania, Governor Edward Martin, running a successful campaign to dislodge Senator Joseph Guffey, constantly hammered at the "Communist" Political Action Committee (PAC) of the CIO. In Detroit rank-and-file members of the CIO refused to contribute to PAC, charging it was Communist. The Gallup poll, gauging campaign issues in late September, found "foreign policy and relations with Russia" ranked the most important. (The other issues, in order, were lowering the cost of living; curbing strikes and regulating labor troubles; working out world peace and making the UN succeed; housing; shortages of food, clothing, and other necessities; and veterans' welfare.)

A major imponderable in the election was "the veteran vote," a supposed bloc estimated at upward of eight million persons. "The hustings ring with cries of concern for the . . . demobilized GIs," Sam Stavisky wrote in the Washington *Post*. "Every platform and virtually every speech promises the former serviceman a panacea for his readjustment problems." The Democrats took credit for every piece of veterans' legislation passed since the Revolutionary War—a somewhat dubious claim, since the benefits would have passed anyway, given the veterans' special postwar standing; indeed, a Mississippi congressman named William M. Whittington was the lone man in either house to vote against terminal leave pay for enlisted men. The Republicans promised to do the same things, only better.

Several incidents in the summer of 1946 displayed veterans' potential political clout, and raised fleeting fears that they would use guns rather than ballots to achieve their goals. The most dramatic episode came in Athens, Tennessee, when supporters of the "G.I. Nonpartisan Ticket" felt the entrenched Democratic machine cheated them during a primary ballot count. Rival mobs gathered, the machine politicians took refuge in the courthouse, under protection of eighty-three deputy sheriffs, and hundreds of angry, armed GIs milled around outside.

After six hours the veterans blasted away the front of the courthouse with dynamite, and the deputies surrendered. The veterans set up an interim government and called for new elections. Encouraged by their example, GIs in three adjacent Tennessee counties started organizing against their own local machines, and dissidents from throughout the South met in a "convention" at Alamo, Tennessee, to discuss a national political party. But Brigadier General Evans F. Carlson, famed Marine raider and much respected by organized veterans, dissuaded them: work within the frame work of the national parties, he said, lest you create a fatal cleavage between ex-GIs and other citizens.

Nonetheless, any candidate who carried a war record into the 1946 campaigns began with a distinct advantage. In Pennsylvania, Republicans tried—but failed—to get native-son General Carl A. "Tooey" Spaatz, the air corps hero, to run for governor. DeLesseps Story Morrison, who won the Legion of Merit as a thirty-three-year-old colonel in the transportation corps, was in a separation center when New Orleans politicians asked him to run for mayor. He won and the victory pictures had him still in uniform. In Massachusetts, John F. Kennedy, running for Congress, frequently recalled a "promise" he had made while a PT-boat skipper in the Solomons: "When ships were sinking and young Americans dying . . . I firmly resolved to serve my country in peace as honestly as I tried to serve it in war." In California, navy veteran Richard M. Nixon reasoned that a majority of veterans had been enlisted men for whom a politician campaigning in officer's uniform held little appeal. So Nixon threw out the military pictures, and the words "Dick Nixon" replaced "Lieutenant Commander Richard M. Nixon" on his literature. But Nixon did let voters know where he had been the last four years. Campaign literature described him as the "clean, forthright young American who fought in defense of his country in the stinking mud and jungles of the Solomons," while incumbent congressman Jerry Voorhis "stayed safely behind the front in Washington."

Even a pro-veteran voting record was not enough to save many incumbents who had not gone away to war. In Oklahoma, three ex-GIs mounted an offensive against Congressman Lyle Boren, and beat him in the Democratic primary. In Wisconsin Joseph R. McCarthy demonstrated how to make the most of the "issue." He distributed 750,000 copies of a twelve-page brochure depicting him in the rear seat of a bomber and emblazoned with the slogan: *Washington Needs a Tail-Gunner.* Newspaper advertisements read:

Joe McCarthy was a tail-gunner in World War II. When the war began Joe had a soft job as a Judge at eight grand a year. He was exempt from military duty. He resigned to enlist as a private in the Marines. He fought on land and in the air all through the Pacific. He and millions of other guys kept you from talking Japanese. Today Joe McCarthy is home. He wants to serve America in the Senate. Yes, folks. Congress needs a tail-gunner.. . . . America needs fighting men. . . .

The McCarthy literature contemptuously dismissed the record of incumbent Robert M. La Follette, Jr., who had been in the Senate since 1925: "sat out the war in Washington, lived on his Virginia plantation," enjoying his Senate salary and "fat rations" while "15,000,000 Americans were fighting the war and 130,000,000 more were building the sinews of war." McCarthy won by 5,396 votes.

By autumn *Army Times,* a service publication, counted 183 Second World War veterans who had hurdled the primaries to represent the major parties in congressional elections: 110 Democrats and 73 Republicans. Of these, 69 were elected, or about one out of seven members of the new Congress.

Harry Truman went to bed early election night, on a special train bringing him from Missouri, where he had gone to vote, back to the capital. He woke up the next morning with a bad cold and a Republican Congress—the House split with 246 Republicans and 188 Democrats; the Senate 51 to 45.

The Chicago Tribune puffed with joy the morning after the election; for the first time since 1928 Republicans had cause to be happy in the wake of a national election. "The New Deal is kaput," gloated the New York *Daily News*. The Washington *Daily News*, in similar vein, attributed the Republican success in part to the "deep American conviction that it is unhealthy in a free government to keep one crowd in power too long."

Regardless of the reasons, Harry Truman faced two years as an "accidental" and most unpopular President, opposed by a Congress eager to assert its own voter mandate. With such a vote of nonconfidence, why shouldn't Truman speed up the inevitable and permit a Republican to take the presidency? Marshall Field, publisher of the Chicago *Sun-Times*, a Truman supporter, suggested he step aside. So, too, did Democratic Senator J. W. Fulbright of Arkansas, who said Truman should appoint a Republican as secretary of state, and then resign. Since there was no vice-president, the Republican would accede to the presidency.

But Harry Truman intended to cling to office, even if under the most adverse political circumstances ever to confront an American chief executive. The Eightieth Congress whetted its knives, and Truman was a lame duck ready for the carving.

CHAPTER 14

ENTER THE EIGHTIETH CONGRESS

Several days after the Republican-controlled Eightieth Congress convened, Representative Clarence Brown of Ohio looked over at the Democratic minority and announced his plans with a gloat: the Republicans, he said, intended to "open each session with a prayer and close it with a probe." The Republicans had campaigned on the thesis that the Democratic government was riddled by "communism, confusion and corruption"; soon the GOP had no fewer than thirty-nine investigative committees and subcommittees looking for confirmatory evidence. In the House, Representative George H. Bender of Ohio handed each new

GOP member a new broom tagged, "Here's yours—let's do the job."

Yet exactly what was the "job" to be done? Reflecting the negative tone of the 1946 campaign, the GOP policy committees in the Congress laid out three main tasks: "Clear away the rubble of the New Deal and the war," which in translation meant returning the government to pay-as-you-go financing; curbing labor; and reducing spending and taxes by as much as twenty percent. For congressional Republicans the taste of power had broader meanings as well. The next two years they were to show the nation how *Republicans* ran things, the first such opportunity afforded their party since 1932. An uncountable number of these persons caressed thoughts of the presidency, either outspokenly or in their private moments. Power was there for the seizing. As a party of losers the Republians swore fealty to no leader. Those from the party's Midwestern heartland suspiciously crossed their arms across vests at the approach of New York Governor Thomas E. Dewey, who had lost in 1944, and who looked toward 1948 with the infuriating expectation that the party "owed" him the presidency. The Easterners, conversely, thought the outlanders stupid and dated, typifying Republicanism that had died along with Warren G. Harding.

It was through Congress, however, that the Republican Party had the opportunity to show its face to the nation. And the 1946 landslide propelled a peculiar mélange of characters into power—some of them considered downright peculiar even by persons and periodicals that spent considerable energy propagandizing the Republican cause.

To the general public, the Eightieth Congress was personified by Senator Robert A. Taft of Ohio—son of a President, "Mr. Republican" to many in his party, who as GOP policy chairman was the intellectual and ideological voice of the majority. Specifically, Taft was responsible for devising alternative programs to the New Deal and the successor Fair Deal, and in packaging acceptable both to the eastern moderates and the Midwesterners. Taft's chief attributes were smartness and a belief in principle: as one observer put it, he absorbed complex legislative issues as swiftly as most congressmen could understand the dialogue in comic strips. He had led his law class at Yale, and before his move to Washington, he had earned a comfortable living in Cincinnati doing the dullest, driest, most technical corporate and civil cases imaginable. Taft's chief drawback was his dour personality. Somber-faced, most comfortable in a dark, double-breasted suit with vest and a tight necktie, Taft came across to the public more as a conservative banker than a politician. He professed little sympathy for the downtrodden; his motivation, in the words of one contemporary observer, was the "historically deep-seated, experienced sense of responsibility for the whole community characteristic of the genuine aristocrat." Executing such a role without appearing condescending is a ticklish feat, and one that Taft could not accomplish. Though many senators respected Taft, few liked him.

Lacking charismatic leadership, the GOP congressional bloc was forced back upon the issues. And although they boasted of a "mandate," the Republicans went slowly in making any use of it. In terms of concrete legislation, the Republicans and conservative Democratic outriders did push through ponderously complicated legislation intended to "curb the powers of big labor"—the Taft-Hartley Act, named after Senator Taft and Representative Fred Hartley of New Jersey. An amalgam of more than one hundred antilabor bills that had kicked around Congress for a decade or more, Taft-Hartley was designed to outlaw a plethora of "unfair labor practices" by unions, just as the Wagner Act had barred "unfair management practices" at the start of the New Deal. Taft-Hartley proscribed the closed shop, jurisdictional strikes (in which rival unions contended for organizational rights in a plant or industry), and the secondary boycott (in which a union that is striking the Acme Company persuades other unions to strike the Bacme Company, with which Acme does business). Taft-Hartley revived the injunction to end strikes, although only on motion of the government. It provided wide governmental intervention in internal union affairs, on the assumption that rank-and-file members needed as much protection from their officers as they did from employers. Extensive financial reports had to be filed with the Labor Department. Officers of national unions were required to swear affidavits they were neither members nor sympathizers of Communist groups. Labor unions could not spend money directly or indirectly in national elections or primaries. On and on rolled Taft-Hartley, an act so complex that few union leaders understood it, much less the lay citizen; a generation later, it still provided work for a troop of labor-law specialists and federal bureaucrats.

In its pursuit of "corruption," the GOP had little success. The closest they got to Truman's official family was the disclosure that Brigadier General Wallace Graham, the White House physician, speculated in the commodities market at the very time Truman was denouncing speculators for unjustifiably puffing up consumer prices. "Five-percenter" and "deep-freeze," words that came to be synonymous with Truman Administration corruption, had not been heard by 1948. So, in the end, the GOP turned to the last refuge of ambitious politicians: national security and communism.

CHAPTER 15

RECONSIDERING THE RUSSIANS

In February 1945, as Russian troops sped westward across Germany toward a linkup with other Allied forces, seven of ten Americans were so enthused about the Soviets that they endorsed the idea of sending German men to the USSR to help rebuild cities devastated by war. By the middle of 1946, disillusionment had begun: almost six of ten Americans felt Russia's actions in Eastern Europe and elsewhere portended an ambition to rule the entire world; about one in four was ready to go to war immediately to stop her. According to a study by public opinion specialist Alvin Richman: "By early 1948, approximately 70 percent of the American public viewed the Soviet Union unfavorably."

During wartime, American policy toward the Soviets was ambiguous, perhaps necessarily so. President Roosevelt went into negotiations at Teheran and Yalta, in 1943 and 1945, with the notion that the Soviets could be cajoled and soothed into good behavior. Recognizing Moscow's historic fear of invaders, FDR leaned over backward to heed demands that she have friendly powers on her borders when postwar Europe took shape. Fourteen times since 1800 invading armies had swept across the naked plains to Russia's west; Minsk had suffered 101 foreign occupations. Quite obviously the Soviets wished to fight any future wars in buffer states, not on their homeland. Winston Churchill, conversely, took a much darker view of the Soviets, arguing that the U.S. and Britain should begin preparing for how to cope with probable Russian designs on Europe. Churchill was doing just that on his own; in exchanges in 1943, he and Stalin reached tacit agreements that British influence should remain dominant in Greece; that Britain and the USSR would share Yugoslavia; and that the Soviets, through dint of occupation, could do what they wished in Rumania, Bulgaria, and Hungary. Neither kept his word, choosing to use these "agreements" as the starting point for further bargaining.

Truman, too, was swiftly backing away from the openhanded policy of Roosevelt and following his instinctive feelings that the Soviets should not be trusted. Averell Harriman, ambassador to Moscow, warned soon after Truman's succession to the presidency that the Soviets would seek to impose their foreign policy and police-state system upon any nation they occupied and would likely ignore any "agreement" not to their advantage.

The first test came over Poland. Contrary to his Yalta promise, Stalin flatly refused to permit any members of the government-in-exile to join the provisional regime created by the occupying Soviet army. The United States and Britain, in turn, refused to permit seating of the "puppet" Polish delegation at the United Nations founding conference, which opened with great fanfare and expectations in April 1945 in San Francisco. Truman was furious.

Stalin then recalled twenty of the leading London exiles to Moscow, ostensibly to talk about their roles in a new government. No sooner had they arrived than he put sixteen of them on trial for inciting underground resistance to the Soviet occupation troops. As a sop to Truman, Stalin put the other four into the government, one as vice-premier. Unwilling to see the UN die over the Polish issue, and under pressure from other governments, Truman reluctantly agreed to recognize the puppet Warsaw delegation.

The Polish question also haunted the opening of the Potsdam Conference, in July 1945. The Big Three kicked the "Polish question" into the future, to be resolved during drafting of an overall German peace treaty. (Three decades later, no such treaty has been written.) Stalin took a similar attitude elsewhere in Eastern Europe: what the Soviets held, the Soviets intended to dominate through docile "governments" that systematically excluded all save Communists. The Soviets hampered American and British members at every hand, ignoring their presence and so restricting their movements that they were effectively isolated from the countries they ostensibly were supposed to be running.

On Germany, the most important issue, the Big Three made no progress whatsoever. At Yalta, Stalin had demanded $10 billion in reparations; at Potsdam $20 billion was the top bargaining goal. All the while the Soviets busily dismantled entire factories in their zones of occupation— not only in Germany but in the Nazi satellite states, including oil refineries in Rumania that had been owned by British and American companies before the war. When Truman protested, Stalin replied it was a "trifling matter"; after all, the Russians needed refineries to replace those that the Germans had destroyed. Potsdam was a failure, although one cloaked from all but the handful of lay citizens with the insight to sense failure beneath the language of the final communiqué.

With peace, and the end of censorship and boosteristic propaganda, the U.S.-Soviet differences no longer could be pushed out of sight. Almost daily the newspaper headlines told the public of yet another example of Soviet intransigence: the tightening of Communist regimes in Eastern European nations that passed swiftly from Nazi vassalage to the Soviet bloc; Russian support of guerrillas in Greece; Russian refusal to withdraw troops from the northern part of Iran; the incessant Russian demands for control of the Straits of the Bosporus, which, if permitted, would have meant the end of Turkey as a nation. From Moscow's viewpoint, the preceding sentence could be restated as follows: the purging of Eastern European nations of the vestiges of the fascist governments that brought them into the war on the side of Nazi Germany; friendship toward insurgents attempting to overthrow an archaic monarchical rule in Greece that remained upright only because of the supporting prop of British imperialism; an attempt to end the Anglo-American monopoly of Middle Eastern oil; and a continuation of Russia's historic quest for warm-water access to the oceans of the world, for commerce and self-defense.

But American patience stretched past the snapping point. Americans had spent four years fighting and working for a brave new world of peace; such had been promised them by their government, and in the swirl of postwar euphoria people tended to believe what they were told. Americans did not wish to burden themselves with the intricacies of unintelligible issues in far-away places; they wanted strife and war purged from the front pages. Our former allies "seemed to be going back to the old methods of seizing territory, dominating smaller nations, preparing strategic positions, restoring colonial nations," wrote John C. Campbell of the Council on Foreign Relations. "The greatest offender in American eyes, was the Soviet Union." The shortcomings of Soviet society, the deep differences of the United States and Soviet economic and political systems, had been glossed over in the interest of the common war effort. The propaganda offensive against Nazi totalitarianism, as Campbell has noted, "was in many respects applicable also to the doctrines and practices of Soviet Russia." Hence, when the Soviets pressed ahead with their own political and strategic offensives, unilaterally and in violation of the principles of its wartime allies, "American opinion was conditioned to react strongly against them." The Russians stood as the most visible obstruction to world tranquillity.

For months Truman refused to share his own mounting anxieties with the American people. When Molotov harassed the hapless Secretary of State James Byrnes at a foreign ministers meeting in October 1945, Truman poo-poohed the significance—merely a single step on the path toward an overall peace settlement, he told a press conference; the international scene would soon quieten, much as the domestic labor-management strife would run its course.

Stalin felt no such restraints. He publicly disavowed the wartime alliance in a speech to a party congress on February 9, 1946, that officially labeled the western nations, and especially the United States, as a graver threat than even Nazi Germany. Drawing upon the Marxist axiom that capitalism is fated to repeat boom-bust cycles, each worse than the last, he said the "capitalist ruling class" eventually would resort to aggressive war in quest of a solution for its economic problems. Stalin blamed the two world wars on such crises, and said a third must be expected because peaceful resolution of economic strife "is impossible . . . under present capitalist conditions of the development of world economy." Stalin announced a new Five Year Plan of economic development to bring the USSR to a war footing. "Only under such conditions," he said, "can we consider that our homeland will be guaranteed against all possible accidents." He predicted the confrontation would come during the decade of the 1950's, when America would have sunk into a disastrous depression.

Washington received Stalin's speech somberly. Supreme Court Justice William O. Douglas, a pillar of American liberalism, called it "the Declaration of World War III." A month later Truman publicly reverted to a get-tough policy himself, in a manner that was indirect—and, by the account of his daughter, Margaret, unintended. In March 1946, Winston Churchill, now a private citizen—although certainly no ordinary one—accepted an invitation (endorsed by the President) to make a speech at Westminster College, in Fulton, Missouri. Truman rode with Churchill on the train from Washington, and introduced him with these words:

I had never met Mr. Churchill personally until a conference we had with Mr. Stalin. I became very fond of both of them. They are men and they are leaders in this world today when we need leadership. . . . . I understand that Mr. Churchill is going to talk about the sinews of peace. . . . *I know he will have something very constructive to say to the world..*

Churchill's speech, a harsh and eloquently phrased denunciation of Soviet aggression, contained a terse and evocative description of what lay ahead for the world:

From Stettin in the Baltic to Trieste in the Adriatic, an iron curtain has descended across the continent. From what I have seen of our Russian friends and allies during the war, I am convinced that there is nothing they admire so much as strength, and there is nothing for which they have less respect than for weakness, especially military weakness.

Churchill pleaded for a resumption of the British-American "fraternal association" to discourage Soviet expansionism.

Truman, sitting on the speaker's stand behind Churchill, applauded at several points, and his staff told reporters he had read the speech enroute to Missouri. The special circumstances of the speech—Truman's role in the invitation, and his introduction—led to the conclusion that he endorsed what Churchill said, and that the event signaled a hardening of the U.S. stance toward Moscow. Bert Andrews of the New York *Herald Tribune,* one of the better-informed Washington correspondents, wrote, "Mr. Truman went along largely with what Mr. Churchill had to say, if not entirely." Margaret Truman, in her memoir of her father's presidency, insists this was not the case; that Truman in no sense considered the speech a break with Russia. And, indeed, Truman did write his mother and sister a day or so later that while he thought the affair "did some good . . . I am not yet ready to endorse Mr. Churchill's speech."

Stalin thought otherwise. He denounced the Fulton speech as a "call to war against the USSR," and the whole Soviet propaganda machine busied itself with a barrage of vituperation against Churchill and his "fascist friends in Britain and America." (Three years later, in a newspaper interview, Truman revealed that Stalin sent him a private note protesting the Churchill speech. Whereupon Truman handwrote the Soviet leader a letter offering to send the battleship USS *Missouri* to bring him to the United States, and to escort him personally to Fulton for "exactly the same kind of reception, the same opportunity to speak his mind." Truman said Stalin refused.) Internally, the Soviet press did not report what Churchill said, only what Stalin replied. John Fischer, traveling in Russia at the time, wrote later, "Dozens of war-weary little people—farmers, train porters, bookkeepers, who normally took no interest in politics— asked me anxiously why these evil men were trying to set the world aflame again. And why didn't President Truman denounce these warmongers as Stalin had?" Thereafter the Soviet press carried items almost daily about America's "imperialist" motives in establishing bases in the Pacific and Iceland, and the soft treatment of "quisling war criminals" in refugee camps the United States ran in Germany. These statements were widely publicized in the United States, along with an article by P.F. Yudin, an authoritative spokesman for Marxist doctrine, who demanded a strengthening of the Red Army "because the Soviet Union is surrounded . . . by capitalist states which are constantly sending in a stream of diversionists and spies."

The same week Churchill spoke in Missouri, U.S. correspondents succeeded in entering Soviet-occupied Manchuria for the first time since the war ended. They did not report pleasant things. Factories were being dismantled and carted away to the Soviet Union by the veritable trainload.

The populace was cowed. A factory manager who gave the correspondents an interview was shot within hours. The Russians kept the reporters cooped in their hotel and refused them transport; if they ventured outside, snipers fired at them. "The tommy gun is king and you see it everywhere," wrote A. T. Steele of the New York *Herald Tribune*. Robert Martin of the New York *Post* sensed a "studied and cynical freeze" directed against newsmen.

The journalist-editor John Fischer, who began studying the Soviets while at Oxford in 1933 and who spent several months in the USSR in early 1946 on a mission of the United Nations Relief and Rehabilitation Administration (UNRRA), tried to remain objective. In articles in *Harper's, Life* and *The New Yorker* in 1946, he explained the Soviets' pathological fear of outside invaders, wrote about the Russians as human beings, and counseled patience in dealing with them during the uncomfortable postwar years. Yet Fischer's exasperation leapt from his articles. He recounted talking with a Soviet official who argued that it would be an unfriendly act for the United States to direct shortwave broadcasts into the USSR, although the Soviets should feel perfectly free to broadcast its propaganda to America. Why? asked the befuddled Fischer. "A perfect example of reciprocity," he quoted the Soviet as replying. "Your laws provide for free speech, and we observe them. Our laws do *not,* and it would be improper for you to disregard them." Again, he told of a Russian official's explanation about why planes were not equipped with de-icers: "Sure we have a few more crack-ups. Maybe ten percent more than if we had all those safety devices. But by leaving them off, we can build fifteen or twenty percent more planes a year. So we are still five or ten percent ahead." Fischer thought it "characteristic that human life didn't enter into this calculation."

Because of the special audience of intellectuals and college-trained professionals and academicians who read *Harper's,* Fischer's articles had profound impact upon American opinion makers. Fischer was no belligerent yahoo, bellowing animosity at "Rooshian commies," a notable talent of the Hearst newspapers and the Chicago *Tribune:* he was one of the thinking class's very own, he had examined the Soviets with the objective eye of the scholar-journalist, and he found their system sorely wanting in human decency. More than any single writer Fischer had seminal effect upon America's postwar thinking about the Soviet Union, and especially upon liberals who had wanted to believe the best about Russians and were rapidly changing their minds.

Concurrent with Fischer's gloomy reportage, Brooks Atkinson of the

New York Times also wrote off the Soviets. Returning from a ten-month tour in Moscow in mid-1946, he called for drastic changes in the U.S.-Soviet relationship. "The familiar concepts of friendship" should be abandoned in attempts to establish workable relations with Moscow. "Friendship in the sense of intimate association and political compromise is not wanted, is not possible, and is not involved. . . . The Russian people are admirable people . . . but between us and the Russian people stands the Soviet government. Despite its sanctimonious use of the word 'democracy' it is a totalitarian government. . . . There are no freedoms within the Soviet Union. . . . [T]he government is a machine for generating power within the Soviet Union and as far outside as the power can be made to extend; and all attempts to deal with it in terms of friendship are doomed to failure.

"Although we are not enemies, we are not friends, and the most we can hope for is an armed peace for the next few years. . . ."

For younger veterans who came out of the war with idealistic hopes about world harmony, the Soviet break was an acutely painful wrench. Once sympathetic, Bill Mauldin now drew a cartoon of two Soviet bullies approaching an emaciated man in a dungeon. One carried a noose and said,"There's nothing to it, excellency. Comrade Popoff and I have committed hundreds of successful suicides." The same week Mauldin wrote a *mea culpa* letter to *Time:*

I guess I'm a disillusioned fellow traveler. I'm angry with our former great Allies. It's an accumulation of many things, but principally it's because of Russia's behavior in the United Nations. The Russians are determined to break up the UN. We could take a lot of slaps at our own foreign policy, we've lost a lot of our moral right to criticize. We're all wrong, but Russia is wronger.

Soviet-U.S. détente a failure, the Truman Administration fell back upon a double-pronged strategy of nuclear superiority and military and economic aid to any nation willing to oppose the Russians.

CHAPTER 16

THE WORLD POLICEMAN

The nuclear issues America faced in 1945 were complex: whether the United States, through the United Nations, should share the nuclear secret with allies and potential foes; under what auspices, military or civilian, atomic energy should be developed for peaceful purposes; and whether scientists should be allowed to contrive more horrifying versions of the bomb.

The first issue, civilian control of nuclear energy, was resolved in short order. President Truman wanted it. So, too, did atomic scientists chafing under generals more interested in making bombs than power plants. The Atomic Energy Commission, created in 1946, declared that development and utilization of atomic energy, "so far as practicable," should be for civilian purposes, "subject at all times to the paramount objective of assuring the common defense and security." The AEC swiftly became a major industrial force in America, and despite the emphasis on peaceful uses of atomic power, the military placed such demands on the AEC that at least ninety percent of its program was military.

Hopes of putting the atomic bomb under international control succumbed rapidly to U.S.-Soviet distrust, internal congressional politics, and Truman's unwillingness to run patently grave risks with the century's most important military development. The Soviets, meanwhile, were receiving a steady flow of information on the U.S. program from espionage rings in the United States and England, and Stalin apparently was willing to risk developing his own bomb without American help rather than enter into a controls agreement that would violate the Russians' xenophobic fear of foreign inspection.

The Truman Administration, meanwhile, kept its nuclear monopoly on conspicuous display. In July 1946, the military staged two public tests of the bomb on a tiny atoll called Bikini, in the Marshall Islands, 2,000 miles southwest of Hawaii. Doomsayers—and many scientists—predicted the explosions would send an enormous tidal wave rushing across the Pacific to inundate San Francisco. Others warned darkly about what might happen to the ocean when stung by the atom. The first bomb, decorated with a picture of the love goddess Rita Hayworth, was dropped from a B-29 into a flotilla of seventy-three ships—U.S., Japanese and German battleships, transports, landing ships, destroyers, even an aircraft carrier—from 30,000 feet. An audience of congressmen, reporters, and scientific observers from all nations gawked as the water boiled into a cloud of fire and foam. The vessels heaved and pitched; many burst into flames, but only five sank. A second blast three weeks later, however, this one underwater, showered the target fleet with a heavy contamination of radioactivity. The skeptics raised new specters: of a bomb exploding in a lake, a reservoir, a river, to snuff out an entire city beneath a deadly mist of radioactive haze during the night. The net result of the tests, however, was to soothe the fears of the American people almost as much as the bombs dropped on Japan had aroused them.

But who *could* control the bomb? Labor declined. Scientists declined.

The military in 1946 let it be known it intended to spend $125 to $175 million annually, a high percentage on secret work. *Time* reported that "thoughtful scientists are thoroughly alarmed" at the change. "Is the military about to take over U.S. science lock, stock and barrel, calling the tune for U.S. universities and signing up the best scientists for work fundamentally aimed at military results . . . ?" Yes. Universities had greatly expanded their scientific departments and laboratories with wartime funds: the researchers wanted to keep them open, even if the price was purely military work.

With new designs of bomb in hand in 1948, the military and the AEC set up a new series of tests on Eniwetok Atoll, some 200 miles west of Bikini. Three bombs in all were detonated, this time under circumstances of utmost secrecy; no longer did the United States deign to invite Soviet observers. The only public statement emitted by the AEC was a single terse sentence: "Operation Sandstone [the code name for the tests] confirms the fact that the position of the United States in the field of atomic weapons has been substantially improved." A few weeks later Senator Edwin C. Johnson of Colorado inadvertently gave the the true dimensions when he boasted in an interview that U.S. scientists "already have created a bomb that has six times the effectiveness of the bomb that was dropped at Nagasaki"—that is to say, a bomb with an explosive power of 120,000 tons of TNT.

The inevitable happened one afternoon in late September 1949. Charles Ross, Truman's press secretary, called in reporters for a brief announcement in the name of the President: "I believe the American people are entitled to be informed of all developments in the field of atomic energy. That is my reason for making public the following information. We have evidence that within recent weeks [i.e., the third week of September] an atomic explosion occurred within the U.S.S.R." The nuclear race was on.

The immediate precipitant for military and economic aid to countries threatened by the Soviets was a sudden crisis in Greece in the spring of 1947. When the war ended, the British, dominant commercially in the country, reinstalled King George (whose unpopularity was enhanced by the fact that he was not even Greek) and brought in troops to suppress the resistance movement. A truce was finally called, and non-Communists won parliamentary elections of dubious authenticity.

The Communists took to the hills as guerrilla fighters, and the British army spent millions upon millions of pounds futilely trying to contain them. Its economy near ruin because of postwar domestic problems, on February 24, 1947, the British government told the United States it could provide no further economic or military aid. The Truman Administration decided to take up the burden the British were casting away. On March 12 the President asked a joint session of Congress for $400 million in aid for Greece and Turkey, as well as authority to detail military advisers. The speech was tantamount to a declaration of global policy that committed the United States to undertake a job of world policing and economic aid to any nation opposing communism and the Soviet Union.

The Senate Foreign Relations Committee began hearings the next day, and skeptics raised a host of questions and objections. The toughest questions put to the Administration concerned its decision to bypass the United Nations, and whether Truman meant the United States intended to become a world policeman. The UN bitterly disappointed persons, in Congress and elsewhere, who had taken the grandiose charter language at face value, and felt the Greek situation should be handled by the international community, and not by the United States acting alone.

In making its case the Administration presented testimony from ambassadors to the two recipient nations; both stressed the pragmatism of Truman's decision. To the Administration's relief, the general public accepted the Truman Doctrine, even if unenthusiastically and without signs they understood its full implications.

Two parallel developments followed closely upon the Truman Doctrine to extend even further the policy of Soviet containment—the Marshall Plan, indirectly, through economic aid to Europe; and the North Atlantic Treaty Organization (NATO), a military alliance intended as a defensive shield against the Russians. Enacted against a backdrop of brutal Soviet crackdowns on democratic dissidents in Eastern Europe (notably Hungary and Czechoslovakia) the U.S. initiatives in 1947–48 ended any lingering public optimism about the postwar world.

Thus began the era of Pax Americana, a policy devised not so much by free choice of the public as by the lack of a palatable alternative; and one that led inexorably to U.S. involvement in such unforeseen places as Guatemala, the Dominican Republic, the Middle East, Chile—and Indochina. Stripped of diplomatic verbiage, the Truman Doctrine meant that the United States would use dollars and armed might to contain communism, with right-wing governments as partners if necessary.

CHAPTER 17

THE SPY SEARCHES

In early 1945 an analyst for the Office of Strategic Services, the espionage and intelligence organization that was to grow into the Central Intelligence Agency, read with rapidly rising eyebrows an article in *Amerasia,* a scholarly journal on Asian affairs. The article on British-American relations in the Orient, closely paralled a top-secret report the analyst had written on the subject for OSS superiors. Entire paragraphs had been abstracted from his report; others were loosely paraphrased. Quite obviously the writer had had access to a document that should not be in public circulation.

On March 11, a raiding party entered the vacant *Amerasia* offices. They found sophisticated photocopying equipment and briefcases crammed with classified OSS reports. The details eventually went to the FBI, who put the *Amerasia* principals under tight surveillance for several months, with agents making several surreptitious entries into the offices to find even more documents. Within a week six persons were arrested on charges of conspiring to violate the espionage act.

Then the same month the *Amerasia* case went to court, another "espionage" episode involving Soviet spies and subversion began unfolding in Canada. The central figure was Igor Gouzenko, ostensibly a twenty-six-year-old civilian clerk in the Soviet embassy in Toronto, in actuality a Red Army officer assigned to transmit encrypted espionage reports of his superior, Colonel Zabotin. Originally a dedicated Communist, Gouzenko became disillusioned with the Soviet system the more he compared it with Canada's open democracy. Soviet hypocrisy distressed Gouzenko. Although Canada was directing hundreds of millions of dollars of military aid to Russia, he knew from Zabotin's cables that the embassy concurrently spied on its hosts through a wide network of agents. His two-year assignment to Canada nearing an end, Gouzenko purloined scores of documents from Colonel Zabotin's files, went to a newspaper office, announced he was defecting. Would the paper be interested in such a story?

Incredibly, no. Gouzenko packed up his papers and went home to his apartment in frustration. The next day he tried again, at various government offices and to a new face at the newspaper. He was unable to find anyone who would take him seriously. Knowing his absence from the embassy would be noted, and fearing for his wife and young son, Gouzenko sought refuge with a neighbor, a sergeant in the Canadian air force. In due course two Soviets beat down the door of Gouzenko's apartment, the police were called, angry threats were exchanged, and the Canadian government finally realized a defector of some importance had fallen into its lap.

Gouzenko's story was staggering. The Soviet embassy was a mare's nest of spy rings, with military intelligence and the NKVD directing separate but parallel operations. The targets ran the gamut of Canadian military and political secrets—not only of the Canadians but of the United States and Great Britain. One person pinpointed fairly early was Alan Nunn May, a British scientist given temporary wartime assignment to atomic energy research in Canada. Unbeknownst to the British, May was an ardent, if secret, Communist, and through prearrangement Colonel Zabotin took him into tow under the code name "Alek." Arrested in Britain in February 1946, the trigger for the first public exposure of Gouzenko's information, May admitted giving his Soviet contact wide information on Canadian nuclear research and tidbits on the U.S. program he gleaned from his work. He also handed over samples of uranium 233 and 235.

May pleaded guilty, and was sentenced to ten years imprisonment. May's material gain, in addition to ideological satisfaction, was $700 and two bottles of whiskey.

CHAPTER 18

THE MOOD TURNS SOUR

If Soviet spy rings existed in the United States, did they rely upon supporting networks of covert American agents and fellow travelers, as had the Canadian networks? In Congress, the responsibility for ferreting out and exposing foreign agents rested with the House Un-American Activities Committee (HUAC).

Oddly, HUAC began its odyssey in Hollywood, capitalizing on the glamour of the movie industry to bring itself klieg-light publicity. Communists undeniably had made strong inroads in the movies during the 1930's and 1940's, for several reasons: the glamour of celebrity endorsements sells cigarettes, beer, and soap; it can also sell political ideas. The Communists wanted a base in Hollywood labor unions. Followers could neutralize or eliminate anti-Soviet and anti-Communist tones in American films.

The party activity, however, did provide the foundation for use of "the Communist issue" in violent labor disputes that erupted in Hollywood in

1945, and led directly to the HUAC probe. Movie unions long carried smelly encrustations of both corruption and communism. The largest was the International Alliance of Theatrical Stage Employees and Motion-Picture Operators of the United States (the IA). Anti-IA unionists gravitated to the Conference of Studio Unions (CSU), chiefly due to the vigor of a rather abrasive and cocksure painters' union leader named Herb Sorrell, who concentrated on bread-and-butter issues. Sorrell readily formed alliances of convenience with the Communists, and his IA opponents charged (and he denied it) that he was a party member. As the CSU grew, it inevitably quarreled with the IA over jurisdiction, and in March 1945 Sorrell ordered a strike.

Now enters a new figure in the "anti-Communist" crusade: Roy M. Brewer, an AFL troubleshooter who had worked with the War Labor Board. The IA imported him to direct strategy in the fight with Sorrell and the CSU, and he chose to campaign against communism, associating himself and the IA with an ad hoc group called the Motion Picture Alliance for the Preservation of American Ideals, which had been formed in 1944 to combat "the growing impression that this industry is made up of, and dominated by Communists, radicals, and crackpots." Despite its broad industry base, the Motion Picture Alliance was largely financed and controlled by studio heads, who saw it as a vehicle for "pro-free enterprise" messages.

In early 1947 the Motion Picture Alliance sent emissaries to Washington to persuade Chairman J. Parnell Thomas of HUAC to hold hearings to expose "Communists" in the industry. And, finally, there emerged William Randolph Hearst—aging, his once-powerful press empire slipping both in influence and affluence, reclusive and eccentric, but nonetheless a newspaper baron and one whose opinions could break a politician or an industry.

During the 1940's writer Adela Rogers St. John worked in the epicenter of the movie industry—as a story scout for Metro-Goldwyn-Mayer, responsible for locating suitable material for Clark Gable; as a personal troubleshooter for MGM head Louis B. Mayer, nursemaiding the drug-troubled young star Judy Garland; as a writer for the Hearst organization, frequently on movie subjects; and as a close confidante of William Randolph Hearst. Hence she observed at first hand Hearst's role in spurring the Hollywood investigation.

"Hearst had spent millions of dollars of his own money before Congress moved in with that committee. Everybody in Congress, in those early

days, got all their material from us [the Hearst organization]. We had two floors of the Hearst magazine building on Eighth Avenue in New York devoted entirely to the testimony and investigative answers we had gotten. The Hearst crew put all the material together—chiefly through a man named Jack Clements, who knew more about communism than anybody else, and J. B. Matthews—and then the committee got into it. Mr. Hearst forced that.

"Mr. Hearst had always had a keen interest in movies, but I don't think that just because he liked the picture business he was willing to let Communists run it.

"Out of this, of course, came the Hiss case and the breakup of the group in the State Department. We made one fatal mistake—and how could anybody have known it? We were looking for a senator to carry the ball. I went down and tried to get Millard Tydings, the great senator from Maryland [Mrs. St. John's enunciation of the word "great" was not complimentary]. He said, 'Nooooo, noooooo, they'd beat you to death before you are through. I am willing to die for my country, but not that way.' Other senators wouldn't come anywhere near it. They saw the material, they knew we had it, no question.

"The only guy who would go was [Joseph] McCarthy. We didn't know he was a drunk. If McCarthy hadn't been an alcoholic, the whole story would have been different, because we had the material, but he kept blowing it. He'd get drunk and say things he shouldn't.

"We had stuff on a man in China, a man we had just about pinned down, and McCarthy got drunk in a hotel in New York one night and told the whole tale, and messed it up. He made so much commotion we couldn't get it back together. Someone said, 'Why don't you take McCarthy out to New Jersey and lock him up and get him sober?' But it was no use—take your eyes off him, he'd go get drunk again."

At the same time Mrs. St. John and other Hearstlings worked to move HUAC into Hollywood, lawyer Robert Kenny worked to keep it out. A former attorney general of California, defeated by Earl Warren when he sought the governorship in 1944, and an activist in the budding presidential campaign of Henry A. Wallace, Kenny for more than a decade was the ranking figure in California's non-Communist left. Kenny detected Hearst's influence in HUAC's hearings, and ascribed it to somewhat less lofty motives than those cited by Mrs. St. John.

"I was attorney for the Screen Writers Guild, an organization riddled with many professional jealousies, but nonetheless blessed with a number of very progressive citizens, most of whom lived very well. Someone once *called them the 'swimming pool pinks,' which says a lot about their ability to be good liberals and make a decent living at the same time.*

"When HUAC began prowling here, Metro-Goldwyn-Mayer and some of the other studios threw out several of our members who had long-range contracts. We filed a lawsuit, and we began taking depositions early enough [before the hearings, when the industry went into a shell] that everyone was still speaking freely. When we asked Louis B. Mayer why he fired these people, he said it was 'his friend Mr. Hearst' who did it.

"Hearst would not support any movie studio that did not blacklist people he considered to be 'Reds.' Hearst thought he had been mishandled in the 1944 campaign, when he worked hard against Roosevelt, and that 'leftists' in the movie industry had reelected FDR through their favorable publicity for him.

"There was a personal pique as well. Some studio people continually made snide remarks about Hearst's relationship with Marion Davies, and about what an awful actress she was, and that if she wasn't screwing Hearst she wouldn't be able to work.

"Hearst became quite reactionary in his old age, and he had enough papers left to make life hell for people he disliked. He put out the word the Hearst newspapers would boycott any pictures from studios that did not 'check out Reds'—no reviews, no publicity, no advertising. And, to make it short, the studios turned tail and ran."

Despite the union turmoil, and the lobbying of the anti-Communist Motion Picture Alliance for the Preservation of American Ideals, Hollywood was not of a single mind on the hearings. Given its demonstrated penchant for irresponsible handling of witnesses and its suspicion of social ideas, HUAC could well torment the movies for months, destroying public confidence in the industry and forcing censorship.

The first round of public hearings, in Washington, confirmed the skeptics' worst suspicions. Using witnesses supplied by the Motion Picture Alliance for the Preservation of American Ideals, HUAC let prominent Hollywood personages lay the groundwork for charges of systematic and massive "communization" of the film industry. Producer-director Sam Wood (*For Whom the Bell Tolls*) named a long list of writers and other creative people as Communists.

The veteran character actor Adolphe Menjou cheerily identified himself as a "Red-baiter" and added, "I make no bones about it. I'd like to see them all in Russia. I think a taste of Russia would cure them." Menjou said he had an infallible method of detecting Reds: "attending any meetings at which Mr. Paul Robeson appeared, and applauding or listening to his Communist songs." Lola Rogers, mother of actress Ginger Rogers, said the Communists were wickedly subtle. She noted *None but the Lonely Heart,* with its "despair and hopelessness." Its background music, by Hanns Eisler, a German Communist before emigrating to the U.S., was "moody and somber throughout, in the Russian manner."

During this first phase of the hearings, HUAC accumulated names of nineteen persons—writers, directors, and producers—who supposedly served the Communist cause. Parnell Thomas laid out a course of action. The nineteen would be put on the stand and be asked directly whether they were Communists. Then the industry would be asked whether it would support legislation barring Communists from employment in the movies.

At this point HUAC had nothing other than hearsay evidence about Communist influence in Hollywood, and no proof that they affected the content of a single picture. Besieged, the anti-HUAC forces mobilized. Dozens of stars organized "The Committee for the First Amendment" under producers John Huston and William Wyler and writer Philip Dunne, declaring in a manifesto that "any investigation into the political beliefs of the individual is contrary to the basic principles of our democracy." The adherents included such names as Henry Fonda, Ava Gardner, Paulette Goddard, Benny Goodman, Van Heflin, Katharine Hepburn, Myrna Loy, Burgess Meredith, Gregory Peck, Barry Sullivan, Cornel Wilde, and Billy Wilder. The committee laid down a careful strategy. A select delegation would appear at the hearings to take the publicity away from Chairman Thomas and his sympathetic witnesses. Yet they would make plain they were not defending any Communists—only attacking HUAC's abuses of due process.

But the committee outsmarted the actors. On the day they appeared HUAC was to have heard Eric Johnston, the president of the Motion Picture Producers Association. Instead, Thomas craftily produced writer John Howard Lawson, a writer whom several witnesses had already named as the grand old man of Hollywood Communists.

Each time he was asked about past associations, Lawson declared HUAC had no right to make such inquiries, Thomas punctuating his objections with smart raps of the gavel. Lawson's stormy behavior and his extensively documented record of Communist associations shocked many of the stars who had come to Washington to protect their industry. None expected Lawson to cozy up to the committee, assuredly, but his shouting and doctrinaire denunciations made many in the group wonder whether HUAC just might be on to something. At a press conference after Lawson's testimony, the questions made plain to the delegation their presence was being interpreted as support for him. The same day the Washington *Times-Herald,* an unflinching HUAC supporter, stated that Sterling Hayden, one of the organizers of the trip, had a Communist background. William Wyler called a meeting to raise funds for a libel suit on Hayden's behalf. Hayden embarrassedly told them not to bother: the newspaper was correct; he in fact had been a party member for six months. After a couple of other witnesses emulated Lawson's performance, the actors' committee quietly withdrew to Hollywood. In all, HUAC summoned ten of the nineteen industry figures, none of whom would testify. Each was cited for contempt, and the "Hollywood Ten" went away to federal prison.

Despite its plethora of old party membership cards and lists of people who sponsored front-group affairs, HUAC never produced anything to justify an affirmative answer to a somewhat central question: did Hollywood Communists get anything into films that spread the party line? "The contents of the pictures constitute the only proof," said industry spokesman Eric Johnston. "It is the obligation of the committee to absolve the industry from the charges against it." This, of course, HUAC did not attempt to do. And the "evidence" of propaganda was thin. For instance:

In a script about a boys' school, Lester Cole used a paraphrase of the old line "better to die on one's feet than live on one's knees." A handful of moviegoers perhaps would have recognized the source: the Spanish Communist La Pasionaria.

When pressed by committee critics for chapter and verse on Communist taints in movies, Parnell Thomas fell back upon three wartime films that were undeniably pro-Russian. *Mission to Moscow,* about Joseph E. Davies' service as ambassador to Moscow, was depicted by critic James Agee in *The Nation* as "almost describable as the first Soviet production to come from a major American studio . . . a great, glad two-million dollar bowl of canned borscht." In the end, however, even *Time,* whose coverage was generally friendly to HUAC, concluded the committee "had failed to establish that any crime had been committed—that any subversive propaganda had ever reached the screen."

The uncertain ending notwithstanding, Hollywood capitulated to HUAC. All during the hearings Eric Johnston and other industry leaders denounced attempts at censorship and swore blood oaths they would not turn their backs on HUAC's targets. Within a month, however, fifty members of the three leading industry groups (the Association of Motion

Picture Producers, the Motion Picture Association of America, and the Society of Independent Motion Picture Producers) met for two days at the Waldorf Astoria Hotel and adopted a policy statement intended to appease HUAC. Those under contract would be suspended without pay; none would be rehired until he was acquitted "or has purged himself of contempt and declared under oath that he is not a Communist." The movies would not employ Communists or anyone else belonging to a group advocating forceful or illegal overthrow of the government. "In pursuing this policy," the producers reassured themselves, "we are not going to be swayed by hysteria or intimidation from any source."

The Waldorf Declaration satisfied Congress and the hearings trailed off, although they did revive again in the early 1950's, when yet another group of movie people took the stand to admit involvement with the Communists, and to plead for absolution. The Waldorf Declaration marked the beginning of a potent new weapon for "anti-Communists" to use in the entertainment industry: the blacklist.

By 1948 anti-Communist militancy was sweeping the country, spearheaded by the American Legion, such newspaper chains as Hearst and Scripps-Howard, and any number of ad hoc business and "patriotic" organizations. Information on the Communist conspiracy, and the people composing it, was marked with commercial success. "American Business Consultants, Inc." formed by three former FBI agents in a Madison Avenue office reachable only by freight elevator, put together files (from HUAC and other investigative bodies, the *Daily Worker,* and the multitude of fliers issued by the Communists and their front groups) and offered their services to the business community. Did an employer have a question about a man's loyalty? For a fee, ABC would screen its material and "clear" the person.

Harry Truman watched HUAC's work, and the spreading anti-Communist drives, with much apprehension. He felt that "the security agencies of the government are well able to deal quietly and effectively with any Communists who sneak into the government, without invoking 'Gestapo methods.'" But the Gouzenko spy revelations, and the incessant din of HUAC, prompted Truman to do something publicly about "subversives in government." In 1946 he created a committee of subcabinet officers to review loyalty programs, both for prospective and existing employees, and recommend tightening where necessary.

After a year's work the committee called for an intricate system of loyalty review boards, which Truman promptly instituted, even though with misgivings. Under the system, a person accused of belonging to a subversive organization, or engaging in subversive activities, was given a first hearing before a board in his own department, with the decision reviewed by the department head. If the findings were adverse, the person could appeal to a national Loyalty Review Board, under the Civil Service Commission.

The system, with a misleading superficial fairness, contained grave civil liberties flaws. Although the accused was provided a résumé of the charges, anything considered secret was omitted. Confidential informants of the FBI and other investigative agencies were not required to testify, or even to be identified.

In its first year the loyalty program resulted in firings of 793 government employees; eighteen others quietly resigned under investigation. Reasons for the disloyalty findings varied, but the War Department said 158 of the 190 civilians it fired were "ineligible for employment for disloyalty involving Communism."

The loyalty panels' dragnets reached deep into American life. One guideline they used for judging loyalty was something that came to be called "the Attorney General's List." When serving as attorney general, Francis Biddle compiled a list of subversive organizations for agencies to use when evaluating prospective workers. Biddle wanted some uniformity among agencies, and the list was intended as a guide, not a blacklist. It was strictly confidential. However, Representative Martin Dies, while chairman of HUAC, obtained a copy and put it into the *Congressional Record*. In his executive order establishing the loyalty boards, President Truman said membership in any of the organizations was nothing more than a "factor to be taken into consideration" in determining loyalty. As a practical matter, however, membership in a group on the Attorney General's List could—and did—cost a person his government job, his teaching position, his pulpit, his position in private industry.

CHAPTER 19

THE HISS CASE: AN IDEAL TARNISHED

During HUAC hearings on physicist Edward U. Condon in the spring of 1948, a New York journalist quietly passed a tip to Robert E. Stripling, the gaunt-faced, methodical Texan guiding HUAC's work as chief counsel. The New York grand jury, the reporter said, had been talking with a *Time* editor named Whittaker Chambers. According to corridor gossip, Chambers was spewing big names. Stripling dispatched two investigators to talk with Chambers, and on Tuesday, August 3, HUAC put him on the stand for a public hearing.

Chambers was a little-known figure even at his own magazine, a man who avoided office confidences, worked with his door closed, and spent his off time at a farm in remote rural Maryland. A brilliant writer, equally at ease writing lush, baroque prose about medieval theology and chatty Timese about current events, the fact is that Chambers had spent the bulk of his adult life in the domestic Communist underground, and he had carried the secretiveness with him when he left the party—first, by his account, to avoid feared party retribution; later, as a matter of personal choice. Chambers' biography, *Witness*, reveals a tortured neurotic, a man incessantly pondering suicide, choosing to remain alive only because of what to him was a God-given mission to save western civilization.

Reporters described him variously as "rumpled, moon-faced"; "perpetually rumpled and disheveled"; "a fat, sad-looking man in a baggy blue suit"; and "drab, middle-aged, hesitant of speech and manner." But Chambers' testimony, not his physique, was what counted. His story, in this initial public appearance, was as follows:

Chambers joined the Communist Party in 1924 because he felt western civilization "was doomed to collapse or revert to barbarism"; and "as an intelligent man I must do something," and thought he had found the answer in the economics of Marx and the politics of Lenin. Much of this time Chambers spent "in the underground, chiefly in Washington, D.C." He worked mainly with an underground organization developed "to the best of my knowledge, by Harold Ware, one of the sons of the Communist leader known as 'Mother Bloor.'" Chambers said he knew seven men at its top level:

The head of the underground group at the time I knew it was Nathan Witt, an attorney for the National Labor Relations Board. Later, John Abt became the leader. Lee Pressman was also a member of this group, as was Alger Hiss, who, as a member of the State Department, later organized the conferences at Dumbarton Oaks, San Francisco, and the United States side of the Yalta Conference.

The purpose of this group at that time was the Communist infiltration of the American government. But espionage was certainly one of its eventual objectives.

Chambers said that "in 1937" he repudiated communism because "experience and the record had convinced me that [it] is a form of totalitarianism, that its triumph means slavery to men wherever they fall under its sway, and spiritual night to the human mind and soul." For the next year he lived in hiding, "sleeping by day and watching through the night with gun or revolver within easy reach."

In 1939, two days after the Hitler-Stalin pact, Chambers went to Adolph A. Berle, then the assistant secretary of state with security responsibilities, and told "what I knew about the infiltration of the United States government by Communists." Berle acted shocked, but nothing happened. Chambers said he was especially galled to see Alger Hiss continue to rise through the State Department bureaucracy, from a minor post in the Trade Agreements Division to the director of the office in charge of United Nations affairs. In subsequent years FBI agents often called on Chambers (fourteen or fifteen times, in all, he later computed) but nothing happened to Hiss, who resigned from government in 1947 to become president of the prestigious Carnegie Endowment for Peace.

In going after Hiss, Chambers struck at the sort of man generally regarded as the best America has to offer. Born of Baltimore gentility, he attended Johns Hopkins University and Harvard Law School, and won the most cherished position available to a fledgling lawyer, a clerkship to the esteemed Justice Oliver Wendell Holmes. He came to Washington as counsel to the Nye committee investigating the munitions industry, worked at the Agriculture Department, and then moved to State. His government service, culminating in administrative groundwork of the United Nations, put him on a career track that carried into the heart of the American establishment. He was selected for the Carnegie foundation post by none other than the redoubtable Wall Street lawyer/diplomat John Foster Dulles. Only forty-four years old in 1948, Hiss had reason to anticipate even greater prestige and position—conceivably the post of secretary of state.

Certainly Hiss was not a man who could ignore Chambers' stain on his name. So Hiss telegraphed HUAC a strong denial of the charges, and asked the opportunity to appear publicly to refute them. And this he did, on August 5, in a skillful blend of subdued outrage and pained bemusement. Physically, Hiss was the antithesis of Whittaker Chambers. Slim, graceful, composed, articulate, with the lawyer's insistence on precise phrasing. And under risk of perjury indictment he declared:

I am not and never have been a member of the Communist Party. I do not and never have adhered to the tenets of the Communist Party. I am not and never have been a member of any Communist-front organization. I have never followed the Communist Party line, directly or indirectly. To the best of my knowledge, none of my friends is a Communist. . . .

To the best of my knowledge, I never heard of Whittaker Chambers until in 1947, when two representatives of the Federal Bureau of Investigation asked me if I knew him and various other people, some of whom I knew and some of whom I did not know. I said I did not know Chambers. So far as I know, I have never laid eyes upon him, and I should like to have the opportunity to do so.

When counsel Robert Stripling showed Hiss a photograph of Chambers, he replied he would rather see the man than his picture, and that he would not care to testify that he had never seen him. When Stripling asked directly, "You say you have never seen Mr. Chambers," Hiss said, "The name means absolutely nothing to me, Mr. Stripling."

To the Hiss partisans, predominant in the hearing room, his statements came across as unequivocal denials. Hiss left the room in a cluster of admirers and friendly reporters, and one committee member muttered, "We're ruined." An irrefutable citizen had put the lie to a HUAC-endorsed witness in direct terms, and sentiment was strong for getting away from the Hiss-Chambers case as rapidly and gracefully as possible. But Representative Richard M. Nixon, the freshman Republican from California, demurred. He argued he detected distinct hedges throughout Hiss's testimony; the "denials" were not that he knew Whittaker Chambers, but that he did not know *a man named Whittaker Chambers*. Hiss's opening statement denying Communist Party membership or allegiance was also subject to negative interpretation: if Hiss truly was a deeply implanted agent, as Chambers charged, he likely was not a formal party member, and certainly would keep his public distance from identification with any Communist causes. "It is a little too mouthy," Nixon said of Hiss's looping sentences. At Nixon's insistence the committee decided to seek proof of whether Chambers had actually known Hiss, as he claimed. It created a subcommittee, with Nixon as chairman, to question Chambers in closed session to discover what hard facts he knew about Hiss, his family, his personal life, the Georgetown houses he lived in. Then it would separately quiz Hiss on the same points and compare the answers.

The separate interrogations swiftly brought the committee back to total belief in Chambers. Answering brisk questions from Nixon, he ticked off detail after detail about the Hiss household. Much of the information was trivial and a matter of record in *Who's Who* and other standard reference works. But Chambers had a knack for flavorful details that went beyond public knowledge. Not only did he know that the Hisses were amateur bird watchers (a fact noted in several biographical reference books), he also recalled "once they saw, to their great excitement, a prothonotary warbler," rare in the Washington area. Others of Chambers' firm assertions were outright wrong. Chambers estimated Hiss's height at "five feet eight or nine"; actually Hiss is an even six feet. Shown a hearing-room picture of Hiss with a hand cupped over his ear, Chambers responded, "Mr. Hiss is deaf in one ear." He is not. Chambers called the Hisses teetotalers. Hiss is not. But the bulk of his answers indicated great familiarity with the Hiss household.

Given the tight coordination between HUAC and the FBI, it is probable, though it has never been proven, that Nixon primed himself with bureau reports of Chambers' many interrogations and of earlier background investigations of Hiss. In any event, one question cut to the core of Hiss's carefully hedged denials that he knew anyone by the name of Whittaker Chambers. Asked if Hiss knew him in that guise, Chambers responded, no, "he knew me by the party name of Carl."

How did Chambers know Hiss was a Communist? "I was told by J. Peters, the head of the entire underground" in the United States. Could Chambers provide "any evidence" to support his claim? No, "nothing beyond the fact" that Chambers knew him as a "dedicated and disciplined Communist" who faithfully paid his dues monthly for two years. As an underground agent, Hiss didn't carry a party card. Chambers made no mention of any espionage.

When Hiss went before the subcommittee on August 16 for private testimony, much of his previous self-assurance had vanished. Newspaper leaks of Chambers' supposedly secret testimony irked him. Accused of "hedging" he expressed indignation that Chambers, "a confessed former Communist and traitor to his country," should be given weight equal to his own. But under Nixon's lead, members took the unwitting Hiss over the household and personal material previously given by Chambers. Much of it jibed. What members considered a "clinching point" came when Hiss talked about bird watching.

McDowell: Did you ever see a prothonotary warbler?
Hiss: I have right here on the Potomac. Do you know that place? . . . They come back and nest in those swamps. Beautiful yellow head, a gorgeous bird . . .

A sudden hush fell over the subcommittee. How could Chambers possibly know such a fugitive detail from the past—unless he in fact had enjoyed a close relationship with Hiss? Nixon hastily asked another question to fill the void of silence.

After a recess, Hiss abruptly stated he thought he could resolve at least part of the conflict. After sifting through his memory, and the leaked testimony that Chambers claimed to have lived in his house during the

1930's, he felt the man in question could have been a ne'er-do-well free-lance writer named "George Crosley," whom he had met in 1935 while working for the Nye committee. "Crosley" sought out Hiss for information on the munitions industry for use in an article. Hiss took a mild liking to the man, let him and his wife and small child stay in his apartment a few nights during their move to Washington. Because Hiss and his wife were changing their own Georgetown residence at the time, they even let the Crosleys have their old apartment for a period when the leases overlapped, lent them some furniture, and gave them the use of a dilapidated 1929 Ford. Crosley, Hiss said, turned out to be a deadbeat who never paid rent on the apartment nor returned several small loans, and Hiss maintained he eventually drifted away. Hiss repeated his demand that he be brought face to face with Chambers. And even if Chambers and "Crosley" were the same man, he denied knowing him as a Communist agent. The subcommittee thought Hiss's surge of memory was play acting. Its interpretation was that the nature of the questions alerted Hiss that Chambers had told so much about their relationship that a blanket denial would no longer suffice. Hence the change of strategy in mid-course.

The committee promised the long-sought personal confrontation would be arranged and nine days later staff members hustled Chambers to New York, and a cryptic telephone call to Hiss's office told him to report to Room 1400 of the Commodore Hotel in Manhattan.

The two men stared at one another across the hotel suite—Hiss thinking that "I saw Crosley in the added pounds and rumpled suit," but uncertain until he heard his voice; Chambers considering it "great theater," Hiss's "performance . . . made . . . shocking, even in its moments of unintended comedy, [by] the fact that the terrible spur of Hiss's acting was fear." At Nixon's direction Chambers stated his name, and Hiss walked quizzically toward him, staring at his face, and asking "Would you mind opening your mouth wider?" By Hiss's account he wanted a clearer view of Chambers' teeth, since one of "George Crosley's" distinguishing characteristics had been blackened, jagged front teeth. Congressmen and the HUAC staff watched with fascination. When Hiss said he wished to hear more of Chambers' voice Nixon handed him *Newsweek,* and he began reading. After further straining and hesitations, Hiss said he could "positively" identify Chambers as the man he had known as Crosley. And he dared Chambers to repeat his charges outside the libel-proof forum of HUAC: "I challenge you to do it, and I hope you will do it quickly."

The hearing ended with a decision to bring Hiss and Chambers together publicly in Washington on August 25.

August 25 was a day of infernal heat, a discomfort that did not deter the curious from cramming the caucus room of the old House Office Building far beyond capacity an hour before the opening gavel. The strange new medium of television, adding its blistering lights to the torment, beamed most of the ten hours of proceedings to viewers along the eastern seaboard.

A point subjected to tedious haggling was exactly how Hiss disposed of a ramshackle 1929 Ford. Chambers' story was that he used the car briefly while living with Hiss, and that later Hiss insisted on giving it to the Communists for their use. Chambers said Hiss made the gift through a Washington used-car company that the Communist underground regularly used as an unobtrusive channel for auto transfers. Hiss's story was somewhat different. The car had sentimental value only and was deteriorating in the street. So he "threw it in" when he let Crosley take his old apartment, as he by then had a new Plymouth. (Earlier Hiss had said he "sold" the Ford to the man he recalled as Crosley.)

The committee, however, had registration records showing that Hiss didn't buy the Plymouth for some months after he said he gave the old Ford to Chambers, and that he in fact had transferred the Ford via the "Communist underground" car firm by July 1936, a full year after the car supposedly was made available to Chambers. Pressed by Nixon to explain the discrepancy, Hiss replied he had testified from memory, not from records. Impatient, Nixon tried to elicit a direct answer.

NIXON: Now . . . did you give Crosley a car?
HISS: I gave Crosley, according to my best recollection—
NIXON: Well, now, just a moment on that point, I don't want to interrupt you on that "to the best of my recollection" but you certainly can testify "yes" or "no" as to whether you gave Crosley a car. How many cars have you given away in your life, Mr. Hiss?

Hiss, for the first time in the sessions, heard the ridiculing sound of unfriendly laughter. All he could (or would) say was, "I have no present recollection of the disposition of the Ford."

The committee, of course, was trying to lead Hiss into a flat answer on the car that could be proved a lie by its documentary material. But Hiss carefully avoided the bait. By committee count, on 198 occasions Hiss qualified his answers with a phrase such as "according to my best recollection."

The Hiss affair now took on a momentum of its own. His virtuoso HUAC performance notwithstanding, Chambers clearly was expected to accept Hiss's challenge: to make his charges publicly and risk a libel suit; or to be considered an untested witness. Chambers threw down the gauntlet to Hiss on a *Meet the Press* broadcast on August 27, declaring flatly Hiss was a Communist, but declining to say whether he "now is or is not a member of the party." Chambers said he did not think Hiss would sue. And he chose his words carefully during a long series of questions aimed at eliciting whether Hiss acted as an espionage agent.

The ball now was in Hiss's court, and when he did not sue immediately the Washington *Post* reminded him he had created "a situation in which he is obliged to put up or shut up." In late September he filed, asking $50,000 damages; when Chambers, in a press statement, alluded to the "ferocity or the ingenuity of the forces that are working through him," he upped it by $25,000. Chambers now had to substantiate his charges in a courtroom, to the satisfaction of a jury.

The preliminary proceedings went poorly for Chambers, by his own admission. His lawyers did not put the same credence in his story as had HUAC, and for the first time Hiss, through his attorneys, had the opportunity to examine him under oath during the depositions. Chambers' lawyers warned him that "if I did have anything of Hiss's" that would help prove the case "I had better get it."

By his story, Chambers made a weekend trip to Brooklyn, to the home of his wife's nephew, and found a cache of documents and microfilm he had hidden away as a "life preserver" when he broke with the Communist Party. The material included sixty-five typed pages, memos handwritten by Hiss and Harry Dexter White, and microfilms of papers from the State Department's Trade Agreements Division, in which Hiss had worked. Chambers gave the typed copies to his libel lawyers, which were put into evidence at the depositions and (at Hiss's insistence) then surrendered to the Justice Department for safekeeping, because of their confidential nature. The microfilms he hid away on his farm, eventually in a hollowed-out pumpkin. HUAC got wind of their existence, and after some legalistic jockeying Chambers led committee investigator Don Appell into the field late the night of December 2, guided by flashlight, and pulled out what came to be known as "the pumpkin papers."

The appearance of the papers cast the Hiss case in an entirely new light. Now Chambers was offering *documentary proof* that showed Hiss to be not a mere intellectual follower of communism, but an active Soviet agent as well. Such was the thrust of the newspaper shouts the first weeks of December 1948; public sentiment crystalized against Hiss overnight. The New York grand jury intensified its work, with HUAC members charging, darkly, that the Justice Department seemed eager to prosecute Chambers for perjury, but not Hiss.

The dates on the documents posed another problem for Chambers. In HUAC testimony Chambers said that he left the Communist Party in 1937. He gave the same date in interviews with the FBI and State Department security agents. Later, during the public confrontation with Hiss, he edged the date forward to "early 1938." But the "pumpkin papers" bore dates as late as April 1, 1938; most were dated after January 1, 1938. Further, internal markings on many of the papers showed that they had never been handled in the offices where Hiss worked. All Chambers could do was revise his early testimony, claiming his "break" in 1937 was ideological, not actual, and that he did not leave the party until 1938.

When HUAC began leaking the papers in early December, Hiss partisans had much sport with the committee's description of them as "vital to the nation's security." The papers contained such harmless chatter as the fact that the Italian and German armies had exchanged staff officers; that the Japanese were trying to buy a a manganese mine off Costa Rica where the mineral was known not to exist. But the Democratic chortles faded when Hiss revealed that some of the documents "were of such importance" that he had asked the Justice Department to take possession of them. And Sumner Welles, the undersecretary of state at the time the papers were stolen, said certain of the papers had been transmitted in the "most secret code" and their possession by a foreign power could have caused the United States great harm.

Hiss spent eight days, off and on, before the grand jury. On the last day of its eighteen-month existence, it indicted him on two counts of perjury: for denying that he had given any government documents to Chambers; and for denying that he had seen Chambers after January 1, 1937. Congressman Nixon called the indictments a "vindication" of HUAC—a statement that Hiss termed "a frank admission of the committee's investment in the result." Liberal sympathy remained strongly on the side of Hiss. But most progressives and liberals saw the deeper significance of the trial. In the public mind, the New Deal stood in the dock with Alger Hiss.

During the six months between indictment and trial, the defense succeeded in locating what it accepted as an old Woodstock typewriter that had been in the Hiss household at the time he knew Chambers and that had been passed on to two young black brothers who helped the family move. Scientific tests showed that many of the "pumpkin papers" had been typed on the Woodstock; Hiss could offer no logical explanation, but this damaging evidence was made known to the prosecution. A drumbeat

317

of hostile publicity intensified in the weeks preceding the trial. Two concurrent trials kept public attention on the Communist issue on the eve of Hiss's trial—that of leaders of the Communist Party, USA, for violation of the Smith Act, which began on January 16 in the same building where Hiss was to be tried; and the trial of Judith Coplon, accused of acting as a spy courier, in Washington on April 25. New York newspapers frequently paired stories on the Smith Act and Hiss trials.

The Hiss trial itself produced little new evidence; after two days' deliberation the jurors reported themselves hopelessly deadlocked, and Judge Samuel H. Kaufman discharged the panel. The Justice Department announced it would bring Hiss to trial again as rapidly as possible.

In the interim, however, an angry storm of vituperation broke over Judge Kaufman's head—one touched off by Congressman Richard Nixon the day after the jury locked, with a demand for an investigation of the jurist's conduct of the trial. Kaufman's "prejudice . . . against the prosecution" had been "obvious and apparent," said Nixon, who never set foot in the courtroom during the trial. To the *Journal-American,* Nixon hinted that jurors might be subpoenaed before HUAC. The *Daily Mirror* told why: "Those who voted for acquittal could not be convinced otherwise. . . . There might have been a Communist sympathizer in the group." Nixon declared, "When the full facts of the conduct of this trial are laid before the nation, the people will be shocked."

Citing the chilling impact of these attacks on prospective jurors, and the very real danger a fair trial was no longer possible in New York, the Hiss defense tried futilely to move the trial to Vermont, but the motion was denied and Hiss went on trial again on November 17, 1949, this time before Judge Henry W. Goddard.

Little new substantial evidence was developed, and once again the jury debated two days. This time the verdict was guilty, on both counts, and Judge Goddard sentenced Hiss to the maximum five years. The Second Circuit Court of Appeals rejected his appeal, and the Supreme Court refused to review the case. On March 22, 1951, fourteen months after his conviction, Hiss went to prison at Lewisburg, Pennsylvania.

In terms of its impact upon American political life, the Hiss case stands as the most important trial in the United States history. The shoddy tactics of HUAC in the initial phase of the case (in permitting Chambers to make a public accusation without giving Hiss proper opportunity for rebuttal); the right-wingers' gusto in twisting the affair into a blanket assault upon all the New Deal stood for; Richard Nixon's assault on the integrity of the judicial system after the first trial—all these factors encouraged liberals reflexively to throw a protective circle around Hiss and claim him as one of their very own. The guilty verdict left these people and their tradition in an awful position of exposure: the liberals had identified themselves with a convicted agent of what the right wing called "the Communist conspiracy."

A congeries of horrors is directly attributable to Hiss's fate. A native American, a man groomed for national leadership, was shown to be susceptible to subversion for a foreign power. HUAC's shabby cadre of Red hunters could now boast the special virtue of verification by jury. J. Edgar Hoover's FBI, under the umbrella of loyalty programs, acquired staggering powers of inquiry into the personal lives and political beliefs of hundreds of thousands of citizens.

The jury voted Hiss's conviction on January 21, 1950. On February 9, Senator Joseph McCarthy of Wisconsin, who had been actively scouting Washington for "an issue that can get me reelected in 1952," spoke to the Republican Women's Club of Ohio County, West Virginia, in Wheeling. According to the account in the Wheeling *Intelligencer* the next morning, McCarthy brandished a document selected from a pile before him on the podium and said:

While I cannot take the time to name all of the men in the State Department who have been named as members of the Communist Party and members of a spy ring, I have here in my hand a list of two hundred and five that were known to the Secretary of State as being members of the Communist Party, and who, nevertheless, are still working and shaping the policy in the State Department.

Thus was a squalid legacy passed from the 1940's into the 1950's, one that could be exploited for four tormented years, years that would bear the name "McCarthyism."

CHAPTER 20

OF GIDEON, DIXIE, AND IKE

In late 1947 a temporary surge of popularity attributable to the Marshall Plan pushed President Truman's standings in the polls to a "favorable" rating of 55 percent, highest in months and a welcome turnaround, but nonetheless a thin cushion to carry into an election year. The Gallup poll ran him in a trial heat with the two top Republican contenders, Governor Thomas E. Dewey of New York and Senator Robert A. Taft of Ohio, and he beat them decisively. The wise men of the Democratic Party took Truman's renomination for granted, although he was not to announce his candidacy formally until March 8 of the following year.

By the time of the announcement, things had fallen apart for Harry Truman—in Congress, in the left wing of the Democratic Party, in the Jewish community, in the ranks of big-city leaders wary of entanglement with a "loser," in the polls, which in a short three months showed him dropping from 52 to 36 percent favorable. If Harry Truman was to be elected President of the United States, he must do it on his very own.

On the Left: Gideon's Army

Journalist Dwight Macdonald, dissecting Henry Wallace in the fall of 1947, was tempted to declare the man a political corpse and be done with him. But three times previously the pundits had buried Wallace—after he failed to get the vice-presidency in 1944; after his firing from the cabinet in 1946; after a European trip in 1947 devoted chiefly to praising Russia and denouncing U.S. foreign policy. That Wallace still possessed political vitality was a symptom of the anxiety gripping America. Macdonald concluded "so long as he remains a symbol of hope and of dissidence, so long will he retain a mass following."

Wallace's promised "loyal opposition" to Truman's foreign policies evolved, by gradually heightening bounds, to a third-party candidacy. As editor of the New Republic he enticed readers with such Wallacese sentences as "New frontiers beckon with meaningful adventure."

Wallace set out on a speaking tour under the sponsorship of the Progressive Citizens of America, an umbrella group of leftists ranging from popular fronters to non-Marxist progressives. The crowd turned out en masse, and they loved him. At the outset he insisted all he intended to do was to "scare the Democratic Party leftward." But as the tour neared its end he had progressed to a near declaration of his candidacy: "If we can't make the Democratic Party liberal, we'll have to take what action is appropriate." He proposed a 10 percent reduction in taxes; increased wages to be financed from the "swollen profit structure"; a no-strings-attached handover of U.S. atomic weapons to the United Nations; a ten-year reconstruction program for the USSR, to be financed by the United States. Robert Kenny, the former California attorney general, defense lawyer for the Hollywood Ten, and the state's most prominent liberal, saw in the Wallace crowds "a mounting tide of popular opposition to the politics and leadership of both political parties." Kenny felt a new party would give voters "a clear choice between progressive and reactionary candidates for president." He and Wallace spoke of nationalizing coal mines, railroads, electric power facilities. By midsummer Wallace's vigorous campaigning, and his obvious charm for younger people, forced Democratic strategists to take a serious look at him.

In January 1947 a strong cadre of veteran New Dealers—Chester Bowles, Paul A. Porter, John Kenneth Galbraith, to name a sampling—gathered in Washington to form an organization that would have a sizable impact on American politics: Americans for Democratic Action. The purposes were broad: to extend New Deal programs, protect civil liberties, stabilize the economy, work for world peace through the United Nations. A key sentence in the statement of principles read: "We reject any association with Communists or sympathizers with communism in the United States as completely as we reject any association with Fascists or their sympathizers." Thus was the line drawn between ADA and the Progressive Citizens of America. In a very telling gesture, Eleanor Roosevelt, long a Wallace admirer and friend, opted for ADA: so, too, did such labor leaders as James Carey, Walter Reuther, David Dubinsky, and Emil Rieve, each in a struggle with Communists in his own union and desperate for support.

The liberal unions' alliance with ADA was a turning point for Wallace because it forced him to the farthest-left fringes of labor for manpower and dollars—almost invariably, Communist-dominated factions in CIO unions. Thus was the die cast for Wallace. On a national radio broadcast the night of December 29 he announced his candidacy, declaring:

There is no real fight between a Truman and a Republican. The bigger the peace vote in 1948, the more definitely the world will know that the United States is not behind the bipartisan reactionary war policy which is dividing the world into armed camps and making inevitable the day when American soldiers will be lying in their arctic suits in the Russian snow. . . .

We have assembled a Gideon's army, small in number, powerful in conviction, ready for action. . . . We face the future unfettered by any principle but the general welfare. . . . By God's grace, the people's peace will usher in the century of the common man.

A week later Wallace acquired a runningmate, the flamboyant Glen H. Taylor, a freshman Democratic senator from Idaho. An isolationist, he opposed the Marshall Plan and voted to cut foreign aid funds by more than half.

Wallace and Taylor sputtered their separate ways in quest of votes.

No one of substance expected Wallace to win, but many Democratic leaders did fear him as a spoiler: the polls showed Wallace with a tentative grip on almost 10 percent of the people, votes Harry Truman needed.

On the Right: The Dixiecrats

"That the United States is very nearly ten percent a black nation is known to everybody and ignored by almost everybody—except maybe the ten percent," John Gunther wrote in 1947. The civil rights "issue" simply did not exist in the early 1940's because the vast majority of Americans ignored blacks, but the war brought race relations out of the shadows. About one million blacks served in the armed forces, and although the bulk of them were in segregated units, they moved around and saw new things and heard much talk from the government about the "rights of men" and freedom and democracy. Southern whites, concurrently, also became acutely conscious of the black, through the influx of black soldiers and defense workers to facilities located in warm climes.

The confrontations were inevitable, swift, and brutal. But federal interventions were rare, for prosecutions of such crimes as murder were matters for individual states. The Department of Justice could enter a case under federal civil rights statutes only if an official or agent of the state was involved. Notoriously touchy on the subject of "states' rights," southern officials did not readily admit such involvement. Even if a case could be brought to trial, juror sympathies were solidly with the local citizen. "There has never been a successful federal prosecution for lynching, per se," the New York Times noted in 1946.

The South vigorously excluded blacks from the polls, using the poll tax and stringent property requirements to disenfranchise blacks (and poor whites as well, unless their votes were needed by the dominant machine). Some statistics illustrate how well the system worked. In 1946 Mississippi had about 1,250,000 citizens of voting age, of whom only around 180,000 went to the polls. In 1944 South Carolina had 989,841 citizens over twenty-one; only 99,830 of them voted. But South Carolina had six members in the House of Representatives—identical with the state of Washington, where 793,833 persons voted of a total voting population of 1,123,725. Liberals fumed about "political immorality" but could do nothing to change things. Three times the House passed a bill abolishing the poll taxes; three times the Senate killed it with filibusters.

Born of Confederate stock and raised in Jim Crow country, Harry Truman nonetheless considered official discrimination and racial hatred to be repugnant to the Bill of Rights. In December 1946 he appointed a committee to investigate and report on the status of civil rights in America. They recommended sweeping advances: an anti-lynching law; abolition of the poll tax; laws ending discrimination in voter registration; an end to segregation in the armed forces and in transportation and school facilities; establishment of a Fair Employment Practices Commission; and creation of a permanent Commission on Civil Rights, a Civil Rights Division in the Justice Department, and a joint Congressional Committee on Civil Rights.

As a political realist Truman certainly realized the recommendations had little chance of enactment. But he had them drafted into specific bills, which were introduced in February 1948. By Truman's account, basic morality left him no choice: every Democratic convention since 1932 had "stressed the devotion of our party to the constitutional ideal of civil rights. . . . The platform of a political party is a promise to the public. Unless a man can run on his party's platform—and try to carry it out, if elected—he is not an honest man."

A week after the civil rights message the annual meeting of the Southern Governors Conference bristled with threats of rebellion against Truman and the Democratic Party. After four days of blustery oratory about the "carpetbagger" Truman and his many shortcomings, the conference sent a six-governor delegation to Washington to find out how serious the Administration was about civil rights. Governor Strom Thurmond of South Carolina put the question direct to J. Howard McGrath, the Democratic national chairman:

Will you now, at a time when national unity is so vital to the solution of the problems of peace in the world, use your influence . . . to have the highly controversial civil rights legislation, which tends to divide our people, withdrawn from consideration by the Congress?

McGrath stared back at Thurmond and replied, "No."

The southern revolt was on. Bills were introduced in Dixie legislatures taking the names of presidential candidates off the ballot, leaving only electors for each party. A postelection convention would instruct them how to vote in the electoral college. The threat was clear: Truman must withdraw civil rights bills, or the South would deny him the presidency.

The Dixiecrats roared on, putting together a two-part strategy. First, they would attempt to block Truman's nomination and substitute a prominent Southerner such as Senator Harry F. Byrd of Virginia. Failing, they would convene immediately after the Democratic National Convention to choose a third-party candidate who would siphon off enough votes to deny a majority to either Truman or the Republicans, thus throwing the election into the House of Representatives, where each state would have one vote. There, the Dixiecrats felt, the South would dictate a president of its liking.

Whatever the outcome, Truman faced grave trouble below the Mason-Dixon Line.

In the Center: Who Likes Ike?

Dwight D. Eisenhower came out of the war a truly popular hero. The popularity, and the presidential talk, followed Eisenhower into his post-war positions as army chief of staff and president of Columbia University. Ike reacted testily each time someone suggested he seek the White House. As early as January 1947, with "Ike for President" buttons sprouting over the country, the Washington *Times-Herald* broke out eight-column banner headlines to go with a supposed Eisenhower quotation: "I will run for President if the people of this country want me to run." "You know it's a lie," Eisenhower replied angrily. "I never said anything of the kind."

The public hunger for Eisenhower was remarkable for several reasons. The people talking about him for President were not even sure whether he was Republican, Democrat, or neither (although the initial support was from the GOP). Eisenhower's views on national issues were totally unknown; as chief of staff, he had testified for universal military training, but beyond that the public record was barren. Nor, for that matter, did he display any obvious qualifications for the presidency. But public and professional politician alike scented a winner in the hero-general; regardless of his "qualifications," he would be a better national leader than the slumping Harry S. Truman.

So the Ike-for-President talk continued and gained momentum. In January 1948 a branch of the Draft Ike Committee announced it would enter Eisenhower in the Pennsylvania primary on April 27.

Things were clearly out of hand, so Eisenhower moved again to squelch the political career that people kept trying to push upon him. In early February he wrote a public letter to a New Hampshire newspaper stating ". . . . I would not accept nomination even under the remote circumstance that it was tendered me." And so the Republicans reluctantly gave up on Eisenhower.

The Republican boom for Eisenhower had been dead but for a month when anti-Truman Democrats took up his cause, signaled by a statement by the national board of Americans for Democratic Action that the party needed an open convention.

Wallace on the left. The Dixiecrats on the right. Eisenhower in the center. Could Harry Truman survive the Democrats' intraparty contests, much less the November elections?

CHAPTER 21

HST: THE UNDERDOG PLANS

Yes, he could, because as President he still controlled the machinery of the Democratic National Committee, and through it the convention. By early May, Truman had 423 of 620 delegates named by state conventions, only 195 short of a majority; many of the unpledged could be expected to vote for him. Thus weeks before the convention Truman had clinched the nomination. The splinter candidates could provide a noisy convention, but they would have to seek the presidency under a different banner.

Truman, therefore, looked beyond the convention to the campaign, planning for which had begun in earnest after the 1946 congressional debacle. Truman strategists worked from a thirty-three page single-spaced memorandum entitled "The Politics of 1948," written in September 1947 by James Rowe, a presidential assistant, after weeks of interviewing politicians and others about the main problems facing Truman and how he could overcome them.

The bulk of the document was incisive analysis and point-by-point scenarios for exploiting Republican weaknesses and capitalizing upon the many powers of the presidency. A Democratic victory, Rowe wrote, depended upon maintaining the "unhappy alliance" of the "three misfit groups" comprising the traditional Democratic majority—southern conservatives, western Progressives, and big city labor. Rowe forecast that the sole important domestic issue would be the high cost of living, with neither party likely to do anything to curb inflation because of fear of alienating the farmers. Rowe urged cultivating labor while rank-and-file members (political neuters in prosperous times) were still receptive because of anger over the Taft-Hartley Act. Labor leaders "must be given the impression that they are once more welcome" at the White House, with the stroking done by Truman personally. "The mere extension of an invitation to William Green, Dan Tobin, Philip Murray, [David] Du-

binsky or any of the prominent leaders to 'come in and talk with me' has a
stupendous effect on them and their followers. One by one they should
be asked to 'come by' and the President should ask them for their advice
on matters *in general*. (This is a question of delicate 'timing'—it is dangerous to ask a labor leader for advice on a *specific* matter and then ignore
that advice.) No human being—as every President, from Washington on,
has ruefully learned—can resist the glamour, the self-important feeling of
'advising' a President on anything, even if it is only his golfing backswing."

Rowe recommended that Truman deliberately antagonize the Republican-controlled Congress on the assumption no White House programs
would be approved under any circumstances in an election year. "Its [the
White House's] recommendations—in the State of the Union message
and elsewhere—must be tailored for the voter, not the Congressman;
they must display a label which reads 'no compromises,' the strategy on
the Taft-Hartley Bill—refusal to bargain with the Republicans and to accept any compromises—paid big political dividends. That strategy must
be expanded in the next session to include all the *domestic* issues." The
White House should propagandize its economic programs through the
press so that "by the time Congress convenes the people will know thoroughly what the President has been asking of them. He won't get it, his
program will not get very far, but whatever *is* done will be regarded as a
Democratic gain; and the Republican Party will be a sitting target for having been obstructionist." Even if the Republicans proposed good legislation it should be opposed: ". . . In terms of 1948 the Administration simply cannot afford to allow a bill with Taft's name to pass." Rowe would
also go after the special interest groups working with the Republicans.
For instance, he advocated promoting a grass-roots movement against
realtors because of their opposition to housing bills: "It is the essence of
politics to wage an attack against a personal devil; the Real Estate Lobby
should be built into the dramatic equivalent of the Public Utility Lobby of
1935. Purely on the merits, the performance of the real estate interests in
their postwar gouging fully deserves everything they get in the way of retaliation. There can be no possible compunction about using such a tactic against them." Rowe doubted that a current Justice Department anti-
trust probe would be useful because of a "widespread suspicion that the
department's motivation was purely political. . . . However, the useful
material already gathered by the department's investigators should be
made available to those who can make propaganda use of that material."

On black voters, Rowe cited the conventional political theorem that
blacks held the electoral balance of power in New York, Illinois, Pennsyl-

vania, Ohio, and Michigan. Roosevelt tore the black vote from the Republicans in 1932; now it showed signs of slippage, especially in New York, because of assiduous cultivation by Governor Dewey, who insisted that "his controllable legislature pass a state anti-discrimination act." Rowe warned that the black voter, "a cynical, hardboiled trader," would return to the Republicans because southern Democrats had a hammerlock on Congress. "The Negro press, often venal, is already strongly Republican." The standard Democratic protestation about the blacks' improved economic lot "has worn a bit thin with the passage of the years. . . . Unless there are new and real efforts (as distinguished from mere political gestures which are today thoroughly understood and strongly resented by sophisticated Negro leaders) the Negro bloc, which, certainly in Illinois and probably in New York and Ohio, *does* hold the balance of power, will go Republican." Rowe made no civil rights recommendations. Clark Clifford, in forwarding his version of the memo, suggested that "it would appear to be sound strategy to have the President go as far as he feels he possibly could go in recommending measures to protect the rights of minority groups. This course of action would obviously cause difficulty with our southern friends but that is the lesser of two evils."

So what should the Democrats do? One key suggestion was "to create in the public mind a vote-getting picture of President Truman." The "honeymoon" period had ended; so, too, had the months of "violently critical . . . public opinion. . . . Emerging instead is the picture of a man the American people like. They know now that he is a sincere and humble man and, in the cliché so often heard, that he is a man 'trying to do his best.'" Nonetheless Truman still came across as a politician, a person who "does not hold first place in the ranks of American heroes. Today's public picture of President Truman is not sufficiently varied. The people want something more." Rowe went on to say that the public pays little attention to what the President does as chief of state: "They really form their lasting impressions from watching his incidental gestures—when he appears as the representative of all the American people." Illustrating, Rowe noted that on a state visit to Brazil, Truman received more warm publicity from a comic equator-crossing ceremony in which he was "changed from a pollywog into a shellback" than from formal conferences.

Yet the public wanted more than "stereotyped gestures" of visits with "a round-the-world flyer, or the little girl with the first poppy, or the Disabled Veterans, or the Eagle Scout from Idaho." Needed, Rowe said, were "gestures of substance" which through repetition "form a carefully drawn

327

picture of the President as a broad-gauged citizen with tremendously varied interests." Specific suggestions followed:

—The President could lunch with Albert Einstein; it will be remembered he was the man who prevailed upon Roosevelt to start the atomic bomb project. At his next press conference he can explain that they talked in general, about the *peacetime* uses of atomic energy and its potentialities for our civilization. He can then casually mention that he has been spending some of his leisure time getting caught up on atomic energy; he has been having "briefing sessions" from the AEC; and has also been doing some reading purely from the layman's point of view. He suggests to the newsmen it would do them no harm at all to read such and such a book (as long as he picks the right one) which he has just read. . . .

—Henry Ford II . . . is often in Washington these days. The President should casually invite him to lunch to just talk over matters "generally." This picture of the American President and the Young Business Man together has appeal for the average reader. Many other business leaders should be called in occasionally. . . .

—The President should concentrate on other fields. The literary field, for example, has its uses. A novelist with the latest best seller is just as good as an international banker for these purposes. Outstanding *women* in various activities should be invited.

Because custom dictated that Truman not do anything political until after the convention he "must resort to subterfuges—for he cannot sit silent. He must be in the limelight." Rowe concluded, "In national politics the American people normally make up their minds irrevocably about the two presidential candidates by the end of July. If the program discussed here can be properly executed it may be of help in getting them to make up their minds *the right way*."

Beyond the strategy document, the Truman campaign planners started with several assumptions. The press would be hostile. Truman expected fully 90 percent of the media to oppose him "as most were owned, operated, or subsidized by the same private interests that always benefited from Republican economic policies." Businessmen and corporation executives, especially utility moguls, would help the Republicans through advertising attacks on New Deal and Fair Deal programs. Truman's poor standing in public opinion polls was directly attributable to the drumfire of adverse press comment (or so the President felt, anyway); they did not represent farmers and workers. Overcoming the "false propaganda" would require taking the Democratic program directly to the voters.

One professional politician who sensed the impact of Truman's man-to-man rapport was Gael Sullivan, a young Chicago liberal working as staff director of the Democratic National Committee. In mid-1947 he advised the White House how to "capitalize fully on the President's impact on the people."

Sometime before the National Convention in 1948 the President should show himself to the nation via the back platform of a cross-country train.

The easy manner of speaking when speaking informally has been lost in translation to the people via radio and speaking tours.

The White House began casting around for an excuse for the President to make a "nonpolitical" cross-country tour. With the Democrats flat broke, the trip would have to be made at public expense, hence the White House needed some nonpartisan draping. By happenstance, Dr. Robert Gordon Sproul, president of the University of California in Berkeley, wanted a commencement speaker, and when he called the White House to inquire whether Truman was interested, the President literally jumped at the offer. So on June 3 an eighteen-car train, the *Presidential Special,* rolled out of Washington's Union Station in one of the more thinly disguised political trips of the century.

Truman talked tough, both at the Republican-controlled Eightieth Congress and at stay-at-home Democrats who cost the party the 1946 election. Speaking to a convention of the Communication Workers of America in Seattle, Truman said he shared unionists' dislike for the Taft-Hartley Act, but he wouldn't take blame for it. "You know the reason for that is in November 1946, just one-third of the population voted. The people were not interested in what might happen to them. . . . We have the law now, and I am the President and I have to enforce it. Your only remedy is November 1948, and if you continue that law in effect, that is your fault and not mine, because I don't want it." All along the route Truman lashed at congressional inaction on housing and rent controls, its refusal to raise the minimum wage, its agricultural policies, its restrictive immigration legislation. Station-by-station he lambasted the 80th Congress as the "worst" in history.

Tacoma: "Congress is interested in the welfare of the better classes, and passed a rich man's tax bill."

Olympia: "If you want to continue the policies of the 80th Congress, it'll be your funeral. . . . The Republican Congress believes in the theory of Daniel Webster that the West is no good and there is no use spending money on it."

Albuquerque: "The issue in this country is between special privilege and the people."

East St. Louis: "I think they are hunting for a boom and bust."

329

Butte, Montana: Referring to Senator Robert A. Taft, "I guess he'd let you starve. I'm not that kind."

The trip had its rough moments as Truman's inexperienced entourage learned the tricks of cross-country campaigning. In Omaha, poor advance work brought only 1,000 persons into the cavernous Ak-Sar-Ben Auditorium, and press photographs showed Truman staring at row upon row of empty seats. In dedicating an airport at Carey, Idaho, the patriotic decorations misled the President, and he spoke of the "brave boy who died fighting for his country." There was an awkward silence, and a tearful woman standing near the President interrupted: the dedicatee was her sixteen-year-old daughter. Embarrassed, Truman said he was "more honored to dedicate the airport to the young woman who bravely gave her life to her country." The mother tugged his arm again. "No, no, our Wilma was killed right here," in the crash of her sweetheart's private plane while joyriding. All Truman could do was apologize to the shaken parents. During the off-the-cuff speech in Eugene, he said of Stalin, in a remark the Republicans were to hurl back at him for months, "I like old Joe. He's a decent fellow, but he's a prisoner of the Politburo."

But these incidents didn't diminish Truman's zest for political combat. He told his audiences he was on the road to "dispel the lies and misinformation" the press was spreading about him. "I am coming out here so you can look at me and hear what I have to say and then make up your mind as to whether you should believe some of the things that have been said about your President." The crowds were large (50,000 in Berkeley; in Los Angeles a million saw him between the railroad station and the Ambassador Hotel, where he spoke) and responsive, shouting "Pour it on!" when he talked tough about Congress. In Spokane, cub reporter Rehea Felknor of the Spokane *Spokesman Review* was in the midst of an impromptu trainside interview with Truman when Democratic Senator Warren Magnuson passed the President a copy of the paper. Truman skimmed it as Felknor asked, "How does it feel to invade a Republican stronghold?" Felknor wrote Truman's reaction:

Raising his head to glare down on the lone newspaperman, he asked, "Do you work for this paper, young man?" The President's voice became raspy for virtually the only time during his appearance here as he declared:

"The Chicago *Tribune* and this paper are the worst in the United States. You've got just what you ought to have. You've got the worst Congress in the United States you've ever had. And the papers, this paper, are responsible for it."

Senator Robert Taft derided Truman for "blackguarding the Congress at every whistle stop in the country." Whereupon the Democratic National Committee polled mayors and chambers of commerce in thirty-five cities visited by Truman and asked for comment on Taft's statement. Some of the replies:

Eugene, Oregon: "Must have wrong city. As the lumber capital of the world . . . our whistles never stop blowing."

Laramie, Wyoming: "Characteristically, Senator Taft is confused, this time on whistles."

Pocatello, Idaho: "If Senator Taft referred to Pocatello as 'whistle stop' it is apparent that he has not visited progressing Pocatello since time of his father's 1908 campaign. . . ."

Most newspapers treated Truman's trip as a crass vaudeville performance that demeaned his office. Even friendly editorialists chided him. But journalists who listened closely divined exactly what Truman was doing. "The New Deal—its preservation, perpetuation, and completion is what Harry S. Truman is pinning his hopes on," Barnet Nover wrote in the Denver *Post.* "He has begun to make an impression." The crowd response convinced the White House political strategy board that Truman could sell himself—if only he could get through to the voters.

CHAPTER 22

THE GOP: DEWEY, AGAIN

The Rowe strategy predicted flatly that Thomas E. Dewey would be the Republican nominee, a prognosis seemingly sound at the time; titular leader of his party by virtue of his losing the 1944 race with Roosevelt, Dewey was the country's best-known Republican. And even the defeat was no disgrace: reluctant to make a suicidal race against a popular wartime commander, he did his duty to the GOP, campaigned hard and well, and held the plurality to a surprising 3,600,000 votes, smallest in FDR's four campaigns. Dewey rebounded to win reelection as New York governor in 1946 by almost 700,000 votes, largest in the state's history. Moreover, Dewey enjoyed a superb public image. New Yorkers first knew him as the racket-busting young district attorney who put corrupt Tammany chieftains in jail and broke the famous "Murder, Inc." ring. Dewey made a premature run for the GOP nomination in 1940 but was crushed beneath the Wendell Willkie bandwagon. Lowering his sights to a more realistic level, he won the governorship in 1942 and ran a clean, efficient administration slightly to the left of traditional Republicanism. He pushed through New York's first law barring racial and religious discrimination in employment, and he managed to cut both business and personal taxes and still end the war years with a $623 million reserve in the state treasury. Energetic and young (Dewey was forty-six in 1948), he seemed just the man to appeal to progressive urban voters who traditionally favored the Democrats. Yet his conservative credentials were good enough to pass inspection by all but the most neanderthal of Republicans.

And yet, Dewey had a major handicap—his personality. In the often-quoted words of the wife of Kenneth Simpson, GOP leader in New York County, "You have to know Dewey really well to dislike him." Priggish, self-important, brusque, smarter than most people and unwilling to conceal it, Dewey acted as if holding high public office was a personal divinity-granted right. Dewey's world seemed divided into two parts: the press, servants, and the "lesser public"; and people who could help him politically. Politicians endured his haughtiness of necessity; after all, the man won elections, and a party exists for that purpose. But the stories circulated, and many of them got into print. One midnight Dewey and Republican leaders of the legislature sat before a blazing wood fire in the governor's mansion. A burning log rolled out onto the stone hearth, and one of the men instinctively reached for a poker. Dewey halted him with a silent motion, and pressed a buzzer. He resumed the conversation. The servant finally came, brushing sleep from his eyes, and restored the fallen log to the fire. As one of the legislators remarked later, "A thoughtful man would have handled the situation in a few seconds without getting some poor servant up from bed. Dewey just didn't think that way." Then there was the lady reporter from a Republican paper who received an ungallant brush-off from Dewey on Election Night 1944. The lady had traveled on the campaign train with Mr. and Mrs. Dewey and was on a first-name basis with them. She happened to get into an elevator at the Roosevelt Hotel with the Deweys and nodded and spoke. Mrs. Dewey said, "Good evening." Dewey looked above the door of the elevator and said chillingly, "We don't want to see any newspaper people." The morning after his nomination in 1944 Dewey was having breakfast in a Chicago hotel with Governor John Bricker of Ohio, who was to be his vice-presidential running mate, and movie and still cameramen tried to get pictures of the conference. "Shake hands with Governor Bricker, will you please?" a cameraman asked. "One does not," Dewey replied, with a certain reproof in his voice, "shake hands across a breakfast table."

Warren Moscow, a political writer for the *New York Times* who knew

Dewey well, said of him, "Mr. Dewey is a strange character—or perhaps I might say, he's a strange *lack* of character." According to Moscow, soon after Dewey became governor he received a report about an outbreak of amoebic dysentery at a state mental hospital. One patient had already died. A legislative leader asked Dewey privately what he intended to do. Dewey replied, "Oh, we'll let it slide a bit, let it coast for a little while, and then we'll make a bigger splurge when we clean it up." Seven deaths later Dewey acted, depicting the hospital situation as "typical of twenty years of dry rot and incompetence" of preceding Democratic administrations. "In my opinion," Moscow said, "it boils down to seven people dying so that Mr. Dewey could get his name in bigger headlines."

One acutely sensitive subject for Dewey was his height. Although at five feet eight inches he was about average for the American male, the impression of shortness perhaps came from the fact that his head was somewhat large for his body, or that unadmiring photographers deliberately shot him from unflattering angles. Finally, the Dewey staff circulated a fact sheet trying to put down the unkind remarks about his youth and height: he was three inches taller than Joe Stalin, and only three-quarters of an inch shorter than Harry Truman; that Alexander the Great was governor of Macedonia at nineteen, and that Napoleon at thirty-five was master of all of Europe.

Dewey's initial strategy was to await, rather than pursue, the Republican nomination, the same course he had followed in 1944 when he won without opposition. And indeed the field appeared clear for him in 1948. The Rowe campaign memorandum, for instance, wrote off Senator Robert A. Taft as hopeless because his policies had alienated so many large voter blocs. Completely overlooked was another youthful figure of Republican politics, Harold Stassen: elected governor of Minnesota at age thirty-one; a wartime naval officer; a delegate to the founding conference of the United Nations, by appointment of President Roosevelt. Now forty-one, the hulking, moon-faced Stassen, who exuded a Midwestern warmth comparable to Eisenhower's, held no public office, which meant he had to campaign hard, and early, just to keep his name before the voters. Stassen formally declared his candidacy in December 1946 and during the next eighteen months traveled in forty states and made more than 250 speeches. Stassen spread a message of liberal Republicanism—confidence in the free enterprise system and international peace through the United Nations; social programs far to the left of anything ever contemplated by Taft; a mixture of toughness and conciliation toward the Soviets. The experts laughed at Stassen as he gradually built a campaign organization run from Minneapolis by a husky, handsome forty-year-old St. Paul lawyer named Warren Burger.

The 1948 primary drew additional interest because of the belated entry of General Douglas MacArthur, then commanding occupation forces in Japan—an inscrutable war hero whose views on domestic issues were even less known than those of Eisenhower, but who enjoyed the loud backing of the Chicago *Tribune* and the Hearst newspapers, which called for MacArthur's candidacy in a three-column front-page editorial calling him "The Man of the Hour." Republican right-wingers poked at the reclusive general for weeks, attempting to recruit him to halt the detested Dewey. They finally succeeded in mid-March, four weeks before the primary, when MacArthur elaborately announced his availability.

Once in the race, MacArthur could not run. As an active army officer, he was barred from campaigning, and indeed, he issued no further statements, relying instead upon the *Tribune* and the Milwaukee *Journal,* the Hearst outlet, to publicize him. Wisconsin supporters managed somehow to present him as a "favorite son," by virtue of the fact that he briefly attended a high school in Milwaukee, and received his West Point appointment from the state. But just what MacArthur would do as President no one deigned to suggest (after all, the general hadn't even set foot in the United States since 1937).

Stassen, meanwhile, whirled around Wisconsin in a Greyhound bus, speaking from sunup to midnight. The GOP state organization supported him, and freshman Senator Joseph R. McCarthy headed his slate of delegates. The aloof Dewey responded to Stassen's frenzied campaigning by visiting Wisconsin for two brief days. Most observers gave the nod to MacArthur, predicting the week before the election he would win at least fourteen of twenty-seven delegates.

The experts were wrong. Stassen got nineteen delegates, MacArthur eight, Dewey none. The New York governor's noncampaign was suddenly in deep trouble (MacArthur's died outright). As the New York *Herald Tribune* editorialized, Stassen was "no longer a dark horse. All at once Mr. Stassen has emerged from the fringe of interesting possibility. From now on he is in the first division of contenders for the Republican presidential nomination." Naturally concerned, Dewey moved into Nebraska, the next primary state, this time facing Taft as well as Stassen. Dewey campaigned three days, Taft, four; Stassen, in Nebraska frequently for two years, came in for the final days. Once again, a Stassen upset: more than 43 percent of a record vote, with Dewey second and Taft a weak third. Next, Ohio, and Stassen's first stumble.

For Dewey, Oregon would be decisive; for he would have to balance the losses in Wisconsin and Nebraska and to prove he was attractive to voters outside New York. Stassen opened an early lead in the polls, then the Dewey money-blitz began: a barrage of billboards, newspaper ads, and radio spots that cost an estimated quarter of a million dollars, an astronomical sum by 1948 standards. Sensing the nomination slipping from him, Dewey imitated Stassen's bus-stop campaigning with a vigorous effort that covered 2,000 miles in three weeks; often he worked sixteen hours a day. At inestimable cost to his dignity, he even performed some of the foolish rituals demanded of a candidate. He posed in a ten-gallon hat and in an Indian headdress.

The pivotal event, however, was a Dewey-Stassen radio debate broadcast live from Portland to some 900 stations around the country, the first ever in a presidential campaign. The subject: whether the Communist Party should be outlawed, a subject of intense national interest because of the Mundt-Nixon Bill then before the House of Representatives. Stassen took the affirmative, Dewey the negative, and the former prosecutor chewed the former governor into forensic pieces. Dewey won 53 percent of the votes, and all twelve delegates. Harold Stassen's eighteen-month pursuit of the presidency was in grave trouble.

At the convention, which opened in Philadelphia on June 21, the Dewey opposition was so fractionated it could not gather around a single candidate. Dewey came to town with 300 to 350 "sure votes" of the 548 needed, with many others secretly tucked away.

The Dewey forces pursued fence straddlers with promises of federal judgeships and other patronage, and even cash (in the instance of a black delegate from Mississippi). The first ballot gave Dewey 434 votes, Taft 224, Stassen 157, favorite sons and fringers had the rest. An hour later the second ballot gave Dewey 515, Taft 274, Stassen 149, with minor candidates bringing up the rear. The total left Dewey 33 votes short of a majority. The anti-Dewey forces forced an overnight recess. Taft and Stassen talked; Stassen refused to withdraw until after the third ballot; Taft sat down and wrote a concession statement, releasing his delegates to Dewey.

Facing the convention that evening, Dewey gave an address that foreshadowed the oratorical style he was to follow in the fall: rotund profundities which no one would question; no mention whatsoever of Democrats or Truman; no outline of the programs he would pursue if elected. Dewey's main theme was unity. "The unity we seek is more than material. It is more than a matter of things and measures. It is most of all spiritu-

al. Our problem is not outside ourselves. Our problem is within ourselves. . . . Spiritually, we have yet to find the means to put together the
world's broken pieces, to bind up its wounds, to make a good society. . . ." And so it went on, in the vein of a man who had won the presidency, not simply the nomination. Later that night Dewey completed the
ticket by picking Governor Earl Warren as his running mate. The Republicans were ready for November.

CHAPTER 23

HST: THE UNWANTED MAN

Although it was a heated convention the Democrats held in Philadelphia that July, Truman won on the first ballot, with 947½ votes.
Next the delegates formalized Truman's choice of Senator Barkley for
vice-president. Truman brought the wilted convention to life with a roar
when he declaimed, in high, strident tones, "Senator Barkley and I will
win this election and make the Republicans like it—don't you forget it.
We will do that because they are wrong and we are right." Ad-libbing in
short, punchy sentences, Truman flailed the Republicans as the party of
"special privilege" and scorned its record in the Congress. Then Truman
threw out a surprise challenge. On July 26 he intended to call Congress
back in special session. "Now, my friends, if there is any reality behind
that Republican platform, we ought to get some action from a short session of the Eightieth Congress. They can do this job in fifteen days, if
they want to do it. They will still have time to go out and run for office."

The immediate postconvention script went as anticipated. Angry Dixiecrats gathered in Birmingham for a loosely run convention, waved
Confederate flags, and chanted support of Governor Strom Thurmond
for President and Governor Fielding Wright of Mississippi for vice-president. The platform called for "the segregation of the races and the racial
integrity of each race."

The Dixiecrats' racism, their failure to entice southern titans such as
Harry Byrd out of the Democratic Party, their embracing of super bigot
Gerald L. K. Smith (who said in a convention speech that "there are not
enough troops in the army to force the southern people to admit the Ne-
groes into our theaters, our swimming pools, and homes") caused most
editorialists to sniff disdainfully and look away.

"Gideon's Army"—that is, the Wallace people—occupied Convention

Hall a few days after the Democrats left Philadelphia, with Communist-liners swiftly taking control of the new Progressive Party. The platform committee, steered by Lee Pressman (who was fired as general counsel of the CIO for leftism, and who was to admit later he had been a Communist), repudiated the Marshall Plan in language closely tracking that passed by the Communist Party at its convention earlier in the summer. Wallace, who spent much of his time meditating in his hotel room, professed not to see any evidence of Communists at the convention. "I would say that the Communists are the closest things to the early Christian martyrs," he said at a press conference.

Unfortunately, Wallace spent much of convention week—and the following months as well—bogged down in questions as to whether he had the intellectual stability demanded of a President. The questions harked back to an early episode in Wallace's New Deal days. While secretary of agriculture, Wallace had developed an interest in a Russian mystic named Nicholas Konstantinovich Roerich, guru of a religious sect devoted to theosophy: a charlatan to serious theologians, though venerated by such devout followers as the composer Igor Stravinsky. In 1934 Wallace hired Roerich as a government consultant and sent him on a mission to Outer Mongolia, supposedly to search for a strain of drought-resistant grass. Wallace and Roerich eventually fell out, and Wallace dismissed him from the government job.

These events transpired without public notice. Then politicians turned up a sheaf of letters that Wallace supposedly wrote to Roerich. Stated charitably, the letters sounded peculiar. A typical sentence read:

I have been thinking of you holding the casket—the sacred, most precious casket. And I have thought of the new country going forth, to meet the seven stars under the sign of the three stars. And I have thought of the admonition, "Await the stones."

Columnist Westbrook Pegler happily put them into print without the benefit of comment from Wallace, so the columnist sought to raise questions directly at Wallace's first press conference in Philadelphia. Wallace flushed and his voice tightened at the sight of Pegler. "I do not answer questions put to me by Westbrook Pegler," he said. Whereupon Martin Hayden of the Detroit *News* asked the same question: Did Wallace write the letters? "I don't answer questions put to me by a stooge of Westbrook Pegler, either," Wallace replied. H. L. Mencken arose and asked, "Mr. Wallace, do you consider me a stooge of Westbrook Pegler?" Wallace didn't. Mencken continued: "Then I should like to hear, did you or did you not write the Guru letters?" Wallace would not answer. Other reporters persisted, with Wallace shouting back that he would answer in his own way and his own time. Eventually the reporters got up and left, leaving Wallace alone with writers for Communist publications.

Thus was the Wallace campaign sidetracked onto the twin rails of communism and personal idiosyncrasy, to the dismay of uncountable thousands of Americans who wanted a true alternative to Truman.

CHAPTER 24

THE LONELIEST CAMPAIGN

Nothing came of the special session of Congress. The Republicans recognized the Truman move as a political mousetrap, denounced it with suitably harsh oratory and ignored Truman's program. The only legislation passed during the truncated two-week session was a $65-million loan for construction of the United Nations headquarters building and two minor bills on powers of the Federal Reserve Bank. A few days after the session ended Truman picked up a reporter's phraseology and agreed it had been a "do-nothing" Congress. Harry Truman was ready for the fall.

"It looks like another four years of slavery," Harry Truman wrote his sister on September 2, when everyone in the country was predicting his defeat. "I'd be much better off personally if we lose the election but I fear the country would go to hell and I have to try to prevent that." For Truman, "trying" meant a campaign modeled on his western trip of the spring—to get on a special train, stop it wherever people would gather to listen, stage formal rallies in larger cities, and aim at groups with the votes to keep him in office: big-city blacks and union members, farmers, Southerners so ingrained with the Democratic tradition that they would not vote Dixiecrat, and progressive-minded Westerners.

Harry Truman worked. Six times during the next two months his special train rolled out of Washington's Union Station—sixteen cars plus the *Ferdinand Magellan,* a lavish armored suite the railroads had given to President Roosevelt—a combined traveling White House, political headquarters, and press room, with sleeping accommodations of varied comfort for the President, his wife and daughter Margaret, twenty-odd staff members, and three to four dozen reporters. Truman spent all or part of forty-four days away from Washington roaming America like a frenzied

Flying Dutchman. Often he made his first rear-platform talk before six o'clock in the morning. Even after night rallies the train would stop at a smaller town down the line, and he would come out (frequently in a bathrobe) and talk to people waiting in the darkness. On one day alone he gave sixteen speeches. By Truman's computation he traveled 31,700 miles by rail and made 356 speeches, averaging ten per full working day.

The morning Truman left on his long western trip Senator Barkley, his running mate, came down to wish the President well. "Go out there and mow 'em down," Barkley said.

"I'll mow 'em down, Alben," Truman replied, "and I'll give 'em hell."

Reporters heard the exchange and used it in their stories, and by the time Truman reached the West Coast people in the crowds were shouting, "Give 'em hell, Harry."

Truman smiled, and Truman obliged. Truman ran against business as hard as he did against the Republicans—"Wall Street reactionaries," "gluttons of privilege," "the economic tapeworm of big business." Truman constantly denounced his adversaries in the Eightieth Congress. In Fresno, California, he told an audience that "you have got a terrible congressman here in this district. . . . He is one of the worst obstructionists in the Congress. He has done everything he possibly could to cut the throats of the farmer and the laboring man. If you send him back, that will be your fault if you get your throats cut."

Most of the platform speeches were extemporaneous; in blunt, sassy, Anglo-Saxon speech Truman told the American people what he thought they should hear, and apparently they agreed with him.

But wasn't Harry Truman wasting his time? On September 9, a week before his long western trip, pollster Elmo Roper wrote that "Thomas E. Dewey is almost as good as elected" and that the chance of an upset could be largely disregarded. Roper gave Dewey 44.2 percent, Truman 31.4 percent, Wallace 3.6 percent, Thurmond 4.4 percent.

Fletcher Knebel spent much of the campaign on the Truman train as a reporter for the Cowles newspapers. As was true with most reporters, he accepted the polls about Dewey's "insurmountable lead" as gospel, a feeling reflected in his daily stories. Yet there were times when Knebel wondered whether he should stop listening to policitians and public opinion experts and trust his reportorial instincts.

"Early on in the campaign we visited this plowing contest in Iowa, a hell of a big mob of people spread out as far as you could see in a hot, inde-

scribably dusty field. The reporters stuck fairly close to the campaign train, for Truman didn't speak from a text, and we wanted to be sure to get what he said. One man who did go out into the crowd was a Scripps-Howard reporter and he came back shaking his head. These were Midwestern farm people, the bankers and grain dealers as well as the farmers, and you weren't supposed to find more than one Democrat every hundred miles or so. But the Scripps-Howard man talked to a hundred people, and he found a solid majority behind Truman. We decided it was a statistical fluke, that he had wandered into a chance gathering of Democrats, and we laughed; I don't think he even wrote the story himself. He was going to lose. We believed it, because we wrote it every day."

So, too, did Tom Dewey, who didn't even begin campaigning until September 19, only six weeks before Election Day, and who behaved more as an incumbent than a challenger for a party that had been out of office for sixteen years. He ran as a statesman, calling for national unity, never mentioning Truman, and avoiding issues that could cause trouble in his own party. The polls and the Wallace/Dixiecrat defections gave Dewey an ample supply of confidence.

As did Truman, Dewey traveled by train, but the differences were profound. For one thing, he made only about half as many rear-platform appearances; Dewey started his campaign day in gentlemanly leisure at 10 A.M. Not even a crowd could arouse Dewey from his slumbers ahead of time: when the Dewey campaign trail rolled into Terre Haute, Indiana, at 7 A.M., a crowd was on hand in the expectation he would appear and say a few words, as Truman had done earlier. Many of the farmers had driven for miles to see Dewey. When word was passed he would not come out, they pelted his car with tomatoes and cabbage heads. Dewey tended to be forced and awkward when speaking from the rear of a train. Although he was a superb public speaker on formal occasions, a master of pace and modulation, in the impromptu talks he seemed determined to say as little as possible, and even that in high-sounding platitudes festooned with clichés.

Only once did Dewey show any emotion in public, and that moment was remembered. On October 12 he had just begun to speak from the rear platform in a small Illinois town, when the train suddenly moved backward into the crowd a few feet. No one was injured, and most persons took the mishap good-naturedly. But Dewey's temper flared. "That's the first lunatic I've had for an engineer," he said. "He probably ought to be shot at sunrise but I guess we can let him off because no one was hurt."

The Democrats, of course, promptly capitalized upon the incident, Truman saying with a dead pan that "I was highly pleased when I found out . . . that the train crew on this train are all Democrats. . . . We have had wonderful train crews all around the country and they've been just as kind to us as they could possibly be." In a radio broadcast a few days later (financed by a union) Truman said, "We have been hearing about engineers again recently from the Republican candidate. He objects to having engineers back up. He doesn't mention, however, that under the 'Great Engineer' [a popular nickname of former President Herbert Hoover] we backed up into the worse depression in our history."

Dewey yawned and stayed on the high road, so sure of victory that his staff was uncertain whether he should "waste" the last week of the campaign with another trip.

The fringe campaigns, meanwhile, spluttered along ineffectively, of interest mainly as curiosities certain to siphon Democratic votes from Truman. Truman kept out of the South altogether and made no attempts, overt or otherwise, to win segregationist support. In fact, he did just the opposite. Advance men invited blacks to a Truman rally at the Dallas baseball park, the first integrated political rally ever held there. When reporters traveling with Truman didn't mention the fact in their stories, the Truman staff quietly advised them of the historic first.

Candidates Thurmond and Wright whooped around the South, denouncing Truman as a "carpetbagger" and worse, but adding nothing of substance to the denunciations of the spring. By late autumn it was obvious the Dixiecrats were dead except in the four states where citizens were not able to vote for Truman even if they wished to do so.

So, too, was Henry Wallace, who suddenly found himself running without the labor and liberal support crucial to his campaign. Crowds melted. In September he embarked upon a trip to the South intended to challenge racist mores: he would insist upon holding unsegregated meetings, and he would challenge Jim Crow in his own roost. Bull Connor of Birmingham warned, "I ain't going to allow darkies and white people to segregate together." Oddly, however, Wallace had minute pockets of support scattered throughout the South—labor organizers in the textile mills; the few civil rights activists; blacks who risked their lives to participate in the political process; students whose social consciences had been stirred by wartime experiences.

Despite its surface appearance of an in-progress disaster, the Truman campaign was buoyed by two circumstances either overlooked or discounted by the press and the professional politicians: farm discontent and feverish labor activity on behalf of the President.

The farm situation was grotesquely complex. Under the price support system began in the New Deal, the government guaranteed farmers a certain "support price" for such basic crops as wheat and corn. If the market price proved higher, the farmer sold his produce through commercial channels without government involvement. But if prices dipped below the support level, he could obtain a loan based upon the guaranteed level, and pledge his crops as collateral. If the market recovered, he sold the crop and repaid the loan; otherwise, he simply forfeited the collateral and kept the money. To be eligible for the loan, however, the farmer had to store his crop in a facility approved by the government—either a commercial bin or one operated by the Commodity Credit Corporation. And here arose the problem. At the end of the war CCC began liquidating its storage space, dropping from 292 million bushels capacity to less than 50 million. When CCC's charter came up for renewal in the middle of 1948, the economy-minded House Banking and Currency Committee, noting that CCC was selling, not buying, space, prohibited it from acquiring any new storage bins. When the bill reached the floor, two farm-state Republicans objected briefly about the provision but it passed; not a Democratic voice was heard in opposition. Nor did any of the major farm organizations say anything.

Then came the deluge. The 1948 corn crop of 3,681,000,000 bushels was the largest in history, 55 percent above 1947. The wheat crop was the second largest in history. The bumper crops quickly filled all available commercial facilities; when the farmers turned to CCC, the traditional overflow storage, no space was available. Concurrently, prices plunged. Corn went from $2.46 a bushel in January to $1.78 in mid-September; wheat, from $2.81 to $1.97. Hence farmers faced the paradox of financial disaster during a bonanza year. And, incredibly, as tempers rose in the farm belt, the Republicans, through Harold Stassen, attacked the Truman Administration for shoring *up* farm prices through big grain purchases for export.

The Stassen statement conceivably pleased a handful of housewives who had the acumen to link up the farm support program with supermarket prices but it was a disaster in the farm states. Democrats distributed texts of the speech by the scores of thousands, and Truman came down hard on the issue, blaming the Republicans in speech after speech. "Farmers all over the country are being forced to drop their grain as distress grain or let it rot on the ground because the CCC no longer has the power to provide emergency storage space for a bumper crop," he said.

Dewey strategists tried to warn their candidate of the volatility of the issue; not until three weeks before election did the Dewey command create a farm division and it accomplished nothing. Dewey brushed aside entreaties that he make a strong statement, and as late as October 25 Tom O'Neill of the Baltimore *Sun* reported that only a "trace of concern" existed on the campaign train and that the farm issue could help Truman.

Similarly, Dewey did not bestir himself for labor votes. Besides the erratic John L. Lewis of the mine workers, the only major union leader to back Dewey was Alvanley Johnston of the Brotherhood of Locomotive Engineers, whose 80,000 members were one-third the number of *active* workers fielded by the CIO's Political Action Committee (PAC).

Labor's main contribution to Truman was manpower. The PAC concentrated first on voter registration, then on getting unionists and friends to the polls. PAC used as an incentive Taft-Hartley and other Republican congressional actions. The PAC hired fleets of cars to carry people to Truman's whistle stops, and it helped produce crowds for his rallies. The Democratic debacle in the 1946 congressional elections, and labor's subsequent failure to find enough votes to sustain Truman's veto of the Taft-Hartley Act, brought the AFL into national politics with a roar. Joseph Keenan, a veteran of Chicago politics, signed on as director, and cajoled and goaded the big national unions to free manpower and money for Truman.

Joseph Keenan began to realize by mid-October that the election would be closer than the "experts" predicted. So, too, did the PAC's Jack Kroll, who made public predictions that Truman would win.

Few other persons in America would agree. During the last week of the campaign, *Newsweek* polled fifty top political writers; all gave victory to Dewey, with an average of 366 electoral votes, a flat hundred more than he needed. The *New York Times* predicted 345. Drew Pearson's column the day before the voting said a Truman victory was "impossible." The insider pieces were seemingly endless. "Government will remain big, active, and expensive under President Thomas E. Dewey," the *Wall Street Journal* told its readers. *Changing Times,* published by the Kiplinger organization, proclaimed on its cover "What Dewey Will Do," and gave a full issue of predictions. A note on the last page suggested the special issue "will have historical value in the future. Perhaps you should put a copy away for your children or grandchildren."

But the size and enthusiasm of the Truman crowds nagged many persons, even among Dewey strategists: 50,000 in Dayton; 60,000 in Akron, many of whom stood two hours to await the train; 55,000 in Duluth, half the population of the town along a two-mile route; 15,000 in the auditorium at St. Paul, and another 6,000 outside; 200,000 in Miami. Dewey attracted 1,500 to the rail yards in Hammond, Indiana, Truman 20,000. In Chicago, Democratic chieftain Jacob Arvey turned out a crowd of half a million persons to line a motorcade route from the Blackstone Hotel to Chicago Stadium, where Truman spoke to 23,000 people.

Editorally, the vast majority of the nation's press supported Dewey—65 percent of the dailies, with 78 percent of the circulation. Only 15 percent supported Truman; the rest were neutral. The *New York Times* and the Cleveland *Plain-Dealer,* which had opposed Dewey in 1944, now moved behind him. The St. Louis *Post-Dispatch,* in Truman's home state, said he did not have the "stature, the vision, the social and economic grasp, the sense of history required to lead the nation in a time of crisis." The Oregon *Journal* said that Truman, "in descending to his Missouri training in campaign vilification, has lost leadership of the nation."

Working newsmen, conversely, worried about the sort of President Dewey would make. The cold efficiency of his staff, the lack of any human depth in Dewey, his ego and his unwillingness to discuss the issues raised by Truman, an overall shallowness of character and mind—should this man become President?

CHAPTER 25

NATIONAL CROW FEAST

On November 2, Harry Truman voted in Independence, lunched with friends at a country club, then slipped away to a resort hotel at Excelsior Springs for a Turkish bath and relaxation. About 4:30 in the afternoon, hours before the polls closed, Herbert Brownell, Dewey's campaign manager, confidently announced that the record vote meant that Dewey had been overwhelmingly elected.

Truman had a light snack and went to bed in the early evening.

Dewey dined with family and friends in a New York hotel and began scratching out early vote totals on a pad. Downstairs, an early and confident crowd gathered, and the Dewey staff mimeographed hundreds of copies of the victory statement. Six secret service agents arrived to protect the new President.

The radio networks had hoped to announce the Dewey victory by 9 P.M., prime time in the East. They decided they had best wait. Truman was winning not only in the South (except the four Dixiecrat states) but was making a strong run in the Republican Midwest.

At 11 P.M. Truman led in Illinois and in the farm states of Iowa and Wisconsin. Although Truman carried New York City by half a million votes, Henry Wallace siphoned away enough support to threaten to throw the state to the Republicans. Herbert Brownell said a "pattern indicative" of Republican victory is developing."

At midnight, Missouri time, Harry Truman rolled over and turned on the radio. Commentator H.V. Kaltenborn reported he was leading by 1,200,000 votes, but that he could not win: rural votes would turn the tide. Truman grunted and went back to sleep.

At 4 A.M. James Rowley, head of Truman's secret service detail, could not stand any more suspense. He shook Truman awake and turned on the radio. H.V. Kaltenborn, in his excited Germanic tones, said Truman now led by 2,000,000 votes, but could not win because the "rural vote" would soon be in. Truman knew otherwise. He dressed and returned to his Kansas City headquarters. Dewey, meanwhile, had gone to bed.

At 10:30 A.M. Dewey arose to find he had lost Ohio, Illinois, and California—and with them, the election. He talked with Brownell and other aides for perhaps half an hour; what disappointments he expressed, if any, are lost to history. At 11:14 A.M. Dewey sent the telegram: "My heartiest congratulations to you on your election. . . ." A couple of hours later, at a brief meeting with the press, Dewey displayed no outward signs of chagrin at having lost a "can't-lose" election. "I am as much surprised as you are," he told the reporters. "I have read your stories. We were all wrong together." Herbert Brownell could not be found for comment.

Truman had won twenty-eight states with 304 electoral votes, Dewey sixteen states with 189 votes, Thurmond his four Dixiecrat states with 39 votes. In the popular vote Truman polled 24,179,345 to Dewey's 21,991,291, a plurality of 2,188,054. Wallace received a mere 1,157,326 votes, Thurmond, 1,176,126. But these were enough to deny Truman a majority: he got 49.6 percent of the popular vote to Dewey's 45.1 percent. Paradoxes abounded. Truman lost four of the largest industrial states (New York, Pennsylvania, New Jersey, and Michigan) that had been central to Roosevelt's victories. Yet he won three states (Iowa, Ohio, and Wisconsin), dominated by farm votes, that Dewey had won in 1944.

For the Republicans, the sting of defeat was mitigated by the knowledge that probably 95 percent of the people in the country had guessed wrong. Recriminations were few, and mostly confined to intrafamilial griping by the Republicans. But the rest of the country laughed at—and with—itself. When Truman returned to Washington his motorcade passed the Washington *Post* building, festooned with a sign:

MR. PRESIDENT, WE ARE READY TO EAT CROW
WHENEVER YOU ARE READY TO SERVE IT

Truman laughed and waved at *Post* employees in the windows.

Harry Truman's many shortcomings as a President notwithstanding, the 1948 election must rank as the most significant of modern American political history. His victory meant the majority of the voting public accepted the social reforms of the New Deal as institutionalized national standards. It ended, for all practical purposes, the South's death grip on the moral throat of the Democratic Party. It demonstrated that a Democratic candidate could fashion a winning majority from components other than the traditional city/labor/black/South coalition. It forced the Republican Party away from blind conservatism and toward the mainstream of American politics; not until 1964 did the conservatives gain enough force within the party to nominate their own candidate. And, perhaps most important, Truman's victory was one of *issues* over *power*. Truman beat more than Thomas E. Dewey. He beat the established centers of American power—industries and banks, the rich and the professional, the press and the academic elites. Harry Truman indeed was democracy personified.

As it turned out, Truman's election in his own right brought only fleeting respite from the wide public belief that he was a narrow politician, unsuited temperamentally or intellectually to be President. Truman's stubborn loyalty to his friends, even when they were wrong, added to his problems. General Harry Vaughan, the White House military aide, caused Truman serious problems because of his involvement with people caught up in what came to be known as the "five-percenter" scandals.

Embarrassing disclosures tumbled out of the Senate for months. Albert Joseph Gross, a minor-league industrialist from Wisconsin admitted sending deep freezes to such Truman intimates (and officeholders) as Vaughan, John Snyder, Matthew Connelly, and James K. Vardaman, as well as the White House staff dining room. In Senate testimony in September 1949 he denied doing favors for anyone; he called the deep freezes and other gifts "an expression of friendship and nothing more." The committee could not prove otherwise, and Vaughan stayed on Truman's staff until the day the President left office. In less than two years the luster of the 1948 election victory had vanished, and Truman had so fallen in public esteem that Republican congressional candidates could campaign against him in the fall of 1950 (as did Dwight D. Eisenhower two years later) on grounds of "corruption."

As the best years neared the end of the decade, the mass public had its eyes fixed on material comfort. Happiness cannot be measured by statistics alone, but fruits of the postwar era were suddenly available for the picking. Some raw data suggested the economic situation of Americans in 1950 as compared with 1945. In July 1945 the average weekly salary for a worker in manufacturing was $45.42; for nonmanufacturing, $47.47, ranging from $59.64 in the auto industry to $24.40 for retail trade workers. In midsummer 1950 the manufacturing wage was $60.32, up almost $15; for nonmanufacturing, $65.41, up almost $18. Auto workers earned $75.74 weekly; retail clerks, $42.17. Overall, wages and salaries had increased about 23 percent.

Employment was at an all-time high, 61,400,000; the unemployment rate was 5.2 percent. Retail prices increased 49.6 percent; the cost-of-living index 36.2 percent. After-tax corporate profits increased 104.6 percent—more than four times as much as wages and salaries. The average single-family house cost $7,950 in 1950, exclusive of land costs. An electric washing machine sold for $168; six twelve-ounce bottles of Pepsi-Cola for twenty-five cents (nineteen cents on weekend specials). A hamburger cost a dime; gasoline eighteen or twenty cents a gallon; bread seventeen cents for a pound-and-a-half loaf; a bottle of beer twenty or twenty-five cents; five pounds of sugar, forty-nine cents; a best-selling novel such as *Prince of Foxes,* by Samuel Shellabarger, $3; a one-year subscription to *Life,* $5.50; a carton of cigarettes, $1.79; a Dr. West toothbrush, fifty cents; a Van Heusen dress shirt, $2.95 to $4.50; a package of Ex-Lax, ten cents. Between 1945 and 1950 Americans bought 5,500,000 passenger cars; 5,076,800 houses; 20,207,000 refrigerators; 17,549,000 vacuum cleaners; 5,451,000 electric ranges.

Yet history must be known for its spiritual progeny as well as by its physical relics. And what did Americans carry out of the best years?

EPILOGUE: HOW WE ENDED

In the Prologue I wrote that the title *The Best Years* posed an implicit question that I would attempt to answer in due course, that is, was the period 1945-50 indeed "the best years" of the American experience? America did achieve a material well-being unsurpassed in the prior history of mankind. Mass production techniques, economic planning at the national level, a new appreciation for research and applied science—America came out of the decade with the mechanical capability for comfort and prosperity.

During countless interviews in the last three years I asked person after person whether those years were in fact "the best years" for them personally, in terms of general satisfaction with life. The responses fell into a pattern: a review of "what I was doing then"—in college after the military, starting a business, establishing a home and family; an attempt to remember "what was happening"—the landmark events tended to be Truman beating Dewey, the end of rationing, the first postwar automobile, such trivia as the 1946 World Series between the St. Louis Cardinals and the St. Louis Browns, and movie actresses; then a quantum jump to foreign affairs—The Bomb, trouble with the Russians, the Marshall Plan, the Berlin blockade. And almost invariably the interviewees came around to the same answer, couched in roughly the following language:

Yes, they *were* good years, because I was putting my life together, and making enough money to get by on, and we weren't fighting a war. I didn't have all the things I wanted; those came later, in the fifties and the sixties, but the postwar period was the necessary preparation.

The HUAC investigations disturbed me, for I thought many people were mistreated. But like a lot of people, I was scared of the Communists, and I was happy that someone was trying to get spies out of government. Besides, nobody I knew personally got into trouble with HUAC.

I would have preferred that we not go back into the war business, but someone had to take on the job of stopping the Russians, and we were the only country around. It didn't make me especially happy, but it didn't worry me an awful lot either.

Yet the best years left memories elsewhere that were not nearly so pleasant. What followed thereafter, essentially, is that for a full decade, that of the 1950's, America went into a holding period—intellectually, morally, politically. Perhaps the pause was inevitable, even necessary; the nation was weary from depression, war, and reconversion, and the Eisenhower years proved singularly undemanding. The result, regardless, was a generation content to put its trust in government and in authority, to avoid deviant political ideas, to enjoy material comfort without undue worry about the invisible intrinsic costs. America misplaced, somewhere and somehow, the driving moral force it had carried out of the world war.

That America's foreign policy came to be built around the Truman Doctrine, rather than the United Nations, was possible because American leaders in and out of government "bombarded the American people with a 'hate the enemy' campaign rarely seen in our history." The elite community of American policy makers "fell in love with its Cold War plan," in the opinion of James P. Warburg, a conservative analyst of foreign affairs, and sold it to the public.

The Cold War, by its very nature, inescapably became a protracted conflict without visible battlefields or discernible results, one in which the individual citizen felt he played no direct part—and with which, consequently, he soon became bored. Thus succumbed the national unity that marked the collective adventure of the Second World War. Another phenomenon—this one detected by the public opinion polls and professional sociologists—was the demise of the devil-may-care attitudes found in homecoming veterans in 1945-46. Disgusted with the ultimate regimentation of the military, a majority of the veterans had declared they intended to work for no one but themselves; they wanted their own farms, their own insurance agencies, their own shops. But as the decade ended the same veterans thought differently. The social scientist Harvey Olsen, after a study of 8,900 veterans, reported, "Many of these men came out of the service with a 'ho-ho' attitude towards life; they learned they could be the sole proprietors of their fortunes. They were not bound by pre-war dogmas as their fathers; they opted for their own lives." Unfortunately, reported Olsen, most of the vets quickly reverted to pre-war thinking, settling into the "familiar old patterns rather than seeking out what they really wanted." But he found that "the ones who are the happiest, the most-balanced, in the long run, are those who obeyed their instincts and made new lives, even at the cost of passing psychic discomfort." *Fortune,* in a survey of graduating college seniors in June 1949, found the class "has turned its back on what its elders automatically assume is . . . one of the most cherished prerogatives of youth. Forty-nine is taking no chances." Only 2 percent of the graduates planned businesses for themselves. "The men of Forty-nine everywhere seem haunted by the fear of a recession. . . . 'I know AT&T might not be very exciting,' explains one senior, 'but there'll always be an AT&T.'" The graduates seemed little concerned with making vast amounts of money. "Forty-niners simply will not talk of the future in terms of the dollar. In terms of the Good Life, however, they are most articulate." The Good Life meant marriage, three children, a comfortable home, "a little knockabout for the wife," a summer cottage, an annual income of $10,000 a year (the median family income in 1950 was $6,405 for white families; $3,449 for blacks). The blandness of the graduates worried *Fortune:* Would they "furnish any quota of free-swinging s.o.b.'s we seem to need for leavening the economy? The answers will be a long time in coming."

Harry Truman, in a "nonpolitical" whistle-stop tour of western states in the spring of 1950, preparing for the congressional elections, happily told his audiences, "The world is more settled now than in 1946." Perhaps it was. Western Europe had apparently stabilized, with the Communists losing pivotal elections in Italy and France. The Communists had prevailed in China, to be sure, an inevitability the Administration had expected since 1946. The blockade of Berlin had been broken by the air lift.

But worries nagged Washington nonetheless. In late April 1950 Dean Acheson, the secretary of state, confided that he feared trouble in South Korea, Berlin, and Burma. The likely trigger spot, Acheson said, was Berlin, where the Communists were expected to try to march half a million youth organization members into the western sector to oust the Allies. The United States, France, and Britain were ready to resist with force if necessary, Acheson said. Francis Matthews, secretary of the navy, warned, "There is nothing in the current international picture to justify the assumption that we shall not again be called upon to defend ourselves."

The first week of May the military staged a training exercise at Fort Bragg, North Carolina, that pointed up the depleted status of U.S. strategic might. The exercise was built around some 32,000 ground soldiers from the 82d and 11th Airborne Divisions, both at reduced strength, and a regimental combat team from the 3d Infantry Division—"just about all the Sunday punch the United States can mobilize in the first critical hours after a Cold War opening shot," in the words of one observer. The Carolina exercise assembled virtually all the troop carrier and cargo planes that would be available should the United States come under attack; getting the men and planes into place took four months. Military strength elsewhere included two half-sized Marine divisions; the 2d Army, so widely deployed at domestic posts as to be 'wholly unready"; four occupation divisions in Germany and Japan; and twenty-seven National Guard divisions, a year from combat readiness. In 1950 the United States was spending $12.5 million for guided missiles for the army, and $34.1 million for peanut price supports.

But why should America worry? Truman's strategy of containment was working, for the media said so. In its cover story for May 29, 1950, *Time* told the American public even more supportive news:

The United States now has a new frontier and a new ally in the Cold War. The place is Indo-China, a Southeast Asian jungle, mountain and delta land that includes the Republic of Viet Nam and the smaller neighboring kingdoms of Laos and Cambodia, all parts of the French Union.

A week later *Time* expressed optimism about events in yet another part of Asia:

Six months ago South Korea, bedeviled by guerrilla raids, galloping inflation and the daily threat of invasion from the North, looked like a candidate for the same mortuary as Nationalist China. Now the Republic of Korea looks more like a country on its way to healthy survival. . . . It has trained and equipped a first-rate ground army. . . . [U.S.] advisers have tried to give the Koreans Yankee self-sufficiency as well as Yankee organization and equipment.

The policy has paid off. . . . Most observers now rate the 100,000-man South Korean army as the best of its size in Asia. Its fast-moving columns have mopped up all but a few of the Communist guerrilla bands . . . and no one believes that the Russian-trained North Korean army could pull off a quick, successful invasion of the south without heavy reinforcements.

On Sunday morning, June 25, 1950, Mrs. Ida Hamme wept as she stood before her Sunday school class at the First Methodist Church in Weslaco, Texas. A gentle woman in her thirties, with two young sons, Mrs. Hamme talked about the strange war that had begun during the night in a far-away place called Korea. She asked her class, all preteen children, to pray that peace would be swiftly restored.

Mrs. Hamme's grief so disturbed two of the children, Jody Corns and Anne Caskey, both twelve, that when class ended they went home instead of to church services. They found Maurine Corns, ten, and Kindred Caskey, eight, and walked the seven blocks to the Corns home. They spread the Sunday newspapers on the living-room floor and read the war news, and tried to understand what was happening and why.

"Our main question," Jody Corns remembered a quarter of a century later, "was whether our daddies would have to go back to war."

The best years were over.

A WIND TO
SHAKE THE WORLD

THE STORY OF THE 1938 HURRICANE

A condensation of the book by

EVERETT S. ALLEN

Book I

NEW JERSEY, NEW YORK CITY
AND LONG ISLAND

CHAPTER 1

Nobody expected anything to happen on that September day in 1938. It was not as it is now, when almost nothing, however awful, would be surprising. In those days, if there was a disaster, it always occurred in one of those vague locations where they didn't wash and built their houses out of straw. There was no reason to assume that this Wednesday would be appreciably different from any other September 21; the people who had watched the weather in this place all their lives knew what they knew about it.

It is appalling, in retrospect, to reflect upon how little we expected what happened, to discover how little we knew about what was going on elsewhere on the day of the storm and to realize how long it was before we did know. That was because New Bedford, where I was starting my first day as a waterfront reporter, was not the first to get the hurricane. It came from the south. Consider then, those who were to the south of us.

New York City and, for that matter, much of the state—excluding Long Island—and neighboring New Jersey were not immediately aware of the vastness of what occurred on the twenty-first because the hurricane's full fury was for other places. Yet the explosion of weather left its mark here.

The peak of the storm passed over New Jersey in the late afternoon. It was the worst in fifty years and met the home-going commuter just in time to disrupt his return from New York to examine the damage.

At Manasquan, the sea tore the entire fourteen blocks of the boardwalk off its foundations and distributed it two blocks inland. On the way, the breaking sections crashed into casinos and pavilions fronting the ocean and into cottages on the side streets. Porches were torn away and doors and windows were smashed open to the wind, and the slashing rain and sea left behind a three-foot deposit of sand, burying Ocean Avenue its full length. Nature's onslaught cost Manasquan a quarter of a million dollars.

The bridge across Absecon Inlet, separating Atlantic City and the island of Brigantine, a one-million-dollar structure, had already been weakened by high winds and heavy seas; it collapsed with the high tide that followed, marooning more than two thousand people at Brigantine.

From Cape May to Sussex, the storm delivered a final blow to the 33,000-acre tomato crop and caused widespread damage to the forty percent of the state's 3.5 million bushels of apples still on the trees. The combined pressure of wind and rain on the laden boughs broke them down and uprooted thousands of trees in ground that had been softened by the steady downpour of the previous four days. In North Haledon, Fred Yahn's flock of four thousand young pheasants were so jammed together by the wind and panic in the run that a thousand of them were smothered before he could pry the birds apart and get the survivors under cover. The birds were worth two dollars apiece.

New York City did not officially have a hurricane, since average intensity of the gale was 65 miles an hour and a hurricane must be at least 75. Yet because of the wind, high tides, and a four-and-a-half-inch rainfall, the routine of city life was virtually at a standstill from 3 to 6 o'clock in the afternoon.

Thousands of office workers, seeking to return to their homes, were marooned in business buildings because transit schedules had been disrupted by washouts. At 8:45 P.M., a power failure on the lines of the Consolidated Edison Company left parts of Manhattan and all of the Bronx in darkness.

All the lines of the Independent Subway System except those running to Queens were affected. Hospitals without emergency apparatus turned to candles, as did thousands of residents. The power failure stemmed from a breakdown of the Hell Gate plant at 133rd Street and the East River, one of the largest in the world and the chief source of supply for most of the electrical energy consumed in Manhattan and the Bronx. The breakdown was caused by overflowing of the East River, which flooded three blocks inland to Willow Avenue, where it was four feet high at nine at night. By then, access to the power plant was possible only by boat.

The flooding made it impossible to operate the boilers, and the generators had to stop for lack of steam. Since the Hell Gate station was built well above ordinary high-water marks, it was immediately obvious that the tide which flooded the plant had broken all records.

Along the waterfront, both in the afternoon and evening, there was, of course, a more acute awareness of what was going on. The French liner *Ile de France,* due to arrive at quarantine at 1:45 in the afternoon, was awaited by the Coast Guard cutter *Navesink,* with about seventy-five customs inspectors, immigration agents, visitors, and newspaper representatives aboard. In driving rain that reduced visibility to less than one hundred yards, the cutter searched in vain for the ship and finally returned to dock at the foot of Whitehall Street.

Shortly thereafter, the liner appeared at the entrance to the Hudson River, the force of the wind then so strong that, as she proceeded to the French Line pier, the big ship listed sharply to starboard. At the pier, where five or six tugs normally were used for docking, a dozen were on hand, and even with these at bow and stern, warping the ship in against the wind, Captain Jules Chabot had to drop his port anchor to aid in swinging the vessel around.

Warned by the Coast Guard that the *Queen Mary,* scheduled to sail from New York at 4:30 P.M. with 868 passengers, might encounter the center of the hurricane, officials of the Cunard White Star line postponed her departure until 5 the next morning.

Near-panic occurred on the Staten Island ferryboat *Knickerbocker* at 6 P.M. when the storm-lashed waters of the bay rolled the vessel down in her slip at the Battery and left her hanging at a 45-degree angle, her port guard rail caught under an iron bumper attached to the piling. The cries of two hundred passengers on board mingled with those of hundreds of homeward-bound commuters waiting to take the ferry to Fort George on Staten Island as they saw the craft assume and retain her alarming slant. It required two tugs and nearly a half-hour to work the *Knickerbocker* loose so that her passengers could be landed safely.

Offshore, one liner met the hurricane and one did not. The Red Star's *Königstein* nosed into it forty miles off Block Island and was consequently nine hours late in reaching Hoboken. Her skipper, Captain Alfred Leidig, said the ship's barometer had fallen to 28.40 and the wind had risen to 100 miles an hour during the worst of the storm. None of her 294 passengers suffered injury. The *Conte di Savoia* of the Italian Line, bound for New York from the Mediterranean, was fortunate in having aboard a passenger who predicted the hurricane two days in advance—that is, on the nineteenth. The passenger was the Reverend Ernest Gherzi, sometimes referred to as the "Father of Typhoons," an Italian Jesuit who had been a meteorologist for twenty-three years at an observatory near Shanghai. On the Monday morning preceding the hurricane, Father Gherzi went to the ship's bridge and remarked, "One of my children will be around in about three days."

In relating the story, he added that the passengers had jovially suggested he be thrown overboard because of the forecast. From then on until Wednesday, he spent long periods on the bridge, examining weather charts and predicting the hurricane's course.

"The path of the hurricane and our path seemed to be converging," Father Gherzi said, "but after studying the warning from the Naval Observatory in Washington, as well as the signs at sea, I was able to assure Captain Alberto Ottino, commander of the liner, that the hurricane, reportedly passing rapidly northward, would go by before we reached it, so we did not have to change our course or reduce speed when we ran into the outer edge of the disturbance and encountered squalls on the night of the twenty-first. The squalls were not dangerous."

Captain Ottino praised Father Gherzi's forecast for its accuracy and said the worst the ship struck was a forty-mile wind for a brief period Wednesday night.

Some beavers also received due credit. At Stony Point, sixty colonies, numbering more than five hundred beavers, manned their dams in the park's 42,000 acres when the storm broke. There were sixty dams in the beavers' defense line, the principal restraining force against rain-swollen river, streams, and ponds.

The size of the problem confronting the animals was impressive. Long Mountain beaver pond, for example, was created by a dam in what normally was a three-foot-wide stream; the pond ordinarily covered about five acres in the center of the park. On Wednesday night, with a rolling stream widened to almost twenty feet and the pond doubled in size, the beaver dam, made of mud, sticks, stones, and sod, withstood the pressure and fed eighteen inches of fast-moving water over its top. That particular dam, five years old at the time of the hurricane, was one hundred and fifty yards long, with a fourteen-foot base and a height of six feet at the midpoint.

In the west central station of the park, Cedar Hill Pond, made by a dam at Stony Brook, doubled its normal four acres when the stream widened from five to twenty feet. Over this dam, which was only forty feet wide, water rose two feet.

Another dam of critical importance was wedged between boulders thirty feet apart; as with all the others, it was completely submerged at the storm's peak, yet never showed a sign of yielding to the strains of the water upon it. John J. Tamsen, superintendent of Bear Mountain Park, and William H. Carr, director of the Trailside Museum, maintained by the American Museum of Natural History, credited the beavers—who cut down trees all through the night of the hurricane to reinforce their wood-and-mud bulwarks—with having saved three arterial highways from serious flooding, preventing the certain destruction of at least one bridge, and retarding the erosion of hundreds of acres of soil.

Carr said had it not been for the beaver dams "backing up perfectly terrific bodies of water, in some cases, more than two hundred yards across," Long Mountain Road, U.S. Highway 6, and the Johnstown Road would have been transformed into rivers for distances of up to a quarter of a mile and the same would have held true of U.S. Highway 9-W, the main road along the west shore of the Hudson, and Route 17, linking Tuxedo Park and Harriman, to the north.

Consider what it was like on that Wednesday if you were driving the length of Long Island, say from Times Square, starting at 3 in the afternoon, to the ocean's edge at Southold. There was hardly more than a nasty blow in New York City in midafternoon. Traffic was proceeding normally through the streets, across the bridge and over the boulevards of Queens, and it was not until one reached the World's Fair site that anything approaching flood conditions was in evidence. Here, automobiles were parked in puddles that reached to the hubcaps.

At Westbury, the Northern State Parkway was more wet and slippery than usual and here and there, a tree was uprooted. The wind was accelerating with disturbing persistence and there was now an unnatural whine about it, such as no ordinary Long Island wind ever made. Traffic was slowing and Grand Central Parkway was beginning to fill with water. The time was about 4:30. It was apparent that a bad storm was getting under way.

A little farther on, the picture got worse. Jericho Turnpike revealed the first real evidence of devastation. Here, the passing motorist looked anxiously at bending trees and fallen branches which began to strew the highway. The wind kept picking up. Drivers felt their cars begin to jump a little under the more forceful gusts, and even tightly closed automobile windows dripped moisture as the gust-driven rain began to pelt from a variety of directions.

One now passed old villages caught in the full rip of the gale. Shutters and awnings were dangling; trees were beginning to fall over the streets. All manner of sodden debris, curiously unidentifiable and shapeless, was being thrown about. Drivers moved ahead at ten miles an hour, peering through the meager hole left by the swishing wiper blade. Darkness was settling over the countryside.

By this time, the wind was roaring; car headlights pierced the torrents of rain no more than fifty feet. Over and over, a tree would appear unbelievably across the road—sometimes flat, in a massive heap, sometimes at a threatening angle—and three or four cars would halt, their lights puny in the turmoil. The drivers, half-soaked, forced car doors open against the wind, braced and struggled to get to the downed tree, yelled some word of advice and then, clothing whipping, battled back to their vehicles and, with luck, drove gingerly around the obstruction. Now and then, a car slipped into a water-filled ditch and there it stayed.

At Laurel, huge trees were not only down across the highway, but thrown against houses and even shoved through walls of buildings. Telephone poles began to give way, bringing down tangles of wires. More and more, cars were forced to leave the roads, bumping, jumping, and slipping in mud, to forge new routes across lawns or even far out in fields in order to bypass the wreckage on the highway.

Just beyond Laurel, two towering trees leaned over the road, falling slowly. A driver stepped hard on the gas and sped under them; they fell in slow motion just behind, blocking the route totally. Others were not so lucky; at least a half-dozen cars were scattered along the road, crushed under heavy trees; at the time there was no way of knowing what happened to their occupants—or whether they were dead or alive.

The few cars still moving crawled through darkened villages; there were no electric lights anywhere. Occasionally one might see the tumbled ruins of houses and barns. Shards of glass were everywhere; roofs were piled up on lawns and streets, and chimneys had disintegrated into heaps of bricks. The wind screeched. Emergency crews pulling away at trees or attempting to prop falling buildings were pathetic in the face of such elemental malevolence.

At Southold, the wind blew every nut off a horse chestnut tree and through the windows of a house; the chestnuts riddled the panes like machine-gun bullets. The ocean moved up into the town; it crawled into cellars; it washed around ground floors; it lapped at foundations.

Elsewhere on the north side of Long Island, dramatic and tragic events of several kinds were in process. In the Port Washington area, something like four hundred craft, ranging from rowboats to seventy-foot yachts, were ripped from berths and moorings when the storm struck at 2 P.M. Seven sloops were carried over a seawell and dropped into the swimming pool of the Manhasset Bay Yacht Club. A forty-foot power boat came to rest with its bow inside a grocery store; the water that carried it there also floated a one-ton delicatessen display case.

Ninety thousand homes on Long Island in the Glen Cove area were without refrigeration because the Long Island Lighting Company had to suspend services at its No. 2 plant, only seven years old and one of the most up-to-date in the country.

Near Northport, the First Lady of Brooklyn and the First Lady of the City of New York were stranded in their homes, six hundred feet apart, yet unable to communicate with each other or with the outside world. Mrs. Raymond V. Ingersoll, wife of the borough president, alone in her Duck Island home, was trapped as high water covered her lawn, making it impossible for her to leave without a rowboat. A broken telephone line prevented her from calling Mrs. Fiorello LaGuardia, who was stranded on the second floor of her home at Asharoken, while furniture floated about in the first-floor rooms below. Local firemen finally rescued them, both uninjured.

At Port Jefferson, the 150-foot steam ferry *Park City* left her dock at 2 P.M. for the customary two-hour run across the sound to Bridgeport. Shortly after 4 P.M., when it had not arrived, word was passed that it was missing, and anxious calls were made to Coast Guard stations on the Connecticut and Long Island shores for possible sightings. Aboard were nine crew members and six passengers, including Mrs. George St. John, Jr., of Wallingford, Connecticut, and her two-month-old baby, and Mrs. H. L. H. Fry of New York City.

The *Park City* was having her problems. When she was well out into the sound, the sea became so heavy that Captain Ray Dickerson, a veteran skipper, attempted to turn back shortly after his vessel approached the Middle Ground Light, but a shift of wind made it impractical to attempt to remain under way, so he decided to anchor.

Then the storm broke upon them, bringing with it dense fog and heavy rain. The seas drove green water over the steamer's bow, gradually filling the hold until the water reached a height of five and a half feet in the fire and engine rooms. This extinguished the fires under the boilers, stopping the steam pumps, which had been operating up to that time to keep the water down in the hold. That was about 3:15 P.M.

"As the gale reached its height, the ship started to drag anchor and we had plenty of worries," Dickerson related, "although the ship was at no time in danger of going down. Our main worry was wondering just where we were going to be blown. The waves kept pounding over the deck and the boat shipped plenty of water."

With the generators knocked out by water below decks, passengers and crew members were provided with lanterns. There were no other lights in the darkened ship. The engineer, Frank Smith, assisted by oiler Percy King and fireman Edward King, worked in water up to their waists in a futile effort to keep the fires and engines going. After the steam pumps failed, all of the crew and two of the male passengers worked on the hand pumps and used buckets to keep the water down.

At 7:30 Wednesday night, the anchor finally caught and held and there they stayed, without heat or food, six miles off Middle Ground Light, through what Dickerson said was "the worst weather I ever experienced in all my sea career and one of the longest nights I can remember." The passengers stayed in the reception room of the *Park City* or in their automobiles. For Mrs. Fry, it was "a harrowing night. I never expected to get back alive. The crew was magnificent. We prayed and prayed fervently."

The next morning, about 7, the Eastern Steamship Line's *Sandwich*, bound for Boston, reported the *Park City*'s location to the patrolling Coast Guard cutter *Galatea,* commanded by Lieutenant Commander A. W. Davis. It took an hour in the still-heavy sea for the cutter to get a line aboard the ferry and three hours more to tow her to Port Jefferson because she had three feet of water in the hold and was listing heavily. A thousand people were on the dock to greet the ferry after her 21-hour drubbing. Captain Dickerson said, "Our chief worry was about Mrs. St. John's baby, but there wasn't a whimper out of the child."

At Greenport, where the anemometer of the big Vanderbilt yacht *Vara* disintegrated after registering a wind velocity of 91 miles per hour, Herman Ficken, manager of the Metro Theater, became uneasy as the storm crisis came at about 3:45 P.M. He halted the showing of the film and asked the sixty men, women, and children in the audience to leave. The audience filed out in orderly fashion and just as the last one left, the front entrance and the rear of the building were blown in, the roof fell, and the structure collapsed.

Sag Harbor's greatest loss was the spire of the Presbyterian Church, called the Old Whalers' Church. The steeple, 125 feet high, regarded by many as one of the most beautiful in America, was torn off close to the roof and blown to the ground.

Of the steeple and its destruction, Ernest S. Clowes wrote, "[It] had stood for nearly one hundred years . Built in a curious medley of architectural styles, yet harmonious and graceful, it had been a welcome sight to the old whale hunters of eighty years ago, returning, perhaps, after a three-year voyage around the world.

"For three generations, it had dominated by its height and singular grace the landscape of Sag Harbor. In the worst of the storm, a great lifting gust tore it whole and bodily from the church, carried it about twenty feet and then dropped it, a crashing mass of shapeless ruin, fortunately clear from the church, which was not otherwise damaged.

"That great crash, preceded by the melancholy tolling of the bells as it fell, was one sound which people who lived nearby heard above the vast roar of the storm."

As bad as all of this death and destruction was, the awful truth of what was happening on the south shore of Long Island was not yet generally known.

CHAPTER 2

From Long Beach on the west to Southampton on the east, there is a thin dune barrier that ordinarily holds back the Atlantic Ocean. Behind it lie usually placid bays and beyond those, the mainland of Long Island's south shore. In the fall of 1938, this dune barrier was well settled; its several colonies of beach homes ranged from modest to pretentious.

Dr. William T. Helmuth of East Hampton wrote, "About three P.M. on September 21, a southeasterly wind reached hurricane force and it rose to a peak about six P.M., at which time the local barometer reached its lowest point at 28.55.

"An unusually high tide coincidentally also reached its highest point almost at the time of the hurricane's greatest intensity, helping to produce the first, and less gigantic, of the several hurricane waves, called by most people 'tidal waves.' By far the greatest amount of damage was done at this time. When the sea broke through the barrier of sand dunes in hundreds of places, inundating land which had previously been protected by them, many dunes were literally blown away to the northward [and] salt water engulfed the coastal bays and ponds, turning them into open arms of the sea. . . ."

Six miles south of Bay Shore, across Great South Bay, lies Fire Island, with its summer colonies, including Saltaire, Kismet, Fair Harbor, Ocean Beach, and Point o' Woods. In this area, within two hours' time, the barometer tobogganed from a high reading of 29.78 to 27.43. As it dropped, the velocity of the wind mounted from a warm zephyr at noon to a forty-mile-an-hour blow at 1:30 P.M. to a ninety-mile-an-hour hurricane at 3. By that time, Coast Guardsmen at Fire Island station, surrounded by water, reported that the beach was "raging like the ocean." One hundred twenty-seven houses were destroyed at Saltaire, 91 at Fair Harbor, and 29 at Oak Beach.

This is Coast Guard headquarters in Bay Shore on the night of September 21.

The only light in the offices is from candles; there is no electric power. As the anxious, many from New York City, come stumbling up the dark stairs seeking information about relatives who are on Fire Island, they face the gray-haired, mild-mannered Commander William M. Wolff.

"What about Ocean Beach?" they ask. "What about Saltaire?"

Wolff speaks quietly, trying to reassure, "The ice cutter [BA-25] has gone over to Saltaire to help the people in that vicinity. They appear to be most badly off. The ocean has apparently cut through in several places and one is between Saltaire and Fair Harbor. The ice cutter is a powerful boat and will be able to help these people if they need it. The crew over there is also trying to get through by using a tractor on the beach."

The hours pass, with no word from the icebreaker. With power lines down in Bay Shore, it is not possible to contact the vessel by shortwave radio. Efforts to get in touch with her through the Rockaway Point Coast Guard station also have been futile. You can feel the rising apprehension among those who stand there, waiting, especially after word comes through from Center Moriches that Westhampton Beach has been hard hit.

At 11 o'clock, power is restored in Bay Shore. Harold G. Cogswell, chief motor machinist, begins to twirl the dials of the headquarters' shortwave radio apparatus. Out of the first crackles of static comes a hoarse, initially indistinct voice that gradually clears and grows louder. It is Paul Long, machinist's mate aboard the icebreaker. Communication across Great South Bay to the cutter, plunging and rolling in the stormy night sea near Saltaire, has been established.

"BA-25, this is Bay Shore, Fourth District Office. Come in, come in, BA-25."

"Fourth District Office, BA-25 standing by, Bay Shore."

"What is the situation at Saltaire?"

"Conditions at Saltaire very bad. Half the houses are down, two women are lost, about seventy-five people are waiting to be taken off the island."

"Are the people waiting at Saltaire safe?"

"They are assembling in the town hall."

"Do you know the conditions of any other places along the beach?"

"No, but they must be approximately the same."

"Take off all who want to leave. Can a boat leave Bay Shore and go over to Saltaire dock now?"

"No, it would be impossible because of floating wreckage."

"Find out the exact number lost. Try to send someone to the town hall to get the names of the dead women."

"We will get you all the information we can."

The conversation ends. One of the waiting men in the office says to another, "Are you going across the bay?" The other replies, obvious strain in his voice, "Yes. But first I want to hear those names."

There is no sound, no movement in the office as communication is resumed with the cutter. "We have the names of the women who died," the voice crackles from offshore. "We have the names. Mrs. Angeline Bazinet, 501 West 122nd Street, New York. Mrs. Max Haas, 38 77th Street, Brooklyn. Three other persons unaccounted for, no names."

"Good God," one of the waiting men says, "Mr. Haas has been here for hours. He just left in a boat for Saltaire."

At Saltaire, the morning after the storm, a blond girl sat on a box, which rested precariously on a tilted remnant of one of the boardwalks. As Chief Assistant District Attorney Lindsey R. Henry arrived to survey the damage, she stood up and walked over to him.

"Could you assist us in the search for a body?" she asked.

"Of course," he said. "Whose body is it?"

The girl shut her eyes tightly for a moment and then said very carefully and slowly, "My mother's."

Her mother was Mrs. Haas, who, with Madame Bazinet, had clung to a tree as the wind-lashed sea swept across the island. The Haases had just built a new house on the ocean front at Saltaire; on this Thursday morning, there was nothing left where it had stood but wet sand, flat and hard from the ocean's pounding.

Soon after 3 o'clock on Wednesday, the situation on the beaches became critical, especially on that long strip from Shinnecock Bay to Moriches Inlet, where the dunes were mostly low and had at their backs a succession of bays and canals. Clowes noted, "By half past three, [the sea] was breaking over and through the dunes in many places and sometime toward four o'clock, the final catastrophe occurred. Before the on-slaught of that terrible tide, itself about ten to fifteen feet above the nor-mal height and crested with breakers towering fifteen feet higher or more, the whole barrier of the dunes crumpled and went down. . . .

"In a few minutes, along the stretch of beach from Quogue Village to Moriches Inlet, there remained of one hundred and seventy-nine sum-mer homes only twenty-six battered shells of houses, of which hardly a dozen will ever be habitable again."

Westhampton, with twenty-eight dead and four missing a month later, with at least one hundred and fifty houses destroyed and a property loss of two million dollars, was the worst hit of all the Long Island communities. The storm dealt death indiscriminately; among the victims were promi-nent members of the colony along with their servants.

Agnes Zeigler was the governess of twenty-three-month-old Ann Renée, daughter of the Countess Charles de Ferry de Fontnouvelle, wife of the French consul general in New York. The countess, her daughter, Miss Zeigler, and the family cook were in their Westhampton home.

"About four o'clock, our house began to tremble," Miss Zeigler said. "I was never so frightened in my life. The wind was howling and the water was up to the floor of the living room, having already flooded the base-ment. I waded through the water to a nearby house, where I found a chauffeur and a maid in the basement. I asked them to come and help us, but they wouldn't, so I went back to the house."

The countess said her first thought was of an earthquake, and when the building began to shake, she knew they could not remain there. When Miss Zeigler returned, the countess bundled the baby in a blanket and the four of them set out to seek a place of safety. They struggled along the beach through water up to their hips; the countess, holding the baby to her breast, had to discard the overalls she was wearing because they impeded her flight; she waded on in the sea and gale, clad only in her un-derclothing.

Planks, branches, and even doors were flying through the air; heavy boards and timbers swirled past them on the crests of the seas. "It was only by the grace of God that we were not killed," said the countess. Once they looked back, in time to see the big rambling frame house they had left collapse with a roar.

After traveling a half-mile, they reached the storm-battered residence of William Ottman, Jr. The Ottmans were not there, but their household staff was, including Arne Bendicksen, a Norwegian who had been their butler for two years. Mr. Bendicksen, who already had given shelter to twenty other refugees before the countess and her party arrived, took charge of the situation, and assumed responsibility for all of them. His incredible composure strengthened them; so thoroughly was he in command that not one of the twenty-odd in his care even asked him his name, nor did they know it the next day.

Bendicksen sensed that the situation was getting worse. He went upstairs and out through a scuttle to the roof and attempted to signal the mainland; he thought there was an answer but decided they did not have time to wait for help to come to them. Accordingly, he fought his way to the bridge that crossed to the mainland; here he found three husky boys, Stanley Wilson and Charles and Michael Goy, and they returned to the Ottman house with him.

With the four males to guide and sustain, the refugees linked arms and started for the bridge, which, already weakened by the flood, was threatening to break up. Somewhere along the way, the butler's chin had been cut badly and was bleeding, but he made no mention of it.

All of them crossed the bridge safely, and with little time to spare before it was impassable. "I am convinced we were spared because of the baby. Providence looked down upon us through her eyes," the countess said. The Ottman house collapsed as they struggled to gain the bridge.

And there were others.

The experience of George E. Burghard offers an extraordinary insight into what crossing the bay on storm-driven wreckage meant to hurricane victims at Westhampton.

He and his wife had rented a cottage on Dune Road so that he could carry out some radio experiments. For this purpose, he had installed several large poles, two more than 50 feet in height, to support antennae.

The cottage was 75 feet from the top of the dune on the south and 100 feet from the Dune Road on the north. On the west, 100 yards away, was the Coast Guard station, No. 75. In the vacant space between were the radio poles.

The house was well-built, with concrete foundation and wooden bulkheads on the surf side. The distance from the bulkhead to the normal water's edge was 200 feet, making the normal distance from the road to the surf about 150 yards. The dune itself was 8 or 9 feet high. East of the house was the Livermore residence, which was an identical building; between the two houses was a large bathhouse. Each house had a boardwalk to the dunes.

There were four people in the Burghard household: Burghard and his wife, Mabel, and Carl Dalin and his wife, Selma. The Dalins were in their mid-sixties. The Dalins took care of the house and had been with the family for many years. In addition, there were two dogs, a wire-haired fox terrier named Bitzie and a cocker spaniel, Peter. The Livermore house was vacant—the Livermores had gone to town for the tennis matches— but their 30-foot power cruiser was fastened to her mooring in the bay, off the dock between the houses.

For the Burghard household, as in many another, the day began almost routinely.

10 A.M. The wind was strong from the north, with a heavy sea and sultry weather, but there was no cause for alarm. In fact, the surf was not nearly as high as it had been the afternoon before. The sky was overcast and it was raining slightly.

11 A.M. The wind started shifting toward the east and grew considerably stronger, until at 11:30, it blew almost a gale from the northeast, with heavy rain. It looked like a good northeaster, which was to be expected at that time of year and caused no concern.

Then Dalin reported water bubbling up through the concrete floor of the garage, which was situated under the house on the ground floor opposite the servants' quarters and furnace. Burghard and Dalin went down to investigate and found water coming up in two places. They thought at first it was bay water backing up because of the wind, but after tasting it, they found it was quite salty and decided it must be seawater. Up to this time, no waves had come over the dune, so they concluded it was seepage from the surf through the sand.

All this time, the wind was increasing in strength, and Burghard looked out the window to see if the poles were still standing. The large poles, holding a V-antenna, were in good shape, but the dipole on the 30-foot mast nearest the house was swinging so much that Burghard thought it might be carried away any time. It was raining very hard now, but was quite warm.

12 noon. Dalin saw Livermore's boat start drifting with her mooring, and Burghard called Chief Boatswain's Mate James Ketcham, who commanded the Moriches Coast Guard station about three miles west on the dunes. This was the only station open up to Shinnecock, ten miles east; all the others were closed and No. 75 had only one lookout in the tower; its other buildings were shut. Ketcham said he would come right down and get the boat.

1 P.M. The Burghards' radio was going and tuned to WEAF. The Ar-

lington time signals came on and Burghard went to the radio room to set his chronometer, as he did each day. After the time signals, the announcer gave the following weather report: "The West Indies hurricane is in mid-Atlantic." This was said in such a casual way that Burghard paid no further attention to it. He said, "It seemed impossible anyway. The electric power was still on."

1:30 P.M. As Burghard looked out of the sunroom windows, he noticed that the dipole antenna was in bad shape, so he put on his rubber waders and a slicker coat and went out on the boardwalk to tighten up the guy rope, which was fastened to the railing near the dune. When he stepped onto the walk, the wind was so strong and full of sand and rain that it cut his face. Twice he was lifted off his feet, but by crawling along the railing, got the job done and managed to get back to the house safely. He tried to reach the top of the dune and look at the surf, but it was impossible to keep one's footing. He said, "I tried to phone Bill Ottman, who was coming over to watch the storm, and tell him not to come over, because the wind was so strong it would blow his car off the road, but the phone was dead. I couldn't get the operator. About ten minutes later, he called us. Mabel answered and he said he wasn't coming because his garage had just blown into the bay."

2 P.M. Up to now, no waves had come over the dunes, but the wind was shifting more to the east and growing stronger all the time. Burghard judged it to be at least 90 miles an hour. He and Dalin went down to the garage, finding the water about 2 feet deep, both there and in the servants' quarters. Things didn't look good, but they both thought it would let up very soon and they went back upstairs.

Burghard said, "Mabel had been sitting in the sun porch sewing, with her back to the easterly windows. Mrs. Dalin told her to change her seat, because the windows might blow in. She left, and went into the kitchen to press the dress she had been sewing, but the power was off and the iron wouldn't heat up. Just at this moment, the window where she had been sitting blew out completely and showered glass all over the place."

He and Dalin got an old door from below and lashed it up in front of the window. The wind was so strong that it was all they could do to hold the door against it. They finally secured it with half-inch rope and screw eyes in the casement. Then they spent some time sweeping up the glass, sand, and rainwater.

2:30 P.M. The wind and rain were increasing, always turning more to the east—in fact, the wind was almost due east by this time. The sky was dark, but the air was still quite warm. Burghard went to the leeward windows and saw that the 50-foot mast to the northwest was leaning at an angle of about 30 degrees. The dipole was still standing, although much bent. As he looked, he saw the first wave come over the dune, right in front of the house. It was all white water, but about 4 feet deep, and with plenty of force. All kinds of wreckage came with it, but it was difficult to see distinctly through the sand- and rain-covered windows.

The next wave came a few seconds later, and he saw the bathhouse lifted up in the air and swept around the west end of the house into the Dune Road; he estimated that it moved at about 20 miles per hour.

3 P.M. Burghard told Dalin to go below and get what clothes he could and bring them up to the third floor to the guest room, where he and Mrs. Dalin could spend the night. Burghard helped him with a suitcase and other clothes and then went into the servants' quarters. The water was about 2½ feet deep and all white and swirling like the surf. He went to the rear door, picked up some shoes and other things that were floating around, when suddenly a wave broke through the back door and swept him along the hall. Luckily, the door to the stairway was open and he managed to squeeze through.

He went through the garage, which had 3 feet of boiling water in it now, and got to the leeward side of the house, where the cleats that held the halyards on the V-antenna were located. Just as he got there, a big sea came over the dune and he had to hold onto the pole to stand against it. Between waves, he managed to clear the halyard and lower the V-antenna, but the northwest pole was almost down anyway.

3:30 P.M. After he had finished, he noticed John Avery, the Coast Guardsman who had been on watch in the tower, coming across the meadow. As Burghard watched, the meadow between his house and the Coast Guard station became completely covered by white water, but Avery managed to get through it. Burghard asked him, "Well, lad, do you think it's getting better or worse?"

Avery replied, "The whole dune is going. We'll have to walk for it. I had to leave the tower because all the windows blew out. Is there anybody in the house?"

"Yes, three. Two women and an old man."

"Let's get them moving quick," Avery said. "There is no time to lose."

Every wave was now coming over, and the white water bounded down the slope of the dune like a snowslide. It was then that Burghard realized that the tide had just started to come in. High tide was scheduled for 6:10, E.D.S.T., and if the surf was that high now, where would it be at 6:10?

They went into the house and everyone was quite calm—no trace of panic. Mrs. Dalin kept saying that this storm wasn't as bad as the storm of two years ago, which, of course, was not so, but if she felt that way, it might help matters.

Avery said they would all have to leave the house and try to walk to the bridge, a half-mile to the east. This was their best chance and even if they couldn't make it, the bay there narrowed down to about a hundred feet, which would be only a short swim at most. Where they were, it was well over a mile across to the mainland. Burghard told the Dalins they had to abandon ship; he gave the old man a pair of boots and sent Mrs. Burghard upstairs to put on shoes—the walking would be hazardous because of wreckage.

"My pet barometer, which I had had for years, was hanging in the radio room not fifteen feet away," said Burghard, "but for some unaccountable reason, I never once during that day consulted the glass. It seems a pity, because I had always wanted to see a barometer go below 28."

The surf was now running through the bottom of the house—all white water. The Burghards went up to the third-floor bedroom to see what they could find to take with them. Strange things happen in such unusual situations. Mrs. Burghard put on a pair of sandals, her lorgnette on a chain about her neck, and her handbag on her arm. Her husband, disregarding his watch, keys, and cuff links nearby, put only two season tickets for the tennis matches at Forest Hills in his trousers pocket, thinking, "I must have these because I have to see the semifinals tomorrow."

Burghard came downstairs. Dalin was coming up from below with a suitcase and some clothes. Mrs. Dalin was still working in the kitchen, and Burghard upbraided them for not hurrying.

"Do we really have to go?" Mrs. Dalin asked, and her husband said, "Can't I take my car?"

The Burghards had given Dalin a new car early in the summer, and he took great pride and pleasure in it. Both Dalins were reluctant to leave the house; they seemed stunned.

Burghard told them that the cars were useless because the engines had been under seawater for an hour and that, moreover, even if they had not, the force of the waves and the storm wreckage would wash a car off the road and into the bay. He added, "We must leave at once before the house caves in, and try to walk to the bridge."

4 P.M. Mrs. Burghard came downstairs, and picked up Peter. Her husband followed with Bitzie, after telling the Dalins to hurry, and leaving Avery to help them along. When they arrived at the door to the garage, which was the only exit, they found themselves in white water up to their

waists and, what with dogs and all, could not get the door open against the tide. Avery came to the rescue and they jammed the door open so it would stay. The Burghards floundered out into the driveway, and Avery went back into the house to hurry the Dalins.

The wind was now due east and blowing all of 100 miles an hour. The driveway was full of holes gouged out by the surf, and each wave brought more wreckage. After several spills, the Burghards finally reached Dune Road, which was a roaring torrent, awash with logs and boards. There, in the lee of the house, they exchanged dogs, because Mrs. Burghard had the heavier one. He took her arm and they walked east along the road to the Livermore fence and hedge, which afforded some protection from surf and debris. They put the dogs on the hedge and waited for the rest of the party.

Avery came out the house leading Mrs. Dalin. He virtually had to drag her to the Burghards. She was very frightened, and Mrs. Burghard tried to comfort her by telling her to grab a telegraph pole, which she did. All this time, the surf was coming over the dune with every wave and washing into the bay. They had to hold on to one another to keep from being washed away, and to duck the floating wreckage at the same time.

Burghard looked back and saw Carl Dalin walk out of the driveway, get to a fence post on the road behind the house, and sit down. He was only 75 feet west of where they all were together. They called to him, since he was to leeward and could have heard, but he never even moved his head—he just sat there with his head down, looking at the water.

Time was getting short, so Avery and Burghard, with much difficulty, worked Mrs. Dalin loose from the pole and started to walk east. Then it happened. The wind shifted to the southeast and the surf seemed to be lifted right over the dunes to the road where they were standing. Green waves—some 50 feet high—came over, and the surf began breaking on top of them. They resisted the first of it, but then had to get hold of the telephone poles to duck the boards, planks, and timbers. Mrs. Burghard fell a few times, but they managed to haul her out, and the dogs strangely stayed in the hedge. Mrs. Dalin became hysterical and dragged Avery and Burghard to another pole near her husband—who never moved—and took a death grip, screaming and yelling.

4:15 P.M. Burghard said, "Now we knew we could never walk. The wind was southeast, at well over 110 miles per hour. The rain had let up to a great extent, but the sand in the air was terrific. The sky was as dark as at dusk, the atmosphere heavy and warm, and the temperature of the water almost tropical. Avery and I had a council of war, and decided we had to swim the bay. So we told Mabel and kicked off our boots, threw off our coats, and cut off our trouser legs with a penknife.

"I looked at the Coast Guard station and asked Avery if the large building, which was two stories high, would stand, suggesting that we might all get in there. . . . He said there was no use trying, that everything would go. I looked toward the Livermore dock, and saw the small boat still tied fast and made a run for it. Just as I reached out to get the painter (quarter-inch line), it snapped like a violin string, and the boat went across the bay at a 50-mile clip. I thought perhaps we could drag the Dalins over and send them off in the boat, but that was that. As I was fighting my way back through surf and wind, a big wave caught the Coast Guard station and all five buildings, the steel lookout tower, and the 100-foot steel mast seemed to rise right off their foundations and were washed into the bay.

"It was a terrible sight, but more so because of the absence of noise. The main building—60 by 50 and two stories high—hit the bay and smashed to pieces, throwing the lifeboats in all directions. But the effect was that of a silent movie—there wasn't a sound. I had heard stories of the silence of hurricanes, but was always skeptical. Here now I got the full effect. Although only a few hundred feet to leeward, we could hear none of the break-up crash—the 110-mile-an-hour wind took care of that.

"As the station went, I could think of only one thing—the large building would knock down the poles carrying the high-tension power lines, and we, all being up to our waists in salt water, would surely be burned to a crisp. I yelled to everybody, the Dalins in particular because they were right under the poles, to get away, but the chimney of the large building cut all the lines just as clean as a razor blade cuts twine, and left all the poles intact. Of course my warning was silly, as the power had been cut off hours before.

"When I had worked my way back to where Mabel and Avery were standing, the waves were still higher, and the Townsend house, 100 feet east of Livermore's, cracked up and was blown and washed into the bay in a thousand pieces. This made us realize that we had to take to the bay at once, because anything might happen from now on. We decided to go out on the Livermore dock, which was still intact, and lie down and wait for a big wave to wash us, dock and all, into the bay.

"The surf was so strong by this time that it was all anyone could do to keep a footing. We called to the Dalins to follow us, but no response. Mrs. Dalin was screaming and holding to the pole, and the old man was still in the same position, not even looking at his wife. I still think the poor fellow was either so stunned he couldn't move, or had had a stroke. There was nothing we could do, as it was now so bad you could walk only with the wind and water.

"We decided to abandon the two dogs, and put them on the hedge, but at the last second, little Peter looked at me so helplessly that I took him under one arm, and Mabel with the other, and so we virtually floated to the dock, with Avery on Mabel's other side. As we sat down on the dock waiting for a good wave, I suddenly noticed Bitzie, who had swum up all by himself and joined us. We stood up and yelled and waved at the Dalins to let go and float over to us, but no response. Then the thought came to us that they were now in the lee of the house and as neither of them could swim, if the house and poles held, they were safer where they were. Also, we felt sure that this couldn't last much longer, and that when we got over to the mainland we could come back in a boat and get them. It never occurred to us that this was a major catastrophe.

"Just then, the Livermore bathhouse, which was quite a substantial structure, was lifted up by a huge wave and came right at us. Luckily, it hit some poles and cracked up. A beautiful flat piece came right toward us on the dock. Avery grabbed one end and I the other. Mabel, who was perfectly calm, jumped on the center and the dogs followed. Avery climbed on the rear and I got on the front, and waited for the next wave. The wind had driven the bay water across to the mainland to such an extent that for about 200 feet, the bay bottom was dry, but only between waves. When a wave came, which was every few seconds, there was about five to six feet of white water.

"We looked at the Dalins, but they were still in the same position, and we could do nothing. The next big wave was a dandy and we shoved off just like a surfboard and went about 200 feet into the bay, where we grounded. Avery and I climbed off and waited for the next wave, then gave a shove and jumped aboard and we were off for the deep water. Of course we had a little trouble keeping the wave from throwing the raft over us, but we were lucky.

"The wind was still southeast and blowing us toward the Old Moriches inlet to the west. I said, 'Well, lad, we're going to sea.' Avery answered, 'Yes, I believe we are.' Mabel had overheard us and asked, 'What was that?' So we told her we were just having a little sail. The raft we were on was almost submerged and the waves in the bay, at least six feet high, would wash us off with each breaker from the sea, but we always managed to swim back again."

The flotsam following them was very bad. Halves of houses came floating by, with many large nails protruding. Roofs, second stories, which had a larger "sail" area than their raft, passed them like motorboats. It was quite dark and the visibility was low, although the rain was slight; to look back was almost impossible, due to the wind and sand. Several automobiles followed them. The surf picked the cars up, the wind caught them underneath and threw them a hundred feet or more until they finally struck deep water, where they sank out of sight. As far as the Burghards could see, their house was still standing. The air and water remained very warm.

Mrs. Burghard, looking west, saw what appeared to be a motorboat traveling at about 60 miles an hour and said, "There is a boat going after the Dalins." The men had to destroy her illusion; the "boat" was the corner of a house that had grounded and the wind and tide made it look as if it were moving. A huge black fuel tank, 50 feet long and 10 feet in diameter, passed close by. (It was found next morning on the golf course, two miles inland.) Doors flew over their heads, 50 and 100 feet up, and planks 20 feet long were lifted out of the water by the wind and hurled over their heads.

As they drifted into deeper water, their raft began to sink, apparently because some of the bottom of it had fallen off on the way. "Mabel was perfect all the way," said Burghard. "Every once in a while she would be washed off and I would stick out my foot so she could grab it and haul her back to safety." With the gradual sinking of the raft, the dogs became troublesome. Peter was fine, but Bitzie, the wire-haired terrier, climbed on Mrs. Burghard's neck to get out of the water and pushed her head under.

Avery and Burghard found the dogs "a nice little raft," put them aboard, and shoved them out ahead. When they were about 100 feet away, both dogs jumped off and swam back against the 110-mile wind to the Burghards, who pulled them onto their raft again.

Burghard estimated there was 40 feet of water in the channel, and the waves became constantly higher. Holding onto the raft was steadily more difficult. Several times, as they scrambled back aboard after having been washed off, both dogs swam back with sticks in their mouths, in a playful mood, dropping the sticks on the raft and waiting for somebody to throw them. Once, Bitzie was washed off and Peter jumped in after him, towing him back by the ear.

Just as their raft was going down, along came a very large piece of a house, well-studded with nails, but flat. Avery said, "Somebody better get onto that and lighten the load." Burghard, being the heaviest, climbed

Wreckage of houses swept into piles at Westhampton, Long Island. The ocean resort town with 28 dead, 150 houses destroyed, and property loss of two million dollars, was the worst hit of all the Long Island communities.

377

over and found it so large that both his wife and Avery came aboard, with the dogs. It was big enough so that they could sit above water for the first time since they had left the beach, which was a great relief; there was even a place to brace their feet, which lessened the danger of being washed off.

They were now beyond the channel and the danger of their situation increased. Large chunks of houses, with spikes sticking out, were chasing them on every hand. The two men picked up long pieces of boards and pushed the raft around all the big hunks of debris. By paddling and pushing, they managed to get between the houses and roofs and let them all go by to leeward. A flock of ducks appeared, trying to fly against the wind, which was impossible; the birds were blown backward at about 40 miles an hour while flying at full speed.

"By this time," Burghard said, "we could see the houses on Oneck Point distinctly, but there was so much wreckage that we didn't know whether we were going to miss the point or not. We could see Harold Medina's boat across the cut to the west, apparently on her side, on the lawn.

"There was a house on the point just west of Oneck, which we afterward found out belonged to Mr. Steinbugler, and it looked as if we were going to land there. We were still about 300 yards out in the bay but, for the first time, saw people on the front porch—about ten of them. This was a welcome sight and we thought surely they had seen us and were waiting with a drink and blankets to warm us up, as the strong wind blowing on our bare backs had tended to chill us a bit, although the water was still very warm. We all waved to them with a great feeling of relief, but not one of them responded. They just kept milling about on the porch, which was well underwater.

"From then on, we were so busy keeping the wreckage from crushing us that we had no more time to look. The waves were getting higher as we neared the shore, and we had all we could do to avoid things that were washed and blown at us. One huge plank came over with a wave and rode right across the raft between Mabel and me. I was busy pushing off a roof, and she put her hands on the plank, guiding it safely between us, but sprained her wrist badly doing it.

"The wind and waves swept us on, and we finally grounded in a clump of berry bushes about fifty feet from the Steinbugler house. We looked for the people we had seen on the porch, but to our disappointment, they had all disappeared. No one was in sight to give us a hand—we were all alone again. Avery and I helped Mabel off the raft. He took her around the bushes; there was about three feet of water and we had to go quickly as all the houses and roofs were piling up behind us. Peter swam off and followed them, but Bitzie grew panicky and jumped on a roof to the east. The roof floated into the brush about 100 feet away. I called and whistled to him, but he wouldn't move. I tried to get him, but the wreckage was coming in so fast I couldn't walk. Then he jumped into the bushes and although we looked everywhere, that was the last we ever saw of him.

"I followed the others around the bushes, which were very sharp and scratched us up badly. But we finally reached the road, which was three feet under water. After ducking around and over wreckage, we made the fairway of the Westhampton golf course, the eleventh hole of which was just across the road and high and dry. Peter came along and joined us, tickled to death to be on land; so were we.

"A woman came out of the Steinbugler house and waded through the water to us. She was more or less hysterical, but upon questioning, told us there were two babies in the house. Avery said he would get them and I took Mabel by the arm and we started walking up the golf course.

"On the chart, from our house to where we landed, one point west of Oneck, is a little over a mile, but we figured that with the detour, we floated about two and a half miles. How long it took us to get across will never be known, but I imagine we were traveling at least ten miles per hour.

"The wind had shifted to the southwest by now and was still blowing just as hard, and boards and things were still flying through the air. Trees were blowing down all around us, but we were in an open space on the fairway and in no danger.

"As we walked along, we took account of ourselves. Mabel wore just a bathing suit, but the lorgnettes were still around her neck, and her handbag, dripping water, was still on her arm, with cruel welts showing where the handles had bruised her flesh on the way over. We were both in our bare feet, I with just the remains of a pair of trousers, and our legs bruised and bleeding from many cuts and scratches, but nothing broken, although Mabel's ankle and wrist were badly swollen. Nevertheless, we walked on—where, we didn't know, because we had never been there before. I had Mabel by the arm, but the wind was so strong that several times she was taken right off her feet and I had to pull her back by the wrist. Peter was running about having a grand time."

As they walked along, the darkness lifted somewhat; the sun tried to come through the clouds. The rain had stopped but the wind was bone-chilling. They walked about two miles and, seeing a house over a hedge, finally came out on the main road from Westhampton to Remsenburg. Burghard now knew where he was and said, "I'll go into that house and telephone." The house was unoccupied; even if it had not been, there was not an operable phone in miles.

They stood there, half-naked, bleeding, and shivering in the wind. A woman came out of a house and paid no attention to them, apparently being too frightened, or preoccupied to have time for anyone else. A car drove up, and although the driver appeared not even to notice their condition, he asked how he could get to Westhampton. He was looking for his family and had been trying to get there for two hours. They all jumped into the car, including the dog. After trying road after road blocked by trees and downed utility poles, they came at last to Montauk Highway and found a way into Westhampton.

There was no one in sight, and in the center of town, there was at least 6 feet of swirling water, which was still coming up. A man walked by, leading an old woman. Burghard called to him: "Where can we get warm?" The man replied, "Follow me to the Howell House; it has a stove." When they walked in, with bare feet and bleeding legs, some of the people—frightened, because they thought it was the end of Long Island and the water was still rising—asked, "What do you want?" Burghard replied, "We just swam across the bay," and the people looked at them skeptically.

Finally, someone took them to the kitchen, and they stood dripping there before the warmth of a coal range and had coffee and brandy, Peter getting dried out with them.

In about a half-hour, the water in the village, which had risen to 8 feet in Main Street, receded as quickly as it had come. Burghard got some shoes and dry clothes from the manager of the hotel and went to the third floor to look at the dunes. It was about dusk, but from what he could see, there wasn't a house left standing. He went back downstairs, for the first time looked at a barometer and found that at about 6:30 P.M., it was 28 inches. Somebody put disinfectant on the Burghards' cuts; they had a drink and a sandwich.

Immediately after that, Burghard went looking for his friend, William Ottman, and the Dalins, having borrowed sneakers, blue jeans, and a sweater. Main Street was deserted; he walked through the dark, stumbling over wreckage, without a flashlight, and finally arrived at police headquarters. He said, "They were glad to see me, since we had been reported missing. I asked about Bill [Ottman] and they knew nothing. There was no report about the Dalins. Discouraged, I went into the Patio and there found Jack Face, Bill's chauffeur, who told me Bill and the baby and all were safe. This was a great relief, so we all had a drink.

"Then I made my way to the country club, which had been turned into an improvised morgue, and there identified the body of C. Dalin. It appears that he washed up on the golf course, right where we had landed, and they found him about 9 P.M. His son, Alvin, was there and we identified his father at about 12:30 A.M. It was a gruesome business, as there were no lights and we had to look the bodies over with flashlights.

"Of course we didn't sleep after that, and searched for Mrs. Dalin. At 5 A.M., we found her body in the undertaker's. They had picked her up about a half-mile east of where he landed, at 2 A.M.

"By way of aftermath, to the east and west of where our house stood, there is nothing left but sand, where over sixty houses stood before the storm.

"After many days of searching, we found practically nothing of value. The roof and attic of our house was washed up a swale behind the first hole of the Westhampton golf course about three miles from where it started. Part of the Livermore house landed some 300 feet farther on. The largest radio pole, with halyards intact, was found on the first green of the golf course, and a vest to one of my suits was nearby, 20 feet up in a tree. We found both of Mabel's riding boots, one at least a half-mile from the other. One of my slippers was perched near a Coast Guard lifeboat, a mile inland. Incidentally, there was a piece of shingle driven through the side of this boat with the force of a rifle.

"On the beach where the house used to be, we found part of a loudspeaker, the kitchen sink, a card table on its back, with only one leg broken, Livermore's beach umbrella, and a sweater of old man Dalin's.

"Two weeks afterward, they found my briefcase and some papers, checkbooks, etcetera, belonging to Mabel and me, under ten feet of wreckage on the golf course."

On September 24, Coast Guard Commander Wolff at Bay Shore cited Surfman John R. Avery, the lone lookout at Westhampton Beach, for bravery.

Southampton suffered heavily along the shorefront. From the bathing station to the municipal beach, only two cottages remained standing after the sea swept Dune Road. Among the shattered landmarks was St. Andrew's Church on the Dunes, the scene of many society weddings over the years. The storm left the church in ruins; its south and west walls were battered down and pieces of the organ, pews, and other furnishings were scattered over an area of a mile. An inscription on the church's east wall, which remained standing, lent a touch of irony; it is a verse from the

Psalms: "Thou rulest the raging of the sea; Thou stillest the waves thereof when they arise." A stained glass window in the church, presented about a year before by Mrs. Henry E. Coe, in memory of her husband, was discovered intact, frame and all, under a hedge a quarter-mile away.

At Bridgehampton, the farmers were heavy losers; nearly fifty barns went down from Water Mill to Wainscott and north to the line of the Scuttle Hole Road or a little beyond. Potato farmers near the ocean found many acres washed out, washed away, or buried deep beneath sand from the beach. On other fields that had been flooded with seawater, the potatoes rotted soon after being dug. Farmers lost garages, chicken houses, and outbuildings, as well as barns; there were more than eighty places with such losses. An estimated 3,500 trees were lost in the Bridgehampton-Sagaponack-Hayground area alone.

Trees went down everywhere the hurricane struck, but perhaps nowhere was this phenomenon of the storm more heartbreaking than it was to the residents of East Hampton. The elms and locusts that formed an arch a half-mile long over Main Street had been planted before the American Revolution; they can still be seen in the canvases of many important painters, including Childe Hassam and Thomas Moran.

The trees were among the town's most cherished historical landmarks, but when the storm was over, 42 percent of the Main Street elms were gone. From the Hedges Inn on the east side of Main Street to the Methodist parsonage, counting only trees outside private property lines or just on the line, there were sixty-eight down.

The grim communications traffic concerning bodies—trying to locate the missing and identify the found—was beginning. "To Corporal William Brockman, State Police, Montauk: Body of a man, apparently a fisherman, washed ashore at Block Island and a child's body has been found at Moonstone Beach, South Kingston, Rhode Island. The man was six feet tall, weighed about one hundred and eighty pounds, was bald and clean-shaven and bore no scars or discernible tattoo marks. Wore brown khaki pants and a brown denim shirt and was barefoot. Portions of an inner tube wrapped around his ankle. In his pocket were a brass padlock key, a pocket knife and a portion of a pink celluloid comb. . . .

"The little boy found was between 36 and 37 inches tall, weighing forty pounds and was between two and three years of age. His hair was medium brown, inclined to be wavy. His undergarments were of white cotton, bordered at the neck and bottom with very fine lace. The underwear reached to the neck with fine embroidery stitched down the center of the garment. He wore a dark blue suit with white pearl buttons and green jacket with white celluloid, saucer-shaped buttons. The jacket was lined with black cotton material and bore no labels."

The message was addressed to Corporal Brockman because Montauk was to windward, in terms of the hurricane.

Not all of Corporal Brockman's news was bad. There was the situation of the *Ruth R.*

Captain Dan Parsons owned the *Ruth R.* and her skipper was Captain Charles Landry, who had worked for Parsons eighteen years. The boat, 41 feet long, of 16-foot beam, and drawing 6 feet, had been built twenty-nine years before by Percy Tuthill, of Greenport, and she was considered one of the most substantial vessels operating out of Montauk.

On the day of the hurricane, the crew of the *Ruth R.* was off Culloden Point, working on a fish trap. As the wind increased, Captain Landry signaled for his crew—Cleveland Noels, Wilfred Fougere, and Joseph Guyetche, who were in two trap boats—to come back aboard the sloop.

Before the men could get to the vessel, Noels's boat had capsized. Swimming to a stake a hundred yards away, Noels clung to it while Fougere and Guyetche fought to reach him against a wind that had by then reached hurricane proportions. They were forced to row ashore and hastily bail the water out of their boat—a heavy sea had half-filled her—before they could reach Noels to pick him up. Gaining the side of the sloop, the three leaped aboard, making fast their painter—which proved to be a futile gesture. The wind immediately smashed the boat against the *Ruth R.*, shattering the smaller craft. Left without either small boat, the four men now had to fight for their lives aboard the sloop; she was their only hope.

With her engine hooked up to the last notch in an effort to keep her head into the wind's eye and to stem the thrust of the rushing flood tide, the big sloop nevertheless was forced steadily toward Gardiner's Island. Driving rain made it impossible to remain on deck or to see a boat-length ahead. With the island close at hand, they finally got two anchors down; the wind shifted almost immediately and snapped both cables. An effort to start the engine again proved futile; water had gotten to it.

Now they were adrift and helpless, having neither power nor anchors; they were being driven with the full force of the hurricane in the general direction of Block Island. The sloop was not leaking, but she was taking aboard hundreds of gallons of rainwater. With their clothes soaked, suffering from exposure and fatigue, and in constant danger of capsizing as they drifted broadside to wind and sea, the crew—without heat, food, water, tobacco or matches—pumped continuously all night to keep the *Ruth R.* afloat.

They were adrift for eighteen hours before they sighted Block Island. Then they managed to get the engine started, and tied up in New Harbor at 9 o'clock Thursday morning. There they found that thirty-five out of fifty fishing boats were wrecked and the village shattered. Yet from what was left, they obtained food, a dry, one-burner gas stove, and they ate, grateful to be alive, praising as only seamen can the virtues of the boat and her builder that had made survival possible.

Back in East Hampton, Captain Parsons knew only that his boat and her crew had been swept out to sea during the hurricane; over the hours, he had maintained a constant vigil, knowing very well that each passing hour made it more likely that the *Ruth R.* and all aboard were lost. From every source, the terrible casualty figures were mounting; Parsons was haggard and worn by anxiety.

Finally, it was Friday, and it was State Trooper Brockman who reported to Dan Parsons: "The *Ruth R.* has been sighted. She's on her way home."

Parsons found the news incredible. Even when he first saw the sloop, inbound, he thought his eyes were playing tricks on him. It was not until he threw his arms about Captain Landry, tears of relief streaming down his cheeks, that he accepted as fact the survival of the crew of the *Ruth R.*—something little short of a miracle. In fact, a miracle without qualification.

On the day following the storm, Lieutenant Theodore Harris of the Coast Guard flew the length of Long Island for eight hours; his job was to spot bodies and report their location.

From the air, the coast of Long Island presented a scene of unbelievable wreckage and desolation. There were roofs floating without walls, walls without roofs, and whole houses adrift. There were a thousand small boats capsized, cast upon the land, or pounded to pieces against the shore.

Pat Grady, who was in the plane, said, "At Ocean Beach, 300 houses were crushed and scattered about. At least 100 houses had been demolished at Fair Harbor and about the same number at Saltaire. There were about 40 houses largely inundated at Little Cap Tree Island.

"Approaching Westhampton, the land had the appearance of a child's room on New Year's Day, with all his toy houses and automobiles broken and warped. At least 100 automobiles were washed up in inland waterways and will be searched for bodies. We flew low and even from the air, pathetic scenes were visible as families searched in what was left of their homes for their possessions or for the dead.

"At Moriches Bay, we began to see the dead—the body of a man clad only in shoes and socks was lying face down on a sand dune. The wind had blown off the rest of his clothing. . . ."

There is one aspect of this storm which literally picked up the water of the sea, tore it into shreds, and flung it across the land so that there was no separating driving rain and salt spray that was extraordinary: the noise.

"Despite all the destruction," Ernest S. Clowes recalled, "few people heard anything but one sound: the voice of the storm. It was like nothing else, although it could be analyzed into three parts; the lowest on the scale was the deep bass of the sea, the highest was the shout of the wind through the trees, rising at times almost to a scream. Between them both in pitch and exceeding both in volume was a steady, almost organ-like note, of such intensity that it seemed as if the whole atmosphere were in harmonic vibration. No sound rose above it. It was something one not only heard, but felt to the core of one's being.

"A woman whose house was literally barricaded by fallen trees said afterward, 'I never heard one of them go.'"

Book II

CONNECTICUT

CHAPTER 3

On Saturday, September 24, three days after the hurricane, the New York *Herald Tribune* reported on Page 1 that author Elmer Davis was missing from Mason Island, off Mystic, Connecticut. Actually, he wasn't; he did, however, share with thousands the extraordinary experience of being forced to accept the reality of the hurricane.

"When the wind began to blow about 2 o'clock Wednesday afternoon, most of the inhabitants of these parts were convinced that it was only the traditional 'line storm,' the three-day blow that comes every September when the sun crosses the equator," Davis said. "Even as the wind rose and its tone changed to the ee-ee-ee that well-read persons recognize as the mark of the hurricane, even when the rain came in horizontal sheets, and tightly closed windows began to leak streams of water, traditionalists insisted that this couldn't be a hurricane because there never had been a hurricane in these latitudes. . . .

"And then all at once in a thousand households, the argument stopped and everybody began to nail up all the doors and windows and hope that with all the air shut out, the wind would not take the whole house along in one piece. With every window, every door fastened as tightly shut as you could get it, you sat in the living room and watched the shingles on the garage roof ruffle up like a hen's feathers blown in the wind and then, one by one, tear off and whirl away. You saw nearby trees slowly lean over and go down; you listened to the crash of breaking windows; the steady ee-ee-ee of the wind, you felt the floor waving under you like a shaken carpet."

When the sea rose 14 feet above normal at Mason Island, Carolyn Wilson, a former Chicago correspondent, looked up, while trying to plug leaks in her wall, to find the ocean at her door when it ought to have been one hundred yards away. She had to get out and tried to take her cat with her, but he refused to go, so she kissed him a dolorous good-bye and swam a half-mile over drowned shrubbery to high ground.

Y.E. Soderberg, the etcher, opened his house to relatives who had to abandon their own, but presently the water was three feet deep in his house and the family had to seek refuge in the second story, watching all the ground-floor furniture floating away out of the windows. Herbert Stoops, the New York illustrator, living a scant half-mile from the main highway, had to climb over seventy-nine fallen trees when he made his way out the next morning.

But it was not until the Mason Islanders plodded over the shattered causeway to the mainland, seeking food and candles, that they learned what the hurricane had done to Connecticut.

It was in the New Haven area that New Englanders began to realize the magnitude of the storm's impact upon their natural heritage. Five thousand trees lining the city's streets were destroyed and as many more damaged so extensively that they had to be removed. At least a sixth of the city's trees were gone. They had proved especially vulnerable to the wind because heavy rains preceding the hurricane had left the ground like a filled sponge, weakening the turf holding down the roots. Tree Superintendent Fred Eaton predicted it would be twenty to forty years before the city looked as it had before the hurricane.

It was five years later that the U.S. Forest Service in Willimantic was able to announce that the last of the hurricane timber in Connecticut had been sawed and salvaged, and to close its office there.

And there were the rampaging rivers, already bursting from days of rain. It was at Hartford where man and river fought their fiercest, most prolonged, and most costly battle; the roily, swollen Connecticut River provided disastrous counterpoint to the hurricane.

Howling out of the southeast at four in the afternoon, an 80-mile-an-hour wind, the highest ever recorded in Hartford, spread death and destruction, ripping off roofs, toppling buildings, uprooting trees, disrupting traffic and communications, shattering brick walls, and tearing up fences, which one resident described as "floating in the air like paper." Rain was driven through the city in great sheets, and the *Courant* noted that "few people ventured on the street to brave the wind; at times, their feet were whipped away from under them. . . ."

The clock in the Old State House stopped at 4:10. Pigeons, unable to fly with their beaks to the wind, were smashed against the windshields of automobiles. Store windows buckled in the wind and shattered. Simultaneously, the Connecticut River was rising at the rate of 4 inches an hour; by midnight on Wednesday, it had reached 24.7 feet and was expected to crest at 28 feet by Thursday noon. As rain continued to spill out of gray skies, the residents of the lower East Side stolidly watched their old river foe lapping upward to threaten their homes and their well-being. They made their preparations. Chairs and couches were taken to second floors. Pictures were removed from the first floors. Clothing was packed in case evacuation became necessary.

One woman on Potter Street said, "I was born in a flood and so was my mother. I lived here during the 1936 flood. I'm not afraid. They come every so often." Bushnell Park became a watery wilderness; by night, the lamp-post bulbs glowed like floating Japanese lanterns. But the critical points as the rain-swelled Connecticut rose were at the dikes.

From Hartford's Travelers Insurance Company Tower at noon on Thursday, the view presented a stark contrast.

Overhead shone a benign September sun, and a hazy blue sky dotted with white cloud puffs. Below, the landscape had two faces. One of them complemented the sky. West, southwest, and northwest lay a landscape full of calm and peace, mellow in the mood of early autumn. The other half of the horizon was menacing, and from north to south there stretched a scene of desolation.

The inexorably rising Connecticut River seemed to lie within its banks as it rounded the bend near Windsor, but then, like the contents of a broken paper bag, it sprawled in unsightly disarray over miles of lowlands. The brown, swiftly moving flood, thick with its freight of half-submerged trees and the wreckage of Wednesday's hurricane, stretched from the new concrete Windsor Street extension on the west to the distant meadows of South Windsor on the east.

A few strings of freight cars, temporarily abandoned, stood in the vast lake which covered the freight yards north of the city. To the east of the Willimantic railroad bridge, a foundationless building squatted in the flood, and a long line of coal cars held down the East Hartford trestle.

The entire western section of East Hartford, with the exception of the boulevard, lay inundated by river waters, which had crept up to the sills of first-floor windows. Several scores of dwellings, a school, and an apartment house were cut off entirely from the rest of the town, and there was no sign of life about them. Prospect Street, north and south of the boulevard, was the "beach" of a rapidly advancing shoreline. The pier and the gasoline pumps of the Hartford Yacht Club had gone down the river at 9:45 A.M., carrying with them a private craft. Other boats, huddled in awkward clusters, were flanked by driftwood in the upper branches of trees which stood where the river's edge had been only a few days ago.

Memorial Bridge was covered with black crawling lines of slow-moving cars and trucks; the urgent blare of automobile horns below the Travelers Tower indicated the anxious feelings of the drivers, pushing toward the remaining route to their homes east of the river.

A deserted barge loaded with scrap iron, perhaps bound for some foreign war, stemmed the river's current; once it had been berthed alongside the dock at the foot of State Street. Now it was more than 100 feet from dry land.

Here and there in the streets between the Travelers main building and the western rim of the flood, the scars of Wednesday's storm were apparent. The yellow boards of roofs whose shingles had been ripped off by the hurricane and the white jagged points of shattered tree tops reminded one acutely that the city had barely had a chance to draw its breath after the impact of one catastrophe before it was being forced to face another.

There was a reassuring sight in the southeast, where Brainard Field, a pale green oasis, stretched dry and unscathed, protected by its wide encircling dike and by Colt's dike to the north, which, while its durability was in doubt, still held back the river to this moment.

All day, tensions over the flood increased. When the relentless upcoming of water caused street after street to be inundated, and hundreds to be homeless, predictions of the crest changed several times and always to a higher figure. Boat patrols were set up and took many to safety. Workers in threatened industrial plants, fighting against time, moved millions of dollars' worth of property to higher ground.

And now began the struggle by 1,200 WPA workers, World War I veterans, college students, and other volunteers in the southeast section of the city to save the homes of 5,000 and to protect the semi-industrial area, where two-thirds of the $6 million damage occurred in the flood of 1936.

This is Thursday night:

A thousand men crack their backs to keep a million tons of water out of the south end of the city. A hundred trucks slam over the pitted, pitch-black roads. They dump bags half-filled with sand along the Colt and Clark dikes, raising the low spots, stopping up the street ends.

Under the hiss of flares, a hundred crews grunt to throw the fifty-pound sacks in place. "Place 'em right; pack 'em carefully," the foremen shout.

On the land side, there is furious work, shouting, din, and sweat. On the other, no haste. Just the river, leisurely climbing up and up, seeping through, no more noise than an occasional, ominous lapping. The water creeps up over the 33-foot mark. Three square miles of a city is imperiled; if this army of a thousand is defeated, if the dikes go out with a roar for the second time in two years, the whole of that three square miles will be the scene of flood, devastation, tumbled wreckage, and ruin.

From Springfield, Massachusetts, where the river has been at a standstill for three hours, comes bad news; the water is rising again. In Hartford, the American Red Cross headquarters, already caring for 1,500 evacuees at six relief stations in the city, is notified by the city government to prepare for 3,000 refugees, ordered to evacuate their homes in the area back of the dikes south of Sheldon Street and east of Main Street. Some go fearfully; some debate going; some have to be forced out of their homes.

All during the evacuation, the diking goes on. The people may not be gotten out in time. Even when they are moved to safety, there are still millions of dollars' worth of property, thousands of homes and businesses to be protected, if protection is possible.

A crest of 34.5 feet is predicted for sometime Friday morning. At Springfield, the upsurge of water accelerates to a rate of one-tenth of a foot an hour. U.S. Army Engineers say there is only a fifty-fifty chance that the Hartford dikes will hold.

All night, the engineers roar in automobiles along the dike areas from Commerce to Sheldon Street to Wawarme Avenue, evaluating the constantly changing situation, ordering quick countermeasures against the creeping waters. As early as 9:30 P.M., the two most critical spots are obvious: the junction of Sheldon and Sequassen, near the Colt Firearms Company office, from which the battle against the water is directed, and at Sheldon and Commerce; here at the low levels of these street ends, the river makes its major threat to overwhelm the city's south end.

Sandbags are piled, quickly, surely, with tireless haste, into the depressions made by the low roadways. A triple row for a foundation, and then a single row. Bag upon bag, a slender buttress, half a bag wide against infinite pressure of water. Where the water does not simply press, quiet and deadly, it seeps, and by 11 o'clock, small streams ooze from the sandbagging, trickle across Sheldon and spill into the gutters on the sharp declines of Sequassen and Commerce, the perimeters of the great three-square-mile area that is menaced.

It is more than a mile over pockmarked roads to Brainard Field airport, where a roaring digger throws up earth at the "burrow" and sweating men shovel it into bags. Squads of trucks are backed to the spot, and none waits to be more than half-filled. Time is precious. A few bags can do a lot of good if rushed to vital spots. The trucks bound over roads as black as the inside of a pocket. They dodge between red lanterns and shoot by trooping workers en route from one bad spot to another. The workers scuttle out of the way, their electric torches flashing, as they make their way past holes in the road and tangles of tree branches sent down by Wednesday's storm.

Slam-banging into the lower end of Sheldon Street, the trucks slow down into single file and as they pass the laboring crews, the foremen cut them out as needed. With shouts, they are guided up close to the sandbag walls, the dump body rises with a roar of gears, the bags of sand slide to the ground and without stopping to lower the dumpers, the trucks charge down the side streets and off to the pit for another load.

After each clatter that announces the arrival of a truck, after the noise of unloading, silence once more falls over each crew, broken only by an occasional order barked by the foreman. These men work without talk, in part because they were hours ago tired enough to rest, yet there is not time for rest; they work tensely, but without excitement, to bag up each dangerous spot, higher and higher. They work swiftly but with deliberation and care; one sack out of place and enough water might seep through to start the fatal breach.

When each truckload of bags has been laid, they walk back and forth over the tops of the bags, settling them into place; the foreman watches with a critical eye; this bag needs readjustment, square that one up. Now the water is rising at the rate of two-tenths of a foot per hour. Opposite the Colt office and about twenty feet beyond the dike there is a white post nearly covered with water. It is a stake marking the 35-foot level. There are 800 men working in this area; the call goes out for 200 more. Thomas

F. Foley, local WPA representative, is the man in charge of the battle. Sleepless and with a sprained right ankle, he answers a battery of phones in the Colt office, patrols endlessly between the Commerce and Sequassen weak spots, receives half-hour readings from the yellow-chalked post in the swollen stream just beyond the soaked sandbags, and is grimly noncommital.

Beyond the stake, the murky expanse of rampaging river stretches away into the dark. Some small buildings can be seen dimly in the flickering lights, water halfway up to their single-story roofs. The water makes no sound, and as you look over the top of the sandbagging, it hardly seems to move. It is a sullen river, brown with churned-up earth, and the smell of oil rises from it.

There is some little talk to break the silence when the reserves arrive, with truckloads of shovels. They line up on the porch of the Colt building, waiting to be assigned to gangs. From the dark, there is a loud haloo from some distant foreman, calling for trucks. The wind off the water is cold; it is more comfortable to stand near the flares—at least they give an impression of warmth. By midnight, the water has reached to within a few inches of the tops of the bags in some places and 200 nearby Legionnaires are trying to persuade remaining residents to leave and to assist those who are willing to go.

At 10 o'clock Friday night, the Connecticut River gave up its fight. Reaching a height of 35.1 feet, it began to recede. The U.S. Army Engineers, who had taken over direction of the defending forces, under Colonel John S. Bragdon of Providence, reported that the first recession of the water had been noted and that the level was then 35.09, a drop of 1/100 of a foot. By midnight, the reading was 35.02. The little army, blistered and exhausted, watched by thousands, including the refugees, and prayed for by thousands more, had won the "Battle of Colt's Dike."

It was not until Sunday, when all danger was past, that Mayor Thomas J. Spellacy disclosed that an emergency plan had been set up to dynamite the Clark dike along Brainard Field and the South Meadows at the moment that the Colt dike or its long Sheldon Street emergency sandbag extension gave way. The theory was that if the sandbagging effort had not been successful and the water had broken through, the force of the pent-up river, unless relieved by immediate creation of another outlet to the south, might have swept away the Colt factory buildings and all other structures in its path. City officials anticipated it would have torn oil storage tanks in the area from their moorings and slammed them against the South Meadows generating plant of the Hartford Electric Light Company, and hoped that the dynamiting would have prevented this.

In all of this time of crisis, the most extraordinary phone call received by the Hartford *Courant*—one among a bombardment of hundreds made by those concerned about roads, property, missing persons, and the state of the Connecticut River—came Wednesday night as the city lay shocked and battered after the hurricane. "Can you tell me," the caller asked, "on what date the blizzard of 1888 occurred in Russia?"

Stafford Springs (population 5,500) was typical of many of Connecticut's towns, hit by both flood and hurricane. Undermined by flood waters, Tuesday, when Buck's Dam let go, then knocked down by wind, Stafford Springs was getting its provisions Thursday night chiefly by way of a single-plank bridge, 20 feet long, 8 inches wide. No word came out of the town after the storm Wednesday, and almost no one could get out of it Thursday, but a visitor got in.

"The borough has its main street through Haymarket Square caved in," he reported, "its railroad station foundations washed out, its railroad bed bordering Main Street scooped away, factories undercut, and sections of several highways carried away.

"As incoming goods, ordered before the town lost its telephones, trains, mail and wire service, began to pile up at Barlow's store, west of the break in the road, it was decided to try to bridge the torrent that poured through the gap. Just one plank in width, precarious to cross, the bridge was serving its purpose Thursday night. With power off, bakeries in the town could not provide bread. Bread made up many of the loads carried across the plank.

"Before the hurricane hit, the borough had been flooded. Its Main Street ran with five feet of water in some places. Never had this happened since the Stafford Hill reservoir gave way back in 1877. All over Stafford, no one could smile or laugh Thursday, in the face of all the wreckage.

"St. Edward's Church, made widely known by the late Rev. Felix J. O'Neill, the poet-priest of New England, had shingles blown from its roof and trees toppled at its doors. Father O'Neill spoke of 'fair Stafford—the gem of the vale' in some of his poems and told of its beauty. Today, it is a horribly-battered beauty. . . ."

The story of the storm over a broad Connecticut River area—including Suffield, Hazardville, Enfield, Scitico, Somersville, and Somers—was the story of the tobacco sheds, all of them filled with the year's crops. In Somersville and Scitico, twenty-four sheds were knocked down within an area of two square miles. They looked as if they had been stepped on. Five out of five down was the score of the gale against the tobacco sheds in one spot in Scitico. Four out of seven was the most damaging hit in Poquanock, where the sheds also burned; charcoal was burning in many of the sheds full of drying tobacco that were destroyed, and the helpless owners watched the buildings go up in smoke after going down in the wind. On the day after the storm, not even the owners would give an estimate of damage, although for the area, for the tobacco lost alone, $2 million was thought conservative.

In the inundated South Windsor Meadows, eight men who were working in tobacco sheds were stranded by high water. Charles Davis left his companions in water up to their waists and swam for help. Early Thursday morning, State Troopers Robert Erdin and Joseph Saksa, in a motorboat, were able to reach the marooned men—four of whom were clinging to the bottom of an overturned boat—and rescue them. The sheds in which the eight had been working were leveled.

When a steeple toppled on the Poquanock Congregational Church, Edward Barkal, next door, saw it. The steeple came to rest along the ridgepole of the church. Barkal was asked what he thought when he saw it happen. "Didn't think anything at all. Just ran," he said. He ran from the barn into the house. Then a tree fell on the house and he ran out into the yard again. When he saw no more trees could hit the house, he went in.

In Windsor Locks, a very old man sat looking at two fallen trees on his lawn. "My grandfather planted them," he said.

CHAPTER 4

For New London, it was holocaust: hurricane, flood, and fire combined to leave hundreds homeless and jobless, the city in ruins, with damage estimated as high as $4 million after a destructive interlude of several hours that constituted the greatest disaster in the history of eastern Connecticut.

The Thames River and Long Island Sound broke over their banks along the entire shorefront, while flood waters from inland rivers, brooks, ponds, and lakes rushed down upon the city from several directions. Within minutes, the ordinarily placid Thames was a maelstrom and the Sound a tormented sea. In both river and sound, waves came pounding in; wharves collapsed beneath eight feet of flood water; tugs, barges, and yachts were driven from their berths and moorings, slammed ashore, holed, sunk, and left in shambles, their stacks and wheelhouses just above water, their masts poking skyward at grotesque angles.

The 300-foot five-masted barkentine *Marsala,* training ship of the American Nautical Academy—a school for merchant marine officers—was moored in the stream off the Custom House wharf. She had down a ten-ton anchor with 680 feet of chain on the starboard side and a port anchor of eight tons and 540 feet of chain. Despite this substantial ground tackle, the big ship started to drag, placing her in grave danger because of her size and the relatively confined area. With her master, Captain Oliver Bohld, her chief officer, Commander George Terry, and seventeen midshipmen aboard, the *Marsala* drifted toward the Shaw's Cove railroad bridge, a helpless juggernaut before the withering blast, a threat to the craft to leeward—some anchored, some adrift—and facing the prospect of being seriously damaged herself, either by collision or grounding.

Somebody on a beleaguered yacht, trying to hold on with anchor down and engine all ahead full, saw her coming, got his anchor up, and steamed to windward of her, in the nick of time. Nearing the railroad bridge, the barkentine seemed certain to collide with a barge up against the trestle. But the wind shifted and swung *Marsala's* stern about, so that she cleared both the barge and a tugboat seeking a haven there. The training ship finally fetched up off the Chappell Lumber Company wharf, where her crew succeeded in making her bow fast to one dock and her stern to another. Here, she blocked the offshore end of a large slip between the wharves in which were trapped thousands of board feet of lumber washed overboard, which otherwise would have gone to sea.

By 3:30, the official anemometer at New London registered wind of 98 miles an hour, at which point the wind cups of the instrument blew away.

One man died on the waterfront. Ingvald Beaver was a crew member of the barge *Victoria,* and the roof of his quarters started to peel off. The sea at that time was pounding with great force off the Custom House, where the barge was lying, and Beaver got on top of the cabin in an effort to tie down part of the roof. Before he could secure it, another blast carried it away, and he was last seen reentering his living quarters.

Fire broke out in the stricken city at 4:30 P.M., in a business section near the waterfront; water, flooding the building of the Humphrey-Cornell Company (wholesale grocers), short-circuited electric wires. The blaze raced in several directions and within a few minutes a conflagration that raged for hours and completely destroyed more than a dozen commercial buildings and houses was in progress. Every available piece of fire apparatus in the city was called out to fight New London's worst blaze since that September day in 1781 when the British under Benedict Arnold burned the city. Firemen, floundering in deep water, struggling against a gale that blew the streams from their hoses back into their faces, turned desperately to the battle, soon realizing that New Londoners must save their city themselves, for efforts to obtain assistance from nearby communities proved fruitless. All telephones were out and it was impossible to contact the fire departments in Westerly, New Haven, Norwich, Mystic, Noank, Old Lyme, and Niantic.

The fire alone caused $1 million worth of damage; in addition to the buildings and their contents, at least twenty vehicles, including trucks in two coalyards, were destroyed. As late as Friday—two days after the storm—many burned buildings still smoldered and firemen were overhauling the coal piles of the Central and F. H. and A. H. Chappell Coal companies to get at the flames that burned deep within them.

Of all that befell New London, one of the most awe-inspiring sights created by the storm was provided by the 190-foot steamer *Tulip,* thrust ashore by wind and storm tide near the U.S. Lighthouse Service wharf, in the rear of the Custom House. On September 22, New England officials of the Bureau of Lighthouses informed H. D. King, commissioner, in Washington: "The principal casualty so far reported is that to the lighthouse tender Tulip, 1,057 tons, which was driven ashore at New London, as per attached telegram [received from her]: 'Tulip driven ashore northeast side of dock at New London, nearly broadside, with bow across railroad track. Attempts to float unsuccessful, apparently will roll over at low tide. Have sent entire crew ashore.' Unable to get in touch with New London. Am proceeding there by rail. (Signed) Yates."

Tulip's grounding was observed by few, but thousands came to see her (her bow was on the eastbound tracks of the New York, New Haven and Hartford Railroad) and to watch salvage operations that were started on the fourth day after the storm. The task was at once taxing and delicate. Black-hulled *Tulip* was heavy; she was also resting on her port bilge and there was always a possibility that any effort to pull her free would roll her over, as her commanding officer had noted in the telegram.

George W. Tooker of New York, salvage officer for Merritt, Chapman and Scott Corporation, was in charge of getting her afloat, and he set crews to work night and day cutting a waterway in which to launch her. They dredged 5,000 yards of mud, sand, and rock to shape a basin about 15 feet deep near the lighthouse wharf and 20 feet farther out, to accommodate her stern, which was closest to the water.

At 5 o'clock in the morning of October 7, the floating operation began, with the wrecking steamer *Willet,* the tug *Alert,* and the big derrick *Commodore* on hand. Lines were made fast to the *Tulip,* whose portside ports were battened, in case she should roll over, and the *Alert* took up the slack and churned the waters of the basin near the wharf. *Willet* set up a steady pull on the line offshore and cables creaked through block sheaves on the *Commodore. Tulip* moved, ponderously; her bow came free, and suddenly, she was on an even keel for the first time since the storm. The *Alert* whistled a blast of accomplishment; *Commodore* moved out to take stern lines passed under *Tulip* and made fast to the lighthouse steamer on the shore side to get a better pull. The stern was still on the bottom, but not for long.

Salvage officer Tooker's signal was as shrill as a football referee's. *Commodore* piped a note of instruction to *Willet* and there was the steady, deep throb of straining screw against the sea. *Tulip*'s stern was free; she was afloat, and the lighthouse steamer *Hawthorne* nearby sounded several joyful and fraternal blasts of her whistle.

Harrison McDonald of Lafayette, Indiana, traveling by train, saw New London immediately after the storm, although he had had no intention of doing so. He left Albany at 8 o'clock Wednesday morning on the Wolverine, bound for Boston.

"We got to Springfield [Massachusetts]," he said, "and they told us there was a washout and the train had to be rerouted. So we started off for Hartford, creeping very slowly, with the water lapping around the tracks at various points. We made it all right, and started off for New London. Within about three miles of the town, at 3:15 Wednesday afternoon, the hurricane and flood stopped us.

"The engineer, a smart fellow, pulled ahead to a sharp curve in the track and stopped there. He figured the curve of the cars against the wind would help us and I guess it did. I don't think the train could have stayed upright if it was broadside to the wind and in a straight line. A pullman car weighs sixty-seven tons as it was, the cars were rocking from one track to another—not just shivering and shaking, but literally rocking.

"The Yankee Clipper pulled up behind us and we spent the night there. We were comfortable and had plenty to eat, but the trains ran out of water and finally they were passing coals from the engine back to the dining car in order to get a fire and quick food.

"The next morning, we were taken into New London in buses. The first thing we were given was a card from the National Guardsmen warning us not to drink water or to pour milk without boiling it. The first store I saw was a five and ten cent one. It had been flooded out, but one counter had been set up on the sidewalk and they were selling candles only. We walked down to the business district and found the firemen still pouring water into the smoldering embers.

"Parents were crowding the newspaper office and police station in search of schoolchildren. They had been missing for sixteen hours. They told us that school had let out just before the flood. By then, it was a hopeless hell for them. One man had managed to get forty girls out of his factory after the wind had lifted the roof off it and a moment before the flood and fire had hit it. Another had several missing from his factory still and the factory was gone.

"I was standing at the desk in the Western Union office when a young schoolgirl came in. She was looking for her younger sister, who had not been heard from since school let out the afternoon before. The clerk said they had no report on her. A moment later, a businessman came in. 'Can I get a wire through to New York?'

"'No,' said the clerk.

"'Well, I don't suppose it's essential,' he said. 'I'd just like to let my company in New York know that they haven't got any New London factory any more.'

"They had no electricity, no lights, no heat, no power of any kind. There was also no accurate estimate of the dead and missing. The editor of the New London *Day* said 100 summer cottages were swept to sea in five minutes at Ocean Beach."

At least one vessel sought without success such sanctuary as the port of New London offered in the hours after the storm. Mr. and Mrs. Frank F. Douden of Guilford, Connecticut, were aboard.

They had spent a couple of days visiting Mrs. Douden's relatives on Long Island, in and about East Hampton. On September 21, they had planned to take the Port Jefferson-Bridgeport ferry in the morning and go to their summer cottage at Madison, Connecticut, to stay overnight. Instead, they decided to stay over for a drive to Montauk in the morning and to take the ferry from Orient directly to New London. The vessel was the *Catskill*, Captain Clarence Sherman of Shelter Island; it sailed from Orient at about 1 P.M. Wednesday, with eight passengers, including the Doudens, and three automobiles, one of which was theirs.

The steamer was about three-quarters of the way across the sound when Captain Sherman, a ship handler of ability, realized that the increasing intensity of the storm would make it dangerous to try to get into New London harbor. He put the vessel about and butted back into the heavy sea and wind toward Long Island, continuing to steam beyond Orient. At 6 P.M., he gave the orders for all hands to put on life preservers, having decided they would have to spend the night on the Sound.

There they stayed, pitching and rolling. Faulkner's Island light, which they could see, gave them mixed feelings of frustration and relief. On the one hand, it was a staunch beacon of hope, but on the other, its presence did nothing to improve their situation. To the Doudens, watching it through the long dark hours of the storm, "The cheerful thought occurred that if we were washed ashore, our bodies would be easily identified."

Early the next morning, the *Catskill* steamed into New London. Because of the flood and fire, there was no dock left on either side of the harbor at which the passengers could be landed. Captain Sherman decided to try Groton, and there was finally able to tie up at a coal dock. When the lines were secured, passengers and officers stood in a close circle and sang ("With teary voices," said the Doudens): "Praise God, from whom all blessings flow; / Praise Him, all creatures here below; / Praise Him above, ye heavenly hosts; / Praise Father, Son, and Holy Ghost."

Once ashore and in their automobile, it took the Doudens from 7 A.M. to 12: 30 P.M. to find clear roads and pick their way through blocked roads to their home in nearby Guilford. And the final chapter of their experience was still to come: as soon as they were able to get to their beach cottage at Madison—where they had planned to spend Wednesday, rather than on the ferry—they found it had been reduced to a pile of kindling.

Ernest G. Bushnell, who had long experience with boats, was in charge of a 30-foot cruiser belonging to J. C. Edwards of Chester. He kept the cruiser at a small pier running into North Cove at the foot of Little Point Street. Alarmed by indications of an unusual storm, Mr. Bushnell, assisted by his brother, Edwin, got out extra lines and made everything as secure as possible. The boat rode out the storm without injury, despite the fact that great trees were knocked down near where she was moored and a summer house on the Bushnell place only a short distance away was blown from its foundation.

After the worst of the storm was over, about 6 o'clock, Mr. Bushnell came ashore. He had fallen into the water and he went home to get dry clothes. He returned to the pier about 6:30 and went on board the boat again. Apparently he feared that the storm was not entirely over and he decided to take the cruiser out into the cove and anchor it where there would be no danger of its being blown ashore.

He started the engine and was seen by Mrs. Edwin Bushnell heading out into the cove. Warren Roberts and a companion in a schooner moored above Dauntless Shipyard on the east side of the North Cove channel saw Mr. Bushnell cruising about in their part of the cove, saw him throw his anchor and apparently go overboard with it. They went immediately to help him, but failed to find him. His anchor rope was not attached to the boat and they concluded he had either slipped and fallen over or the line had fouled around his leg and pulled him over, or he had had a heart attack. The boat swiftly disappeared in the gathering darkness. About an hour later, it was found by William Suda, who lived at the head of the cove, a mile or more away. The engine was still running. Mr. Bushnell's body was found in a mass of wreckage floating in North Cove not far from the spot where he went overboard.

At Stonington, the marine disaster was of another kind, for the fleet there was commercial, not pleasure. Of the Point Judith-to-New London fleet totaling one hundred fishing craft, employing 650 men, only three boats were working immediately after the hurricane and they were fishing so that the families of the boatless could eat.

As late as October 7, a waterfront observer reported, "One of the most touching examples of the brotherhood of the sea is enacted here each day when the fishing smack *Gloria* returns from the fishing grounds and distributes food free of charge to the mothers and families whose source of livelihood were swept away by the hurricane.

"The sturdy *Gloria,* owned by Dinny Seidell, is the only smack working since the storm drove the Stonington fleet of fifty-two craft ashore."

Captain John W. Smith, president of the Southern New England Fishermen's Association, to which the one hundred boats belonged, said, "Every night, half of the town comes down to the wharf to get a mess of fish from the *Gloria.* The other townspeople, as well as the fishermen, take it for the asking." He said that what fish were left over after the housewives had taken their dinners home was shipped in the usual course to the New York market but that "up to now, there hasn't been enough surplus to think about."

"Isn't it unusual for a man to give away his source of livelihood as Captain Seidell is doing?" he was asked.

"Oh, the fishermen are that way," answered Smith.

It was about five days later before a big New York lighter, obtained through efforts of the Red Cross, raised George Grogan's *Louise*—the first of the Stonington fleet that went to the bottom or aground to be salvaged. It was some time after that before the port received the "jacks to lift our boats and good greased timber to slide them overboard" for which Captain Smith called on the federal government, and even then they had to replace all the shoreside gear, including the barrels used for shipping fish—which had been swept back into the woods.

It was in the Stonington area that the most extraordinary railroad incident of the hurricane occurred.

The Bostonian, a regular Shore Line express, left Grand Central Station in New York City at noon on Wednesday. After the storm was over, the New York, New Haven and Hartford Railroad issued a statement late on Wednesday saying that all its trains had been accounted for. In fact, one of them had not. The Bostonian thus was officially "lost" for the time being, although Connecticut's Governor Wilbur L. Cross said later that even if he had known of the company's announcement, it would have been "humanly impossible" for contact to have been made immediately with the area in which the Bostonian was located.

Three days later, on September 24, the New York, New Haven and Hartford Railroad issued the following statement: "Upon arrival at Stonington on September 21, No. 14 stopped on signal from the tower man at that point on account of the train ahead. Windows of the tower had been blown out by the hurricane and water had reached the level of the track. Engineer Harry Easton got out of his engine and walked over to the tower to find out what conditions were and before he could return the 1,000 feet to his engine, water was already waist-deep from the tidal wave, which was driving up.

"Meantime, the track under the rear cars had started to give way. The crew were making every endeavor to get the passengers moved up to the forward cars. Some passengers, however, insisted on opening the doors and jumped into the rapidly rising water, fighting their way to higher ground. In the meantime, wreckage driven by the hurricane crashed against the train and broke some of the brake apparatus, making it impossible to release the brakes of the rear car. All of the passengers were thereupon moved up into the head car and then William F. Donoghue, general chairman of the Brotherhood of Railroad Trainmen of the New Haven system, working shoulder-deep in water, succeeded in uncoupling the head car from the rear of the train.

"The engineer then pulled the train ahead through the water and wreckage until he reached dry land. Telegraph wires were down across the engine and as he forced his way forward, the engine pulled down pole after pole, and forced a house from its path which had been thrown upon the tracks by the wind and water. But the engineer kept his throttle open until the place of safety was reached.

"Only last night when a complete report was available was it revealed that a checkup found one passenger and a pantryman of the dining car missing. Their bodies were subsequently recovered." The statement named the victims as Mrs. William B. Markell of Hartford and Chester A. Walker of New York.

Harry Easton of West Haven, engineer of No. 14, was at the throttle at 3:20 P.M.; wind was clocked in the area as high as 120 miles an hour; his train had been struck by numerous storm-driven vessels, including a schooner, as well as by heavy flotsam. At that point, the railroad—hampered by crippled communications systems that soon failed completely—was ordering all its trains to halt.

Just west of Stonington, taking a battering from wind and sea, Easton braked his train to a stop when he saw a "red block" set against him in the signal tower. He was careful to pull the train to high ground before he halted it.

Easton said, "I had been running over rails that were underwater at various points and had been proceeding with extreme caution." Anxious to ascertain the reason for the stop signal, Easton, accompanied by his fireman, D. C. Horan of Guilford, left the engine and walked toward the signal tower, an estimated five minutes' distance. Meanwhile, the flagman had gone to his post at the rear of the train.

"As we started to walk around a curve," Easton said, "we saw another train that had been stopped, apparently by bad conditions of the road. We knew that the Boston and Albany road was using our right-of-way and were doubly anxious about the 'red block' for that reason. Seeing the other train ahead, we turned and started back for our engine. We had taken but a few steps when water was up to our ankles. A few more stops and it was up to our knees.

"You can get some idea how fast that water came up from the fact that we started running and before we got to the engine, the water was above our hips."

Reaching the engine, they observed that the three rear cars of the train were listing toward the Sound. The tracks were being undermined by the surging water; the passengers had to be evacuated quickly from the rear cars, and if any part of the train was to be gotten out of there, it had to be accomplished swiftly.

Joseph C. Richards of West Haven was the conductor. "The rear of the train was on the bridge trestle," he recalled. "The heading of the train was at the signal at the old water tank, alongside a tennis court. The water was so high that boats from everywhere, Narragansett Bay, Westerly, were coming in and slamming against the train. A big yacht landed on a bank opposite the trestle; that was a good 150 yards from the normal low-water mark.

"I went through the train, warning everybody to move up ahead. I told Johnny [John P. Cooke of North Haven, dining car steward] to get his crew out of there, out of the dining car. As I notified those fellows in the kitchen, Chester Walker went out the side door on my left. He headed for the highway about a quarter-mile away. I watched him swimming in the water. He got almost halfway there and there was a timber floating. It must have been eight by ten. It hit him in the back of the head, in the base of the brain, and he went down and never came up.

"In one coach, there were some prep school kids, and they wouldn't move. They didn't take the thing seriously. I ripped open an emergency case and got an ax. I threatened to pin 'em with it if they didn't move. They got up and went into the car behind the baggage car. Some headed for the tunnel. The water was waist-high then. They were smart; they went on the side so that the wind was blocked by the train, so they made it."

Easton added, "By this time, the water was shoulder-high on the slope on which the train stood on the rails. Passengers were leaping in terror from windows, doors, and platforms into the water. The train crew yelled to them to get back into the train and forced all the passengers forward. We packed all the women and children we could into the engine. The rest of the passengers were packed into the front car."

Richards resumed, "I had heard the brakes go into emergency [which locked them]. A big timber hit the air hose and that put them in emergency. I heard air escaping from the train, bubbling in the water. I saw the Oriental [the parlor car at the end of the seven-car train] tipped, as I pushed on through. We had to turn off the air to get pressure enough to move the train to high ground. Five minutes more, with the way the water was rising, and it would be impossible.

"Bill Donoghue was there and I said, 'We got to cut this train off,' and he said, 'I'm younger than you' and he jumped into the water. He had to turn off the air so we could build up air pressure to move. In water up to his chin, he turned the air off and pulled the pin [uncoupling the locomotive and first car from the remainder of the train]. I reached over and grabbed him as he come up on his belly on the vestibule." (One eyewitness described Donoghue as "finally emerging half-strangled, after prolonged submersion at the rear platform.")

Cooke said, "When Joe [Richards] started moving the passengers up front, he said to me, 'When we're ready, I'll tell you,' so we kept up the dining car, putting the tablecloths on and that sort of thing so that the passengers passing through wouldn't get panicky. Then Joe came in and he said, 'Get that little Irish ass of yours out of here!' The dining car was third from the last on the train. When we started to walk out, it had begun to tilt."

Richards added, "We had about a dozen in the dining car and two of them objected strenuously because they had paid for their meal and hadn't finished it. I said, 'Get out or I'll throw you out.'

"This will show you the force and the weight of the water against the train. As that tidal wave came, it was about ten feet above the roadbed. The weakest spot was on the trestle. When the trestle was hit, it weakened the spiles and tipped the cars over, and behind the last car, there were no rails, no ties, and no roadbed.

"When I first got off the train at that tennis court, the water was chest-high. The train blocked the wind for me. There was a garage with a Cadillac automobile in it. I noticed when the wind hit it, it shattered the garage to splinters. It raised the car thirty feet in the air and slammed it into hard dirt upright; it went into the ground past the hood.

"We had 252 passengers. About eighty got off the train because progress was slow in moving up to the head car, some didn't know how to open the doors, and others panicked when a boat hit the side of the train. It was a dragger and it hit three times, starting at the engine tank.

"I had about 160 people in the [head] coach on top of each other. I gave the engineer the signal. His firebox was cooled off in the water and he didn't have much fire. But he had steam enough to move the engine and the one car to a lumber yard, about 250 feet, to higher ground. We went ahead, against the signal."

In addition to the uprooted utility poles, which Easton's engine dragged along until the wires snapped, he found a house in his way, deposited on the tracks by the flood. He edged his locomotive gently up to the structure and nudged it slowly aside; as its sills cleared the rails, the house toppled over and vanished into deep water.

When the train was halted at Stonington, the passengers were informed that a 40-foot schooner was on the trestle ahead. The engineer advised the women to jump to safety.

"An elderly, well-dressed woman who stood beside me jumped into the swelling water," recalled Mrs. Richard Auguste of Hewlett, Long Island, "and I saw her disappear. We threw our coats, hats, and purses into the water, then my daughter and I jumped. The wind churned the water into a whirlpool; there was a strong undertow. I think we had to swim about three hundred yards. Some of the time, water was over our heads, but occasionally, we were able to walk."

Her daughter was struck by a floating tree limb and fractured her leg as they swam away from the flooded cars; they were assisted in escaping by Stephen Glidden, sixteen, of Dover, a pupil at Noble and Greenough, and by Edward Brown, a student at the Massachusetts Institute of Technology, fellow passengers. Mrs. Auguste said women and children "clustered like flies" on the engine as it moved toward high ground and that she saw Harry Easton rescue a woman and child and place them safely on the coal tender.

Edward M. Flanagan, chairman of the Providence Democratic City Committee, and Mrs. Flanagan were sitting in the diner. "We got as far as the trestle west of Stonington where the water was hurling boats and houses up against the side of the train. The roof of a house crashed into the side of the dining car. The train stopped where it was, right on the trestle, and everyone was ordered to go forward," Flanagan said.

"The people then began to grow panicky and even those in charge of the train appeared panicky. As the water began to beat against the train, we were ordered off. We walked the trestle up to the locomotive but could get no farther because of the rush of water. Passengers clung to the cables, engine wheels, and everything else they could get hold of. Some of them were finally swept away. I saw them go with my own eyes.

"My wife held onto me until a powerful Negro took charge of her and left me to take care of a little boy who was on his way to a private school in Massachusetts. I had never seen the boy before. Some of the women climbed into the locomotive. The boy and I hung onto the wheel of the locomotive. Finally, I was able to join my wife.

"When the storm began to abate, the engineer started the train after we climbed aboard. We reached the far side of the trestle, pushing boats, telegraph wires, and other debris ahead of us. When we reached Stonington, we got off the train and the people of the town opened their homes to us. . . ."

Mrs. Milton Smernoff of Brighton and her three-year-old son, Jerry, had boarded the train at New Haven. "The wind was blowing furiously and it was raining even then," she said. "The train held up in New London, but continued on with additional cars. Waves dashed against the train as we struggled along near the water and debris hammered at the sides of the cars. As windows began breaking, the conductor asked us to go over to the left side of the train to avoid injuries from flying glass and debris, which was hurtling into the car.

"Entering Mystic, water covered the tracks, and boats tossed onto the tracks with the fury of the storm bumped against the train. Passengers were asked to move into the forward cars as one of the rear ones was listing dangerously. The waves became so high that it looked as though we were about to ride under them rather than through or over them. More of the coaches began to tip as the hurricane lashed the water, and the engine slowed down gradually and finally stopped.

"The conductor ordered us to leave the train, to step into the three or four feet of water that engulfed us. Some jumped into the raging waters and attempted to swim to shore; others waited fearfully, thinking it safer near the train. A man took my small son in his arms and we started to wade through the water, which nearly reached our waists.

"Biting spray lashed our faces and surging waves tugged at our legs. The man carrying Jerry fell into a hole and they both went down. An engineer noticed their plight and went to their rescue. It was a furious gale that swept over that exposed strip of railroad bed and some who attempted to get to shore lost their lives.

"As we came back into the cab of the train, I noticed the rear car tipping over. Trainmen detached the rear cars to save the rest of the train; all that was left was the engine, tender, and one coach. The engineer tried to start the train again, but debris blocked the way. A huge wave driven on by the gale swept the track clear and we moved slowly for a few hundred feet and stopped again. This time, we were all told to leave. Since we were only about fifty feet from shore, we made it safely into Stonington. I lost all my baggage, but I saw too much to mind a little thing like that."

Conductor Richards said, "I stayed with those people on the vestibule [of the coach that was hauled to high ground] until the wind died down. I had the dining car crew with me. I asked, would they walk out with me and get what supplies we could from the dining car to relieve the passengers. So Johnny [Cooke] and the dining car crew volunteered to go back with me. We saw the rear parlor car, the 'Oriental,' was tipped on its side on the trestle; the car was full of water and the windows were smashed. I found a carton of brandy on the train to take back to the people."

"It was Martell's," said Cooke.

"I found Chester Walker under the weeds," said Richards, "when the water receded at that point. And there were two big vessels on the highway."

Cooke and his crew succeeded in getting a fire going in the dining car and made five gallons of coffee and a hundred sandwiches. They started back to the coach full of passengers.

"Just before we got to the high ground," said Richards, "this fellow Nicholas Pridges [a member of the dining car crew] had hold of a bag of emergency food over his shoulder and he stepped in a hole. I was behind him. It was just getting dusk when he went down. He hollered and he had this tablecloth full of stuff, but he never let go of it. I got under his armpits and he came up. We got back to the coach and my shoes were white with salt, my pants were ripped. We passed the booze around in the car.

"If we'd been five minutes later in turning off the air to get pressure enough to move the train to high ground, it would have been impossible to do it. And if we'd stayed where we were fifteen minutes longer, a good many of those people would have been drowned. A lot of lives would have been lost. I guess the whole operation, from the time we stopped for the signal and I went back to the rear end, until we got the one car to high ground, took about twenty-five minutes."

Most of the passengers eventually straggled into Stonington in a body and went to the Town Hall. Stonington was equal to the situation.

Selectman Ralph P. Wheeler, Elvin B. Byers, and John J. Donohue, Town Clerk Fred J. Moll, Tax Collector Joseph Law, Assistant Town Clerk Ann Ward, social worker Mary Shannon, and just about every occupant of the town hall offices turned to aid the refugees. James Lynch, the town hall caretaker, went below to start the furnace, the residents in the area made sandwiches and took several of the stranded passengers into their homes.

The Westerly *Sun* reported that "emergency measures were used in securing coffee, cans of meat, and bread and soda from the Cutler Street A & P store." Conductor Richards elaborated, "When I went walking uptown, I met about fifteen men [who were among the passengers]. They had broken into a store. They kicked the door down and took canned groceries to the church."

The church was St. Mary's and the pastor was the Reverend Patrick J. Mahoney. "We hugged each other," said Cooke; "I had been his altar boy." Father Mahoney ordered St. Mary's Hall opened as a refuge for the passengers and accommodations also were set up there to feed them. A hundred blankets stored in the hall for distribution to the needy were given to the elderly members of the group. And so they were fed, and given a place to sleep—some sleeping on floors, some on benches and some even on the stage in the Town Hall.

Book III

RHODE ISLAND

CHAPTER 5

Now it was Rhode Island's turn.
Watch Hill, on that Wednesday, was totally oblivious to danger. The late Charles F. Hammond, publisher of *Seaside Topics,* who was responsible for collecting and preserving invaluable first-person accounts of some of those who survived in this area, recalled, "The shops were open and many cottages still occupied by those who loved to stay into the fall. The morning had been mild and hazy, with a brisk breeze blowing. Many went bathing as usual and remarked how warm the water was. Mrs. John McKesson Camp was hostess at a luncheon on the rocks at Weekapaug and her guests gathered at about one o'clock and noticed only that the sea looked restless and spoke of a strange yellow light over it."

Deterioration of the weather thereafter was rapid; it was blowing wildly by 2 P.M. Some remarked on unusual pressure in the ears. Rain became torrential. Man-made things started to break.

"Forty-two persons were still in the houses on the Fort Road when the final act of the tragedy was reached," Hammond wrote. "Fifteen were killed, twenty-seven survived after their houses were demolished by the monstrous seas and they were swept to the Connecticut shore. Thirty-nine cottages on the Fort Road were destroyed, in addition to the yacht club, beach club, and bathing pavilion. The yacht club split in two, and a piano came flying twenty feet into the air like a big bird."

At Misquamicut, the hurricane spent itself in swift death and desolation. Hundreds of cottages were smashed and their lumber piled up in neat windrows like wheat in a newly mown field.

The speed at which disaster struck was breathtaking. One young man loaded his family into the car just before the tidal wave struck their summer place and headed up Winnapaug Road. He kept the car moving as fast as he could. The wave, an estimated twenty feet high, tossing telephone poles and houses before it, was less than a stone's throw behind the automobile. He went forty miles an hour, with the wave still gaining, creeping nearer the car every second. At fifty miles an hour, the foam-topped, curling wave was moving closer. At fifty-five, as the higher ground was approached, the vehicle managed to hold its own, although the water was no more than a few feet from the rear tires. Finally, the car reached the Shore Road and safety—at a mile-a-minute clip.

Some who might have been expected to survive did not; some who might have been expected to die did not. A dozen women from Westerly's Christ Episcopal Church were having a picnic at the Lowry cottage, Misquamicut; Mrs. David Lowry was a member of the group. Just before the storm broke in full force, they moved to the cottage of William D. Wells for safety. It was washed away and all the women perished. Their pastor, the Reverend G. Edgar Tobin, had to leave the picnic early to attend a funeral; it probably saved his life.

In the same area, two babies, each about a year old, were placed on floating wreckage by their parents, who stayed with them, holding them fast as the wind blew flying fragments of boats and houses past them. Both infants safely crossed the turbulent inland sea that was normally Brightman's Pond; one had breathed in a great deal of water, but emerged fine after brief hospitalization, and the other did not have so much as a sniffle.

Assistant Fire Chief E. L. Reynolds, a Misquamicut real estate dealer, said, "It started from the east and suddenly shifted to the south and sent a tremendous wall of water over the beach. I didn't have five minutes' chance to get into my car. People on the beach were laughing and joking, trying to put up shutters and fasten windows to keep curtains from getting wet. They thought it was lots of fun. Then suddenly, before anybody knew what happened, their homes were under twenty to thirty feet of water. Some of the houses just blew up like feathers. I saw one leap seventy-five feet into the air and collapse before it hit the water.

"I succeeded in rescuing six persons, including my father, who is seventy-five years old."

Sylvester Regucci was a handyman at Misquamicut; when it began to breeze, he secured some boats that were lying at the dock. Then he went home to join his wife; they were both fifty-five, and they lived in a two-story house at 10 Winnapaug Road, about seventy-five feet from the ocean front.

During much of the storm, they were in water up to their necks, but they thought their house would hold, even though they saw all the others going. It was, in fact, the last to go; at about 3 in the afternoon, just when they thought they were going to make it, a big house came floating by and bumped their's off its foundation. Standing in the water inside their home, they grasped a small statue, a replica of the old Notre Dame de la Garde that stands in the harbor of Marseilles, and prayed.

The sea ripped away the first story of the house and flung the second story, with them (and their two dogs, Teddy and Lucky) in it, a mile back from the shore. The building landed along the shore road and Mr. and Mrs. Regucci were the only ones found alive in any house struck by the storm along Westerly's eight-mile beach front. Searchers pulled out crushed bodies of storm victims within fifty feet of their newly located home. The only family casualty was Teddy; he survived the hurricane, but died of exposure. "When we prayed, the water went down," said Mr. Regucci. "It was the prayers that saved us."

When they finally touched bottom, watchers along the road shouted to them and they waded ashore, where their milkman found them, and gave them refuge for the night. Later, returning to their wrecked house, they discovered looters had stolen $250 from a bureau drawer, but Mr. Regucci said, "At least we are alive."

For four hours on the evening of the storm, Henry M. Morris, twenty-seven, a five-foot-six, 170-pound carpenter, who was a senior Red Cross lifeguard, with others had been aiding hurricane victims in an area a mile from the inn. With Morris was his nineteen-year-old brother, William; Patrolman Arthur Kingsley and Lieutenant George Madison of the Westerly police; Walter Marshall, Edward Green, and two brothers named Clark.

At 1 in the morning of September twenty-second, this group was standing on the road leading to Weekapaug Beach from the Shore Road. They observed a candle flickering weakly in one of the inn windows and ran toward it, discovering that the storm-cut channel and another similar breachway of surging water east of the inn had left the shattered building on an island.

The west breachway, on whose western bank they stood, was seventy-five feet wide; wadable water in the channel extended four feet from each bank, and elsewhere in the channel, the depths ranged from eight to ten feet. The tide was falling, and in this channel there was a current toward the ocean of 8 to 10 miles an hour; scattered debris also was surging in the same direction. The wind was still blowing 25 miles an hour and visibility was poor, because of heavy mist.

Morris and the others walked to the channel bank; they had a couple of flashlights and they attracted the attention of the group within the inn, all of whom came to the east bank; they were frantic and shouting in desperation to be rescued.

Kingsley, a former seaman, who engineered the rescue, said, "We called a huddle. We tossed a mattress in the channel to see its strength. The mattress disappeared the second it touched the water. We decided that was no place for a boat."

Morris, although fatigued from previous exertion during the evening, offered to swim across. He removed his clothing, except his trousers and jacket. "We got a rope that was just barely long enough to reach across," said Kingsley, and they tied a loop of it loosely around Morris's chest, with a life preserver at his back. Kingsley instructed him that if the rope should break or those on the bank should lose their grips, he should get hold of anything he could and that if he should drift to the ocean, he must swim east or west in an effort to find a rock to which he could cling.

Morris entered the channel and started swimming southeast as hard as he could. Because of the current and mishandling of the rope, he was pulled under the surface of the water briefly after he had gone thirty feet. He was then hauled back to the west bank, where he removed his jacket. Entering the water again, he struck out for the east bank; the group on the west shore payed out line and walked slowly south, keeping abreast of him; because of the strong set of the current, he had to swim considerably more than a hundred feet before he reached the east bank.

The rope then was tied around Miller's chest also, two feet ahead of Morris. The two walked fifty or sixty feet north to allow for the current and entered the water; as the group on the west bank hauled on the rope, Morris and Miller drifted southwesterly, Miller holding to the rope with both hands and Morris holding with one hand and stroking with his free arm and his legs to preserve his balance. They were pulled to the west bank after having drifted southerly about thirty-five feet during the crossing. Morris was aided to the bank; he removed his trousers, which had hampered him, re-entered the water, and once more swam and drifted across to the east bank, while those on the west side payed out the line to which he was attached.

In this fashion, Morris aided Wheeler, Mrs. Rewick, Bliven, and Billings in getting to the west side of the channel. While rescuing Bliven, who was hampered by his hip-length rubber boots, Morris was submerged briefly, and at the conclusion of the fourth trip, he said he was very tired. Kingsley offered to make the last trip, but Morris said he was better able, because of his weight and experience. After the fifth and final trip across, Morris was so exhausted that he had to be hauled out of the water; his shoulder had been struck and bruised by flotsam, and he was assisted to an automobile and taken to the hospital, where he remained until the following day.

In Westerly, it was some hours after the storm before the extent of the tragedy and destruction in the nearby shore resorts was learned, piecemeal. Survivors told of a tidal wave forty feet high that mounted from the ocean, struck broadside against the houses and swept them from their foundations. Louis J. Rossi, Town Engineer, brought back some of the first definite reports from Misquamicut; houses from the beach, he said, were piled up in the fields.

Because of fallen trees across the roads, it was impossible for nearly two hours after the hurricane's height to get to the beaches, but as soon as relief workers did get there—the wind was still blowing freshly—they began to find bodies among the acres of litter. At daybreak, the proportions of the catastrophe were first realized; Misquamicut had been wiped out. Only a desolate space remained, broken by what was left of the Atlantic Beach Casino, the Wigwam Hotel, the Pleasant View House, and a handful of other damaged structures.

As scores of the dead were taken to the temporary morgue in the Westerly High School, state police got in touch with Leo R. McAloon of the State Embalming Board by radio, the only communication available. He appealed to James Heffernan, president of the Rhode Island Funeral Directors Association, who rounded up two emergency crews. The first crew of ten, including McAloon, a Pawtucket undertaker, worked by day; they were relieved at night by a team of five organized by Heffernan. As soon as the bodies at the high school were identified, they were taken to funeral homes for embalming.

This is how the morgue looked to a resident of Westerly: "Where once gay, laughing students prepared themselves for their life's work, dazed, weary relatives look over row upon row of whitesheeted bodies for signs of their loved ones. The old Westerly High School, only a few months ago the cradle of education, is now a huge coffin of death; it is the morgue.

"'Where is the morgue?' You can hardly take a step down the street in Westerly's business section without being asked that question by some anxious friend or relative. You point to the high school.

"It is strange that school buses used to drive up the long concrete drive to the vine-covered building and now hearses are going in and out of the yard. A few are forced to wait while they remove their gruesome load, smashed bodies of mothers, fathers, sons and daughters.

"Inside, Coroner Herbert Rathbun, bearded after long hours of toil, affixes tags to those identified. Some, you can't identify. The same sea gulls that point out to searchers the location of bodies have pecked at them until they are unrecognizable. Those identified are taken away.

"Westerly's five undertakers long since have run out of embalming fluid; more has been rushed from Providence. The toll of death will run up to more than one hundred, but people display a marvelous type of courage. Sometimes you have to rush to support a tottering husband who has just lifted a sheet to find the black and blue remains of his wife. But mostly, people just stare. No tears, just stares."

The nation first knew the tragedy that had befallen the Westerly area because of Wilson E. Burgess and George "Bill" Marshall, two amateur radio operators.

Telephone and electric service were inoperative, trains were halted, and highways blocked. Burgess, clerk in a local store, recalled, "When the power failed, I was still at work and, thinking there might be some use for the machine [his radio equipment], I gathered together a bunch of dry cells and a large storage battery and other bits of equipment.

"I ran into Bill Marshall, another ham, at the police station, and together we carried the equipment up Granite Street hill against the storm to my home. We were able to borrow a South County truck to carry some of the equipment, but that only got halfway home before the way was blocked.

"We managed to rig up a haywire aerial in the storm and finished this job just about dusk. Since we had no power off the street lines, we had to practically rebuild the set for the dry cells and storage battery power. Marshall returned to his home and picked up parts of his set to substitute and we finished putting the thing together in the dark with candles. Then, under low power, we sent out our distress signal by code."

The Westerly *Sun* reported, "It was picked up by another ham in New Jersey and he in turn hooked them up with Hartford, headquarters of the American Radio Relay League. Thus was started the chain of messages which brought relief and rescue workers by the hundreds into this stricken town. . . ."

One of the first messages was to national headquarters of the American Red Cross. Burgess said, "They didn't believe us at first in Washington, but we made them realize what we were talking about. . . ."

The two youths became the official means of communication for the Red Cross and this was the beginning of a fifty-six hour vigil for them; they stayed by their machine for two and a half days, sending out more than 1,100 messages. Some were calls for assistance—funds, food, clothing, volunteers, medical supplies—some were to notify friends and relatives of death, injury, or miraculous survival; others were to ask for the National Guard, or for more undertakers, or more embalming fluid.

It was Burgess who sent the first newspaper story out of Westerly after the hurricane, an account written by four Providence *Journal* reporters. The dispatch went initially to an amateur operator in Chevy Chase, Maryland, then to the Associated Press in Washington, next to Woonsocket via the AP, and it was taken from there to Providence over the highway.

Burgess was given the Paley Award, the highest honor possible for an amateur operator, for his extraordinary public service.

And finally, William A. Batchelor of Woonsocket, former police commissioner of that city, was alive because he refused to obey the doctor's orders. The physician warned Mr. Batchelor that his health would not permit him to make the trip from his summer cottage at Misquamicut to his home on Oakley Road in Woonsocket. Mr. Batchelor decided that his guess was as good as the doctor's, so he went home to Woonsocket on Tuesday, September 20, and felt no worse for the trip. On the following day, his cottage was swept out to sea.

CHAPTER 6

The hurricane roared up Narragansett Bay, leaving its toll of death and destruction written in the shambles of the beaches at Warwick Cove, Oakland Beach, and Shawomet. There was one at Oakland Beach who was rescued and yet who was not. He shall remain nameless, but there are those still who know his name. He was not included in any list of the dead or missing; when the storm had passed, his home still stood and his possessions remained remarkably intact, but his life was over nevertheless and his worldly goods useless to him.

He had been a blacksmith for many years; he had a wife and one son. In 1932, the boy was accidentally drowned in nearby Brushneck Cove and the parents were inconsolable in their grief. Time did not heal the wound; the mother's health failed rapidly and she died three years after the loss of the son.

The man chose to remain where his memories were. He stayed in the house at Oakland Beach, living in solitude. When the hurricane ripped across the beach, his neighbors went to help him. They found him sitting there, oblivious to the seas that shook his home. All he said, over and over, was: "He's come for me. My boy has come back at last."

When that day ended at stricken Oakland Beach, many of its refugees found shelter in the local schoolhouse and fire station. He was not among them. He had been admitted to the State Institution for the Insane.

However, as brutal as was the assault upon the outlying beaches of the bay, it was the city of Providence that suffered most dramatically from the storm's blow. For Providence lies at the bay's head, and there was no place for the high water to go but into the city.

At the climax, the Providence River was 17.60 feet above mean low water and the 100-mile-an-hour hurricane, coinciding with high tide, drove water 8 to 10 feet deep through the city's low-lying business section. Thousands starting home during the 5 o'clock rush hour stepped out into a storm that was at its worst between 5 and 5:15. Hundreds fled to the nearest shelter as soon as they discovered what was happening.

There were no trolley cars and few buses. The great glass skylight of the Providence Public Library crashed. Within minutes, scores of buildings were unroofed and heavy chimneys and cornices came thundering down into the streets. Ponderous signs were ripped from steel moorings and carried down. A power cable parted, and its dangling end spat fire in the faces of marooned pedestrians leaning against the wind or huddled in the lee of doorways.

As the city struggled with the hurricane, the storm wave struck, ripping hundreds of boats from moorings, battering ships and commercial craft, sinking many and smashing piers. A battering ram of water slammed against the underpinnings of Providence bridges, swirled through low-lying streets, inundated lower floors of business buildings and parked automobiles.

Power and lights failed almost completely at 5:15. Thousands were stranded in the high office buildings, stores, hotels, and theaters. For blocks along Fountain, Westminster, and Washington streets and in the cross streets, men and boys organized rescue teams and helped women through the onrushing waters. A boy waded along the sidewalk and carried a dog on his shoulders.

Chester Hayes, thirty, was drowned in the center of the city. Robert Whitaker, who was marooned four hours with fifty others in the Tribune Building, saw Hayes die. "He was clinging to a submerged automobile," Whitaker said. "Before a line could be thrown to him, a parked car floated down the street on the still-rising flood and lurched into the automobile to which he was clinging. He was swept into the swift current. A strong swimmer, appearing as if from nowhere, set out for Hayes as he was carried away, but was unable to reach him. The swimmer disappeared around the corner. Hayes was in water dotted with white caps. He drowned in Turks Head Square."

Between 5:05 and 5:10 P.M., the Weather Bureau instruments on the Turks Head Building recorded a velocity of 85 miles per hour. Then a skylight blown from the roof demolished the recording instruments.

"The crowd marooned at Thompson's Restaurant stood on tables until the water crept up to the table tops," F. Arnold McDermott said. "Then they climbed out onto a fire escape and went to the bakery above, but it wasn't large enough and the water was still coming up. They climbed out onto the fire escape again and went into vacant rooms on the third floor. In the crowd was a woman who had been blown against a brick wall in the alley outside the restaurant. They thought both her legs were broken and when they lifted her through the window, she screamed with pain.

"Another woman had been thrown through the big plate glass window of the restaurant. Her thumb was dangling off and blood was streaming all over her body. And there was a pretty blond woman, between 25 and 30; her front teeth had been knocked out and she was vomiting. Between her heaves, two men were trying to stop the flow of blood.

"In the restaurant at the foot of Waterman Street, across from the Baptist Church, the corpse of a middle-aged woman lay for four hours. She had been sitting in a car outside when the chimney of the building crashed down through the top of her car and crushed her skull.

"A dead woman was swept down the mall in the current of the flood. Rescuers from the Hotel Biltmore weren't able to buck the currents to get to her. She went past."

The inundated downtown stores, their windows smashed by the wind, yielded heterogeneous merchandise to the murky waters that flowed through the streets. Footballs, dolls, furniture, pillows, and automobile tires were washed along with the wreckage of buildings, pieces of smashed trees, and chunks of broken boats.

On the Rhode Island Hospital Trust Building, there was a bronze plate bearing this legend: "In the great gale of September 23, 1815, the wind-driven waters around the walls of this building rose to the level of this line—11 feet, 9¼ inches above mean high water." On September 21, 1938, the water rose to the line on the plaque—and then went three feet above it.

Van Wyck Mason, the author, was en route from Nantucket to New York to deliver a new manuscript to his publisher on the day of the hurricane. "It was beautiful sailing until our steamer, the *New Bedford,* passed Martha's Vineyard," he said. "From there on, it blew so hard that when we got to New Bedford, the steamer missed the slip and smashed into the next pier."

Discovering that no planes were flying out of New Bedford because of the deteriorating weather, novelist Mason left the city by bus, bound for Providence. "Experience No. 1 was a live wire falling on top of the bus, but luckily, the flaming end missed the roof," Mason later said. "Next, two trees fell directly in front of the bus. Then we got into water up to the running board. Still, we made Fall River safely and were going along fairly well just outside of Providence when, on a narrow, circuitous road, trees began crashing down like ninepins. I had with me this manuscript for a 700-page historical novel on which I had been working for a year and a half, and that was my chief concern."

As he alighted at Providence, a chimney fell nearby with a roar and shower of bricks, and he decided it would be prudent to use his suitcase as a helmet. He halted at one point to help extricate a woman from an overturned car and then hurried on to the railroad station. "Just as I got there," Mason said, "the roof of the station came off with a roar like a boiler factory." Standing in the remains of the station, he watched water rise "to a height of ten feet over the square. A woman seeking refuge on the top of her car was swept away before our eyes and drowned; there was nothing we could do. Another woman was wading to safety when she popped out of sight just like a jack-in-the-box; she evidently stepped into an open sewer.

"The lights of automobiles stayed on under the water, giving an eerie glow. Then the horns of automobiles all over the city short-circuited and kept up a deafening din all through the night."

Mason said it was impossible to sleep that night and he sat up by candlelight at the Hope Club. "For the first time in its history, women— refugees, of course—were admitted within its doors. The oldsters at the club didn't like it. They said no good would come of it."

Although Providence was largely isolated by the storm, at least one outgoing telephone line remained. From his room on the second floor of the Crown Hotel, in the heart of Providence, Charles Toomey, a visiting businessman, described to a New Yorker what was happening:

"As I look out over Weybosset Street, one of the city's main thoroughfares, all I can see is desolation, submerged autos, abandoned streetcars hurled up onto the sidewalk. There's not even a rowboat in sight. Water high enough to cover a bus is rolling through the streets at the rate of six or seven miles an hour. A wind of about sixty miles an hour in velocity is still blowing.

"Across the street, clerks and customers of the Outlet Company, Providence's largest department store, are huddled on the second floor. I can barely discern their shapes from where I stand. The wind is so strong that it is blowing out windows and carrying glass fragments through the street in front of it. No one can venture out for fear of being cut down by flying glass.

"The water is still rising as I talk to you. It is pitch-dark and I have not yet seen a single light. No one is drinking water because it may already be contaminated.

"It started when a terrific gale and rainstorm hit the city shortly after three o'clock. The wind must have been traveling seventy miles an hour. At about five-thirty, the rivers began to back up into the city. Nothing like it has ever been seen by the local people. Within a few minutes, the wall of water was fully five feet high and in a half-hour, it was high enough to submerge automobiles."

In Dyer Street, a New England Transportation Company truck was floated from its parking space and grounded near the Wachusett Creamery, on the same street. The driver, who could not swim, yelled for help and employees at the creamery tied tableclothes together until they had sufficient length to reach him, when they hauled him up to the second floor of their building.

In East Providence, Manuel Azevedo, once a horse dealer but now, in his old age, reduced to one horse, prepared to flee the rapidly rising water. He had to think of his horse, as well as of himself. That is why, at the worst of the storm, he was in the barn.

When the water came up to the barn door, he knew it was time for action. The old man led his horse across the railroad tracks to the higher ground of Boston Street, on the far side of the tracks from the river. But by now, even Boston Street was underwater; it surrounded both of them and it was coming up rapidly.

Mr. Azevedo, seeking a way to safety, led his horse northward, along Boston Street, parallel to the river. At the northern (or depot) end of Boston Street, there was a steep and high iron stairway, typical of such railroad station structures, that led up to Watchemoket Square. With all other exits cut off, the old man headed for the stairway and his trusting horse following him without a moment's hesitation—up they went, horse and master, up those thirty or forty iron steps, the animal never faltering or fearing, to the dry land and safety of the square above.

For six years, Ralph Rivers, his wife, Mary, and their family—nine children by 1938—had been living in the cabin of an old barge at Sabins Point, Riverside; the craft was fast to a dock and a two-ton anchor buried six feet in the mud. It made them a good home, Mr. Rivers remarked, a better home than a lot of folks have, "and on washday, it always looked like a flagship flying signals in a fleet." On the day of the hurricane, Mary and six of the children, Ralph, thirteen, Elsie, eight, Raymond, seven; Frank, six; Joan, three, and Helen, one and a half, were aboard the barge. "I was picking apples for Mrs. Charles Redding on Taunton Avenue [in Providence] about 3:30 o'clock Wednesday afternoon," Rivers said later. "I was up in the top of the tree when I heard a kind of moaning in the air. I've been to sea off and on all my life and I know the sound a hurricane makes when it's making up. I said to myself, 'This looks like something pretty bad; I'd better be getting home,' so I climbed down out of the tree and I got in my car.

"Mrs. Redding said to me, 'Ralph, won't you have a cup of tea before you start back?' but I told her, 'No, I want to get back to the barge.' If I'd taken that tea, I wouldn't have any family.

"I guess I was doing seventy in my old car when I passed Moore's Corner. By the time I got to Sabins Point, the gale was hitting ninety. There was the barge anchored at the end of the long wharf that jutted out from the beach. I crouched low and ran and got aboard. I said to Mary and the kids, 'We've got to abandon ship.'

"Just then, the boards of the wharf began to fly. I knew Mary and the kids couldn't make it across the stringers, so I said, 'Well, here we are and it looks bad and we'll have to ride it out, how about some supper?'

"Mary had supper about half-cooked, when the seas came piling up the bay. They hit the old barge with a smash like a battleship's broadside. Water came sloshing into the cabin and I forgot what we were going to have for supper; all I could think of was getting Mary and the kids into the pilothouse. There were six life preservers hanging on the outside of the cabin and I took them into the pilothouse, along with the children. I put five of them on the children and the other one on Mary.

"She wanted me to put hers on the baby but I said, 'No, what would be the use? She would only slip through it.' By this time, the old barge was taking the worst of it. The waves were slamming her over on her beam ends until the kids were almost standing on the walls of the pilothouse. It was dark and howling and all the downriver wreckage was hammering the barge with piledriver blows. I looked out of the pilothouse door and saw a big piece of piling go straight through the cabin, in one side and out the other. Everything that came up the bay hit us.

"The worst was a great mess of wreckage; I guess it must have been part of the wharf at Crescent Park. It hit us with a slam and I was afraid the seas would pike it over on us and smash the pilothouse in, so I grabbed an iron bar and went out into the shrilling wind and the flying spume and somehow I pried the mass of timbers loose. Then I went back inside and it was about that time that Raymond said to me, 'Papa, we're going to die, ain't we?' I said to him, 'No, son, you're not gonna die. Look at those lights up the bay; that's a towboat coming to take us off.'

"I was pretty proud of those children. No whimpering, no crying. A couple of the littlest were seasick and that was all. And Mary, there never was a woman like her. When it was getting bad, she said to me, 'Ralph, how about it, have we got a chance?' I said to her, 'Mary, we've got one chance in a million; if you haven't forgotten your prayers, you'd better say them.' She just closed her eyes a second and then she opened them and said, 'All right, Ralph.'

"I could hear the barge breaking up. When the deck went, up forward, I said to Mary, 'When you see me throw the first kid overboard, you jump!' They all had on life preservers. The seas would carry them right up the bay; they wouldn't land on the beach, but they'd be killed in the pilot-house anyway.

"Just then the tide turned. I looked out and the shore was bright with lights. When the tide went out, it took every last bit of the wreckage that had piled up on the barge and left her high and dry—what was left of her—and what used to be the boatyard, but we could get off only amid-ships because the deck forward was gone and there was about four feet of water there. So I got a heaving line and lowered the children down and Mary and I got down the best way we could. . . .

"We don't have any home now, because nobody will ever live on the barge again, but I guess Mary and I and the children will make out all right."

CHAPTER 7

Although the loss of life at Newport was not heavy, mountainous seas engulfed the beach, crashed over the seawall, roared through buildings, and surged across the roadway into Easton's Pond, which, during the storm, resembled a white-capped ocean itself.

On the waterfront, damage to fish traps was estimated at more than a million dollars, the fleet of the Smith Meal Company took a pasting, and the 130-foot fishing vessel *Promised Land* was blown across the harbor and driven up onto City Wharf. Four hefty lines, each six inches in diameter, which held the New England Steamship Company's freighter *Pequonnock* at Long Wharf were sheared like shoestrings and the vessel was driven ashore.

The rescue of Pierrepoint Johnson, Jr., three-year-old son of Mr. and Mrs. Pierrepoint Johnson of New York and Newport, and the three adults who were with him involved both the Army and Navy. Miss Elsie Searles, a family employee who had been with the baby for two and a half years; Mary McManus, the household cook, and Andrew Healy, gardener, were stranded with the child in a seaside cottage when the storm tide inundated the first floor, demolished their automobile, and washed the garage out to sea.

Moments before the phone went out of commission, Healy phoned for help, reporting that they could not leave unaided and that the house was in danger of being demolished. His message was passed to Lieutenant Commander E. H. Kincaid, U.S.N., of the Naval Training Station. Kincaid discovered that communication with the local Coast Guard was impossible and that proceeding to the scene by boat was out of the question because of heavy seas. He then contacted Fort Adams, which dispatched Captain Harold S. Ruth and Lieutenant William F. Meany and a detachment of enlisted personnel to the scene.

By this time, waves were thundering against the foundation of the house, which was showing signs of collapsing. Healy tied bed sheets together and lowered the nurse and child, then the cook, and finally himself, from the second story to a nearby rock. He guided his party through shallow water to a house close by which appeared more substantial.

Commander Kincaid and Captain Ruth and his rescue group arrived; Healy signaled to them, so they would know that his party had moved to another house. The rescuers ran lifelines to three houses, and along these lines, Lieutenant Meany and three enlisted men waded and swam several hundred yards, risking death all the way. They reached the stranded group and, with Healy's help, started back. A heavy sea broke over all of them, and Miss Searles, who had handed the baby to Healy cried, "Don't let water get in the baby's mouth!" as she was swept away. Meany, an excellent swimmer, immediately detached himself from the lifeline and tried to reach her, but could not. Her body was recovered later at Viking Beach.

One of the bitterest tragedies of the hurricane occurred at Jamestown on Conanicut Island.

Norman Caswell, driver of the school bus, had aboard eight pupils from the Thomas H. Clark elementary school and was taking them home. At Mackerel Cove, it was necessary to cross a low causeway; several vehicles were already stalled on this road and the tide was exceptionally high and still coming.

On the bus were Marion Chellis, seven; her brother, Clayton, twelve; Constantine Gianitis, five and a half, and her brother, John, four, both of whom had moved from Newport only two weeks before, and four children of Mr. and Mrs. Joseph Matoes—Joseph, Jr., thirteen; Teresa, twelve; Dorothy, eleven; and Eunice, seven.

A storm wave thundered up the cove, wiped out a beach pavilion and bathhouses, and swept the bus overboard, off the causeway. Joseph Matoes, Sr., was an eyewitness. "In the afternoon, I got to listening on the radio about a storm coming. So I started for the schoolhouse. For my kids," Matoes said. "They had already left on the bus, so I started to come back and when I hit the beach, the water was about four feet high. At Mackerel Cove, the waves were getting worse and worse, the wind was getting stronger, and pretty soon the pavilion went just like that, and the water was so high that my car and two others were swept into the water. I jumped overboard; my car was in a deep spot right near the cemetery, and I got ashore alongside a stonewall, all soaking wet.

"There was a woman and a boy in a car [Mrs. William Ordner and her son, William] and she drove down the hill and they were washed overboard too, and both drowned. I was still by the wall; I saw Norman Caswell coming around the bend with the bus and I waved him back. I don't know whether he saw me or not. I saw the school bus go over—with the kids. Caswell opened the doors, let the kids out. Well, I had two daughters on top of the roof of the bus, screaming their heads off. I saw them get swept off."

A huge sea struck all of them. It was impossible to reach them immediately or even to see clearly what was happening; the wind still blew hard. "I saw something coming through the water," Matoes said, "something moving and stretched out, so I took a chance and went down from the wall to the water. I got knocked down twice because the wind was so strong, but when I got there, it was Norman Caswell.

"He was laying on his stomach. So I took my boot and kicked him, you know, in the ribs. He grunted. 'Well,' I said, 'he's still alive.' He says, 'Please let me die. I lost a whole bunch of the kids I had in the school bus. Everything's gone. Please don't move me. Let me die.'

"I picked him up and threw him on my shoulder and I walked up the road where there was a wall to divide the roads. I said, 'You stay there until I get onto the other side and I'll take you into my house.' I put him down on the wall and he just turned over and rolled off and I had to pick him up again. Then I took him to my house. He said, 'Where's my bus?' I said, 'Down there in the pond.' I gave him some dry clothes and I changed myself; he stayed until nine o'clock. Then the tide went down and we went down and looked at the bus."

Caswell said later, "I saw that we would have to leave the bus or be drowned like rats. I told the children to grab each other tightly. I had hold of several when the huge wave came over us. I went down twice. When I came up, I saw Clayton Chellis swimming around. He was the only one who was saved besides me. Joe Matoes [Jr.] could have saved himself but he was drowned trying to rescue his younger sister."

While Caswell and Matoes stood there beside the pond looking at the bus, Mr. and Mrs. Chellis came up. Matoes recalled, "Caswell said to him, 'I got your boy, but your daughter's dead—gone' and Chellis got mad and he went down to the road and he took some rocks and he just crashed them windows out of that bus until he busted them all. He was really mad."

Matoes, in his early eighties when I talked with him at Jamestown—a strong, handsome native of the Azores and a fatalistic man of the soil—said, "We never did find one of my children—all but one. Four or five days later, Mrs. Chellis called to her husband and she said, 'Carl, what's that going down the bay there, half white and half red?' Well, she didn't know at the time; she didn't ask my wife, but she thought it might be a lobster buoy.

"But there was a kid who asked my wife, 'What kind of clothes was Dotty wearing?' and my wife told her, a white blouse and a red skirt. She went out to sea.

"Well, so that's the way it went. Took me three years to get over it, took a lot, go through a lot of hard labor—there's a lot of stuff, you know. Ah, ahh!" Here, his voice broke, he paused to regain his composure, and I ended the interview.

There were equally tragic footnotes to the school bus incident.

Edward Donahue lived next door to the Chellis family. He recalled, "The boy who survived said that when the bus driver let them out of the bus, he was holding his little sister's hand; she was only seven, and the last thing he remembered was that she told him, 'Clayton, don't let the water get in your eyes.'"

A Jamestown resident of many years commented, "Norman Caswell was descended from old, old Jamestown settlers. When they got to Mackerel Cove on that day, nobody knew what a hurricane was or that this storm was anything of the kind. They got to the east side of the [Beaver] Neck and the seas were so high that Caswell stopped the bus. By this time, they couldn't get back. He told the children to hold hands, in a line. He put the Chellis boy at one end of the line, because he was the biggest of the children, and he put himself at the front end.

"When the great wave came, it washed over them and the littler children couldn't hold on. The line broke in the middle.

"What happened left Norman Caswell in very bad emotional shape and actually, he died from the shock of this thing.

"The Gianitis family, they were a young couple. They simply disappeared after the accident. They left as soon as you could cross the Neck, after the water went down. They left everything in their house just the way it was. They didn't take anything with them and when we went down to the house afterwards, there were all their things, including some stamps they were collecting and all the little things of a household.

"The Chellis boy who had helped Caswell came out in good shape. The Lord had saved him from this, you see, and he wasn't drowned. When he got to the proper age, he joined the Navy and he was out on the West Coast and went swimming in somebody's pool and he drowned for no reason at all in that pool. Now if that isn't a story. It makes you cry, but God was after him, somehow or other, right?"

At Sakonnet Point, the storm wave flooded the land to a height of twenty feet. It swept away fifty of the seventy-five cottages and shanties that made up the Sakonnet fishing colony. Nine men and a woman sought refuge in a two-story garage on the F. F. Grinnell estate; four died. Allen Kimpel, one of the survivors, still bearing scars on his face from being crushed between the garage and a boat that saved his life, was mending fishing net with a twine needle—sitting in the middle of a great net spread in a sunny field—when he talked about what happened.

"The water was washing out the bricks from under the garage," Kimpel said, "and finally a big sea that broke just before it hit the building knocked it off its foundation.

"The wave ripped off our part of the building and flung us and it into the river. As we floated up the river, I kicked out a window in the peak and some of us climbed out. The garage was starting to break up and we thought the end had come, but we kept a weather eye open for something we could jump to.

"As we floated along, the *Wahoo*, owned by Edward Brayton of Fall River, loomed up and as the building was passing it, I jumped and caught onto the mooring head fast. I was thrown between the building and the boat and squeezed there until they separated; my face was badly cut. I got into the boat and started the motor. Bill Lewis of Tiverton Four Corners, Maynard Blades of Nova Scotia (Blades went to the hospital with broken ribs and head injuries), and Ernest Vanasse got into the boat with me. Frankie Henriques grabbed a piece of wreckage and hours later floated up on the shore with all his clothes ripped off and bruised and cut all over.

"The four who drowned—Al Sabins, Ebenezer Keith, and Mr. and Mrs. Vasco F. Souza of New Bedford—hung onto a piece of the broken building. When they were last seen, only two of them were still holding onto it.

"It's a good thing the *Wahoo* was a staunch craft or it never would have weathered the awful seas. We had all we could do to stay in the boat and we were using both hands to hold on. In the worse part of the storm, the lines broke, and she parted from her mooring, but we were ready and with the order from Bill Lewis, who was the engineer, I gave it full speed ahead and I don't mean maybe.

"Boy, did we come in. People on the Point who were watching the sea from a safe elevation saw the *Wahoo* come in and they said it looked like an airplane. We thought of the ledge and avoided that, although we ran into some submerged wreckage, but that didn't slow us up. We put her into the lee side of the wharf and climbed up on the dock; the *Wahoo* drifted onto the beach and was one of the few craft to survive the blow.

"If there's another hurricane," said Kimpel, "I want to be up where the hills are high."

That was the manner of the hurricane in Rhode Island. One thinks, at last, of the two men at Newport Beach who gathered from the sand two cans of pennies, these being all that was left of their investment in an amusement arcade. One sees the red brick base of Whale Rock Lighthouse, where Walter B. Eberley, father of six, died alone when thundering seas destroyed the beacon. And recalls the story of the Coast Guard cutter *Tahoe*, reaching Prudence Island after the storm. One of her officers called out on the loud hailer, "Where are the dead?" A voice from the shore replied, "All washed to sea."

424

Book IV

MASSACHUSETTS

CHAPTER 8

Now, the hurricane was coming to us.

The New Bedford *Standard-Times* city desk tried to place a long-distance call and the operator was vague about whatever the difficulties were, but it wasn't placeable.

In the wire room, the teletype machines still clacked, and occasionally their bells rang with the urgency of the message, but the stories were little more than bulletins. Increasingly, one sensed that the stories were hours behind the events. Eventually, the last bell rang and the machines quit all together. The ties with the world were being cut and we were coming to face our ordeal alone, as Westhampton had faced it alone, as Westerly had faced it alone.

Outside, the hot wind was wild; the weather lay lower upon the land, as if to smother it.

Even as late as this, the outlying sections beyond New Bedford knew what was happening before the city did.

Reporter Joseph Slight of the *Standard-Times* covered the suburbs. He was making his afternoon police checks on September 21, at sometime between 2:15 and 3 P.M. It had been a run-of-the-mill day; children back in school, workers returned to their jobs, and vacations over.

The wind was freshening. He phoned Dartmouth Police Chief Clarence H. Brownell: "Anything doing, Chief?"

"You better get here quick! Three or four big yachts have broken loose from their moorings in Padanaram Harbor and are smashing up against the Padanaram bridge!" Brownell replied.

Slight said later, "The wind buffeted the light sedan I was driving. At first, there were only broken branches in the streets, but by the time I had gone a mile, great elms were crashing to earth. Wires were coming down; trees began to block the roads.

"When I got to the bridge, men in oilskins and sou'westers were struggling to save three large sailing craft that were smashing against the concrete and steel span. I bucked the wind to a point about one-third of the way across, salt water drenching me, held onto a post with one hand and with the other tried to take a picture of a big sloop that was hitting the bridge with sickening crunches. The water was coming up rapidly; it was up to my ankles. I called the office to give them a bulletin and went back to the waterfront.

"I got there just in time to see a big restaurant that featured a roof with a huge lobster designed in the shingles float out into the harbor and break up. It was virtually raining shingles torn from roofs and walls. Trees and utility poles were coming down and the waters of the harbor were churned into a white froth dotted with overturned and sinking pleasure boats and the mastheads of sunken craft. It was about 3:30. That was the beginning. . . ."

Beyond Dartmouth, there was Westport—Westport Harbor and Horseneck Beach—where twenty-three died and dozens of substantial dwellings were demolished; the West Beach was left a jumble of wrecked cottages and the East Beach, swept clean of its summer settlement.

Ann Mills, twelve, daughter of Mr. and Mrs. Everett B. Mills of Fall River, was standing at the window of their Westport Harbor home when the storm wave struck; beside her was the maid, Miss Mary Frances Black. Ann dove out a window, grabbed a piece of floating wreckage. Miss Black, who had a fear of the water, called to her, "Good-bye, Ann!" The youngster eventually abandoned the wood to which she was clinging because it was not taking her in the direction of safety. She swam a considerable distance and finally reached higher ground and was assisted from the water. The maid, last seen holding onto a pole, as the sea dislodged the house, was drowned. On September 23, the Mills house was found on the sixth fairway of the Acoaxet Golf Club in Westport. The Mills's dog was discovered alive in an upstairs cupboard of the house.

Dr. Andrew F. Hall of New Bedford was one of the early colonists at Horseneck; he had had extensive property holdings at Allen's Point for years. When two small cottages near his home were washed away, he became concerned for the safety of Mrs. Mark Sullivan of New Bedford and Mrs. John de Nadal of Fall River and her baby, who were in Mrs. Sullivan's house about 100 feet down the beach.

Ali Aberdeen, proprietor of the Point Breeze Restaurant at the intersection of East and West Beach roads, came to help him. Hall tied a line to a steel stanchion of his house and Aberdeen struggled through the surf and fastened it to a post on the Sullivan home. The post lasted less time than it took to tie the knot; the next sea carried it away and slung it onto the main highway, but the iron stanchion held. Hall and Aberdeen worked their way across the open stretch of water to the Sullivan house, got Mrs. de Nadal and her baby, and made the trip back safely by holding onto the rope.

Aberdeen went back for Mrs. Sullivan; the water was well above his waist. He got her partway to the Hall house when the sea tore her away. He recovered her and tried again. A wave knocked them both down; the seas were getting heavier, Aberdeen gave up temporarily, after getting Mrs. Sullivan back to her home. He made his way alone to the Hall house.

Meanwhile, the ice cream concession on Town Landing was swept away, crashing into the front of Aberdeen's restaurant. The force of the blow drove the restaurant from its foundation and once afloat, it destroyed the De Nadal cottage. Where the restaurant had been, there stood a pole, bearing a vertical white sign reading "Clambakes." A white board, about the width of the sign, borne by the wind, struck the pole in a horizontal position about three-quarters of the way up the sign, forming an almost perfect white cross. As if it had been nailed there, the board remained against the post and did not drop until the wind let go.

After an hour had passed, Mrs. Hall glanced out the window at the storm and saw Mrs. Sullivan holding onto a telephone pole which was directly in front of her home on the West Beach road. She was waist-deep in water and apparently had been washed off her porch. Using the pole as a shield against the debris-filled waters, she was moving from one side to the other, dodging planks and timbers. Even as they watched from the Hall home, the flood waters became nearly shoulder-deep, rampaging across the land with equal force from the southwest and southeast.

Mrs. Sullivan, whose survival hung on a miracle a moment, as wreckage that could have killed her—tons of it—shot by her on the crests of the muddy seas, was no more than 150 feet away from those who were helpless to aid her, yet she was frequently out of sight behind solid water and stinging spray that clouded the air. Again and again, they were certain that she had lost her grip and been carried away, yet each time that they could see across the troughs and the air cleared momentarily, there she remained. Until finally, they could not see her at all.

Minutes passed; she was not at the pole any more. Then suddenly, they saw her on hands and knees, moving along the edge of a wall on the north side of the Hall property. In a moment, she was reachable; Aberdeen and Hall crawled across the intervening stretch—surrounded by cement walls that acted as a breakwater—and dragged her back to the house. She said later she had no idea how she got from the pole to the wall, a move that undoubtedly meant for her the difference between life and death.

James Gill was an employee on William Almy's Quonsett Farm. When the storm began to assume major proportions, he left the farm in his automobile and drove along flooded East Beach Road, headed for his Reed Road cottage to assist his wife and baby.

"While driving along the beach—there was no road, the water had washed it away—my car was blown over several times, with me in it. I got out somehow," Gill said.

"Houses were floating across the road. I started to walk and saw people on the porch of an East Beach house. They called me to come with them. I was exhausted and glad to be with someone. These people were from New York. There were three couples. I didn't know their names.

"I had only been there fifteen minutes when there were three huge waves and the third was the tidal wave, which crushed the house like a paper bag. All the people were drowned. I was the only one left.

"As the house fell in, I got on part of the roof of the porch; it broke loose from the house. As soon as I got on it, away it went, up the river. I was going so fast I could hardly hang on.

"I saw a boat and I swam to it and said, 'My Lord, if anything would stay on top of water, it would be a boat.' It was getting dark and I crawled in and stayed all night. I was so cold. Half of my clothes were torn from my body.

"The next morning, I got out of the boat and looked around; at first, I didn't know where I was. Then I recognized some places and walked back to Mr. Almy's farm."

Although Mr. Gill did not know until the morning after the hurricane how his wife and infant son—whom he had started out to help—had fared, Mrs. Mary E. Hart did; she lived on John Reed Road. "A young woman who had a bathing suit on came to the door and said that water was coming down the road," Mrs. Hart related. "I had just started getting supper for my children; one was eight months and the other, 1½ years. I was nervous because it was windy, the screening had blown in on the porch, my husband wasn't home, and we had no phone.

"When I went out to look, the water was up to the house next door. John Pettey's house was across the street; it was on a rise. I went over there; he was lying down, and I told him and he got right up and said he would go help the people in Mosher's Lane. Henry Gidley went with him. [The Gills lived in Mosher's Lane.] They told me afterward they had trouble because so many people wanted to get in the boat.

"They picked up Mrs. Gill and her baby, Fred White, and Kate Rogers, who had a broken arm, and they took them to a cottage on higher ground, about three-quarters of a mile back from East Beach. They had

One of the sandbag dams at Hartford that held back the Connecticut River. Below, the lighthouse tender Tulip thrust ashore at New London.

At Providence, Rhode Island, dockhouses are inundated; a tug lies trapped in the crib of the railroad bridge. Below, Fort Road, Watch Hill, Rhode Island, is covered by the monstrous seas. On this road fifteen people lost their lives.

At the height of the evening rush hour, Providence, at the head of Narragansett Bay, was hit with 100 m.p.h. winds, flooding much of its downtown area. Below, the Dorchester yacht fleet being pounded at Boston, Massachusetts.

no milk for the Gill baby, so they gave it strips of cloth wet in sugar to suck on.

"When I got out of my house, I didn't think of myself; I thought of my children. The water was swirling around the backyard. The house did move some, but it stayed there. I wanted to get back into the house and get some food but the water was flowing across and I couldn't get to it. Through the efforts of John, I and my children got into a car. We went to the Midway Road. Another car came along in the water with the spray flying over it. It was my husband.

"His car got stuck west of the Midway Road. We stayed there and the men put markers out so they were able to tell when the water stopped rising and started to recede. I was worried about my baby when the water was coming up; I was afraid it couldn't live if we had to get out and leave the car because the wind took your breath away.

"I had two quarts of milk in the car and as soon as the water went down, my husband, Roger, and John Pettey—they had to hold onto each other because they kept falling into potholes made by the storm—took a quart to the Gill baby.

"And when the water went down, all those people came out from the dunes to Midway Road. We didn't realize even then how bad it had been. It was 5 P.M. when the woman came to the door to tell me about the water. It was 8:30 P.M. when all the people began coming out of the dunes and when I had a chance to look at East Beach. I didn't believe it, I couldn't believe it. . . ."

To the northeast lay Martha's Vineyard.

In Edgartown, the tide rose until it flooded summer homes along the harbor front. Piers were under water, fences went adrift, and so did boathouses and boats. Captain Fred Vidler, keeper of the harbor light, said that at least twenty and probably more boats of various sizes went out past the lighthouse in the tide. Seven or eight were battered against the lighthouse bridge, a number sank, with only their masts visible, and the Chappaquiddick ferry lay shattered. Water rose halfway to the eaves of the Edgartown Yacht Club; within, the piano was afloat.

Thomas P. F. Hoving, now director of the New York Metropolitan Museum of Art, summered in Edgartown; his family had a house on Pease's Point Way. "I remember the smell of the eye of the hurricane," Hoving said. "It smelled like six billion air-conditioning sets dispensing ozone."

He was seven years old, small enough to fit under a card table. "That was where my mother put us while the hurricane was going on. To keep us children calm, she put two or three card tables together and laid blankets over them, and my sister was instructed to tell us all the ghost stories she knew. She stretched the one about the screaming skull over about three hours. We were so scared of her ghost stories we forgot about being scared of the storm till it was all over.

"When the smell went away and the storm had subsided, we went out to see what damage it had done. Where Vincent's drugstore is was the waterline. The 125-foot, steel-hulled *Manxman* had been torn loose from her mooring and had knocked down the top of the coal dock."

In Vineyard Haven, water was knee-deep over the steamboat wharf. The lower streets of the town were flooded to a depth of two or three feet and the harbor-front lawns were strewn with boats and wreckage. Antone Silvia was marooned at the Tashmoo home of Katharine Cornell, where he was at work, and he became concerned for the safety of Miss Cornell and her guests, Miss Caroline Pratt and Miss Helen Marot, Menemsha summer residents.

Waves were washing through the Cornell house when Silvia went out to attempt to cross the nearby Herring Creek, which lay between them and the road to the village. Breakers were rolling through the creek; he could neither wade through it nor jump it, so he attempted to swim. The flood immediately swept him before it; half-drowned, he managed to clutch a clump of tall beach grass on top of the bank and haul himself to safety. When Vineyard Haven police officer Simeon Pinkham arrived shortly afterward, checking the shore danger areas and assisting in evacuation, he suggested to Miss Cornell that the situation might easily have become dangerous. She replied, "Oh well, I guess I could have grabbed hold of something and held on."

It was "up-island" where the greatest damage was suffered and the Vineyard's only loss of life occurred.

My father, Joseph Chase Allen, wrote his story for the Vineyard *Gazette* immediately after the storm with his car headlamps for lights.

"The ruin at Menemsha Creek constitutes something unbelievable, with virtually everything along the waterfront except the grocery store wiped out completely . . . the inrushing tide was so strong that it cut the sand away from pilings, while huge breakers reared above the jetties, foaming and racing clear across the anchorage basin and sweeping everything before them. Boats, buildings and docks, together with tangled masses of fishing gear, went swirling up into Menemsha Pond, some of the men sticking to their boats and going with them. . . ."

Boats torn from their moorings in the creek were stranded high up in the fields, in many cases, hundreds of yards from water. My father concluded, "The scene of destruction goes beyond anything recalled by the oldest inhabitants. Indeed, there were some who doubted if there would ever again be a harbor at Menemsha, but within twenty-four hours, the indomitable fishermen were planning the salvage of their boats and restoration of the waterfront."

There was one death on Martha's Vineyard because of the hurricane.

At about 4:15, Benedict Thielen, summer resident of Chilmark, left his shack on the beach and went to his house. The sea was high, but the wind was nothing extraordinary. He stood at the window with his wife and they both looked out at the sea. Bits of foam were blowing over the top of the dunes and, after a while there was a little trickle of water. This trickle increased and later, there were two streams, one on each side of the house, but the water was not more than an inch deep.

Mr. and Mrs. Thielen had tea and, as time passed, they continued to watch the storm, and still there was nothing of a frightening nature. As the water increased, however, they decided to leave the house and walk to dry land. They put on boots, sweaters, and oilers and prepared for a walk in the storm. Their maid, Mrs. Josephine Clarke, thirty-eight, of Jamaica, went with them, wearing a raincoat. As they left the back door of the house, the water was about eighteen inches deep. Then, when they had walked perhaps a half-dozen steps, a wave came, overwhelming the land, and the water was up to their necks. In another half-minute, the next great wave broke, and the water was over their heads. There was nothing for it but to swim. Mrs. Thielen reached a sort of knoll and managed to get her boots off. Mr. Thielen was struggling in the sea with great difficulty, because of his boots and heavy clothing.

Both Mr. and Mrs. Thielen were good swimmers, but the blowing spray was blinding and choking and the drag of Mr. Thielen's clothing was a great handicap. He was giving support to Mrs. Clarke, who could not swim, and trying to guide her toward land, but in a desperate effort to free himself of his boots, he had to let go momentarily and she was swept away. Mr. Thielen managed to swim again, and finally made his way through wind and water to safety, but Mrs. Clarke was gone.

This is how Mr. Thielen remembered it. "We watched the hesitant, then rapid, then pausing, then flying-forward, yellow flecks of foam. It looked like the vomit foam of a sick animal. Finally, the water for which we had been waiting, came. A little trickle, as if someone had emptied a glass, flowed gently over the crest of the dune and was quickly soaked up by the sand. A moment later, there was a second one, but this was a little longer and a little wider than the one before. Presently, a dozen narrow threads of water were running across the sand on all sides of the house. Then a small stream was flowing down a hollow on one side, and then another, until on both sides of the house, there was water flowing. But it was only an inch or two deep, and we knew that, since the house was built high, even a few feet of water passing beneath it would do no harm. We kept watching the slowly increasing flow of water.

"And it is the slowness that stands out. There was no sudden crash of overwhelming waves but only a gradual drop-by-drop addition to the volume of the waters. But now the tops of the waves sent up spray from the dunes, and all over our land the water was flowing to the pond behind it. It was no more than ankle deep, and there were many higher places that were still dry. But in the swishing sound of the flowing water there was now something different. There was a thin clicking of pebbles being carried along by the sea. This sound soon deepened until it became a dull rumbling as the stones which were beneath the sand were also uncovered and borne away. The heaviness and deepness of the sound increased, and now, from time to time, there were hard thuds against the foundation of the house as boulders struck it.

"The water still was deepening only slowly, but there was a sense of increasing strength, and the sound of it was different from any we had ever heard before. It was then that we decided to leave—reluctantly, because we felt it was like deserting a ship in distress. As we were putting on sweaters, boots, and oilers unhurriedly, there was a crash of glass somewhere in the house. There was something incredible about it, as though a new and perfect machine should suddenly, for no reason, develop a flaw, crack, and begin to disintegrate.

"We stepped off the back porch into a foot of water and began to wade towards the high ground beyond the shore. Virginia went ahead, and I followed more slowly, holding our cook by the hand. It was not difficult, although by now the water was flowing fast and you had to brace yourself against the wind. We took five or six steps in the shallow water. But now the tempo of the sea and tide changed. There was no slow, gradual increase of the water. There was a swirl and a noise of rocks and splintering wood, and the water was up to our waists. There was a second wave and it was up to our necks. Josephine could not swim. I held on to her. Something huge rushed from the beach, and the water rose above our heads.

"Up to a point you can describe things consecutively, but beyond that there is no sequence of events. The things that happen have their reality only in the manner in which they exist in or momentarily impinge on the mind of the person caught up in their midst. The mind of that person does not see consecutively: it is impressed by a series of images which in themselves have no logical connection but exist only as isolated, unrelated phenomena. The mind, in art and in life, feels a basic need for some kind of arrangement of these unrelated phenomena. Suddenly deprived of this, it finds itself facing a horror and a loss that is far deeper than any mere physical distress of the moment. There is a kind of eerie surrealist dream quality about it. It is like this:

"The poor frightened black face rises, then disappears in the gray whirling water. Above it is a blue felt hat with a green feather pointing upward. An immense surge of current sweeps in from the sea. But I am a very good swimmer. I was brought up by the sea, and I have always felt that water was my natural home. I still have her wrist tightly in one hand, but my boots are filled with water and I can't kick to swim. My sweater is like lead on my arms, and my oilers are stiff and heavy with the cold. Also, I am looking for my wife. I see her sitting on the last bit of dry land, a hummock covered with the pale gray-green of dusty miller. I call to her to swim towards the pond shore, and I see her take off her coat and boots and start.

"There is a screaming in my ears of this sinking woman and the wind blowing at ninety miles an hour—across this water where there was once land. I know about lifesaving and try to swim backwards holding her with one arm on my chest. I cannot move my legs with their water-filled boots. To get them off, I must submerge completely, lean down, and pull at each one with both hands. I must let go my hold on this dark reaching hand. A bathhouse drifts by, half over on its side. I see the dark face sink in the water, then rise again. I dive under, twice, once for each boot, then undo the buttons of my oiler and then go under again to pull off the trousers and their tangled braces around my shoulders. I see my wife swimming slowly ahead of me. The other face is gone. A woman's hat with a green feather is floating, spinning slowly around in the water.

"In the filthy water—the water is yellow, filled with slowly turning clumps of bushes with muddy roots. The clear water that we knew is the color of stale weak coffee and soured milk. My wife turns about, and her face, her mouth, is smeared with black mud. I lean back for a moment to float and rest before swimming to the pond shore, but when you lean your head back the wind drives the spray with the force of a vaporizing gun down into your throat and lungs. The small house behind ours, which my wife used as a studio, is floating ahead of us. I had not seen it go past. It is floating neatly, on an even keel, like a houseboat. Each time I lift my arm to swim, the water-soaked sweater pulls it back. I don't want to submerge again if I can avoid it. But I find I must, to get the sweater over my head. Timbers and parts of houses are floating past, but not near us. After every few strokes I turn my head towards the ocean, into the wind, to see if any are coming towards us. I come up to Virginia, and we swim slowly along together.

"Out in the pond the waves are smaller than they were back there on the beach. It is not hard swimming. It feels almost quiet now except for the driving spray. We swim towards the nearest point of land, but the current carries us past it. Suddenly I have a strange and unbelievable sensation: I wonder if we shall get to the shore beyond. It is something that never occurred to me before, because we are both good swimmers.

"The filthy yellow water streams by, and a big clump of bushes in which my arms get entangled for a moment. The only color anywhere—in the water and in the sky—is this smear of dirty yellow. Everything else is in shades of gray and white, like a movie. It reminds me then of all the silly movies that I've ever seen, of all the broken dams, floods, storms, and charming young women (with neat hair and perfectly made-up faces) and stalwart young men battling for life. 'I'm struggling for my life. Yes, that's what I'm really doing. I—' The words go over and over in my mind, and I feel embarrassed, as though I had been cast in some fatuous part in amateur theatricals. But it is true. I feel utterly exhausted, and it is still far to the tossing bushes on the shore. There is a sense of wondering unbelief at the sight of the high and solid land and the green of the swelling fields. But slowly, like a small limp worm, I crawl nearer.

"Some cows stand shivering in the spray—looking strangely firm and secure on the ground. Moving slowly in the heavy water, I know what the bushes at the water's edge will feel like in my hands. They are wild rose-bushes and briars and bayberries, hard and coarse and thorny. They are just beyond the deep slime and tangle of mud and grass and broken roots. Then I feel them, the hard thorns, the gnarled stems, strong and tough against the hands, like rope by which you can pull yourself up from a deep place.

"Then, to get warm, you can drink all the rum they hand out to you and you can get drunk on it, but it won't make you sleep. The wind cries all night long around the house, and every time you close your eyes you see the immense slavering arch of the oncoming wave, the yellow spittle dripping down, and a dead face in the sullied waters."

Across Vineyard and Nantucket Sounds, the storm belted Cape Cod and, although deaths occurred and damage was extensive, one of the most important, and largely untold, aspects of the Cape's hurricane experience concerns the deaths that did not occur and why they did not.

Cape Codders, wise in local weather lore, sensed the approach of a natural catastrophe, and the forethought and quick action of such authorities as Chief Ray D. Wells of the Falmouth Fire Department, Police Chief Harold L. Baker of Falmouth, and Police Chief William R. Crump of Bourne were credited with preventing at least 100 deaths.

At 1:30 Wednesday afternoon, Chief Wells made a tour of the shore, noted the conditions of the sea at low tide and anticipated what was to happen six hours later at high water. He telephoned State Police, Troop D headquarters in West Bridgewater, informed them that the Cape shore would be inundated and asked that boats, equipment, and volunteers be sent without fail immediately.

The alarming message, so incredible at that hour, prompted the State Police to verify its authenticity. Five minutes later, they telephoned Chief Wells at Falmouth to make certain that he had called. Wells impressed upon them the danger that he foresaw, and the West Bridgewater headquarters relayed the appeal by teletype to Cape stations.

At 3:45, the storm wave thundered in, and all communication with the Cape was cut off at the Cape Cod Canal. But the call for help had brought response and already volunteers with dories, rope, floodlights, and trucks were rolling over the highways, bound for the stricken area just as the emergency commenced.

The Falmouth police log recorded: 6:35, bridge at West Falmouth to Old Silver Beach out. Call from Woods Hole. Family on roof, house flooded. 6:36, Henry W. Maurer reports Alice H. Maurer in car on Beach Road. Car washed off road into pond. Doesn't know if she went in or not. 6:45, call State Police, help from anywhere, SOS. . . . 7:11, call Massachusetts Department of Public Safety, no connection. 7:13, Barnstable radio off until further notice. 7:13, sergeant called radio station, Chatham, for weather. Nothing. . . .

But help was on the way.

Barnstable sent a crew with trucks and dories which arrived first and aided Chiefs Wells's and Baker's forces in rescuing 38 people who undoubtedly would have lost their lives otherwise. The Chatham Naval Reserve unit which went to Bourne arrived in time to assist Chief Crump in rescuing approximately 50 people in danger of drowning, who spent the night in hastily arranged quarters in the town hall. At Woods Hole, 15 people were rescued from an inundated house on Gardiner Road. At Maravista, firemen and volunteers found a man and woman marooned in an automobile and took them to safety; the couple then revealed that they had placed their three children in a cottage that they thought would be safer. The water was making up so rapidly that on the return trip the firemen had to take a skiff to get to the house and after rescuing the children had to row inland nearly a mile before landing.

Chief Wells commandeered every available boat and man for rescue work, while Chief Baker called out reserve policemen and civilians to aid his department.

In at least one instance, hurricane tragedy required the courts to determine which is the weaker sex.

Mr. and Mrs. Andrew F. Jones of Dorchester were pioneer colonists at Silver Beach, North Falmouth; they had been going there for thirty-seven years—there were only two cottages there during their first summer, and they were instrumental in the organization of the Silver Beach Association. When they observed their golden wedding anniversary in the summer of 1937, invitations were sent to more than 250 Cape friends, and about 400 were served in the recreation room of their Silver Beach cottage, which stood on the waterfront. It was called "The House That Jack Built." It was directly in the path of the storm.

Both Mr. and Mrs. Jones were seventy-one; he had not been in good health since he broke a leg during the previous winter. When the waves inundated his yard, at 6 P.M., he tried without success to start his car. The sea continued to rise; Mr. and Mrs. Jones went to the second floor of their home and finally managed to climb to the roof.

When the house went to pieces, the roof floated off with them on it. Neighbors in a nearby tearoom saw the Jones's roof sweeping past their building and tied blankets together, in an effort to throw a lifeline to the elderly couple, but the wind swept away the frail effort. The roof, driven inland, finally was smashed as it struck another house; husband and wife were thrown into the water.

Both bodies were recovered, that of Mrs. Jones bearing thousands of dollars' worth of diamonds and other jewelry she had put on immediately before fleeing to the roof, in the hope of saving her life and some of her valuables. On September 27, the wills of Mr. and Mrs. Jones were filed in Suffolk Probate Court.

Mr. Jones's will had been written March 11, 1915; it left all his belongings, including the cottage at Silver Beach, to his wife. The will of Mrs. Jones was drawn on February 9, 1933, and left all her money and possessions to her husband. Jones asked that his wife be named executrix and Mrs. Jones asked that her husband be named executor. The question arose as to who was next of kin, as there was no mention of any children in either will.

At the time of filing of the wills, an attorney commented, "There is a natural presumption in law that the man, being the stronger of the two, probably survived the storm longer than his wife. Unless this can be rebutted, it is reasonable that the heirs of Mr. Jones would obtain possession of the property. . . ."

Miss Alice H. Maurer, forty-two, a retired private nurse, was a summer resident of The Fells, Falmouth; she had been going there seasonally with her family for fourteen years and planned to return to her winter home in Rochester, New York, on the Monday following the hurricane.

Early on the afternoon of the storm, she and her nephew, Henry W. Maurer III, went to Falmouth and did some shopping. Mr. Maurer mentioned that the car might need gasoline but Miss Maurer, in a hurry to reach home, thought there was sufficient for the short drive. The car ran out of gasoline when they reached the road by Oyster Pond.

Shortly afterward, E. Gunnar Peterson of Falmouth came driving by. He offered to take Mr. Maurer for gasoline and urged Miss Maurer to go with them, but she said she preferred to wait in her car and watch the surf. When they returned, the Maurer car was in the pond and Miss Maurer could not be found, either in the car or in the water nearby.

A group of sightseers who also went to the Falmouth shore to watch the surf were only a few yards away, near the Moors Pavilion, but were horrified and helpless witnesses to Miss Maurer's tragic end.

The sea was sweeping across the shore in waves of muddy water; a huge comber smashed through the pavilion, the seas broke over its roof, showering the nearby road with thick spray. Watchers on the beach suddenly found the water well above their knees and moved hurriedly toward the higher section of the road. Somebody directed attention to two cars stalled near the bathhouses and expressed the hope that their occupants had left in time.

"Suddenly, we realized there was a figure moving slowly, pulling itself along the highway fence—it was made of cement posts and steel cables— that bordered the beach road," said Miss Eleanor Brooks, one of the group. "I ran to a car that had just driven up and sent its driver back to the fire station for help."

The figure—they could not tell whether it was a man or woman—remained by the fence, not moving one way or another. Higher surf was rolling in across the road. Intermittently, the rain and spume blotted the person in the water from the view of those who watched. The pavilion was breaking up under the sea's pounding.

Two boys drove up and the beach watchers ran to tell them that someone was caught in the surf. One of them removed his shoes, rolled up his trousers and waded into the water; it rose to his armpits and a sea knocked him off his feet. He tried once more, although because the rolling seas were much higher now and the spray thicker, it was impossible to tell whether either the fence or the figure was still there. Overwhelmed by the water again, the boy gave up and had all he could do to swim back to safety.

Firemen arrived, and two of them tied themselves together with a rope, but the stretch of surf was now so wide and the breakers so high that although they went into the water up to their shoulders, being able neither to make headway nor retain their footing beyond that point, it was obviously futile and dangerous to make further effort.

Chief Baker's men made extensive search after the storm, and at 2 o'clock on the following Sunday, Miss Maurer's body was found near the center of Salt Pond, off the Moors. When it was towed ashore, a warm sun was shining; the pond and sound were a gently rippled blue. Sunday strollers gathered to watch the arrival of Chief Baker and the undertaker. Some turned away as the body was brought to shore; others took photographs.

Woods Hole caught the full force of the storm. At 4 o'clock on Wednesday, the first rush of water came. As it neared the top of the steamship wharf, station agent Robert C. Neal grew uneasy; he had never seen it that high other than at exceptional flood tide. He phoned the Falmouth *Enterprise* office, learned that high tide was not due for at least three hours, and gave orders to have all tickets and money removed from the office, which was located near the end of the pier. In the relatively short time that it took to clear the office, the water rose three feet and Ronald Densmore, ticket seller, had to be helped from the swaying building.

Swiftly the waters came up. Books and valuables were taken out of Samuel T. Cahoon's fish market when water reached the floor. Fishermen whose vessels were lying nearby fought to keep their boats from floating onto the steamboat dock as the sea lifted them. By 5:45, Woods Hole's entire Main Street, as well as Millfield Street, Spencer Baird Road, and Penzance Road, were flooded. Firemen waited until water reached the fenders of their engine before moving the apparatus up the hill to the post office. Still the water rose.

On Dyer's dock, the second largest wharf in Great Harbor, struggling men gave up their effort to pull automobiles clear; they retreated slowly, to higher ground, with the rush of water pouring behind. Automobiles parked on the dock were thrown into the water; other vehicles parked near the harbor were submerged, and the dock itself was beaten to pieces; a large gasoline tank that had been used to provide yachts with fuel spun in a great whirlpool over the place where the dock had stood.

At the Woods Hole Oceanographic Institution, the crew of the big ketch *Atlantis* ran out additional hawsers to nearby buildings as she rose above the wharf spiles. Small boats were being destroyed all about the ketch; a party boat was sunk under her stern, and nearby, a yawl was pounding a sloop that was being wrecked against a seawall. From the roof of Community Hall, Eel Pond and Woods Hole harbor looked one and the same—a flood of turbulent water.

At 6:15, the cry went up from those gathered at the drawbridge that it was being washed away. As one side of the bridge started to lift, Sidney Peck, the draw tender, yelled, "Look out for the planks! Those who can manage better come across now." Women in light housedresses were carried across to the high ground past Rowe's Drug Store. Sheets of rain made it impossible to see across the street in the gathering dusk. The Naushon landing, Crane's pier, the Bureau of Fisheries dock all were reported smashed by the heavy seas that continued to roll in. Near the Oceanographic building, the water turned black when the coal in the rear of the Penzance garage washed to the surface. Somebody passing hollered that Penzance Point was cut off in two places. "It's an island now, but if the water keeps coming, it won't even be there!" one man shouted, his voice hardly audible above the wind.

On Penzance Point, P. Milton Neal and his father, Albert W. Neal, caretaker for many years of the Hector J. Hughes summer estate there, were attempting to board up doors and windows. The wind and tide changed, sweeping water from Buzzards Bay back through Great Harbor. Realizing that the foundation of the house had begun to sag and that the building offered no sanctuary, the son aided his sixty-year-old father in getting to a nearby utility pole, to which he clung. The son made his way to another pole a few yards away and they hung on, while storm and sea battered them, for about two hours. At the end of that time, a large wave swept over them, and the older man, weakened by long exposure, lost his grip; he was swept away and drowned while his son watched. Milton clung to the pole for nearly two hours more until a rescuer, tied to a rope held by others, was able to reach him.

Mostly, the lower Cape escaped; the heaviest damage was to its fish traps—after the hurricane, only 19 out of 58 were operable. The lowest tides in the recollection of the oldest inhabitants saved the area; before the storm broke, the tide had retreated far from shore, leaving sandbars and shallows where normally water would have been several feet deep.

On a hilltop in Truro, a late-staying summer resident was writing to his wife when the storm came. He said, "As I wrote, the wind became a moan, as if great quantities of air were sucked up and suddenly let go. A neighbor described it as being like a dog worrying the end of her house like a bone. Presently, I looked at the water below me. It had become a whirlwind of flying spume; piled lumber was being flung about. . . ."

"I opened the door a crack, but flying sand cut my face like ground glass and I slammed it shut. I knew that safety lay in the event that none of that furious wind found its way inside. Once it did, the house would go like seaweed. Through the floor of the sun porch, the wind came up like knife thrusts.

"I found myself changing that letter from badinage to seriousness and ending it finally with a message that if I were not alive when she found it, the note would be self-explanatory."

The writer lived to mail his note.

At the "gateway" to the Cape, in Wareham, the water rose on lower Main Street to a level twelve feet above ordinary tide levels; it crippled the town's business section, caused damage of more than one million dollars and took nine lives in the outlying beach areas. Both the Narrows highway bridge and the railroad bridge were swept away. A floating gas stove out of the Wareham Coffee Shop was used as a raft by two exhausted men trying to swim to safety in Main Street. David Wilcox, who had carried the mail from the post office to the railroad station, became stranded there on top of a baggage truck and was rescued by two men in a canoe.

William L. Ross, Jr., was manager of the Warr Theater. "Charlie Hatch was crippled and operating a tiny eatery," Ross said. "He was hollering, sitting on top of the counter, with water all around him, pots and pans, etc. Two doors down, the Chinese man was also screaming, in the same condition. My projectionist and I rescued these people with a boat we found floating near the railroad tracks. Water peaked at about 9 feet in this area on Main Street."

In the Onset Fire District, more than $1 million in property damage was reported, including $300,000 for pleasure craft, together with the loss of 325 houses, rendering 400 homeless.

Because of the rapidity with which the storm wave charged up the Wareham River (within moments placing upon the railroad bridge a burden it could not bear), a major tragedy might have resulted there had it not been for the alertness of a New York, New Haven and Hartford Railroad engineer.

William Reed was proceeding on his regular Hyannis-to-Boston run with sixty passengers aboard. Reed was within a few hundred yards of the Wareham bridge when he saw a boat float over its rails. Until that moment, he had not realized the force of the growing storm. Even as he watched, water surged over the bridge and started flowing toward the train. Reed reacted instantly, recognizing the quickly growing danger. (The flood ripped up whole sections of ties, twisting and bending the steel rails attached to them.) He backed the train a distance of two miles to the Onset station. He was unable to go farther because tracks to the rear had been washed away.

Train crew, passengers, mail, and baggage were taken to Boston over the highway the next day, but the trackless train remained marooned at the Onset station for about three weeks.

Donald G. Trayser, Boston *Globe* correspondent in Hyannis, had to drive all the way to Middleboro before he could find a telephone that worked, in order to call his newspaper on the night of the storm. He had to go through Onset back roads to get around Wareham. Returning after midnight, he saw the lighted train, with steam up, on the track at Onset. "Where are you going?" he called to Reed. The engineer replied, "Buddy, I can go back two miles or forward a mile, and that's all."

At Swift's Beach, where three died, approximately ten acres of waterfront was swept clear and the wreckage left in heaps so that it was impossible to tell one house from another. At 6 P.M. on the twenty-first, just before the hurricane obliterated the colony, a deed to one of the cottages was delivered to its new owner by an attorney. The latter said, "It's all yours now, and here are the keys." Shortly afterward, the new owner watched the sea smash the building to pieces.

Publisher Lemuel C. Hall of the Wareham *Courier* interviewed one of the rescuers at Swift's Beach; without their efforts, the death toll there unquestionably would have been higher. "Black and blue and cold from five hours of immersion in the tidal wave that swept [the colony] into oblivion, 18-year-old Northfield [Massachusetts] Seminary graduate Miss Marguerite Bryant of Worcester is the heroine of this beach community," he reported.

Miss Bryant's father was an invalid. At about 5 o'clock, when she saw the ocean "suddenly appear to rise up and come towards the shore in a wall-like mass of water," she ran from the house for help. A Wareham police ambulance responded; its crew, up to their waists in water, carried her father out of the house on blankets, and led other members of the household onto high ground.

After Miss Bryant had gotten her own family to safety, she learned that the postmistress and her two children [Mrs. Victor Brown, her son, Richard, eleven, and a seven-month-old infant] were not out of the flooded area. She attempted to wade and swim through the wreckage-filled waters, found she could not, got a boat, and finally made her way to the post office, where she took aboard the mother and two children, as well as a second woman, all of whom were on top of the building, which soon after was destroyed.

At Hamilton Beach, Miss Elizabeth I. Holliday and Mrs. Fanny Butler were occupying a beach cottage with Mrs. Clarence Willard. Miss Holliday said, "There was no warning of the storm in the way of rain. We were in an exposed section and the wind blew increasingly. Finally, the tidal wave came at us, it seemed, from three directions. At first, we tried to save the steps of the cottage, which were whirled this way and that with the force of the wind and the current.

"Mrs. Willard went for help with her car. Then, it became clear that we could save nothing. By this time, the water pouring into the cottage was waist-high. With things we found at hand, we forced up a screen on a rear window. As we climbed over the window ledge, the house tipped, like an unbalanced boat.

"Outside, Mrs. Willard, who had been forced to abandon her car because of the water and trees strewn everywhere, was calling to us. She had become afraid we were lost and was upset and crying. We made our way on foot for over a mile until a car took us to the little settlement and post office that served the beach. The owner of a little rooming house invited all the wet and frightened people into his kitchen to dry themselves. Everyone was splendid; they were confused and fear-struck, but it was a revelation to see the consideration everyone displayed. I put on another woman's shoes and she put on mine and we never noticed. . . .

"Then people came to check among the survivors, looking for missing members of their families. One old man was looking for his wife and daughter. He found their bodies, one under the steps of his cottage, the other beneath the porch, both drowned. . . ."

Wareham Police Chief Chester A. Churchill phoned his wife from Police Department headquarters on Main Street, shortly before communications failed. He said, "The water's up to my waistline." She replied, "You'd better get out of there." Afterward, she recalled, "I didn't see him for the next three days."

Churchill said, "We lost the people on the beaches because the water came in behind them, cutting them off from the mainland. We couldn't get to them and they couldn't get out. One husband and wife had planned to leave for Ohio the day before, but they postponed leaving because the weather was bad. They were both drowned."

Leroy P. Ellis lived on Onset's East Central Avenue. "I looked out toward the lowland flats and the firemen were taking people out of the second-story windows," he said.

"East of the pier, there was a big black schooner anchored; she was about 60 feet and belonged to Hamilton Garland. She was all provisioned for a long cruise. She started to drag and somebody came to me and said Garland was offering $1,000 to anybody who would get hold of her and keep her from going ashore. If I'd had my boat, I'd have given a try but she was in a good safe place and I didn't want to move her. That schooner must have drawn 6 feet, but the water came in so fast it floated her over a wall and left her in the middle of a paved road east of the Point Independence bridge. I'm sure it cost him more than $1,000 to get her floated again; house movers had to cradle her and roll her over the wall.

"Every house on Onset Island broke up and floated; there was eight feet of water over the island and one woman and son saved themselved by staying up a tree until the water went down. Captain Harold Hatch was on the motor sailer *Goosander*, off the yacht club; a house floated down on him from Onset Island, driven by the southeasterly wind, struck his boat, and it split on his bow, half of it drifting by on the port side and the other half on the starboard.

"There must have been at least twenty big boats ashore after it was over and I believe it would have been a lot worse if it hadn't been for the Cape Cod Canal, which took a lot of the high water—water went through the canal at a speed of at least 15 knots.

"There was a man and some other people drowned in a house in the canal when it smashed up against the Bourne Bridge. The man had a small cabin cruiser, 25–30 feet, tied out in front of his house at Gray Gables. It was in a sheltered place and it didn't take any harm. Two or three days after the hurricane, I got a call asking if I would tow the boat to a boatyard. His widow didn't want to have to look out the window and see the boat anymore. . . ."

The drowning of the people in the house in the Cape Cod Canal was one of the most crushing single tragedies which the storm inflicted.

The home of Mrs. Elizabeth Lane, seventy-four, on Jefferson Road, Gray Gables, was a two-story frame building located a couple of hundred feet east of Buzzards Bay and about fifteen feet south of the canal. The house rested on a foundation of concrete blocks, but was not attached to the foundation; the south bank of the canal at this point rose approximately nine feet. In the house with Mrs. Lane were Mabel V. Wells, sixty-one, of Mount Vernon, New York; Emily Needham, sixty-two, of Vineland, New Jersey; and Joseph Needham, eleven, a schoolboy, who was Emily Needham's adopted son. None of them could swim.

Hayward Wilson, fifty-four, a boatman and a good swimmer, lived on high ground nearly 300 feet southeast of the Lane home. The canal in this area was 540 feet wide, with a normal depth in midstream of 35 feet at high tide; the Lane house was 30 feet high.

At about 3:30 P.M., the tide was rising and was already unusually high; the wind was more than 50 miles an hour, and increasing; in the canal, there was a strong current to the northeast, and wind-blown spray reduced the visibility greatly. Wilson, observing the storm conditions, visited a house east of the Lane residence to make certain that two elderly people there were all right. He then went to a nearby cove, pulled several rowboats up onto the bank for greater security, and checked the lines on his own boat at a landing. Because of the wind, he had difficulty maintaining his footing and part of the time lay flat and clung to the landing.

Conditions became worse, and about 4:20 P.M., Wilson noticed that water 3 to 4 feet deep was moving northeast in waves, nearly 300 feet east of the normal shore of the bay and south of the Lane home. He knew the normal tide would be high at 5:45 and expected still higher water. The occupants of the Lane home were new residents. He thought there was at least one woman in the home besides Mrs. Lane and he told his wife that he would visit the women to make sure of their safety.

Wilson could swim 250 feet; he could tread water and float. He was familiar with local wind and tide conditions. He did not indicate to his wife that he thought the Lane house was in danger of being washed away.

He walked rapidly northwest from his home to the north side of a house that was east of the Lane house and then for about 40 feet more; he was observed walking west downgrade, and holding onto trees and bushes. At that time, he was on dry ground, but the water may even then have been about a foot deep in front of the Lane house. So far as is known, Wilson was not again observed outside the Lane house.

Fifteen minutes later, he telephoned to his wife from the Lane house and told her he was safe, but that he would be unable to leave until about 7 P.M., when the high tide would have receded somewhat. He told his wife to telephone for a man to bring a rowboat to the Lane house to get the women out. He also instructed her to telephone people in Boston and Brockton to send someone to save their launches, which were in the cove. Wilson spoke calmly and firmly, and Mrs. Wilson felt relieved. He did not say anything about the Lane house, but he did say, "I'm going to wait here until the water goes down. It's impossible to get back."

Mrs. Wilson telephoned to a family three miles away for aid; the message was relayed to a man who started toward Gray Gables. Blocked roads and high water prevented him from reaching there. Meanwhile, the storm increased in violence. Mrs. Wilson wanted to telephone to her husband but was unable to get the number at the Lane house.

Shortly before 6 P.M., the tide rose to 10 feet above normal and the water extended to within 10 feet of the Wilson house. Very soon afterward, the Lane house drifted northeast into the canal, submerged to within a few feet of the top of the roof. No one was observed on or in the house. After drifting 2 miles, the house lodged against a pier of the Bourne bridge. It was sighted there at 11 P.M. by Katherine Keene, a Buzzards Bay telephone operator, as it lay grounded against the abutment.

A work force led by Bourne Police Chief William R. Crump, Fire Chief Thomas Wallace, and Naval Reservists headed by Lieutenant Samuel Freedman of Chatham risked their lives to break through the roof to get to the occupants. At midnight, they found five bodies on the second floor; all had drowned. A bloody bruise was on Wilson's forehead and his hands were badly bruised and lacerated; he had made a last desperate effort to break through the roof to get the women and little boy out of their water-filled prison. Wilson was awarded the Carnegie Medal for Heroism, the reverse side of which reads: "Greater love hath no man than this, that a man lay down his life for his friends."

Raymond A. Dennehy, professional at the Kittansett Golf Club in Marion, had a golf date at 1 P.M., September 21, with Charles Peirson, the club treasurer, and John McDonald, a member. "It was only blowing and cloudy to begin with, but pretty soon, it got serious. We hit some of the longest damned shots with the wind," Dennehy said, when I talked with him.

Undoubtedly, the most extraordinary shot of the afternoon was made by Peirson, who, with a surprisingly strong southeast wind at his back, decided to chance carrying the trees that guard the corner of the dogleg at the fourth hole. This is a shot that requires tremendous carry to reach the fairway beyond the thick woods. The distance from tee to green is 350 yards; the trees on the corner are 250 yards out and about 40 feet high. Peirson hit the ball perfectly; it was high and well-carried, and all three of them saw it clear the woods on the corner and head for the green. It bounced once in the fairway and disappeared into the woods on the far side. Few golfers in the club's history had ever successfully reached the fairway on that shot. Peirson had carried the woods beyond. "We never found the ball," Dennehy said, "but there is no doubt that it carried the corner, went over the green and into the woods."

But hitting against the wind was impossible. (Golfers in Dartmouth, a few miles to the west, who were playing at about this time on the twenty-first, told of hitting balls that went straight up in the air.) The three Marion players decided to quit and walk in; they soon discovered when they got to the clubhouse that they were cut off from the mainland because the ocean had poured across the point.

MacDonald had a brand-new Chrysler. When the water came in over the road, he was still showering and had no chance to drive it to higher ground. All its windows were closed, making it tight, and the waves picked up the car and floated it right out into the bay. He was in time to see that and remarked, "Damn, there go my golf clubs."

"I got into my car on the 18th green and parked it there," Dennehy said. "That's the highest land on the point. MacDonald waded through shoulder-high water to the club. I thought I would be better off in the car because buildings were beginning to go. Also, I had a German shepherd with me and I didn't want to risk letting him get loose in the storm.

"At Bird Island Light, just off shore, there was a two-story house. I could see that being smashed up. Water was at least two-thirds of the way up on the lighthouse itself. Pretty soon, I saw the wreckage of the building on Bird Island come floating by. My whole golf shop started to disintegrate.

"The [Beverly] yacht club was a substantial two-story building, on cement posts. The water rose around it and, bit by bit, it just caved in and

449

broke up, and three of the club cottages, too. It wasn't too long after that before I saw the wreckage of the yacht club come by. The clubhouse was demolished in much less than an hour.

"My car was sitting in four feet of water. It was over the floorboards. I was one scared guy. I don't like water much.

"With all the buildings going down, I thought the clubhouse would be next. Its first floor was flooded and everybody in it went to the second floor, except that there were a couple of women and they grew so nervous, feeling the building wouldn't last, that they persuaded somebody to put them into an oak tree next to the building. They didn't know it, but the tree was covered with poison ivy; they got a terrible case of it.

"I think I was probably in the car about four hours. Finally, the tide went out, awfully fast, and the water was full of wreckage. Everywhere, there were boulders, sand, and debris. There was a bathtub on the fairway; it came out of one of the cottages.

"That was Wednesday. We were supposed to have our big four-ball tournament for 150 golfers on Friday. I called my boss in Andover (Golf Committee chairman Rodney W. Brown) and told him we couldn't have it because everything was ruined. They hadn't gotten much storm there and he didn't believe me. He said, 'Have you been drinking?' and I said, 'No, but I wish to hell I had.' He spent all the next morning getting down to Marion to see for himself, because there were trees and everything in the roads. We didn't have the tournament."

All the boats at Marion did not go ashore. Jakob M. Svendsen was aboard Otto Braitmayer's 65-foot yacht *Fearless II,* which was lying in Planting Island Cove. As the wind increased in intensity, various small craft, power and sail, broke loose and drifted down toward him. Fending these craft off kept him busy for some time, until he realized the painter on his skiff had parted and the boat had drifted down the cove.

The cove is very shallow; its narrow channel is only 7 feet deep at low tide. Water safe for *Fearless* was sharply limited, and the cove by this time was extremely rough. Suddenly, the swivel below the mooring buoy let go. It was imperative to get rid of the mooring line to prevent the buoy from punching a hole in the hull.

"I immediately started the engines to hold her up," Svendsen said. "I eased up as close as I dared to Planting Island. The water was now on the causeway and you could not see Meadow Island at all. When I reached a point as close as I dared to go, I disengaged the clutches and prepared to get the buoy away. Since there was only a low single wire rail on the foredeck, I stripped down to pants in case I went overboard. I then went forward and discarded the mooring line, allowing the buoy to drift away.

"By this time, we had drifted back to a dangerous position and I again proceeded to work my way back to Planting Island under power. I realized I would have to get the anchors out as soon as possible. We carried one small mud hook in one hawsepipe and two 135-pound anchors on deck. One was attached to the chain in the port side hawsepipe and the other was a spare. In order to use the spare, I had to retrieve a long cotton line which was stowed in the lazaret in the afterdeck.

"I then proceeded to move up close to the island, disengage the clutches, rush aft to obtain the anchor line I required, watch my position as I drifted back, and rush forward to the pilothouse to move up again. I continued this—moving up under power, then drifting back, time after time after time. I was, of course, completely soaked and extremely cold by now. By the time I retrieved the anchor line for the spare anchor, attached one end to the anchor and the other to the capstan, placed the stocks in both anchors and put the port side one in the davit ready to drop, I probably made 25 to 30 trips to the island.

"When all was ready, I had to use the sounding lead to determine where I wanted to end up, not knowing how far the tide might drop going out. There were no more landmarks visible for me to use. After deciding where I hoped to end up, I eased forward to where I believed the anchors ought to be. I then made my way to the bow again and threw the spare anchor over the bow and released the two anchors attached to the chain in the hawsepipes. I allowed the cotton line to play out to get as much scope as possible and then adjusted the remaining two with the winch.

"I now had three anchors and I was still using the engines to ease the strain, but kept an eye on the temperature gauge since the water was extremely dirty with all the stirring up from the storm. When the engines started to heat up, I immediately shut them down to prevent overheating and possibly freezing them up tight. At this point, the anchors appeared to be holding, with waves breaking over the bow.

"I then went to the engine room and proceeded to turn the engines over by hand to prevent them from binding up from excess heat. The warmth of the engine room was a blessing, since I was very cold from my activity out on deck in the wind and waves.

"My wife and son were constantly at the water's edge with a light that enabled me to get some bearing on my location. As soon as the storm subsided, I pulled in the anchors and made my way into Marion Harbor and deeper water, where I anchored. Some sections of the anchor chain were literally tied in knots and the anchor stocks were all bent."

Dr. Raymond H. Baxter was the medical examiner of Marion. "My street was blocked by downed trees so an ambulance could not get in," he recalled. "A man put his arm through a broken window and severed the radial artery. This is an operating room job, but it was up to me to do something in the light of flashlights and candles. My twelve-year-old son was watching the breakers coming up my street and at the height of my sweating, he announced, 'The water's only a little way from our house, Daddy.' By the grace of God, I got a clamp on the artery practically in the dark and got a suture around it. My office looked like an abattoir the next morning from the bloody spurts. . . ."

Mrs. Parker Converse was on Converse Point, Marion, which has been owned by the family since 1898. Although the sea had begun to pile over the seawall and dock (which was eventually under eight feet of water), she prepared to drive to meet her husband's train at Wareham. She wrote in her diary, "Took son (he was six) and general maid across the road to caretaker's house, which was on higher ground. As I turned back to the house, Tony Cruz, the caretaker, and I were appalled to see a tidal wave lift the 35-foot sailer that was tied to the dock, carry it over the pond, and deposit it in the woods."

Finding the Wareham road underwater, she drove back to Converse Point and wrote later, "Met by breakers, abandoned car. Told that it was impossible to get to the Moorings, as the end of point [where her home was] was underwater. Managed to get to garage. The caretaker took his two small girls and I, my small son. We ran with them until we got to low land, put them on our backs and struggled through the breakers, with furniture sweeping and tumbling by us. Reached dry land just as our strength was giving out."

I asked Benjamin D. Dexter of Marion, who described himself as an "old-timer," what he remembered about the storm.

"I had a thirty-foot boat pulled up in a field about six feet above mean high water," Dexter said. "Soon, the water was up to her and I was concerned that she would float and smash into a stone wall nearby. So I got an anchor and line and proceeded out into the field to secure the anchor in the ground. I was wearing hip boots, a long raincoat and a sou'wester. As I bent over to hook the anchor in the ground, the thought came to me that I must be dreaming. 'Here I am anchoring a boat in the middle of a vegetable garden,' I said to myself. Just then, a wave broke over my head, but I had hooked the anchor, so I held on and the wave passed.

"A Mr. Fernandes living off Route 6 [the waters of Marion Harbor rose over Route 6] had his barn floated away. Later, he found the barn intact and his cow still in its stall chewing hay.

"At Great Hill, Arthur Griffin, then superintendent of the Stone estate, had a new boat in a boathouse. As he watched, the boat came up through the roof and took off for Wareham, where he later found it, with barely a scratch. As for the height of the water, I saw a story and a half house sitting on Dummy Bridge in Onset. That bridge is some 10 to 12 feet above mean high and that house must have floated at the eaves, making about 20 feet of water there.

"Steven Watts was caught outside in his power boat. He sought refuge behind Ram Island, but so much refuse began to come off the island as the water rose, he decided to make a run for the shore. He ran his boat ashore at the Marion campgrounds in Hammett's Cove. There, he learned that his boat shop was burning; some live wires had ignited the shop, and the Fire Department had responded but with several feet of water, the firemen had to take to boats. One boat capsized with a fireman holding a nozzle. He went under holding the hose and the force of the nozzle sent him zagging about in all directions. He said that only the hose kept him from being jetted out into the harbor. This man must have been the first, and probably the last, jet-propelled fireman."

CHAPTER 10

At Mattapoisett, Dr. Austen Fox Riggs, internationally famous psychiatrist and head of the well-known Stockbridge, Massachusetts, foundation bearing his name, was in his seashore cottage in the Hollywood Beach area. Including his chauffeur, secretary, and household help, he had with him a staff of six.

By 4:30 in the afternoon, the tide was 3 feet higher than Dr. Riggs had ever seen it there; he knew that high tide was not until two hours later. Within ten minutes, he told the household they would have to leave, and his chauffeur had discovered Riggs's station wagon was in the water and useless.

"I got all the help to hold hands. The water was up to our armpits. Only a few of the party could swim. Miss Leary [Susan Leary, sixty, the cook], a woman about 5 feet tall, was so short that we had to carry her. The water was about 6 feet high on the tennis courts," Riggs said in an interview.

"I got to the garage and backed out a larger car. My portable office had been swept away and I saw another portable house smashed to pieces. I packed everyone into the car, only to find the drive flooded. The car stalled and a large swell came in. Mrs. LaFarge [Mrs. Warden LaFarge, his literary secretary] and I managed to get out and open the door. My chauffeur [Harry Bell], Mrs. LaFarge and the others clung to pine trees. I lifted Miss Leary to the top of the car. As the water continued to rise, I got her to swim on her back and got her to the gate post and to the wall. We left her there.

"I swam 150 yards to get help. By this time, the water was 8 feet deep. I reached the home of William Corey, a neighbor."

Corey and Raymond Winslow found oars in a nearby house and set out in what Captain Walter E. Bowman, a licensed Buzzards Bay pilot for a half-century and an eyewitness, described as "breaking surf" to rescue the stranded members of the Riggs household. All survived but one. Riggs said, "When I got back, I discovered Miss Leary had been washed from the wall. She got back to the top of the automobile and Bell clung to her arms for more than an hour before a wave swept across them and he lost his grip. Two days later, they found Miss Leary's body under a lilac bush near the gate, 100 yards from the house."

Mattapoisett Constable Frank P. LeBaron estimated immediately after the storm that 170 cottages were destroyed at Crescent Beach and 15 more at adjoining Pico Beach. Revised figures ranged from 125 to160. But whatever the exact total was, it meant that the Crescent Beach settlement was no more.

The storm wave at Crescent Beach was described as a fourteen-foot wall of water that drove inland a quarter of a mile. When it retreated, the search for the dead began. In the following days, hundreds of WPA workers, townspeople, twenty-eight members of the First Baptist Church of New Bedford, and twenty-seven Worcester men, including thirteen members of the city government, searched through the heaps of timbers, planks, and pieces of houses strewn five and six feet thick over a mile-long strip of waterfront.

Of the total settlement, only five cottages remained. Along the shore and even back into the woods were strewn the details of disaster: smashed crockery, plumbing, broken toys, soaked furniture spewing its stuffing, curled books, their pages puffed and stiff from salt water. In one cottage standing on end, there was a letterhead bearing an address written in a masculine hand. Below it was written, "Dear Al:" the remainder of the page was blank.

The evidence suggests that John Pyne gave his life in attempting to save his six-week-old son; their bodies were separated by only a few feet. The bodies of Mrs. Albert Norlander and Mrs. Harry P. McAllister were recovered under tons of wreckage on September 29 by National Guardsmen; they were about three hundred yards from the site of the Norlander cottage.

Carl B. Forman, who lived at Crescent Beach, was recovering from two recent operations. Despite this, he rescued Joseph B. Ellis of Attleboro, who was partly paralyzed, and whose home was swept away, and Mrs. Walter Pratt, whose leg was in a cast. "The screams were terrible. You could hear people in all directions calling for help. I tried to get in to Mr. Fred L. Heyes but I couldn't reach him because of the water and wreckage," Forman said.

Later, volunteer workers found a belt on a heap of debris; it bore Mr. Heyes' initials.

The newspaper account concerning Mrs. Jennie Brown was brief; it said, "Reported among the missing, [she] was first discovered beneath the roof of a collapsed cottage at Crescent Beach, Mattapoisett, when her voice was heard by searchers. Pinioned beneath the housetop, Mrs. Brown was released when poles were used to pry the boards from her body. It was feared that she had suffered broken legs and body bruises, and contusions were numerous. Her clothing was cut from her body. She was wrapped in coats and carried more than a half-mile through remnants of cottages to a waiting Army truck. She remains at the hospital, where she is under treatment for chest injuries."

The man who found this seventy-five-year-old woman under the wreckage and undoubtedly saved her life was Edwin L. Perkins of Mattapoisett. Of the night of September 21, he recalled, "That evening was a bright moonlight night. I guess it was a near full moon. I was in the plumbing and heating business and the superintendent of the town Water Department contacted me to see if I would go to Crescent Beach and shut off as many water services as I could find, so that we wouldn't lose so much water.

"I drove down as far as the Cedars, right at the curve to go to the beach, in my truck; I could go no farther because the debris was in sheets. I remember I got out and started toward Crescent Beach. There was no road to see, just pieces of houses, doors; they covered the road.

"I crawled over what I could and headed toward the middle of the beach. That night was so bright all I could see was a stone house across from Bill Raymond's store. The store was demolished. I walked over tops of houses, furniture; there didn't seem to be a bare spot of ground. I had to go on everything, from houses to furniture.

"By the time I got to the middle of the development, I heard a voice. I did not know at first whether it was a woman or a man. The wind was blowing a little and it was hard to tell, but it said, 'Get me out, get me out.' I started to go toward where I heard the voice. Then I didn't hear it. Then I recognized that it was a woman's voice, saying, 'Please get me out.'

"I traveled sort of a circle, bigger and bigger. I found out after why she didn't say anything all the time. She was in and out of consciousness. Then she said, 'I am Mother Brown. Please get me out.' I was five, maybe ten, feet from the voice. There was debris everywhere, four to five feet thick, halves of roofs, chairs, doors, everything. She heard me walking over the debris; that's how she knew I was there.

"I said, 'Are you all right, Mrs. Brown?' and she didn't answer. For a couple of minutes, there wasn't a word. That was an awful feeling. Then she said again, 'I am Mother Brown; get me out.'

"I said, 'I am Mr. Perkins, the plumber. I know you.' I reached down with my right arm between the debris until I touched the top of this woman's head. She said, 'Mr. Perkins, please get me out.'

"I suppose it sounds funny now, but I said, 'Mother Brown, don't move; I'll get help.' She couldn't have moved if she had tried.

"So I said to her, 'I'll go get help,' and I said to myself, 'How will I ever find her again?'

"I had on a black and white plaid shirt from L. L. Bean in Maine, and I found an oar and I put the oar handle down in the sleeve of the shirt, then I stuck the oar in a loose place in the debris to mark the spot. I walked way up to where the road was clear; they were allowing only the State Guard and police there. I told one of the State Guard men and he said, 'We'll get a crew and follow you.'

"Eight or ten National Guardsmen then came along. We found her again, we spoke to her and there was no answer. I was afraid she was dead. The men started hauling away the debris.

"When we got to her, she was on a slant, sort of huddled down there. The only thing she had on was a piece of cloth around her left arm and shoulder. Everything else had been ripped off her body. She came to then, but she couldn't move. Two of the National Guardsmen found a door ripped off something and they used that as a stretcher and took her from there way up to the cars, where the road was clear. They got her to the hospital.

"She was very bruised; no bones broken, but shocked. They took sixty-eight pieces of wood out of Mrs. Brown's body—they weren't ordinary splinters—and we figured the water must have pushed and pulled her, back and forth, because it not only ripped off all her clothing, but some of those splinters were in as if she had gone against them going down and some as if she had gone with them, in the same direction. She was in the hospital for some time and had to go back in again. I went to see her.

"As we found out later, Mrs. Brown had started from her cottage to Angelica Avenue after the water came up to her piazza. 'I think I better go to dry ground,' she said. She got part way and she said, 'I left all my jewelry, watch, and diamonds in the cottage.' So she went back. By the time she got the jewelry and had started for high ground again, the big wave came. She couldn't go anywhere. Houses were going to pieces. How that woman ever lived through it, I don't know. That big wave, with debris, must have overwhelmed her. She must have been washed back and forth. And her jewelry was never found.

"The hurricane hit at about 4 P.M. I found her about 10 P.M., so she must have been in there five or six hours."

When I interviewed Mr. Perkins in 1974, he showed me a gold wristwatch inscribed, "J. M. B. to E. Perkins, 9-21-38." He said, "About a year after the storm, James Stowell, a friend who knew her well, brought this watch and a letter, and gave them to me."

The letter was as follows:

September 19, 1939

My dear Mr. Perkins:

In appreciation of your efforts in locating me after hearing my voice and then your continued effort in my behalf by bringing aid who made possible my rescue, I present you this token of my sincere appreciation.

With kindest regards and sincere best wishes, I am,

Most sincerely,
Jennie M. Brown

The storm of September 21, 1938.

To the west, in Fairhaven, the entire stretch of Sconticut Neck suffered; whole neighborhoods of cottages on the peninsula were wiped out, and more than 40 police, former servicemen, and other volunteers rescued at least 200 people from the remains of houses and from trees, utility poles, and boats. First reports, after the Acushnet River had risen to 11.53 feet above mean high water, indicated that the Greater New Bedford area had 69 known dead, 40 still missing, and damage of at least $5 million.

Fifteen-year-old Edward Minnock was at the family cottage at Pope Beach, with his five-year-old brother, Thomas. Their father was at work;

Mrs. Minnock had gone to New Bedford to arrange to have the cottage's gas and lights turned off, since they were moving back to their winter home the next day.

"Tommy and I were getting quite a kick out of the high tide when we felt the house move," Edward said. "Then I noticed Mr. Flanagan's house next to ours was right up to our windows. And before I could move, the tidal wave came roaring in through the house.

"I grabbed Tommy and we were pushed by the water to the back door and I noticed our steps breaking away. I put Tommy on my back and jumped. The water was up to my neck. I managed to get over a pile of rocks. The water was getting higher and higher and there was no one around but us. We jumped in the water and I swam as good as I could, with Tommy on my back. Tommy wasn't scared; he was getting a lot of fun out of it.

"We had a good 200 yards to go and the water was getting deeper and very rough. I was terribly scared and I didn't think we could make it. I was swimming toward the store at the corner and I was losing my strength fast.

"We got to the store and I was just going to grab it when it let go and floated down the street. That was when I gave up hope and I was praying for my brother and myself when a big log came floating right up to me. I grabbed that and we went right on to Hathaway Street, where the water was only knee-deep. Then we were noticed by people at the head of the street and they came running to help us.

"The police were trying to locate us; Dad and Mom were trying to find us. It was 10:30 when we were reunited and we were all crying. I can still hear that water roaring."

At Shore Acres, Sconticut Neck, John Rimmer, seventy-nine, realized that his cottage was about to be swept out to sea and that he could not save himself. He opened a window, leaned out, and fired his rifle as a signal for help. The shot was heard by seventeen-year-old Eugene Barboza, who waded and swam to Rimmer's house, got him out through a window and carried him to safety. The Rimmer house broke up and was washed away.

Lena K. Arden, my friend of many years, was a New Bedford school-teacher, a serious musician. As a child, she had played juvenile roles on the English stage in plays with her mother, Kate, who was known professionally for nearly two decades as Katie Peerless. At the time of the hurricane, Miss Arden was engaged to marry Charles A. Fernandes, a prominent New Bedford pharmacist. On the afternoon of the twenty-first, they went to her cottage at Winsegansett Heights, Sconticut Neck, to make sure that everything was in place and locked up.

"I began to gather a few things to take back to the city. I looked out the front window. The waves were over the top step; the sea struck my 15-foot rowboat and smashed it against the wall. I ran out to tell Charlie and he said, 'We're getting out of here,'" Miss Arden related.

They had driven no more than a few feet in his car when the water was over the hood. There was a stone wall back of the house and they thought they could walk along it to higher ground, where they could see other people standing. "We began walking, one behind the other," Miss Arden said, "and holding on tightly. We were doing quite well when a tremendous wave came right over the top of a house and crashed into us.

"I came to in the water and began to scream for Charlie. I couldn't see him. A piece of fencing came floating by. I climbed on it. The fencing bumped into a garage. I climbed on the roof. I lay down on my stomach and held on tightly. I saw a little bantam hen sitting calmly on a nest which rose with the water. I sometimes wonder what became of her.

"A young man came swimming and he said, 'Put your hand on my shoulder and don't fight.' I said, 'I won't fight,' and he took me to land. There were two priests there who had come for the fishing and I said to one of them, 'I want to see Charlie.' The priest said, 'Be calm and grateful for what has happened to you. You will see Charlie someday.' I looked into his eyes and knew what he meant. . . .

"After that, I saw my cottage go floating on the swamp water, north out of sight. Charlie's body was found three days later. He was carried into a small hollow near a clambake pavilion. The doctor said that when the wave threw us into the air, he had evidently landed headfirst on his car and that was the cause of his death."

There were occasional small miracles.

At Knollmere Beach, Mahlon Faunce, Sr., of New Bedford went to the assistance of a Mr. and Mrs. Logan and their dog. Mrs. Logan was partly paralyzed; she was lying on her bed with the water lapping over her. Faunce, though husky, knew that swimming with them was impossible and wished that he had a boat.

A small sailboat, with mast gone, and full of water, raced by. He caught it and wondered how he could bail it out. Then some buckets he had left at his own back door about two hundred yards away bobbed by; he grabbed one and bailed out the boat. And at that time, his garage went to pieces, releasing his oars; he caught two when they floated past him, and paddled the Logans and their dog to safety in the boat.

Book V
NEW BEDFORD AND THEREAFTER

CHAPTER 11

The late edition of the *Standard-Times* on the twenty-first had a page 1 bulletin of several paragraphs, reporting that "the city was struck late today by a 45-mile-an-hour windstorm. A driving rain hit New Bedford for a few minutes after 3:30. Awnings were torn and reports of damage increased.

"The highest span of the roller coaster at Acushnet Park collapsed. Tree branches were broken over a wide area and there were reports of a large yacht on the rocks beside Padanaram Bridge. A young woman who refused to give her name was blown off her feet in front of the Free Public Library and stunned."

It was I who provided the sentence about the young woman; that was my first contribution to the newspaper. When I saw her—she was wearing something red—I had just emerged from City Hall and did not realize what was happening to the weather. I thought she was simply running. As she came closer, I realized that she was struggling to keep from being blown flat, that her face was contorted with fright and exhaustion, and that she was weeping.

I started toward her, but there was no running against the wind. I hung onto a telephone pole and reached out to grab her as she passed me, but a yard beyond my reach, she lost a shoe, stumbled and fell, tearing her stockings. She sat there, doubled up on the sidewalk, both knees bleeding, sobbing and weaving her head and shoulders back and forth, and crying, "No! No!" The contents of her handbag were strewn over the sidewalk. The lighter articles blew away; I grabbed for one, a white scarf, but it was gone. I helped her to her feet, picked up her things and put them in her bag. I asked her if she wanted a doctor and she brushed me away, shouting, "No! No!"—more as if she could not believe, rather than as if she were answering me. Once standing, she blew on down the street, weeping.

That was the way it began, for me, with a prelude of unbelievable wildness, something gone incredibly and abruptly wrong.

I ran up the three flights of iron stairs to the newspaper's city room to find out what the hell was happening. "It's the hurricane," said George L. Geiger, the city editor. He handed out flashlights to us. "We don't know much about what it's done anywhere else, but it's bad. We expect to lose power and lights. If it does here what it seems to have done elsewhere, there will be heavy damage and loss of life. You probably won't be able to phone us, but the night side will be here. Day people ought to be back here by six tomorrow morning at least, to start writing. If we lose our power, we'll try to arrange to print somewhere else. Take care of yourselves."

I walked out of the building feeling personally afraid—the last radio broadcast I heard urged everyone to stay under cover—and professionally incompetent. I did not own a hat or raincoat, and I was damp already. I ran from the lee side of one building to the next, headed for the waterfront. The uptown streets were largely empty by now; the storm was upon the city.

I stood in the shelter of an old brick building and put no more than half my face and one eye around the corner to stare into the storm, southerly down the harbor and across the bay. Rain struck my face like pebbles and poured down my shirt; mixed with spray, it was salt to the taste. You could not look long, but I saw what appeared to be a wall of water coming toward the harbor; it was like a purple brush stroke. The harbor itself was full of craft in contortion. A naked man who straddled a broken piece of white masthead, was blown past me, up the Acushnet River. He clutched the spar with arms and legs, leaning low over it; his mouth was open and I do not know whether he was yelling or just trying to breathe. In a moment, he was out of sight in the spume. I never found out who he was or what happened to him.

The 60-foot dragger *Winifred M.* parted her lines at Pier 3, a short distance to the south. She was driven north to the Nye Oil Company wharf—an old stone-faced pier of the whaling era—whacked by a half-dozen heavy seas that laid her open like a split mackerel, and she sank. The whole business took about fifteen minutes.

Frank Murphy and Horace Neagus were manning the drawbridge at the head of the harbor. "We knew there was one thing we had to do," Murphy said, "and that was to turn off the hydraulic pressure under the bridge. The pressure operates the big wedges and the four 100-ton jacks that turn the draw; it's 2,800 pounds per square inch and if it let go in the storm, it would be like dynamite."

Leaving the operators' shanty on the end of the bridge pier, they ran over the planks to the platform steps. They had hardly left the little building when the sea reduced it to splinters, lifting the catwalk they had just run across, and carrying it overboard at the same time. A minute later, as they reached the hydraulic base and were turning off the pressure, the platform steps were washed away. But the job was done.

"After that, Neagus and I hung onto the bridge rail all night to keep from being swept into the water, patrolling back and forth and picking up what few poor devils we could from the decks," Murphy said. "But some of the boats went into pieces so fast that God only knows what became of the sailors. Some of the biggest boats cracked against the bridge so hard that it would almost shake your grip loose. We thought the draw might go but we knew that if the bridge was letting go, the vibrations would warn us. And there was gasoline in the water, so much that every time a wave hit you in the face, it would burn your eyes."

Just east of the draw was the Pope's Island station of the New Bedford Yacht Club, a two-story building that was part of the city's waterfront heritage, familiar to countless shore people and thousands of sailors. I saw its end, and as with the America's Cup defenders in Bristol, its passing was more than a matter of wood and fastenings; when it went, all of the echoes and shadows went, too.

Now, as I watch that same clubhouse, the wind builds the sea. The harbor, open to the south, is vulnerable to both. The yacht club, at the harbor's head, is precisely in the target area. Before long, there is a pattern to the waves, as there is in the deeper water offshore; they come crooked, black and curling, their tops crumpling, but not breaking. One or two pleasure craft still in the anchorage are hawsing in frantic fashion, leaping as the sea rolls under them, falling into the troughs, and rolling their dark bottoms out as they attempt to recover.

The water raised the float stages, already abnormally high, and they surge and yank at their chains. The sea is rough even close to the beach; it slams against the stonework, throwing spray; it inches higher on the docks and their decks are already soaked and slippery. As every sea hisses past the spiles on its way to smash on the beach, its top thunders and splatters up through the cracks between the wharf planks, flooding in yellow foam across the deck.

The wind begins to sound like mad music. It is impossible to look into it, the eyes run streaming; it rips at the clothes. Such few clouds as there are blow in harried strings. The air is horizontal. Things are beginning to let go; plate glass buckles and smashes. All of the boats are dragging; two have parted their gear and wallow broadside like wounded birds, bound for disaster to leeward. The white water of the harbor is full of vessels adrift, their mastheads rolling in quick arcs, and when they drop into the troughs, the masts are all that show.

Docks and stages have been torn adrift; the best-driven oak pilings were not meant for this. Water has risen around the yacht club; it is up to the wheels of the automobiles in the parking lot and rising fast. Some vessels are aground; there is a big sloop in the surf in front of the club; she is hove down and being pounded and when the sea strikes her, the spray flies a hundred feet.

And now the Pope's Island station of the New Bedford Yacht Club is inundated. The sea has flooded the island, has overrun the bridge, and is hammering at the building that artist-architect Nat C. Smith took such pains with only eight years ago: "Rebuilt and Renovated Throughout— Greatly Improved Facilities Obtained Without Loss of Accustomed Atmosphere," said the headline. No building could stand the punishment being inflicted by the tons of gale-driven water pounding against the front of the clubhouse. Everytime the sea hits, something smashes; every time it falls back for another blow, something drops—in pieces.

That clubhouse—which had been substantial enough to have withstood all the waterfront weather since 1877—disintegrated as I watched it. The sea hammered in the front, the roof fell, and the building collapsed, abruptly reduced from a snug monument to a half-acre of junk, strewn, as one member observed, "from hell to breakfast." And beside it, equally symbolic, the wreckage of the little schooner yacht *Lizzie* lay against the stonework that had destroyed her, the bottom driven out of her and her masts leaning against the iron railing of the bridge.

In midharbor at New Bedford is Palmer's Island. It is about 1,000 feet long and 460 feet wide and its highest point is between 30 and 40 feet above sea level. In 1938, Captain Arthur A. Small had been keeper of the lighthouse on the north end of Palmer's Island for nineteen years; he and his wife, Mabel, lived in a white story-and-a-half house on the island.

Small and his wife were alone on the island on September 21. Having been through a number of hurricanes, being weatherwise in the manner of all deep-water sailors, he knew what the heavy atmosphere and the color of the sky meant. Shortly before dark, he prevailed upon Mrs. Small to go to the oil house, the highest point on the little island, where the water was already 3 feet deep. Palmer's Island was beginning to flood; the wind was stiff, and the sea was rolling across it, burdened with all manner of lumber and driftwood.

Leaving her in the upper part of the oil house, he forced his way through the water toward the lighthouse; it was time to light the lamp. The seas knocked him off his feet; he was hurt, and was being swept overboard. He swam, but with difficulty, because of his injury.

Mrs. Small, seeing that he was in trouble, left her place of safety and ran to the boathouse. She was an excellent oarsman and was going to row to him; he was already in deeper water than she could wade in. Small, by swimming underwater to dodge the wreckage, got his footing again, and was struggling to regain the station. He could see his wife going to launch a boat and then watched in horror as a heavy sea slammed into the boathouse. It collapsed upon her. The next wave swept the building away.

"I was hurt and she knew it," Small said later. "Seeing the wave hit the boathouse was about the last thing I remember. I must have been hit by a piece of timber and knocked unconscious. I came to some hours later, but all I remember was that I was in the middle of some wreckage. Then I must have lost my senses again, for I remember nothing more."

Nevertheless, even though suffering from both shock and injury, he somehow retained enough strength and consciousness to haul himself back to the lighthouse, and he kept the light and the fog signal operating throughout the hurricane and Wednesday night.

At 7:45 in the morning on September 22, observing that the keeper's house and other buildings on Palmer's Island had been swept away, Captain William D. Raymond and Captain Fred W. Phillips—both close friends of Small—rowed out to the island with food. Raymond contacted the Lighthouse Service for permission to have Small relieved from duty, for the rule of the service stated: "No keeper may leave his post until relieved, if he is able to walk." Raymond and Phillips arranged for a police escort over to New Bedford-Fairhaven Bridge—closed to traffic because of grounded boats and debris—and took Small to St. Luke's Hospital.

On September 23, the following letter was sent from the hospital to the Superintendent of Lighthouses in Washington:

In reporting the destruction of and loss of building and equipment at Palmer Island Light Station, New Bedford, Mass. on September 21st, 1938, the keeper made preparations all during that day, securing everything so far as possible, carrying extra oil and lamp equipment to the tower. This station felt the full force of the gale, the seas reaching clear across the island. . . .

Keeper swept overboard, but by swimming underwater, made the station again. Mrs. Small, the keeper's wife, was seen by the keeper while he was overboard. She left the oil house where he had told her to stay and evidently she tried to launch a boat to save the keeper, but she was swept away and drowned. . . . There is no shelter to be had at the station, except in the top of the tower.

Keeper remained on duty until properly relieved. The light and fog signal were in good order. Keeper removed to St. Luke's Hospital suffering from exhaustion and exposure.

(Signed) Arthur A. Small, keeper. Dictated by Arthur Small, keeper, recorded by Wesley V. Small, keeper's son.

Three days later, in Washington, Commissioner Harold D. King of the Bureau of Lighthouses described Captain Small's performance during the hurricane as "one of the most outstanding cases of loyalty and devotion that has come to the attention of this office."

E. H. Tripp of Fairhaven wrote a tribute to Mrs. Small and, implicitly, to her husband, which unquestionably reflected the feelings of many:

"A happy and courageous companion through thirty years of married life in the Lighthouse Service, in Wednesday's storm, she abandoned her refuge in an attempt to help her valiant husband, struggling for his life, to reach his post of duty and thereby lost her own.

"The manner of Mrs. Small's death shocked the community and her loss is deeply felt and mourned by her family and very wide circle of friends. A great number of people in all walks of life have visited Captain and Mrs. Small, the noted, as well as the obscure, and have met with a sincerely cordial and generous hospitality. Mrs. Small and her husband shared their enjoyment of people and books and art with their friends. And those who have been welcomed to the home circle and who enjoyed their company will grieve that, with the gracious mistress gone, the home is no more.

"All express their deepest sympathy for Captain Small and his two stalwart sons, Wesley and Allan. Wesley is skipper of the two-masted schooner *Adventure,* lying at Gloucester, and Allan spent the summer as one of the crew of the three-masted schooner *Sachem* of Essex, Connecticut.

"Mrs. Small's forty-eighth birthday came two days after the catastrophe. Mrs. Small was a member of the Fairhaven Mother's Club, for which she and Captain Small had given talks. Living by and on the sea and knowing full well the might of God's awful elements as well as sunshine on a sandy, rock-strewn isle, the brave wife of a brave man, casting aside all thought of self, nor by wind or tide dismayed, she tried to bring succor to her mate, who struggled in the raging flood.

"We, her friends who weep, may pause and say, 'There is no greater love than this—her dear memory to us a treasure will be always.'"

On September 30, there was a classified advertisement in the *Standard-Times* of New Bedford, which read: "LOST—IN HURRICANE FROM PALMER ISLAND, large sum of currency in canvas pouch about 6 x 8 inches. Substantial reward for return in whole or part. Wesley V. Small." In the files of the newspaper, attached to that clipping, there is a handwritten notation that reads: "Reported $7,000-$8,000 on Mrs. Arthur Small at time of hurricane drowning."

Captain Small visited Palmer's Island on either October 15 or 16, 1938, the first time he went there after the hurricane and perhaps the last time. He informed the Fairhaven police that he had been granted a long furlough by his superiors in order to regain his health and that he would be living in Dorchester.

About two weeks later, he wrote the following letter from Dorchester to the Superintendent of Lighthouses, Second District:

Referring to the superintendent's letter of October 4, 1938, requesting that this office be furnished with a report listing personal effects lost as a result of the hurricane:

The list enclosed herewith is a report covering only the outstanding items lost at this time.

All buildings except light tower and oil house [where he had placed Mrs. Small for safety] were destroyed and carried away in the heavy sea that swept the entire reservation and all personal property was lost. None of the personal effects belonging to Mrs. Small, my wife, who lost her life as a result of this hurricane, are included in the list herewith.

Respectfully,
Arthur Small

Essentially, what Captain Small listed was "Personal library of several hundred volumes, many out of print, and the result of about thirty years of careful selection, $75;

"The value of the following cannot be estimated, as my personal records and data of sailing ships were sketches and notes, the result of thirty years' work and used for reference in painting the history of sailing ships, a spare-time hobby, $100."

Two things are noteworthy. In characteristically modest fashion, Captain Small asked for no compensation for a number of his paintings that were lost in the Palmer's Island house, although, as a matter of record, his work had marketable value. Further, records in the National Archives reveal that someone, not identified, recommended he be given $100, rather than the $175 he had asked for.

By March 20, 1939, the *Standard-Times* reported, "That Captain Arthur A. Small, for many years keeper of the light at Palmer's Island, never will return to New Bedford in his official capacity, is the information just received by Frank Ponte, temporary keeper of Palmer's Island light, in a letter written to him by Captain Small from the Canal Zone.

"Reading between the lines of Captain Small's letter, Mr. Ponte is of the opinion that the U.S. Treasury Department has granted Captain Small a leave of absence with pay for the next two years, at the end of which Captain Small will be retired from the Lighthouse Service on pension.

"Captain Small, following the death of his wife by drowning, the loss of $7,500, which she had with her when she attempted to save his life in the tidal flood and hurricane last September, and the injuries he sustained, was sent to the Marine Hospital at Chelsea for treatment.

"When convalescent, Captain Small was granted an indefinite leave of absence on full pay and upon his discharge from the hospital, went to Panama, where his son is employed on a millionaire's yacht."

In August of 1939, a visitor to Palmer's Island observed, "The present light keeper has a small rocky terrain, with only hurricane wreckage for company; crumbled bricks which were once the foundation of a house . . . are mute evidence of New Bedford's lighthouse tragedy."

Slightly more than forty-eight hours before, I had come to New Bedford on the steamer *Martha's Vineyard,* in search of my fortune. It was a pleasant, uneventful trip, such as thousands of tourists have known, aboard that same vessel. But at 4:30 on the afternoon of the twenty-first, the *Martha's Vineyard* and those aboard were on the threshold of trouble.

She came rolling up to Pier 9 minutes ahead of the rush of water into the harbor. Her fifteen passengers, once off the vessel, discovered that they were not going any farther; behind them, the river was rising and out beyond the dock shed, the driving rain and wind had shut everything down. They went into the company office at the head of the dock; when the first floor was flooded, they went to the second and were trapped there, watching the water still coming up. Crew members of the steamer, including porters, manned two skiffs, battled their way across the slip, and took the passengers out of the inundated building through a second-story window, rowing them across deeply flooded streets to higher ground.

As the water poured into the harbor, it picked up the *Martha's Vineyard* and suspended the steamer by its guardrail from the roof of the pier building. The guardrail, 7 feet above waterline, held the big vessel to the roof; all during the period of high water, the ship pounded the shed and threatened its own destruction as well. When the water receded, as rapidly as it had risen—throughout all the waterfront streets of the city, you could hear it going with an awful sucking noise like a giant drain—the steamer dropped off the roof, but her guardrail caught on the tops of four wharf spiles. There she hung, listing at a frightening angle and with her steel hull under terrible strain.

That is how I came upon her, paddling through the muck, the broken fish boxes, the hundreds of cans of motor oil floated off somebody's dock, dodging the open manholes whose covers had been blown off by the high water; I, coming with flashlight in the dripping dark to see who and what was left.

There was the good round-faced Dutchman, Albert F. Haas, the steamboat company superintendent, standing stalwart and chunky in the yellow blob of the battery-powered emergency lighting hooked up to the caplog, watching his steamer, wondering if she would break in half before they could help her.

In the weak light, the arc of her steel guardrail overhead hung like a scimitar and that is what it was for the steamer's crew who set to work with saws and axes to cut off the spiles on which she was hung. Working underneath those tons of vessel, with each stroke weakening the wood that held her suspended, they kept one hand for the blade and one for themselves, alert with each stroke for that last cracking of spile which would signal that the steamer was coming down. There was no way of knowing what she would do at the moment when her hull was freed.

It was ringing bite of the ax, steady risp-rasp of the saw, the bent backs, rising and falling with effort, the figures half in light, half in dark, chips and sawdust gathering on the dock, one man spelling another, so through the hour. Then the crack of timber came, somebody yelled a warning, they all jumped, and down came the *Martha's Vineyard,* transformed in an instant from incongruous cripple to her customary grace. Sweaty-faced, they cheered. Haas said softly, "They saved the vessel and the pier as well. As far as I am concerned, that was heroic. They did not know what might happen."

East of the yacht club and across the highway, there was a diner. I waded toward it, past an automobile agency with its plate glass windows shattered and the new showroom models wheel-deep in salt water. From somewhere in the darkness, two men came splashing; one wore a bathing suit and shoes, the other khaki trousers and a life jacket. I assumed they were off some boat—perhaps the schooner yacht *Gallant,* which lay hove down in the nearby park—but they were looking for a couple of fellows who had been in the diner.

"What do you think happened to them?" I asked.

One of them looked toward where the sidewalk in front of the diner ought to be. Water still poured over it and a big chunk of the steel bridge rail was gone. "I suppose they're overboard somewhere," he said, and sloshed off. "I suppose they're dead," he yelled back.

They were overboard, but not the way he thought.

Halfway down the harbor, Enos E. Days, Jr., had a 38-foot cabin cruiser, *Prudence*, berthed on the north side of Union Wharf, Fairhaven. On the south side of the wharf were lying several laid-up holdovers from the port's rumrunner fleet of Prohibition days; they were heavy boats, 50 to 60 feet long. When the water rose, the rum boats floated over the wharf and parted all of *Prudence's* lines, setting her adrift.

Meanwhile, to the north, the owner of the bridge diner, Antone J. Viau, and an employee, Edward Riendeau, were having a hard time. Water flowed through the restaurant so rapidly that by the time they got to the front door, it was too high and running too hard for them to risk getting into. As they stood there, in increasing danger every minute, *Prudence*, unmanned, and broadside to the flood and wind, was hastening to the rescue.

The cruiser was blown up the Acushnet River, over flooded Marine Park, where deeper vessels grounded, and across Route 6; she fetched up momentarily broadside to the brick front steps of the diner where Viau and Riendeau were stranded. They jumped aboard and broke a cabin door to get to the wheel, hoping to be able to steer the cruiser if the sea washed her free of the restaurant. For a moment, it looked bad; *Prudence* pounded against the steps and punched a hole a foot-and-a-half in diameter in her port side. Fortunately, most of it was above the waterline and it did not cause her to leak much.

The next series of waves carried *Prudence* clear of the diner, but the two aboard discovered immediately that there was no steering her because her rudder had been smashed. So they rode her helplessly, northeast across the upper harbor to the Fairhaven shore. There, she sheared the piazza off one house and came to rest on the lawn of another, at least a hundred feet from the water in ordinary times. Neither Viau nor Riendeau was injured. I reported both "probably drowned," and was pleased to be found in error.

Inevitably, the night provided a little humor. Aboard Thomas Kearn's big steam yacht *Neelia,* aground at Marine Park, there were lights, because she had her own power plant. In a dark and damaged world, the glow through the cabin windows was both incongruous and cheering. I made my way there carefully, each step oozing, to see what was going on.

There was a ladder leaned against the side of the vessel. I arrived at the foot of it, at which moment, the glare of a bull's-eye lantern flashed upon me and a voice said, "Freeze or I'll shoot!" I froze. A police officer walked out of the darkness, revolver in hand.

I said, rather lamely, "I'm a reporter for the *Standard-Times.*"

"Got any credentials?"

"This is my first day. All I have is a Social Security card."

"Goddam." Then he said, without putting away his gun, "We have orders from Boston to shoot looters. This area is out of bounds, as of a half-hour ago. I had no idea who you were or what you were doing. I would have been justified in taking extreme action." He put his gun away. "And you get a goddam press pass and you come down to the station house and show it to me tomorrow morning. D'you hear?"

Then he left and let me go aboard the *Neelia.* I remember to this day how he said "extreme action." After he left, I was somewhat unraveled.

That was not what was funny.

Once aboard the yacht, aware of my muddy feet and damp clothes, I discovered that Mr. Kearns—totally undisturbed by the fact that his vessel was high and dry on the storm-littered grass of the park—was host at a small supper. He and guests were "quite comfortable." That was funny.

On the east side of the Acushnet, the fleet took a savage battering. At Fairhaven's Union Wharf, little Joe Pinto, master of the freight boat *Eben A. Thacher* of Vineyard Haven, saved her, and very possibly the lives of her crew, when he decided it was less dangerous to try to cross the swollen river full of junk than it was to stay at the exposed dock. "When the water took her above the level of the wharf, I knew the spiles were likely to go," Joe said. "I started my engine, sent a man forward and one aft with axes, and when I threw in the clutch, I yelled at them to cut the lines.

"I didn't know whether we could dodge the wreckage and the vessels that were being swept up the river, but I had to take a chance. My keel scraped the caplog on the wharf and my propeller chopped a big piece of concrete off the top of the dock, but we got out of there. We got across the river and I saw lee, on the north side of Pier 3. Just as we were easing in, the Cuttyhunk boat *Alert* washed right over the wharf and into the slip where we were heading. A minute more and she would have dropped on top of us. We hauled out of there and found another place. . . ."

Captain Phillips, a gentleman mariner of the old school, was newly master of the *Lochinvar,* the large, twin-screwed vessel recently purchased by Amory Houghton of Corning Glass; she was undergoing repairs at the Pierce and Kilburn yard, the most southerly in the harbor and the most exposed. "We were all lying on the south side of the dock. We were on the outside, in the *Lochinvar.* Between us and the wharf lay the schooner *Quita,* and the Swedish sloop *Gladje,* with Captain Edward Coffin of Nantucket aboard her," Phillips said to me.

"The sloop parted her lines first and came down onto us under the bowsprit of the *Quita.* The *Quita* parted next and sawed our bow line right off. It was blowing hard then and all three of us were about ready to go adrift in a bunch.

"The *Lochinvar* still had a spring line and a stern line fast, and we carried the stern line forward, threw out two anchors, and let her hang off the end of the dock. Coffin had been jumping back and forth between us and his vessel and if he'd known we were going to cast off, I know he would have stayed aboard his own craft. He wanted to get back aboard her and was going to try it when she was carried down by us, but he couldn't make it.

"It's lucky he didn't, because she went right across the harbor, hit the Hathaway dock and sank after two seas had smashed her to pieces. If Coffin had stayed aboard his vessel, he never would have come out alive.

"It was one hair-raising night. Everything went by us. I saw a paint shop driving down on us, rolling end over end, but it sank before it got to us. There must have been a hundred cradles and all kinds of gear from the railways that went by us. But the worst scrape occurred when Andrew G. Pierce's 110-foot schooner *Palestine* came down on us. She poked her bowsprit right through the stateroom window, took out two panes and their frames, and went on by. That was close."

Palestine was lost, and when the storm had passed, only the masts of Warren Burbridge's schooner *Caroline* and the cabin top and stack of Joseph Cudahy's steam yacht *Innisfail* were above water. The 100-foot dragger *Leretha,* hauled out on the ways for repairs, was hurled across the tracks, stove on her port side, and dumped on her beam ends.

CHAPTER 12

There are a few other things that ought to be said.

When Harrison McDonald of Lafayette, Indiana, finally arrived in Boston on September 23, he observed, "you don't know how queer it seems to be in a normal city with lights, heat, and telephones running."

The suggestion that Boston had escaped the hurricane was born of relativity; compared to New London and Providence, from which Mr. McDonald had just come, the city was fortunate. Yet there was the matter of the city's North End to be considered; this was the home of those Italian fishermen who made up the crews of the so-called "mosquito fleet," the little boats. Ordinarily, six boats, with a total of thirty men, would have docked early Wednesday evening. When the hurricane had thundered its way past Boston, when darkness had fallen, the six boats had not come home.

It was a bad night in the North End, and no time for sleeping. These people were close; many were related; the families were large, and the fate of the six vessels affected a lot of them. Through the night, the women, children, and old men stood and talked quietly in little knots in the streets; in Fleet Street, North Street, and Moon Street, they waited, tautly and quietly, their parish priests with them. The small stores—neighborhood gathering places crammed in fragrant disorder with fat lumps of mozzarella, strings of garlic, golden crusted loaves, and black oil-cured olives—were crowded all through the dark hours. They had telephones; there might be some news come by them. A group of youngsters remained on duty at the Eastern Packet Pier, where the Italian fleet berthed, ready to rush home with the glad tidings if any of the missing boats came up the harbor.

A report came—the *4C554*, a 45-foot vessel, had gone down off Finn's ledge in Boston Harbor. The women, fingering their prayer beads, passed the word. They knew that number; they knew the names of the four men aboard; they knew them by their first names. The hours wore on.

Coast Guard headquarters relayed a radio message received from the British freighter *Baron Dechmont*. Outward bound from Boston, she had observed a small fishing vessel capsize off Finn's Ledge. Only one survivor had been sighted and rescued. When last seen, the capsized vessel was drifting toward Nahant.

Only one man rescued? Was it Frank Marino? Or Joe Sciafano? Or Frank's brother, Tony, the father of six, or Tony Ciulla, the father of eleven? Waiting in the streets, they looked at each other, holding back grief until they knew who it was.

At daybreak, the Eastern Packet Pier was crowded with the anxious. The sun rose; the entire fleet that had made it home safely put to sea to search the waters of the bay for survivors of the *4C554*. As the morning passed, some better news came. Some of the little boats, scattered in the gale, had made it. The *St. Joseph,* with a crew of six, and the *Maria,* with five, both safe at Portsmouth, New Hampshire. The *Josephine F.,* with six, arrived at Gloucester, with all hands. The *Maria Giuseppe,* five aboard, wrecked off Nahant, all safe. And at 10 in the morning, the stalwart *Anna Madre,* her port bulwarks carried away, her crew of four worn out from the battle, chugged up the harbor and the hundreds on the pier greeted her with a rousing cheer as she nosed into her berth.

Then Frank Marino came home. He was suffering from shock, his face was lacerated, several of his teeth had been knocked loose, and he staggered so, still weak from immersion and his ordeal, that he could hardly get to his house on Prince Street. He had only a hazy idea of what happened when the hurricane overtook the $4C554$ as she was running for the shelter of Boston Harbor.

He said he was barely conscious after a sea struck him and washed him overboard from the deck of the vessel. He struggled to stay afloat and thought he was in the water about fifteen minutes before someone aboard the *Baron Dechmont* threw him a line. He lost consciousness after he was hauled aboard the freighter; he came to his senses early Thursday morning as he was being transferred from the British vessel, off the harbor entrance, to an inbound trawler. Landed at the Fish Pier, he walked home, praying all the way that the other three aboard the $4C554$ had somehow made port safely. None had; none ever did.

Surveying Boston's \$6-million loss, the Boston *Globe*'s "Uncle Dudley" editorialized, "After lives and houses, our worst loss from the hurricane is trees . . . there they always were, some for a century and a half, and the assumption was that there they always would be. Then, in two hours, thousands of them are laid low.

"Did you see the fight they put up? It was game. They roared like goaded animals and mostly, they fell slowly, fighting to the end. One old fellow, an elm, at least 150 years old, if not 200, on the exposed ridge of a seaward headland, was delivering a splendid battle. He met the buffets of the hurricane with contempt. 'Pfugh,' said he. 'To hell with you.' And he won; only a minor limb of him went down. But his neighbors, younger and not so strong, were less lucky. . . .

"A creature that has established and maintained itself on a spot of land from ten to one hundred years is a citizen. What is more, any orchardist or forester will tell you that a tree manages its affairs far more sensibly than do most people. It does less harm to its neighbors and gets into fewer scrapes of its own. This realization that trees are people and have rights, when it first comes home to one, is startling. In 'Specimen Days,' Walt Whitman speaks of walking out on Boston Common and sitting out underneath the great trees along the Beacon Street Mall, until he has made himself acquainted with 'their personalities.'

"Mourning will not bring back the dead. . . ."

Worcester counted seven dead, and the toll might have been higher had it not been for the quick action of a school janitor and a teacher. Classical High School, built in 1892, was one of the city's oldest; on the afternoon of the storm, twenty-five pupils were in the school auditorium. A double window blew out, and janitor Charles W. Carrick and Miss Margaret M. Walsh, an instructor, had the pupils leave the room immediately and, because of the heavy rain, go to the basement for shelter.

Mr. Carrick went to his office and telephoned his wife. Just as he was about to hang up the receiver, the upper part of the building began to collapse; a heavy board came through the ceiling of his office and he had just time to jump under a beam for safety. Teacher and janitor quickly evacuated all the pupils, housing them in a nearby store.

They had hardly arrived there when, about 5 P.M., with a roar that rocked houses for blocks around, the massive slate roof of the school collapsed, crashed through the third floor into the assembly hall on the floor below, and ripped away much of the rear of the brick structure. As the upper part of the building disintegrated, sheathing was flung into windows of nearby houses, an immense section of wreckage crushed the porch of an adjacent dwelling, bricks were scattered the length of the street, heavy timbers were thrown about, and falling brick crushed and buried three automobiles.

The *New York Times* of September 22 reported from Northfield, Massachusetts: "Two students at Northfield Seminary, Miss Norma Stockberger and Miss Audrey Lucas, were killed instantly and two others were seriously injured—Miss Mary Kidder and Miss Lucille Carle—when a tall brick chimney crashed during the height of the hurricane. The chimney crashed through the roof of the school dining hall at 6:15 o'clock, while the students were eating dinner. There were 140 girls in the hall at the time and it is considered miraculous that many more were not killed or seriously injured."

Harold B. Ingalls was chaplain of the school at that time and he recalled: "Suddenly [in the afternoon of the twenty-first], the storm became ferociously worse and threatening; some trees and hundreds of branches fell. My wife and I lived in a house owned by the school, but just across the street from the campus. We went from window to window on all four sides of the house and marveled that, at that point, we could not see that any building had been damaged. Of course, visibility was poor and most of the campus buildings were not within sight of our windows. Electric power in the town had failed by that time.

"Suddenly two girls from Gould Hall appeared at our door. Elizabeth Colvin and Margery Smith, roommates, had somehow managed to get across the campus to report the tragedy in Gould. I immediately got raincoat, etc., and called to our neighbor, Russel Roberts, a school employee who lived in the apartment above us, to do the same and come with me, telling him there had been a bad accident at Gould Hall.

"We were there quickly—either the first, or among the first four or five men to arrive. I am not sure whether the school power plant was still operating or we were dependent upon our flashlights, but we could see at once the extent of the devastation and managed to get to the most seriously injured persons. I do recall there was no electricity later as we continued to work. Some other men arrived and cars took the injured to the school infirmary.

"The wind at its height hit the large chimney full force and snapped it off at or very near the roof level. It must have been almost horizontal when it crashed through the ceiling of the dining room, leaving (I think I am accurate) a clear pattern of its shape overhead. Most, if not all of those killed or seriously injured were at one table for ten, I believe.

"Quick work by an intelligent, dedicated group of faculty members present (all women at the moment) was responsible for saving at least one life, possibly more. Miss Elizabeth Homet, biology teacher, quickly saw that one girl was lying on her back with blood gurgling out of her mouth, turned her over and administered first aid. There were others who helped in similar ways, while some went for professional medical help.

"Miss Annie Milfred Herring, dietitian, was aware that there was a possibility a second chimney—not as tall or wide as the first, but quite large—might topple, and she rounded up all who could walk and sent them to the basement, where there was a large, safe area.

"I recall having stopped at the school infirmary to see if any help was needed. The school physician and two or three nurses, aided by faculty and community people who had had some nursing or first-aid experience, had things well under control, though they were overworked. I cannot recall how many patients there were there or how many injured and placed in a dorm until the next day. I remember, of course, the four mentioned in The *New York Times* story. Lucille Carle, 'Bushy'—loved by all—did not make it. Eleanor Shedd was very seriously injured, hospitalized for months, but finally made a good recovery.

"There was no possible way to get to any hospital that night, nor could any help get in from any direction. Nor was communication elsewhere possible. Later that night, I was asked to try to get to Greenfield by truck, with a crew of men who went ahead and hand-sawed or chopped enough space between fallen trees and branches so that we could get through. It was my sad responsibility to call and notify parents of the dead girls and those most seriously injured of what had happened. (I think I managed to get The *New York Times* also, but I am not sure.) It took some round-about routing, but we managed to reach nearly all of the parents, although it took the rest of the night.

"I wish I had kept a daily record of events immediately following September 21 and for months thereafter. The problems resulting from the storm were many. Most related to structures, etc., were quickly solved, temporarily at least. But the emotional and intellectual (especially theological) problems required longer periods and a vast amount of counseling and guidance. I suspect that not all of them were solved and that there are still scars. . . ."

Miss Betty Goff was a student at Northfield; she escaped injury, and in a letter to her parents, Mr. and Mrs. W. W. Goff of Westerly, Rhode Island, shortly after the storm, she said that forty girls were hurt when the chimney fell. Miss Goff wrote: "Wednesday, two chimneys fell over and through the roof at Gould Hall. As it was, they fell through the dining room and all the girls were just eating. Two girls were killed and fifteen taken to a hospital out of town and twenty-five here in the hospital. A lot more were cut and bruised.

"They took the girls out of the cellar (where they finally landed) and wrapped them up in blankets and sent them in bunches all over the campus to different buildings. I was drying dishes when they came in here. It was awful to see them, all cut and crying and fainting. We went into the living room and they were lying all over the room, wrapped in soaking wet blankets. Most of them went to the hotel to sleep but a lot slept here.

"It's just like being on an island here. All the wires are down and nobody can get across the river or send any mail except by air. Last night we were given stamps and told to write home a very short letter saying we were all right and the mail went out in five minutes.

"None of the girls from Gould Hall have been back to their hall, so we lent them clothes to wear. I think tonight they are to go back, but not eat there. I just can't explain any more about it here, but everyone is in a daze and has been in a daze since Wednesday."

On September 24, the Boston *Transcript*'s Washington bureau reported, "Although granting that New Englanders had scant warning to prepare themselves against the tropical hurricane, Dr. Charles C. Clark, acting chief of the U.S. Weather Bureau, said today that the bureau forecasters, on the basis of the data on hand, could hardly have given any greater advance warning, for the tropic storm—the worst in the history of the Northeast—was a freak; it did not follow the usual pattern. . . .

"Up to the time it reached Hatteras, there was no indication that it would be particularly dangerous, and it seemed quite likely that it would go out to sea well off the Atlantic Seaboard. However, from Cape Hatteras, the storm center headed north with enormously increased momentum, covering on Wednesday six hundred miles in twelve hours, an average of fifty miles an hour. This is believed to be the fastest movement ever recorded by a major tropical disaster."

Owing to the unusually rapid rate of progress of the storm across New England, the winds on the right or east side of the path were very destructive, while strong winds did not extend far to the westward. At the Harvard Meteorological Observatory at the top of Blue Hill, Milton, Massachusetts, gusts of approximately 173 and 186 miles per hour were recorded during the storm's height. Wind velocity of 111 miles an hour was recorded on the summit in three five-minute periods at 6:05, and 7:12 P.M. The gusts of 173 and 186 miles an hour occurred during the passage of 7 miles of wind in 2½ minutes at 6:59 P.M. and the passage of 4 miles of wind in a little over a minute at 6:15 P.M.

The most sensitive recorder on the hilltop, a French windmill anemometer, started to disintegrate when registering a five-minute velocity of 80 miles. It broke under a gust of 100-mile-an-hour velocity.

Damage to property along the coast was largely due to the storm wave. At the Battery, New York City, it was 6.44 feet above mean sea level. Along the coast of Connecticut, Rhode Island, and on the shore of Narragansett and Buzzards Bay, the highest tide ranged from 12 to 25 feet above mean low water, being highest on the southern shores of Massachusetts, where the maximum stage occurred about 5 or 6 P.M. At Point Judith Coast Guard station, the water rose 18 feet above mean low water; at Fairhaven, it was estimated at 25 feet.

Even to this day, statistics concerning the hurricane, especially concerning lives lost, vary considerably. It is generally accepted, however, that there were 680 lives lost and property damaged to a total of $400,000,000. Comparable figures for the San Francisco earthquake and fire of 1906 were 450 lives and $350,000,000 property damage, and for the

Chicago fire of 1871, 200 lives and a $200,000,000 loss.

Seven hundred and eight suffered injuries; 4,500 homes, summer cottages, and farm buildings were destroyed, 15,139 homes, summer cottages, and farm buildings were damaged; 2,605 boats were lost and 3,369 were damaged. A total of 19,608 families applied for emergency help or assistance in rehabilitating themselves.

Twenty-six thousand automobiles were smashed; 275,000,000 trees were broken off or uprooted, amounting to 2.6 billion board feet of timber downed, and nearly 20,000 miles of electric power and telephone lines were blown or knocked down. A total of 1,675 heads of livestock and between 500,000 and 750,000 chickens were killed. Railroad service between New York and Boston was interrupted for seven to fourteen days while 10,000 men filled 1,000 washouts, replaced nearly 100 bridges, and removed thousands of obstructions from the tracks, including a number of houses and 30 boats. More than a half-million telephones were silenced, isolating 240 communities. In order to repair these, Bell System crews rolled into New England from as far south as Virginia, from as far west as Arkansas and Nevada; more than 2,300 trained men and 615 motor vehicles were loaned by 14 telephone companies.

The Bell System listed materials needed to effect hurricane repairs as: 400 miles of cable, 31,000 poles, 72 million feet of wire, and 50 carloads of telephone hardware.

The storm destroyed $2,610,000 worth of fishing boats, equipment, docks, and shore plants. Orchardists also suffered greatly. During the first part of September, it was anticipated that the total apple crop would be 2.8 million bushels from Massachusetts, 1.8 million from the orchards of Connecticut, almost one million from Maine, and lesser amounts from New Hampshire, Vermont, and Rhode Island, in that order. Agriculturists estimated that at least half of the total apple crop was still on the trees when the hurricane struck and that growers received from $1 million to $2 million less than they had expected earlier in the month.

CHAPTER 13

After it was over, there were comments of several sorts.
Bernard DeVoto said, "The face of New England had been changed forever . . . But one had seen, had listened in darkness, had realized the community rallying."

As for John Q. Steward, associate professor of astronomical physics at Princeton Univeristy, he concluded that "newspapers, especially outside New England, gave the stupendous hurricane of September 21 very inadequate treatment. For two or three days immediately following the disaster, bits of it were front-page items, but the whole account was not available until the neurotic interests of editors had jumped to fresher happenings. . . .

"A seaboard as wealthy as any in the world and its hinterland . . . felt the shock. There had been no warning worth the mentioning. . . . A sophisticated population died by hundreds, with little or no knowledge of what raw shape of death this was which struck from the sky and the tide. In the long and laudable annals of the government's weather forecasters, that day's record makes what must be the sorriest page."

Then there was the question of God's involvement. The Reverend Dr. Arthur Lee Kinsolving of Boston's Trinity Church said, "There is no valid evidence that Christianity ever assumed the world would provide maximum security and comfort. The guest at a hotel may make such demands, but we are in no such position to expect this sort of attention from God." In Springfield, Massachusetts, the Reverend Dr. Earl Vinie, speaking at East Church, rejected the notion that the storm was an act of God. He said, "These so-called 'acts of God' you find referred to in your old insurance policies are a direct carryover of certain outgrown religious teachings found scattered throughout the pages of the Old Testament. Those who taught those things were mistaken."

As for me, I walked the docks and beaches during the following days, attempting not so much to discover the truth of why it had happened as to accept the reality of what had happened. If the dark wildness of Wednesday remained unbelievable (Thursday dawned benign, quiet, its water characteristically gentle), the miles and acres of destruction over which I crawled and stumbled were equally incredible even when one walked them in the unforgiving light of day.

It takes some time to sort out an experience like this. If you have seen the sea sun-sparkled and glassy, clear and clean, swirling about the bare feet of a child and have watched it in the same place, only hours later, dirty, ugly, and as high as a two-story house, crushing things and people, it stretches the mind to accept the contradictions.

And there are so many other things—the row of boathouses, shops, and shanties, silvered by generations of weather, that had been a fundamental of childhood; it might not have been so bad if something had been